Elementary School Mathematics

Elementary School Mathematics

Activities and Materials

George F. Green, Jr.
Indiana State University

D. C. HEATH AND COMPANY
Lexington, Massachusetts   Toronto   London

Preface

This book was written primarily as a textbook for use in methods courses for prospective teachers of elementary school mathematics. Although written mainly for those preservice teachers who have already studied the corresponding mathematics separately, two other potential uses for the book might be considered. First, although this is not a "math book," the mathematics of each topic in Part II is reviewed in some detail, and the book could be adapted for use in courses which blend mathematical and pedagogical instruction. Second, the book was written with an eye toward being as practical as possible, and could serve as a reference for in-service as well as preservice teachers.

The chief purpose of the book is to identify some basic activities and materials for teaching the major topics found in most contemporary elementary mathematics programs. Of course, we can neither include all topics that might appear in a given elementary school textbook, nor can we identify all possible activities and materials for teaching any given topic. Learning to teach mathematics effectively must, in fact, be viewed as a continuous process, for which a book such as this can at best provide a beginning.

The interested reader will find it necessary to look elsewhere for detailed discussion of the mathematics, the theories of learning, the research findings, and the administrative concerns which affect the teaching of elementary school mathematics. It would be impossible to ignore these crucial topics, but we have attempted to assimilate them into practical teaching suggestions rather than elaborate upon them in detail per se.

Preliminary versions of the book have been used with university students and have been carefully and critically reviewed by several colleagues. Based in part on their reactions, two comments on the organization of the book, including some suggestions for using it, follow.

First, Appendices A and B appear at the end of the book but should be introduced at the beginning of the course. The enjoyment and appreciation of mathematics can be developed only from "doing mathematics." Games and problems such as those found in Appendix A should be used regularly, we believe, beginning with the first day. The now familiar adage,

"I hear and I forget, I see and I remember, I do and I understand" applies not only to children but to all of us, including university students and their teachers. The materials suggested in Appendix B (and throughout the book) are basic instructional tools. Collecting or constructing such materials is rather time-consuming and so should begin early in the course. Insofar as possible they should be available to students during class sessions and/or during adjunct laboratory sessions. Furthermore, such materials — and suggested activities which employ them — can best be understood and evaluated if prospective teachers have the opportunity to try them with children.

Second, the projects, questions, and suggested activities at the end of each chapter were not intended as test items. Rather, they were intended to extend the reader's understanding of the chapter. They should at least be skimmed before reading the chapter, and in most cases are appropriate for use while the chapter is being studied rather than after a unit is finished. Similarly, the appearance of suggested readings at the ends of chapters is not necessarily intended to suggest that they should be considered only after the chapter has been read. Many times such readings (or updated alternatives provided by the instructor) should be read as the chapter is being studied or even beforehand.

Before this book was written, I made several resolutions about it. As a final introductory remark on the intent of the book, a few of those resolutions are summarized here:

- Keep the book practical, one worth keeping as a reference.
- Provide a variety of alternatives from which serious, intelligent students may choose, but don't presume to tell them how to teach. Don't preach.
- Don't belabor students with excessive background material. Write for your students, not your colleagues: let your writing reflect your understanding of learning processes, of significant historical facts, of research, of important people and philosophies; but address yourself as directly as possible to the more immediate needs of beginning teachers.
- Don't forget your own experience with children and teachers. Remember and report those ideas that work. Discard those that seemingly ought to work but do not.
- Don't pigeonhole activities and materials in terms of grade level or purpose. If an activity makes sense, then it may be equally appropriate for initial instruction, remedial instruction, or enrichment. Let teachers decide for themselves when to use a particular activity for a particular purpose.
- Assume that an instructor using the book has convictions about the scope and sequence of his course and about the evaluation of students. Let the book be flexible enough to be useful. *Suggest* activities and readings, but leave assignments, exercises, and tests up to the judgment of the instructor.
- Avoid jargon. Say what you mean as clearly and concisely as possible. Remember Mark Twain's admonition never to use a paragraph if a word would do as well.

Contents

Elementary School Mathematics

I. BACKGROUND FOR THE PROSPECTIVE TEACHER

The student preparing to teach mathematics in tomorrow's elementary schools should be aware of the "state of the art" today. This includes some understanding of how contemporary programs have evolved in the recent past, current issues in the field, broad objectives of school mathematics, teaching principles which should be followed in teaching any topic, requirements for effective instruction, and classroom organization. Part I is an introduction to these important topics.

What mathematical topics do today's children need to learn? What are they capable of learning during the elementary school years? How should mathematics be presented to them? Such fundamental questions—and hypothesized answers—have perennially determined the content and methodology of elementary school mathematics programs. These and other questions were pursued widely and vigorously during the 1960s; the so-called "new math" or "modern math" movement which resulted has had a profound influence on current programs. In Chapter 1, then, that movement will be examined as a means of providing some perspective for the beginning teacher.

Why is mathematics taught in elementary schools? What are we trying to accomplish in the long run? What needs to be done in order to accomplish these objectives? The specific day-to-day decisions a teacher makes in the classroom are—or should be—influenced in part by his or her convictions about these broader questions. Chapter 2 examines some of those key issues about which teachers must make daily decisions and suggests some principles which the author believes should guide the everyday practices of the beginning (and the experienced) teacher.

What is the best setting for mathematical instruction? What materials are needed? How should the classroom be arranged? How should children be grouped and how should their instruction be presented? While it would be presumptuous to attempt definitive answers to these questions, Chapter 3 examines some of the options for the beginning teacher to consider, with special emphasis on the "math lab" concept and on the issue of individualized instruction.

The material in Part I, particularly in Chapters 2 and 3, should be viewed as largely suggestive rather than prescriptive. It is necessarily broad and general in nature and will become particularly meaningful if it is reexamined periodically as the reader considers the specific mathematical topics of Part II.

1. Perspectives

1. Forces Affecting the Mathematics Curriculum

Various authors have pointed out that the mathematics curriculum has rightfully reflected at least three basic considerations: the logical, structural nature of mathematics itself; theories of learning and the psychological nature of the children to be taught; and the needs and expectations of society. While each of these factors is important, there are always people who see one as more important than the others, so that the relative influence of each factor varies from time to time. One hundred and fifty years ago, for example, social utility seemed to dominate. In the relatively static society of that time, this emphasis was quite reasonable; one could predict with considerable certainty the kinds of mathematical needs and problems children would face as adults. In subsequent, rapidly changing times, however, the "mathematical future" has become increasingly clouded. We can safely conjecture, in fact, that today's children will need to solve mathematical problems as adults, which have not even been identified today. This realization is undoubtedly one reason why mathematical structure has recently received more emphasis than it did in the past; the argument is that if a person fully understands the basic underlying principles of a subject, he is more likely to succeed in applying those principles to solve new and unfamiliar problems.

Such a point of view seems sound. Yet the pendulum continues to swing, with questions being raised about the abilities of children to become "little mathematicians" capable of absorbing and comprehending generalizations that became synthesized in mature minds only after painful centuries of struggling. And the question of "relevance" persists: are sophisticated principles and structural basics really necessary—in fact, do they even help—in solving current problems?

In any event, it seems both fair to agree that contemporary mathematics programs are influenced by the same three forces, and logical to concur with those optimistic enough to foresee a healthy balance approaching among them.

3

2. The "New Math" of the 1960s

It is clear that the nature of today's elementary mathematics program has been influenced, more than anything else, by the reforms—some of them very sweeping—of the past decade. Let us try, then, to characterize that important era.

How Did Mathematics Programs Change in the 1960s?

In 1961, the National Council of Teachers of Mathematics published a document called *The Revolution in School Mathematics*, whose very title underscores the magnitude of the changes then emerging in the field. What were some of these revolutionary changes? One can classify them in two categories: Changes in mathematical content and changes in teaching methods. Two things should be kept in mind considering these changes: First, many of them would have been more properly labeled "evolutionary" than "revolutionary." They were by no means all new and dramatic. The phrase, "new math," which became commonplace, was a misleading one which people tended to apply to *all* changes then taking place in mathematics programs; thus, the term meant different things to different people. (Mathematics teachers are still occasionally asked, "Do you teach the New Math or the Old Math?" This writer's response would be "I don't know" [what *you* mean].) Second, not all the changes were found in *all* the new programs, i.e., there was not a universal, common "housecleaning"—some changes appeared here, others there, and so on. Some of the more common characteristics of several new programs of the 1960s follow.

Changes in Content

Many topics that had been studied in pre-1960 programs were now viewed as essentially nonmathematical, uninteresting to children, and unnecessary for them to learn in elementary or junior high school. Such "dead wood" as reading an electric meter and balancing the family budget was thrown out. Other topics, judged as being in need of reorganization but still worthy of study, were placed on a firmer mathematical basis. Still other topics were judged worthy of being added to the elementary curriculum, either to help accomplish the desired reorganization and mathematical beefing up or for their own sake; some were shifted from junior high and even high school programs to the elementary level.

Today's textbooks still reflect these changes. Children are now commonly introduced, at least intuitively, to the rudiments of algebra, geometry, set theory, logic, numeration systems (other than just the familiar Hindu-Arabic decimal system), exponents, number theory, graphing and coordinate systems, sequences, inequalities, probability, functions, and integers, to name a few. The extent to which such topics appear or are developed varies considerably, but their presence can be quickly verified by a cursory examination of the table of contents of nearly any elementary mathematics textbook on the market today.

Rarely, if ever, is the inclusion of such topics in the elementary curriculum intended to replace more formal study at the higher levels. Rather, a "spiral" approach is generally employed in curriculum planning: topics are introduced very intuitively at low grade levels, reintroduced more formally at middle grade levels, and presented still more formally in the higher grades.

Changes in Pedagogy

Perhaps the most basic characteristic of the "new math" programs was the emphasis on helping children understand the mathematical rationale behind the familiar computational processes. It is now generally considered as important to teach *why* we "bring down the 2" in a division problem, for example, as it is to know how to perform the computation. *Justification*, *proof*, and basic mathematical *axioms* have become new additions to the language of elementary school mathematics. It should be hastily pointed out, however, that the emphasis on explaining "why" is not intended to replace the teaching of "how." Children will always need to know how to compute skillfully.

A logical accompaniment to the trend emphasizing understanding was the trend toward increasing the use of manipulative devices in teaching. After all, elementary mathematical ideas generally are abstract descriptions of physical situations; it seems only reasonable that children should first encounter the ideas in a premathematical context using physical objects. This exposure naturally helps them to understand the related mathematical concepts later on.

Another significant trend emphasized in the teaching of elementary school mathematics during the 1960s was an increased use of instructional strategies, collectively known as "discovery teaching." Like "new math," this expression is perhaps unfortunate because it means quite different things to different people; in general, though, so-called discovery tactics are marked by the absence of initial "how-to" directions from the teacher when introducing a new skill or idea. A basic objective of the method is to provide children with suitable experiences aimed at leading them to discover—or at least conjecture—how to do it. In the next chapter, this concept will be discussed more thoroughly.

Finally, the language and vocabulary of elementary mathematics became more exact. Words and expressions which tended to be misleading, inadequate, or actually inaccurate were largely eliminated and replaced by more precise terms. This trend, like discovery, will be discussed in more detail in Chapter 2.

None of the aforementioned pedagogical innovations of the 1960s could truly be considered new—it is not difficult to trace each of them well back into the history of mathematics teaching. What *was* new in the 1960s, perhaps, was their simultaneous reemergence into the thoughts and actions of leaders and practitioners in the field. The final trend which we shall consider from this revolutionary era is also an old but rekindled notion: an increased concern and awareness with regard to individual differences among children and teachers. Teachers have long acknowledged the existence of extensive differences among children with respect to factors that can significantly affect learning. A long-standing pedagogical axiom has been that, since differences do exist, teachers should endeavor to identify them and give them appropriate consideration when working with individual learners. All too often, this ideal has received less than lip service in the teaching of mathematics. While elementary teachers long ago developed techniques of intraclass grouping in the teaching of reading (including "individualized" instruction), seldom did they consider comparable strategies for mathematical instruction. In the late 1960s and early 1970s, however, teachers began considering such strategies just as appropriate for teaching mathematics as for teaching reading. Efforts are now being made by individual teachers, by school systems, and by large research groups, to find ways to adjust the pace, level, sequence, or content of mathematical instruction to correspond more appropriately to individual children and their needs.

Similarly, individual differences among teachers are being more carefully considered. More and more efforts are being made to take advantage of particular skills, interests, and training among teachers. Key teachers with above average qualifications for teaching mathematics, for example, are being assigned more responsibility in that subject. Elementary schools are devising various forms of departmentalization, differentiated staffing, and team teaching as ways to make optimum use of staff members.

Why Did Mathematics Programs Change in the 1960s?

This question has no simple answer and, as with most revolutions, no real starting date can be identified. Several factors—some still present—can be cited as collective "causes" of this revolution. Many of the changes, both in content and pedagogy, simply evolved, as would be expected, out of combined experience, accumulated research, and collective scholarly thought and effort. But it was no doubt a unique blending of other factors with this otherwise ponderous process which (accidentally?) triggered the new math.

First, there really *is* a great deal of new math. People tend to view mathematics as a relatively static science, unlike say, atomic physics, where dramatic new discoveries are almost commonplace. But in fact, man's knowledge of mathematics has exploded recently in much the same way as his knowledge of other sciences. Several mathematical subjects have evolved in this century, notably topology, abstract algebra, and functional analysis. Methods in older mathematical subjects have furthermore become more sophisticated, and new applications are constantly being found for mathematics. Mathematicians, like medical doctors, must specialize and must constantly keep informed about new developments to avoid becoming outdated and uninformed. (It has been said that Euclid was the last man who was able to include in his writings all of the accumulated mathematical knowledge of his time.) Such rapid advancement at the "frontiers" of the subject inevitably affects what must be taught at the lower levels, even down to the elementary grades.

Moreover, the decade of the 1960s was a tense one politically. It was a highly competitive era, marked by massive power struggles among major nations. Success — even survival — in vital space and defense programs was seen to rest largely on superiority in mathematics and its applications. The advent of Russia's "Sputnik" aroused responsible leaders to a vital concern about the status of the mathematical education of our students, and massive efforts were made to evaluate, update, and strengthen mathematics programs at all levels. An extensive international study of mathematical achievement suggested that students from the United States ranked eleventh out of the twelve nations studied, plus they didn't *like* math as well as did students from other countries.

In 1963, a group of mathematicians and people in related fields met to consider the school mathematics situation. This first "Cambridge Conference" resulted in a report which, while widely and energetically debated, came to be extensively quoted as an ideal for remodeling school mathematics programs at all levels. The overall recommendation of the group was that the thirteen-year (K–12) school mathematics program should, in time, incorporate what was then — and essentially is now — equivalent to three years of top-level college mathematics. They submitted that this three-year gain could be accomplished by a total reorganization of the subject and virtual abandonment of the time-consuming classical drill for drill's sake, replacing it with drill in the context of learning new subject matter. The list of proposed new topics for the elementary school still causes many prospective elementary teachers to squirm!

Finally, the 1960s was an era of suddenly increased awareness of the need for higher levels of mathematical literacy as a requirement for intelligent citizenship. Many decisions which people generally make were coming to depend increasingly on an understanding of applied mathematics: television commercials contained rather subtle statistical "messages"; credit purchasing reached all-time highs; important political, social, and economic news became saturated with mathematical data, which people needed to interpret correctly in order to make vital decisions in our democratic society. While all of the mathematical competence for making these decisions cannot and should not be expected to be fully developed in the elementary school, certainly it begins there. Children today are very much aware, whether we like it or not, of some of the central problems of our time — drugs, international mistrust, the search for well-defined "morality"; ecology, crime, political credibility, and so on. Their information comes to them in largely mathematical terms and their important opinions — some of which will not change appreciably with time — are shaped largely by the depth of their mathematical understandings.

Who Determined What Changes Were to Be Made?

This question, too, has no simple answer; but it is frequently asked, and reasonably so. While in the final analysis, an accurate answer would consist of names of many *individuals*, it may be more instructive to identify the groups that have most influenced curricular changes. These would include mathematicians, the Federal government, educators, industry, publishers, and parents.

As a group, mathematicians previously tended to appear virtually unconcerned with school mathematics, and with elementary school mathematics in particular. However, in the 1960s there was evidence of a reversal of this tendency. Top level mathematicians became involved with planning, writing, and even teaching elementary school mathematics. The Mathematical Association of America (MAA) appointed a committee, The Committee on the Undergraduate Program in Mathematics (CUPM) which makes recommendations for the improvement of college and university mathematics curricula. The so-called "CUPM Level I" recommendations, for instance, concern the mathematical preparation of elementary school teachers, and have been a powerful influence in shaping college and university courses in the field. (The original CUPM Level I recommendations were revised early in the 1970s. The reader may be interested in comparing the two quite different sets of recommendations.)

The investment by the Federal government in education during the 1960s is well known. Government funds from the National Science Foundation (NSF), the United States Office of Education (USOE), and other divisions provided extensive support for meetings, workshops, research, teacher training, the writing of textbooks, and the dissemination of new curricula. Among the more notable examples of funding were the above mentioned Cambridge Conference of 1963 and CUPM, and the School Mathematics Study Group (SMSG), a large team of mathematicians, teachers, psychologists, and others who collectively wrote, and rewrote, exemplary mathematics textbooks for high school, junior high school, and elementary school.

The influence of mathematics educators on the emerging curriculum should go without saying. In particular, The National Council of Teachers of Mathematics (NCTM), through its newsletters, conventions, pamphlets, its two journals, *The Mathematics Teacher* and *The Arithmetic Teacher* (the latter is the only professional journal in this country devoted exclusively to the teaching of elementary school mathematics), and its many other publications, has had a profound influence on the daily professional practices of teachers all over the country. In addition, a number of universities have housed and supported major projects aimed at developing improved materials and strategies. Some of them still exist. Particularly notable programs, some oriented toward the high school but still influencing subsequent elementary projects, were developed at the Universities of Illinois, Maryland, Syracuse, Minnesota, and Wisconsin as well as at Boston College, Ball State Teachers College, and Stanford University. A few characteristics of these projects will be discussed in the next section.

The increased need for mathematically competent employees led industry to put pressure on the universities to modify their programs (with consequent pressure exerted on high schools, junior high schools, and finally elementary schools). Another kind of influence by industry was its own development of training materials and techniques, many of which found application in more academic settings. Much progress in programed instruction can be attributed to industrial development and support. Particular influence has been exerted, of course, by the industries using mathematics most directly — the space-related industries, communications, and computer-oriented fields, for example. One specific curricular topic that has emerged largely through the influence of the scientific and industrial community relates to measurement: teaching children to use those units of measure established by the International System of Units (SI). In this modernized version of the metric system, measures of length, for example, are expressed in meters or in decimal multiples and submultiples of the meter. This system will be discussed further in Chapter 8.

Daily teaching procedures of the typical teacher of elementary school mathematics are usually most directly affected by the basic textbook being used. This, of course, suggests that textbook publishers can exert much influence on school mathematics programs through their choice of what to put into their texts. Teachers are strongly led by the textbook to teach a particular topic in a particular way. Many school publishers provide not only textbooks but extensive teacher's guides, consultant services, in-service training programs, teaching aids, and supplementary publications.

A certain amount of influence (both positive and negative) on mathematics programs has been exerted by properly concerned parents. In particular when, in the 1960s, an ever-increasing percentage of youth were planning to attend college, parents demanded better school mathematics programs to enable their children to meet stiffer college entrance requirements. While individual parents usually do not influence the specific nature of curricular change in any major way, they do persistently motivate the schools to provide the best possible programs; collectively, of course, parents' voices create a greater impact.

In addition to the groups just described, it should be noted that other forces, agencies, and developments have influenced curricular changes in various ways. These would include, for example, the development of the uses for computers in teaching and the impact of testing agencies such as the College Entrance Examination Board.

Experimental Programs of the 1960s

As mentioned earlier, a number of experimental programs developed in the 1960s, each aimed at improving the materials and techniques for teaching mathematics. Programs directed, at least partially, at the elementary school level include the previously mentioned SMSG program, the Greater Cleveland Mathematics Program (GCMP), the Madison Project, the Minnesota Elementary Curriculum Project, the University of Illinois Arithmetic Project, and the Stanford Project(s). Detailed information on these programs can be found in Edwina Deans's *Elementary School Mathematics: New Directions.* Many of today's commercial texts are still patterned after the materials that evolved from these 1960 projects.

Most of the programs had several things in common. They frequently involved large teams of writers. The previously mentioned SMSG project, for example, included mathematicians, teachers and other educators, psychologists, representatives of government and industry, and others. The projects were usually funded quite adequately with grants from the government, private foundations, or other sources. This meant that, unlike many endeavors in education, excessive compromises in quality were not necessary because of lack of money. Most of the projects had dual objectives—to improve the textbooks mathematically and to seek improved pedagogical techniques so that, among other things, the attitudes of children toward the subject might improve. Extensive efforts were made by some projects to provide in-service training to help teachers preparing to use the unfamiliar project materials. Finally, most of the projects were genuinely exploratory and experimental in nature; materials frequently appeared first in mimeographed form for trial use, after which they were subjected to careful evaluation and subsequent revision by project staffs.

Although little conclusive research emanated from these so-called "experimental" projects, three claims were frequently reported: first, that the attitudes of children toward the new materials were generally favorable (in sharp contrast to past attitudes); second, that children were able to learn much more mathematics than had been thought possible, and that they could do so at an earlier age (consistent with opinions long held by many psychologists); third, that the emphasis of these materials on mathematical structure improved and economized instruction; in other words, that children learned more quickly and more thoroughly when new content was related to known content by reference to basic underlying principles.

3. Current Questions and Issues

So much for the past, particularly the immediate past. What are *today's* issues? Are there new ones? Do we still need to resolve old ones? What are the basic priorities of elementary mathematics teachers today? What major questions will you, as a teacher, be facing? What judgments will you be called upon to make?

We believe the fundamental issues today and for the immediate future relate primarily to the improvement of *teaching* rather than content. Should instruction be "individualized"? To what extent? In what manner? For whom? What should be the role of computers, programed instruction, and multimedia "systems"? What, if any, special teaching strategies are best for low achievers? Inner-city children? High achievers? What are the best ways to put teachers, materials, and children together? Should elementary teachers "specialize"? Is team teaching the answer? Teacher's aides? Is the "open" classroom the answer? Math labs? Behavioral objectives? Behavior modification? Prescriptions? Are the activities we have children engage in consistent with what is known about how they learn? What kinds of things really "turn kids on"?

On the other hand, some serious questions are being raised with regard to *content* as well as pedagogy. Does what we now teach children lead to global understanding or is the picture we give too fragmented and disjointed? Can they use the mathematics we teach them? Do they? Is it too formal? Too informal? Is there too little drill? Too much? What should be the role of geometry in the elementary school? Probability and statistics? Logic? Computers? Should mathematics and science be correlated or integrated? Is there convincing evidence that the money and effort expended for curricular innovations over the past several years is paying off in terms of learning?

There is enough debate going on over many of these issues to convince this writer that they will remain unresolved, in the sense of general consensus, for some time to come. Answers will only come slowly and gradually, from experience and from combined efforts of classroom teachers, mathematicians, psychologists, administrators — and the public. One should be suspicious of enthusiastically heralded panaceas that will allegedly solve all the problems, yet be open-minded enough to consider and try new ideas — even an occasional panacea.

Projects, Questions, and Suggested Activities

1. Report on the Brownell, Burns, and Junge articles (see Suggested Readings) — individually or collectively.
2. Look at a textbook series from the 1950s; compare and contrast it with a current series. This can be done in several ways — e.g., compare the

general nature of each series; compare topics covered; compare a particular grade level; compare the treatment of a single major topic, such as fractions or division.

3. Find out and report on some of the details of Husen's international achievement study (Suggested Readings). Besides the two-volume report itself, see also the March 1971 issue of *Journal for Research in Mathematics Education*; *New York Times*, March 12, 1967, p. E-11; or "The Price of Mathophobia," *Time*, March 17, 1967. Several other periodicals reported on the study at the time.

4. Debate some of the questions in the last section of the chapter. For example, you will probably have no difficulty finding a classmate who disagrees with you on one of the questions, "Should elementary teachers specialize?" or "Should instruction be individualized?"

5. Suppose you are a teacher. A confused parent comes to you and says, "I notice a lot of strange things in my child's math book. What's going on these days? Why is math so different from when I was a kid?" Answer him.

Suggested Readings

Adler, Irving. "The Cambridge Conference Report: Blueprint or Fantasy?" *The Arithmetic Teacher*, March 1966, pp. 179–86.

> Summary of the 1963 Cambridge Conference, together with some excellent suggestions for implementing their recommendations. Highly recommended.

Brownell, William A. "The Revolution in Arithmetic." *The Arithmetic Teacher*, February 1954, pp. 1–5.

> Identifies some basic changes in teaching arithmetic from 1900 to midcentury.

Burns, Paul C. "Development of Elementary School Mathematics Teaching in the United States." *The Arithmetic Teacher*, May 1970, pp. 428–34.

> Title is self-explanatory. Comprehensive. Emphasizes recurring issues since the midseventeenth century.

Cambridge Conference on School Mathematics. *Goals for School Mathematics: The Report of the Cambridge Conference on School Mathematics.* Boston: Houghton Mifflin, 1963.

> This is the complete report. Chapters 2, 3, and 5 are of particular interest to the elementary teacher.

Deans, Edwina. *Elementary School Mathematics: New Directions.* Washington: GPO, U.S. Department of Health, Education, and Welfare, 1963.

> A good summary of the "new math" programs of the 1960s as well as descriptions of experimental programs of the time.

Edwards, E. L., Jr.; Nichols, Eugene D.; and Sharpe, Glyn H. "Mathematical Competencies and Skills Essential for Enlightened Citizens." *The Arithmetic Teacher,* November 1972, pp. 601–7.

> A carefully thought out analysis, by an NCTM committee, of this important aspect of mathematics education.

Husen, Torsten, ed. *International Study of Achievement in Mathematics: A Comparison of Twelve Countries.* 2 vols. Stockholm: Almqvist and Witsell, 1967.

> Complete report of the international achievement study discussed in this chapter.

Inskeep, James E., Jr. "Building a Case for the Application of Piaget's Theory and Research in the Classroom." *The Arithmetic Teacher,* April 1972, pp. 255–60.

> Just what the title suggests. Should be read in conjunction with the articles by Weaver (pp. 263–70), Lovell (pp. 277–82), Sawada (pp. 293–98), and Rosskopf (pp. 309–14), in the same issue.

Junge, Charlotte W. "What's Old About the New Mathematics?" *The Arithmetic Teacher,* October 1970, pp. 475–81.

> Observes that many "modern" ideas and techniques have at least been *proposed* for a long time. Several quotes from textbooks of the 1800s. Clauson's article (pp. 461–72) in the same issue is related. Both recommended.

Major, John R. "Science and Mathematics: 1970's — A Decade of Change." *The Arithmetic Teacher,* April 1970, pp. 293–97.

> A case for the ultimate correlation of science and mathematics programs — and for introducing decimals before common fractions. In the same issue, Johnson and Cohen (pp. 305–10) give many examples of the fundamental concept of function.

National Council of Teachers of Mathematics. *The Revolution in School Mathematics.* Washington, D.C.: The Council, 1961.

> Well worth reading to identify the causes and nature of the "revolution."

Suydam, Marilyn N. "Teachers, Pupils, and Computer-Assisted Instruction." *The Arithmetic Teacher,* March 1969, pp. 173–76.

> An informative and concise introduction to the potential role of Computer Assisted Instruction in elementary classrooms. Related articles describing activities and some research results can be found in the same issue: McDermott (pp. 177–78) and Thompson (pp. 179–81) describe a few upper grade activities; Fejfar (pp. 184–88) discusses the computer's potential for providing individualized drill; Jerman and Suppes (pp. 193–97) describe one way the com-

puter can be used to individualize instruction. In another vein, Phillips (pp. 203–11) provides a serious and very thought-provoking essay on some of the critical issues in mathematics education today. Highly recommended reading.

Suydam, Marilyn N. "What's the Answer?" *The Arithmetic Teacher,* November 1971, pp. 439–41.

> Sound advice on viewing "panaceas." In the same issue, Cruikshank and deFlandre (pp. 443–47) present several sensible curriculum guidelines.

Van Engen, Henry. "The New Formalism." *The Arithmetic Teacher,* February 1971, pp. 69–70.

> A plea for paying less attention to mathematical formality and more attention to children.

Van Engen, Henry. "The Next Decade." *The Arithmetic Teacher,* December 1972, pp. 615–16.

> Views of a respected mathematics educator on major issues of the 1970s.

Van Engen, Henry. "Twentieth Century Mathematics for the Elementary School." *The Arithmetic Teacher,* March 1959, pp. 71–76.

> One of the early pleas for a "new math." Identifies many things which were inadequate about pre-1960 programs and makes some suggestions for change.

Walbesser, Henry H. "Behavioral Objectives, A Cause Célèbre." *The Arithmetic Teacher,* October 1972, pp. 418, 436–40.

> Should be read together with the companion article by Nichols (pp. 419, 474–76) for two divergent points of view on this issue.

2. Basic Principles

It would obviously be futile for anyone to attempt a comprehensive blueprint of "methods" for teaching elementary mathematics. There are, however, some basic principles that apply in teaching any topic at any grade level. We will attempt to identify such principles in the context of some key pedagogical issues such as drill, discovery, planning, and so on. But all teaching practices, and certainly the basic principles guiding such practices, must reflect, among other things, our underlying purposes for teaching mathematics.

1. Objectives of a Modern Elementary School Mathematics Program

Every successful teacher will acknowledge the positive relationship between careful planning and effective teaching. Careful planning, in turn, cannot be accomplished without considering one's aims or objectives. This applies whether we are planning for tomorrow's classes or for a whole curriculum. The former plan must, of course, be very specific and detailed, whereas the latter permits the inclusion of broader, more general, even "idealistic" statements. Success in teaching requires consideration of both kinds of objectives, but we will examine here only the broadest educational aims, those which each mathematics teacher probably needs to think about only intermittently, but then very carefully. They may be summed up as what we expect (or hope) each child will gain as a result of his total (K–12) mathematical experience. Each teacher should strive to contribute as much as possible toward the accomplishment of four basic aims.

Problem-Solving Proficiency

Many authorities would argue that the most important outcome of a mathematical education is the ability to solve problems. We generally think of a mathematical problem as a question, involving numbers or other mathematical concepts, that cannot be answered by simple recall or by simple application of a memorized algorithm. Solving a problem requires, among other things, the ability to decide what data is needed and what operation(s) can be used to answer the question. Thus an equation such as $3 + 2 = n$ is not generally thought of as a problem, since both data and operation are clearly specified. Most textbook "word problems" are artificial in the sense that they are hypothetical, intended only to teach certain patterns and basic procedures which can be applied to actual problems.

Many children who are apparently competent and skillful with computational procedures are nonetheless unable to solve "word problems." This all too common condition suggests at least two things—that those computational procedures were probably taught in a rote manner, without sufficient reference to the physical situations of which they are abstractions, and that children need to be *taught* how to solve problems, a difficult task which too many teachers do not even attempt (a child who encounters problem-solving difficulty is often simply told to "think harder").

Computational Proficiency

Certainly almost everyone would agree that a basic task of the elementary teacher is to develop children's skill (i.e., speed and accuracy) in computation. By the time a child has completed the sixth grade, we would like to assume that he can add, subtract, multiply, and divide any whole numbers or any fractional numbers, including those expressed as decimals. Furthermore, he should be able to unhesitatingly perform such "operations" as renaming numbers (e.g., "reducing" fractions, expressing fractions as decimals, "borrowing," "carrying," and so on).

Such computational skill necessarily involves rote memorization of at least two kinds—memorization of the 390 "fundamental facts" (see Chapter 5), and memorization of the basic *algorithms* or *approaches* to computation. Several things should be emphasized with regard to this objective. First, memorization should ultimately be as *absolute* as possible. A child should not need to waste his time by "figuring out" that 7×9 is 63. The association between 7×9 and 63 should be as automatic to the child as the association of a good clarinet player between a printed note and the correct fingering of it on his instrument. The association should not call for any thinking; in fact, to the extent that a child must *think* about the product of 7 and 9 (or the clarinet player, how to play a B flat), just that much will he be slowed down and frustrated. This objective should not be confused with the means of achieving it. Memorization of the fact, $7 \times 9 = 63$ should *follow* understanding of *why* 7×9 and 63 name the same number. Rote memorization as a teaching procedure has long been deemed both inefficient and ineffective. Finally, in the case of the algorithms, there is probably no "best" way to compute. There are, for example, at least four effective techniques being taught for subtraction and at least two common ways to divide. The "best" method is usually that which the child was initially taught, although some teachers still insist on forcing children to follow "their way."

Understanding Basic Mathematical Concepts

As already emphasized, mere memorization of facts and procedures, devoid of understanding, is neither efficient nor effective. Each mathematical idea presented to children should be related to other concepts they already have; if this is done, mathematics will be a cohesive, related, sensible collection of ideas rather than a fragmented, disjointed jumble. Although children should be *able* to rely on their memories for performing many of the routine activities of mathematics, they should never *need* to do so without other recourse. It is necessary to know *why* 7×9 is 63 if memorization of that fact is to make sense.

The understandings we usually hope children will acquire include continually deeper comprehension of (1) the structural properties (closure, commutativity, identities, and so on) of the various number systems; (2) relationships and patterns between related mathematical ideas, such as the inverse relationship between addition and subtraction; (3) the distinctions between and the relationships connecting physical entities or situations and their abstract mathematical counterparts; (4) both the powers and limitations of mathematics; and (5) "correct" (conventional) use of the basic language and symbolism of mathematics.

"Positive" Attitudes Toward Mathematics

In teaching mathematics, we usually aspire to develop certain "positive" attitudes, including these:

Open-mindedness. While there is certainly a strong need for children to categorize newly encountered concepts, relating them to previously encountered ones, there is too often a tendency to overformalize this by emphasizing formulas and "trick" phrases. It would be far better to lead children to approach new problems and new ideas in as flexible a way as possible, with open minds, willing both to accept new ideas and to modify existing ones. This is often a very difficult attitude to develop, particularly for teachers who themselves are "set in their ways" mathematically, but it is one which is nonetheless worthy of aspiration.

Curiosity. Mathematics abounds in curios: strange and intriguing patterns (and near-patterns), unsolved problems, paradoxes, historical tidbits, puzzles, and the like. Exposure to such curios cannot help but generate curiosity and lead children to experience at least some measure of the aesthetic pleasures of mathematics. Children are said to be "naturally curious," and this is no doubt at least partially true, but teachers should strive to encourage and extend this natural curiosity and certainly avoid stifling it.

Self-confidence. Children should never be intimidated by mathematics (though this frequently seems to happen). Rather, they should develop confidence in their ability to solve new problems or to recall forgotten facts; such confidence is dependent upon in-depth understanding of basic concepts, of course.

Finally, we should consider the attitude that "mathematics is fun." Attempting to develop such an attitude in children is subject to some question. Mathematics really *isn't* "fun" to most people. It's usually hard work, satisfying, hopefully, with a sufficient investment of effort, but not "fun." Rather than trying to develop the attitude that "mathematics is fun," we should strive for the healthier and more realistic attitude that "mathematics is rewarding." There should, of course, be times for fun in every mathematics classroom, and we certainly want to prevent negative feelings, but mathematics time should normally be regarded as a time to work, not to play. A skillful teacher can make this work pleasant, satisfying—and sometimes "fun."

2. Key Pedagogical Issues and Principles

Effective teaching of elementary school mathematics can be described quite well by identifying a surprisingly small number of the everyday practices of good teachers. It will be convenient to discuss these "principles of good teaching" in the context of eight key issues of concern to teachers of mathematics: structure; levels of understanding; readiness and motivation; drill and practice; discovery; language; problem solving; and planning.

Structure

What is meant by the expression "structure" (or "mathematical structure"), so frequently heard in discussions involving mathematics or the teaching of mathematics? Any attempt to precisely define "structure" would inevitably lead to at least some disagreement. In general, the term is used to designate continually recurring concepts that provide the framework around which a mathematical subject is developed. In this sense, new or unfamiliar concepts are explained and absorbed into the structure by relating them to existing structural concepts. What are these fundamental structural concepts? Again, not everyone would agree on any given list; but at least insofar as elementary school mathematics is concerned, it should include the ideas of set, number, equivalence, function, operation, identity, and inverse, as well as those ideas that can be expressed as patterns and occur in many contexts, i.e., commutativity, associativity, and distributivity. Consider the significance of commutativity, for example. There is an obvious conceptual relationship between the notions that the union of two sets is unaffected by order and that the sum or product of any two natural numbers is similarly unaffected; or that this pattern occurs also with whole numbers, integers, rational numbers, and (beyond elementary school) the real and complex numbers. Such patterns as commutativity can generate productive intellectual stimulation even in their absence—it is as instructive to note that subtraction and division are *not* commutative in these number systems as it is to observe that their inverse operations, addition and multiplication, *are* (or that the difference or quotient of two numbers *is* affected in a very systematic way when order is reversed, i.e., that $a - b$ is the additive inverse of $b - a$, if both exist, and that $a \div b$ and $b \div a$, when both exist, are multiplicative inverses of each other).

Mathematically, one encounters such structural concepts continually in the study of any number system. Why, though, are they important in teaching? Two pedagogical hypotheses, not unrelated, are commonly advanced. The first of these is that learning is accomplished most effectively, thoroughly, and permanently when emphasis is put on relationships that exist between a new idea and previously learned ideas. The second is that emphasis on such structural principles enhances the ability of the learner to apply, transfer, or extend what has been learned to new and unfamiliar situations. These hypotheses are widely accepted. If they are indeed valid, then they suggest the following basic teaching principles.

Structural Properties Should Be Taught

Children should be taught that addition of whole numbers is commutative, for example. Whether a child can verbally describe the property or identify it by name is of no particular consequence, particularly at lower grade levels. He should, however, come to know the property and to recognize particular instances of it. This can be accomplished in many ways. For example, drill and practice can be so designed that structural properties are likely to become apparent. This will alert children to be on the lookout for patterns and shortcuts. After many specific instances of one or more properties have been encountered in this way, the children can be asked to examine patterns, make hypotheses, and express each property in general terms.

Structural Properties Should Be Used

Children should be encouraged to think about new topics in terms of previously learned topics and their properties. As an example, when introducing division of fractional numbers, one can help children to understand the ideas involved by having them first recall such basic ideas as the relationships between multiplication and division (of whole numbers); relationships between division and subtraction; the effect of dividing a nonzero number by itself or one. Structural properties can be used whenever there is occasion to teach, review, or justify any of the standard computational algorithms.

Levels of Understanding

A child's understanding of any mathematical idea (e.g., the commutative property of addition) can range from ignorance of it to relatively complete mastery of it. Between those two extremes is a hierarchy of "levels of understanding" which might include (in approximately this order) having a vague awareness of it, being able to recognize specific instances of it, being able to describe it in terms of specific numbers, being able to express it in relatively abstract terms, and being able to apply it in unfamiliar situations. Presumably, understanding of an idea normally evolves in order through each of the several levels of understanding.

This suggests that children will learn mathematical ideas best when those ideas are first introduced in very real, very concrete, specific, and understandable situations; such situations can be expected to generate lower order levels of understanding. Higher levels of understanding should logically evolve later, through increasingly abstract experiences. Thus, *teachers should generally introduce a concept by providing for concrete, manipulative experiences, followed by a sequence of successively less concrete, more abstract experiences.* For example, in teaching an addition fact, such as $2 + 3 = 5$, children might first be shown the results of uniting two sets, such as a set of two children and a set of three children (the sets being chosen to be disjoint, of course). As the children observe that the result is a set of five children, they are *beginning* to learn the desired fact. Other manipulative devices should be used at this time: blocks, toy money, poker chips, pencils, etc. Later, at a slightly higher, semiconcrete level, the teacher might direct attention toward pictures of sets; at a still higher, semiabstract, level, nonrepresentational pictures (e.g., tally marks, geometric shapes, etc.) might be used to show the fact. Finally, children will learn, at the abstract level, that "two plus three equals five," and will learn the associated symbolism "$2 + 3 = 5$."

While it may be acknowledged that teachers should generally proceed gradually in this manner from concrete to semiconcrete to semiabstract experiences, it should be pointed out that there are considerable differences among children with respect to the amount and level of concrete experience they need prior to handling an idea at a higher level of abstraction. Deciding when to shift from one level to another is both difficult and crucial—shifting too fast or too slow can result in confusion, boredom, frustration, or rebellion.

Readiness and Motivation

The expressions "readiness" and "motivation" are used extensively in educational circles to identify two related ideas. *Readiness* generally refers to a student's condition with respect to whatever prerequisites are deemed necessary for a specified learning. *Motivation* refers to the desire of a student to learn and can be regarded as a part of readiness. We will therefore discuss these two ideas together.

Whether a student is ready to learn a given mathematical topic (assuming that he has matured sufficiently in the cognitive sense) probably depends more than anything else on how well he has mastered the mathematical prerequisites of that topic. The subject matter of elementary mathematics is commonly regarded as a collection of neatly and logically ordered topics, and "learning mathematics" is thought of as mastering each topic in its turn. While this is certainly an oversimplification, it has some basis in fact and it provides a convenient way to think of "readiness." That is, for a given mathematical topic, we can normally identify other mathematical topics that a student should have already mastered to a reasonable extent (complete mastery is rarely a realistic expectation). It is widely believed that the extent of a child's subject-matter readiness to learn a topic will affect the intensity of his effort in the learning situation, how thoroughly he learns it, his retention of it, and his ability to "transfer" it to new situations. Ignoring subject-matter readiness is likely to lead to short-lived understanding at best.

The motivational aspect of readiness is also an important prerequisite to effective learning. The desire to learn is commonly described as being either intrinsic or extrinsic, the former referring to those desires generated by the learner himself to satisfy some internal need; the latter referring to desires resulting from external pressure of some sort. Both kinds of motivation can be equally wholesome and effective, and both can be directly influenced by the actions of teachers; but research suggests that, from the learning point of view, intrinsic motivation is generally preferable.

When proper consideration has been given to a student's subject-matter readiness to learn a given topic, the likelihood of his being successful at that learning is enhanced. Success, in turn, is likely to help develop his self-confidence and his enjoyment of mathematics. On the other hand, excessive failure, which is an almost certain consequence of neglecting readiness, usually leads to negative attitudes, especially lack of confidence.

A number of teaching practices should be self-evident from the preceding remarks. For example:

Before teaching a new topic, analyze that topic in terms of prerequisite subject matter. Give students a diagnostic pretest covering that material, and provide remedial help for those who are not ready for the new work.

Such tests can frequently be short, informal, oral tests, or can even be part of an achievement test from a preceding topic.

Give careful consideration to children's interests. While current interests of children cannot be used as a basis for what to teach in general, a skillful teacher can tell when to capitalize on them. When a child really wants to know about a topic, he is ready from the motivational point of view. If he is also ready mathematically, it can be quite appropriate for the teacher to depart from whatever else may have been planned.

Teachers can arouse student interest in a number of ways: Interest, curiosity, and enthusiasm are contagious, so a teacher's own attitudes toward mathematics (whether positive or negative) are often picked up by children. A teacher who is genuinely interested in mathematics usually transmits this to students. It should be pointed out, however, that artificial "interest" is usually obvious to children. It is particularly important that introductory lessons on a given topic be as interesting, challenging, and well-organized as the teacher can make them. Initial excitement and enthusiasm often help children get through subsequent hard work, whereas a dull start is frequently very difficult to overcome. We have already mentioned that mathematics abounds in intriguing patterns and curios, many of which can be readily understood by children. Frequent use of these fascinating devices can be very helpful in motivating children to want to learn more about mathematics in general.

Drill and Practice

The importance of computational proficiency and the need for rote memorization of certain facts and processes go undisputed. Certainly proficiency and, particularly, memorization can come only after considerable practice. This is the basic role of drill in elementary mathematics. Realizing the role of drill in the development of proficiency, educators at one time reasoned, in effect, that drill should be the essence of teaching. Unfortunately, drill as a teaching method proved to be ineffective on many counts: it is time-consuming, it does little to assure understanding and transfer, and it can lead to very negative attitudes toward mathematics on the part of justifiably bored students. Perhaps in overreaction to the above, drill was then frequently ignored in favor of understanding; i.e., the prevailing attitude came to be that if students sufficiently understand a process, proficiency will automatically follow. This, too, has proven to be an inadequate philosophy, generally leading to poorly developed skills. Drill seems to be a necessary, but not sufficient, component of effective teaching.

Our past mistakes, recent research evidence, and serious professional judgment suggest a new role for drill in today's elementary mathematics programs. In order that drill be effective in terms of its purpose, that it be efficient in terms of time and energy expended by teachers and students, and that it not lead to negative attitudes, the following guidelines are proposed.

Understanding Should Precede Drill

Drill should not be used to teach an idea. It should be used as a means of reinforcing ideas that are already understood. This is in sharp contrast to the philosophy that understanding will be an automatic result of drill. Drill will, of course, increase the level of understanding in most cases, but at least a reasonable level of understanding should come first.

Drill on a given topic should be spread over a long period of time, occurring in *brief* but *frequently held* sessions. This takes into account both the apparent advantages of the spiral approach to teaching and the motivational disadvantages of lengthy repetitive drill.

Drill Should Be Done in the Context of Learning Something New

One of the major recommendations contained in the report of the 1961 Cambridge Conference on School Mathematics was that drill for drill's sake should be virtually abandoned, since there is always the opportunity to provide abundant drill in the context of doing exploratory exercises designed to teach a new concept. Consider, for example, the multiplication and division practice a child can obtain as he learns to determine whether given numbers are prime or composite; the addition practice involved in filling in rows of Pascal's triangle; the practice in multiplication and subtraction involved in an ordinary division example; or the practice in whole number multiplication involved in multiplying or dividing fractional numbers. There can be little doubt that if drill for drill's sake were to be replaced by carefully designed teaching exercises, there would be time to teach considerably more subject matter without sacrificing the development of computational proficiency. It should be kept in mind, on the other hand, that exploratory exercises lose their significance if the student has to concentrate so heavily on the mechanical aspects of computation that he has little mental energy left over to see (or even to look for) the new idea.

Drill Should Be Varied

If the recommendation of the preceding paragraph is followed, this will certainly be the case, for children would encounter multiplication practice, for example, in many contexts. Mathematical games are also a good way of providing variety in drill. Although games designed to provide drill should be fun because part of their purpose is motivational, there are other criteria to consider. A game should, for example, involve each individual. Types of Bingo games are good in this respect. "Spelling bee" games, by contrast, tend to involve only one child at a time; in a class of thirty children, each child may be inactive and nonparticipating for up to twenty-nine-thirtieths of the time! Also, a game should be carefully analyzed to verify that it in fact provides effective drill on the needed skills.

Drill Should Be Accurate

The results of a child's efforts should be checked as soon as possible and he should know immediately (when possible) whether he is on the right track or whether he needs help. Too often children work a large number of drill exercises repeating a single error over and over again on each example. The absurdity of this is compounded when the teacher does not check the work (or delays doing so), or does not analyze the error, or does not prescribe remedial action. One simple way to prevent such waste is to check each child's work on the first problem or two of each type to be assigned before he is allowed to continue.

Drill Should Make Sense to the Child

He should be helped to see and to accept the need for practice, and he should have evidence that it is "paying off." Simple record-keeping schemes can be devised to keep the child informed of his own progress. For example, a child may take timed fundamental facts tests each day for several weeks, recording the number of correct responses he makes each day. In most cases, some progress is inevitable, and evidence of that progress can do much to bolster the child's confidence in himself and to increase his determination to succeed.

Discovery

The widely used expression "discovery teaching" is interpreted in different ways to different people, and like many new labels in education, has probably been subjected to both unwarranted praise and unwarranted criticism. We will briefly examine here a rather general description of discovery teaching, consider some of its advantages and limitations, and examine some commonly used procedures.

Mathematics instruction of the past frequently began with the teacher's explanation of rules for solving a particular type of problem, with emphasis on "how to do it," followed by plenty of drill. Some people call this "tell-do" teaching. Most people regard discovery teaching as the antithesis of tell-do teaching. That is, in discovery teaching, initial explanations by the teacher are deliberately avoided. Instead, the teacher attempts to lead the child, in various ways, to investigate his own methods, to formulate his own rules and generalizations, and to find his own solutions. Before outlining more specifically what is involved in this approach, it should be pointed out that discovery teaching does *not* mean turning children loose to let them drift aimlessly about in the naive hope that they may "discover" something by some lucky accident. Unfortunately, the word "discovery" has this connotation to some critics who no doubt think of it in the context of the discovery of gold or comets!

While a number of different strategies have been classified as "discovery," in general, discovery teaching follows a definite sequence.

A Problem Is Identified

The problem, which should be very clearly understood by the learner, may be simply to find a specific instance of a generalization he understands. For example, once a child comprehends a general approach for finding the sum of two whole numbers, then to find the sum of two specific numbers could be a simple discovery exercise. More commonly, discovery tactics are used to solve what might be called "basic" problems ("How can we find the product of two fractional numbers?") or "intermediate" problems designed to lead to (or obviate) the solution of basic problems ("How can we find the area of a rectangular region whose sides are measured with fractional numbers?"). Still another type of question that lends itself to discovery is a less general one of an inductive nature which although it could be solved by "awkwardness and brute force," virtually begs to be solved by finding and using a short-cut pattern or generalization ("What is the sum of the first 100 natural numbers?"). In any event, the teacher makes certain that the child understands what his problem is. (The teacher's purpose may well be a more subtle, higher level one than the specific task proposed, but nonetheless, the child must know what is expected of him.) The child must also understand any related conditions (e.g., the meanings of "fractional number," "area," "natural number," or "rectangular region"), and must have a reasonable grasp of all prerequisite skills.

A Solution Is Sought

Much variation can be found here, depending on such things as the nature of the problem and the sophistication of the child, but there are three particularly common approaches to problem solving via discovery. The simplest of these merely involves manipulation of suitable objects according to an understood generalization. For example, assuming that a child has at least a working concept of the array model for multiplication of whole numbers, he can attempt to find the product of, say, 7 and 9 by constructing a 7-by-9 array and by then determining the number of elements it contains.

For some problems, a hit-and-miss approach of simply groping for a solution is appropriate. While this may sound haphazard and disorganized (and *can* be!), a skillful teacher can lead children gradually to refine their guessing techniques and to employ more and more sophisticated, logical, deductive methods. In any event, at this step, the child is looking for an answer—the teacher is not giving it to him.

The approach that most nearly characterizes what most people think of as discovery teaching, however, is what is sometimes called an "inductive" approach (not to be confused with "mathematical induction," which is a specific method of proof). The stated problem (it must be a certain *kind* of problem) can first be reduced to a sequence of simpler, but clearly related, problems, each of which can be solved by "brute force." These solutions are examined in search of patterns that may suggest a solution of the broader problem. To illustrate this approach, consider the previously mentioned problem of finding the sum of the first 100 natural numbers. A teacher might first suggest that the child find the sum of the first two natural numbers, then find the sum of the first three, then the first four, and so on. It is usually helpful to systematically record or display (e.g., on a chalkboard) these first results as they are obtained in order to reveal any relationships or patterns suggesting a solution of the main problem. A table such as the following, for example, might be displayed:

Numbers	How Many Numbers?	Sum
1,2	2	3
1,2,3	3	6
1,2,3,4	4	10
1,2,3,4,5	5	15
1,2,3,4,5,6	6	21

The teacher frequently needs to provide clues, ask leading questions, or rearrange the data in order to help the child to arrive at at least a hunch. (It is assumed, of course, that the teacher knows a way to solve the problem.)

A Tentative Solution Is Reached

Again, many variations appear at this step but the important thing is that the solution or hypothesis (often only a hunch) is the child's, not the teacher's. Furthermore, the teacher usually plays a skeptical, "show me" attitude, neither supporting nor rejecting the child's tentative "discovery." The child is generally not expected to precisely verbalize any generalizations he may reach (there exists significant empirical evidence that verbalization can do more harm than good in terms of learning).

The Hypothesis Is Checked

An important component of discovery teaching is encouraging children to question what they believe to be solutions to problems. They need to learn that three possibilities exist: their solution may be correct, in which case they should try to verify it; it may be partially correct and need to be modified; or it may be completely wrong and need to be rejected. With older children and with certain problems, proposed solutions may lead to generalizations that can be stated as proposed theorems to be proven.

Some of the strongest arguments frequently given in support of teaching by discovery are that a child is likely to remember longer, understand more thoroughly, and use more effectively that which he discovers for himself; that the strategies a child learns to use in such a process (i.e., experimentation, conjecturing, testing, weighing evidence, searching for patterns), are in themselves desirable outcomes of a mathematical education; that the process is inherently active and participatory, which is a trait usually deemed effective in teaching; and that discovery situations tend to be intriguing to children, and thus enhance motivation.

There are limitations to discovery teaching, as well as advantages. For one thing, it requires a great deal of careful planning on the part of the teacher to structure situations in such a way that the child is led to make discoveries. It can also be very time-consuming in the execution as well as in the planning stages, and requires careful supervision by the teacher (a child could easily "discover" that $8 \times 3 = 25$ through an error in manipulation!). Discovery is largely an individual, personal phenomenon, rather than a group one; and it is therefore difficult for a teacher in a conventional classroom setting to direct and pace discovery activities in such a way that they will be optimally effective for all students. (Structuring the situation in which children are expected to seek a discovery is sometimes best accomplished in a group, since one child's remarks, efforts, and questions can benefit and stimulate others. Nonetheless, the very critical time at which the discovery is reached is very much an individual thing.) Finally, discovery teaching is not necessarily the most appropriate strategy for all topics nor for all children. Teachers should choose pedagogical techniques on the basis of their suitability for the topic being taught and should vary their approaches in the interest of maintaining children's interest.

The above discussion suggests these pedagogical principles: *Children should normally be led to make their own mathematical discoveries, rather than be told "how to."* However, this principle should be followed only insofar as it is reasonable and efficient to do so in terms of the children and the mathematical task at hand. Teachers must make the critical decision when to use discovery tactics and when to use others. *Discovery situations must be carefully structured. Teachers can help stimulate children to make their own discoveries by providing appropriate problems, clues, and manipulative materials at strategic times.* Again, critical decisions must be made by the teacher. It should be clear that effective discovery teaching requires skills that can only be developed through practice and experience. At this time, the reader may wish to consider some of the problems in Appendix A to get a better feeling for the strategies suggested above. Problems 5, 13, 14, 15, and 21 are particularly appropriate.)

Language

In a previous section, it was pointed out that one pedagogical trend in "the new math" is toward more precise language. We will now examine some examples of this trend and suggest some principles for teachers to follow.

Consider the verbalization so frequently associated with division. For example, $2\overline{)8}$ is often read "2 goes into 8" or "How many times does 2 go into 8?" or "How many 2s are there in 8?" Such phrases no doubt grew out of efforts to help children associate a certain kind of physical problem situation with division. That kind of situation, technically called "measurement," is exemplified by the following problem: "If 8 children are to form teams of 2 each, how many teams can be formed?" For such measurement situations, expressions like "How many 2s are in 8?" seem quite reasonable. There are three objections to this kind of language, however: first, it can contribute to the confusion which children so often develop between *sets* and *numbers*. It makes some sense to ask "How many subsets of 2 each are there in a set of 8?" (tacitly assuming that a *partition* of the set is meant; that is, a set of 8 is entirely separated, in one of several ways, into mutually disjoint subsets of 2 each). But one *number* cannot be contained in another. To be precise, then, there are *no* "2s in 8." Even if this technical error were deemed insignificant, as it is by many, a second objection is that if children associate division with "How many 2s are there in 8?" they will likely have some difficulty associating division with the second, more subtle, kind of problem situation, called "partition," which is exemplified by this problem: "If 8 children are to form 2 matching teams, how many will be on each team?" We certainly want to teach children to associate such a problem with division, but the problem does not suggest answering the question, "How many subsets of 2 each are there in a set of 8?" (or "How many 2s in 8?") This language, then, is a potential obstruction to teaching the partition concept. A third objection to the "2 goes into 8" sort of language is that children who habitually use such language frequently have difficulty extending the division concept to include problems where the divisor is greater than the dividend. Consider, for example, $2 \div 8$ (i.e., $8\overline{)2}$, or 2/8). Children who reason — correctly — that "there are *no* 8s in 2" or "8 won't go into 2" find it difficult to accept the fact that such problems can be solved at all.

All three of the above difficulties can be easily avoided by simply using more abstract language. The expression "8 divided by 2" is neutral in terms of physical interpretations; it suggests neither the measurement nor the partition situation per se. If children are to associate several kinds of physical situations with a given mathematical operation, it is more reasonable to use language which, by virtue of its abstractness, is flexible, not suggesting any single interpretation to the exclusion of others.

A common expression associated with subtraction can be challenged on similar grounds, i.e., that it suggests only one particular physical interpretation and thus can lead to restricted understanding. We frequently hear $7 - 3$ expressed as "7 take away 3." To recognize a limitation of this expression, consider this problem: "Johnny has 7 marbles and Sam has 3; how many more marbles does Johnny have than Sam?" We want children to associate this "comparison" situation with subtraction, but if they have earlier learned to express subtraction in take-away terms, they could have difficulty. Again, the more abstract "7 subtract 3" or "7 minus 3" has no such physical connotation.

There are many other expressions in traditional arithmetic which, taken literally (as children tend to), suggest inadequate or misleading interpretations of the concepts to which they refer. Consider, for example, "reduce," "invert," "cancel," "bring down the 2," "borrow," "carry," and "*of* means multiply," to name a few. These can easily be replaced by more accurate—if less colorful—expressions.

There is a trend toward simplifying the language of arithmetic and toward using expressions that emphasize relationships. For example, consider this pair of related facts:

$$\begin{array}{cc} 2 & 5 \\ \underline{+3} & \underline{-3} \\ \triangle & \square \end{array}$$

In the subtraction problem, 5 is sometimes referred to as a sum, 3 as a *known addend,* and $\square$ as a missing addend. This choice of vocabulary not only reduces the number of words to be learned (5, 3 and $\square$ have traditionally been called *minuend, subtrahend,* and *difference,* respectively), but more important, it emphasizes the inverse relationship between addition and subtraction. For the same reason, "dividend," "divisor," and "quotient" are sometimes replaced by "product," "known factor," and "missing factor," respectively, to stress the relationships between multiplication and division.

Finally, while teachers are being encouraged to use language carefully and accurately, it must be kept in mind that the purpose of language is communication. If precision of language leads to the breakdown of communication, then it does little good. The age and background of children should obviously be given careful consideration in choosing vocabulary to use with them.

Problem Solving

Inasmuch as one major aim, if not the major aim, of any school mathematics program is the development of problem-solving proficiency, we will consider it in some detail: what is meant by "problem solving," its

role in the elementary school mathematics program, some common difficulties encountered by children, and some suggestions for the teacher.

There are many interpretations of what a "problem" is in mathematics, but to most mathematics teachers, a problem ("word problem" or
"verbal problem" is some sort of a question, accompanied by sufficient
quantitative data for the capable student to use in answering the question.
The problem generally boils down to deciding what to do with the data, i.e.,
choosing the appropriate operation or operations for obtaining an answer.
This is the major distinction between a problem and a computational
example, equation, or inequality.

Many kinds of problems can be used in the mathematics class.
Problems may be *real*, in that they involve actual questions and data, or
they may be *hypothetical*, such as those in a textbook (textbook problems
may be realistic, but they are not real); they may be oral or written; they
may involve a single computation or several; they may involve computation
with specific data ("What is the area of a square whose sides measure 78
inches each?") or they may deal with generalizations ("What happens to the
area of a square if the lengths of its sides are doubled?"). There are "typed"
problems such as time-rate-distance problems; there are collections of
problems where the solution of one is used as data for a subsequent one;
there are problems whose solutions are not even known ("Are there infinitely many prime twins?"); there are problems that require the student
to find his own data or to ignore some of the given data.

Again, many regard problem solving as the essence of a good
mathematics program, the highest level of quantitative thinking. What is
its role in the elementary school mathematics program? Probably the most
important function of problem solving is to introduce new processes or
concepts. Working with word problems gives meaning to new ideas and
helps children to associate concrete situations with their abstract mathematical counterparts. Problem solving is often used continuously during
the development of a process or concept to further illustrate the main ideas
and to broaden the students' understanding. Moreover, problems are used
to stimulate children's imagination, to develop their reasoning skills, and
to lend variety to drill.

Many children, even those who may be quite skillful at computation,
have difficulty with problem solving. Such children juggle numbers, take
wild guesses, perform wrong operations, or simply give up when confronted
with problems. There are, of course, many factors which can account for
this. One of the major sources of difficulty is some kind of reading disability,
such as reading too rapidly for the material, misinterpreting punctuation or
technical terms, lack of attention to detail, or low comprehension in general.
Other common causes of problem-solving difficulty include lack of computational skill, lack of experience with situations described in the problem,
and failure to associate mathematical operations with physical situations.

The emphasis so often put on speed and "getting the answer" in mathematics no doubt causes some children to work too quickly when they should instead reflect carefully about the structure of a problem situation.

There are many things a teacher can do to improve the problem-solving skills of students:

1. Introduce new operations, skills, algorithms, or concepts in problem settings. It is important to use a variety of problems and to use realistic problems, so that children learn to associate physical situations with the corresponding mathematics.

2. Teach children to write equations corresponding to problems. For example, given the problem, "If Mary has $3.00, how much more does she need to buy a $4.98 toy?" the equation $3.00 + \triangle = 4.98$, expresses the sense of the problem, i.e., that an unknown amount, $\triangle$, when added to 3.00 will give the desired amount, 4.98. The student will need to learn separately, of course, that his equation is equivalent to (has the same solution set as) the equation, $\triangle = 4.98 - 3.00$, or to the computational form,

$$\begin{array}{r} 4.98 \\ -3.00 \\ \hline \end{array}$$

3. Reduce, insofar as possible, the stumbling block of difficult language. When constructing problems, try to keep the language consistent with the children's ability. When helping children to interpret textbook problems, it is often helpful to substitute given words, such as names of places or people, with familiar ones, or to replace lengthy phrases with more succinct ones.

4. Encourage children to routinely ask themselves such things as, What is the question I need to answer? What information is given? Can the question be answered directly from that information or are there intermediate questions to be answered? Does the problem sound like others I have solved? How would I solve it if the numbers were different? (Often a child can see a solution if the numbers are rounded or if smaller ones are substituted.) Is the solution I have found reasonable? No single set of questions will work for all problems, nor will be necessary for all problems; but this kind of reflective thinking is generally helpful.

5. Avoid the use of cue words or phrases (e.g., "*of* means multiply") insofar as possible. Such phrases are generally inadequate, unreliable, and often lead to mechanical, unthinking habits. Similarly, when making up problems, avoid excessive use of any single phrase such as "How many were left?" Children need to learn to cope with questions phrased in various ways.

6. Except to illustrate different applications of a given operation, problems should normally not be referred to as for example, "subtraction problems." To do so destroys the essence of what the child needs to learn to do—i.e., decide which method(s) or operation(s) to use. Similarly, a set of problems should generally be mixed as to type, method, operations involved, and so on.

7. Problems should, as a rule, be as realistic as possible and consistent with situations familiar to the children.

8. Sketching a simple picture or making a chart or table from the data frequently helps children to understand relationships and find methods of solution.

Planning Daily Lessons

That effective teaching requires careful planning at all levels has already been noted. We have, in fact, already compiled some basic aims suitable for guiding long-range planning in elementary mathematics instruction.

There is no standard optimum format for planning daily lessons, however. Individual preferences, administrative requirements, and differences in basic classroom organization account, in part, for the wide variety of formats in common use. Regardless of the format used, however, the four fundamentals discussed below must be considered for any mathematics lesson, at any grade level. It is unnecessary to write them all down as part of each lesson plan, but none should be ignored.

Objectives

Lesson objectives should be stated as realistically and specifically as possible. The now popular expression "behavioral objective" refers to the specific performance(s) expected of the learner, including the exact criteria for measuring whether the objective is fulfilled and the conditions under which this measurement is to be obtained. Objectives stated in such specific, performance-oriented terms contribute to an efficient, effective lesson plan, whereas objectives stated in more vague or general terms can lead to less efficient use of time.

Procedures

Certainly an indispensable component of any daily plan is the formulation of what is actually to be done—by both teacher and students—to accomplish the stated objectives. The *first* step in a lesson is important because a well-planned, impressive, dramatic start can offset even an otherwise mediocre lesson; whereas a dull start is difficult to compensate for, regardless of what follows. The pace of the lesson should be varied as necessary to be consistent with the age and maturity of the children. Younger, less mature children require more varied, rapidly changing activities than older, more mature ones. It is a good idea to plan the amount of time (number of minutes) to be devoted to each activity in the lesson. The teacher should normally read what he will expect the students to read and work each example he will ask them to work. While this is time consuming and not *always* necessary or feasible, it can significantly increase the teacher's insight into potential student difficulties and errors. It is also essential to plan for *all* of the students, i.e., to consider any special difficulties the slower children are likely to face and any special activities the faster ones can undertake. Finally, today's lesson plan should relate to both yesterday's and tomorrow's plan, as much as reasonably possible, to provide continuity. All these procedural considerations obviously require maximum understanding of both the students and the subject matter.

Materials

Visual aids, manipulative devices, textbook pages, or other instructional materials should be carefully specified in the plan. Particularly with young students, it is necessary to consider such seemingly trivial matters as where materials are stored, how they will be distributed, and how they will be put away, since even minor inefficiency in these tasks can divert children and throw off the timing of an otherwise well-paced lesson.

Evaluation

Some provision should generally be made for determining the extent to which lesson objectives have been satisfied. This component of the plan may include consideration of drill and practice or testing activities, and any special provisions for giving students speedy feedback to their responses.

The role of the textbook teacher's guide should be noted here. Most elementary school textbooks are accompanied by teacher's guides providing detailed suggestions relevant to lesson objectives, procedures, materials, and evaluation. Most beginning teachers — and wise experienced teachers — make extensive use of these guides for lesson ideas. When in doubt, doing as the teacher's guide suggests is probably "right."

On the other hand, a sensitive teacher with even a little experience quickly learns when to depart from any plan. Reactions from students tell the teacher when to speed up, slow down, omit, supplement, or drastically alter a lesson plan. Such decisions have to be made quickly yet carefully, because too little attention to students' reactions can result in an uninteresting, ineffective lesson, while too much adjustment frequently leads to aimless, unproductive activity.

Finally, when planning a lesson, careful attention should be given to mathematical accuracy and continuity, always keeping in mind the maturity of the children: the appropriate degree of rigor, the level of abstractness, and the extent of mastery to be expected should be determined carefully in advance.

Projects, Questions, and Suggested Activities

1. Suppose you are a teacher beginning a new school year. Make a list of New Year's Resolutions—things you are going to vow to do (or not do) as a teacher, insofar as mathematics is concerned. Think big. Be idealistic.

2. Outline a plan for a discovery lesson. List some hints you might provide, or show a way to display children's findings as they work on the problem. Some suggested topics:
   a. Is 12734169824737 a square number?
   b. What is the sum of the first 100 multiples of 3 (0, 3, 6, 9, . . .)?
   c. How many segments are determined by 278 distinct points on a circle?
   d. How can we find the area of a right triangle? A parallelogram?

3. Contrast Ausubel's and Hendrix's viewpoints on discovery teaching.

4. Suppose you needed to determine whether a child was ready to learn the idea of carrying in addition, i.e., to solve problems such as $28 + 57 = \triangle$. What would you do?

5. In your opinion, what is the *most* important reason for teaching mathematics in the elementary school? Defend your position.

Suggested Readings

Adler, Irving. "The Cambridge Conference Report: Blueprint or Fantasy?" *The Arithmetic Teacher*, March 1966, pp. 179–86.

   Pages 185–86 contain some sound teaching principles.

Ausubel, David P. "Some Psychological and Educational Limitations of Learning by Discovery." *The Arithmetic Teacher*, May 1964, pp. 290–302.

   A very comprehensive and thought-provoking article on the topic. Read the Hendrix article (cited below) first.

Bidwell, James K. "Learning Structures for Arithmetic." *The Arithmetic Teacher*, April 1969, pp. 263–68.

   Summarizes the theories and research of several widely accepted authorities (e.g., Gates, Gagné, Bruner, and Piaget) on the questions of readiness and levels of understanding.

Biggs, Edith F., and Hartung, Maurice L. "What's *Your* Position on the Role of Experience in the Learning of Mathematics?" *The Arithmetic Teacher*, May 1971, pp. 278–95.

> Two widely respected authorities discuss this question (separately); many examples to clarify the meanings of "discovery teaching" and "activity," and the need for keeping mathematical objectives in mind. Both articles highly recommended. (See also a response from Rappaport, October 1971, pp. 419–20, with a reference to Weaver, April 1971, pp. 263–64.)

Bompart, Bill. "Teaching Concepts Incorrectly." *The Arithmetic Teacher*, February 1972, pp. 137–39.

> On the importance of precision in language.

Cochran, Beryl S.; Barson, Alan; and Davis, Robert B. "Child-Created Mathematics." *The Arithmetic Teacher*, March 1970, pp. 211–15.

> Two definitions of discovery; in the same issue. Bradfield (pp. 239–42) gives nine examples to show that problem solving can be *funny.*

Davis, Robert B. *A Modern Mathematics Program as It Pertains to the Interrelationship of Mathematical Content, Teaching Methods, and Classroom Atmosphere (The Madison Project).* U.S. Department of Health, Education, and Welfare, Project No. D-233, Contract No. OE-6-10-183, pp. 4–45.

> Describes the philosophy of the Madison Project (that mathematics is a process) and gives many examples. Many principles of teaching are included.

Grossman, Anne S. "Mid-Nineteenth Century Methods for the 1970's." *The Arithmetic Teacher*, April 1971, pp. 230–33.

> Suggestions for putting problem-solving and manipulative aids in their respective places. In the same issue, Weaver (pp. 263–64) provides a word of caution about the potential abuse of mathematical curios.

Henderson, George L., and Van Beck, Mary. "Mathematics Educators Must Help Face the Environmental Pollution Challenge." *The Arithmetic Teacher*, November 1970, pp. 557–61.

> Includes examples of real problems which can be presented in the classroom.

Hendrix, Gertrude. "Learning by Discovery." *The Mathematics Teacher*, May 1961, pp. 290–99.

> A description of the process by one of its ardent proponents.

Johnson, David R. "If I Could Only Make a Decree." *The Arithmetic Teacher*, March 1971, pp. 147–49.

> On the fine art of asking questions. Worth reading.

Jones, Phillip S. "Discovery Teaching—From Socrates to Modernity." *The Arithmetic Teacher*, October 1970, pp. 503–10.

> The title is self-explanatory. A thorough and informative summary.

Maertens, Norbert, and Schminke, Clarence. "Teaching—For What?" *The Arithmetic Teacher*, November 1971, pp. 449–56.

> A careful discussion of four levels of learning, and suggestions for testing each of them.

O'Daffer, Phares G. "On Improving One's Ability to Help Children Learn Mathematics." *The Arithmetic Teacher*, November 1972, pp. 519–26.

> Good basic advice for the beginning teacher. The ABC's of teaching: Knowing children, knowing mathematics, and knowing how to involve children with mathematics. Specific examples.

Reys, Robert E. "Considerations for Teachers Using Manipulative Materials." *The Arithmetic Teacher,* December 1971, pp. 551–58.

> A very thorough and important discussion of manipulative materials. Highly recommended.

Reys, Robert E. "Mathematics, Multiple Embodiment, and Elementary Teachers." *The Arithmetic Teacher*, October 1972, pp. 489–93.

> Describes the idea of "multiple embodiment"—using a variety of physical materials to represent a mathematical idea. Points out the need for research on this concept.

Swart, William L. "Number Please." *The Arithmetic Teacher*, May 1970, pp. 441–42.

> A plea for common sense in precision of language.

Trueblood, Cecil R. "Promoting Problem-Solving Skills Through Nonverbal Problems." *The Arithmetic Teacher*, January 1969, pp. 7–9.

> An interesting way to help children solve word problems—eliminate the words! Many other helpful suggestions on this topic can be found in this issue, ranging from theoretical and research-oriented discussions to ideas for teaching problem solving to slow learners; nine helpful articles in all.

3. Instructional Settings

Excellent teaching occurs daily in many contexts: in inner-city schools, suburban schools, and rural schools; in schools old and new; with bright children and slow ones; in poorly endowed schools and well-equipped ones; by generalist teachers in self-contained classrooms and specialists in team-teaching situations; with and without teacher aides; in graded and ungraded schools; before large instruction groups and small and in individualized instruction; with heterogeneous and homogeneous grouping. The beginning teacher needs to recognize that no single factor such as location, a certain grouping procedure, a classroom design, or a *modus operandi* for utilizing teachers guarantees excellent instruction—poor teaching occurs daily in many contexts, too! There are, however, certain conditions in the instructional setting which can be expected to optimize the effectiveness of instruction; teachers should be aware of these conditions and should attempt to provide them regardless of the particular setting. There are also various ways of grouping children for instruction, each of which manifests specific advantages and limitations. In this chapter we will examine both of these aspects of the instructional setting.

1. Requirements for Effective Instruction

There is no blueprint for excellence in teaching. Good teachers can solve or circumvent the problems imposed by limited facilities, inadequate space, meager supplies, administrative restrictions, or "problem" children, while less capable teachers may flounder under the most ideal circumstances. But there are a number of conditions which teachers and administrators should strive to establish in order to maximize the chances that children will enjoy and profit from their mathematical education. These conditions reflect contemporary thinking about how mathematics should be taught.

The Open Classroom and the Mathematics Laboratory

More and more educators are subscribing to an instructional philosophy that has been labeled "the open classroom" method. Closely akin to this in the teaching of mathematics is the "mathematics laboratory" method. Such labels are generally misleading since they not only tend to suggest essentially standardized, well-defined techniques for teaching but also frequently lead to unwarranted and unfortunate emotional reactions, from both overzealous advocates and skeptics. (Enthusiasts and critics are often equally uninformed — or misinformed.) Nonetheless, beginning teachers should be aware of the basic concepts underlying these movements and should recognize the potential advantages and limitations of their essential features.

Both "open classroom" and "mathematics laboratory" suggest certain physical attributes of the classroom or instructional setting, but the essence of each is philosophical rather than physical. The cornerstones of this philosophy, none of them new, bear repeating briefly here.

1. Children learn by doing. The Nuffield Mathematics Project in England underscores this old but frequently ignored adage by recalling an ancient Chinese proverb.

> I hear, and I forget
> I see, and I remember
> I do, and I understand

2. Children gradually arrive at mathematical generalizations by solving many and varied problems.
3. Children learn to solve many problems by manipulating suitable materials.
4. Discovery by oneself of an idea, however crudely and imperfectly it may be verbalized (if at all) is more useful, permanent, and relevant than inheriting it intact.
5. Numerous physical instances of mathematical abstractions can be found not only inside the classroom but also in the other (and much wider) areas of the environment, e.g., at home, outdoors, and in the rest of the community.
6. Learning requires freedom to move about, to try out ideas independently, to make mistakes without fear of reprimand, all in the confidence that help and guidance are available nearby.
7. Freedom to learn requires the child to assume responsibility for his activities, i.e., to schedule his own time (in part, at least), to record and evaluate his progress, and to pace his work (again with the security of adult guidance).
8. Learning is an individual phenomenon, and although it frequently is stimulated or reinforced in group settings, the optimum pace, level of

abstraction, materials, amount of practice, and approach vary widely from child to child.

9. Children are most creative and persistent in their efforts when learning tasks are pleasing to them, genuinely interesting, and initiated by them rather than imposed and entirely directed by others.

It is the aim of the open classroom and the mathematics laboratory approaches to implement these essential conditions. The ways of doing so are many and varied. The degrees of success or failure hinge largely on the teacher's mathematical and pedagogical skill; patience; willingness to work hard; and skill in leading, guiding, reassuring, and when necessary, firmly but patiently controlling children. These skills are more critical in the relatively free atmosphere of this type of teaching than in the authoritarian, teacher-dominated classroom of the past, for without them, student activities can become chaotic, aimless, disruptive, and totally unproductive.

Many strategies such as the following are employed in this approach to teaching mathematics:

1. A group is introduced to a new idea by the teacher, and activities aimed at developing the idea further are suggested or required.
2. A group identifies a problem, e.g., through a discussion or as a result of some activity; and the teacher assigns or suggests activities leading to further understanding.
3. Individually, the children select "activity cards," either in a prescribed sequence or according to their interests. Each card describes an activity to be followed, raises leading questions, suggests records to be kept, etc.
4. Children work in flexible groups of twos or threes on a problem of mutual interest, following either activity cards or the teacher's suggestions.
5. Enrichment or extra-credit activities are available, to be done on a voluntary basis, according to interest, as supplements to routine class assignments.
6. Activities are available to help slower children master necessary prerequisites to routine class assignments.
7. Children work in relatively permanent small groups, independently of other children in the class, on a sequence of activities prescribed by the teacher.
8. Each child works individually through a sequence of activities prescribed by the teacher at regular intervals (e.g., day-to-day or week-to-week) on the basis of individual performance, ability, and interest.

Teachers striving to establish strategies of this kind for the first time should keep several things in mind. Chief among them is the necessity for careful and detailed planning, carried out over a sufficiently long period of time to permit objective consideration of potential problems. In addition, school administrators, children, parents, and fellow teachers should be consulted and informed; rarely can significantly new programs succeed without certain mutual agreements. Then too, new approaches are best introduced gradually, perhaps with small groups of children or for short periods of time, expanding only when both teacher and children are ready to do so. Also, much can be gained by studying and gleaning from the efforts of others (and there is abundant opportunity to do so in the literature), but rarely can one teacher successfully emulate another's model in toto, without some modifications. Lastly, the inevitable problems of beginning a new approach should be faced objectively and patiently as they arise, and modifications made as necessary.

In the next section, we consider some of the physical conditions which are helpful in implementing this "open" or "laboratory" approach to teaching.

Physical Requirements

Mathematics is no longer regarded as a subject which can best be mastered while seated in the second desk of the fourth row, watching a teacher perform at the chalkboard or working an endless collection of paper-and-pencil problems from a textbook (quietly!). Learning mathematics today requires more space than it used to, and it requires different kinds of space. First, there should be space for doing physically active and potentially noisy things: working with manipulative materials such as Cuisenaire rods and Dienes blocks, measuring, constructing, experimenting, and using audio-visual devices individually or in groups. Another kind of space is needed for discussions and demonstrations. Much effective instruction requires that students assemble, generally with a teacher, to discuss a new idea, explore a problem, study an expository display at the chalkboard or projection screen, and so on. The main requirement here is comfortable seating and good visibility. Also, children need space for individual work — desks or carrels with easy access to books, paper, pencils, and other necessary supplies, and with maximum opportunity for privacy.

Perhaps the best solution to these distinct space requirements, particularly in the traditional classroom (designed for about thirty children), is reached through the organization of time as well as space. That is, certain times may be scheduled for activities that can be expected to cause interference, while other times are set aside for discussions, and still others for quiet study. This kind of scheduling requires that children be able to move to an area of the room for discussion, either taking their chairs or sitting on the floor (this arrangement tends to be more conducive to discussion and to preventing distractions from the treasures frequently hidden in one's desk). For independent work, desks arranged around the periphery of the room or in clusters with cardboard dividers will increase privacy, reducing unwanted interaction, while opening up the classroom for the more vigorous activities of "noisy" time. Room dividers, doubling as bulletin boards, can mark off distinct areas of the room.

Larger classrooms designed for about 60, 90, or 120 children, without major partitions, lend themselves to the simultaneous occurrence of several varied activities. Designated areas may be more permanently established for specific activities, thus avoiding the necessity of moving chairs or other furniture. Some classrooms of this sort are adjoined by small, totally soundproof rooms for particularly noisy or distracting activity. Even so, teachers need to consider the potential distractions that can accompany several divergent activities occurring under the same roof.

Every classroom, small or large, has a few basic requirements. Regardless of the activity, adequate lighting and visibility are essential. There is, for example, nothing more futile than an otherwise well-organized demonstration or presentation which some children cannot see because they are sitting too far away or have too many heads in front of theirs or there is a glare from improper lighting or the seating arrangement interferes.

Adequate storage space for equipment, materials, and supplies is indispensable. Shelves, drawers, and cabinets need to be kept clearly labeled, uncluttered, and easily accessible both for removal and return of materials. Many commercial materials are packaged so compactly that teachers need to repackage them in order to facilitate easy access and return by children. Otherwise, much valuable time can be wasted. Most contemporary programs require a variety of books, activity cards, and other materials which are best stored on shelves the children can easily see and reach. Each child should have some private space available for his on-going projects, preferably both a small, permanent locker and some more expansive, temporarily shared, drawer or shelf space as needed.

Every effort should be made to provide for soundproofing. While this is largely beyond the control of individual teachers, acoustical tile, drapes, and carpeting all help to curb distracting noise. Headsets for individual use of tape recorders or projectors, and felt or scrap carpeting on table surfaces where noisy materials such as wooden blocks are to be used are examples of ways to minimize noise.

Consideration should be given, insofar as possible, to the types of desks and other furniture in the classroom. Desks serve not only as units for individual study and use of manipulative materials but, combined in twos, fours, or sixes, they form conference or activity tables. Flat surfaces, therefore, are preferable to slanted ones, and rectangular or trapezoidal shapes are best. Chairs should be separate from desks for maximum flexibility. If possible, classrooms should contain separate work tables so that individual desks need not serve this dual purpose. In fact, children should have access (not necessarily within the classroom) to tables at which they can *stand* to work rather than sit (as some of their fathers do in their basement or garage workshops).

Finally, the room should lend itself to easy housekeeping. This is accomplished in part by adequate storage (and firm agreements about its use), but can be helped also by convenient sinks, smooth work surfaces that clean easily, and floor surfaces that resist the inevitable wear and tear of active children.

The second major aspect of the instructional setting involves procedures for grouping children. Here, again, much variation can be found reflecting each teacher's particular philosophy and teaching style. In this section we will briefly review the rationale and common procedures for schoolwide grouping policies and then examine the three major procedures for within-class grouping and teaching.

Schoolwide Grouping Policies

For reasons of economic feasibility, tradition, and experience, school administrators usually apportion children to teachers in a ratio of about thirty-to-one. When financially possible, most systems try to reduce this ratio. In the interest of efficiency and effectiveness, two major factors are considered in making these assignments: *similarities* among children and *differences* among them. A tacit but questionable assumption is that children of about the same age are likely to be essentially similar with respect to variables that affect learning. Accordingly, children are routinely classified and assigned to "grades." In efforts to overcome some of the inevitable drawbacks of this procedure, educators have, here and there, modified this basic pattern, but it still prevails generally. Another more plausible assumption is that within any so assigned collection of about thirty children, there will be significant individual differences with respect to presumed learning variables: I.Q., previous academic achievement, maturity, aptitude, work habits, socioeconomic background, and so on. Accordingly, when the number of children of a given age/grade level in a school or school system is large, i.e., some multiple of thirty, consideration is given to these factors in making the assignments. Variations on two basic policies can be found, both with inherent advantages and limitations: (1) Random, and therefore heterogeneous, assignment, which leaves teachers with the responsibility to provide for individual differences. (2) Homogeneous assignment, generally based on relative homogeneity with respect to I.Q. and/or achievement. In the latter, the teacher still must provide for other differences and for finer differences within the I.Q. or achievement variables.

A currently popular variation of the two above-mentioned policies is to assign two, three, or four sections to a "pod" type of classroom and to a team of two, three, or four teachers who collectively assume responsibility for grouping and teaching the children.

Within-Class Grouping and Instructional Procedures

No matter how children may be grouped on a schoolwide basis, the teacher cannot ignore the existence of significant individual differences among them and the importance of those differences in the learning process. The skillful teacher both capitalizes on children's differences and compensates for them. There are many ways of doing both, and because of the wide range of individual differences among *teachers*, we find varying emphasis placed on the two.

Some teachers, in their efforts to *compensate* for individual differences of children, attempt to refine any homogenization of the class by some form of within-class grouping. This reflects the assumption that the more nearly the *effective* pupil-teacher ratio (the ratio of "significantly different" pupils to teachers) approaches 1-to-1, the more likely it is that instruction can attain its maximum potential effectiveness. The most common means of accomplishing this are to partition the class into two or three groups for most instruction, and to individualize instruction. The latter implies an *actual* 1-1 pupil-teacher ratio insofar as instruction is concerned and is regarded by many as the obvious epitome of the above assumption. Other teachers, attempting to *capitalize* on children's differences, generally prefer total-class instruction, without grouping. Still others combine these methods at different times depending upon the circumstances of the moment.

Excellent teaching can, of course, occur with *any* of these approaches. Some teachers excel in total-class instruction; others are most effective with small groups. Each teacher should know the merits and potential drawbacks of various grouping procedures and should be given the freedom to choose his own modus operandi, whatever it may be and however he chooses to modify it from time to time. The drawbacks of any one procedure can usually be overcome by the ingenious, industrious, and conscientious teacher.

As we go on to consider each of these grouping procedures and some relevant teaching strategies, it should be emphasized again that much variation exists, and that many teachers combine procedures from time to time.

Total-Class Instruction

Total-class instruction means that all children in a class do essentially the same thing at the same time. New material is presented to the entire class, manipulative and drill activities occur at the same time for all children, and so on. This type of organization is useful as a general routine, particularly with relatively homogeneous groups. It is also useful, when other grouping procedures (small groups or individualized instruction) are normally followed, for introducing new concepts, watching a film, discussing problems, or in discovery work where much student interaction is desired.

When total-class instruction is used routinely, specific procedures vary with the type of lesson being taught. Textbook teacher's guides provide ample guidance for the beginning teacher and need not be elaborately repeated here. One type of lesson, as an example, might begin with the teacher posing a problem or reviewing previous work, followed by students' exploration—via manipulative materials or discussion—of content leading to a new generalization or extension of previous concepts, and ending with a time for drill, practice, or enrichment. The latter can vary from child to child.

Total-class instruction is generally to be recommended for beginning teachers. It helps them learn how children react to various kinds of activities, how to pace instruction, how to present introductory work (and how to reteach it later), and how much drill and practice are appropriate. All of this can best be learned from experience with a variety of children. Total-class instruction has other advantages, even for more experienced teachers. It is easier, for example, for the teacher to develop one basic lesson plan per day than two, three, or more, so in effect more planning time can be devoted to the subject. It is also easier and quicker, when checking and recording children's work, to have one set of answers and one place to record them. This provides extra time for item analysis and can help the teacher identify common misunderstandings, leading perhaps to reasonable adjustments in the next day's plan. Children benefit from the comments, questions, and reactions of others; and often children in large groups pursuing a common problem find approaches and solutions that are far more ingenious and much richer than the teacher had planned or expected. Total-class instruction is basically "democratic" in that it doesn't underscore sometimes embarrassing differences in ability, as is occasionally the case with ability grouping. There is usually sufficient time provided during a class period for teachers to work individually with children and answer their questions. Children's questions during this period are usually lesson-related, which makes them easier to answer and provides the teacher with valuable feedback on the quality of teaching.

There are, of course, potential drawbacks in total-class instruction. Variations in ability and readiness frequently make it difficult to pace instruction effectively for all children, to give suitable assignments, or to establish an appropriate level of abstraction. Slower children tend to be continually pushed while faster ones are held back or bored by repetition. This is particularly true when the class is relatively large or heterogeneous. It sometimes happens that a small number of children dominate the large-group situation by responding more quickly or more frequently. This can fool the inexperienced teacher into thinking that an idea is (or is not) understood by *most* of the children. It also prevents those who may react more slowly from having an opportunity to contribute. One real limitation is that more of each kind of manipulative material is required at a given time for total-class use than for individual or small-group use.

Small-Group Instruction

As an organizational procedure, small-group instruction incorporates many of the advantages of total-class instruction but circumvents some of its disadvantages. Before considering these we will first examine its nature.

Teachers who prefer to work with fewer than thirty children at a time or who note that wide variations in children's abilities, backgrounds, or other factors impede the effectiveness of instruction, sometimes find it advantageous to partition the class into smaller, generally more homogeneous groups. Usually the number of such groups ranges from two to four, and the make-up of the groups is kept flexible, as are the bases for grouping. Some common grouping criteria, aside from subject matter, include achievement rates; abilities, such as the ability to read or to work independently; interest; sex; friendships; and random assignment simply to reduce numbers.

Once the groupings are established, the teacher normally works with one group at a time, while the other groups do something else. Alternately, different assignments are given simultaneously to all groups, and the teacher's time is divided among them on the basis of individual or group needs. Specific teaching procedures are otherwise essentially the same for this approach as for total-class instruction.

Small-group instruction usually has several advantages over total-class instruction. It reduces the pupil-teacher ratio at any given time so that children have more opportunity to participate, ask questions, and receive attention, while the teacher, in turn, has a better opportunity to receive feedback from them. The amount of time a teacher spends with each particular group can vary according to group needs. And since, normally, the groups are relatively homogeneous in some significant respect, it is possible to plan more appropriate instruction. Different groups can pursue different topics or a different sequence of topics, or they can study the same topics at different levels or different rates. Thus alternate textbooks or other materials can be used for different groups; and, because smaller quantities of materials are required, the teacher can provide a wider variety on a given budget.

Small-group instruction is generally recommended only for teachers with some experience, since it requires skills and poses problems less likely to occur with total-class instruction: Some children are not happy with the group to which they are assigned, for various reasons. This is particularly delicate when ability or achievement grouping is employed and some children must inevitably belong to the slower groups. Teachers are rarely insensitive enough to label the groups so bluntly, but no matter what labels are used, children are very perceptive of their assigned status, and this awareness can be psychologically unfortunate for some children. Whenever such groupings are determined, there are borderline decisions to make and these can easily be made incorrectly. Another problem is that the need for multiple class preparations increases the necessary amount of planning time and can therefore decrease its potential effectiveness, while the increased number of teacher presentations can severely limit the time available for helping individuals. If a teacher plans to work with three groups in a 45-minute period of time, then the 15-minute average amount of time he can devote to each allows for relatively little personal interaction with those who may need his help. Finally, if a teacher is working with ten children, some of the twenty others who are independently occupied may encounter difficulties with their work (or their self-control) which can lead to disruptive or at least unproductive class periods. Planning and executing lessons that avoid this contingency requires skill, ingenuity, and usually some experience.

Individualized Instruction

Individualized instruction is certainly the most complex and demanding approach to within-class grouping, and while it has perhaps more theoretical advantages than the other methods in terms of providing for individual differences in children, it undoubtedly has more potential drawbacks.

Basically, the ideal of individualized instruction is to provide educational experiences on a completely tutorial, one-to-one basis. The mathematical content, methods, pacing, choice of materials and activities, record-keeping, amount and kind of drill, level of abstraction — in short, all aspects of the instruction each child receives — are tailor-made according to his unique ability, achievement, interests, and other individual characteristics. Rarely has this ideal been challenged; still more rarely, if ever, has it been fully realized.

Since, for all practical purposes, the concept of individualized instruction is relatively new (actually, it can be traced quite far back in the history of education), its meaning has never approached the degree of standardization that can be associated with the concepts of total-class instruction or small-group instruction. Since it means different things to different people, it is frequently subjected to the same kinds of simultaneous hypercriticism and naive support as concepts like "discovery teaching" and "open classroom." So before we can reasonably consider its advantages and limitations, we should first provide at least one working definition of the idea. In the broadest sense, any instructional situation in which there is communication on a one-to-one basis between teacher and student for the purpose of teaching might be called "individualized instruction": a teacher helping a student solve a problem, a student reading and responding to instructions written by a teacher he may not even know (via a conventional text or programed text), tutoring, a student listening to or watching an instructional audio or video tape, all fall into this general category. But this interpretation is too general to be useful. In the following paragraphs, *individualized instruction* is considered to mean *any established classroom routine in which* basic instruction *is normally presented on a one-to-one basis. Basic instruction* means *that portion of the total program intended to introduce or further develop fundamental concepts and skills*, e.g., the concept of "fraction" or the skill of long division. Basic instruction is thus distinct from, but clearly related to, other *supportive* aspects of instruction, such as drill, testing, enrichment, and remediation. These supportive components must also be built into an individualized program, of course, but its essence is basic instruction.

According to our definition, then, individualized instruction neither means providing occasional enrichment or remedial work nor helping individual children when the basic instruction has been presented in a conventional group context. Individualized instruction is characterized by some built-in provision to vary one or more key aspects of instruction, e.g., pace, level of abstraction, or sequence, according to the individual characteristics of students. If, for example, two students differ in reading ability, then to the extent that basic instruction in mathematics involves the ability to read, a program appropriate for one child might differ from that for the other in this respect. This could be accomplished by preparing instructional materials for a given topic in different forms, each differing in reading difficulty. Or suppose two students differ in how much time they need to grasp a particular topic; then an individualized program might include a provision to vary the amount of time the two students would be expected to spend on that topic. Numerous other possibilities will occur to the reader.

To accumulate the necessary materials for a functional individualized instruction program in mathematics and to establish working procedures to accompany those materials is a formidable task. A few organizations with large staffs have undertaken it and have developed materials and methods already tried out in some schools. Several colleges and school districts have begun experimental projects, again with many people collaborating. Materials are available commercially to individualize drill (but not instruction). Some of the key ideas of the larger efforts have been incorporated or modified in programs developed by individual school staffs, and by a few individual teachers; but, again, the problems involved in originating such a new approach justifiably deter most teachers. The best way to begin such efforts, if at all, is very gradually and after a great deal of consideration, consultation, and preparation.

Any acceptable individualized program for teaching mathematics should satisfy all the criteria for any sound mathematics program; that is, each child should have ample opportunity within the program to approach the limit of his intellectual capacity; the results of the program should include both the understanding of concepts and proficiency with skills; the program should lead children to make their own discoveries of important results insofar as possible; new concepts or skills should not be introduced until all prerequisite skills and concepts have been sufficiently mastered; understanding of any skill should precede drill on it; suitable use of manipulative materials should be included in basic instruction; the program should be logically cohesive, both within and between grades; each child should be kept aware of the status of his progress in general and should receive reasonably rapid feedback on his achievement in specific activities; the teacher should be constantly aware of each child's progress, both in general and in his daily activities; children should find the program satisfying and enjoyable; and children should have sufficient opportunity to interact with each other and with the teacher.

Some of these requirements pose serious problems and raise significant questions to be considered in the development of individualized instruction programs. One such question is, What aspects of the program should be individualized? Certainly it is unrealistic for a teacher to completely design a unique program for each of thirty children. The most common solution is to individualize a single component, and usually the pace of instruction is easiest to vary, keeping other components essentially fixed. That is, each child works through a common sequence of activities, but at a rate that is best for him, independent of the rates of his peers.

If only the pace is to vary, how should the content and sequence be specified? Probably the most realistic way to answer this is to carefully select a single textbook and use it as a guide. The decision as to what should be included at a given grade level, how to develop it, and in what sequence it should occur is best left to the authors of children's texts. On the other hand, the teacher is the only one in a position to determine how quickly a given child can cover the material, when he is ready to begin it, and when he is ready to continue. Typically, individualized programs begin by carefully specifying a definite sequence of assignments, activities, or tasks, based on the contents of a text, for the entire year's work. These are sometimes phrased in terms of *objectives* which specify what student responses are expected in order to assure reasonable mastery of the tasks. (Not all anticipated outcomes of a child's mathematical education can be phrased in this way, of course.) In some programs, children are given a sequential list of assignments covering as much as the entire year's basic work; in others, teachers *prescribe* work on a short-term basis for each child, sometimes varying the assignments from child to child. Such an arrangement could be described as "fixed-content/flexible-pace."

Assuming a relatively fixed-content/flexible-pace arrangement, what happens to the child who either finishes the prescribed year's work early or fails to complete it at all? This has no easy answer. Perhaps the only solution is to have an entire curriculum specified in the above manner, so that these children can pick up next year wherever they may have left off this year. This, of course, requires tremendous schoolwide coordination and planning. Sometimes faster children are given extensive enrichment or in-depth assignments toward the end of the year. This latter practice should be viewed with caution; if one truly subscribes to the philosophy that a child should progress at his own pace, it would seem more reasonable to let him do so. Enrichment should be provided for all children, throughout the year, not as a device to kill time in May and June.

How should basic instruction be implemented and how can a child get help when he needs it? This poses perhaps the most critical challenge to those who decide to individualize instruction. Obviously the teacher cannot personally tutor each child on a one-to-one basis. Furthermore, the majority of textbooks are written to be used with a group of children led by a teacher, not to be studied independently by a single child—as demonstrated by the teacher's guides, with suggested prebook activities, and proposals for using the printed page. Although some children are able to use the textbook or other references independently, most usually need carefully prepared activity cards, programed texts, tape recordings, filmstrips, or other autoinstructional devices. Sometimes one child can help another, or the teacher can assemble temporary groups of children working on a common activity in order to provide instruction.

A final problem area here is, How can the teacher determine whether a child understands an idea before he starts doing drill exercises on that topic? This is a particularly difficult task with a program of individualized instruction because of the range of assignments and activities going on simultaneously, and because it requires both checking students' responses and personal interaction with them. There is a related question: How can the teacher keep up with scoring, analyzing, and recording all the diverse written assignments that are done in a day? Still a third question in this regard is: How should the teacher determine when a student has satisfactorily completed an assignment and is ready to begin the next? Again assuming the fixed-content/flexible-pace pattern, the importance of efficiently controlling drill, providing feedback to students' responses, and determining what to do next cannot be overemphasized. One approach to these final questions has the following pattern: After the basic instruction is believed to be completed, the child attempts to work a specified representative *sample* of the drill exercises, e.g., one of each distinct type, he checks his own answers against a key, then takes his work to the teacher, either to get help if he has made errors, or for a brief interview during which the teacher decides whether the child really understands what he is doing by asking questions and carefully examining his work. The teacher then either prescribes a remedial sequence or clears the student to complete the drill. The drill is completed when the child has done all the exercises, checked the answers with the key, and reworked any examples on which he has made errors until all his answers are correct. The work is then turned in to the teacher, who later examines it and records the results. In this particular system, children record their answers in a column at the left side of their paper; the scoring key is similarly arranged, so the two can be put side by side for easy scoring. (Spacing between answers matches because all children use the same type of paper as the key, which reduces scoring errors). Each key is on a numbered page in a loose-leaf notebook, and there are about ten such notebooks for a class of thirty children, so that excessive time need not be spent waiting to check answers. Periodic cumulative tests, which each child takes as they occur in the sequence of assignments, are scored by the teacher.

It should be pointed out that this is a procedure intended only for certain kinds of activities, i.e., drill and testing. There are many alternate ways to accomplish the same result. Teacher aides are sometimes available to score papers, for example; diagnostic pretests are sometimes built into the system; branching procedures can be used, and so on.

The above paragraphs should suggest some, but not all, of the advantages and limitations of individualized instruction. On the positive side: children are neither held back nor pushed forward by the performance of their peers (this *can* be a disadvantage in some cases!); instruction is, potentially at least, more personal, direct, and efficient since each assignment is begun only when there is evidence of readiness; discipline problems tend to be rare — most can be traced to frustration caused by children being pushed too fast by the program or to boredom caused by the other extreme; children find such programs challenging, yet satisfying and pleasant, so motivation and morale tend to be high; small quantities of many kinds of manipulative materials are sufficient, as with small-group instruction; it lends itself to both heterogeneous or homogeneous schoolwide grouping; and achievement results tend to indicate that individualized instruction is at least as effective as conventional instruction.

If these advantages are to be realized, there must exist very carefully designed procedures that children will understand and can follow smoothly with relative independence. Designing such procedures requires exhaustive planning. Some of the other limitations have already been suggested above.

1. Individualized instruction requires a great deal of energy and stamina on the teacher's part to handle the multitude of brief and frequently unrelated contacts with children during the class time; teachers' aides are almost a "must."
2. It reduces or virtually eliminates valuable interaction between children.
3. Checking students' work and recording their progress is complicated.
4. Effective basic instructional materials are scarce and in some cases expensive.
5. It does not suit the personalities or teaching styles of all teachers, yet must almost inevitably be done cooperatively within a school.
6. It is not equally effective for all students. Primary grade children who have not yet matured enough to work independently much of the time,

or upper grade children who have exceptionally poor backgrounds, work habits, or general ability do not usually function very well in individualized settings.

7. Nor is it equally effective for all mathematical topics, for all types of activities, or for achieving some important educational objectives, such as teaching children to work together cooperatively.

8. Finally, it is somewhat paradoxical that individualized instruction, intended to provide flexibility and to emphasize individuality, is necessarily quite inflexible, rigid, and mechanistic in execution.

Projects, Questions, and Suggested Activities

1. Suppose you were assigned the task of "setting up" a mathematics laboratory for an elementary school (or for a particular grade level, for primary grades, for intermediate grades).

   a. What kind of organization would you establish so that children could use it effectively?

   b. How would you furnish it? You may wish to make a hypothetical floor plan.

   c. How would you equip it? You may wish to start collecting catalogues to get an idea of what is available, what things cost, etc. As you read further in this book, you may modify your plans.

2. Stage a debate on the merits and limitations of various procedures for grouping children for basic instruction, e.g., total class, small group, individualized instruction, etc.

3. Take a current textbook for a grade level of your interest and outline a possible procedure for individualizing instruction for a class of thirty children using that book as a basic guide.

4. Choose a topic you might plan to teach to children of a particular grade level. Try making some activity cards that could be used by a child independently to learn the topic. If possible, try them out with some children.

5. Visit a school and find out the physical characteristics of a given classroom: floor plan, furnishings, and so on. Make a scale drawing showing how you would arrange the room or modify it if you were to teach there.

Suggested Readings

Beuthel, Donald G., and Meyer, Phyllis I. "A Regular Classroom Plus a Mathematics Laboratory." *The Arithmetic Teacher*, November 1972, pp. 527–30.

> Two classroom teachers describe their approach to setting up a math lab—and how it worked. In the same issue, Jacobs (pp.

571–77) discusses some discoveries made in a math lab with egg cartons and other simple materials. Good, practical ideas in both of these articles.

Copeland, Richard W. *Mathematics and the Elementary Teacher.* 2nd ed. Philadelphia: Saunders, 1972.

Chapter 11 (pp. 232–56) contains many ideas for implementing mathematics laboratories.

Davidson, Patricia S., and Fair, Arlene W. "A Mathematics Laboratory— from Dream to Reality." *The Arithmetic Teacher*, February 1970, pp. 105–10.

Just what the title suggests. A how-to-do-it article.

Dienes, Zoltan P. *Mathematics in the Primary Schools.* London: Macmillan, 1964.

Chapter 9, "Classroom Organization" (pp. 202–14) contains many excellent ideas.

Hapgood, Marilyn. "The Open Classroom: Protect It from Its Friends." *Saturday Review*, September 18, 1971, pp. 66–69, 75.

A sensible word of caution for those eager to imitate the British "open classrooms."

Jacoby, Susan. "What Makes Sue Morrell's Open Classroom Work?" *Learning,* February 1973, pp. 58–62.

Descriptive article suggesting that the teacher is the key.

Kidd, Kenneth P.; Myers, Shirley S.; and Cilley, David M. *The Laboratory Approach to Mathematics.* Chicago: Science Research Associates, 1970.

Many, many practical ideas throughout the book.

Leeb-Lundberg, Kristina. "Kindergarten Mathematics Laboratory—Nineteenth Century Fashion." *The Arithmetic Teacher*, May 1970, pp. 372–86.

Is there nothing new under the sun? An excellent article, with many up-to-date ideas for the lower grades. In the same issue, Gibb (pp. 396–402) presents a comprehensive and thoughtful review of individualized instruction dating back to the 1800s. A study of the 1925 NSSE yearbook (her references 3, 9, 13, 14, 15, and 17) is recommended.

Mathews, Geoffrey, and Comber, Julia. "Mathematics Laboratories." *The Arithmetic Teacher*, December 1971, pp. 547–50.

Two leaders of the Nuffield Mathematics Project describe the math lab idea briefly. This issue features math labs. See also the excellent articles by Ewbank (pp. 559–64), Barson (pp. 565–67), Vance and Kieren (pp. 585–89) and Silverman (pp. 596–97).

"Projects on Individualized Instruction." *The Arithmetic Teacher*, March 1971, pp. 161–63. (No author mentioned.)

> Brief descriptions, names and addresses, and grade levels; a follow-up listing can be found in the November 1971 issue (pp. 473–75). In the same issue, Riedesel (pp. 177–79) points out some interesting research findings regarding the use of time, e.g., how much time to spend on drill, etc.

Schaefer, Anne W., and Mauthe, Albert H. "Problem Solving with Enthusiasm—The Mathematics Laboratory." *The Arithmetic Teacher*, January 1970, pp. 7–14.

> Ten specific examples of fifth-grade mathematics laboratory activities including geometry, measurement, and probability. Good ideas.

The Editorial Panel. "Individualized Instruction." *The Arithmetic Teacher*, January 1972, pp. 5–6.

> A summary of the major articles in this issue, which features nine articles on the topic; all nine should be read to get a variety of points of view—and some practical ideas; in the May 1972, issue, Wegener's article (pp. 355–57) also belongs with these.

Young, Carolyn. "Team Learning." *The Arithmetic Teacher*, December 1972, pp. 630–34.

> A case for grouping children in pairs. Many specific suggestions for "almost individualizing" instruction.

II. TEACHING BASIC MATHEMATICS

In the remaining chapters, the emphasis is on activities and materials for teaching topics to children. The basic principles discussed in Chapter 2 should be kept in the reader's mind when studying a given chapter, as they were kept in the author's mind; they will not be repeated in detail. The general plan is to consider activities in a sequence that follows, approximately, the order in which relevant topics are normally developed throughout an entire program. In general, the material is not organized by grades, since many of the suggested activities can be used at several grade levels. Another reason for this organization is that there is considerable variation among programs and textbooks in regard to the grade placement of topics. The reader who is interested in finding out, for example, how much is taught about fractions in the third grade is usually concerned about the coverage in a particular program or textbook series. A fairly quick look at the table of contents, teacher's guide, or scope-and-sequence chart will answer his question. Also, every teacher should become familiar with a broad range of appropriate activities in order to provide variety for all students; an activity that is a remedial experience for one child could be quite challenging for another.

Another feature of the organization of Part II is that each chapter begins with a brief review of its underlying mathematical content. It is assumed that the reader has previously studied the material more thoroughly elsewhere. The mathematics involved is presented for the teacher's background and is not necessarily phrased as it would be for the instruction of children. In general, the material is more rigorous, formal, and comprehensive than would be appropriate for elementary school children. These review sections might be ignored, skimmed, or used as appendixes by the well-prepared reader who is interested only in the pedagogical considerations of each chapter.

Then again, the majority of activities in these chapters can be incorporated into any organizational procedure the teacher may be using. That is, they can be presented to an entire class, to a small group, or to an individual child. They can be presented via teacher-made activity cards, programed units, tape recordings, or other modes of "teaching in absentia." The intent is to describe the activities specifically enough that the teacher can use them, yet generally enough both that they can be modified as needed and that they will suggest additional activities to the resourceful teacher.

Finally, the importance of manipulative materials has been emphasized in preceding chapters; in the remaining chapters, those materials, both commercial and "homemade," that are appropriate for teaching the particular topic under discussion will be described with suggestions about how to use them for that topic. Certain materials are mentioned in several chapters because they are useful for teaching many topics. The reader may refer to the chapter in which the materials are initially described or to Appendix B, where they are summarized along with suggestions for constructing some of them.

4. Teaching the Number and Numeration Concepts

Before children can use numbers with understanding, they must first of all have a reasonable understanding of what numbers are and how to name them. Because these two concepts are technically distinct, we will consider them separately; in practice, however, they are taught more or less together. A prerequisite to understanding numeration is understanding the meaning of the numbers zero through nine, which we will discuss first.

1. Teaching the Concept of Number

Mathematical Review

The "number concept" provides an excellent example of a familiar problem faced by teachers of mathematics: an idea which seems simple and obvious to us, because of much experience with it, can be quite perplexing to children when they first encounter it. On careful analysis, however, it becomes clear that the idea is not as simple as we thought, and our sympathy for children's confusion with it is increased.

What is a *number*? Specifically, for example, what is the *number three*? There are at least two common answers to this, both quite abstract, but both based on a common concept: *matching,* or *one-to-one correspondence* (the terms are synonymous). Before attempting a specific definition of number, then, we will review this concept.

Given any nonempty sets, *A* and *B*, we can *pair* their elements *one-to-one.* That is, we can associate one element of *A* with one element of *B*, then associate another element of *A*, if there is one, with a different element of *B*, and so on until we have "used up" all the elements of one (or both) of the sets. *If* when we do this, every element of *B* is paired with an element of *A*, and every element of *A* is paired with an element of *B*, then we say the sets match or that their elements are in one-to-one correspondence. In the language of functions, a "1–1" correspondence is a function from set A into set B which is both 1–1 (each element of the range is the image of a *distinct* element of A) and "onto" (the range includes *each* element of B). For example, if $A = \{a, b, c\}$ and $B = \{x, y, z\}$, one such function can be represented in several ways. There are six possible 1–1 correspondences be-

tween A and B, but there is no possible 1–1 correspondence between A and a set such as $\{w, x, y, z\}$. We can *classify* sets on the basis of 1–1 correspondence, since 1–1 correspondence is an equivalence relation. That is, for all sets, X, Y, and Z,

(a) Each set X matches itself.
(b) If X matches Y, then Y matches X, and
(c) If X matches Y, and Y matches Z, then X matches Z.

Every set belongs to one — and only one — collection (equivalence class) according to this classification scheme. For example, the set $\{x, y, z\}$ would be classified with the sets $\{a, b, c\}$, $\{d, e, f\}$, and with infinitely many other sets, because they all match each other. Any set in the class could be used to *represent* the class. It should be clear that while the *elements* of any given pair of sets in a class might have some common characteristic or property, the only characteristic that is common to *all* the *sets* in the class is that they match.

We find *number* (whole number) defined in two closely related, equally acceptable ways: First, a number is an *equivalence class* (of sets determined by the one-to-one correspondence relation). The number three, for example, is the collection of all sets which match $\{0, 1, 2\}$. Thus each set *represents* a (unique) number. And second, a number is a *property* or characteristic of sets. *Every* set has a unique "number property" (and *only* sets can have this property of "number"). The number three, for example, is the (only) common property of all sets which match $\{0, 1, 2\}$. Thus each set *has* a (unique) number (or number property).

The assignment of *names* to numbers, whether we think of numbers as classes of sets or as properties of sets, is merely an arbitrary way to distinguish one number from another. Number names are in the form of words such as "three" or symbols called numerals, such as "3," or expressions such as "$5 - 2$".

Every number has infinitely many names. For example, there are infinitely many expressions of the form $a - b$ or $a \div b$ which name the number three. When we write $5 - 2 = 3$, we mean "the expression $5 - 2$ and the numeral 3 name the same number."

The whole numbers, or their names, have a "natural" order, again associated with the matching process. If two sets, A and B, do not match, then either A has more elements than B or it has fewer elements than B. (A has fewer elements than B if A matches a proper subset of B; A has more elements than B if B matches a proper subset of A).

The numbers associated with sets can be ordered accordingly: If a set A has fewer elements than a set B, then the number of A, sometimes abbreviated $N(A)$, is less than the number of B; similarly, $N(A)$ is greater than $N(B)$ if A has more elements than B. The symbols $<$ and $>$ represent the expressions "is less than" and "is greater than" respectively. For example, $3 < 4$, $3 > 2$ or $N(A) < N(B)$.

Each (whole) number except zero has a unique *predecessor* and each number, including zero, has a unique *successor*. These are based on the "one-more-than" and "one-fewer-than" relationships between sets such as $\{a, b\}$ and $\{x, y, z\}$. The predecessor of 3 is 2, for example, and the successor of 3 is 4. It should be noted that the empty set, $\emptyset$, and its associated number, zero, are somewhat special in that

(a) $\emptyset$ is the only set in its equivalence class. Each *non*empty set, on the other hand, is classified with infinitely many others.
(b) 0 is the least whole number. It has no predecessor. Every nonzero whole number is greater than zero.

"Counting" means naming successive *nonzero* whole numbers in their natural order, 1, 2, 3, . . . , n. There are three special kinds of counting. The expression *rational counting* is used to designate the process of determining the number of (elements in) a nonempty set. Here a one-to-one correspondence is established between the elements of the given set and the set of nonzero whole numbers, 1, 2, 3, . . . , n in their natural order, where n is the greatest number needed in the matching. This final number, n, is the "number" of the set. *Rote counting* is distinct from rational counting in that it is done without reference to any set. Rote counting means *only* naming successive numbers in order. *Skip counting* refers to counting, either rational or rote, where a consistent interval is skipped between each name that is called off, such as when "counting by threes."

The uses of number may be classified either as "cardinal" or as "ordinal." The cardinal use of number refers to *enumeration*, that is, counting or expressing the number of elements in a set. For example, "There are *seven* days in each week." A number is used in the ordinal sense when it refers to the order in which a given element appears in a set, providing there *is* some natural ordering of those elements. It should be recalled that when a set is named using braces or other notation, no order is implied. For example, if $A = \{Tom, Bob\}$, then also $A = \{Bob, Tom\}$. There is no "first" element or "second" element based simply on how the set is named. We can only order the elements when we consider them with respect to some common characteristic which can be naturally ordered. If we wish to compare the ages of Tom and Bob, and if Tom is younger than Bob, then Tom is the first element of A. Not every characteristic can be naturally ordered. The characteristic "eye color," for example, does not lend itself to ordering the elements of $\{Bob, Tom\}$. We sometimes (but not always) use special word names for numbers used in the ordinal sense, such as "first," "second," "third," etc. For example, "Today is the *seventh* day of September."

Necessarily, the number concept is one of the first things taught in elementary school mathematics. Although the preceding paragraphs may suggest that the task is formidable because of its complexity, it need not be. A few relatively simple and informal notions, easily within the grasp of a first-grade child, are sufficient to enable him to use numbers meaningfully. These notions cannot, however, be either assumed or ignored. Even a cursory examination of the research done by men like Piaget and Dienes reminds us that a child's concept of number evolves slowly and may be quite undeveloped by the time he starts school. The primary teacher must provide many activities designed to develop this concept before a child can use numbers effectively. Our immediate concern below, therefore, is with prenumber concepts.

Activities and Materials for Teaching Prenumber Concepts

Set and Set Membership

If children are to associate numbers with sets, an obvious prerequisite is the basic concept of set and set membership. The words "set" and "member" are helpful but certainly not essential. The only requirement is that children be able to perceive of objects as *belonging* to particular collections. Some children will have already acquired this idea fairly well before starting school and will need little help. They themselves are elements of an important set, their families. They will have already begun to classify things in their environment and think of things as belonging together—toys, pets, shoes, crayons, and other things that have significance to them. In the classroom, the teacher can further develop the concept by using words like "set," "member," and "belongs to" in talking about collections the children can see—children, books, chairs, pencils, toys, pictures, windows, tables, and the like. At first, elements of the sets should have clearly recognizable common characteristics. Questions and instructions are aimed at helping children develop two specific skills: First, given a characteristic, the child decides whether a specific object is or is not in the set of objects with that characteristic, e.g., "Raise your hand if you are a member of the set of girls in the room" or "Is this a member of the set of books in the room?" And second, given several sets, the child identifies the one having a specific characteristic, e.g., "Point to the set of toys on the table" (there should be several little collections there, each grouped together and separated from the others — a pile of books, a few coins, and some pencils, for example, along with the set of toys). Care must be taken to avoid ambiguity and children at this stage need not be concerned with objects that belong to more than one collection. Grouping things together or "packaging" them, e.g., putting crayons in a box, can afford opportunities to develop the set idea. Loops can be put around small collections to emphasize their "togetherness" — a loop of string around a set of pencils on a table, a loop of yarn around a flannel-board collection, or a loop drawn with chalk around a set of pictures on a chalkboard.

Children should gradually have their attention focused on sets of several kinds and in several contexts, in approximately this order: sets of physical objects that can be seen and touched and whose elements are all the same kinds of things, e.g., books; sets of physical objects whose elements are related but individually different, e.g., toys or dishes; sets of physical objects whose elements seem unrelated except for having been put together, e.g., a set consisting of a pencil, a toy soldier, a book, and a crayon grouped together on a table; pictures of sets of each kind mentioned above; and sets of objects that can be perceived but not seen, e.g., family membership or the days of the week. It should be emphasized that the set concept is best taught by imitation, repetition, and example, *never by definition*, and that an object may or may not belong to a given set, in accordance with the individual child's perception of its membership.

More and Fewer

Once the set concept has been established fairly well, attention can be focused on comparisons between pairs of sets. At first, the teacher should be sure that children have the concepts of *more* and *fewer*. At the prenumber stage, the decision as to whether one set has more or fewer elements than another can only be made on the basis of what *seems* to be the case. Thus, differences in number should be fairly large, e.g., a set of two compared with a set of eight. Essentially, the only question that needs to be raised is, given two sets, which has more (or fewer) elements? At this point, the teacher should be careful to help children distinguish between *more* or *fewer*, in comparing the numerousness of sets by inspection, and *larger* or *smaller*, in comparing the physical size of elements of sets. Deliberate effort should be made, for example, to have children compare a set containing a few large elements with a set that has more but smaller elements, and conversely. It should also be made certain, before going much further, that children recognize that the spatial arrangement of its elements does not affect the more/fewer property of one set compared with another. Many children will, quite naturally, assert that a given set has more elements when those elements are spread farther apart or that a set whose elements are scattered over a relatively large area has more elements than one whose elements are closer together. Research suggests that this is quite natural until children reach a certain level in their development. Until this level is reached, they should not be expected to fully comprehend the activities discussed below, and the teacher should insure that many opportunities are provided that emphasize the distinction between "more" and "farther apart."

1-1 Correspondence

Once the foregoing concepts have been established, children can begin making finer distinctions, based on *pairing elements* of sets on a one-to-one basis. At first, they may be asked to pair elements of sets of related objects (or pictures of objects), such as cups and saucers, dolls and doll carriages, dogs and bones, balls and bats, bees and flowers, etc. Then, with manipulative objects such as blocks, they actually can put elements from two sets side by side, one at a time. A metal surface with magnetized plastic objects (apples, rabbits, stars, etc.) or a felt board is useful for this activity. Later, with pictures, they can draw lines to suggest the pairing. At first, objects should be arranged so the task is quite easy; later they can be arranged to be more challenging. It is when 1-1 correspondence activities are introduced that the third comparative relationship between sets, "as many as," emerges and there should be ample opportunity provided to experience it. There are numerous classroom activities and situations that can lead to the concept of 1-1 correspondence, such as "John, get one piece of paper for each person at your table," or "Are there enough chairs for all the children to sit on?" Again, it should be kept in mind that such situations require only the concept of 1-1 pairing, not rational counting. The "more," "fewer," and "as many as" relations are now based on 1-1 pairing rather than on perception alone. Again, this concept requires experience with various types of sets, including pairs of sets whose elements are the same kinds of things, related things, unrelated things, or abstract things such as geometric shapes.

Order of Sets

Understanding the relationships "more," "fewer," and "as many as" between pairs of sets enables the child still at the prenumber stage to classify small collections of finite sets with respect to the transitive *order* relation. Given several sets, the child should be able to order them in terms of 1–1 correspondence. Again, the suggestions in the preceding sections should be followed: The relative order of a given set relative to others should be based on 1–1 correspondence, independent of relationships between characteristics, including size and spatial arrangement of the elements of the sets. For example, children might be asked to arrange three or four sets of objects so that each set has more elements than the preceding one. The numbers of elements involved should be large enough (beginning with about five or six) and close enough together, e.g., 6, 8, and 9, so that the child must use 1–1 pairing rather than his perception. Such tasks can be set up by the teacher to be fairly easy at first, gradually requiring more and more thought and care on the child's part.

Rote Counting

Many children enter first grade able to "count to" some number, such as ten, twenty, or more. Usually this is a rote skill, developed by playing games, singing songs, or remembering poems designed for the sole purpose of helping children memorize the sequence of word names for the first few natural numbers. This rote counting is helpful, if not absolutely necessary, when the child begins to develop number concepts, particularly the concept of *order*. Such techniques are intended only to familiarize children with the *sounds* of the word names for numbers in their natural order, beginning with "one." Frequently children recall the words but confuse their order, or show evidence of recognizing yet not mastering the inherent patterns of the word names beyond "twelve."

The Stern Structural Arithmetic Materials

Many materials for teaching prenumber concepts have been mentioned in the preceding sections; most of them can be (or should be) found in any primary classroom. Toys, books, pencils, and the like, while not ordinarily designed specifically for teaching these concepts, can be so used. On the other hand, some toys and certain commercially available educational materials *are* specifically designed for this purpose. Teachers can find many such devices by obtaining catalogs from publishers and from companies who specialize in educational materials, e.g., Creative Publications, The Cuisenaire Company, and Selective Educational Equipment, Inc., to name a few (see also Appendix B). We will describe here and in subsequent chapters some representative commercial materials, restricting ourselves to materials that we have used in the classroom, that we believe are appropriate for teaching the particular topic under discussion, and that are quite commonly found in schools. This selection is not intended to suggest that the hundreds of other available materials are not recommended. New materials are marketed continually, many of them of high quality and educationally sound.

The Stern Structural Arithmetic materials are designed for teaching prenumber concepts, among others. "Structural Arithmetic" is a primary grade program first introduced in the 1950s by Catherine Stern. It includes a variety of physical apparatus together with student workbooks and teacher's guides which suggest *numerous* activities for developing pre-number concepts (and many others). The physical apparatus is mostly made of wood or masonite, so it is durable enough to last for years. Color is employed in such a way that it is both pedagogically effective and appealing to children.

The basic piece of apparatus is a set of wooden blocks called *unit blocks*. There are unit blocks of ten sizes, each size a different color. The smallest, called the *unit cube*, which children will later call the 1-block, is a cube which measures 19 mm ($\frac{3}{4}''$) on each edge. The 2-block looks like two unit cubes glued end-to-end; the 3-block looks like three unit cubes end-to-end, and so on up to the 10-block. Several blocks of each size are needed

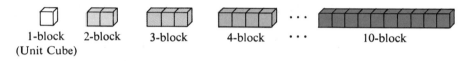

| 1-block | 2-block | 3-block | 4-block | $\cdots$ | 10-block |

(Unit Cube)

for some activities, while others call for several unit cubes or a single block of each size.

The *counting board* consists of a set of ten segmented grooves, one to fit each of the ten sizes of unit blocks. Paralleling the basic row of grooves

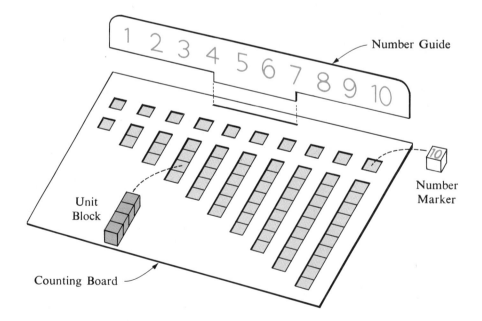

is a set of square grooves which hold blocks called *number markers* with the ten numerals printed on them. These would not be used at the prenumber stage, of course. Similarly, a *number guide* with the ten numerals in order can be attached later.

The materials include a set of ten *pattern boards*, one for each number up to ten. Each board has grooves to match a different number of unit cubes. The grooves are arranged in rows of one or two.

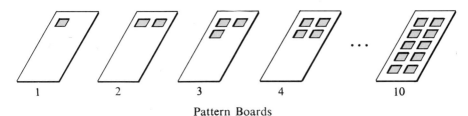

Pattern Boards

The Stern materials include several other kinds of apparatus, but the final prenumber device is a set of ten shallow square boxes called *number cases*. Each number case holds a square number (1, 4, 9, 16, . . . , 100) of unit cubes. The case which holds 100 cubes is also called a *unit box*.

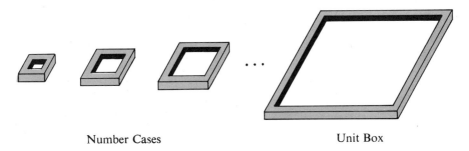

Number Cases   Unit Box

There are many prenumber activities possible with the Stern materials. As a starter, perhaps, a child can be given a counting board and a scrambled set of unit blocks (or unit cubes) and asked to fill a particular groove either using exactly one unit block or unit cubes. This can be repeated for each groove, sometimes in natural order, sometimes in random order, and sometimes "backwards" from 10 to 1. Or, from a scrambled set of unit blocks, children can be asked to identify the *smallest* block, then the next, and the next. This can vary considerably, e.g., by arranging the blocks in staircase fashion or putting them into the grooves of the counting board. With a scrambled set of pattern boards and a set of unit cubes, children can (a) use the cubes to match the groove patterns of a particular board or of several boards and verify their work by placing the cubes in the grooves; (b) pick the board which matches a given set of cubes, arranged in the two-column pattern or otherwise; (c) use both cubes and boards to match pictures of things, e.g., 2 apples or 3 birds; or (d) study a single board, then turn it face down and try to match its pattern with cubes. (These exercises can be made more challenging by increasing the distance between boards, cubes, and pictures.) Using a unit box and some unit blocks, children can be instructed to put one block along the lower edge of the box, then fill the remaining space along that edge with a single block, and to repeat this with different pairs of blocks until the box is full; or make a "staircase" inside the box using one of each size block, then, with another set, fill the remaining space. Children can be directed to nest a set of number cases, or to match each case with the unit block that just "fits" it. And so on—our list hardly exhausts the prenumber activities possible with the Stern Structural Arithmetic materials.

Activities and Materials for Teaching the Numbers Zero Through Nine

Objectives and Basic Activities

Once the prenumber concepts have been developed sufficiently, the child is ready to begin a more formal study of the first few numbers. Usually one or two numbers are taught at a time, starting with *one* (or one and two)—not with zero. Teachers usually introduce a given number by showing children several sets with that number; talking about the number; showing the numeral to them; having them repeat the name; or asking them to point to sets which have that number and count from "one" to the number as they point to sets. Such activities must be repeated over and over, with as much variety as the teacher can provide. Several activities are summarized below, and should be repeated for each number (or pair of numbers). We will use the number 5 as an example. Reasonable mastery of the tasks that follow would indicate an understanding of 5 and should be expected before repeating comparable tasks for 6.

1. Given collections of 3, 4, 5, 6, and 7 things, the child should be able to point to or otherwise identify those collections which have exactly *five* elements. Furthermore, he should be able to identify those with more than or fewer than five elements. Initially, of course, the teacher would need to demonstrate several sets of five, talk about such sets, relate them to sets of four, i.e., a set of five has "one more" element than a set of four. The child should be able to identify a set of five *by inspection*, without counting, as well as being able to count rationally to five. For sets with more than five elements, identifying the number without counting becomes more difficult. It can be made easier by arranging the objects in an orderly manner and by using sets of simple geometric objects. Much varied practice is necessary. For example, the child

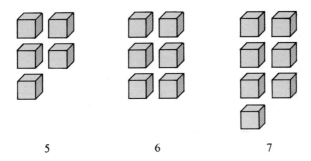

| 5 | 6 | 7 |

should encounter sets with successive numbers arranged as in the preceding picture and as "staircases." And in preparation for learning

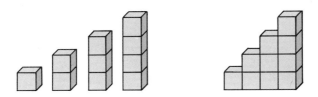

addition, subtraction, and numeration skills involving partition and union, he should encounter sets that have been partitioned in various ways, e.g., a set of five might be represented as illustrated here. He should be encouraged to experiment to see in how many ways he can arrange a set

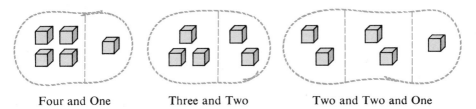

Four and One   Three and Two   Two and Two and One

of five blocks or other small objects. Ultimately, given any one of the following, he should be able to provide the other two: a set of five (or a picture of such a set), the numeral 5, the word five (either spoken or written).

2. Given a set of many objects, say 15 or 20, he should be able to count out five of them, upon instruction from the teacher, and show that he has the desired number (this is rational counting). At first, he should be carefully supervised to be certain that he in fact correctly associates objects one-to-one with the counting numbers in their proper order.

3. He should be able to recognize the word "five" in print as well as verbally. This is accomplished by showing him the word—on a card, flannel board,

chalkboard, etc. — while saying it and showing him an appropriate set (or picture of a set). Later he will need to learn to *write* the word as well as to recognize its sound and its printed appearance. It should be kept in mind that the words themselves are unrelated to each other and to the numbers they name, so that unlike the corresponding numbers themselves, the child is not helped in this task by patterns. On the other hand, (a) except for perhaps "two" and "eight," the words are relatively consistent with phonetic generalizations the teacher is developing in the reading and language arts programs; (b) because the words are short, they are relatively easy; and (c) the child's prenumber exposure to the rote counting games, poems, and songs can help him to learn the words in their more rational context.

4. Similarly, the child should learn to write the numeral 5 correctly. Left on their own to merely copy the numeral as they see it, children might form it in various ways, not all of them efficient. So the teacher needs to carefully guide and supervise them as they practice this skill (as in teaching them to form letters). Correct formation of the numerals can at first be facilitated by "tracing" activities which call for gradually increased independence, e.g.,

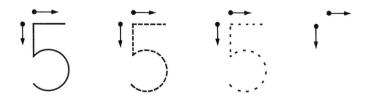

Much practice is usually needed before a child can form the numerals quickly and correctly with respect to both shape and size. Practice is, of course, achieved in the context of *using* numerals (e.g., for addition and subtraction), but considerable early practice is usually given per se.

5. Given a collection of five or more objects in a row, he should be able to identify the *fifth* one. This requires learning the ordinal word "fifth" and rational counting for a different purpose, i.e., to answer the question "Which one?" (as distinct from the question "How many?" which he learned earlier). It should again be noted that this ordinal task only makes sense if the set in question has an inherent ordering of its elements, and if that ordering scheme is clearly understood by the child.

6. In conjunction with his rational counting and other skills, he should be able to correctly order both the word names and the numerals rationally. That is, not only can he say the words "one, two, three, four, five," but he also can associate each number name both with an appropriate set and with an appropriate element of a set, e.g.,

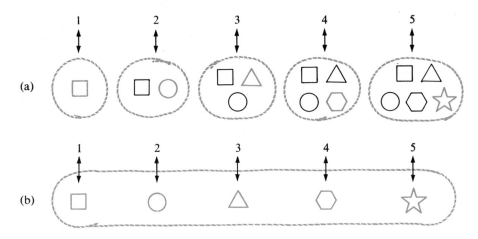

Not only should the child be able to put the numerals in correct order, but he should also be able to fill in any missing ones in a sequence, e.g., 1, 2, —, 4, —, to correctly show, for example, that 4 is between 3 and 5, and to tell which number precedes or follows a given number.

The *number line* (or ray) is a useful device with which to represent the order of numbers. Children should be taught to correctly associate each number with the appropriate point. Gradually, a child learns to associate (intuitively) the geometric order and betweenness properties of the

number line with the corresponding number properties. That is, for example, if point *A* is to the left of point *B*, then the number corresponding to *A* is less than that corresponding to *B*.

Counting rods are frequently used to develop the ordering skill. These are commercially available or can easily be constructed by stringing beads on a wire (e.g., coat hanger). In counting to five, for example, the

beads are first pushed to the left, and as each successive number is called off, the child slides one bead to the right. The number of beads can at first be restricted to five, more being added as the child learns new numbers, or there can be up to ten beads permanently mounted. Children usually find such ten-bead rods easier to use if the rods are placed in two groups of five by color. This facilitates grouping.

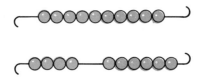

The number zero is usually more difficult for children to understand than are the numbers one through nine, so it is not commonly introduced in its natural order (first). The main source of the difficulty is that the word *set,* or any synonym for it, is most frequently and naturally used to represent collections of "many" things (at least two). A child can fairly readily perceive four books as a *set* of four books, but it is somewhat more artificial to think of *one* book in this way, and still many times more of a strain to imagine a set which contains *no* books. The empty set and its number are both very important, but, as with one-element sets and the number one, extra effort is required on the teacher's part in order to develop the concept meaningfully. One of the most effective strategies for introducing zero is to show a sequence of pictures in which the number of objects (e.g., cookies on a plate, crayons in a box, fish in an aquarium) decreases from, say 3 to 2, then from 2 to 1, and finally from 1 to 0, leaving the empty container (plate, box, or whatever). Since we can ask "How many?" for each of the nonempty pictures, we have a certain motivation to seek a name for the number of objects in the empty container, thus the number *zero* is introduced. Any formal teaching of the empty set should be postponed, if possible, because of its abstractness.

Instructional Materials

Many materials appropriate for teaching the prenumber and number concepts have been suggested in preceding paragraphs. We will briefly consider a few others here. But first it should be recalled that number is an abstraction, and if children are to acquire the ability to abstract the number concept, it is imperative that a variety of models be used. Otherwise, number properties may be confused with the physical attributes of a single set of apparatus.

Sets of wooden or plastic blocks, either homemade or obtained commercially, can provide an efficient and effective model for teaching the numbers one through nine. There are three common types of blocks: (1) sets of cubes, measuring usually 1 cm, $\frac{3}{4}''$, or $1''$ on each edge, and either varnished or painted (with nontoxic paint!) in one color or a variety of colors; (2) sets of blocks such as the commercially available Stern materials; and (3) sets of rods such as the Cuisenaire rods and the Centimeter rods of graduated lengths which provide a *measuring* model for numbers. One set of blocks,

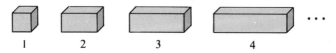

1   2   3   4

the Unifix cubes, combines both (1) and (2) above; they can be used singly or can be snapped together. Most of the commercially available materials are accompanied both by adjunct materials which help to emphasize key patterns and by teacher's manuals, children's texts, or activity cards which suggest effective ways to use them (see Appendix B).

The Stern blocks, in particular, are very effective in developing certain number concepts. Many of the activities already mentioned can be repeated or modified by adding number names to them. For example, given a counting board with some unit cubes and unit blocks, the child can be asked to guess how many cubes will fill a particular groove, then check his guess experimentally; to fill a given groove with cubes, counting aloud (perhaps with the teacher) as he sets each cube in; to fill a groove with cubes, then replace them with the single block of the same length, gradually assigning number names, e.g., "5-block" to replace *color* names, such as "yellow block"; to fill all grooves in order, calling out number names as he goes; to match grooves with number markers, checking his work by placing the number guide on the board; or to call out the number name of a block or groove as the teacher points to it or identifies it in the ordinal sense, e.g., the "fifth" groove. Using pattern boards and cubes, he can be asked to order the pattern boards and name them with numbers, or to count a given set of cubes and then find the board that fits it, again by counting the grooves. Or, given a number case, the child can fill it with cubes, counting as he goes along.

An additional piece of the Stern apparatus can be introduced at this stage. The *number track* is a wooden model number line scaled to match the blocks, i.e., on a scale from 0 to 10. Blocks can set in a continuous groove running the length of the track. A removable "bumper" attaches to either end of the track via dowels and matching holes to help align blocks correctly and to complete the track. Later, the track can be extended in ten-unit sections up to 100. The number track can be used in several ways

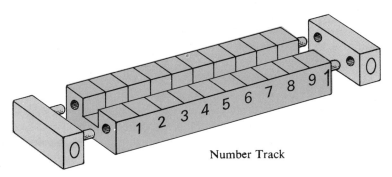

Number Track

once children have learned at least most of the numbers to nine: counting to nine and pointing to the grooves or numerals one at a time; filling the groove with cubes, one at a time, while counting and reading the numerals; putting blocks in one at a time to "measure" them; or finding the block which fits from the "beginning" point to a given point on the track, e.g., the 5-point.

There are many other kinds of number line, both homemade and commercial. The more appropriate ones for the primary grades include the "walk-on" number line, made with chalk (or a roll of narrow paper or tape appropriately labeled) on the classroom floor, with the unit points about one (child's) pace apart; a metal number line that hangs on the wall or chalkboard with magnetized snap-on bars each one unit long (to match the unit distance of the line); a plastic model on which the line is printed, and on which children can mark with crayon or grease pencil; a wooden line with pegs which fit into holes drilled at each unit point.

Finally, various types of flash cards can be made for drill and practice on recognition of names, numerals, or the number of elements in a given set. Such cards can be used, too, in matching games by one or more children, e.g., given five cards each containing a set picture and five cards each showing a numeral, the child matches the pictures with numerals.

As with teaching any topic, the number and variety of possible activities is limited only by the individual teacher's resourcefulness. The preceding ones are only suggestive.

2. Teaching Numeration Concepts

Mathematical Review

Numeration refers to the naming of numbers. Since the earliest days of civilization, man has needed to devise numeration systems in order to keep track of his possessions, to keep records, and to communicate with others about quantities. A *numeration system* consists of a finite set of basic symbols which name certain key numbers and a set of agreed-upon rules for using those basic symbols to name other numbers. Man has devised a wide variety of numeration systems throughout his history, most of them quite crude by today's standards though adequate for the simpler needs of their time. Our numeration system is the Hindu-Arabic system, originated by the Hindus in India and later adopted and refined to its present form, except for minor changes in basic symbols, by the Arabs. The history of numeration systems in general, and of the Hindu-Arabic system in particular, is an excellent source of enrichment and perspective for the elementary school child. It is beyond our purpose to examine that history in detail, but it is worth pointing out here that the Hindu-Arabic system is in universal use today among all civilized peoples (with minor differences in notation), which testifies to its "perfection." This was not true until about the beginning of the sixteenth century; until that time, man's mathematical progress was excruciatingly slow as we look back on it. The Hindu-Arabic system of numeration provided a vital link to progress. It can only be viewed as a profound achievement.

As with many such universally accepted major inventions, e.g., printing, our familiarity with the Hindu-Arabic system sometimes clouds our recognition of its unique advantages. Before we consider these, recall these familiar features of the system:

1. It employs exactly ten symbols, one for each of the natural numbers up to nine, plus a symbol for zero. These are the *digits*, 1, 2, 3, . . . , 9, 0.
2. It is a positional system. This means that in any numeral with two or more digits, the position or "place" of a given digit affects the value it represents. Specifically, the value of a given digit in a numeral is the product of its "face value" or "absolute value" multiplied by its "place value," which is always a particular power of the number ten, which is called the *base* of the system. (The choice of ten as the base also determines the number of basic symbols that are used.) The place values within any given numeral, from right to left, are always successively 10^0, 10^1, 10^2, 10^3, . . . , 10^n for some whole number n. For example, in the numeral 40,368, where $n = 4$, the digits 8, 6, 3, 0, and 4 respectively represent 8×10^0, 6×10^1, 3×10^2, 0×10^3, and 4×10^4, or 8×1, 6×10, 3×100, 0×1000, and $4 \times 10,000$.
3. It is an additive system. The value of a multidigit numeral is the sum of the values represented by each digit according to the above rule. In the example above, then, the numeral 40,368 represents the sum $(4 \times 10^4) + (0 \times 10^3) + (3 \times 10^2) + (6 \times 10^1) + (8 \times 10^0)$ or $40,000 + 0 + 300 + 60 + 8$.

There are three specific advantages of this system over other systems which preceded it.

1. Large numbers can be named with just a few digits. As an example, the equivalent of our 40,368, expressed in an Egyptian Hieroglyphic system which has been revived recently for pedagogical purposes, would be this 21-digit numeral:

and in one modernized version of the better known Roman numeration system, it would be the 11-digit numeral

$$\overline{\text{XL}}\text{CCCLXVIII}$$

2. The Hindu-Arabic system facilitates computation tremendously. Tobias Danzig, in his *Number, the Language of Science* (p. 26), underscores

this by recalling the story of a German merchant who in the fifteenth century sought the advice of a university professor as to where he might send his son for an advanced commercial education. The professor replied that if only addition and subtraction were required, the German universities would probably suffice, but only in Italy could he expect to obtain instruction in the more advanced arts of multiplying and dividing! Whether this story is actually true or not, it is certainly based on fact — computations which today's sixth grader can perform in a few moments once required hours or days of complicated labor by a specialist. The now familiar algorithms for computation could never have evolved in the context of less sophisticated numeration systems than the one we use.

3. A unique advantage of this system — not recognized until the late sixteenth century — is that it can be extended to name fractional numbers and, in fact, all Real numbers, by extending the system to include negative powers of the base, using so-called "decimal" numerals. For example, $\frac{1}{2}$ can be written as .5 or 5×10^{-1} $(5 \times \frac{1}{10})$. Looking at this another way, there are no practical limits to the (Real) numbers that can be represented with the system: Numbers as large as we wish, as small as we wish, or as close together as we wish can be represented in a straightforward way with this extension of the Hindu-Arabic system. This will be discussed in more detail in a later chapter. In the remainder of this chapter, we consider the system as it applies to naming only whole numbers.

Two counting procedures that involve numeration are used by children. The first involves the procedure for rationally "counting out" a specified number (greater than nine) of elements from a set containing more than that number of things, or simply naming successive numbers beyond 9. Whenever the specified goal exceeds 9, the child must be familiar with the order for naming larger numbers. Although he verbalizes — perhaps to himself — in terms of the word names, ". . . eleven, twelve, thirteen, . . . ," he normally thinks in terms of numerals, ". . . 11, 12, 13, ..." Thus he needs to know the pattern involved in naming each "next" number. That is, when he reaches 9, the greatest number he can name with one digit, adding one more can be represented by annexing a new *position*, "tens' place." He enters 1 in that place and 0 in "one's place" to get 10, which he calls "ten." He then returns to the natural sequence from 1 through 9 in ones' place. We leave as an exercise the task of completing a precise description of this iterative process (counting from 1 through an arbitrarily large number).

The second counting procedure involves determining the number of elements in a given set when that number exceeds 9. While this can be accomplished in the preceding manner, it can also be done by partitioning the set into subsets of size 1, 10, 100, . . . , 10^n as needed. A child does this by counting out a subset of 10, calling it "a ten," then another, and another until he has 10 tens. These ten subsets are combined to form *one* subset, "a hundred," and so on. When finished, he counts the number of subsets of each size, e.g., 3 hundreds, 2 tens, and 7 ones, which is recorded as 327.

A related skill may be thought of as the reverse of the preceding one: Given a *numeral*, such as 327, demonstrate a set which has that *number*, where each subset has the indicated number of elements.

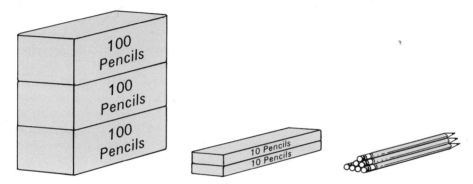

A convention used to facilitate reading numbers beyond 4 digits, e.g., 23240061397, is to separate the numeral into "periods" of 3 digits each insofar as possible, beginning at the right, and separating each period with a comma: 23,240,061,397. This is not strictly a characteristic of the numeration system itself, and in various European countries the convention is different—in some, the periods are 6 digits in length, and in some, the commas are replaced by dots, e.g., 23240,061397 or 23.240.061.397. (Germans use dots where we use commas and commas where we use dots.)

Related to this is our system of assigning word names to larger numbers. Again, this is independent of the basic system, and varies somewhat from society to society. Our system is rather complex. To help appreciate the child's potential confusion with it, we summarize it here in some detail. The numbers from one through nine are named with short basic words. (These same words are later combined, sometimes in modified form, in naming larger numbers.) As was previously mentioned, the words themselves do not bear any obvious order relationship among themselves or to the numbers they name. The same is true for zero, ten, eleven, and twelve, but from thirteen through nineteen the words have the common -teen suffix appended to the root words three through nine. These seven words begin the first repetitive pattern in the system—adding ten ("teen") to the root words, which in the cases of three and five are slightly modified ("thir" and "fif"). The multiples of ten, from twenty through ninety, are derivations of the basic words "two" through "nine," appended with the -ty suffix, interpreted to mean "multiplied by ten." From twenty-one through ninety-nine, excluding the multiples of ten, the names are hyphenated and imply addition, e.g., "twenty-three" means "twenty plus three." Multiples of 100 from 100 through 900 are two-word expressions (unhyphenated), such as "three hundred" which means 3×100. All remaining numbers through 999 (excluding those mentioned above) are represented, without punctuation, as sums of the form "X hundred (plus) Y" where X ranges from 1 through 9 and Y is one of the already mentioned forms, e.g.,

> Three hundred eleven   : $(3 \times 100) + (10 + 1)$
> Six hundred forty   : $(6 \times 100) + (4 \times 10)$
> Eight hundred thirty-two: $(8 \times 100) + (3 \times 10) + 2$

Beyond 999, the word names within each period are verbalized by applying the above rules (except that zeroes in the first and/or first and second positions are ignored) and appended by the appropriate period name, "thousand," "million," "billion," and so on, except that no name is appended to the final period and if each digit in the period is zero, nothing is verbalized. Commas between periods abbreviate addition. It is somewhat curious, perhaps, that this complex system is very repetitive, yet the word "zero" is never used except to name the number zero itself.

Small wonder that children are confused by this word-name system! Expressed formally, the numeral 23,840,061,397 must be interpreted

$$(2 \times 10^1 + 3 \times 10^0) \times 10^9 + (8 \times 10^2 + 4 \times 10^1) \times 10^6 + (6 \times 10^1$$
$$+ 1 \times 10^0) \times 10^3 + (3 \times 10^2 + 9 \times 10^1 + 7 \times 10^0) \times 10^0$$

or

$$(20 + 3) \times 10^9 + (800 + 40) \times 10^6 + (60 + 1) \times 10^3 + (300 + 90 + 7) \times 10^0$$

or

$$23 \times 1,000,000,000 + 840 \times 1,000,000 + 61 \times 1000 + 397 \times 1$$

or

$$23 \text{ billion} + 840 \text{ million} + 61 \text{ thousand} + 397$$

Although period names exist to at least vigintillion (7 vigintillion means 7×10^{63}, or 7 followed by 63 zeroes) numbers of this magnitude are almost always expressed in "scientific notation" rather than either standard numerals or word names.

Numbers are frequently "rounded (off)," particularly when they are especially large or small. Rounding a number "to the nearest n," when n is a power of ten, means naming the multiple of that power of ten *nearest* to the given number, e.g., 23,840,061,397 is rounded to 23,840,061,000 to the nearest thousand, 23,840,000,000 to the nearest million, and 24,000,000,000 to the nearest billion. Normally numbers are rounded only to their largest period — 23,840,061,397 would usually be rounded to the nearest billion — and are commonly expressed with a combination of numeral and word names, such as "23 billion." Fortunately, word names for such large numbers rarely need be *written*, although it is sometimes necessary to verbalize them, e.g., "twenty-three billion, eight hundred forty million, sixty-one thousand, three hundred ninety-seven."

Activities and Materials for Teaching Prenumeration Concepts

Numeration concepts evolve gradually and quite naturally from activities designed for teaching the number concepts for zero through nine. Unlike the number concepts, which normally receive major attention only in the primary grades, the more complex numeration concepts are taught, spiral fashion, throughout elementary school as the child is gradually able to conceptualize larger numbers.

The preceding section should have suggested two essential pre-numeration concepts. Before a child can begin to understand numeration he must first have an understanding of the numbers zero through nine, which were discussed in the first part of the chapter, and the partitioning of sets, which we will now discuss.

Children need to learn that a set can be partitioned into subsets in various ways without affecting its number, e.g., a set of 5 can be partitioned into subsets of 1 and 4; 2 and 3; 1, 2, and 2; and so on. In particular, sets with from 10 to 99 elements can be partitioned into tens and ones.

This prenumeration concept can begin, of course, while teaching the numbers one through nine. But it is particularly crucial in teaching the numbers ten, eleven, and twelve. Suppose we first consider the task of teaching the *number* ten, as "one more than nine." This can be done using the same activities suggested for teaching the numbers zero through nine. There is a crucial difference, however, in teaching the *numeral* 10, the first numeral the child encounters that is significantly different from the preceding ones. The teacher must acknowledge several potential difficulties in teaching children the meaning of the numeral 10. Specifically, it is the first multidigit numeral and as such involves the place-value notion, which has not been used in naming the lesser numbers. Thus understanding the numeral 10, and all that follow it, involves learning a system, unlike the basic numerals. That system involves a possible, if not actual, grouping (partitioning) of the elements of any set it represents. Also, the corresponding word name seems analogous to those for smaller numbers and does not itself suggest a 2-part numeral. (The same is true for 11 and 12.) The numeral names a number greater than nine yet uses the symbols for the *least* two numbers, zero and one, both of which are uniquely difficult, incidentally, for reasons we have seen. A final difficulty lies in that there is a new and rather subtle semantic problem in naming a number with a pair of numbers: Up to nine, the numerals or number words are normally used by children as adjectives, i.e., the child sees, for example, a set of *3 pencils*: *3* identifies a certain property of a specific collection. While the same holds true for 10 pencils or 16 pencils or 24 pencils, we frequently need to use expressions such as, 1 ten and 0 ones (or 1 ten and no ones), 1 ten and 6 ones, or 2 tens and 4 ones. Numbers such as ten and one used in the above way as nouns are new to the child and can be confusing. He hasn't normally had to think of 7 pencils as "1 seven" or "a seven." Efforts must be made to make this new and more abstract use of number seem reasonable and meaningful.

A suggested approach to this problem is to temporarily postpone it. That is, teach the numbers 10, 11, and 12, including their word names, but avoid the numerals until all three numbers are reasonably well understood. Numerous partitioning activities are needed to prepare children for the conventional notation and new vocabulary. A child can be asked, for example, to separate a set of 12 objects into subsets of 3 objects each.

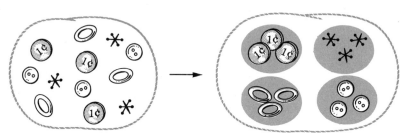

In talking about the grouping, the abbreviated expression "4 threes" can be casually introduced to replace "4 subsets (or sets) of 3 elements each." This activity should be repeated with several different sets and with each factor of 12 except 12 and 1, i.e., 12 can be separated into twos, fours, and sixes. Similarly, 10 can be separated into twos and fives. Eleven is prime, so this particular activity would not be appropriate for it. The converse activity should be practiced, too. That is, the teacher can partition the set and ask the child to describe the partitioning and to tell the total number. The activity can be used with the smaller composite numbers, 4, 6, 8, and 9 as well. It can also be varied by asking the child to determine, for example, how many threes there are in a set of 12. When the child can meaningfully think of 10 as 2 fives or 5 twos and 12 as 2 sixes, 3 fours, 4 threes, or 6 twos, he can be given the task of separating a set of 12, for example, into "3 twos and 2 threes" or "2 fours and 2 twos," and to "fill in the blanks" in one of these ways:

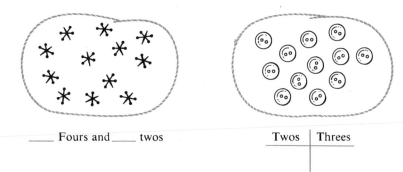

_____ Fours and _____ twos   Twos | Threes

These early partitioning activities should be structured so that both the sub-set size and the number of subsets is greater than 1, and are, therefore, restricted to these combinations:

4: 2 twos
6: 2 threes; 3 twos
8: 2 fours; 4 twos
9: 3 threes
10: 2 fives; 5 twos; 2 twos and 2 threes
12: 2 sixes; 3 fours; 4 threes; 6 twos; 3 twos and 2 threes

Having done these, most children should be ready to understand the more difficult expressions where the number of subsets of a given size is 1, e.g., 1 four and 1 six, and additional combinations can be introduced:

8: 1 two and 2 threes; 1 four and 2 twos; 1 two and 1 six;
1 three and 1 five
9: 2 twos and 1 five; 1 two and 1 seven; 1 three and 1 six;
1 four and 1 five
10: 2 twos and 1 six; 2 threes and 1 four; 2 fours and 1 two;
3 twos and 1 four; 1 two and 1 eight; 1 three and 1 seven;
1 four and 1 six
11: 2 twos and 1 seven; 2 threes and 1 five; 2 fours and 1 three;
1 two and 1 nine; 1 three and 1 eight; 1 four and 1 seven;
1 five and 1 six
12: 2 twos and 1 eight; 2 threes and 1 six; 2 fives and 1 two;
3 twos and 1 six; 1 two and 1 ten; 1 three and 1 nine;
1 four and 1 eight; 1 five and 1 seven

(Adequate performance in these activities is evidence of readiness for addition, multiplication, and division.) The more difficult concept involving 1 as a subset "size" can now be introduced, e.g., 2 ones, 4 ones, etc. The variations this can provide would include:

3: 1 two and 1 one
4: 1 two and 2 ones
8: 1 five and 3 ones
10: 2 fours and 2 ones
12: 2 threes and 6 ones

At this point, by appropriately separating sets into the maximum possible number of subsets, children can be led to see the very important equivalence of 4 ones and 1 four, 8 ones and 1 eight, 1 ten and 10 ones, etc. At a still higher level of difficulty, children can be asked to partition sets into, say, threes and ones where the number of ones is 0, e.g., sets of 6, 9, or 12 elements. This will require careful guidance, but they should soon be able to report that such a set has, for example, 3 threes and no ones, or 3 threes and 0 ones. The choice of ones is arbitrary though purposeful. Alternatively, a child could be asked to partition a set of 8 into fours and twos: 2 fours and 0 twos. Emphasis here, as in the preceding activity, should be on first obtaining the maximum possible number of the *larger* size; otherwise ambiguity can occur, e.g.:

$$8 = 2 \text{ fours and } 0 \text{ ones} \quad or \quad 1 \text{ four and } 4 \text{ ones}$$

Also, it is desirable to include many sets of twelve, eleven, and ten objects (in that order) to be grouped as tens and ones. This activity paves the way for introducing the numerals 10, 11, and 12 as standard abbreviations for 1 ten and 0 ones, 1 ten and 1 one, and 1 ten and 2 ones, respectively.

It should be mentioned that expressions like "1 ten and 2 ones" may be related to multiplication or addition, but need not be. That is, a child's understanding of these expressions does not depend on the more formal interpretations of "1 ten" as 1×10, "2 ones" as 2×1, or "1 ten *and* 2 ones" as 1 ten + 2 ones or $(1 \times 10) + (2 \times 1)$. Such relationships can be made later, when the child's concepts of these operations are developed.

Also, activities at this stage are most effective when the sets chosen to represent the numbers contain simple, relatively small elements of the same kind, which are normally packaged in tens or can be visualized as packaged that way. This includes many things such as pencils, crayons, eggs, matches, hamburger rolls, etc., which may in fact be more commonly packaged in fives, sixes, eights, dozens, or twenties. Ten is a "triangular" number and can be conveniently represented in the triangular configurations:

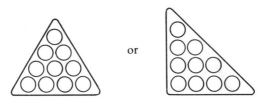

in various stages of abstraction:

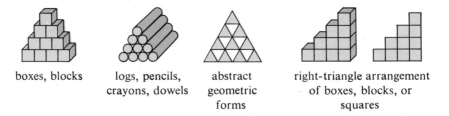

| boxes, blocks | logs, pencils, crayons, dowels | abstract geometric forms | right-triangle arrangement of boxes, blocks, or squares |

Activities and Materials for Teaching Numeration Concepts and Skills

Once 10, 11, and 12 are understood and the processes of grouping objects by tens and recording the number of elements in a set as "tens and ones" is established, the child is ready for more formal instruction. But before considering specific materials and activities for this purpose, a few preliminary remarks and reminders are in order.

There are many devices, models, materials, and activities which lend themselves to developing numeration concepts and skills. These vary widely in their abstractness, in their effectiveness for teaching specific skills, in their appropriateness for particular children, and in their limitations. Encountering an abstract concept in a variety of ways is a key to understanding. Providing this variety and carefully selecting appropriate activities is an important part of the teacher's job.

Numeration as a topic is developed throughout the elementary school, not just in the primary grades. The spiral approach is used to gradually lead children to understanding and to increased skill. At times, numeration is taught per se, but certain aspects are more reasonably developed in the context of learning other things, especially the "renaming" aspects of the addition and subtraction algorithms. Only those activities for teaching numeration specifically are discussed in this chapter; others will be discussed in later chapters.

Once prenumeration skills have been developed, including the numeration involved in teaching the numbers ten through twelve, the varied partitioning activities associated with teaching the lesser numbers can be replaced by partitioning mostly by tens and ones. This type of activity, together with emphasis on the patterns that emerge for the first time between the numerals 3 through 9 and 13 through 19, dominate this next stage of instruction. When this is completed, children generally move more quickly to twenty, then still more quickly through 99, and finally to 100 and the numbers up to 999. Considerable time is spent on the numerals to 999, since mastery of this period sets the stage for subsequent periods. The 1-to-10 and 10-to-1 relationships between successive place values are crucial to understanding larger numbers, and should be extended to include emphasis on the 1-to-100 and 100-to-1 relationships between place values that are *next* to adjacent, i.e., ones and hundreds, tens and thousands, and hundreds and ten-thousands.

A particularly important precaution is warranted relative to the treatment of zero. One frequently hears the misleading statements "zero is nothing" or "zero is nothing but a place holder." On the contrary, zero is a bona fide number; and, like one, two, three, and the rest up to nine, its numeral is used as a "place holder." Its uniqueness as a place holder is evident only when we use it to round numbers as approximations for more precise large numbers such as those expressing national debts, heights of mountains, or distances to celestial neighbors. Otherwise it functions precisely as the other numbers.

Finally, the role of unconventional and nonstandard numeration systems should be mentioned. The role of such systems should be regarded as twofold: To provide added insight into the intricate mechanics of the conventional system, and to provide enrichment, historical perspective, and appreciation for it. Activities with systems patterned after the Hindu-Arabic system except for a change of base can provide valuable insight into the abstract concept of base and its role in our system, but must be used carefully to avoid defeating that very purpose. Similarly, studies of ancient numeration systems can provide enrichment, insight, and perspective, but only if they are treated as such, not as basic subject matter with expectations of skill acquisition.

The materials and activities in the final section of this chapter are intended to develop the essential concepts reviewed earlier. These concepts can be viewed as consequences of acquiring the following *skills*, some of which are normally taught, or introduced, in the early grades, while others would not be appropriate until later. In any event, the elementary school child should ultimately be able to do each of the following:

1. Partition a collection of up to 100 objects or pictures of objects into "tens" and "ones" to determine and report its number. He should be able to describe how the process could be extended beyond 100, even though it would normally be impractical to do so.
2. Describe the meaning of a standard numeral such as 23 as a sum of products, i.e., 23 means $2 \times 10 + 3 \times 1$, or, less formally, 23 means 2 tens + 3 ones. (Here "2 tens" is understood to mean 2×10.)
3. Demonstrate the equivalence of 1 ten and 10 ones via bundling and unbundling appropriate objects. For example, ten pencils, held together with a rubber band, would be a model for "1 ten"; removing the rubber band leaves the pencils intact, but they would then be viewed as "10 ones." The child should be able to describe, if not exhibit, extensions of this notion, e.g., the relationships between 10 and 100, 1 and 100, and so on.
4. Use numeration understandings, so that when given two (or more) different numbers, each greater than 9, he can put them in their natural order; e.g., 1425 < 1435 since 2 (tens) < 3 (tens).
5. Name and be able to write, in their natural order, the numbers from 1 to n, where n is some whole number greater than 9 (how much greater depends on the child's progress, of course). Also, he should be able to write the names of the numbers from k to n where $k \neq 1$, e.g., 28 to 36. That is, he should know and be able to use the patterns in the natural sequence of numerals.
6. Skip count by tens, hundreds, thousands, etc., and describe the relationship between this and "normal" counting from 1, i.e.,

$$10, 20, 30, 40, \ldots$$
$$\updownarrow \quad \updownarrow \quad \updownarrow \quad \updownarrow$$
$$1, \quad 2, \quad 3, \quad 4, \quad \ldots$$

7. Be able to provide several corresponding expanded numerals for a given standard numeral, such as 243:

$$2 \text{ hundreds} + 4 \text{ tens} + 3 \text{ ones}$$

$$200 + 40 + 3$$

$$(2 \times 100) + (4 \times 10) + (3 \times 1)$$

$$(2 \times 10^2) + (4 \times 10^1) + (3 \times 10^0)$$

$$(2 \times 10 \times 10) + (4 \times 10) + (3 \times 1)$$

8. Skip count by 2s, 5s, and 10s and identify resulting patterns.
9. Use an abacus (or similar device) to represent a given number; conversely, name the number represented on an abacus.
10. Write the numerals for whole numbers up to billions, including proper use of commas, and recognition of the 1–10–100 pattern within each period. Be able to read such numerals correctly; i.e., given either the word name or the standard numeral for a large whole number, provide the other.
11. Round a whole number to the nearest (given) multiple of 10^n; e.g., round 847 to the nearest 10, or the nearest hundred.
12. Read and write numerals according to unconventional systems, such as Egyptian, Roman, Base Five, etc.; e.g., given a standard base ten numeral, identify the corresponding Egyptian numeral, and conversely.

Some of the preceding objectives, of themselves, suggest obvious activities leading to their accomplishment. The use of certain instructional materials for some of the others will be discussed in the remaining sections of this chapter. Many or all of these materials are commercially available, with detailed suggestions for their use, and our discussion is intended only as a sampling of possible activities.

The Place Value Chart

The place value chart is designed to focus a child's attention on two key features of the Hindu-Arabic system—place value and face value. Several forms and variations can be selected, according to children's maturity. Typically, these charts are large enough for classroom demonstration-participation activities, but some can be easily devised for individual use. One version is a *pocket chart*, made of tagboard folded into two or three pockets for holding tickets. Place values are indicated by labels, and the number in each place is represented by inserting that number of tickets or a single numeral card in each pocket (or both).

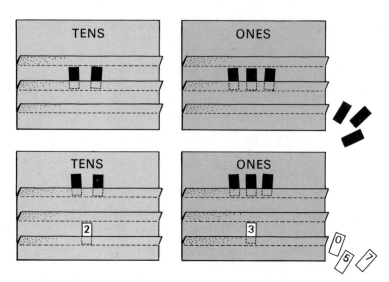

Tickets may be of different colors for different places or, at a more concrete level, each marker in tens place may actually be ten tickets, bundled together with a rubber band. More charts, labeled "Hundreds," "Thousands," and so on, may be added as needed or a single chart may be partitioned into three or more places; labels can be interchanged to change bases, and tickets may include pictures to suggest values.

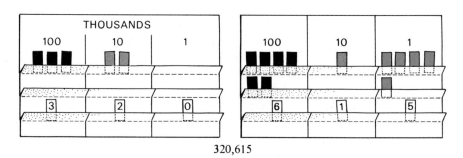

320,615

$132_{(FIVE)}$

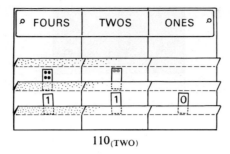

110(TWO)

Other types of place value charts include: charts with brass clips or pegs to hold tickets with holes punched in them;

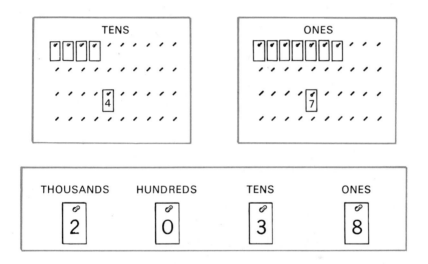

boards with nine lights in each place, any number of which may be turned on;

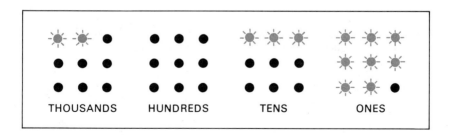

and Papy's "Minicomputer," a device that represents each place value as a square card, partitioned into four smaller squares, each of a different color.

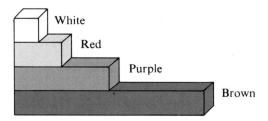

The colors match those of the white, red, purple, and brown Cuisenaire rods

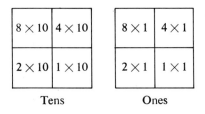

which, when white is used as the unit, represent the numbers 1, 2, 4, and 8, respectively. These colors represent *multiples* of the base. Markers are

8 × 10	4 × 10
2 × 10	1 × 10

Tens

8 × 1	4 × 1
2 × 1	1 × 1

Ones

placed in appropriate small squares to represent the products desired, and the sum of the values shown is the total value of that place.

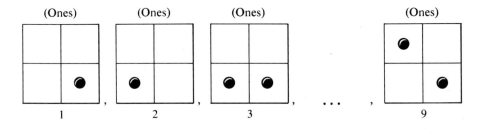

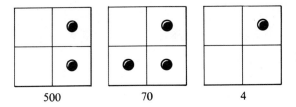

Each child can make his own place value chart by simply labeling one or more sheets of plain white paper appropriately. Numbers can be represented by any kind of small markers, such as chips, coins, corn, etc.

TENS	ONES
● ●	● ● ● ● ●

Experience with place value charts would include activities along the following lines. (a) One child (or the teacher) sets up the chart to represent a number, and a second child is asked to name the number. (b) A child is given a number and is asked to represent it on the chart. (c) Counting can be done by representing each of 1, 2, 3, 4, and so on, in order on the chart; or with a number already set up on the board, the child is expected to represent the next one, then the next, and so on. Or he is asked to represent his count of a given set of objects on the chart as he goes along. (d) Trading activities, where the chart is "overloaded" in one or more places, requiring the child to simplify the board, without changing value:

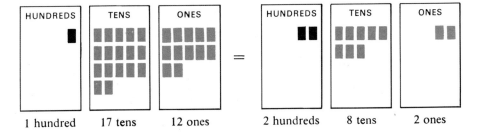

Conversely, given a board with a standard numeral represented, the child is asked to show how he could obtain more ones (or tens, etc.) without changing the *total* value shown on the board:

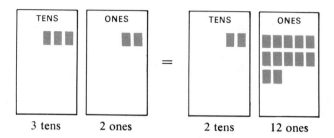

(e) Comparison activities, involving *two* place value charts either of the same or of different types, with numbers represented on each of them (or two numbers represented on different lines, pockets, or rows, of the same chart), and asking the child to identify the larger number.

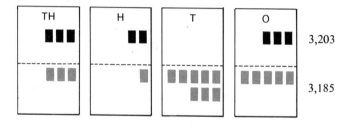

(f) A multiplying activity that involves first showing a number on a place value chart, then shifting each marker one place (or two places) to the left or right, and having children compare the two numbers.

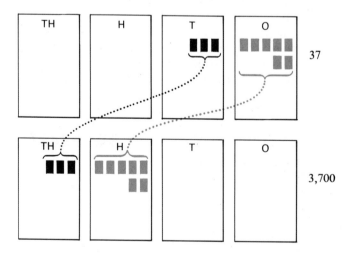

The teacher who experiments with place value charts by himself before using them with children (a strongly recommended procedure) will find that the manipulations can be relatively time-consuming and it is easy to make errors. Children should be carefully observed to assure that they maneuver the device accurately. It should be emphasized that the place value chart is *not* particularly effective for visualizing relative place values — a ticket in thousand's place *looks* just like a ticket in ten's place. In this sense, they are a relatively abstract tool.

Place value charts are useful in teaching computational procedures and decimals. These activities will be discussed in subsequent chapters.

The Abacus

The abacus or counting frame is an ancient device which, although it has appeared in many forms, has remained essentially unchanged for centuries. It is still in relatively common use in the Orient, and those who use it do so with amazing rapidity. The basic instrument used in elementary schools today consists of a frame supporting several parallel wires or strings representing successive place values, and beads or other markers designed to represent "face values." The markers may be permanently strung on the wires or may be added or removed as needed. Each child can have his own abacus consisting of a sheet of plain white paper with "wires" drawn on it and a pile of markers.

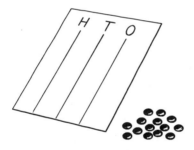

There are several common types of classroom abacuses. The frame type of abacus has either nine or ten beads strung on each strand of wire or

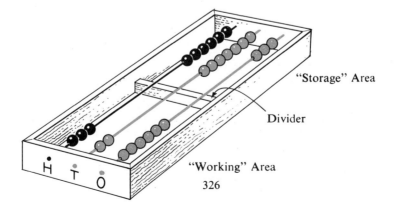

string. These are housed in a box, usually with a wooden divider crossing under the flexible wires midway between top and bottom to separate the "working" beads from those not being used. Beads are moved from "storage" to the working part by sliding them over the divider. (There are numerous equivalents of this basic physical structure.) When ten beads are used, the tenth one, farthest from the working area, is a "reminder." Frequently the beads in one column are all of one color, with a different color for each column; in this case, the reminder bead may be of the same color as those in the next column.

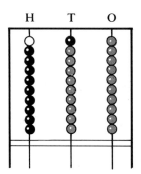

The *spike abacus* consists of a row of dowels or long nails mounted on a board. Markers such as washers or empty thread spools can be strung on the spikes as needed. The spike abacus has an advantage over the frame

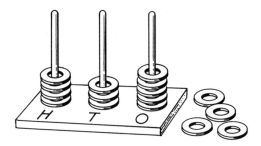

type in that unused markers can be kept aside, where they are less likely to distract and confuse the child. Spikes may be long enough to hold 9, 10, or up to 18 markers.

The *Yoder abacus* has rigid curved strands mounted vertically on a board, with a divider to hide the unused markers. Like the spike abacus, it may have up to eighteen markers, any number of which may be taken out of "storage" by flipping them along the wire over the divider.

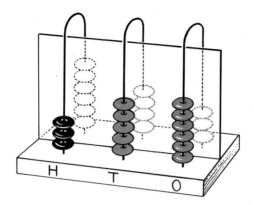

Most of the activities suggested for place value charts are equally suitable, with minor adaptations imposed by the apparatus, for the abacus. "Trading" activities are probably too complex to be feasible on the frame abacus, although they can be performed on the other types, providing there are sufficient reserve markers and space to exhibit them. The same is true for comparison activities, for which clothespins or similar dividers can separate markers used to represent different numbers.

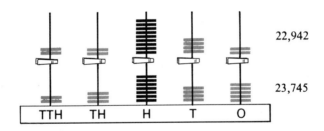

The limitations of the abacus parallel those of the place value chart. For example, the representation of 99 uses eighteen beads, while 100 requires only one. This can be misleading to children unless they are carefully guided. The abacus is highly representative with respect to place values.

Procedures for *counting* with the abacus should be carefully practiced by the teacher before they are demonstrated to children: Counting from 1 to 9 is straightforward, one marker is advanced for each successive number, but going from 9 to 10 requires a two-step move: One marker is advanced in the tens column and the 9 markers are returned to "storage" (or removed, in the case of the spike abacus). On the 10-bead frame abacus, once 9 beads have been advanced there are no additional beads in ones column except the reminder bead which must remain there, serving only as a clue to advance one bead in the next column. The spike abacus and the Yoder type have no such reminder (although on the spike abacus the dowels can be made exactly long enough to hold 9 markers so there is no room for an erroneous tenth one, or the spikes can be painted a contrasting color at the crucial point). A similar two-step move must be made at each multiple of ten, and when both ones and tens are full (99), they *both* must be cleared when advancing the single bead in hundreds place. The same type of manipulation is necessary at each power of ten, of course.

Again paralleling the place value chart, the abacus is useful in teaching some computational procedures, including those with decimals, and will be discussed further in subsequent chapters devoted to those topics.

The Stern Materials

There are a variety of ways in which the Stern unit blocks and number track can be used effectively to develop certain numeration concepts and skills in addition to the prenumber and number concepts already discussed.

1. Given a collection of up to ten 1-blocks and a collection of one each of the unit blocks for 2 to 10, the student is asked to determine, for example, "How many 1-blocks match the 5-block?" This matching can be done by either measuring or counting: He lines up five 1-blocks end-to-end and discovers the equivalence of 5 ones and 1 five, or he counts the sections in the 5-block. This activity is particularly crucial for establishing the equivalence of 1 ten and 10 ones.

2. Given a collection of between ten and twenty 1-blocks and a set of one each of the blocks for 1 through 10, a child can be asked to *trade* the collection for an equivalent collection (one of the same length when put end-to-end) which contains a 10-block and one other block. He learns, for example, that 16 ones are equivalent to 1 ten and 1 six. An important variation of this is to give the student only the ones and a ten, so that he must trade 16 ones for 1 ten and 6 ones. This activity can then be extended by increasing the number of ones to, say, 32 and providing the student with sufficient 10-blocks to discover that 32 ones is equivalent to 3 tens and 2 ones or 3 tens and 1 two.

3. Given a collection of several (up to nine) 10-blocks and at most one different block, the student is asked to determine their combined value. This can be done by *counting* the tens (e.g., 4 tens and 1 six so its value is 46) or by *measuring* the collection by putting it on the number track and reading the result directly. Or, given several 10-blocks and several 1-blocks (up to nine), he can count tens and ones to determine the value to be, say, 4 tens and 6 ones, or 46.

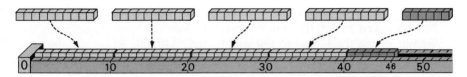

4. Given *two* collections, each containing up to nine 10-blocks and up to nine 1-blocks (or up to nine 10-blocks and at most one block shorter than a 10-block), the student can be asked, "Which collection has more?" This can be determined by matching the collections in various ways: by lining them up end-to-end, with or without the number track; by stacking them up side-by-side; or by lining them up either end-to-end or side-by-side and cancelling the common tens. If the two collections have the *same* number of 10-blocks, then he sees that his decision depends on the remaining ones, but if the number of 10-blocks is *different*, he can decide on the basis of the 10-blocks, e.g.,

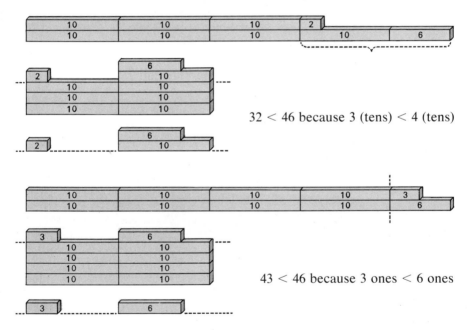

32 < 46 because 3 (tens) < 4 (tens)

43 < 46 because 3 ones < 6 ones

5. Given a fairly large collection (as many as possible) of 2-blocks, 5-blocks, or 10-blocks, and a number track, a child can be asked to record the lengths of each of the successive "trains" made by adding on blocks of the same kind. This can lead to the development of patterns in the ones-place digits of the sequences,

$$2, 4, 6, 8, 10, 12, 14, \ldots$$
$$5, 10, 15, 20, 25, 30, 35, \ldots$$
$$10, 20, 30, 40, 50, 60, 70, \ldots$$

6. Given up to nine 10-blocks, one other block, and a number track, a child can be asked to lay the blocks end-to-end on the track, starting at the 0-point of the track, and to tell which "ten" (10, 20, 30, . . . , 90) the (right) end of the train is nearest to. This leads to rounding numbers, e.g.,

>   4 tens and 1 three is closest to 40 on the track
>   4 tens and 1 seven is closest to 50 on the track
>   4 tens and 1 five is equally close to 40 and 50 on the track

These activities may suggest related ones. It is fairly easy to duplicate the Stern unit blocks and number track from wood, masonite, tagboard, plastic, or paper (see Appendix B). Since these materials can be used for teaching many concepts other than numeration, it is well to consider making them of fairly permanent material.

The Dienes Multibase Arithmetic Blocks (MAB)

The Dienes Multibase Arithmetic Blocks, or Dienes blocks as they are sometimes called, are sets of unpainted wooden blocks, developed by Z. P. Dienes. Each set includes blocks of 4 sizes, called *units*, *longs*, *flats*, and *blocks*, respectively. The *shapes* of the units and of the blocks are similar — both are cubes — but their *sizes* are different. There are six *sets*

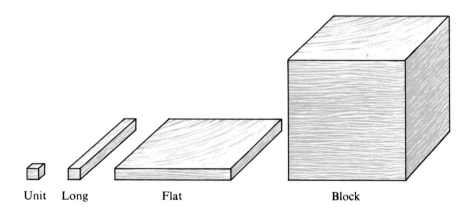

Unit   Long   Flat   Block

of blocks, based on size ratios of 2, 3, 4, 5, 6, and 10, respectively. These are sometimes called the *base two* blocks, the *base three* blocks, and so on. In each set, the unit blocks are of a common size (about 9 mm on each edge). The remaining blocks are segmented, like the Stern blocks, and are scaled in size to represent successive *powers* of the respective bases, up to the 3rd power. Thus in the base 10 set, for example, a long looks like 10 units glued together, a flat looks like 10 longs or 100 units, and a block looks like 10 flats or 100 longs or 1000 units. The workmanship in the materials is very precise, so this image is highly effective.

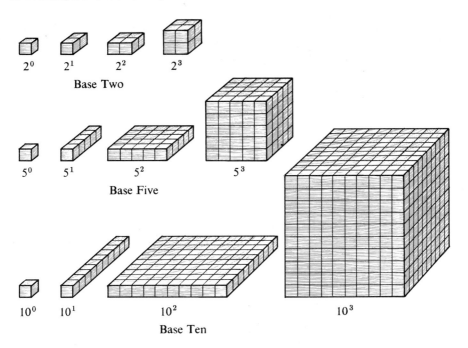

2^0 2^1 2^2 2^3

Base Two

5^0 5^1 5^2 5^3

Base Five

10^0 10^1 10^2 10^3

Base Ten

Still larger numbers can be represented by arranging the blocks into "long blocks," "flat blocks," "block blocks," etc. Using base-ten blocks, for example, a long block is made by placing 10 blocks end-to-end, making a shape that looks like a big long. It represents 10^4 or 10,000. Ten long blocks side-by-side form a flat block, representing 10^5, and a block block contains ten flat blocks. Analogous shapes can be made with each set (base), of course. Although there are physical limitations on the actual construction of some of these, experience with the blocks will lead to their conceptualization — they can be imagined.

The base-ten Dienes blocks lend themselves to the teaching of many specific numeration skills, and the blocks collectively are particularly suitable for developing the more *general* concept of "base" as it is used in numeration. Unlike most devices, such as the place value chart and the abacus, the Dienes blocks provide a concrete visual image of the relative place values up to thousands, and a basis for mentally visualizing values beyond that. By repeating activities with different bases, the more generalized concept of relative values of successive powers of any base can be developed. This is the purpose of the neutral labeling of the materials, for example, as "longs" and "flats" rather than "tens" and "hundreds," or "fives" and "twenty-fives."

Another significant difference between the Dienes material and the place value chart or abacus is that while the blocks provide a good model for the relative place *values* they do not in themselves suggest the left-to-right positional feature of the numeration system. This limitation can be overcome by using the blocks on a wooden or masonite playing board on which specific places for each size block are marked off:

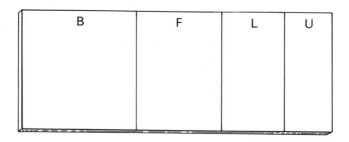

Although full appreciation of the potential usefulness of the Dienes blocks is best accomplished by examining the materials together with the prepared student activities and teacher's guides, a few samples are suggested here. In general, the activities will be most effective if students keep records or notes as they proceed. (The reader should recognize conceptual parallels between these exercises and those for the materials discussed previously.) (a) Given a relatively large collection of units, say 15, trade them insofar as possible for longs of a given base. Trade these, in turn, for flats, insofar as possible, and repeat the trading until the resulting collection contains the fewest pieces of wood possible. Repeat for different bases, e.g.,

> 15 units is equivalent to 1 block, 1 flat, 1 long, and 1 unit,
> > using base two materials
> > or 1 flat and 2 longs, using base three
> > materials
> > or 3 longs and 3 units, using base four materials
> > or 3 longs using base five materials
> > or 2 longs and 3 units, using base six materials
> > or 1 long and 5 units, using base ten materials

For any base, b, this activity can be (theoretically) repeated for up to $b^4 - 1$ units, i.e., up to 15 units with base two, up to 80 units with base three, up to 255 units with base four, or up to 9,999 units with base ten. (b) Given a particular collection from the base ten set (up to 9 each of units, longs, flats, and blocks), ask a child to name the number of *units* to which the collection is equivalent, i.e., how many units are "contained in" the collection. (c) Ask the child to represent a given number using base ten materials. (d) Have a child count from one given number to another, e.g., 1 to 42, or 325 to 347, representing each successive number in turn using base ten materials. (e) Given any standard collection from the base ten materials, ask the child to show how he could trade to get more units (or more longs or both, and so on) without changing the value of the given collection, e.g.,

$$\text{2 flats, 3 longs, 8 units} = \text{2 flats, 2 longs, 18 units}$$
$$= \text{1 flat, 12 longs, 18 units}$$

(f) Given two collections formed from one set, determine which has the greater "value," i.e., which collection is equivalent to more units.

The Hundred Board

A "hundred board" is a 10-by-10 square array. It can take on a wide variety of forms: it can be printed on paper or made of materials such as

```
o o o o o o o o o o
o o o o o o o o o o
o o o o o o o o o o
o o o o o o o o o o
o o o o o o o o o o
o o o o o o o o o o
o o o o o o o o o o
o o o o o o o o o o
o o o o o o o o o o
o o o o o o o o o o
```

wood, cardboard, or pegboard; and its 100 positions can be represented by squares, dots, dowels, circles, golf tees, holes, or nails.

1	2	3	4	5	6	7	8	9	10
11	12	13	14	15	16	17	18	19	20
21	22	23	24	25	26	27	28	29	30
31	32	33	34	35	36	37	38	39	40

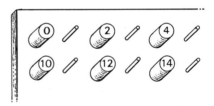

Each position on the board is associated with one of the numbers from 1 to 100 or from 0 to 99. All, some, or none of the numbers may be revealed to the student at a given time, depending on the purpose of the activity for which the board is used. The dowel board (above, right) is accompanied by markers, such as empty thread spools, which slip over the

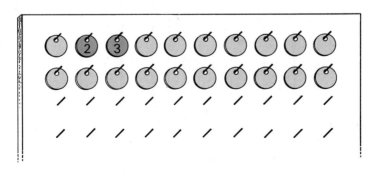

dowels. Numerals are painted on the markers or attached with gummed labels as needed. Similarly, boards can be made with reversible labels such as round or square pieces of tagboard, plastic, aluminum, etc., blank on one side and with numerals on the other. A small hole attaches the label to a small nail on the board (see bottom, preceding page).

The following activities are typical of ways in which the hundred board is used. (a) Using 2, 3, or more rows of squares, on paper, a child may fill in some or all of the squares with the numerals in order. This gives him practice in writing the numerals. More important, it can help him to discover or enforce his understanding of the pattern of their sequence by observing the row and column patterns in that portion of the hundred board. (b) Given an array with reversible labels and with some of the numerals concealed, the child is asked to determine the missing number, then reverse the label to check his answer. (c) A child may identify a sequence, such as the multiples of 2, 3, 4, 5, or 10, in various ways, e.g., putting on labels, taking them off, and so on. (d) The teacher points to a given numeral and asks the child to read it, or asks which number is 10 more, 20 more, 10 less, and so on. (f) String or large rubber bands can be put around, say, five full rows of unmarked pegs and the first four pegs of the next row. The child then determines how many pegs are encompassed and/or the name of the "last" peg. (g) The teacher points to two pegs—in the same row or the same column or elsewhere—and asks which names the larger number and why. (h) The child can use the board to help him count by tens, starting at a number that is not a multiple of ten, e.g., 13, 23, 33, 43, ...

The Counting Board

The counting board resembles the hundred board in that it is essentially a ten-by-ten array, and is called by various names. The Stern version

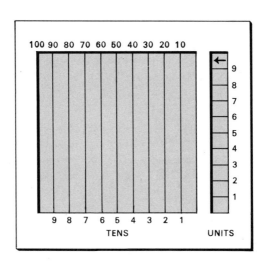

of the counting board is called a *dual board*. It has a 1-by-10 unit opening beside a 10-by-10 unit opening, which will hold a *hundred square*. A hundred square looks like ten 10-blocks glued side-by-side and serves as a visual model for 100, relating it to 10 and to 1. Other forms vary from this in minor ways: some are marked both horizontally and vertically, some are labeled left to right, others not at all, and some do not include the units scale. Counting boards are used with matching blocks such as the Stern 10-blocks and unit cubes, or similar squares and 10-square strips made of cardboard or plastic.

The counting board can be used to demonstrate a given number up to 100 or to name such a number when displayed on the board. The boards with labels eliminate the necessity of counting for this purpose:

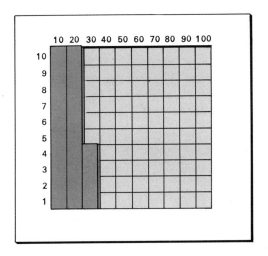

Counting activities involve adding one unit cube or square to the board for each successive number. With the Stern type of model, this is done only in the units column, beginning at the bottom. When the units column is filled, a 10-block is placed in the appropriate column and the units column is emptied before continuing. In models without a separate units column, this process usually begins in the left-most column and proceeds toward the right as 10-blocks replace the units. The counting board can also be used for trading activities, where either a collection of more than ten units is traded, ten at a time, until fewer than 10 units remain, or a standard collection is modified by trading a ten for 10 ones in order to obtain more ones.

Related Materials and Activities

Our discussion of materials such as the place value chart, abacus, Stern materials, Dienes blocks, hundred board, and counting board has covered several common types of activities, particularly counting, including skip counting; trading, with emphasis on the 10–1 relationship between adjacent place values; comparison, which leads to comparing numbers by their numerals; rounding; and interpretation, where a standard numeral is interpreted on a device or, conversely, the student determines the number represented on it.

The reader should be able to modify such activities with related materials, such as real or toy money (pennies, dimes, and dollars for base ten, or pennies, nickles, and quarters for base five). Odometers, the mileage-counting devices on automobile speedometers, exemplify the counting pattern of our numeration system, and effective models of them can be constructed for classroom use. The number line is particularly suited for counting by tens and for rounding activities. The commercially available Cuisenaire rods, centimeter rods, and Unifix cubes have been mentioned briefly; these materials can be used in ways paralleling some of the materials described above in more detail.

Both the Cuisenaire rods and Centimeter rods include rods of ten sizes that represent the numbers 1 through 10. The smallest rod is a cube measuring 1 cm on each edge. The remaining rods of the two sets are similar in that they are unsegmented multiples of the basic cube, measuring 2 cm, 3 cm, 4 cm, and up to 10 cm in length, each rod being a different color. The

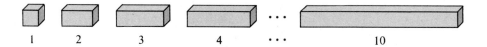

sets differ in that the Cuisenaire rods are made of wood, the Centimeter rods of plastic; the rod colors are different in the two sets; and an individual set of Cuisenaire rods contains several rods of each size, while a Centimeter rod set includes exactly two of each rod size except for the 10-rod, of which there is one. We will leave to the reader assessment of the advantages and limitations in these differences.

The Unifix cubes are varicolored plastic cubes measuring about 19 mm on each edge, except that each cube is constructed so that it can snap together with others. These cubes are accompanied by supplementary materials similar to those of the Stern set, and can be used in the same ways.

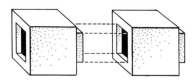

One final numeration device, which can be made or purchased, is the "counting man." This is a plastic, wooden, or masonite caricature of a man with outstretched hands; his fingers are detachable strips of metal attached to magnets in his palms — or clothespins. He represents numbers, as children do, by holding up an appropriate number of fingers. The counting man can be used in teaching numbers up to ten, but for numeration purposes at least two men are needed — a ones man, a tens man, and so on. The uses of this appealing device should be self-evident, as should its limitations.

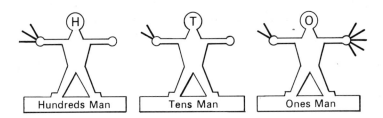

In conclusion, it should be emphasized again that while many devices and materials can be made or purchased for teaching number and numeration concepts, none is complete — all have their advantages and limitations, and the abstract kind of conceptual learning we use them for requires that they be varied. They must be supplemented and complemented with teacher-directed activities, including demonstrations, discussions, and instructions for paper-and-pencil exercises. And, finally, they must ultimately be discarded — and *will* be, quite naturally, by children, each in his own time. When they have served their purpose and a child can function with understanding, independent of physical apparatus, he should be allowed to do so, encouraged to do so, and expected to do so.

Projects, Questions, and Suggested Activities

1. Suppose you are a second-grade teacher and you suspect that a particular child doesn't really understand "his numbers" (zero through nine). Make up a diagnostic test to find out if you are right. Write it as though a teacher's aide is to administer it orally to the child: For each question or activity, tell the aide what materials to display, what directions to give, and what response to expect. (A similar diagnostic test could be constructed based on numeration understandings and skills.)

2. Suppose you have given a diagnostic test on numeration to a fifth-grade child and find that he seems quite weak on one or more of the skills listed on pp. 82–83 of this chapter. Outline a plan of activities that could be used to reteach the skills. Again, assume a teacher's aide is to do the teaching so be specific about materials, directions, and expectations.

3. Try designing and making some of the apparatus discussed in this chapter (see Appendix B). If possible, use them first by yourself and then with

a child to teach or test him on one or more of the topics discussed in the chapter.

4. Identify some merits and limitations of some of the apparatus listed in this chapter.

5. Just for fun, suppose the positions in our numeration system were reversed, e.g., suppose 235 meant 2 ones + 3 tens + 5 hundreds. Try a few computations with this "system," e.g., 432 × 26 or 234 ÷ 86.

6. You have probably had some experience with bases other than ten, such as expressing a given number in base five or finding the standard (base ten) numeral equivalent to a given base seven numeral such as 346. (If not, try it.) What would happen if a fraction were chosen as the base? Or a negative number? Consider the decimal extension as well, e.g.,

$$624.35_{(\text{base } 1/2)} = 6 \cdot (\tfrac{1}{2})^2 + 2 \cdot (\tfrac{1}{2})^1 + 4 \cdot (\tfrac{1}{2})^0 + 3 \cdot (\tfrac{1}{2})^{-1} + 5 \cdot (\tfrac{1}{2})^{-2}$$
$$= 6 \cdot \tfrac{1}{4} + 2 \cdot \tfrac{1}{2} + 4 \cdot 1 + 3 \cdot 2 + 5 \cdot 4$$
$$= 32\tfrac{1}{2}$$
$$624.35_{(\text{base } -2)} = 6 \cdot (-2)^2 + 2 \cdot (-2)^1 + 4 \cdot (-2)^0 + 3 \cdot (-2)^{-1} + 5 \cdot (-2)^{-2}$$
$$= 6 \cdot 4 + 2 \cdot (-2) + 4 \cdot (1) + 3 \cdot (-\tfrac{1}{2}) + 5 \cdot (\tfrac{1}{4})$$
$$= 24 - 4 + 4 - \tfrac{3}{2} + \tfrac{5}{4}$$
$$= 23\tfrac{3}{4}$$

See what you can discover about such systems. Can any number be written in such a system? Are there limits on the choice of base (other than that 0 and 1 cannot be used)?

7. Make a list of each different word a child would need to know in order to be able to read or write any number up to 1 hundred; 1 thousand; 1 million; 1 billion.

Suggested Readings

Armstrong, Jenny R., and Schmidt, Harold. "Simple Materials for Teaching Early Number Concepts to Trainable-Level Mentally Retarded Pupils." *The Arithmetic Teacher*, February 1972, pp. 149–53.

> Accurate title. Contains several good ideas for normal children as well.

Bender, Albert E. "Why Johnny Can't Count." *The Arithmetic Teacher*, November 1972, pp. 553–55.

> An amusing analysis of why children have difficulty with word names for numbers. In the same issue, Morgenstern and Pincus (pp. 569–70) describe a good technique for helping children with place-value patterns involved in this skill.

Brainerd, Charles J. "The Origins of Number Concepts." *Scientific American,* March 1973, pp. 101–9.

> Research evidence that children understand and can use *ordinal* use of number before cardinal. "The conclusion that a new 'new math' emphasizing ordinal notions is called for seems inescapable." (p. 109). Should be read.

Danzig, Tobias. *Number: The Language of Science.* Garden City, N.Y.: Doubleday, 1930. (Doubleday Anchor Book #A67).

> "This is beyond doubt the most interesting book on the evolution of mathematics that has ever fallen into my hands" (Albert Einstein). Need we say more? The first chapter is particularly appropriate here.

Gardner, Martin. "Mathematical Games." *Scientific American*, January 1970, pp. 124–27.

> Some historical anecdotes on the abacus.

Green, Roberta. "A Color-Coded Method of Teaching Basic Arithmetic Concepts and Procedures." *The Arithmetic Teacher*, March 1970, pp. 231–33.

> Money talks: Ones are copper, tens are silver, and hundreds are green. Clever idea.

Hicks, Carl D. "EOPDICA." *The Arithmetic Teacher*, January 1973, pp. 17–23.

> An electronic device that can be used to teach set operations and numeration (and several other things).

McKillip, William D. " 'Patterns' — A Mathematics Unit for Three- and Four-Year Olds." *The Arithmetic Teacher*, January 1970, pp. 15–18.

> Activities for developing prenumber Concepts. In the same issue, Vaughn's article (pp. 55–60) on the appropriate use of the language of sets should be required reading for primary grade teachers. A third article in this issue by Rea and Reys (pp. 65–74) discusses the mathematical concepts and skills kindergarten children have before they come to school — a comprehensive report based on a study of over 700 children.

Moser, James M. "Grouping of Objects as a Major Idea at the Primary Level." *The Arithmetic Teacher*, May 1971, pp. 301–5.

> Prenumeration activities also serve as premultiplication and pre-division ones.

Silverman, Helene. "Teacher-Made Materials for Teaching Number and Counting." *The Arithmetic Teacher*, October 1972, pp. 431–33.

> Simple devices made from everyday objects. In this same issue, see Van Arsdel and Lasky's article (p. 445) describing uses of Papy's Minicomputer.

Sowder, Larry. "A Number Is a Set of . . . ? NO!!" *The Arithmetic Teacher*, March 1972, pp. 177–78.

> A caution against excessive formalism in defining numbers. In the same issue, see Pincus' article (pp. 197–99) on word names for whole numbers, and Rinker's article (pp. 209–16) on a third-grade numeration game.

Steinen, Ramon F. "Abstract (Verb) Versus Abstract (Adjective)." *The Arithmetic Teacher*, April 1971, pp. 257–61.

> Good examples of how to help children *arrive at* abstractions rather than having to *cope with* them; subject matter: bases other than ten.

Swain, Robert L. (revised by Eugene D. Nichols). *Understanding Arithmetic*. New York: Holt, Rinehart and Winston, 1965.

> On page 27 (Table 1–6) is a listing of the period names from "billion" to "vigintillion." Many interesting historical facts about numeration can be found in this chapter.

Unenge, Jan. "Introducing the Binary System in Grades Four to Six." *The Arithmetic Teacher*, March 1973, pp. 182–83.

> Activities and strategy games (using weights to teach binary numeration). In the same issue, see Morgenstern's related article (pp. 184–85) in which lights are used for this topic; and Tucker's article (pp. 188–89) in which liquid measures are used to teach the same thing.

Williams, Elizabeth, and Shuard, Hilary. *Primary Mathematics Today*. London: Longman Group, 1970.

> A valuable source book for this and each of the remaining chapters. Thousands of classroom activities. Highly recommended.

5. Teaching the Fundamental Facts

1. Algorithms and Fundamental Facts

Problems involving addition, subtraction, multiplication, or division of whole numbers are solved in one of three ways—by computation, from memory, or by using definitions of the operations. For example, we solve $5 \times 8 = \square$ by using the definition of multiplication or by having memorized that "$5 \times 8 = 40$"; whereas we solve $35 \times 728 = \triangle$ by performing a computation according to a procedure (algorithm) we learned in elementary school. In this chapter, we consider the teaching of those facts that are normally memorized, the so-called "fundamental facts" or "basic facts." Chapter 6 deals with the algorithms.

The fundamental facts are so called because they are necessarily used in our algorithms, and memorizing them facilitates computation. For example, in the usual procedure for solving

$$\begin{array}{r} 384 \\ \times\ 76 \\ \hline \end{array}$$

we use 6 fundamental multiplication facts: $6 \times 4 = 24$, $6 \times 8 = 48$, $6 \times 3 = 18$, $7 \times 4 = 28$, $7 \times 8 = 56$ and $7 \times 3 = 21$. Memorizing them speeds up the computation.

Consider such a problem with two of its digits concealed:

$$\begin{array}{r} 4a2 \\ \times\ 6b \\ \hline \end{array}$$

We know that a is a whole number less than 10, so there are 10 possibilities for a: 0, 1, 2, 3, . . . , 9. The same is true for b, so there are 100 possibilities for $a \times b$. Thus, in order to quickly solve this or any similar problem, the child needs to know all 100 such facts. These, then, are the *fundamental* multiplication facts: they enable us to solve *any* multiplication problem.

Similar analysis of the remaining standard algorithms for whole-number arithmetic reveals that there are exactly 390 fundamental facts:

100 each for addition, subtraction, and multiplication, and 90 for division. The 100 fundamental addition facts are the true statements of the form $a + b = c$, where $a < 10$ and $b < 10$. Since there are again 10 possible whole-number replacements for a and 10 for b, there are 100 such facts. The 100 fundamental multiplication facts are the 100 true statements of the form $a \times b = c$, where $a < 10$ and $b < 10$. In the remainder of the chapter, we will take the common liberty of using the term "fundamental fact" (or "fact") to refer variously to the entire fact, e.g., $3 + 2 = 5$; to a "combination," e.g., $3 + 2$; to an "open" sentence, e.g., $3 + 2 = \square$; to a general form like $a + b = c$; or even, sometimes, to the "solution," 5. Although, of the above, only $3 + 2 = 5$ is (in fact) a fact (!), the appropriate interpretation will hopefully be clear from the context.

Fundamental facts for subtraction and division can be described in terms of those for addition and multiplication. If $a + b = c$ is any fundamental addition fact, then $c - b = a$ is a fundamental subtraction fact. Since there are 100 fundamental addition facts, there are also 100 fundamental subtraction facts. If $a \times b = c$ is a fundamental multiplication fact and $b \neq 0$, then $c \div b = a$ is a fundamental division fact. Since there are 10 possible replacements for a and (only) 9 for b, there are 90 fundamental division facts. For example,

$5 + 2 = 7$ is a fundamental addition fact, since it is a true statement of the form $a + b = c$, where $a < 10$ and $b < 10$, so $7 - 2 = 5$ is a fundamental subtraction fact.

$8 + 7 = 15$ is a fundamental addition fact, so $15 - 7 = 8$ is a fundamental subtraction fact.

$8 \times 5 = 40$ is a fundamental multiplication fact, since it is a true statement of the form $a \times b = c$, and $b \neq 0$, so $40 \div 5 = 8$ is a fundamental division fact.

$9 \times 0 = 0$ is a fundamental multiplication fact of the form $a \times b = c$, but $b = 0$, so $c \div b = a$, i.e., $0 \div 0 = 9$ is *not* a fundamental division fact.

Each of our algorithms has been invented as a short-cut for the more basic definitions in the processes of addition, subtraction, multiplication, and division. As was briefly mentioned in Chapter 4 (and which will be considered in more detail later), many algorithms have been invented throughout history, but they all reflect and can be explained in terms of two things: characteristics of the *numeration systems* within which they evolved, and characteristics of the number systems with which they deal. Our algorithms, and thus our fundamental facts, are, of course, based on the *whole numbers* expressed in the decimal *Hindu-Arabic* numeration system. It is important to note that much of the background needed for understanding the algorithms — essential *numeration* characteristics and essential generalizations about numbers — can be developed while learning the fundamental facts.

2. Mathematical Review

The Number Systems of "Elementary Mathematics"

Learning the fundamental facts of arithmetic is the first step in developing an understanding of one of several number systems the child will encounter during his mathematical education. The concepts developed at this stage provide the basis for understanding subsequent, ever more complete number systems. Since the elementary child develops these concepts so gradually, only his teachers are in a position to view this development in perspective, recognizing how the initial learnings relate to the more general and useful learnings to follow. This, together with the fact that it is impractical to separate the teaching of *number* concepts from the teaching of *numeration* concepts, requires that teachers should have a global concept of number systems and clearly understand the distinction between number systems and numeration systems.

In Chapter 4, it was pointed out that a numeration system consists of a finite set of basic symbols for naming certain key numbers and a set of rules for using these symbols for naming other numbers. A number system, on the other hand, consists of

1. A generally infinite set of things called "numbers." (These can sometimes be formally defined, e.g., in terms of equivalence relations, but are more practically either left undefined or described in terms of certain of their characteristics.)
2. A set of basic operations defined on these numbers or, more intuitively, described in terms of their characteristics.
3. A set of generalizations, e.g., about the operations, which are either assumed to be true (axioms) or which can be logically proven to be true (theorems).

It should be clear, therefore, that numeration systems and number systems are quite distinct; though any numeration system relates to a particular number system.

It is pedagogically worthwhile to recognize that the number systems of elementary mathematics can be viewed as evolving from one to the next in a rather smooth and systematic order. Beginning with the *Natural* Number System, the next system is the System of *Integers*, followed by the *Rational* Number System, the *Real* Number System, and the *Complex* Number System, in that order. The systems are alike in their *general* structure, but two major distinctions among them should be reviewed. First, beyond the Natural Number System, each system (excepting the complex numbers, which, unlike their predecessors, are not ordered) is successively more "complete" than its predecessor. That is, we can do certain things with a given system that cannot be done with its predecessors. For example, we can subtract *any* pair of integers, but not *every* pair of natural numbers (within the Natural Number System alone) and we can divide any pair of rational numbers (excluding zero divisors) but not every pair of integers. A second distinction among the systems is that both the *numbers* and the *operations* of each system, beyond "the Naturals," are defined so that they are distinct from the numbers and operations of the preceding system. These definitions are, however, *in terms of* the predecessor system. That is, integers are defined in terms of natural numbers (sometimes as ordered pairs of natural numbers), and addition of rational numbers is defined in terms of addition and multiplication of integers.

In spite of this second distinction each system is *isomorphic* to a subsystem of its successor. The Natural Number System, for example, is isomorphic to that subsystem of the integers which includes (only) the *positive* integers, and the System of Integers is isomorphic to that subsystem of the Rational Number System which includes those rational numbers that can be put in the form $\frac{a}{+1}$, where a is any integer. Without reviewing all the details of isomorphism, we should recall that two systems that are isomorphic behave exactly alike with respect to their respective operations; e.g., the sum of the two natural numbers 2 and 3 (as that sum is defined for natural numbers), corresponds to the sum of the integers $^+2$ and $^+3$ as *that* sum is defined for integers. The important thing about isomorphism is that isomorphic systems are identical except for notation. Thus, we can view the system of integers, for example, as being *contained in* the entire Rational Number System. In this way, we can view all of the systems as subsets of the Complex Number System, as shown. Then we may think of certain

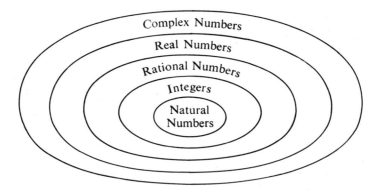

numbers in one system in the notation terms of simpler systems; for example, we can think of the integer $^+2$ as the natural number 2, or we can think of the rational number $\frac{+4}{+1}$ as either the integer $^+4$ or the natural number 4. (-2 and $\frac{+3}{+5}$ cannot be so replaced, however, except that in writing $\frac{+3}{+5}$ as

$\frac{3}{5}$, we are thinking of $^+3$ as 3 and $^+5$ as 5). We can also think of any number in the notation of more sophisticated systems; for example, the natural number 6 can be expressed as $^+6$, $\frac{^+6}{^+1}$, or $6 + 0i$. This intermixing of notation is commonplace because of its convenience. Each system inherits many of the structural characteristics of its predecessors. The fact that addition of natural numbers is commutative, for example, can be identified as the essential factor in proving the analogous characteristic for addition of integers, rational numbers, real numbers, and complex numbers.

The Whole Number System

The elementary school child's introduction to number systems usually begins not with the natural numbers but with the *Whole* Number System. From that system, children have traditionally been introduced to the "Fractional" Number System (the nonnegative rational numbers and their operations). This departure from the sequence described above appears to be based on the pedagogical assumptions that zero is an important number which children should — and can — deal with early; that negative numbers — both negative integers and negative rational numbers — are easier to comprehend after the nonnegative numbers are understood; and that since the arithmetic of integers and rational numbers is performed in terms of the arithmetic of whole and fractional numbers, those systems should be studied first; more formal study of the natural-integer-rational-real-complex sequence can follow later.

Before reviewing the structure of the Whole Number System, we should make one observation: In practice, since fractions quite naturally enter the everyday world, they are introduced long before the child can comprehend the entire structure of the Whole Number System. Similarly, negative numbers cannot be kept hidden from the child's consciousness prior to formal study of the integers, because of such things as below-zero temperatures and game scores which "go in the hole." Some irrational numbers even emerge occasionally in the course of quite normal situations, such as measuring the sides of certain geometric figures. So children quite naturally become aware of and curious about integers, and rational and real numbers in the course of their more formal study of the whole numbers. The logical view of the evolution from the natural numbers to the complex numbers, is, in fact, only a convenient way to organize and synthesize — from the hindsight we are afforded by our historical vantage point — the concepts both man in his collective history and each child in his individual experience more or less "stumble upon" during their corresponding developments. The history of the evolution of the complex number system has been slow and clumsy, marked by a certain amount of resistance and groping for understanding. Children's concepts evolve similarly.

   When considering an evolutionary process such as this, one is led quite naturally to consider beginnings. If the real numbers evolve from the rationals, which are developed from the integers, which in turn "grow" from the natural numbers, where do the natural numbers have their origins? Or, for our purposes, what are the origins of the whole numbers? The answers to these questions are not simple, but in the case of the whole numbers we can view both the numbers and the operations as evolving from elementary set theory. Basic properties of set operations help account for corresponding properties of the whole number operations.

   We will now review the basic structural properties of the Whole Number System as they evolve from intuitive set theory:

Basic Structural Properties

1. The concept of what a whole number *is* — in terms of sets — has been reviewed in Chapter 4 and need not be repeated here.
2. The basic whole number *operations* — addition and multiplication — can be defined in terms of set operations:
    (a) If a and b are whole numbers, then the *sum* of a and b, denoted $a+b$, is that whole number c determined as follows: If A and B are any sets such that $n(A) = a$ and $n(B) = b$ and $A \cap B = \emptyset$, then $c = n(A \cup B)$.
    (b) If a and b are whole numbers, then the *product* of a and b, denoted $a \times b$, is the whole number c determined as follows: If A and B are any sets such that $n(A) = a$ and $n(B) = b$, then $c = n(A \times B)$.
3. The basic properties of the whole number operations correspond to the properties of operations on sets:
    (a) *Closure:* For all finite sets A and B, $A \cup B$ and $A \times B$ are also finite sets, so for all whole numbers a and b, $a + b$ and $a \times b$ are whole numbers (the set of whole numbers is *closed* with respect to both addition and multiplication).
    (b) *Commutativity:* For all sets A and B, $A \cup B = B \cup A$, so for all whole numbers a and b, $a + b = b + a$. While it is *not* true that for all sets A and B, $A \times B = B \times A$, it *is* true that there is a 1–1 correspondence between $A \times B$ and $B \times A$, so for all whole numbers a and b, $a \times b = b \times a$.
    (c) *Associativity:* Similarly, $(A \cup B) \cup C = A \cup (B \cup C)$ for all sets, so $(a + b) + c = a + (b + c)$ for all whole numbers. And since there is a 1–1 correspondence between $(A \times B) \times C$ and $A \times (B \times C)$ for sets A, B, and C, for all whole numbers a, b, and c, $(a \times b) \times c = a \times (b \times c)$.
    (d) *Distributivity:* For all sets A, B, and C, there is a 1–1 correspondence between $A \times (B \cup C)$ and $(A \times B) \cup (A \times C)$, so for all whole numbers a, b, and c, $a \times (b + c) = (a \times b) + (a \times c)$. Similarly, $(a + b) \times c = (a \times c) + (b \times c)$ since there is a 1–1 correspondence between $(A \cup B) \times C$ and $(A \times C) \cup (B \times C)$.

(e) *Identities:* For each set A, $A \cup \emptyset = A$ and $\emptyset \cup A = A$, so for each whole number a, $a + 0 = 0 + a = a$. Thus 0 is the identity element for addition of whole numbers, just as $\emptyset$ is the identity element for the union of sets. There is no identity for the Cartesian product operation for sets, but for any singleton, S (a set with one element), and any set A, there is a 1–1 correspondence between $A \times S$ (or $S \times A$) and A. For each whole number a, $a \times 1 = 1 \times a = a$.

These five basic properties of the Whole Number System, together with basic properties of equality and a few definitions, account for several important generalizations to which children can and should be introduced while learning the fundamental facts.

Basic Definitions

Two important definitions are those for subtraction and division, the so-called "inverses" of addition and multiplication. Recall that "inverse" is used in more than one way: In number systems beyond the whole numbers, a number x has an *additive inverse* y if the sum of x and y is the additive identity, 0; x has a *multiplicative inverse* z if the product of x and z is the multiplicative identity, 1. For example, in the Rational Number System, $\frac{2}{3}$ and $-\frac{2}{3}$ are additive inverses, because their sum is zero; and the multiplicative inverse of $\frac{2}{3}$ is $\frac{3}{2}$, because their product is one. There is little reason to consider this basic property in the context of whole numbers, since no whole number except 0 has an additive inverse, and no whole number other than 1 has a multiplicative inverse.

On the other hand, while whole *numbers* do not generally have inverses, the whole number *operations* do have inverses. This concept can be viewed in several ways, as we shall see, but the basic notion is expressed in the definitions of subtraction and division:

$$\text{If } a + b = c, \text{ then } c - b = a$$

$$\text{If } a \times b = c, \text{ and if } b \neq 0, \text{ then } c \div b = a$$

Looking at these definitions from a slightly different angle, $c - b$, when it exists (for whole numbers, it exists if $c \geqslant b$), is that number which when added to b equals c. Similarly, $c \div b$, when it exists (there is such a whole number whenever $b \neq 0$ and c is a multiple of b), is that number which when multiplied by b equals c. This inverse pattern relating the two pairs of operations is sometimes viewed in yet another way: "adding b" and "subtracting b" are "cancelling" operations. That is, if we start at a, add b, and then subtract b from that sum, we end up at a again. Conversely, starting at c, subtracting b, and then adding b to that difference returns us to c. The same kind of cycles occur with multiplication and division (excluding zero divisors).

There are several pedagogical models for subtraction and division, as we shall see in a subsequent section of this chapter, but the mathematical basis for one interpretation of subtraction should be recalled: If X and Y are sets such that Y is a subset of X, then $X - Y$, the *relative complement* of Y with respect to X, is the set of all elements in X that are not in Y. If $X - Y = Z$, then $Z \cup Y = X$. Since Z and Y are disjoint, the *numbers* of these sets are related in the inverse sense, i.e., if sets X, Y, and Z have numbers x, y, and z respectively, then $x - y = z$ and $z + y = x$.

It is worthwhile to note here an extension of the definition of *order* considered in Chapter 4; i.e., if A and B are sets such that B matches a proper subset of A, then $N(A) < N(B)$. Thus for whole numbers a and b, $a < b$ if any sets A and B representing these numbers have this relationship. Once children learn about addition, this definition can be modified in terms of numbers only: $a < b$ if there is a nonzero number c such that $a + c = b$. The pattern of this definition is more general since it is used in the corresponding order definitions for the higher number systems.

Basic Generalizations

The generalizations that follow are particularly important in children's subsequent work with the whole number algorithms. Some are also directly helpful in developing the fundamental facts or can at least provide variety in the activities aimed at teaching them. The reader should be able to verify these generalizations formally, using the properties and definitions above, together with the cancellation properties of equality (if $a + c = b + c$, then $a = b$, and if $a \times c = b \times c$ where $c \neq 0$, then $a = b$) and the uniqueness properties of equality (if $a = b$, then $a + c = b + c$ and $a \times c = b \times c$). Each of the generalizations is true for all whole numbers, a, b, c, . . . , and the reader may find it helpful to replace the variables in some of the more complex statements with suitable whole numbers to be certain that they are clearly understood.

1. The sum of any number of whole numbers is unaffected by the order in which they are added and by the way in which they are grouped. Recall that, by convention, if an addition expression contains three or more addends, they are normally added in pairs from left to right, e.g.,

$$a + b + c = (a + b) + c$$
$$a + b + c + d = [(a + b) + c] + d$$

This generalization, based on the commutative, associative, and closure properties of addition, says that this convention is not necessary, e.g.,

$$a + b + c + d = (a + b) + (c + d) \quad \text{or}$$
$$[(d + c) + a] + b \quad \text{or}$$
$$b + [(c + a) + d], \text{ etc.}$$

Four numbers can be *ordered* in 24 different ways and for each of these orderings there are 5 possible ways to *group* them in pairs, so there are 120 different ways to add them. The number of possibilities increases rapidly as we consider sums of 5, 6, 7, or more numbers. The analogous generalization is true for the *product* of 2 or more numbers.

2. $a \times 0 = 0$ and $0 \times a = 0$.

3. $a - a = 0$.

4. $a - 0 = a$.

5. If $a \geqslant b$, then $a - b = (a + c) - (b + c)$.
   If $a \geqslant c$ and $b \geqslant c$, then $a - b = (a - c) - (b - c)$.

6. If $a \geqslant b$, then $(a \times c) - (b \times c) = (a - b) \times c$.

7. If $b \geqslant c$, then $(a + b) - c = a + (b - c)$.

8. If $a \geqslant c$ and $b \geqslant d$, then $(a + b) - (c + d) = (a - c) + (b - d)$.
   This generalization can be extended to include 3, 4, or more addends in each part of the expression on the left, e.g., if $a \geqslant d$, $b \geqslant e$, and $c \geqslant f$, then

   $$(a + b + c) - (d + e + f) = (a - d) + (b - e) + (c - f)$$

9. If $a \neq 0$, then $a \div a = 1$.

10. $a \div 1 = a$.

11. If a and b are multiples of c and if $c \neq 0$, then

    $$(a + b) \div c = (a \div c) + (b \div c).$$

    This generalization can be extended to include 3, 4, or more addends in the dividend, e.g., if a, b, and d are multiples of c, and $c \neq 0$, then

    $$(a + b + d) \div c = (a \div c) + (b \div c) + (d \div c).$$

12. If $b \neq 0$, then there exists a unique number q (i.e., there exists one and only one number q) and a unique number r, where $r < b$, such that

    $$a = q \cdot b + r$$

13. If a is a multiple of b, if $b \neq 0$, and if $c \neq 0$, then

    $$a \div b = (a \times c) \div (b \times c)$$

    If also a and b are multiples of c, then

    $$a \div b = (a \div c) \div (b \div c)$$

14. If a is a multiple of b and if $b \neq 0$, then

    $$(a \times c) \div b = c \times (a \div b).$$

The applications of these generalizations to the computational algorithms will be discussed more fully in subsequent chapters.

Functions and Operations

We frequently speak of addition, subtraction, multiplication, and division as the "four basic operations" of arithmetic. Technically this is somewhat inaccurate: Only addition and multiplication are "operations," although this minor liberty with the language is of no particular importance. On the other hand, the concept of *function* (an *operation* is a special kind of function) is of central importance pedagogically and mathematically from elementary school on. There are many ways of defining and thinking of functions; for our purposes the following will suffice:

> If X and Y are sets, then a *function f from X into Y* is a *pairing* of *each* element of X (called the *domain* of f) with some (but only one) element of Y. The set of all those elements in Y that are paired with some element of X is called the *range* of f.

For our purpose in this and in the next three chapters, several things should be reviewed, namely, (a) the sets X and Y *may* be the same set; (b) there is *usually* (but not necessarily) a well-defined underlying relationship or *rule* which determines the pairing; and (c) the domain X may be a set of numbers or a set of *pairs* of numbers (functions may relate other things than *numbers* to one another, but we are concerned here with numerical functions).

The kinds of functions with which we are presently concerned may be classified in terms of their domains. A function such as "addition" or "subtraction" is a *binary* one, which means its domain is a set of *pairs* of things (e.g., numbers). In this context we mean, of course, *ordered* pairs. The notation $\{x,y\}$ suggests a pair but is not intended to suggest any order. The notation (x,y) also suggests a pair, but when this notation is used, x is understood to be the *first* element (or component) and y is understood to be the *second*. The addition function associates each (ordered) pair of whole numbers (a,b) with a whole number according to the "addition rule," e.g., $(7,2)$ is associated with 9. The domain of the addition function—and of the multiplication function—is the set of *all* pairs of whole numbers. The domain of the subtraction function is the set of all ordered pairs of whole numbers (a,b) where $a \geqslant b$, e.g., $(5,2)$ and $(3,3)$. The domain of the division function includes those pairs (a,b) where $b \neq 0$ and a is a multiple of b, e.g., $(12,3)$, $(0,5)$, and $(6,6)$.

Singulary functions are those which associate *individual* things (e.g., numbers) with other things. Functions such as those specified by the rules "adding 2" or "subtracting 1," "multiplying by 3," "squaring," and "cubing" are examples of singulary functions.

Binary operations are functions whose domains include *all* ordered pairs, (a,b) of elements of some set such as W and whose ranges are subsets of that same set. *Singulary operations* associate *each* element of a set with an element of the same set. Both singulary and binary operations as well as singulary and binary functions play an important role in the teaching of fundamental facts, as we shall see.

3. Teaching the Fundamental Facts

Objectives

Four basic objectives for teaching elementary school mathematics were outlined in Chapter 2: problem-solving proficiency, computational proficiency, understanding of basic concepts, and positive attitudes toward mathematics. Discussion of those objectives included several references to the teaching of the fundamental facts, and should perhaps be referred to once again. We consider here three specific objectives, clearly derived from those broader objectives, for teaching the fundamental facts. They are of equal importance, although not normally or necessarily achieved in the order in which they are listed.

First, the fundamental facts should be memorized. The penalties for failure to achieve this are obvious. The child—and adult—uses them *every* time any computation is done, either mentally or on paper; this includes not only computation with whole numbers, but also those involving subsequent number systems—fractions, integers, etc. If the facts are not memorized quite early, the necessity of figuring them out can continually impede the learning of other numerical concepts. Even the simplest mathematical tasks can become needlessly time-consuming and frustrating. Again, it should be emphasized that memorization is not proposed as a *method* of teaching the facts, but as one of the objectives of that process.

Second, given any particular fundamental fact, the child should know how to "figure it out," preferably in several ways. This skill includes the ability to recall a forgotten fact before it has been memorized, and the ability to verify a conjecture or explain his answer. Looking at this objective another way, the child should be able to interpret any specific fact, e.g., $3 \times 8 = \square$, in terms of his understanding of models for the operations or of the generalizations he gradually learns about models. This includes relating the unknown or forgotten fact to facts he knows and remembers. In short, the child should be able to "see"—and tell— in several ways, *why* 3×8, for example, is 24.

And third, the child should be able to *use* fundamental facts to solve appropriate problems. Certainly this objective is related to the preceding one, in that it requires functional understanding of the operations in terms of models and of basic characteristics or properties of the operations. This objective requires the child to use this understanding in reverse order, so to speak. That is, given a problem situation, he should be able to relate it to the appropriate operation and, more specifically, to a particular fact. He needs to know *when* to add or multiply, etc., as well as *how* to do so and *why* his solution is correct. Knowing when to use a particular operation and fact requires him to be able to associate a given situation with one of several basic kinds of situations with which the operations are identified.

The conceptual understanding underlying the second and third objectives is crucial, of course, but it should be emphasized that verbalization of such things as definitions, properties, relationships, and generalizations need not be an objective, particularly in the lower grades. Stating them, particularly in abstract terms, is important only if and when it facilitates communication. Children can use structural concepts, which evolve gradually and slowly, long before they can — or need to — precisely identify them.

Before attempting to teach a given fact or collection of facts, the teacher should be certain that children have sufficient working understanding of prerequisite concepts. For the fundamental facts, those prerequisites are *number, numeration,* and *set operations.* That is, before learning to add 2 and 3, for example, it is necessary to understand the meanings of 2, 3, and 5. Or, in order to effectively cope with the multiplication facts with factors of five, a child must be comfortable with numeration up to at least the forties, and should be able to "conserve" number, i.e., recognize — and be internally convinced — that the number of a set is unaffected when it is joined with another set, or when it is separated into subsets, such as two subsets whose numbers may differ, or into several subsets each with the same number, or into a specified number of matching subsets. Some of the activities for developing this concept, and the associated language ("3 twos," for example), were discussed in Chapter 4. Such activities need not — and, at first, should not — be accompanied by the language and symbolism of the numerical operations.

These prerequisite concepts are not entirely independent of each other, nor need they be fully developed before introducing the fundamental facts. For example, in the process of learning the number 5, the child is led to see that 5 is "one more than 4" and that a set of 5 can be separated into sets of 2 and 3. Learning the "larger" fundamental facts generally rests on previous understanding of the "smaller" ones. One example of the interdependence of these concepts and the relationships between them is seen in a common strategy for teaching fundamental addition facts with sums greater than ten: A combination such as 8 and 5 is represented first as a set of 8 joined by a set of 5; the elements of the two sets are then rearranged to form the combination 10 and 3, leading to the fact $8 + 5 = 13$. The numbers 2, 3, 5, 8, and 10 are clearly prerequisite concepts, as are the fundamental facts $8 + 2$ and $2 + 3$ (or $10 - 2$ and $5 - 2$), but the activity contributes to understanding the associative property of addition and numeration, as well as the particular fundamental fact, $8 + 5 = 13$. While, here, one child may derive the result by using his numeration skill, others may benefit more by using the result to better understand numeration or the associative property or the related prerequisite facts or the numbers 13, 10, or 5.

Models for the Operations

If a child does not know (or cannot remember) the product of, say, 8 and 6, he needs some way to "figure it out," as we have said. Assuming that he is not told the answer and that he does not look it up in a table, he needs to know a general model or interpretation that can be applied to any such multiplication combination. There are several such models for each operation, any one of which will generally work (with a few exceptions involving 0 and 1). He should in time learn *each* of them, because the models have a second purpose: most of them serve as "patterns" of basic *problem situations* that can be solved by the whole number operations. At the risk of oversimplifying (there is no simple "pattern" for problem solving in general), we may broadly classify whole number problem situations as involving either counting or measurement. Most counting problem situations suggest some manipulation of things, resulting in the quantity to be determined. This can be put in the language of sets. The "things" can be thought of as elements of a set A or a pair of sets A and B; the manipulation suggests a set operation, e.g., union, complement, Cartesian product, partition, and so on; and the "quantity to be determined" is the number of elements in a resulting set. That number can always be determined by counting.

Measurement involves the assignment of numbers to entities — distances, weights, times, areas, volumes — as a way of comparing the entities with some standardized *unit*. When measures are expressed only as whole numbers, they represent multiples of the unit and can in fact be interpreted in terms of counting. For example, when we say that the distance between two points is 5, or that an object has length 5, we mean that the object is 5 times as long as, or the points are 5 times as far apart as, some unit distance (with which we associate the number 1). The length of an object, providing it has a straight edge, can be determined by appropriately placing it along a scale on which multiples of the unit length are recorded. The scale eliminates the *need* for counting, but does not prevent it. Linear measurement problems, where measures are expressed in terms of whole numbers, involve relationships between the numbers associated with two or more distances.

Most whole number problems may be analyzed as involving either counting or measuring. Thus, these are the two major types of models for the fundamental facts; although sums, products, and so on, may also be determined by rote counting (without reference to sets), and by using other known operations.

Addition

Counting problems that call for determining the total number of elements in two or more sets considered together, where the numbers of the sets may differ, can be solved by addition. One basic model for addition is an application of the definition of addition based on set union. Thus, to demonstrate the sum, $a + b$, of the numbers a and b, find any set with a elements and another set with b elements, being certain that the sets have no common elements. A child can then form one set from the two and count its elements. Thus, to solve $3 + 5 = \square$, for example, he combines a set of 3 with a set of 5 and *counts* the elements in the new set to find $\underline{8}$.

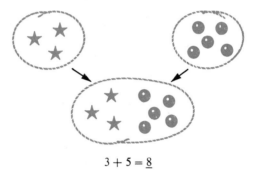

$$3 + 5 = \underline{8}$$

Problems calling for the total length of two objects joined end-to-end, or for the distance from a point A to a point B via an intermediate point C, involve the linear-measurement application of addition and supply a second model for addition facts. Thus, to find $a + b$, find two objects whose lengths are a and b respectively, place them end-to-end and measure their combined length, which is the desired sum. (It should be noted that if $a = 0$ or $b = 0$, this and other measurement interpretations are not particularly useful; if both a and b are zero, measurement, in this sense, is virtually meaningless). If children are familiar with blocks such as those from the Stern, Cuisenaire, or Centimeter rod materials, this problem can be carried on in two ways. One, by placing the appropriate blocks on a *scale* such as the Stern number track, or beside a metric ruler for the other two (familiarity with using such a scale is a prerequisite, of course, as is familiarity with number-names for the blocks). To solve $3 + 5 = \square$, for example, a child can measure the combined length of a 3-rod and a 5-rod. The *scale* tells him that $3 + 5 = \underline{8}$.

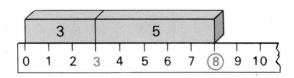

Two, by placing the blocks beside a single block, or set of blocks, of *known* measure and of the same length. For example, the child discovers that $3 + 5 = \underline{8}$ because the two blocks match the 8-block; similarly $6 + 7 = \underline{13}$.

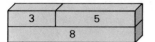 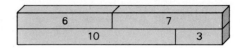

The scale or number line can be used by itself, without matching blocks, to find sums. $3 + 5$, for example, is represented by a "trip" or "jump" (to the right) of length 3, normally starting at the 0-point on the line, followed by a trip (again to the right) of length 5. The "ending" point of the trip, 8, corresponds to the combined length of the two trips and is the sum of 3 and 5. Alternately, $3 + 5$ can be represented as a trip of length 5 *starting* at 3. It should be noted that the length of the *second* trip must frequently involve *counting,* whereas the printed scale on the line serves to measure the first.

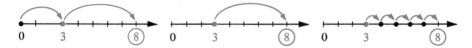

A third way to determine $a + b$ is by rote counting from 1 to a, and then continuing to count for the next b numbers. For example, to solve $3 + 5 = \square$, a child counts "1, 2, 3" and then "4, 5, 6, 7, $\underline{8}$." Thus $3 + 5 = \underline{8}$. More commonly, the counting begins right *after* 3: i.e. "jumping" from 3 to "4, 5, 6, 7, $\underline{8}$." Actually, children who use this method usually are not doing *rote* counting, because they generally use some form of "counters" to help them keep track of the second number. Their fingers make convenient and effective counters for addition fundamental facts. So convenient, in fact, and so effective (with some practice, children achieve amazing skill!) that some find it a waste of time to memorize the facts, much to the chagrin of many an elementary teacher.

Subtraction

Three basic problem situations are associated with subtraction: "take-away" situations, "additive" situations, and "comparison" situations. All three occur both in counting and measuring contexts. A difference can also be found by addition, which is formally used as the basic *definition* of subtraction, and by rote counting. We first consider set (counting) situations of the three basic types.

Take-away situations call for determining how many elements of a set are left after a subset has been removed. This kind of situation is formalized in the "relative complement" operation for sets. Using this model, a child can determine the difference $a - b$ by finding any set with a

elements, identifying a subset of it which has *b* elements, and then determining the number of elements left in the original set when that subset is removed.

Example: $6 - 2 = \square$

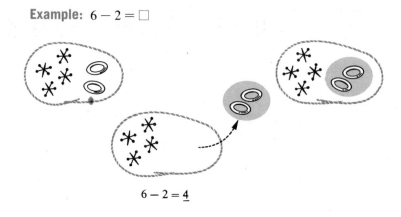

$$6 - 2 = \underline{4}$$

Additive situations raise such questions as "How much more is needed?" or "How many more are needed?" with respect to some "goal." (These are called "additive," of course, because they parallel those situations involving addition, i.e., two sets are joined to form another.) In solving such problems, a child who has learned to write equations corresponding to problems would interpret an additive situation with the equation $b + \square = a$, where *a* and *b* are the "goal" and the "beginning quantity," respectively. Since the two equations $b + \square = a$ and $a - b = \square$ are equivalent, i.e., they have the same solution, he can think of $a - b = \square$ as $b + \square = a$ and solve it by obtaining a set with *b* elements, then increasing the number of elements until he has *a* elements. The number of elements "added" is the solution.

Example: $2 + \square = 6$

$\qquad\qquad\quad 6 - 2 \ = \square$

$$2 + \underline{4} = 6, \qquad \text{so} \qquad 6 - 2 = \underline{4}$$

Comparison problems that can be solved by subtraction are those, as the name suggests, that ask how many more elements there are in one set than in another. Thus, to solve $a - b = \square$, the child can choose a set with a elements and another set with b elements; he then pairs the elements of the sets 1-to-1 and determines how many (if any) elements remain in the set with more.

Example: $6 - 2 = \square$

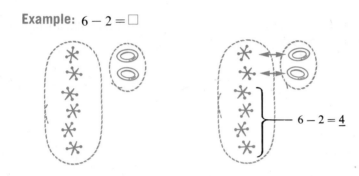

The take-away, additive, and comparison problem situations for subtraction in a measuring context parallel those involving sets and need not be elaborated on in detail. Simple problems of each type (using *linear* measure) are, for example:

1. How much of a 6-inch ribbon is left if I cut off a 2-inch strip? (Take-away.)
2. If I have completed 2 miles of a 6-mile trip, how much farther must I go? (Additive.)
3. How much longer is a 6-inch toy train than a 2-inch train? (Comparison.)

Blocks and number lines can serve as models for subtraction. Solutions of $6 - 2 = \square$ can be found, for example, in various ways.

1. Using Unifix blocks, make a 6-block, then remove a 2-unit strip from it. The difference can be determined by counting the remaining unit blocks or by measuring them against a number line with a 19 mm unit scale.

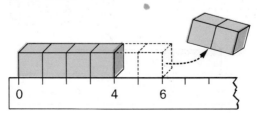

2. Using only a number line, take a "trip" of length 6 to the right, starting at 0; from there, take a trip of length 2 to the left. The "ending" point, 4, is $6 - 2$. (Alternately, skip the first step, starting at 6.)

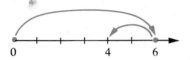 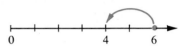

Take a trip from 0 to 2 (or start at 2); from there take a trip to 6. The length, 4, of the second trip is $6 - 2$.

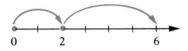

Take a trip of 6 and a trip of 2, both starting at 0. The difference in their lengths, 4, is $6 - 2$.

3. Using blocks whose lengths are known, place a 2-block above a 6-block so they have a common endpoint; then find the block which, when joined to the 2-block, matches the 6-block. Since this is a 4-block, $6 - 2 = \underline{4}$.

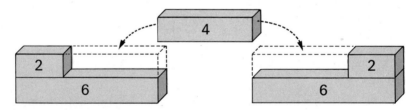

4. Using blocks of known lengths and a number line, place a 2-block on the line, with its left endpoint at 0; then find the block (4-block) which, together with the 2-block, reaches 6 on the scale.

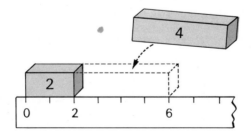

$6 - 2$ is the distance from 2 to 6, which can be determined by finding the block that just fits in the two-to-six space.

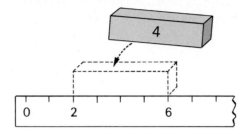

If a 2-block is placed on the line so its right endpoint is at 6, then its left endpoint will be at $6 - 2$.

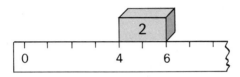

In addition to the above problem-solving models, addition and rote counting can be used by children to figure out fundamental facts. While the inverse relationship is used as the *formal* definition of subtraction, and thus as an "introduction" to it, children usually *discover* this relationship (aided, perhaps, by teacher guidance and structured exercises) as they learn the first few fundamental facts. Once it is discovered and verified that $a - b$ is the number which, when added to b equals a, that fact can be used. So, without sets, blocks, or number line, the child determines that $6 - 2 = \underline{4}$ because $2 + 4 = 6$.

Rote counting is used to solve $6 - 2 = \square$. One may count from 3 to 6, i.e., "(2); 3, 4, 5, 6"—this is commonly done while putting four fingers into 1–1 correspondence with $\{3, 4, 5, 6\}$, and determining the result by counting the fingers. Other rote counting methods involve counting backward from 5 to 2, i.e., "(6); 5, 4, 3, 2" or counting back two numbers from 6, "(6); 5, 4."

Multiplication

Two general classes of counting problems can be solved by multiplication of whole numbers. The more common situation calls for determining the total number of elements in several pairwise disjoint sets when each contains the same number of elements. This type of problem may be viewed in terms of a special extension of the union definition for addition. Children's first introduction to multiplication is usually in the context of such problems, so their first basic model for solving $a \times b = \square$ is to obtain a sets, each of which contains b elements; the elements are then viewed as those of a single set, whose number can be determined by counting. Because multiplication is commutative, the roles of the two factors can be interchanged, i.e., $a \times b$ can be interpreted as b sets with a elements each; but the former interpretation is more common.

Example: $3 \times 4 = \square$

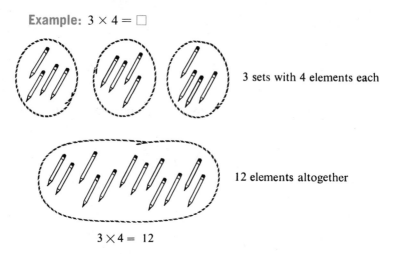

3 sets with 4 elements each

12 elements altogether

$3 \times 4 = 12$

Elements of the sets are generally, but not necessarily, the same kinds of things, such as these 3 sets, each containing 4 pencils. Frequently, problems of this sort concern objects arranged in nonintersecting rows and columns, with the same number of objects in each row (such as seats in an auditorium, desks in a classroom, or a sheet of postage stamps). Thus, one important variation of this model is the rectangular *array*. The solution of $a \times b = \square$, then, can be interpreted as the number of elements in an a-by-b array — an array with a rows and b columns (or b rows and a columns; the former is more common, although the latter is preferable in terms of certain extensions of this concept, such as interpreting Cartesian coordinates).

Example: $3 \times 4 = \square$

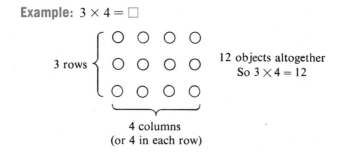

The array model is particularly useful for demonstrating the commutative and distributive properties, as well as for developing several important applications and extensions of whole number multiplication, which will be considered later.

Examples:

(a) $3 \times 4 = 4 \times 3$

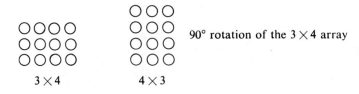

90° rotation of the 3×4 array

$3 \times 4 \qquad 4 \times 3$

(b) $3 \times 7 = 3 \times (5 + 2)$
$\qquad = (3 \times 5) + (3 \times 2)$

$3 \times 7 \qquad\qquad\qquad 3 \times 5 \qquad 3 \times 2$

Another important variation of this first counting model involves *rates*. For example, "If pencils cost 4¢ each, how much do 3 pencils cost?"

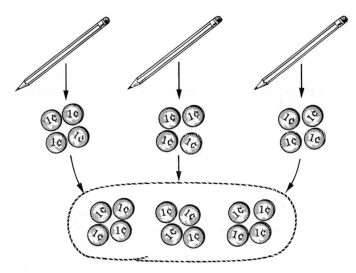

Such rate problems have several important extensions later, such as in developing the ratio interpretation of fractions, and in solving certain problems by using proportions.

A second basic type of counting problem calls for finding the number of ways in which the elements of two sets can be paired. These relate most directly to the formal definition of multiplication stated in terms of Cartesian product. For example, "How many different couples could be formed with two boys and three girls?" While this type of situation is difficult to represent physically, pairings can be represented pictorially in various ways. To solve $3 \times 4 = \square$, for example, the elements of a set of 3 and a set of 4 can be paired in these two ways:

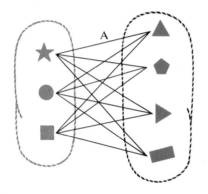

Each line represents a pair. Line *A*, for example, represents the pair (★, ▲).

Each dot represents a pair. Dot *B*, for example, represents the pair (▲, ★).

The number of pairs is 12, so $3 \times 4 = 12$.

Linear measurement problems involving multiplication of whole numbers deal with such things as the total combined length of several objects, each of the same length, or the total distance along several paths of the same length. As with addition and subtraction, such problems can be represented with blocks or the number line (or both), as suggested below with the example $3 \times 4 = \square$:

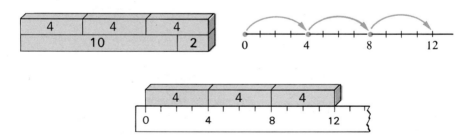

The array model for multiplication can later be used in developing a second measurement concept, that of *area* measure. The area of any region is intuitively defined as the number of adjacent, nonoverlapping unit-square regions (those regions enclosed by squares whose sides each measure 1) that completely cover the region. In the case of rectangular regions, that number is the product of the lengths of two adjacent sides because the unit squares form an array. This measurement concept is not commonly used as an early model for fundamental multiplication facts, but can be used for solving area problems once the basic area concept has been taught. For example, "What is the area of a rug that measures 3 feet wide and 4 feet long?" Since the rug is covered by 12 unit square regions, as indicated below, right, its area is 12; and since the lengths of two adjacent sides are 3 and 4, the same result can be obtained by solving $3 \times 4 = \square$.

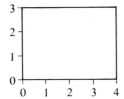 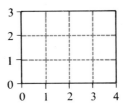

In addition to the models above, which relate directly to problem situations, two additional models are in common use. Their relationship to the physical models should be obvious. The first is "repeated addition," whereby a child solves $a \times b = \square$ by finding the sum of a identical addends, each of which is b. For example,

$$3 \times 4 = 4 + 4 + 4 = 12$$

The second model is rote skip counting by b's, starting with b and continuing for a total of a numbers. The last number is $a \times b$. For example, 3×4 is determined by thinking "4, 8, 12." The latter is a *convenient* way to recall forgotten fundamental facts; and, of course, should ultimately be discouraged in favor of memorization. Experienced teachers will attest that the more convenient models, such as this, are abandoned by children with more reluctance than are those requiring more manipulative effort!

Division

Problem situations that relate to whole number division can be classified into categories sometimes called "measurement" and "partition." Both counting and measuring problems occur in each category. Here again is an instance of a word, "measurement," used in different ways, as was "inverse" previously, so the reader is advised to consider the context carefully. The potential difficulty is compounded by the fact that both basic division situations can be related to the concept of partitioning of sets. (Fortunately, children need not be concerned with these technical and pedagogical labels.)

Before examining the two classes of division problems, recall that set partitioning refers to the separation (not necessarily physical, of course) of the elements of a set into subsets in such a way that each element of the set belongs to one and only one of the subsets (thus, each pair of subsets is

disjoint and their collective union is the original set). Division situations
relating to sets involve the partitioning of a set with a given number into
matching subsets, and we are concerned with two things: the number of
subsets, and the number of elements in each subset. In each case, we know
one of these and must determine the other.

   Partition situations are those in which we know the number of
subsets and must determine the number of elements in each. For example,
"Twelve cookies are to be shared equally by three boys. How many cookies
should each boy receive?" To represent such a problem, a child can begin

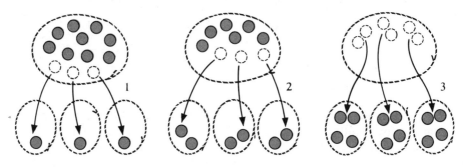

with 12 counters representing the cookies and distribute them into 3 matching subsets; he then counts the number of objects in each subset. Since
there are 4 elements in each subset,

$$12 \div 3 = 4$$

This partitioning process is comparable to dealing cards, and can be done
one at a time, as in steps 1 and 2 above, or more than one at a time, as in
step 3.

   Measurement situations are those for which the number of elements
in each subset is specified and the child must determine how many such
subsets can be formed. For example, "If twelve flowers are to be put into
vases, with 3 flowers in each vase, how many vases are needed?" We may
depict the solution of such a problem as follows:

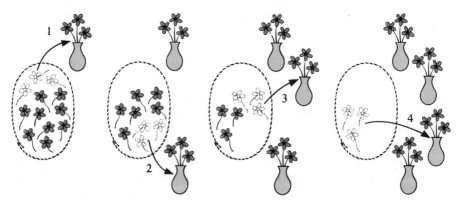

Given any fundamental fact, $a \div b = \square$, then, not associated with a specific problem situation, the child can interpret the *divisor*, *b*, either as the number of subsets to be formed from a set of *a* elements (partition), or as the number of elements in each subset to be formed (measurement). The *quotient* for each type is then interpreted as is the divisor of the other. Measurement frequently appears to be easier for children to interpret at first, but both measurement and partition must be taught because of their common occurrence in problem situations. It should be noted that in counting problems involving fundamental facts (both measurement and partition problems) the original set is entirely "depleted"—*each* element is assigned to one of the subsets. A more general procedure, which should be considered at the fundamental fact stage, involves partitioning the given set into matching subsets *insofar as possible;* in problems that involve open sentences such as $14 \div 3 = \square$, there are necessarily elements "left over," leading to the notion of "remainders." (See Chapter 6.)

Problems involving *rates* occur in both measurement and partition contexts, as do those suggesting arrays, and can be interpreted and solved by the methods we have just discussed.

Examples:

(a) If candy bars cost 3¢ each, how many can you buy for 12¢? (Measurement)

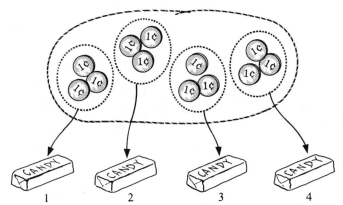

(b) If 3 candy bars cost 12¢, how much is one? (Partition)

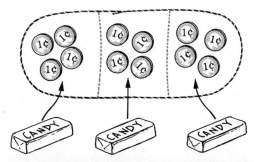

(c) If 12 toy soldiers are put into 3 rows, how many will be in each row?
(Partition)

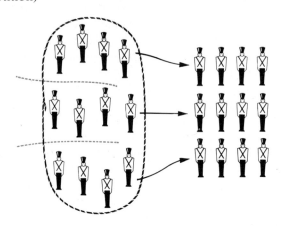

(d) If 12 toy soldiers are put into rows with 3 soldiers in each row, how many rows will be formed?
(Measurement)

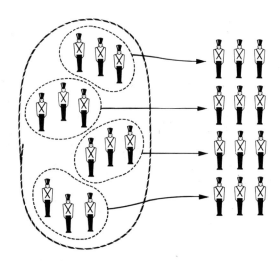

Division problems involving linear measure occur in both measurement and partition contexts, and can be represented and solved using the same materials employed for other measurement problems—blocks or number lines (or both). Procedures for interpreting and solving each type of problem with these tools are suggested below.

For *measurement*, the following question can be posed: How many 3-foot ribbons can be cut from a 12-foot ribbon? The dividend, the length

of the 12-foot ribbon in this case, can be represented by either the interval
from 0 to 12 on a number line or by a standard set of blocks (a 10-block and
a 2-block end-to-end). The number of 3-blocks or trips of length 3 each
which match that length are to be counted. This number is the quotient, 4.
The blocks or the trips can begin at 0 and proceed toward twelve, or begin
at 12 and proceed toward zero. The latter has the advantage, with the
number line, that when problems with nonzero remainders are solved in
this way, the remainder can be determined from the scale. For such problems, of course, the quotient is the maximum number of 3-blocks (or trips)
whose combined length is less than or equal to the length represented by
the dividend.

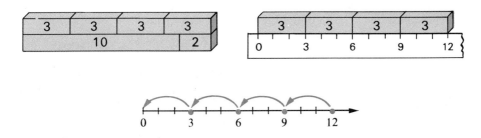

For *partition,* the question can be revised to: If a 12-foot ribbon is
cut into 3 smaller ribbons, each of the same length, how long will each
ribbon be? The 12-foot length is again represented in the same manner.
But this time, the child must find three blocks each of the same length which,
when put end-to-end, cover the distance. The length of each of these is the
quotient, 4. It should be clear that this can involve considerable trial and
error. The child may try 3-blocks, 4-blocks, 5-blocks, and so on, until he
discovers the correct size to use. For this reason, if the child is using the
number line to solve a given division problem without reference to a problem
situation, the measurement interpretation should normally be used rather
than the partition one.

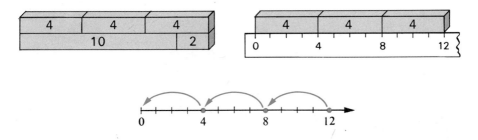

Division facts, like those for the other operations, can be determined
by using three models that do not involve counters, blocks, or number lines.

1. *Rote skip counting* can be used exactly as it is for multiplication except that the terminal number is known. For example, $12 \div 3 = \square$ can be solved by skip counting by 3s from 3 to 12 and counting the skips ("3, 6, 9, 12": 4 skips).

2. The *inverse relationship* between multiplication and division, the basic definition of division, can be used once it is discovered by children and once the fundamental multiplication facts are sufficiently recalled, e.g., $12 \div 3 = \square$ is solved by thinking, "What number, when multiplied by 3, equals 12?"

3. *Repeated subtraction,* which corresponds to measurement interpretation with sets, can be used. Here the child subtracts 3 from 12, then subtracts 3 from that difference (9), and continues until 3 can no longer be subtracted. The quotient is the number of times this can be done:

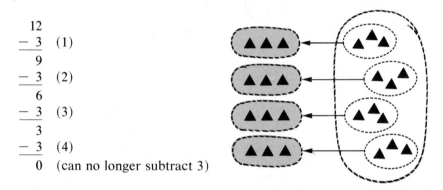

It should be noted that this process can be shortened by subtracting more than one 3 at a time:

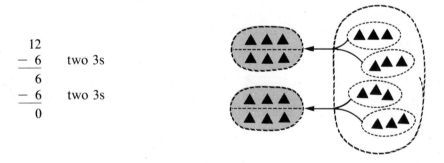

The problem types discussed in this section are intended only to illustrate basic models with which children can "figure out" fundamental facts, not as a survey of all possible problem types. Children frequently encounter more complex problems and other *types* of problems than we have considered here. Teachers should be prepared to help them, when necessary, to relate new problems to these basic models.

Basic Practices

There are certain basic principles and practices to guide the teacher in teaching the fundamental facts. The principles discussed here should recall examples or suggest implications of those outlined in Chapter 2.

Problem Solving

Fundamental facts should be introduced in problem-solving contexts. Simple problems which can be solved by counting, by looking at pictures, or by other rudimentary means can provide the background for introducing abstract operations and specific facts. Problems should be chosen carefully to provide examples of each of the different *basic* situations children must accurately associate with the operations. (See the preceding section.) This principle should be followed not only in introducing new operations but also throughout the extension of those operations as new facts are taught. Only in this way can children be expected to subsequently decide *when* to add, subtract, multiply, or divide when given more complex problem situations.

Symbolism

The transition from "obvious" results, which can be achieved by mere observation, counting, and so on, to the abstract symbolism we ultimately expect children to be able to use should be made gradually, with a minimum of new language or symbolism being introduced at each new step. For example, addition might be introduced first in a situation such as a group of 2 children being joined by 3 others, when the teacher simply raises the question of how many children there are altogether (without reference to addition). Numerals, 2, 3, and 5 can then be attached to pictorial representations of such collections, again without attempting to introduce the vocabulary and symbolism of addition. Numerous more abstract examples, such as Stern blocks; Cuisenaire Rods; or counters such as checkers, pencils, books, or dowels can be used. Later, *sentences* such as "2 apples and 3 apples together make 5 apples" can be introduced, followed by introduction of the still more abstract language, "2 apples *plus* 3 apples make 5 apples." Or, after much variety, "2 plus 3 is 5," then "2 + 3 is 5," and finally "$2 + 3 = 5$." Proceeding too quickly from the obvious to the abstract is probably one of the more common reasons children fail to comprehend and master the fundamental facts. Along these same lines, patience should be exercised in introducing the facts. Children are easily (and rightfully) discouraged by the prospects of having to learn a hundred facts, whereas learning four or five at a time is relatively easy to accept. Particularly in remedial situations, a few facts should be considered at a time, with frequent breaks in the routine.

Sequence

The fundamental facts should be gradually developed from the easier ones to the harder ones. While it is not always easy to determine whether one fact is harder than another, there are a few rather clear guidelines: (a) Addition and subtraction appear to be easier than multiplication and division, so should usually be introduced first. (b) "Small" numbers are generally easier for children than larger ones, so, for example, addition facts with sums less than ten, together with the corresponding subtraction facts, should be introduced long before the others. (c) "Doubles" such as $2 + 2$, $6 + 6$, 2×2, 3×3, and so on, are usually easier than others. (d) Adding a small number to a large one is easier to comprehend than the opposite, e.g., $9 + 2$ is simpler than $2 + 9$; subtracting a small number, i.e., $9 - 2$, is easier than subtracting larger ones such as $9 - 7$; and small multipliers or divisors, such as 2×6 or $12 \div 2$ are easier than those such as 6×2 or $12 \div 6$.

Models

Concrete representations of facts should vary as widely as possible. For example, in adding two numbers, sets of the same kinds of things (e.g., pencils) should be used, but so should sets of different kinds of things (e.g., 2 pencils and 3 crayons). Although *most* applications for the operations involve so-called "denominate" uses of number, it should be kept in mind that neither the number concept nor the operation concepts require that the objects being considered be of the same kind. If the operations and facts are to be *conceptualized,* they must be encountered in many and varied contexts.

Structure

While varied applications and different interpretations are important, even more so are relationships and similarities. Structural generalizations including such things as relationships between inverse operations can only be developed if appropriate groups of facts are viewed together. To accomplish this, facts should normally be taught collectively rather than individually. The 200 separate addition and subtraction facts, for example, can be treated as 38 learning units when they are taught in collections based on common structural characteristics. The 190 multiplication and division facts can similarly be treated as 31 learning units. These learning units, sometimes called "families" of facts, are based on commutativity, the inverse relationship, the identity properties, and so on. For addition and subtraction, the 38 families include:

1. The 19 addition facts of the form $a + 0$ or $0 + a$, and their 19 inverses, the subtraction facts of the form $a - 0$ or $a - a$. This collection of 38 facts can be viewed as essentially *one* "fact."

2. The doubles and their inverses, e.g., $1 + 1$, $2 + 2$, . . . , $9 + 9$, and $18 - 9$, $16 - 8$, . . . , $2 - 1$. Excluding the $0 + 0$ and $0 - 0$ doubles, which belong in the preceding family, there are 18 facts in this special collection. (The characteristic that delineates this family is more pedagogical than structural, i.e., children find these learning units quite easy, particularly the addition combinations).

3. The 36 remaining families, each containing 3 different numbers, such as the family

$$[5 + 3 = 8, 3 + 5 = 8, 8 - 5 = 3, 8 - 3 = 5]$$

The members of these families are related by commutativity and the inverse relationship. There are, altogether, 144 addition and subtraction facts in these 36 families.

The multiplication-division facts comprise 31 learning units:

1. The 19 multiplication facts with 0 as a factor. These can be taught simultaneously by the generalization $a \times 0 = 0 \times a = 0$. Only 9 have inverses because of zero divisors, so there are 28 facts altogether in this family.

2. The 30 facts related by the multiplicative identity, 1, and the inverse relationship (0×1 and $0 \div 1$ may be viewed either in this or in the preceding family).

3. The 16 remaining doubles (the products of which are the square numbers).

4. 28 families based on commutativity and the inverse pattern, such as

$$[3 \times 4 = 12, 4 \times 3 = 12, 12 \div 4 = 3, 12 \div 3 = 4]$$

Grouping the facts in families this way has the advantage of reducing the number of *separate* things to be learned while teaching structural generalizations and how to use them. *Learning* facts in collections does not, however, obviate the need for *practicing* them separately. Ultimately, each child should be able to instantly recall, for example, that $5 \times 8 = 40$ without intermediately relating it to 8×5 or some other pattern such as counting by fives. That is, the understanding of patterns and generalizations must not stand in the way of skill. The organization of facts into the learning units listed previously is not unique nor is it sufficient to introduce all of the patterns and generalizations children must learn — and which, in turn, will help them learn facts. For example, we previously suggested (pp. 116–117) an activity that can teach the associative property of addition while also teaching fundamental facts with sums greater than ten. Another organizational pattern and some associated activities are offered in the following paragraphs. Others will be suggested later.

The addition and subtraction facts can be classified as either "sum families" or "addend families," collections of facts with a common sum or a common addend. There are 19 sum families, one for each sum from 0 to 18, and 10 addend families. For example, the largest sum family is the 10-family, which includes 18 combinations:

$$1 + 9, 2 + 8, 3 + 7, 4 + 6, 5 + 5, 6 + 4, 7 + 3, 8 + 2, \text{ and } 9 + 1,$$

together with their inverses,

$$10 - 1, 10 - 2, 10 - 3, 10 - 4, 10 - 5, 10 - 6, 10 - 7, 10 - 8, \text{ and } 10 - 9.$$

An example of an addend family is the 4-family:

$$0 + 4, 1 + 4, 2 + 4, 3 + 4, 4 + 4, 5 + 4, 6 + 4, 7 + 4, 8 + 4, 9 + 4$$

and their inverses,

$$4 - 4, 5 - 4, 6 - 4, 7 - 4, 8 - 4, 9 - 4, 10 - 4, 11 - 4, 12 - 4, \text{ and } 13 - 4.$$

Multiplication and division facts can be grouped into "product families" and "factor families." Product families are not particularly useful for teaching the fundamental facts (except for the 0-family; there are many interesting patterns related to products, but they are generally more profitably examined later. We will consider some in Chapter 7). Factor families, however, are very useful. Each factor family, excluding the 0-family, includes 20 related facts. The 5-family, for example, includes facts of the form $a \times 5 = b$ or $b \div 5 = a$.

Operation tables provide a convenient way for children to observe factor patterns. Children can construct them—or parts of them—or they can be prepared in advance for children to examine. The entire tables, in their conventional forms, are:

+	0	1	2	3	4	5	6	7	8	9
0	0	1	2	3	4	5	6	7	8	9
1	1	2	3	4	5	6	7	8	9	10
2	2	3	4	5	6	7	8	9	10	11
3	3	4	5	6	7	8	9	10	11	12
4	4	5	6	7	8	9	10	11	12	13
5	5	6	7	8	9	10	11	12	13	14
6	6	7	8	9	10	11	12	13	14	15
7	7	8	9	10	11	12	13	14	15	16
8	8	9	10	11	12	13	14	15	16	17
9	9	10	11	12	13	14	15	16	17	18

×	0	1	2	3	4	5	6	7	8	9
0	0	0	0	0	0	0	0	0	0	0
1	0	1	2	3	4	5	6	7	8	9
2	0	2	4	6	8	10	12	14	16	18
3	0	3	6	9	12	15	18	21	24	27
4	0	4	8	12	16	20	24	28	32	36
5	0	5	10	15	20	25	30	35	40	45
6	0	6	12	18	24	30	36	42	48	54
7	0	7	14	21	28	35	42	49	56	63
8	0	8	16	24	32	40	48	56	64	72
9	0	9	18	27	36	45	54	63	72	81

Although the procedures for using these tables are probably familiar to the reader, they must be explained to children. They are, briefly:

1. Each row and each column is numbered. To find $a + b$ or $a \times b$, find the cell which is in the a-row and the b-column of the appropriate table. The number in that cell is the desired sum or product.
2. To determine $a - b$ or $a \div b$, use the inverse table and locate the cell in the b column which contains a. The row number is the desired difference or quotient; in the case of division, if $b = 0$, this does not work unless $a = 0$; but even then, multiple quotients can be found, so the consideration of zero divisors must be rejected.

The tables should not be used in their entirety until all the facts have been at least introduced. But when children have learned the addition and subtraction facts with sums up to, say, 5, or the multiplication and division facts with factors up to 5, abbreviated tables can be presented:

+	0	1	2	3	4	5
0	0	1	2	3	4	5
1	1	2	3	4	5	
2	2	3	4	5		
3	3	4	5			
4	4	5				
5	5					

×	0	1	2	3	4	5	6	7	8	9
0	0	0	0	0	0	0	0	0	0	0
1	0	1	2	3	4	5	6	7	8	9
2	0	2	4	6	8	10	12	14	16	18
3	0	3	6	9	12	15	18	21	24	27
4	0	4	8	12	16	20	24	28	32	36
5	0	5	10	15	20	25	30	35	40	45
6	0	6	12	18	24	30				
7	0	7	14	21	28	35				
8	0	8	16	24	32	40				
9	0	9	18	27	36	45				

×	0	1	2	3	4	5
0	0	0	0	0	0	0
1	0	1	2	3	4	5
2	0	2	4	6	8	10
3	0	3	6	9	12	15
4	0	4	8	12	16	20
5	0	5	10	15	20	25

Although filling in the tables is not a particularly worthwhile drill activity, because of the patterns within the table (it *is* possible to provide some drill by randomly covering a few cells and asking for the missing number), the tables are useful for discovering or visualizing certain generalizations in that they generate certain questions, thus:

1. Read the numbers in row 3 (or column 3) of the addition table (or multiplication table). What can you say about the numbers?
2. Find all the 5s in the addition table. Where are they?

3. Read the numbers in order along the diagonal from upper left to lower right. What about these numbers? What is the relationship between the numbers on opposite sides of that diagonal?
4. How do the numbers in the 0-row (or column) of the addition table compare with those in the 1-row (or column) of the multiplication table?
5. How many times does 0 appear in each table? Why? How many times do 2, 3, 5, and 7 appear in the multiplication table? Why do 11, 13, 22, 26, 34, and so on, not appear in the multiplication table?

Discovery

Fundamental facts should be discovered by children. The teacher must, of course, provide enough initial instruction when introducing a new operation so that children have a *basis* for discovering facts. Careful guidance should be provided for the use of manipulative or other materials, and the teacher should be available to provide interpretations and models that will help in discovering facts as quickly as possible. For example, counting devices are effective for some easy multiplication facts, such as 3×2 or 3×4 (see preceding section); but finding products such as 8×7 by counting is inefficient (measurement approaches are quicker). Nonetheless, the numbers involved in the fundamental facts are small enough that children can always discover them, given appropriate materials and the understanding to do so. Incidentally, it should be kept in mind that when leading children to discover *facts* or generalizations, the end result is inflexible (whereas some other discovery situations are more open-ended and can lead to different results). The teacher, then, needs to check to see that the correct result *is* discovered, and to provide enough alternate approaches so that children can check themselves. A child could "discover," for example, that $8 \times 7 = \underline{55}$ if he makes an error in using apparatus or in interpreting his manipulations.

Language

Teachers should be careful to use mathematically correct language, which the children can understand; which is not likely to lead to subsequent misunderstanding; and which facilitates learning the facts. Several specific suggestions were made in Chapter 2 in this regard. Use neutral terms, for example, for subtraction and division, because of their multiple interpretations (e.g., "5 minus 2" rather than "5 take-away 2," and "6 divided by 2" rather than "2 into 6"). The same sets of words should be used for both addition and subtraction (addend, sum) and the same words used for multiplication and division (factor, product). This can enforce the inverse relationship. Words such as "divisor," "minuend," and so on, can be introduced more meaningfully after the fundamental fact stage. Avoid expressions such as "We can't subtract 5 from 2" or "We can't divide 3 by 8." Some children have difficulty accepting subsequent work with rational numbers or integers where they *can* subtract 5 from 2 ($2 - 5 = {}^-3$) or divide 3 by 8 ($3 \div 8 = \frac{3}{8}$). Such situations should not be deliberately brought up by the *teacher* unless he is prepared to introduce fractions or negative numbers. When *children* raise such questions, however, the best approach is to answer their questions as honestly as possible (within their ability to comprehend) and to point out that such problems will be studied later, or that such problems do not have whole number solutions because of the basic meanings of whole number subtraction and division.

Equation Form

Fundamental facts should be introduced in equation form rather than computational form, i.e.,

$$5 + 3 = \square \qquad \text{rather than} \qquad \begin{array}{r} 5 \\ +3 \\ \hline \end{array}$$

There are several reasons for this.

1. Equations (mathematical sentences) are consistent in their left-to-right form with ordinary sentences. Primary teachers, concerned with teaching children to read, can thus relate these two skills.
2. Equations provide more flexibility than the computational form in that "missing" numbers, represented by variables such as boxes, triangles, and so on, can occur at any point in the sentence, and can even represent missing operation or relation symbols. E.g.,

$5 + 3 = \square$	sum missing
$5 + \triangle = 8$	addend missing
$\_\_ + 3 = 8$	addend missing
$5 \square 3 = 8$	operation missing
$5 + 3 \triangledown 8$	relation missing

3. If the concepts of *equality* (and inequality) and *variable* are introduced with fundamental facts, they can be meaningfully used in subsequent explanations of more complex ideas.
4. It is at least as easy, natural, and intuitively meaningful to use equations as it is to use computational form.
5. There is no reason to use computational form with fundamental facts — the various computational forms were devised *only* to facilitate those computations involving the algorithms, i.e., involving numbers greater than those used in the fundamental facts.
6. Equations can be used to help children express the "sense" of problems, as was pointed out in Chapter 2.

Computational forms can, of course, be introduced at the fundamental facts stage, as readiness for teaching the algorithms; but their introduction should follow much experience with equation form.

Drill

Teachers must provide adequate practice, drill, and repetition in order for children to memorize the fundamental facts. There is no alternative to drill. (A child can learn some things without repetition, e.g., that stoves are hot and not suitable places to put fingers! Not so the fundamental facts.) The reader is advised to review the principles outlined in Chapter 2 regarding drill. The following suggestions are derived principally from them.

1. Drill is only appropriate after basic understanding has been achieved. The child should always know *why* $2 + 3 = 5$ before he is asked to *recall* that fact.
2. Drill should occur frequently and for short intervals. There is no need to postpone drill until a large number of facts have been learned. Rather, it can be employed as soon as a very few have been discovered.
3. In this same vein, drill should overlap previous learnings. That is, when a few new facts are learned, drill on them, but include previously learned facts as well.
4. Both written and oral drill are important and helpful.
5. Drill can include more than one operation at a time, e.g., $(3 + 5) \times 2$, $(3 \times 2) + (4 \times 2)$, $(4 \times 2) + 2$, and so on. One activity children enjoy in this regard is a mental game where the teacher (or a child) says something like, "Start at 2; add 6; multiply by 4; subtract 2; divide by 5. Where are you?" A similar mental game, useful for providing combined drill while teaching the function concept, is played as follows: The teacher thinks of a "(function) rule", e.g., $2K + 3$, and asks children to name any numbers. If a child says, "2," the teacher responds, "That makes me think of 7." As other numbers are called and responded to, children try to guess the rule. Guesses such as "add 5" or "multiply by 3 and add 1" are eliminated as successive "inputs" and "outputs" are heard.
6. Drill can be structured to introduce or strengthen understanding of important generalizations, e.g.,

$(2 + 3) - 1 = \underline{\hspace{1em}}$ $(2 + 3) + 4 = \underline{\hspace{1em}}$

$2 + (3 - 1) = \underline{\hspace{1em}}$ $2 + (3 + 4) = \underline{\hspace{1em}}$

$(4 + 6) - 3 = \underline{\hspace{1em}}$ $(5 + 2) + 6 = \underline{\hspace{1em}}$

$4 + (6 - 3) = \underline{\hspace{1em}}$ $5 + (2 + 6) = \underline{\hspace{1em}}$

$$\vdots \qquad\qquad\qquad\qquad\qquad\qquad \vdots$$

$(a + b) - c = a + (b - c)$ $(a + b) + c = a + (b + c)$

$$(8 + 6) \div 2 = \underline{} \qquad\qquad\qquad 8 - 8 = \square$$
$$(8 \div 2) + (6 \div 2) = \underline{} \qquad\qquad 7 - 7 = \triangle$$
$$(9 + 3) \div 3 = \underline{} \qquad\qquad\qquad 6 - \triangledown = 0$$
$$(9 \div 3) + (3 \div 3) = \underline{} \qquad\qquad \square - 5 = 0$$

$$\vdots \qquad\qquad\qquad\qquad\qquad\qquad\qquad\qquad \vdots$$

$$(a + b) \div c = (a \div c) + (b \div c) \qquad\qquad (a - a) = 0$$

7. Although much drill can be provided in the context of learning new things, it must sometimes occur per se. Once a child discovers the *pattern* involved in a drill, his answer for the remaining exercises can frequently (and rightfully) be obtained *without* necessarily providing drill on the facts. Thus, drill on facts per se should always be arranged randomly, without any (apparent) pattern, so that the child is required to recall each fact. Tests on fundamental facts should be timed, with gradually more demanding time limits, in order to force children to recall facts from memory. Children should ultimately be able to write the answers to all the facts for an operation within 3 minutes. (This can be an exciting challenge and fun if it is handled carefully by the teacher, or a discouraging nightmare otherwise!) It should be observed that there are $100!$ $(100 \times 99 \times 98 \times 97 \times \cdots \times 3 \times 2 \times 1)$ ways to randomly order 100 facts. ($100!$ is a number with over 150 digits.) There are several undesirable aspects to the practice of using duplicated test papers on which children write the answers, so that the same random arrangement is used over and over: it uses up a great deal of paper in a short time; a great deal of the teacher's time is required for scoring (30 children can produce 3,000 answers in 3 minutes!); and the children soon begin to recall the *sequence* of answers rather than being forced to recall the separate facts. A more effective procedure is to duplicate several alternate forms for each test, print correct answers on the back, and have children cover the test with acetate, using grease pencils to write their answers. If the positions of the correct answers correspond to those where children's answers are written, children can then turn the test paper over, place their answers (on the acetate) over the correct answers, and score themselves. This solves all three problems and is probably well worth the extra time needed to prepare the tests.

Activities and Materials

There is, of course, no practical way to summarize all or even a major part of the many games, activities, and devices described in the literature and available from commercial sources for teaching the fundamental facts. There is probably more written about this topic and more material available for teaching it than for any other area of elementary school mathematics. Certainly one characteristic of the successful teacher is his familiarity with and his use of a wide variety of classroom activities that are both enjoyable and instructive. The best way to accumulate such a repertory is by regularly studying current and past issues of professional journals, such as *The Arithmetic Teacher,* by examining catalogs of educational publishers, and by observing and listening to one's colleagues — in their classrooms, in the teacher's lounge, and at professional meetings. One good idea can generate many more; such is the aim of the balance of this chapter. The interested reader may supplement the following material by consulting the bibliography for this chapter and Appendix B.

Games

Any activity is a game if children think it's fun. What is a game in one child's eyes may be a bore, a drudgery, or even a threat in the eyes of another. Thus, we prefer in general to think in terms of *activities* rather than games. There are, however, many activities that are *intended* to be (instructional) games and which usually are. Many are patterned after familiar recreational games, differing only in that the child is called upon to associate numbers with combinations. For example, games of the Bingo type can be made, in virtually endless ways, by calling off combinations instead of numbers. If a child has a 12 in the appropriate column on his playing board, then he can score if any combination such as 6×2 or $5 + 7$ is called off. Games of this sort are commercially available or easily constructed. The best way to "make your own" is to *systematically* pattern playing boards and the expressions to be called off after the regular recreational game, being certain, of course, that the numbers and combinations correspond appropriately. Other activities in this category can be adapted from almost any game children like to play — card games (like *Fish*), board games like *Monopoly,* relay games, trading games. Cards, spinners, dice, and the like can easily be fashioned to contain the particular fundamental facts to be practiced at a given time.

Arrays

A "magic square" is a square array of numbers arranged so that the sum of the numbers in each row, column, or major diagonal is the same. A "perfect" 3-by-3 magic square contains each number from 1 to 9; and, in general, a perfect *n*-by-*n* square includes each of 1 through n^2, for $n > 2$. "Perfect" 3-by-3 and 4-by-4 squares are illustrated.

8	1	6
3	5	7
4	9	2

1	15	14	4
12	6	7	9
8	10	11	5
13	3	2	16

Magic squares can be used to generate many interesting activities, beginning at the fundamental facts stage: (a) determining whether a given 3-by-3 array is a magic square — there are 12 fundamental addition facts in the 3-by-3 array above; (b) determining what are the missing numbers in a square in which some numbers have been left out — this provides subtraction practice;

8		6
	5	7
4		

8		
	5	7
4		2

(c) finding "sum families" in the square — in a perfect 3-by-3 square, for example, the 10-family, except for $5 + 5$, occurs in a regular way, as does the 17-family in the 4-by-4 array; (d) trying to rearrange the same numbers in different ways to make new magic squares;

4	9	2
3	5	7
8	1	6

8	3	4
1	5	9
6	7	2

2	7	6
9	5	1
4	3	8

6	1	8
7	5	3
2	9	4

(e) finding patterns in such rearrangements; or (f) multiplying each number by 2 (and so on) to see if the result is a magic square. A rather challenging activity is to describe a consistent pattern linking each number with its successor (see Appendix A, problem 4).

Both drill and structural insight are provided by an array such as this, for which the child is asked to find the missing numbers by adding the

5	2	
4	3	

first and second numbers in each row and column to get the third number. He can then be asked to look for patterns, and to explain the number in the

8		6
	1	
5		

Subtract

15		5
3		1

Divide

lower right-hand cell. Any combination of 4 numbers, and different operations, can be used (with careful choice of numbers in the case of subtraction
and division), and various numbers can be deleted.

Still another activity of the array variety is the "crossnumber
puzzle," patterned after crossword puzzles. Numbers are used instead of
letters, and much varied drill can be incorporated.

Across	Down
1. 6×4	2. 2, —, —, —, 1—,
4. 8×8	12, 14, . . .
6. $(8 \times 9) + 10$	3. 4×3
7. 5, —, 15, 20, . . .	5. 7×6

Counters and Numeration Devices

Activities involving the counting interpretation of fundamental
facts can, and should, be done with a wide variety of objects, none of which
need to be special in any way except that they should generally be movable.
Children can move about to dramatize a fact; books, pencils, pieces of paper,
coins, poker chips, paper clips, dowels, blocks, are all suitable devices.
Flannel boards with various felt cutouts or similar magnetized boards provide a good way to display problem situations for a group of children. Sometimes color can be used to advantage, especially in addition and subtraction.
For example, $3 + 2$ might be represented by 3 red checkers and 2 black
checkers, separated by color at first and then pushed together; conversely,
$5 - 2$ could be shown by starting with that same collection and then pushing
away all the black checkers.

Numeration devices such as the abacus, Dienes blocks, place value
chart, hundred board, and counting board (see Chapter 4, pp. 83–101).
have no particular advantage over ordinary counters when the largest
number (the sum, minuend, product, or dividend, usually) is less than ten;
beyond that point they can sometimes be used to advantage, particularly
for multiplication and division, and for providing mathematical readiness
for the borrowing and carrying problems that later occur in addition and
subtraction.

Addition. To solve a fundamental addition fact with sum greater
than ten, such as $8 + 6 = \square$, the child could first represent each addend
separately (using the place value device), combine the addends, where
appropriate, and then simplify by grouping or trading ten ones for one ten.
Some illustrations follow.

(a) Spike or Yoder abacus:

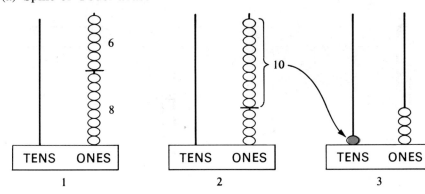

(b) Place value chart:

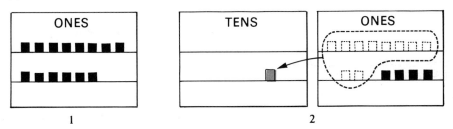

(c) Dienes blocks:

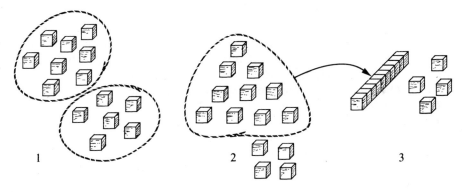

(d) Hundred board:

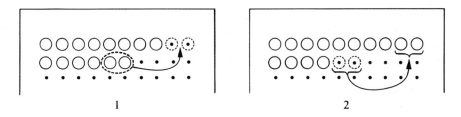

(e) Counting board:

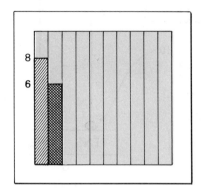 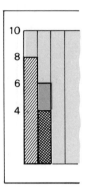 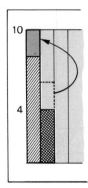

An alternate approach (necessary, in the case of the 9- or 10-bead frame abacus) is to first set up the device to represent the first addend, 8. Then add the 6 counters *one at a time,* stopping to trade or simplify when 10 is reached before continuing to add the remaining 4. Except for the frame abacus, the 6 markers to be added can be *collected* first to avoid losing track of the count in the trading process.

Subtraction. The additive interpretation of the related subtraction problem, $14 - 6 = \Box$, could best be done according to the above alternate approach. That is, represent 6, then add to the collection one at a time, trading when 10 is reached where appropriate, then continuing until 14 is shown. If different colored markers can be used, e.g., with the place value chart, the first 6 can be one color and the added markers another to facilitate the final step, i.e., counting to determine how many were added.

The take-away interpretation of the same problem could be represented with each device by reversing the order of the manipulations for addition: Begin by representing 14 in the *standard* way, as 1 ten and 4 ones; then trade or regroup the ten so that 6 ones can be removed and the remaining 8 counted. (No trading is necessary on the hundred board.) On the counting board, the 1 ten may either be traded for 10 units or regrouped as $8 + 2$, the latter requiring more insight on the child's part. None of these devices is particularly useful for the comparison interpretation of subtraction.

Multiplication. Multiplication facts involving products greater than ten could be represented in the same way as addition, but most of the above devices would be of limited use because of their physical limitations. The single exception is the hundred board, which can be set up as an array to represent the problem and then rearranged to obtain the standard representation.

Example: $6 \times 7 = \square$:

First, set up a 6-by-7 array, starting at the top of the board, to represent 6×7. Each of the six rows will then have 3 empty positions.

Second, fill as many of the empty positions as possible, starting with the *top* row, by taking markers from the *bottom* rows; 4 rows can be filled in this way, with 2 markers left.

Thus, the product is 4 tens and 2 ones, or 42.

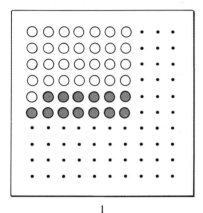

1

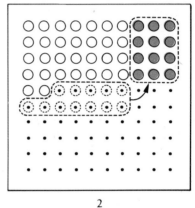

2

Division. Related division problems can be represented, either as *measurement* or *partition,* by rearrangement of the hundred board markers in the reverse order of the above. For example, to solve $42 \div 6 = \square$, the board can first be set up as in step 2 above (or 42 markers can be collected but not set up on the board). The markers can then be put into 6 matching rows (partition) or into rows of 6 each (measurement). The quotient can be found by counting the number of markers in each row in the partition case or the number of rows in the measurement case. The other devices would be relatively cumbersome for division problems, except for relatively simple problems with divisors of 3 or at most 4. Even then the abacus should be avoided.

Cartesian coordinates. Another useful activity can be provided by a hundred board supplied with markers that are labeled with numerals. The rows and columns can also be numbered, each from 0 to 9, starting in the lower left-hand corner. This provides an opportunity to introduce the conventional ordered-pair scheme for identifying points. That is, any given peg on the hundred board can be associated with the pair of numbers (a, b), where a is the number of the *column* it is in, and b is the *row* number. Once children are familiar with this basic orientation, the board can be transformed into a modified addition table or multiplication table by labeling each peg—or selected pegs—with the sum or product of the pair of numbers that identify it, e.g.,

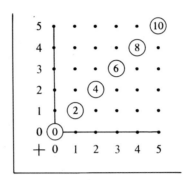

This can provide another, and in some ways better, view of the patterns in the tables (in the context of introducing the standard Cartesian coordinate system). For example, the child can be asked to supply successive labels along specified rows, columns, or diagonals and try to identify resulting patterns, e.g.,

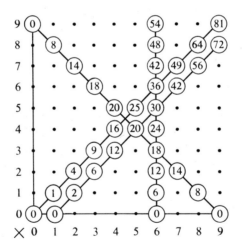

Stern Materials

Together, the Stern unit blocks and number track, referred to earlier, can provide straightforward *measurement* models. (The corresponding Unifix materials are equally effective, except that the cubes must first be clipped together correctly, and care must be taken to prevent the colors from causing distraction.) This combination of apparatus provides perhaps the *quickest* way to "figure out" a particular fact—sometimes a major consideration! Children frequently lose interest, are distracted, and make errors when using the lengthier *counting* models, particularly when the numbers involved are quite large.

A few additional fundamental facts activities with the unit blocks are suggested below.

The *commutative properties* can be easily represented by placing appropriate blocks side-by-side.

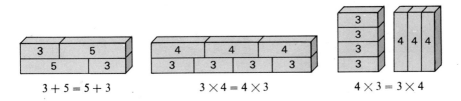

$$3 + 5 = 5 + 3 \qquad 3 \times 4 = 4 \times 3 \qquad 4 \times 3 = 3 \times 4$$

The *associative property of addition* can be demonstrated with the unit blocks, as follows:

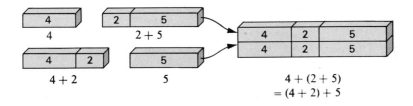

$$4 + 2 \qquad 5 \qquad 4 + (2 + 5) = (4 + 2) + 5$$

The *associative property of multiplication* is a little more difficult, but can be developed in at least two ways:

Examples:

(a) For three relatively small numbers, such as 3, 2, and 4, interpret $3 \times (2 \times 4)$ as a "string" of three 2-by-4 blocks; then there are two possibilities: (1) note that the result is the same as 6×4 and since $6 = 3 \times 2$, conclude that $3 \times (2 \times 4) = (3 \times 2) \times 4$ without

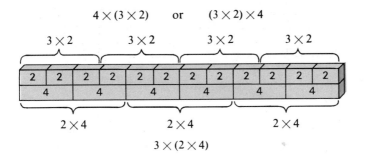

$$4 \times (3 \times 2) \qquad \text{or} \qquad (3 \times 2) \times 4$$

$$3 \times (2 \times 4)$$

further manipulation; or (2) place a string of four 3-by-2 blocks beside the first. [This is cheating a bit, since such a string represents $4 \times (3 \times 2)$ according to the interpretation above, but the commutative property justifies our thinking of it as $(3 \times 2) \times 4$.] Since the two strings are the same length, $3 \times (2 \times 4) = (3 \times 2) \times 4$.

(b) Alternatively, form a 3-by-2-by-4 box from two 3-by-4 arrays (or three 2-by-4 arrays or four 3-by-2s):

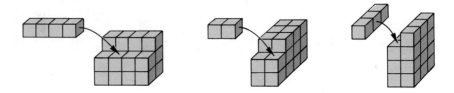

This can be used to introduce the concept of volume. Since $(3 \times 2) \times 4$ and $3 \times (2 \times 4)$ represent only different *views* of the same box, whose volume is constant, the two expressions are equivalent.

The *distributive property* can be represented either in terms of linear measure or the array. For example, that $4 \times (5 + 3)$ is equal to $(4 \times 5) + (4 \times 3)$ can be shown in two ways. (In the first figure the bottom row of blocks can be rearranged into the configuration of the top row, or separate blocks can be used as shown.)

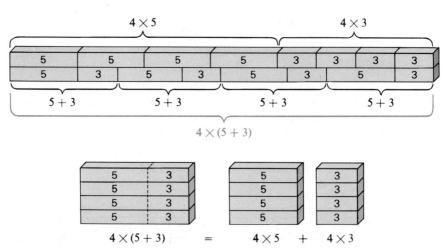

The *equal addition theorem* for subtraction $[a - b = (a + k) - (b + k)]$, which says that the difference of two numbers is unaffected if the same number is added to each of those numbers, can easily be represented by interpreting the difference as the gap which results when the blocks representing the two numbers are placed side-by-side with a common endpoint. That gap can be measured with a block. For example:

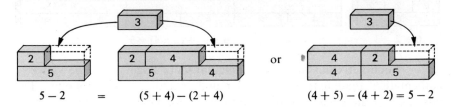

$$5 - 2 \quad = \quad (5 + 4) - (2 + 4) \qquad\qquad (4 + 5) - (4 + 2) = 5 - 2$$

Many of the *other theorems* mentioned in the mathematical review section of this chapter, all of which are important in subsequent work with the algorithms, can be represented with the blocks while children are at the fundamental facts stage. A few are outlined below:

Examples:

(a) $(a + b) - c = a + (b - c)$

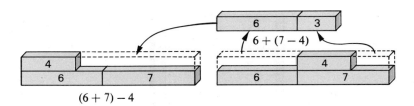

$$(6 + 7) - 4$$

(b) $(c \times a) - (c \times b) = c \times (a - b)$

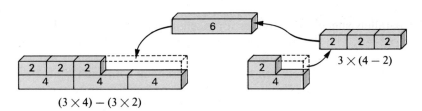

$$(3 \times 4) - (3 \times 2)$$

(c) $(a + b) \div c = (a \div c) + (b \div c)$

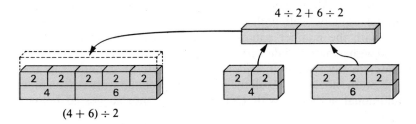

$$(4 + 6) \div 2$$

(d) $a \div b = (a \times c) \div (b \times c)$

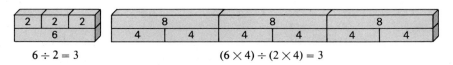

$$6 \div 2 = 3 \qquad\qquad (6 \times 4) \div (2 \times 4) = 3$$

Such activities at the fundamental facts stage should be viewed as mathematical readiness for the fuller understanding which follows. They must be repeated with various numbers in order to lead to any degree of generalization. Two things should be emphasized. First, in doing these activities, children are getting valuable drill in the context of learning something new. And, second, many children will need considerable teacher guidance, and complete mastery of the generalizations is not to be expected at this point; they will need to be repeated in more detail when they are to be *used* in teaching the algorithms.

The *sum families* are effectively represented by the number cases of the Stern materials (see Chapter 4, pp. 65–66). The 6-family, for example, is suggested by this staircase arrangement constructed in the number case:

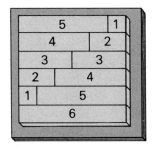

This parallels suggested activities for teaching the number concept (Chapter 4, pp. 65–66, 71); the distinction is that conscious emphasis is now placed on the staircase as representing fundamental addition and subtraction facts and the relationships between those facts. Playing with such staircases can help to create a lasting visual image of the sum families up to ten.

Cuisenaire Rods

The Cuisenaire rods have already been described (Chapter 4, pp. 70, 86, and 100). All the activities suggested above using Stern blocks can be carried on equally well with Cuisenaire rods if children are sufficiently familiar with the number names corresponding to the rods or if they are provided with a metric scale with which to measure them. (Since the Cuisenaire rods are unsegmented, children cannot rely on counting, as they can with the Stern blocks, to recall the number associated with a given block.) A few additional activities with Cuisenaire rods are suggested below. The reader who is not familiar with the rods may find it helpful to examine this table of the ten rod sizes, colors, and abbreviated color-names (other abbreviations can be used):

Dimensions (in cm)	Color	Abbreviated Color Name
1 × 1 × 1	White	w
1 × 1 × 2	Red	r
1 × 1 × 3	Light Green	g
1 × 1 × 4	Purple	p
1 × 1 × 5	Yellow	y
1 × 1 × 6	Dark Green	d
1 × 1 × 7	Black	k
1 × 1 × 8	Brown	n
1 × 1 × 9	Blue	u
1 × 1 × 10	Orange	o

For *addition* and *subtraction* activities, *any* rod can be chosen as the unit—because the rods are unsegmented. While this characteristic is most useful later, when fractions are being taught, it can provide variation in representing addition and subtraction facts. For example, 2 + 3 can be represented in several ways:

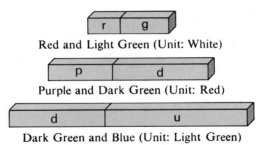

Red and Light Green (Unit: White)

Purple and Dark Green (Unit: Red)

Dark Green and Blue (Unit: Light Green)

Multiplication can be, and usually is, represented in the following way: In order to find the product of, say, 3 and 4, a child selects a 3-rod and a 4-rod. (In the Cuisenaire materials, these are usually first identified by color names rather than number names, but the 3-rod and 4-rod notation is consistent with our previous discussions.) He then represents 3 × 4 by forming a *cross* with the rods, and constructs a *floor* by placing two more

4-rods under the 3-rod so that the width of the floor is the same as the length of the top rod. The top rod is then discarded and the rods of the floor are

put end-to-end forming a *train*, which is then measured against a *standard train* (a "standard train" includes, at most, one rod that is not a 10-rod).

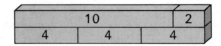

Since the matching standard train represents 12 $(10 + 2)$, the child can see that $3 \times 4 = 12$. This model for multiplication differs from others we have considered in that *both* factors are initially represented with rods; comparable previously mentioned models for this same fact represent *one* factor by a rod (length), and the other is represented by the number of "copies" of that rod that are used.

The reader can readily verify that if any rod other than the white rod is chosen as the unit, this multiplication model will lead to results which are inconsistent with arithmetic. For example, if the red rod is chosen as the unit, 3×4 would be represented as a *dark green* and *brown* cross; the floor would contain six brown rods, which would be matched by the standard train of four orange rods and one brown rod. Each orange rod would represent 5, and the brown rod represents 4, so the result would be 24!

The *distributive property* can be developed with this model by representing one factor as a sum. For example: $3 \times (2 + 4)$ would begin with this cross:

which leads to this floor:

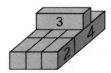

and this chain:

$(3 \times 2) + (3 \times 4)$ would lead to a train of the same length, so

$$3 \times (2 + 4) = (3 \times 2) + (3 \times 4)$$

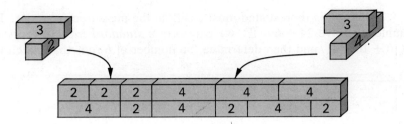

The *associative property* of multiplication can be represented by an extended cross, called a *tower*. Thus, $3 \times (2 \times 4)$ or $(3 \times 2) \times 4$ would be represented by this tower:

To show $3 \times (2 \times 4)$, the 2×4 cross would first be formed, and then (discarding the 2) the resulting $4 + 4$ train would be formed. The $3 \times (4 + 4)$ cross is then formed.

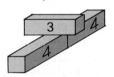

This would result in a $4 + 4 + 4 + 4 + 4 + 4$ train. To show $(3 \times 2) \times 4$, we would first form a 3×2 cross, leading to the $2 + 2 + 2$ train, then form a

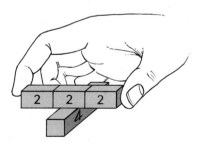

$(2 + 2 + 2) \times 4$ cross, which would again result in a $4 + 4 + 4 + 4 + 4 + 4$ train, so

$$3 \times (2 \times 4) = (3 \times 2) \times 4$$

Division is represented most easily in the measurement sense. For example, to solve $24 \div 6 = \square$, we can form a *standard train* to represent 24 $(10 + 10 + 4)$, and then determine the number of 6-rods that match it:

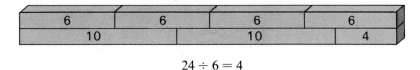

$$24 \div 6 = \underline{4}$$

To show the inverse relationship between multiplication and division, the four 6-rods can then be arranged to form a floor from which the appropriate 4×6 cross (and its equivalent, 6×4) can be made. This can in turn be

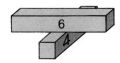

simplified, culminating in the original standard train. Thus, multiplying by 6 "undoes" dividing by 6. This cyclic procedure could be reversed to show that dividing by 6 likewise "undoes" multiplying by 6.

Centimeter Rods

The Centimeter rods (Chapter 4, pp. 70 and 100), like the Cuisenaire rods, can be used for many of the preceding exercises except that unless several sets of blocks are used, different types of exercises are required. (Recall that a one-child set contains only *one* 10-rod and two of each of the rods representing 1 through 9.) These rods are best suited, then, to activities involving the measurement of given shapes by choosing appropriate rods. Addition and subtraction are represented essentially as with the Cuisenaire materials. The Centimeter rods can be used to relate addition, multiplication, and division.

Examples:

(a) Measure this $6 + 4$ string:

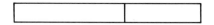

(b) Measure the $4 + 4 + 4$ string and the $3 + 3 + 3 + 3$ string:

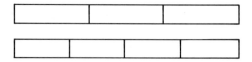

(c) Measure this $4 + 4 + 4$ *folded string*:

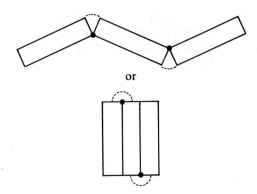

or

(d) This is the shape of a folded string. It could be the shape of a 3×4 string or a 4×3 string.

(e) How many 6-rods cover this shape?

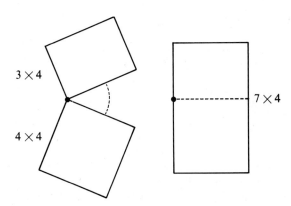

The distributive property can be represented by measuring shapes formed by two or more folded strings:

Balances

Inexpensive balances provide a model for the operations and their properties quite different from the preceding ones: A commercially available model (see Appendix B) has 10 numbered pegs along each side of the plastic beam, and a set of metal markers, each of the same weight, designed to hang on the pegs.

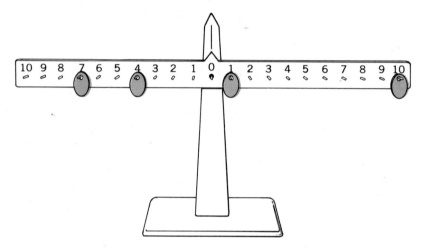

An *equation* is represented by horizontal equilibrium which, because of the design, occurs when the proper combination of weights is placed on either side. The scales are interpreted additively. In the picture above, for example, 7 + 4 is represented on the left side and 10 + 1 on the other. Since these sums are equal, the instrument "balances." Inequalities are registered, of course, by imbalance.

The pegs are long enough to hold several weights. Several weights on one peg would correspond to a product. Thus, 3 weights on the 5-peg would represent 3 × 5, and can be balanced by any corresponding combination on the opposite side, e.g., 5 weights on the 3-peg, or 1 weight on each of the 5- and 10-pegs.

Subtraction and division must be interpreted in additive terms. For example, 14 − 6 = □ would be interpreted as 6 + □ = 14. In its simplest form, this would be set up by hanging a weight on the 6-peg on one side and, on the other side, a weight on each of the 4- and 10-pegs. This creates an imbalance that can be overcome by placing a weight on the 8-peg (or its equivalent) on the same side as the 6. A quotient such as 24 ÷ 4 = □ can be determined by balancing 24 (2 tens + 1 four) either with 4 weights on the opposite 6-peg (partition) or 6 weights on the 4-peg (measurement).

This device, which can be homemade with a little care, can thus be used by children to figure out (or verify) fundamental facts, by trial-and-error at first, but gradually with some finesse as they gain intuitive insight into the physical properties of the apparatus. There are numerous uses for this deceptively simple device beyond the fundamental-facts stage—inequality and betweenness, equivalence of fractions, and so on. Concepts of immediate concern include the commutative, associative, and distributive properties; the identity properties; sum families, factor families, and several of the important theorems already discussed. Serious work with the apparatus (as with any such instructional aid) should be accompanied by student record-keeping, such as filling in blanks, based on manipulative results, in a work sheet designed to lead toward some generalization.

Projects, Questions, and Suggested Activities

1. Make a list of "word problems" that could be used to introduce fundamental facts for a given operation. Include (and identify) as many distinct models for the operation as possible.
2. Classify the fundamental facts for either addition and subtraction or multiplication and division (e.g., the "doubles," those with a factor of 0, etc.). List all the facts in each category.
3. Construct a fundamental-facts test as described on page 141. One way to obtain multiple copies is to prepare a ten-by-ten grid on a Ditto (or other) duplicator master sheet. Each cell in the grid should have an "answer space."

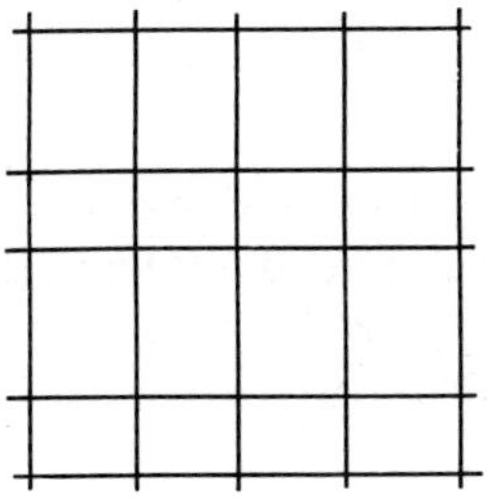

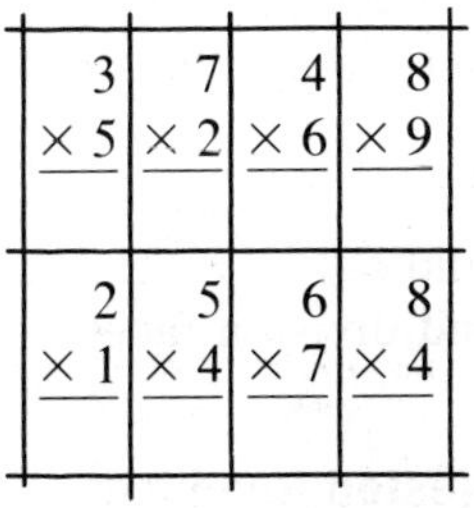

Now run a supply of master sheets through the duplicating machine (one at a time) to imprint the grid on each master. Leave the thin intermediate

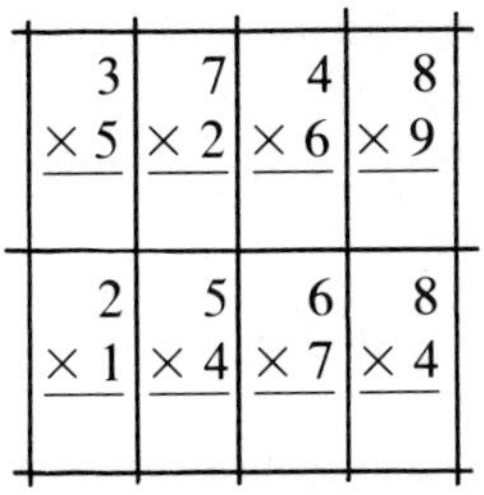

Question Side

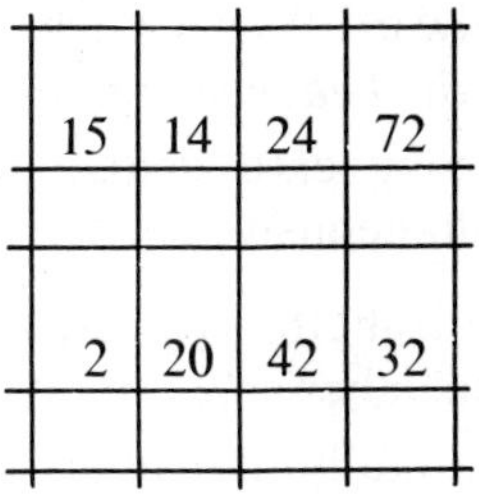

Answer Side

sheet in; the grid will not show in the finished product. Two such masters will be required for each test: One for the "question" side and another for the "answers." Be sure the facts are selected randomly, e.g., by shuffling a set of flash cards and drawing them one at a time. If this is done as a class project, each person can have a very useful collection of facts tests to use with children.

4. Survey *The Arithmetic Teacher* to find games for teaching or practicing fundamental facts. Record directions, materials needed, and so on, for each game on a separate sheet of paper. A few games are included in the Suggested Readings, but you will find many more. Again, if this is done cooperatively and the results duplicated, each beginning teacher can start with a very useful collection. You may wish to make up some games of your own. Most of those in *The Arithmetic Teacher* were invented by teachers.

5. Practice using a set of Cuisenaire rods, Centimeter rods, or a balance to solve some fundamental facts.

6. Make a set of blocks patterned after the Stern blocks and a matching number line (one is described in Chapter 6, p. 226). Ordinary 1-inch lumber, even clear fir, is quite inexpensive, and most lumber yards are willing to slice it into strips for you. You will find that a "1-by-6" (or "1-by-*n*") board is actually $\frac{3}{4}$-inch thick, so have it sliced into $\frac{3}{4}$-inch wide strips, which you can then saw to the necessary lengths. About 10 blocks of each size, with a few extra tens and ones, and a matching number line about 100 units long will be a very useful teaching aid to keep.

7. Debate this: subtraction and division are not fundamental operations. They should not be taught per se and children need not learn the 190 subtraction and division facts.

Suggested Readings

Andrews, W. S. *Magic Squares and Cubes*. LaSalle, Ill.: Open Court, 1917.

A classic on the topic.

Arnsdorf, Edward E. "A Game for Reviewing Basic Facts of Arithmetic." *The Arithmetic Teacher*, November 1972, pp. 589–90.

An easy card game; provides practice with all four operations simultaneously.

Fennema, Elizabeth H. "Models and Mathematics." *The Arithmetic Teacher,* December 1972, pp. 635–40.

A carefully documented, thorough discussion of concrete and symbolic models and how to use them. Summarizes many research studies on the subject. In the same issue, Jencks and Peck (pp. 642–44) reinforce this idea.

Hampton, Homer F. "The Concentration Game." *The Arithmetic Teacher,* January 1972, pp. 65–67.

> Adapting the television game to drill on fundamental facts.

Hervey, Margaret A., and Litwiller, Bonnie H. "The Addition Table: Experiences in Practice-Discovery." *The Arithmetic Teacher,* March 1972, pp. 179–81.

> Patterns in the addition table.

McCombs, Wayne E. "Four-by-Four Magic Square for the New Year." *The Arithmetic Teacher,* January 1970, pp. 79–80.

> A process for generating many such squares from one basic pattern. Don't neglect the editor's note.

Schloff, Charles E. "8 = Turkey." *The Arithmetic Teacher,* April 1971, pp. 268–70.

> A good example of how children can learn new multiplication facts from those they already know—by doubling.

Shafer, Dale M. "Multiplication Mastery via the Tape Recorder." *The Arithmetic Teacher,* November 1970, pp. 581–82.

> Good idea for drill and a particularly helpful idea for analyzing children's responses.

Sherrill, James M. "Egg Cartons Again?!" *The Arithmetic Teacher,* January 1973, pp. 13–16.

> A way to teach addition and subtraction facts (plus some other things).

Thiessen, Richard. "Magic Squares." In *More Chips from the Mathematical Log.* Josephine P. Andree, Ed. Mu Alpha Theta, University of Oklahoma, 1970, pp. 21–25.

> Interesting description of how to construct magic squares and some extensions, e.g., magic cubes, triangles, hexagons. . . .

Van Arsdel, Jean, and Lasky, Joanne. "A Two-Dimensional Abacus—The Papy Minicomputer." *The Arithmetic Teacher,* October 1972, pp. 445–51.

> How to use this device for teaching fundamental facts.

Werner, Sister Marijane. "The Case for a More Universal Number-Line Model of Subtraction." *The Arithmetic Teacher,* January 1973, pp. 61–64.

> Advocates one particuiar number-line model for subtraction in preference to others, because of its transfer later on to subtraction of integers.

Wills, Herbert. "Diffy." *The Arithmetic Teacher,* October 1971, pp. 402–5.

> An interesting open-ended game for subtraction facts (and much more). Are shapes other than a square possible for a playing board?

6. Teaching the Algorithms for Whole Number Operations

Teaching children how to perform whole number computations with proficiency and understanding is a major objective of the elementary mathematics curriculum. Some specific activities and materials for accomplishing this are considered in this chapter. The prerequisites for learning these procedures — understanding of the essential characteristics of our numeration system and the understandings and skills associated with learning the fundamental facts — were considered in Chapters 4 and 5. We begin here by reviewing the way in which the material in those chapters is applied to the algorithms.

1. Mathematical Review

Any algorithm (or algorism) is a process involving the repetition, for a variable but finite number of times, of certain steps, terminating in the result for which the algorithm was invented. The first step in each of the standard algorithms of whole number arithmetic is to write down the numbers in a specific *computational form* which, based on the structure of the number and numeration systems, is designed to make the computations relatively simple, requiring essentially only the manipulation of fundamental facts (and a few "renaming" generalizations). The remaining steps involve repeated and systematic mental additions, subtractions, and so on, of the numbers named by the individual *digits* of the number concerned, according to a specific pattern (determined by place value), and recording the sums, differences, and so on, in their appropriate places. In the cases of addition and multiplication, this frequently requires mentally renaming the sum or product, recording part of it, and "carrying" the rest of it to the next place. Subtraction and division generally require renaming one of the numbers *before* doing the computations.

The familiar computational forms for addition, subtraction, and multiplication can be viewed as arrays: The ones-place digits of the numbers (i.e., their numerals) to be added, subtracted, or multiplied are aligned vertically; this aligns the digits similarly for *each* place, of course. This alignment is crucial for each of those algorithms. The nature of the division algorithm is such that aligning corresponding digits is not helpful, so the dividend and divisor are aligned side-by-side horizontally. For each algorithm, answers are recorded one digit at a time — in general, multiplication and division computations require the recording of intermediate numbers, also one digit at a time. Place values for the digits in answers and all intermediate digits correspond to those of the array in the cases of addition, subtraction, and multiplication, and to those of the dividend in the case of division.

We will now analyze each algorithm separately. In doing so, we will normally use the words "number," "numeral," and "digit" interchangeably, as most people do, assuming that the actual meaning is clear from context. In those cases where it seems necessary to distinguish specifically between numbers and numerals, we will follow the convention of using single quotation marks to indicate a *numeral,* e.g., '3' or '47' (no such punctuation is used to indicate the corresponding *numbers,* e.g., 3 or 47). Also, in order to generalize the discussion somewhat, lower-case letters will be used as variables for numbers 0 through 9; corresponding capital letters will be used to represent *products* of such numbers and a power of ten. When placed in juxtaposition, as $ABCD$, addition will be implied, as with standard numerals, i.e., $ABCD$ means $A + B + C + D$, where $A = a \times 10^3$, $B = b \times 10^2$, $C = c \times 10^1$, and $D = d \times 10^0$ (and $a \neq 0$). This parallels the conventional "abbreviation" involved in standard numeration. For example, '4703' means

$$(4 \times 10^3) + (7 \times 10^2) + (0 \times 10^1) + (3 \times 10^0)$$

Thus the power of ten by which a number e is multiplied to obtain E should be clear from the context in which it appears.

The Addition Algorithm

The addition algorithm can be used to find the sum of more than two numbers at one time, unlike the other algorithms, which always involve exactly two. The basic procedure is the same regardless of how many numbers are being added and regardless of their magnitudes. We will arbitrarily analyze it, then, in terms of finding the sum of four numbers, which we will abbreviate $ABCD$, EFG, $HIJK$, and $LMNO$. Placing the four numbers in computational form is done as follows according to the previously mentioned procedure:

$$
\begin{array}{r}
A\,B\,C\,D \\
E\,F\,G \\
H\,I\,J\,K \\
+\,L\,M\,N\,O
\end{array}
$$

It should be clear that the sum of these 4 numbers is in fact the sum of 15 numbers:

$$(A+B+C+D)+(E+F+G)+(H+I+J+K)+(L+M+N+O)$$

The commutative and associative properties, taken together, assure us that the sum is unaffected by the ordering or grouping of the individual numbers; and, in particular, we can think of them in terms of their columnar arrangement:

$$(D+G+K+O)+(C+F+J+N)+(B+E+I+M)+(A+H+L)$$

The four "partial sums" $(D + G + K + O)$, and so on, are *consciously* determined by adding the corresponding numbers:

$$(d+g+k+o)$$
$$(c+f+j+n)$$
$$(b+e+i+m)$$
$$(a+h+l)$$

Each of these 15 numbers is less than ten, of course. The distributive property is involved here since these groups of numbers represent *products* with common factors. For example,

$$D+G+K+O = (d \times 10^0) + (g \times 10^0) + (k \times 10^0) + (o \times 10^0)$$
$$= (d+g+k+o) \times 10^0$$

and

$$C+F+J+N = (c \times 10^1) + (f \times 10^1) + (j \times 10^1) + (n \times 10^1)$$
$$= (c+f+j+n) \times 10^1$$

Determining the sums $(d + g + k + o)$, $(c + f + j + n)$, and so on, generally involves a skill beyond the fundamental facts stage. To illustrate this, suppose that $d = 8$, $g = 4$, $k = 6$, and $o = 7$. Then

$$(d+g+k+o) = 8+4+6+7$$

If these are added in the order in which they appear (although this is not imperative), we have $[(8 + 4) + 6] + 7$, i.e.,

$$8 + 4 = 12$$
$$12 + 6 = 18$$
$$18 + 7 = \underline{25}$$

The first of these, $8 + 4 = 12$, is a fundamental fact; but $12 + 6 = 18$ and $18 + 7 = 25$ are not. These are examples of what are sometimes called *higher decade* addition facts, which are of the general form $x + y = z$ where $x \geqslant 10$ and $y < 10$. Such sums must be found with skill if children are to become proficient with the algorithm. We will consider the teaching of higher decade facts in section 3.

Let us assume that the four sums that are consciously determined are

$$d + g + k + o = \mathcal{S}$$
$$c + f + j + n = \mathcal{R}$$
$$b + e + i + m = \mathcal{Q}$$
$$a + h + l = \mathcal{P}$$

Then

$$(D + G + K + O) + (C + F + J + N) + (B + E + I + M) + (A + H + L) =$$
$$\mathcal{S} \times 10^0 + \mathcal{R} \times 10^1 + \mathcal{Q} \times 10^2 + \mathcal{P} \times 10^3$$

If each of $\mathcal{S}, \mathcal{R}, \mathcal{Q}$, and $\mathcal{P}$ is less than 10, i.e., s, r, q, and p, then the desired sum is $PQRS$. However, one or more of these partial sums is generally greater than or equal to 10. In such cases, the sum is renamed according to the following carrying generalization: By the *basic division relation* (see pp. 173–174), every number greater than 9 can be expressed in the form $10x + y$, where $y < 10$. If z is such a number, i.e., if $z = 10x + y$, then for any power of 10, 10^k,

$$z \cdot 10^k = x \cdot 10^{k+1} + y \cdot 10^k$$

Thus, if $z = 25$, then $x = 2$ and $y = 5$; and, for example,

$$25 \cdot 10^2 = 2 \cdot 10^3 + 5 \cdot 10^2$$

that is

$$25 \text{ hundreds} = 2 \text{ thousands} + 5 \text{ hundreds}$$

Or, if $z = 172$, then $x = 17$ and $y = 2$,

$$172 \cdot 10^0 = 17 \cdot 10^1 + 2 \cdot 10^0 \qquad 172 \text{ ones} = 17 \text{ tens} + 2 \text{ ones}$$

If the sum, z, of the *digits* in a given column (place) is greater than 9, z is renamed as $10x + y$. Then 'y' is recorded in that place and x is "carried" to the next place and added with the numbers in that place—if there are any— if there are no digits in the next place, x is recorded in that place or those places in the sum.

Again, the commutative and associative properties suggest that the partial sums can be obtained in any order. However, the general necessity of carrying makes it simpler to add from right to left, i.e., add *ones*, then *tens*, and so on, since this leads to simplifying the sum as we go along.

The addition algorithm can be summarized as follows:

Step 1:

Record the numbers to be added in computational form.

Step 2:

Add the numbers named by the digits in ones place.
(a) If that sum is less than 10, record it in ones place.
(b) If that sum is greater than 10, think of it as $10x + y$. Record
'y' in ones place and "carry" x to be added with the numbers
in tens place.

Step 3:

Repeat step 2 for each place (replacing "ones place" in the discussions of step 2 with "tens place," "hundreds place," and so on, in turn) until all numbers in each place have been added and their sums recorded.

Example:

Step 1:

Let

$$
\begin{array}{ll}
\begin{array}{l}
A\,B\,C\,D \\
E\,F\,G \\
H\,I\,J\,K \\
\overline{L\,M\,N\,O}
\end{array} & \text{be} \quad
\begin{array}{l}
2418 \\
304 \\
5736 \\
\overline{8627}
\end{array}
\end{array}
$$

that is,

$A = 2000$	$B = 400$	$C = 10$	$D = 8$
	$E = 300$	$F = 0$	$G = 4$
$H = 5000$	$I = 700$	$J = 30$	$K = 6$
$L = 8000$	$M = 600$	$N = 20$	$O = 7$

and

$a = 2$	$b = 4$	$c = 1$	$d = 8$
	$e = 3$	$f = 0$	$g = 4$
$h = 5$	$i = 7$	$j = 3$	$k = 6$
$l = 8$	$m = 6$	$n = 2$	$o = 7$

Step 2:

$(8 + 4 + 6 + 7)$ ones $= 25$ ones $= 2$ tens $+ 5$ ones; record '5' in ones place, and "carry" 2 to tens place.

Step 3:

$2 + (1 + 0 + 3 + 2)$ tens $= 8$ tens; record '8' in tens place.

$(4 + 3 + 7 + 6)$ hundreds $= 20$ hundreds $= 2$ thousands $+ 0$ hundreds; record '0' in hundreds place, and "carry" 2 to thousands place.

$2 + (2 + 5 + 8)$ thousands $= 17$ thousands $= 1$ ten-thousand $+ 7$ thousands; record '7' in thousands place and, since there are no numbers in ten-thousands place, record '1' in ten-thousands place.

The sum is

$\underline{1}$ ten-thousand $+ \underline{7}$ thousands $+ \underline{0}$ hundreds $+ \underline{8}$ tens $+ \underline{5}$ ones

or

$$17085.$$

The Subtraction Algorithm

Like addition, algorithms for subtraction generally proceed place-by-place, beginning with ones place. The result is recorded, in standard form, as one proceeds in order — from ones to tens to hundreds, and so on. Unlike addition, however, no single subtraction algorithm has become entirely standardized; there are basically two algorithms currently taught in this country. The two differ in the way in which an impasse is resolved. (An impasse is a situation where, in a given place, the indicated numbers a and b cannot be subtracted with whole numbers; i.e., given $a - b$, where $b > a$.) The two common methods of resolving an impasse are *borrowing* and *equal additions*. Of the two, "borrowing" is by far the more commonly taught, probably because it is easier to teach meaningfully. We will consider only this algorithm here and briefly consider the other subsequently.

The two numbers to be subtracted are first recorded in computational form, e.g.,

$$\begin{array}{r} ABCD \\ - \ EFGH \end{array} \quad (a \neq 0, \ a \geqslant e)$$

The basic procedure is derived from the generalization that if $a \geqslant c$ and if $b \geqslant d$,

$$(a + b) - (c + d) = (a - c) + (b - d)$$

This generalization can be extended to any number of addends. Here,

$$(A + B + C + D) - (E + F + G + H)$$
$$= (A - E) + (B - F) + (C - G) + (D - H)$$

providing each of the differences is defined. As with addition, a distributive principle (multiplication over subtraction) is involved, e.g.,

$$A - E = (a \times 10^3) - (e \times 10^3) = (a - e) \times 10^3$$
$$B - F = (b \times 10^2) - (f \times 10^2) = (b - f) \times 10^2.$$

Thus we mentally compute, in turn, $(d - h)$, $(c - g)$, $(b - f)$, and $(a - e)$, if they exist, and record the differences in the corresponding places. First, let us assume that each difference *does* exist, i.e., that $d \geqslant h$, $c \geqslant g$, etc. If

$$d - h = l$$
$$c - g = k$$
$$b - f = j$$
$$a - e = i$$

then

$$ABCD - EFGH = IJKL$$

That is,

$$[(a \times 10^3) + (b \times 10^2) + (c \times 10^1) + (d \times 10^0)]$$
$$- [(e \times 10^3) + (f \times 10^2) + (g \times 10^1) + (h \times 10^0)]$$
$$= [(i \times 10^3) + (j \times 10^2) + (k \times 10^1) + (l \times 10^0)] = IJKL$$

In computational form:

$$\begin{array}{ll} (a \times 10^3) + (b \times 10^2) + (c \times 10^1) + (d \times 10^0) & \text{Example:} \quad 8674 \\ - (e \times 10^3) + (f \times 10^2) + (g \times 10^1) + (h \times 10^0) & \qquad\qquad\;\, -2320 \\ \hline (i \times 10^3) + (j \times 10^2) + (k \times 10^1) + (l \times 10^0) = IJKL \\ \quad I \qquad\qquad J \qquad\qquad K \qquad\qquad L \end{array}$$

In the more general case, however, an impasse may occur in any place. To illustrate, suppose $d < h$, e.g.,

Let $ABCD$ be (a) $\begin{array}{r}8652\\-4326\end{array}$ or (b) $\begin{array}{r}8602\\-4326\end{array}$ or (c) $\begin{array}{r}8002\\-4326\end{array}$
$\quad\;\, -EFGH$

where $2 < 6$. If the next digit is nonzero, as in (a) where $c = 5$ and $d = 2$, we can use the borrowing generalization

$$(m \times 10^k) + (n \times 10^{k-1}) = (m - 1) \times 10^k + (n + 10) \times 10^{k-1}$$

where $m \neq 0$. (This can be easily verified.) If, as in (b) and (c), the next digit is zero or the next several digits are zero, this generalization can be applied repeatedly, as needed, beginning in the first place with a nonzero digit

(b) $8000 + 600 + 0 + 2 = 8000 + 500 + 100 + 2 = 8000 + 500 + 90 + 12$
(c) $8000 + 0 + 0 + 2 = 7000 + 1000 + 0 + 2 = 7000 + 900 + 100 + 2$
$$= 7000 + 900 + 90 + 12$$

Thus, a given impasse in any place can always be resolved by renaming the minuend via the process commonly referred to as "borrowing."

A minor variation on the above occurs when the two numbers being subtracted have a different number of digits, e.g.,

$$\begin{array}{r} 8462 \\ -\ \ 124 \end{array} \quad \text{or} \quad \begin{array}{r} 670235 \\ -\ \ 2172 \end{array}$$

In such cases, we annex zeroes so that the numbers of digits correspond. This is done tacitly, without actually recording them:

$$\begin{array}{r} 8462 \\ -\ 0124 \end{array} \quad \text{or} \quad \begin{array}{r} 670235 \\ -\ 002172 \end{array}$$

The Multiplication Algorithm

Given two numbers, say ABC and DE, to multiply, we first record them in computational form:

$$\begin{array}{r} ABC \\ \times\ \ DE \end{array} \quad \text{e.g.,} \quad \begin{array}{r} 327 \\ \times\ \ 14 \end{array}$$

This provides a convenient format for using the distributive property, which is an important key to the algorithm. This property, in its *simplest* form, says that the product of two numbers, a and d, can be found by expressing (either) one of the factors as a sum of two numbers, say $d = (b + c)$; the product $a \times d$ can then be found by adding the two products $a \times b$ and $a \times c$, i.e.,

$$a \times d = a \times (b + c)$$
$$= (a \times b) + (a \times c)$$

This distributive property can be extended in two ways: Either *both* factors can be expressed as sums, e.g.,

$$a = e + f \quad \text{and} \quad d = b + c$$

and therefore

$$a \times d = (e + f) \times (b + c)$$
$$= (e \times b) + (e \times c) + (f \times b) + (f \times c)$$

that is, each addend of a is multiplied by each addend of d and the *sum* of those four products is the desired product, $a \times d$. Or, either factor can be expressed as *more* than two addends (as many as desired), e.g.,

$$(g + h + i) \times (j + k + l + m)$$
$$= (g \times j) + (g \times k) + (g \times l) + (g \times m) + (h \times j) + (h \times k) + \cdots + (i \times m).$$

Thus, since '*ABC*' and '*DE*' are abbreviations for the sums $A + B + C$ and $D + E$, $ABC \times DE$ can be found "in parts," i.e.,

$$ABC \times DE = (A + B + C) \times (D + E)$$

$$= (A \times D) + (A \times E) + (B \times D) + (B \times E) + (C \times D) + (C \times E)$$

Both addition and multiplication are commutative and associative, so the order of finding these sums and products can be — and is — changed in computation, thus:

$$\begin{array}{r} ABC \\ \times \ \underline{DE} \end{array}$$
$$= [(E \times C) + (E \times B) + (E \times A)] + [(D \times C) + (D \times B) + (D \times A)]$$

The two addends, $[(E \times C) + (E \times B) + (E \times A)]$ and $[(D \times C) + (D \times B) + (D \times A)]$, are called *partial products*.

Each of $A, B, C, D,$ and E is itself an abbreviation for a product, e.g.,

$$(E \times C) = (e \times 10^0) \times (c \times 10^0)$$

$$(D \times A) = (d \times 10^1) \times (a \times 10^2)$$

Using the commutative and associative properties of multiplication, the six products can be expressed as

$$\begin{array}{c} (e \times c) \times 10^0 \times 10^0 \\ (e \times b) \times 10^0 \times 10^1 \\ (e \times a) \times 10^0 \times 10^2 \\ (d \times c) \times 10^1 \times 10^0 \\ (d \times b) \times 10^1 \times 10^1 \\ (d \times a) \times 10^1 \times 10^2 \end{array}$$

Each of the expressions on the left, i.e., $(e \times c)$, $(e \times b)$, and so on, is a fundamental multiplication fact; those on the right can be simplified using the rule for multiplying powers: $a^b \times a^c = a^{b+c}$. Thus the above expressions simplify as follows:

Let

$$\left. \begin{array}{l} e \times c = \mathcal{F} \\ e \times b = \mathcal{G} \\ e \times a = \mathcal{H} \end{array} \right. \left. \begin{array}{l} \mathcal{F} \times 10^0 \\ \mathcal{G} \times 10^1 \\ \mathcal{H} \times 10^2 \end{array} \right\} \begin{array}{l} \text{1st partial} \\ \text{product} \end{array} \Big\} \ (\mathcal{F} \times 10^0) + (\mathcal{G} \times 10^1) + (\mathcal{H} \times 10^2)$$

$$\left. \begin{array}{l} d \times c = \mathcal{I} \\ d \times b = \mathcal{J} \\ d \times a = \mathcal{K} \end{array} \right. \left. \begin{array}{l} \mathcal{I} \times 10^1 \\ \mathcal{J} \times 10^2 \\ \mathcal{K} \times 10^3 \end{array} \right\} \begin{array}{l} \text{2nd partial} \\ \text{product} \end{array} \Big\} \ (\mathcal{I} \times 10^1) + (\mathcal{J} \times 10^2) + (\mathcal{K} \times 10^3)$$

The two partial products are recorded as with column addition. That is, if any of the products $\mathcal{F}, \mathcal{G}, \mathcal{H}$, and so on, above is less than ten, it is recorded in the place determined by the power of ten by which it is multiplied. If it is greater than or equal to ten, it is renamed, as in column addition, as $10x + y$; 'y' is recorded in that place and x is added to the next product.

Example:

```
 327
× 14
1308
```

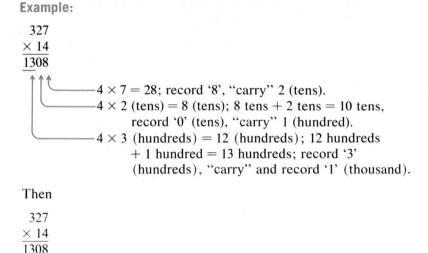

—— $4 \times 7 = 28$; record '8', "carry" 2 (tens).

—— 4×2 (tens) $= 8$ (tens); 8 tens $+$ 2 tens $= 10$ tens, record '0' (tens), "carry" 1 (hundred).

—— 4×3 (hundreds) $= 12$ (hundreds); 12 hundreds $+$ 1 hundred $= 13$ hundreds; record '3' (hundreds), "carry" and record '1' (thousand).

Then

```
 327
× 14
1308
 327
```

—— 1 (ten) $\times 7 = 7$ (tens); record '7' in tens place.

—— 1 (ten) $\times 2$ (tens) $= 2$ (hundreds); record '2' in hundreds place.

—— 1 (ten) $\times 3$ (hundreds) $= 3$ (thousands); record '3' in thousands place.

The final step is to add the partial products. This is done by the addition algorithm; the single difference is that the second partial product has no digit in ones place; if there were a third partial product, it would have no digits in ones place or tens place, and so on. The absence of a digit is treated as though there were a '0' in that place.

The Division Algorithm

"Long division" is by far the most complex of the algorithms. Both teaching and learning this process involve several potential sources of difficulty, some of which are considered below.

Whereas the addition, subtraction, and multiplication algorithms are performed almost entirely in terms of the fundamental facts that appear in the problem, the division algorithm generally requires a considerable extension of fundamental facts mastery. Take the following example: in solving

$$\begin{array}{r} 36 \\ + 52 \end{array} \quad \text{or} \quad \begin{array}{r} 46 \\ - 12 \end{array} \quad \text{or} \quad \begin{array}{r} 82 \\ \times 46 \end{array}$$

we first determine the value of $6+2$, $6-2$, or 6×2, respectively. In each case, the digits 6 and 2 appear in the problem and indicate what the initial step is. On the other hand, in each of these cases,

$$2\overline{)7} \qquad 19\overline{)596} \qquad 189\overline{)6927}$$

the appropriate fundamental fact to be used is $6 \div 2 = 3$; yet 6 and 2 do not appear in the problem as a "cue." The student must be able to perform somewhat sophisticated interpolation at times before applying appropriate fundamental facts.

Division, unlike addition, subtraction, and multiplication, generally involves *guessing* when the divisor is greater than 10. The first (or second) step in solving $48\overline{)34926}$, for example, is to *guess* at the first partial quotient. Is it 800? 700? 600? Various techniques can help us guess more accurately, but unfortunately there is no *certain* way to insure our guessing correctly the first time. Needless to say, guessing leads to errors and thus to frustration.

The other operations are "right to left" processes, i.e., they involve manipulations beginning with *ones* place and proceeding place-by-place to the largest place (we add ones, e.g., then tens, then hundreds, . . .). With division, we begin with the largest place and proceed toward ones place.

The division algorithm requires accuracy in both multiplication and subtraction, yet both are normally done in unfamiliar and at first confusing formats. For example:

$$264\overline{)\begin{array}{r}3\\\hline\end{array}} \qquad\qquad \begin{array}{r}\overline{)89064}\\-792\\\hline 98\end{array}$$
$$792$$

Multiplication step   *Subtraction step*

The sophistication and complexity of the division algorithm make it difficult to explain in such a way that the *reasons* for each step are clear to children. The difficulty is frequently compounded by the use of short cuts and of vocabulary such as "bring down the 6," which are not always explained in mathematical terms.

There are alternate ways of treating nonzero remainders, all of which must eventually be learned, because *problem* situations calling for division differ. Thus, the answer to a problem question involving division cannot always be determined in as straightforward a way as are corresponding questions involving the other computations. To take a simple example, consider these four questions:

(a) If 2 hungry boys are to share 17 cookies, how many cookies should each boy receive? (*Answer:* $8\frac{1}{2}$ cookies.)

(b) If 2 boys are to share 17 marbles, how many will each boy receive? (*Answer:* 8 marbles.)
(c) If a 17-foot ribbon is cut into 2-foot strips, how much will be left? (*Answer:* 1 foot.)
(d) If candy bars sell at 2 for 17 cents, how much would you need to pay if you bought just *one*? (*Answer:* 9 cents.)

All of these call for the computation:

$$
\begin{array}{r}
8 \\
2\overline{)17} \\
-16 \\
\hline
1
\end{array}
$$

Yet the answers are all *different*. In problems of comparable difficulty involving addition, subtraction, or multiplication, the child's computation leads *directly* to the answer, without the necessity for making additional judgments.

In this same vein, the common practice of expressing such an answer as "8R1" (8 remainder 1) frequently leads to misunderstandings. For example, if $17 \div 2 = 8R1$ and $25 \div 3 = 8R1$, then it must be that $17 \div 2 = 25 \div 3$. But this cannot be true since also $17 \div 2 = 8\frac{1}{2}$ and $25 \div 3 = 8\frac{1}{3}$. This fallacy results from thinking of 8R1 as one number, when it is in fact *two*. (Nor is 8R1 the same as $8 + 1$, as is sometimes asserted!)

Of the alternate ways of teaching long division, we will consider here the so-called "quotient estimation" algorithm; "repeated subtraction" will be considered later (pp. 240–242). We will examine a *particular* problem, $264\overline{)89064}$, in detail. Before we do so, however, it is worth recalling that the quotient, q, for a given division computation is in general determined "in parts." In the above problem the quotient is $300 + 30 + 7$.

$$
\begin{array}{r}
337 \\
264\overline{)89064}
\end{array}
$$

Each of 300, 30, and 7 is called a *partial quotient*. The single nonzero digits of a partial quotient, i.e., '3', '3', and '7', above, are called *partial quotient figures*. The partial quotients are found in reverse order as compared with the procedures for finding sums, differences, or products; that is, we first find the partial quotient for the largest place and proceed in turn from that place to the ones-place partial quotient. At each place we must find the *maximum* possible partial quotient, since otherwise we would ultimately have a remainder which is greater than or equal to the divisor.

Three key mathematical generalizations (reviewed in Chapter 5) form the basis for this algorithm. The first is the theorem sometimes called the *division algorithm* theorem or the *basic division relation*. (We will use the latter to avoid dual use of the word "algorithm.") The theorem says that if a and b are any whole numbers, except that $b \neq 0$, then there exist unique whole numbers q and r, where $0 \leqslant r < b$, such that $a = (q \times b) + r$. The expressions a, b, q, and r are called the *dividend, divisor, quotient,* and *remainder*, respectively:

$$
\begin{array}{rl}
& 337 \quad \leftarrow \quad q \text{ (quotient)} \\
\text{(divisor) } b \quad \rightarrow \quad 264\overline{)89064} & \quad \leftarrow \quad a \text{ (dividend)} \\
-\underline{88968} & \quad \leftarrow \quad (q \times b) \\
96 & \quad \leftarrow \quad r \text{ (remainder)}
\end{array}
$$

In order to understand the algorithm, it is important to emphasize that the remainder, r, *must* be less than the divisor, b, and to note that $a \geqslant (b \times q)$ since $r \geqslant 0$. Also, it should be noted that in the computational procedure, the remainder is determined by subtraction, i.e., $r = a - (b \times q)$.

The second key generalization is the distributive theorem which says that if a and c are each multiples of b, then

$$(a + c) \div b = (a \div b) + (c \div b)$$

Several things about this generalization merit attention.

(a) It can be extended to more than two addends, e.g., if a, c, and d are multiples of b, then

$$(a + c + d) \div b = (a \div b) + (c \div b) + (d \div b)$$

as in

$$(200 + 60 + 4) \div 2 = (200 \div 2) + (60 \div 2) + (4 \div 2) = 100 + 30 + 2$$

which is

$$
\begin{array}{r}
132 \\
2\overline{)264}
\end{array}
$$

or

$$
\begin{array}{l}
(2 \text{ hundreds} + 6 \text{ tens} + 4 \text{ ones}) \div 2 \\
= (2 \text{ hundreds} \div 2) + (6 \text{ tens} \div 2) + (4 \text{ ones} \div 2)
\end{array}
$$

which is

$$
\begin{array}{r}
1 \text{ hundred } + 3 \text{ tens} + 2 \text{ ones} \\
2\overline{)2 \text{ hundreds} + 6 \text{ tens} + 4 \text{ ones}}
\end{array}
$$

(b) If the *digits* of the dividend are not each multiples of the divisor, then the divisor can *sometimes* (if there is a zero remainder) be renamed to satisfy the conditions of the theorem, as in

$$2\overline{)356} \rightarrow 2\overline{)3 \text{ hundreds} + 5 \text{ tens} + 6 \text{ ones}}$$

$$
\begin{array}{r}
1 \text{ hundred } + \quad 7 \text{ tens} + \quad 8 \text{ ones} \\
\rightarrow 2\overline{)2 \text{ hundreds} + 14 \text{ tens} + 16 \text{ ones}}
\end{array}
$$

For relatively large divisors, this renaming of the dividend is not as simple as above nor is it as simple as the renaming involved in addition, subtraction, and multiplication. For example:

$$13\overline{)3198} \rightarrow 13\overline{)3\text{ thousands} + 1\text{ hundred} + 9\text{ tens} + 8\text{ ones}}$$

$$\rightarrow 13\overline{)\begin{array}{c} 2\text{ hundreds} + \quad 4\text{ tens} + \quad 6\text{ ones} \\ 26\text{ hundreds} + 52\text{ tens} + 78\text{ ones} \end{array}}$$

In fact, the renaming cannot in general be conveniently done *prior* to the separate divisions; rather it is a *consequence* of the computation, as we shall see.

(c) If the dividend is not a multiple of the divisor, i.e., if there is a nonzero remainder (the most general case), then the generalization takes the following form: If $a = c + d + e + r$; if $b \neq 0$; and if c, d, and e are multiples of b, and $r < b$, then

$$a \div b = (c + d + e + r) \div b = (c \div b) + (d \div b) + (e \div b) + (r \div b)$$

c, d, and e may be called *partial dividends*; r is, of course, the remainder. The number of partial dividends is irrelevant, but corresponds with the number of partial quotients. Note that $c \div b$, $d \div b$, and $e \div b$ are whole numbers because c, d, and e are each multiples of b, and $r \div b$ is a fraction, $\frac{r}{b}$, where $\frac{r}{b} < 1$. For example:

$$264\overline{)89064} \rightarrow 264\overline{)\begin{array}{c} 3\text{ hundreds} + \quad 3\text{ tens} + \quad 7\text{ ones} + \frac{96}{264}\text{ ones} \\ 792\text{ hundreds} + 792\text{ tens} + 1848\text{ ones} + \quad 96\text{ ones} \end{array}}$$

$$
\begin{array}{r}
337 \\
264\overline{)89064} \\
- 79200 \quad \leftarrow 3\text{ hundreds} \times 264 \\
\hline
9864 \\
- 7920 \quad \leftarrow 3\text{ tens} \times 264 \\
\hline
1944 \\
- 1848 \quad \leftarrow 7\text{ ones} \times 264 \\
\hline
96 \quad \leftarrow r
\end{array}
$$

The third key generalization is the definition of division, i.e., $a \div b = c$ means $c \times b = a$. This is used (indirectly) as each partial quotient (and thus each partial dividend) is determined. For example, in the preceding problem,

$$
\begin{array}{lll}
79200 \div 264 = 300 & \text{because} & 300 \times 264 = 79200 \\
7920 \div 264 = 30 & \text{because} & 30 \times 264 = 7920 \\
1848 \div 264 = 7 & \text{because} & 7 \times 264 = 1848
\end{array}
$$

The following paragraphs outline the rather complex steps of the standard division algorithm and their mathematical bases. The first two steps are sometimes interchanged, although there are some advantages to the sequence listed here.

Step 1:

Determine the *place* of the first partial quotient. That is, determine whether the first partial quotient is in "the ones" (from 0 to 9), "the tens" (from 10 to 99), "the hundreds" (100 to 999), and so on. Since the place of the first *partial* quotient is the largest place in the *entire* quotient, q, this question is equivalent to finding the "yes" answer in this sequence:

Is q at least 1 but less than 10? (i.e., in the ones)
Is q at least 10 but less than 100? (i.e., in the tens)
Is q at least 100 but less than 1000? (i.e., in the hundreds)

$$. \qquad\qquad .$$
$$. \qquad\qquad .$$
$$. \qquad\qquad .$$

Is q at least 10^k but less than 10^{k+1}?

$$.$$
$$.$$
$$.$$

These questions are equivalent, in turn, to finding the first "no" answer in this sequence:

Is q at least 1?
Is q at least 10?
Is q at least 100?
Is q at least 1000?

$$.$$
$$.$$
$$.$$

Is q at least 10^n?

The basic division relation can be used to answer these questions. We know that the product of q, whatever it may be, and the divisor, b, is less than or equal to the dividend, a, because $a = (q \times b) + r$ and $r \geq 0$. If $r = 0$, then $a = q \times b$ and if $r > 0$, then $a > (q \times b)$. Thus $a \geq (q \times b)$ or, equivalently, $(q \times b) \leq a$.

We can (mentally) multiply the divisor by 1, 10, 100, 1000, and so on and compare each of these products with the dividend until we find one that is *greater* than the dividend. For example:

$$264\overline{)89064} \qquad 264\overline{)\begin{array}{l} 1 \\ 89064 \end{array}}$$

$$\underline{264} \leftarrow 1 \times 264 \leq 89064, \qquad \text{so} \qquad q \geq 1$$

$$\frac{10}{264\overline{)89064}}$$
$$\underline{2640} \leftarrow 10 \times 264 \leq 89064, \qquad \text{so} \qquad q \geq 10$$

$$\frac{100}{264\overline{)89064}}$$
$$\underline{26400} \leftarrow 100 \times 264 \leq 89064, \qquad \text{so} \qquad q \geq 100$$

$$\frac{1000}{264\overline{)89064}}$$
$$\underline{264000} \leftarrow 1000 \times 264 > 89064, \qquad \text{so} \qquad q < 1000$$

The last two comparisons tell us that q is at least 100 but is less than 1000 ($100 \leq q < 1000$). That is, q is a 3-digit number. Thus the *place* of the first partial quotient is hundreds, and there will be 3 separate divisions to perform altogether, to obtain partial quotients whose places are, in turn, hundreds, tens, and ones.

Step 2:

Determine the first partial quotient. This is where the guessing begins. Since the quotient of our sample problem is at least 100, but is less than 1000, the first partial quotient must be one of 100, 200, 300, 400, 500, . . . , 900. It suffices, of course, to find the first partial quotient *figure*: 1, 2, 3, 4, 5, . . . , 9.

Most guessing techniques are essentially based on the reasoning that the quotient of two given numbers is about the same as the quotient of other numbers which are close to them. By rounding the given dividend and divisor we can find numbers close to them that can help in making the guess. There are several ways to do this. For example, since 264 is between 200 and 300, we can round 264 to either of these; similarly, 89064 is between 80,000 and 90,000 so it can be rounded to either of these. (The expressions "rounding down" and "rounding up" are sometimes used to describe these processes.) Since 264 is close to 200 and to 300, and since 89064 is close to 80,000 and to 90,000, then $89064 \div 264$ should be close to one of these:

$$200\overline{)80000} \qquad 200\overline{)90000} \qquad 300\overline{)80000} \qquad 300\overline{)90000}$$

The first partial quotient *figure* for each of these can be approximated by considering only their significant (nonzero) digits and finding the corresponding quotient:

$$\frac{4}{2\overline{)8}} \qquad \frac{4}{2\overline{)9}} \qquad \frac{2}{3\overline{)8}} \qquad \frac{3}{3\overline{)9}}$$

Using one of these rounding methods leads us to try 200, 300, or 400 as the first *trial* partial quotient. (Of the four approximations above, $264\overline{)89064}$ is closest to $300\overline{)90000}$, so 300 is the most likely to be correct.)

If the first digit of the divisor is greater than that of the dividend, as in $437\overline{)36254}$, then the procedure can be modified by considering the first 2 digits of the dividend:

$$437\overline{)36254} \rightarrow 400\overline{)36000} \rightarrow 4\overline{)36}^{\,9}$$

or

$$400\overline{)37000} \rightarrow 4\overline{)37}^{\,9}$$

or

$$500\overline{)36000} \rightarrow 5\overline{)36}^{\,7}$$

or

$$500\overline{)37000} \rightarrow 5\overline{)37}^{\,7}$$

Up to this point we can only guess at the first partial quotient. The process of checking the correctness of that guess is a complex one:

(a) Multiply the trial partial quotient (200, 300, or 400) by the divisor, 264, to determine the first partial dividend. If the trial partial quotient is correct, the partial quotient, partial dividend, and divisor will be correctly related according to the definition of division.

(b) First check: If this product is less than or equal to the dividend, then the *trial* partial quotient is less than or equal to the *correct* (maximum possible) partial quotient, and we proceed to step (c). If we guess 200, we compute:

$$\begin{array}{r} 200 \\ 264\overline{)89064} \\ \underline{52800} \leftarrow 200 \times 264 \end{array}$$

and since $200 \times 264 \leq 89064$, the correct partial quotient is at least 200, i.e., 200, 300, 400, . . . , 900. (This involves the same kind of reasoning as in step 1.) If we guess 300, we find that $300 \times 264 \leq 89064$, so the first partial quotient is at least 300, i.e., 300, 400, . . . , 900. On the other hand, suppose we guess 400:

$$\begin{array}{r} 400 \\ 264\overline{)89064} \\ \underline{105600} \leftarrow 400 \times 264 \end{array}$$

Since $400 \times 264 > 89064$, the first partial quotient must be *less* than 400, i.e., 300, 200, or 100, because if 400 were the correct first partial quotient, the entire quotient, *q*, must be at *least* 400, so $q \times b$ would be at least 105600. But then $a < (q \times b)$, contrary to the basic division relation. (Recall that the dividend, *a*, must be greater than or equal to $q \times b$). Thus if our guess is 400 (or larger) we must try a *smaller* guess (300, 200, or 100) and return to step (a), above.

(c) If the product of the trial partial quotient and the divisor passes the first check, subtract it from the dividend to determine the sum of the remaining partial dividends and the remainder.

$$
\begin{array}{r}
200 \\
264\overline{)\,89064} \\
-\ 52800 \\
\hline
36264
\end{array}
\qquad \text{or} \qquad
\begin{array}{r}
300 \\
264\overline{)\,89064} \\
-\ 79200 \\
\hline
9864
\end{array}
$$

If 200 is the correct first partial quotient, then 52800 is the correct partial dividend; and, by the relationship between subtraction and addition, $89064 = 52800 + 36264$, so the sum of the remaining partial dividends and the remainder is 36264. If 300 is correct, that sum is 9864. Since not both 200 and 300 can be correct, we must perform a second check:

(d) Second check:
   (i) If this difference is greater than or equal to the product of the divisor and the place value of the partial quotient, then the correct (maximum possible) partial quotient is greater than the trial partial quotient. Thus we must make a *larger* guess and return to step (a), above. To see why this check works suppose our guess were 200:

$$
\begin{array}{r}
200 \\
264\overline{)\,89064} \\
-\ 52800 \\
\hline
36264 \leftarrow \text{compare with } 100 \times 264 \quad (26400)
\end{array}
$$

Since $36264 > 26400$, we can subtract 26400 (100×264) from 36264. This in turn means that we can subtract at least 300×264 from 89064. Looking at this another way, to see why we must find the maximum possible partial quotient, suppose 200 were considered to be the correct partial quotient. Then the maximum possible value for the entire quotient would be 299. But $89064 - (299 \times 264) = 10128$, so 10128 would be the *least* possible remainder, and it is greater than the divisor. This is contrary to the basic division relation, which requires that $r < b$. Since for $a = (q \times b) + r$ the dividend and divisor, *a* and *b*, are fixed, with *q* and *r* to be determined, the only way to obtain a sufficiently small remainder, *r*, is to obtain a sufficiently large quotient, q. Thus to make $r < 264$, we make $q > 299$ by increasing the first partial quotient.

(ii) If the difference is less than the product of the divisor and the place value of the partial quotient, then the trial quotient is correct, for similar reasons. For example, if we guess 300, then $89064 - (300 \times 264) = 9864$, and since $9864 < 26400$ (100×264), we cannot subtract 26400 from 9864. That is, the quotient is at least 300 but cannot be as great as 400.

$$
\begin{array}{r}
300 \\
264\,\overline{)\,89064} \\
79200 \quad \leftarrow 300 \times 264 \\
\hline
9864
\end{array}
$$

Having determined that the first partial quotient is exactly 300, since it is neither too large (first check) nor too small (second check), we can proceed with the algorithm. Now since $89064 - 79200 = 9864$, $89064 = 79200 + 9864$, and since $300 \times 264 = 79200$, by the definition of division $79200 \div 264 = 300$. Thus the distributive theorem can be used as follows:

$$
\begin{aligned}
89064 \div 264 &= (79200 + 9864) \div 264 \\
&= (79200 \div 264) + (9864 \div 264) \\
& \ \ 300 \quad\quad + (9864 \div 264)
\end{aligned}
$$

So the procedure for checking the trial partial quotient also leads us to the next step in the process, which is to perform a new division.

Step 3:

Determine the remaining partial quotients in order by repeating steps 1 and 2. Recall that in our sample problem, it was determined at step 1 that it would be necessary to perform 3 divisions. In general, if d_1 is the *difference* obtained in steps 1 and 2, then the next partial quotient is found by dividing d_1 by b. In our case, then, the *second* partial quotient is determined by finding the first partial quotient for

$$264\,\overline{)\,9864} \leftarrow d_1$$

such that the *next* difference, $d_2 < (10 \times 264)$.

Repeating steps 1 and 2, we find (by guessing and checking) that the second partial quotient is 30:

$$
\begin{array}{r}
30 \\
264\,\overline{)\,9864} \leftarrow d_1 \\
-\ 7920 \\
\hline
d_2 \rightarrow 1944
\end{array}
\qquad
\begin{array}{l}
\text{Check 1:} \quad (30 \times 264) \leqslant 9864 \\
\text{Check 2:} \quad d_2 < (10 \times 264)
\end{array}
$$

In practice, this division is performed cumulatively.

$$
\begin{array}{r}
30 \\
300 \\
264\overline{)89064} \\
-\,79200 \\
\hline
9864 \\
-\,7920 \\
\hline
1944
\end{array}
$$

Thus, up to this point we have

$$
\begin{aligned}
89064 \div 264 &= (79200 + 7920 + 1944) \div 264 \\
&= (79200 \div 264) + (7920 \div 264) + (1944 \div 264) \\
&= \quad\;\; 300 \quad\;\; + \quad\;\; 30 \quad\;\; + (1944 \div 264)
\end{aligned}
$$

The next repetition, then, is to obtain the third and final partial quotient by solving

$$264\overline{)1944}$$

such that $d_3 < (1 \times 264)$, i.e., $d_3 = r$. This partial quotient must be 7 according to these two checks.

$$
\begin{array}{r}
7 \\
264\overline{)1944} \\
-\,1848 \\
\hline
96
\end{array}
\quad
\begin{array}{l}
\leftarrow (7 \times 264) \qquad\quad \leq 1944 \\
1944 - (7 \times 264) < (1 \times 264)
\end{array}
\qquad
\begin{array}{r}
7 \\
30 \\
300 \\
264\overline{)89064} \\
-\,79200 \\
\hline
9864 \\
-\,7920 \\
\hline
1944 \\
-\,1848 \\
\hline
96
\end{array}
$$

Thus $89064 \div 264$

$$
\begin{aligned}
&= (79200 + 7920 + 1944 + 96) \div 264 \\
&= (79200 \div 264) + (7920 \div 264) + (1944 \div 264) + (96 \div 264) \\
&= \quad\;\; 300 \quad\;\; + \quad\;\; 30 \quad\;\; + \quad\;\; 7 \quad\;\; + (96 \div 264) \\
&= 337 + (96 \div 264)
\end{aligned}
$$

Therefore, $q = 337$ and $r = 96$.

In discussing fractions and decimals in subsequent chapters, we will examine procedures for continuing the algorithm to obtain results such as

$$
89064 \div 264 = 337\tfrac{96}{264} \qquad \text{or} \qquad 89064 \div 264 = 337.\overline{36}
$$

The procedure for solving this particular problem can be applied to the solution of any division problem, although it would require quite complex notation to summarize the algorithm in general terms. Several short cuts traditionally employed in using the algorithm are described below.

At each repetition except the final one, those digits of the dividend beyond the place of the partial quotient under consideration can be ignored, since they do not affect it:

$$
\begin{array}{r}
300 \\
264\overline{)89064} \\
79200 \\
\hline
9864
\end{array}
\qquad \rightarrow \qquad
\begin{array}{r}
300 \\
264\overline{)89064} \\
79200 \\
\hline
9864
\end{array}
$$

$$
\begin{array}{r}
30 \\
264\overline{)9864} \\
7920 \\
\hline
1944
\end{array}
\qquad \rightarrow \qquad
\begin{array}{r}
330 \\
264\overline{)89064} \\
-79200 \\
\hline
9864 \\
-7920 \\
\hline
1944
\end{array}
$$

In doing so, only the partial quotient figure is recorded at each repetition; the multiplications are abbreviated by not recording the terminal zeros. The second check is abbreviated to comparing the difference with the divisor itself rather than with, for example, 100×264 or 10×264. The subtractions are abbreviated and done in two "interrupted" parts: For example, subtracting 79200 from 89064 is abbreviated to subtracting 7920 from 8906, first by subtracting 792 from 890, then performing the second check (comparing that difference, 98, with 264), and finally subtracting 0 from 6. Because $a - 0 = a$ for any number a, this is sometimes verbalized "bring down the 6."

$$
\begin{array}{r}
89064 \\
-79200 \\
\hline
\end{array}
\;\rightarrow\;
\begin{array}{r}
890 \\
-792 \\
\hline
98
\end{array}
\;\rightarrow\; \text{Compare 98 with 264} \;\rightarrow\;
\begin{array}{r}
890\;6 \\
-792\;0 \\
\hline
98\;6
\end{array}
$$

Abbreviated, the steps of the standard division algorithm are: *First*, compare the divisor, 264, with the dividend, 89064. Since

$$264 > 8 \qquad 264 > 89 \qquad 264 < 890$$

the *place* of the first partial quotient is *hundreds* (the place of '0' in 89064). *Second*, guess that the quotient for $264\overline{)890}$ is 3; record it in the appropriate (hundreds) place; and use it to multiply the divisor. Check that

$$3 \times 264 \leq 890$$

Subtract 792 from 890; check that

$$890 - (3 \times 264) < 264$$

and "bring down" the '6'. *Third,* guess that the quotient for $264\overline{)986}$ is 3; record it in tens place; and use it to multiply 264. Check that

$$3 \times 264 \leqslant 986$$

Subtract 792 from 986. Check that

$$986 - (3 \times 264) < 264$$

and "bring down" the '4'. *Lastly,* guess that the quotient for $264\overline{)1944}$ is 7; record it in ones place; and use it to multiply 264. Check that

$$7 \times 264 \leqslant 1944$$

Subtract 1848 from 1944. Check that

$$1944 - (7 \times 264) < 264$$

Since there are no digits to "bring down," the computation is finished, with quotient 337 and remainder 96.

$$
\begin{array}{r}
337 \\
264\overline{)89064} \\
792 \\
\hline
986 \\
792 \\
\hline
1944 \\
1848 \\
\hline
96
\end{array}
$$

2. Basic Procedures for Teaching the Algorithms

The algorithms are all quite complex and must be developed gradually, beginning with the easiest possible cases and proceeding slowly to the most general ones. Authors of children's textbooks take this into consideration; and, in general, teachers should make use of a given textbook's step-by-step sequence of development, since it is designed to produce ultimate understanding of, and proficiency with, the general forms of the algorithms. Nevertheless, children normally need review or reteaching of previously introduced stages—sometimes including those they were "taught" but did not master at previous grade levels. It is important, therefore, that teachers be familiar with and be able to use effective strategies of their own for teaching *each* stage of the procedures. Before a new stage in the development of an algorithm is introduced, teachers should carefully analyze it, try to anticipate the difficulties children are likely to encounter with it, and be certain—by pretesting and review, if necessary—that necessary mathematical prerequisites are understood.

The number of different stages in developing an algorithm should be kept at a minimum. Once a key idea is introduced it should be extended as quickly as possible in order to emphasize basic understandings. For example, once children *understand* "borrowing" between ones and tens, there is no reason to postpone teaching them to borrow between hundreds and tens, thousands and hundreds, and so on (unless the prerequisite numeration has not been developed, of course). Similarly, treatment of 3- or 4-digit factors or divisors is *conceptually* no different from that of 2-digit ones (they only require more repetitions of the same basic steps) and should not be treated as something new. Also, emphasis should generally be placed more on the reliability of the algorithms to solve *any* problem than on a need for specific variations to take care of special "cases."

Standard computational forms can be *introduced* while children are learning the fundamental facts, as readiness for encountering them with the algorithms. It is as important in teaching the algorithms to precede the use of the computational forms with manipulative experience and equations as it is in teaching the fundamental facts. Additionally, various expanded computational forms should precede the final forms. An expanded computational form is a temporary form in which the numbers involved are expressed or recorded in nonstandard ways, such as expanded numerals (see Chapter 4, p. 83), for the purpose of preparing the students for some of the subtle short cuts of the algorithms. For example,

$$
\begin{array}{r}
3 \text{ tens} + 4 \text{ ones} \\
+\ 2 \text{ tens} + 2 \text{ ones} \\
\hline
5 \text{ tens} + 6 \text{ ones}
\end{array}
\quad\rightarrow\quad
\begin{array}{r}
34 \\
+\ 22 \\
\hline
56
\end{array}
$$

Expanded computational forms are intended to develop understanding of the procedures of the algorithm and to emphasize the role of fundamental facts in the processes.

Structural principles should be emphasized continually when teaching the algorithms, so that children understand *why* as well as *how* they work. Children should view the algorithms as logical applications of the same generalizations they have encountered in studying numeration and the fundamental facts. The algorithms for addition and subtraction can and should be developed in parallel. Similarly, relationships between multiplication and division should be emphasized, but the algorithms are quite distinct and are therefore normally taught separately. Nonmathematical terms and expressions such as "borrow," "carry," "bring down the six," and so on, should either be avoided or postponed until they can be introduced as abbreviations for maneuvers that are based on mathematically valid principles. (We use such terms here because they are commonplace,

but with quotation marks as a reminder that they be used with caution!)
No step in an algorithm should be a mystery to children based only on a
teacher's authoritarian dictum.

As children become skillful with any algorithm, they begin to perform it mechanically, and this is as it *should* be, for the algorithms are only
tools that enable them to work on more interesting mathematical problems.
However, once they begin to perform the algorithms by rote, there is an
increased tendency to make errors. They should, therefore, be encouraged
to check their computations regularly, and to estimate answers before the
computation is done. There are many familiar ways of estimating and
checking. In the upper grades increased insight into the mechanics of the
algorithms, and thus, potentially, a decrease in errors, can result from work
with "denominate numbers" and with bases other than ten. Both require
children to consider numeration principles, particularly those involving
renaming, very carefully, an approach that may sometimes carry over to
their work with more conventional computation. Examining some of the
historical predecessors of our algorithms and some alternate contemporary
algorithms can be interesting and can provide additional insight into the
standard algorithms.

Children need to practice the algorithms, like everything else with
which they are expected to become skillful. As children begin to learn the
algorithms, there are more and more opportunities to place drill in the
context of learning new and interesting things, solving more complex
problems, and discovering new relationships, because knowing the algorithms allows for the use of a broader range of numbers than is available
with fundamental facts alone. It is well to keep in mind that each of the
algorithms includes certain subskills that should be introduced and practiced
per se before children are expected to use them in algorithms. (For example,
the kinds of renaming involved in "borrowing" and "carrying," or the multiplication form used in long division.) Although teaching of the algorithms
can begin long before children have mastered all the fundamental facts, and
although practice on the facts is provided by practice on the algorithms, care
should be taken to see that quite easy facts are used when the algorithms are
first introduced, and that those facts have been fairly well mastered. Otherwise attention to learning the processes of the algorithm may be diverted to
a consideration of fundamental facts.

Finally, since the algorithms are not entirely standardized and since
they are normally developed over a period of several years, it should be
mentioned that if a child's initial instruction has been oriented toward a
particular algorithm, teachers in subsequent grades should generally try to
continue that approach rather than try to change it. This sometimes necessitates special grouping or individualized instruction and requires the teacher
to be able to teach various algorithms, particularly in subtraction and division.

3. Materials and Activities for Teaching the Algorithms

The remainder of this chapter will examine the key stages in the development of each of the algorithms. Addition and subtraction will be discussed together, since this is how they are normally taught. Multiplication and division algorithms will be examined separately.

The Addition and Subtraction Algorithms

Adding and Subtracting More Than Two Numbers

The first step in teaching the addition and subtraction algorithms normally begins after children have become reasonably proficient with the 64 fundamental facts that have sums and minuends up to 10 and with the numeration of tens and ones, e.g., that 45 means $40 + 5$ or 4 tens $+ 5$ ones. Also, in the case of addition, the fundamental facts are extended to include addition of three numbers each less than 10, where the sum of the three does not exceed 10, e.g.,

$$(2 + 1) + 4 = \square$$

$$(3 + 2) + 2 = \triangle$$

Any of the materials and activities appropriate for teaching fundamental addition facts are equally appropriate for teaching children to find such sums. In equation form, children would need to be introduced to the meaning of the parentheses as grouping symbols. That is, $(2 + 1) + 4$, for example, means "add 2 and 1, then add that sum to 4." Thus

$$(2 + 1) + 4 = 3 + 4 = 7$$

It is generally useful to structure such exercises as follows:

$$(2 + 1) + 4$$
$$= \underline{\hspace{1cm}} + 4 = \square$$

If children know the two facts $2 + 1 = 3$ and $3 + 4 = 7$, no manipulative activity is necessary. Otherwise, sets, blocks, or other materials can be used as suggested in Chapter 5.

Such problems lend themselves to teaching the associative property of addition, of course. Several pairs of examples such as

$$(2 + 1) + 4 \qquad\qquad 2 + (1 + 4)$$
$$\underline{\hspace{1cm}} + 4 = \square \qquad 2 + \underline{\hspace{1cm}} = \square$$

can quickly lead to the discovery that, in general,

$$(a + b) + c = a + (b + c)$$

In computational form, children can be provided with similar grouping directions at first:

$$\begin{array}{r} 2 \\ 1 \\ +\,4 \\ \hline \square \end{array}\!\!\Big\}\triangle \qquad\qquad \begin{array}{r} 2 \\ 1 \\ +\,4 \\ \hline \square \end{array}\!\!\Big\}\triangledown$$

Once children realize that grouping directions do not affect the sum, they can be deleted and the problems can be worked without regard to order.

Although not essential to development of the subtraction algorithm, related exercises (in equation form) can provide variation in fundamental facts practice while enforcing the notion of how to use parentheses. Some children will also discover important generalizations by working exercises such as these:

(a) $8 - (5 - 2)$ $(8 - 5) - 2$ $a - (b - c) \neq (a - b) - c$
   $= 8 - \underline{\hspace{1cm}} = \square$ $= \underline{\hspace{1cm}} - 2 = \triangle$

(b) $(6 + 4) - 2$ $6 + (4 - 2)$ $(a + b) - c = a + (b - c)$
   $= \underline{\hspace{1cm}} - 2 = \square$ $= 6 + \underline{\hspace{1cm}} = \triangle$

(c) $7 - (3 + 2)$ $(7 - 3) - 2$ $a - (b + c) = (a - b) - c$
   $= 7 - \underline{\hspace{1cm}} = \square$ $= \underline{\hspace{1cm}} - 2 = \triangle$

(d) $9 - (6 + 2) = \square$ $(9 - 6) + 2 = \triangle$ $a - (b + c) \neq (a - b) + c$

Column addition can easily be extended to include four or five numbers, with or without grouping directions, although in constructing such exercises care must be taken at this point not to let the sums exceed 10. Children should ultimately be led to recognize that neither the order in which addends are considered nor the grouping of them affects the sum:

$$\begin{array}{r} 2 \\ 1 \\ 3 \\ +\,4 \\ \hline \end{array}\!\!\rightarrow \qquad \begin{array}{r} 2 \\ 1 \\ 3 \\ +\,4 \\ \hline \end{array}\!\!\Big\}\!\!\begin{array}{c}\triangle \\ \square\end{array} \qquad \begin{array}{r} 1 \\ 2 \\ 3 \\ +\,4 \\ \hline \end{array}\!\!\Big\}\triangledown \qquad \begin{array}{r} 1 \\ 2 \\ 3 \\ +\,4 \\ \hline \end{array}\!\!\diamond$$

Higher Decade Facts Without Bridging

Higher decade addition facts (see section 1) are solved as a direct extension of *fundamental* facts. For example, knowing that $2 + 3 = 5$ enables a child—in time—to find sums such as $12 + 3$, $22 + 3$, $42 + 3$, $92 + 3$, $102 + 3$, $142 + 3$, and so on, in a *single step*, where the ending (ones-place digit) of the sum is the same as that of the related fundamental fact. While such skill is not, strictly speaking, essential to understanding the place-by-place *mechanics* of the algorithm, it is extremely important, ultimately, in *using* the algorithm. Furthermore, higher decade facts are also used in multiplication. For example, the next mental step in the computation

$$\begin{array}{r} 65 \\ \times\ 7 \\ \hline 5 \end{array}$$

is solving $(7 \times 6) + 3 = \triangle$, i.e., $42 + 3 = \triangle$, a higher decade fact. Children need to become skillful in obtaining such sums mentally, in a single step, in order to develop computational proficiency.

If the sum of a fundamental fact is less than 10, then the tens place digit (and any digits in larger places) in the sum of any higher decade fact generated by that fact is unchanged from the first addend. For example,

$$\underline{3}2 + 5 = \underline{3}7 \qquad \underline{86}2 + 3 = \underline{86}5$$

If the sum of a fundamental fact is greater than or equal to 10, on the other hand, sums of related higher decade facts increase by one in tens place, compared with the first addend, e.g.,

$$\begin{array}{r} 38 \\ +\ 7 \\ \hline \underline{4}5 \end{array} \qquad \begin{array}{r} 868 \\ +\ 7 \\ \hline \underline{87}5 \end{array} \qquad \begin{array}{r} 48 \\ +\ 2 \\ \hline \underline{5}0 \end{array}$$

The latter situation has traditionally been referred to as "bridging" or "bridging the tens." Thus, higher decade facts can be put into two categories: Those with bridging and those without bridging. Both are of equal importance. (There is no need to use such terms with children.)

Higher decade facts without bridging can be (and commonly are) taught as soon as children have learned the fundamental facts with sums less than 10. The rationale for their solution depends also on the associative property and on numeration skills, so both of these should be reasonably well established first. The teaching of such problems and those of subsequent stages of the development, should normally proceed in about this sequence (we use a single fact, $32 + 4 = 36$, as an example; in practice, several facts should be used at each step):

Physical objects. Two collections of objects can be displayed on a table — one containing 32 objects grouped as 3 tens and 2 ones, the other containing 4 objects (or 1 four). The child is asked first to tell how many objects are in each collection; to identify the suggested numerical expression, $32 + 4$; to find how many objects there are altogether; and finally to identify the *fact,* "$32 + 4 = 36$." The objects can be counters such as dowels; blocks such as the Stern, Dienes, or Cuisenaire blocks (with or without number lines); coins (dimes and pennies), and so on. At first, grouping and regrouping should be emphasized by physically moving the 2 ones or by putting a loop of string first around the 32, then moving it to the (2 + 4). Children frequently will *count* the 6 objects, but should be encouraged instead to use the fundamental fact 2 + 4 = 6, which they should know.

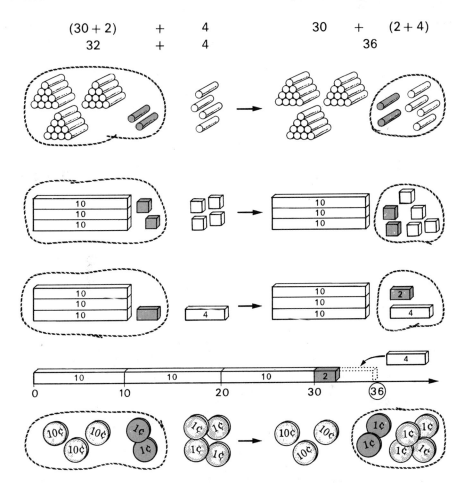

$$(30 + 2) \qquad + \qquad 4 \qquad\qquad 30 \qquad + \qquad (2 + 4)$$
$$32 \qquad\qquad + \qquad 4 \qquad\qquad\qquad 36$$

With a number line and matching blocks, 32 + 4 can be represented in an abbreviated way by placing the left endpoint of a 2 + 4-train at the 30-point of the line. The *line* "tells" the child that 32 + 4 = 36, but the *blocks* strongly suggest the fundamental fact. The train can be similarly oriented at 20, 40, 50, 60, and so on. The child soon recognizes the relationship between the fundamental fact and the family of higher decade facts it generates. In like manner, extra 10-blocks, bundles of sticks, or dimes can be added to the original collections of 32 until the desired relationship is established. Once such problems have been done manipulatively, they can be represented pictorially with other examples.

Place value devices.   A place value chart, abacus, hundred board, or other place value device (see Chapter 4) can be set up to represent 32. The child is asked to identify the number and then 4 more counters are added. Again the child is asked to identify the "number situation," $32 + 4$; the result, 36; and the fact, $32 + 4 = 36$. As with physical objects, additional markers can be put in the tens place to emphasize that the ones-place digit of the sum is unchanged. The hundred-board representation of 32 can be

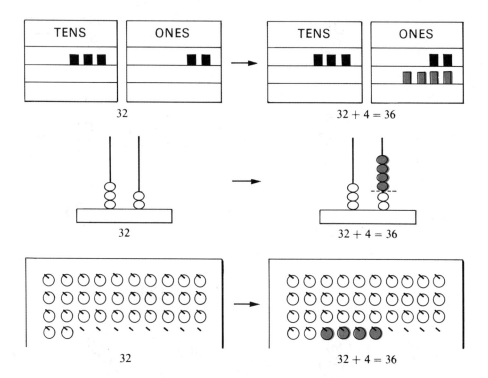

abbreviated by putting 2 markers in the fourth row, to save time, with the agreement that the top 3 rows are *imagined* to be full. This again focuses attention on the fundamental fact; the six markers representing $2 + 4$ can be shifted up and down (i.e., to the 2nd row, the 5th row, and so on) to represent a family of higher decade facts. Similar activities on other place value devices should be apparent.

Equations.   Once the above have been done—or, at first, *while* they are being done—children may be asked to write equations corresponding to the solutions of higher decade facts. They should be able to provide justifications (in their own words) for each step in the proof and relate each step to the preceding activities:

$$32 + 4 = (30 + 2) + 4 \qquad \text{Place value}$$
$$= 30 + (2 + 4) \qquad \text{Associative property}$$
$$= 30 + 6 \qquad \text{Fundamental fact}$$
$$= 36 \qquad \text{Place value}$$

Expanded computational forms. Two expanded computational forms can then be used to represent the fact:

$$\begin{array}{r} 3 \text{ tens} + 2 \text{ ones} \\ + \qquad 4 \text{ ones} \\ \hline 3 \text{ tens} + 6 \text{ ones} \end{array} \qquad \begin{array}{r} 30 + 2 \\ + \qquad 4 \\ \hline 30 + 6 \end{array}$$

Final computational form. The fact can now be expressed in standard computational form:

$$\begin{array}{r} 3 \text{ tens} + 2 \text{ ones} \\ + \qquad 4 \text{ ones} \\ \hline 3 \text{ tens} + 6 \text{ ones} \end{array} \rightarrow \begin{array}{r} 32 \\ + \ 4 \\ \hline 36 \end{array}$$

$$\begin{array}{r} 30 + 2 \\ + \qquad 4 \\ \hline 30 + 6 \end{array} \rightarrow \begin{array}{r} 32 \\ + \ 4 \\ \hline 36 \end{array}$$

Practice. If each of the above has been developed with understanding, which generally requires some informal questions and discussion about the relationships involved, children will finally be ready to practice the facts and to solve problems involving them. It is important that they associate higher decade facts with *fundamental* facts, thinking "thirty-two plus four equals thirty-six because two plus four equals six." At this stage, children should *not* be led to think of two separate additions (tens and ones), because, first, they have not yet learned to do so, and second, they should not do so when using the facts later in column addition or multiplication. That is, no *computation* should actually be done. The process is entirely mental. The child writes:

$$\begin{array}{r} 32 \\ + \ 4 \\ \hline 3 \end{array} \rightarrow \begin{array}{r} 32 \\ + \ 4 \\ \hline 36 \end{array} \quad \text{not} \quad \begin{array}{r} 32 \\ + \ 4 \\ \hline 6 \end{array} \rightarrow \begin{array}{r} 32 \\ + \ 4 \\ \hline 36 \end{array}$$

Plenty of oral drill should be provided to increase speed, and practice problems in *equation* form ($32 + 4 = \square$) are preferable to those in computational form. The facts should be quickly generalized to include sums such as $432 + 5$, providing the numeration of hundreds has been developed. (Dienes blocks provide a good *physical* model for numbers up to thousands.)

Corresponding subtraction facts, e.g., $36 - 4 = 32$, can be developed simultaneously, of course, using the same basic steps and activities. It is useful for children to be able to solve such problems mentally, although they do not occur in the subtraction algorithm. The take-away interpretation of subtraction is sufficient for developing this and subsequent stages of the algorithm; the other two can be used later.

It is generally helpful to overlap activities of one stage with activities of the following stage or stages. For example, if *both* blocks and place value chart appear together at first, children are more likely, with guidance, to correctly associate the physical with the more abstract materials than if the blocks are put away before beginning the place value chart work.

Adding and Subtracting Tens and Hundreds

Since the addition and subtraction algorithms in their ultimate forms involve the addition or subtraction of the digits in tens place, hundreds place, and so on, as though they were *fundamental* facts (or higher decade facts in the case of addition), the rationale for this must be taught if the algorithms are to be made meaningful as well as habitual. Later, in subtracting 23 from 86, for example, the child should *consciously* think "eight minus two," but he should nonetheless *know* that he is finding "eighty minus twenty."

$$\begin{array}{r} 86 \\ -\ 23 \\ \hline 63 \end{array} \qquad \begin{array}{r} 80 + 6 \\ -\ (20 + 3) \\ \hline 60 + 3 \end{array}$$

"$8 - 2 = 6$" $80 - 20 = 60$

As we have seen in section 1, such abbreviations are justified by distributive principles and numeration characteristics, i.e.,

$$\begin{aligned} 30 + 20 &= (3 \times 10) + (2 \times 10) & &\text{Place value} \\ &= (3 + 2) \times 10 & &\text{Distributive principle} \\ &= 5 \times 10 & &\text{Fundamental fact} \\ &= 50 & &\text{Place value} \end{aligned}$$

$$\begin{aligned} 80 - 20 &= (8 \times 10) - (2 \times 10) & &\text{Place value} \\ &= (8 - 2) \times 10 & &\text{Distributive principle} \\ &= 6 \times 10 & &\text{Fundamental fact} \\ &= 60 & &\text{Place value} \end{aligned}$$

Thus, we can *think* "$3 + 2 = 5$" or "$8 - 2 = 6$" and then "multiply" 5 or 6 by 10 merely by recording it in tens place. Even though most children have not encountered multiplication at this point, the relationship of facts such as

$80 - 20 = 60$ to corresponding fundamental facts such as $8 - 2 = 6$, can be made as meaningful to them as is the related numeration. That is, they think of the '8' in '86' as 8 tens or 80, harmlessly unaware as yet that both "8 tens" and "80" mean also 8×10.

Activities for teaching children to solve problems such as $30 + 20 = \square$, $300 + 200 = \triangle$, $80 - 20 = \nabla$, and $800 - 200 = \square$ should closely parallel those for teaching the higher decade facts. Here, it is assumed that children know only the fundamental facts with sums and minuends less than 10. Obviously, many repetitions at each level would normally be required, although we will use only a single pair of inversely related problems as illustrations.

Physical objects. To prepare for the problem $30 + 20 = 50$, collections representing 3 tens and 2 tens (bundled sticks, dimes, 10-blocks, and so on) can be displayed on a table. Children are then asked to identify

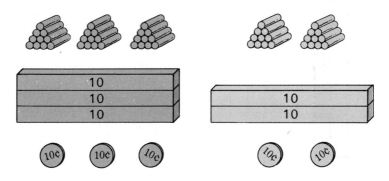

the corresponding numbers as, e.g., both "3 tens" and as "30." The collections are then joined together and the children are asked to identify suggested expressions (here, $30 + 20$ and 3 tens + 2 tens); the result of same (as 50 and as 5 tens); and the fact (as $30 + 20 = 50$, and as 3 tens + 2 tens = 5 tens). The related inverse fact, $50 - 20 = 30$ would then be treated similarly; the number line could be used in connection with the blocks or by itself:

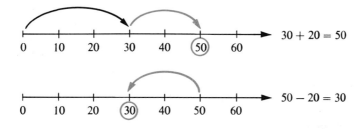

Place value devices. A place value chart, abacus, counting frame, or counting man could next be used to represent the facts (the hundred board would not be particularly useful).

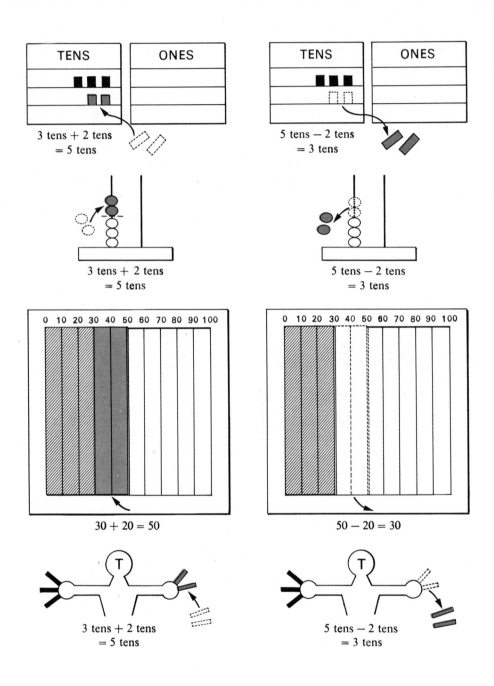

TENS	ONES
■ ■ ■	
▬ ▬	

3 tens + 2 tens
= 5 tens

TENS	ONES
■ ■ ■	
▭ ▭	

5 tens − 2 tens
= 3 tens

3 tens + 2 tens
= 5 tens

5 tens − 2 tens
= 3 tens

0 10 20 30 40 50 60 70 80 90 100

30 + 20 = 50

0 10 20 30 40 50 60 70 80 90 100

50 − 20 = 30

3 tens + 2 tens
= 5 tens

5 tens − 2 tens
= 3 tens

Equations. By now children should be able, perhaps with some help, to read, write, *and understand* corresponding equations:

Example:

$$30 + 20 = 50 \qquad 3 \text{ tens} + 2 \text{ tens} = (3 + 2) \text{ tens} = 5 \text{ tens}$$
$$50 - 20 = 30 \qquad 5 \text{ tens} - 2 \text{ tens} = (5 - 2) \text{ tens} = 3 \text{ tens}$$

Expanded computational forms. Again, expanded computational forms can represent the facts:

Example:

$$
\begin{array}{r}
3 \text{ tens} \\
+ 2 \text{ tens} \\
\hline
5 \text{ tens}
\end{array}
\qquad
\begin{array}{r}
5 \text{ tens} \\
- 2 \text{ tens} \\
\hline
3 \text{ tens}
\end{array}
$$

Standard computational forms. As before, expanded computational forms lead directly to the standard forms:

Example:

$$
\begin{array}{r}
3 \text{ tens} \\
+ 2 \text{ tens} \\
\hline
5 \text{ tens}
\end{array}
\rightarrow
\begin{array}{r}
30 \\
+ 20 \\
\hline
50
\end{array}
\quad \text{and} \quad
\begin{array}{r}
5 \text{ tens} \\
- 2 \text{ tens} \\
\hline
3 \text{ tens}
\end{array}
\rightarrow
\begin{array}{r}
50 \\
- 20 \\
\hline
30
\end{array}
$$

Practice. With sufficient emphasis in the above activities on the '3', '2', and '5', children should understand the relationship between the fundamental facts and the given problems. They are then ready for drill and practice, including problem solving, on similar facts. Such practice can easily include adding hundreds, e.g., $300 + 200 = \square$, and in the case of addition can include more than two numbers, such as $30 + 20 + 10 = \square$, or $100 + 400 + 300 + 100 = \triangle$. These problems also should be solved by *only* considering the significant (nonzero) digits. Place-by-place manipulation is neither necessary nor appropriate, i.e., the child should think "$30 + 20 = 50$," not "$0 + 0 = 0$; $3 + 2 = 5$."

Adding and Subtracting Both Ones and Tens: No Renaming

The next stage of instruction, adding and subtracting both ones and tens, involves little more than combining what children have learned in preceding steps, so it is normally quite easy to teach. It is a crucial step, however, because it introduces the place-by-place nature of the two algorithms. Children need not have learned any of the fundamental facts beyond those required for the preceding steps; in fact, if they have learned them, they should not be used at this point. That is, at this stage we should be concerned only with teaching the basic mechanics of the algorithms, omitting the mechanics of renaming (borrowing and carrying), which should be deferred. At this point, we would be interested in teaching children how to do problems such as these:

$$
\begin{array}{r}
24 \\
+ 32 \\
\hline
\end{array}
\qquad
\begin{array}{r}
86 \\
- 24 \\
\hline
\end{array}
\qquad
\begin{array}{r}
21 \\
43 \\
+ 25 \\
\hline
\end{array}
\qquad
\begin{array}{r}
347 \\
+ 421 \\
\hline
\end{array}
\qquad
\begin{array}{r}
834 \\
- 413 \\
\hline
\end{array}
$$

As with preceding stages in the development of the algorithm, children should have experiences at each of the levels, in turn: physical objects, place value devices, equations, expanded computational forms, standard computational forms, and practice. Extension to 3-place numbers and to 3 addends should occur shortly after the simplest cases have been experienced; teacher guidance is necessary, of course, including sufficient overlaps between levels. It should not be necessary here to elaborate in detail on appropriate activities for this stage, since they so closely follow the preceding ones, but a few notes should be made.

In the case of addition, physical objects should at first be arranged somewhat as are the corresponding digits in the final computational form, e.g.,

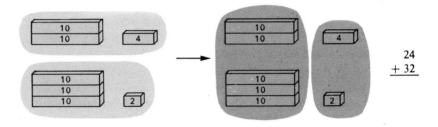

rather than, for example:

Similarly, counters on a place value chart representing the numbers to be added should be in separate pockets or of different colors (or both):

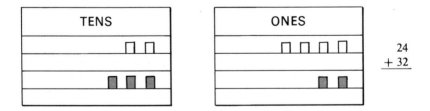

If blocks are used with the number line, there are advantages to each of these physical manipulations: (1) Collect the appropriate blocks as before and then place them on the number line, beginning with all of the *tens* blocks:

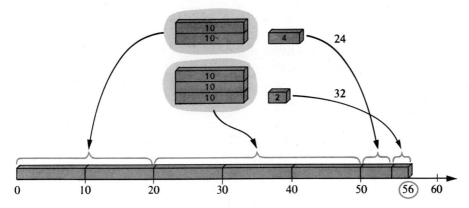

And (2) put the blocks on the line end-to-end beginning with all of the blocks of the first addend; then rearrange the ones blocks:

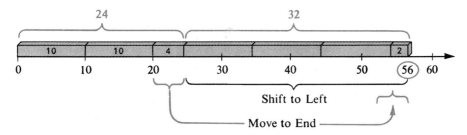

Equations for both addition and subtraction are quite complex and will require considerable guidance. They should be presented slowly, step-by-step, and should be accompanied at first with physical models or place value devices so that the equations make sense.

$$24 + 32 = (20 + 4) + (30 + 2) \qquad 56 - 32 = (50 + 6) - (30 + 2)$$
$$= (20 + 30) + (4 + 2) \qquad \qquad = (50 - 30) + (6 - 2)$$
$$= 50 + 6 \qquad \qquad \qquad \quad = 20 + 4$$
$$= 56 \qquad \qquad \qquad \qquad = 24$$

Subtraction equations, in particular, as well as the expanded computational forms, can be confusing because of the addition signs:

$$(5 \text{ tens} + 6 \text{ ones}) - (3 \text{ tens} + 2 \text{ ones}) = (5 \text{ tens} - 3 \text{ tens})$$
$$+ (6 \text{ ones} - 2 \text{ ones})$$

$$\begin{array}{r} 5 \text{ tens} + 6 \text{ ones} \\ - (3 \text{ tens} + 2 \text{ ones}) \\ \hline 2 \text{ tens} + 4 \text{ ones} \end{array} \qquad \begin{array}{r} 50 + 6 \\ - (30 + 2) \\ \hline 20 + 4 \end{array}$$

These signs can be deleted or replaced with commas without any particular loss of understanding if the first form, above, is used:

$$\begin{array}{r} 5 \text{ tens } 6 \text{ ones} \\ - 3 \text{ tens } 2 \text{ ones} \\ \hline \_ \text{ tens } \_ \text{ ones} \end{array} \qquad \begin{array}{r} 5 \text{ tens, } 6 \text{ ones} \\ - 3 \text{ tens, } 2 \text{ ones} \\ \hline \_ \text{ tens, } \_ \text{ ones} \end{array}$$

Variations on an activity suggested in Chapter 5 (p. 143), based on filling in cells of an array, can provide insight into the algorithms in an interesting way:

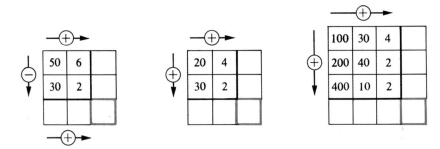

Zero should be included in both developmental and practice exercises, and should be treated like any other number rather than *ignored* as is sometimes done (justifiably, for problems at *this* level). Children should regard computations involving zero as *easy,* but not *special.*

$$
\begin{array}{cccc}
 & & & 406 \\
34 & 840 & 876 & 123 \\
+\,20 & +\,136 & -\,102 & +\,460 \\
\end{array}
$$

By the time children reach the practice level, they should be consciously *thinking* in terms of fundamental (or higher decade) facts but should be able to *explain* what they really mean when they say, for example, "5 − 3" rather than "50 − 30."

Computations for problems at this level can proceed either left-to-right or right-to-left. At first there is no harm in permitting this, but the teacher will want to gently promote the right-to-left approach since it becomes necessary later.

Higher Decade Facts with Bridging

The higher decade addition facts with bridging can be taught as soon as children understand the fundamental facts with sums or minuends of 10 or greater (see Chapter 5, pp. 144–146). Each of these fundamental facts generates many higher decade ones, each of which the child should be able to solve, again, in a single step. Examples of higher decade facts with bridging include:

$$
\begin{array}{cccc}
28 & 43 & 179 & 65 \\
+\,6 & +\,7 & +\,2 & +\,5 \\
\hline
34 & 50 & 181 & 70 \\
\end{array}
$$

Such facts are slightly more difficult than those discussed previously because of the bridging, and the teacher will normally need to spend a little more time at each instructional level.

Physical devices. Physical representations of these facts can involve either counting or measurement models. Counting models require grouping the ones together, *bundling* 10 ones as 1 ten, or *trading* 10 ones for 1 ten (sometimes bundling, as in (1) below and sometimes trading as in (2)):

(1) $28 + 6 = \square$

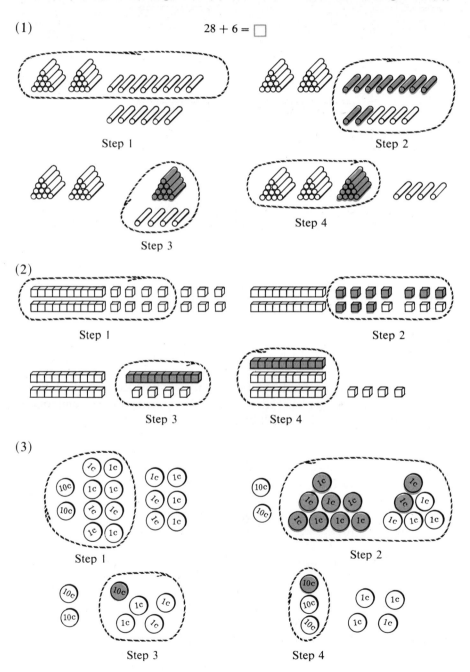

Measurement models, e.g., Stern or Centimeter rods, require similar regrouping, but the process is a little quicker.

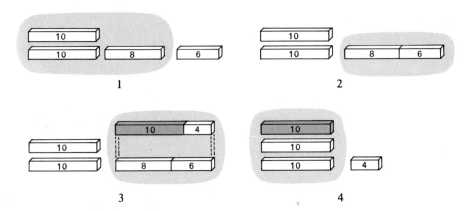

Probably the best physical representation in terms of efficiency is to use blocks *with* the number line, since regrouping is not required (the line indicates the answer directly). This model is also preferable to others, first,

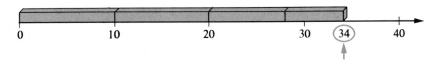

because its objective is to have children solve problems in a single step *without* conscious thought to regrouping or renaming; and second, because the relationship of the fundamental fact to a whole collection of higher decade ones can be emphasized, as before, by aligning the left endpoint of the 8 + 6-train with various multiples of 10 on the line:

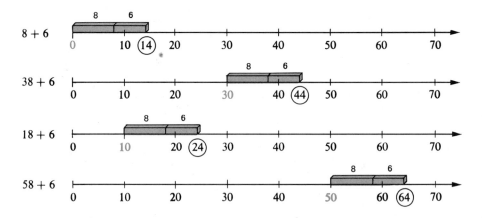

Place value devices. For similar reasons, the best place value representation of these facts is the hundred board using the modification of "imagining" the initial tens, e.g.,

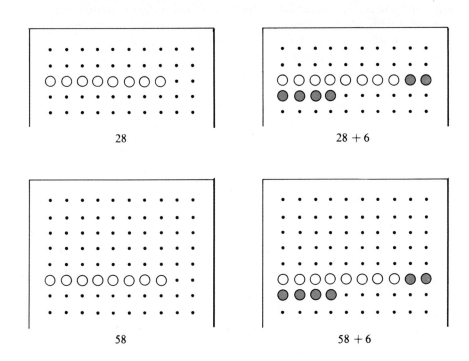

Equations and computational forms. Extensive work with multistep equations and computational forms should be minimized so that children do not tend to use computational procedures with bridging problems later. Although quite complex, the relevant equations and computations help to explain, in structural terms, the mathematical basis for the mental calculation.

$$28 + 6 = (20 + 8) + 6$$
$$= 20 + (8 + 6)$$
$$= 20 + 14$$
$$= 20 + (10 + 4)$$
$$= (20 + 10) + 4$$
$$= 30 + 4$$
$$= 34$$

$$20 + \ 8$$
$$\underline{+ \ 6}$$
$$20 + 14 = 30 + 4$$

2 tens + 8 ones
$\underline{\qquad + \ 6 \text{ ones}}$
2 tens + 14 ones
= 3 tens + 4 ones

Practice. The suggestions regarding practice on higher decade facts without bridging also apply here. Subtraction problems, e.g., $34 - 6 = \square$, should probably *not* be developed in detail at this point.

Borrowing and Carrying

It should once more be emphasized that we use the terms "borrow" and "carry" here because they are relatively standardized, brief expressions, and the reader understands their meaning. In manipulative activities associated with teaching these concepts to children, expressions like *group, regroup, bundle, unbundle, trade,* and so on, should be used when talking about objects. In computational activities, the expression *rename* should be used when referring to the corresponding manipulations with the names of numbers.

Before these processes are introduced in the context of addition and subtraction problems, considerable time should be spent on activities involving the processes per se, to which the balance of this section is devoted.

Using Stern, Unifix, Dienes, Cuisenaire, or other *unit* blocks, place several (more than ten) blocks on the table. Using a nearby supply of 10-blocks, ask the child to figure out how he could *trade* some of the blocks (for tens) in such a way that he ends up with the least possible number of

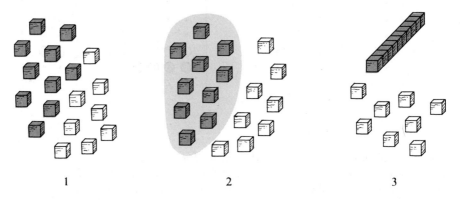

1   2   3

blocks. Several variations of this basic activity can and should be introduced:

(a) Bundling dowels by tens with rubber bands.
(b) Trading pennies for dimes.
(c) Boxing pencils by tens.
(d) Clipping Unifix blocks together in tens.
(e) Starting with more than 10 tens, and trading for hundreds, e.g., Dienes longs and flats, dimes and dollars.
(f) Starting with more than ten of each of ones and tens so that two kinds of trading are necessary.
(g) Starting with more than 20 of each kind.

Gradually the number of objects of each kind should be recorded with markers on a place value chart or with expanded numerals:

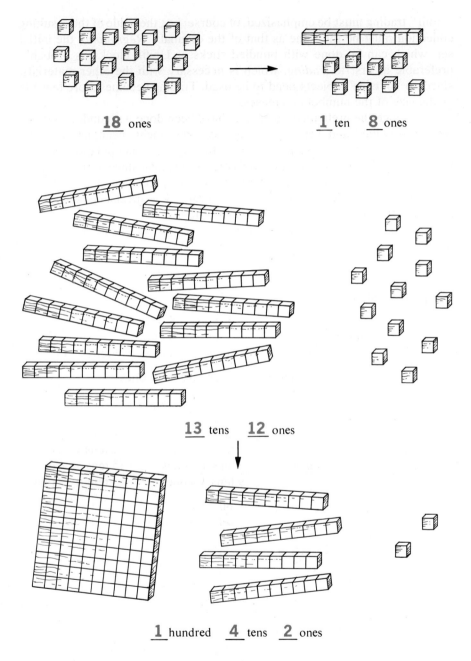

18 ones   1 ten   8 ones

13 tens   12 ones

1 hundred   4 tens   2 ones

Conversely, display a "standard" collection (less than ten of each kind) of, e.g., blocks or dowels; ask the child to trade, unbundle, or whatever, to obtain *more* of a given kind. For example, given 3 tens and 4 ones, ask him to trade so that he has more ones (2 tens and 14 ones). The several variations above have their obvious counterparts with this type of activity.

("Fair" trading must be emphasized, of course; i.e., the value of the resulting collection must be the same as that of the original.) *Regrouping* the initial set, which can be done with bundled sticks or Unifix blocks, is probably preferable at first to *trading,* which is necessary with the other materials, since no "outside" objects need to be used. Trading becomes more feasible as the size of the numbers increases.

Once the preliminary activities have been done with understanding, the "borrowing" and "carrying" steps can be taught meaningfully. The sequence of experiences, beginning with physical manipulation, should be presented in the usual order. Activities at this final stage in the development of the algorithms closely parallel those of preceding stages and will not be repeated in detail. There are, however, a few special considerations regarding the "borrowing" and "carrying" steps.

First, several expanded computational forms can be introduced in preparation for the final form.

Examples:

(a) $\begin{array}{l} 3 \text{ tens} + 8 \text{ ones} \\ + 5 \text{ tens} + 6 \text{ ones} \end{array}$ → $\begin{array}{l} 3 \text{ tens} + \ 8 \text{ ones} \\ + 5 \text{ tens} + \ 6 \text{ ones} \\ \hline 8 \text{ tens} + 14 \text{ ones} = 9 \text{ tens} + 4 \text{ ones} \end{array}$

$\begin{array}{l} 9 \text{ tens} + 4 \text{ ones} \\ - (5 \text{ tens} + 6 \text{ ones}) \end{array}$ → $\begin{array}{l} 8 \text{ tens} + 14 \text{ ones} \\ - (5 \text{ tens} + \ 6 \text{ ones}) \\ \hline 3 \text{ tens} + \ 8 \text{ ones} \end{array}$

(b) $\begin{array}{l} 3 \text{ tens} + 8 \text{ ones} \\ + 5 \text{ tens} + 6 \text{ ones} \end{array}$ → $\begin{array}{l} (1 \text{ ten}) \\ 3 \text{ tens} + 8 \text{ ones} \\ + 5 \text{ tens} + 6 \text{ ones} \\ \hline 9 \text{ tens} + 4 \text{ ones} \end{array}$ $\begin{array}{l} 8 \text{ tens} + 14 \text{ ones} \\ \cancel{9 \text{ tens}} + \ \cancel{4 \text{ ones}} \\ - (5 \text{ tens} + \ 6 \text{ ones}) \\ \hline 3 \text{ tens} + \ 8 \text{ ones} \end{array}$

(c) $\begin{array}{l} 30 + \ 8 \\ + 50 + \ 6 \\ \hline 80 + 14 = 90 + 4 \end{array}$ $\begin{array}{l} 80 + 14 \\ \cancel{90} + \ \cancel{4} \\ - (50 + \ 6) \\ \hline 30 + \ 8 \end{array}$

(d) $\begin{array}{l} (10) \\ 30 + 8 \\ + 50 + 6 \\ \hline 90 + 4 \end{array}$

$\begin{array}{l} 38 \\ + 56 \\ \hline 14 \leftarrow 8 + 6 \\ + 80 \leftarrow 30 + 50 \\ \hline 94 \end{array}$ or $\begin{array}{l} 38 \\ + 56 \\ \hline 4 \\ 10 \\ 80 \\ \hline 94 \end{array}$ or $\begin{array}{l} (10) \\ 38 \\ + 56 \\ \hline 4 \\ 90 \\ \hline 94 \end{array}$

Expanded forms such as these can lead to meaningful use of the usual "scratching" most children do with these two algorithms:

$$
\begin{array}{cc}
\xrightarrow{} 1 & 8\ 14 \\
38 & 9\!\!\!/4\!\!\!/ \\
+\,56 & -\,56 \\
\hline
94 & 38
\end{array}
$$

These crutches are helpful, and should not be frowned upon by teachers, although children should be encouraged to do the renaming mentally as soon as they can.

One special subtraction problem is exemplified by

$$
\begin{array}{ccc}
304 & & 3006 \\
-\,126 & \text{or} & -\,1285
\end{array}
$$

That is, when an impasse occurs in a given place and there is "nothing" in the next place to "borrow" from, what can be done? This kind of multiple renaming problem should not be treated as a *mechanical* extension of the basic renaming process. Instead it, too, should be foreshadowed by manipulative trading activities, expanded forms, and so on. For example, the teacher can display 3 flats and 4 units from the Dienes materials and ask the child to figure out how to trade to obtain more units (trade 1 flat for 10 longs, then trade 1 long for 10 units). Several repetitions of this sort should lead gradually to the final process in computation.

$$
\begin{array}{l}
3 \text{ hundreds} + 0 \text{ tens} + 4 \text{ ones} \\
-\,(1 \text{ hundred} + 2 \text{ tens} + 6 \text{ ones})
\end{array}
$$

$$
\xrightarrow{}
\begin{array}{l}
2 \text{ hundreds} + 9 \text{ tens} + 14 \text{ ones} \\
-\,(1 \text{ hundred} + 2 \text{ tens} + 6 \text{ ones})
\end{array}
\xrightarrow{}
\begin{array}{c}
2\ 9\ 14 \\
3\!\!\!/0\!\!\!/4\!\!\!/ \\
-\,126
\end{array}
$$

Lastly, it is only when borrowing and carrying are involved that it becomes necessary—or, rather, *efficient*—to compute right to left, beginning with ones place. Children should have the chance to discover this. One way to help them do so would be to display a collection such as 5 flats, 6 longs, and 2 units. Then ask a child to remove from that collection 3 flats, 2 longs, and 4 units, recording "what's left" as he goes along. Some children (if not *most* of them) will begin with the flats, recording "2 flats" and "4 longs," and then discover that it is necessary to change what they have written because of the trading they must do next. Those who begin with the units and trade first find that it is unnecessary to change what they have written. (See illustration on following page.)

Alternate Subtraction Algorithms

The subtraction algorithm is not entirely standardized. Most commonly, the borrowing approach is taught. One alternate approach that is

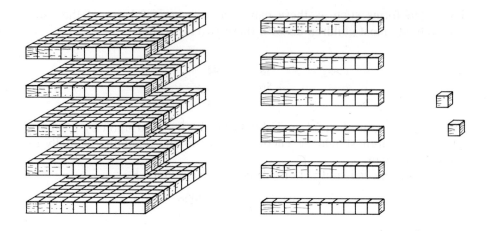

still sometimes taught, and has certain advantages, is the *equal additions* algorithm. It is based on the generalization that the difference, $a - b$, of two numbers, a and b, is unchanged if the same number, k, is added to both a and b, i.e.,

$$a - b = (a + k) - (b + k)$$

For example,

$$9 - 2 = (9 + 8) - (2 + 8)$$

In practice, this generalization can be used in two ways, one an "organized" way, which can lead to a new algorithm (the equal additions algorithm) and the other a "disorganized" way, which leads to an approach that is useful and quite flexible, depending on the particular digits in the example.

First, consider the example $36 - 19 = \square$. It is easy to see that the difference, interpreted in the comparison sense, is unaffected when the same number, no matter what that number may be, is added to both 36 and 19, e.g.,

$$(36 + 2) - (19 + 2) = 38 - 21 = 17$$
$$(36 + 8) - (19 + 8) = 44 - 27 = 17$$
$$(36 + 1) - (19 + 1) = 37 - 20 = 17$$

This generalization can be demonstrated by using blocks (see opposite page), e.g.,

$$36 - 19 = (36 + 1) - (19 + 1) = 17$$

Or, given a subtraction example in which an impasse occurs, such as $83 - 26 = \square$, it may be used by adding 10 to each term: First, 10 ones are added to the 3 ones of 83; then 1 ten is added to the 2 tens of 26. This resolves the impasse.

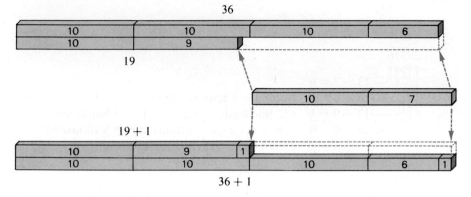

$$
\begin{array}{ll}
83 & \quad 8 \text{ tens} + 3 \text{ ones} \\
-\,26 & \rightarrow \quad -\,(2 \text{ tens} + 6 \text{ ones})
\end{array}
$$

$$
\rightarrow \quad
\begin{array}{l}
8 \text{ tens} + (3 \text{ ones} + 10 \text{ ones}) \\
-\,(2 \text{ tens} + \quad 1 \text{ ten}) + \quad 6 \text{ ones}
\end{array}
\quad \rightarrow \quad
\begin{array}{l}
8 \text{ tens} + 13 \text{ ones} \\
-\,(3 \text{ tens} + \quad 6 \text{ ones}) \\
\overline{5 \text{ tens} + \quad 7 \text{ ones} = 57}
\end{array}
$$

In using this algorithm, a child thinks at first as follows:

$$
\begin{array}{r}
83 \\
-\,26 \\
\hline
57
\end{array}
$$

(1) "3 + 10 = 13; 13 − 6 = 7"

(2) "Since 3 was increased by 10,
I increase 2 tens by 1 ten;
8 tens − 3 tens = 5 tens."

With practice, the conscious thought process is:

$$
\begin{array}{r}
83 \\
-\,26 \\
\hline
57
\end{array}
$$

"13 − 6 = 7"
" 8 − 3 = 5"

For examples involving an impasse in a place other than ones place,
the *conscious* thinking is the same although the actual numbers being added
are higher powers of ten:

```
  58263
− 28947
  29316
```

$13 − 7 = \underline{6}$
$6 − 5 = \underline{1}$ (6 tens − 5 tens = $\underline{1}$ ten)
$12 − 9 = \underline{3}$ (12 hundreds − 9 hundreds = $\underline{3}$ hundreds)
$18 − 9 = \underline{9}$ (18 thousands − 9 thousands = $\underline{9}$ thousands)
$5 − 3 = \underline{2}$ (5 ten-thousands − 3 ten-thousands = $\underline{2}$ ten-thousands)

The same problem can be solved by applying the same generalization in a less standardized way.

(1) 58263 − 28947 Add 3 to each term: 58266 − 28950

(2) 58266 − 28950 Add 50 to each term: 58316 − 29000

(3) 58316 − 29000 Add 1000 to each term: 59316 − 30000

(4) 59316 − 30000 Subtract: 59316 − 30000 = 29316

Conscious subtractions can be done, once impasses are resolved, either in take-away terms or in additive terms (e.g., 8 − 2 may be thought of as "8 minus 2 = □" or as "2 plus □ = 8"). Thus there are, in a sense, four basic ways in which children may perform subtraction computations: resolving impasses by "borrowing," then subtracting in take-away terms; "borrowing," then subtracting in additive terms; resolving impasses by equal additions, then subtracting in take-away terms; or resolving impasses by equal additions, then subtracting in additive terms.

The Multiplication Algorithm

While the sequence of stages in which the addition and subtraction algorithms are developed is relatively standardized, the same is not true for multiplication and division. Any two different textbook series may approach these algorithms in rather different ways. Again, this need not be of particular concern to the practicing teacher, who generally follows whatever sequence occurs in one particular series. It is important, however, that the teacher recognize the rationale of the *entire* development in that series, which generally spans two or three grade levels. An hour or two devoted to examining the various books in the series for this purpose is generally time well spent. It is instructive to consider *why* the algorithm is developed as it is. We will do so here for one typical development.

Consider the problem:

$$\begin{array}{r} 523 \\ \times\ \ 47 \\ \hline \end{array}$$

It is representative of the kind of computation children would be expected to do, with understanding, by the *end* of the development of the multiplication algorithm. The solution of this problem involves several skills and understandings, e.g., multiplying 7×523 and 40×523. Finding each of these partial products, in turn, involves understanding how products like 7×500, 7×20, 40×20, and so on, are obtained from fundamental facts. Furthermore, as these separate products are found — in a specific order — they are automatically added by recording them according to numeration principles. This addition generally involves renaming products such as 21, recording the ones digit in the appropriate place, and "carrying" the tens digit to the next place, as in column addition.

Each of these skills must be developed, and in a logical order. In the following paragraphs we will consider activities for teaching each of them. The first steps can begin once a reasonable number of fundamental facts have been learned. For discussion purposes, we will assume here that children have reasonable proficiency with all of the facts before beginning the algorithm. Prior to introduction of the standard form and practice at each of the six stages, problem types should be introduced in problem settings, including physical manipulations insofar as possible (although this becomes increasingly difficult as larger numbers are involved), followed by representation on place value devices, equation forms, and expanded computational forms.

Powers of 10 as Factors

Powers of 10 as factors occur commonly in mental computations and are at least tacitly used in finding and recording separate products when using the multiplication algorithm. Furthermore, understanding such products is necessary for complete understanding of our numeration system. Problems concerned with application of this concept are relatively easy to teach, and are commonly introduced quite early. For example, replacing expressions such as "5 hundreds + 2 tens + 3 ones" with "$5 \times 100 + 2 \times 10 + 3 \times 1$" or "$500 + 20 + 3$" involves understanding that $5 \times 100 = 500$, $2 \times 10 = 20$, $3 \times 1 = 3$. And understanding products such as 7×20, 7×500, 40×3, 40×20, and 40×500, as in the computation for

$$\begin{array}{r} 523 \\ \times\ \ 47 \\ \hline \end{array}$$

involves multiplying by powers of 10, e.g.,

$$7 \times 20 = 7 \times (\underline{2 \times 10}) = (7 \times 2) \times 10 = 14 \times 10,$$

$$40 \times 20 = (4 \times 2) \times (10 \times 10) = 8 \times 100$$

In particular, products where both factors are powers of 10 (other than 1) occur in such steps of the algorithm as

$$40 \times 20 = 8 \times \underline{10 \times 10} \qquad \text{and} \qquad 40 \times 500 = 20 \times (\underline{10 \times 100}).$$

Children need to understand that in the step at which they consciously think "$4 \times 2 = 8$", they are in fact determining $(4 \times 10) \times (8 \times 10)$, that the actual product is 800, and that it can be recorded as '8' in hundreds place.

Introductory problems for this concept are typically like

$$\begin{array}{r} 10 \\ \times\ 3 \\ \hline \end{array}$$

Since such a problem is so close to the fundamental facts stage, it can be introduced by using any of the activities appropriate for teaching fundamental multiplication facts. In particular, 10-blocks can be arranged either as arrays or trains on a number line. The family $1 \times 10, 2 \times 10, 3 \times 10, \ldots ,$ 9×10 should be considered together; practice should be provided orally, where the factor of 10 occurs both as the first factor and as the second. Written practice should be similarly structured, both in equation and computational form:

$$3 \times 10 = \underline{\quad} \qquad 10 \times 5 = \underline{\quad} \qquad \begin{array}{r} 10 \\ \times\ 3 \\ \hline \end{array} \qquad \begin{array}{r} 5 \\ \times\ 10 \\ \hline \end{array}$$

Most children quickly discover the relationship between the products and the factor that is not 10, and that the product can be found mentally by annexing (not "adding") a zero to that factor. This short cut, once understood, leads to extending the skill to finding products where one factor is 10 and the other is greater than 9, e.g., $12 \times 10,\ 863 \times 10,\ 10 \times 10,\ 20 \times 10$. Place value devices can be used to emphasize relationships; one particularly useful activity in terms of preparing for the algorithm is suggested by such instructions as: "Determine 5×10 and record the product on the place value chart," or "Determine 12×10 and record the product on the abacus." Conversely, given the standard representation of a multiple of ten, such as 50 or 120 on such devices, children can be asked to express them as products (5×10 and 12×10).

Once 10 as a factor is reasonably well understood, similar activities can be used with 100, and later with 1000, and so on. Multiplying by 10 can be used to strengthen children's concept of 100, and to introduce powers of 10 beginning with 1000. Physical models such as Dienes flats or blocks, number lines marked in hundreds or thousands, boxes of small items packaged in hundreds, e.g., rubber bands, toothpicks, paper clips, or thumb-tacks can all be useful prior to the practice stage.

Multiples of 10 as Factors

One key to understanding the final form of the multiplication algorithm involves products where one factor is less than 10 and the other is a multiple of some power of 10, such as 3×20 or 6×400. Closely related to this are those products where both factors are multiples of powers of 10, such as 30×20 or 200×40. At this stage, each multiple of 10 should contain a single nonzero digit, since the immediate objective is to teach children to solve problems by *inspection,* not by computation.

If one factor is less than 10, there are many ways to represent these problems with manipulative and place value devices. Consider, for example, these ways of representing 2×40:

Examples:

(a) Use 2 sets of 4 dimes each; since each set represents 40, by the set union interpretation of multiplication, 2 sets of 40 means 2×40. There are 8 dimes altogether, so $2 \times 40 = 80$; other models for 10 besides dimes should be used in the same way, e.g., 10-blocks from the Stern, Dienes, or Cuisenaire materials, bundled sticks, boxes of 10 pencils each, and so on. The materials can be arranged in 2-by-4 arrays:

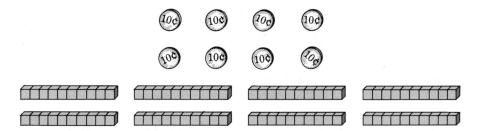

(b) Two sets of four 10-blocks each can be placed on a number line; the first four extend from '0' to '40' on the line, and the second four reach from there to '80', so $2 \times 40 = 80$:

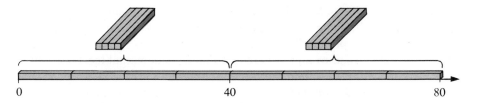

(c) Two rows of 4 tens each on the place value chart or two sets of 4 markers in the tens column of the abacus can be viewed either as 2 × 40 or as 80, so 2 × 40 = 80:

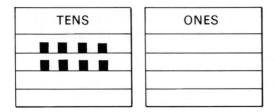 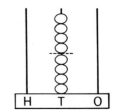

Whatever representations are chosen for 40, in such situations, the child should be led to see *four* things, not forty, e.g., four dimes is more appropriate than forty pennies, since he should be led to think in terms of *fundamental* facts. Physical models can be related to the repeated addition interpretation of multiplication: 2 × 40 means 40 + 40 so, since 40 + 40 = 80, 2 × 40 = 80. Also expanded computational forms and equations can emphasize the relationship to fundamental facts:

$$2 \times 40 = 2 \times 4 \text{ tens} = 8 \text{ tens} = 80$$

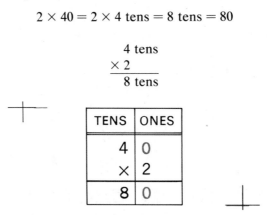

Two important generalizations can and should be introduced (or reintroduced) and emphasized at this point: the associative property and the factor rearrangement generalization (i.e., that the product of three or more factors is unaffected by order or grouping). Both are essential to understanding subsequent stages of the algorithm. There are relatively few opportunities to practice either when children are at the fundamental facts stage because in multiplying three numbers an intermediate product must be found, and if that product is greater than 10, the second product is one they have not yet learned to find. There are only 6 fundamental facts with products less than 10 (other than the rather simple ones with a factor of 0 or 1). For example, at the fundamental facts stage, children can find (3 × 2) × 4 and (4 × 2) × 3, but not (4 × 3) × 2. Once they learn to solve problems of the form $(a \times b) \times c$ where one of a, b, or c is 10, however, the number of possible examples increases considerably.

Children can be led to discover both of these generalizations by solving sets of problems such as these:

$$2 \times (4 \times 10) = 2 \times \underline{\qquad} = \underline{\qquad}$$
$$(2 \times 4) \times 10 = \underline{\qquad} \times 10 = \underline{\qquad}$$
$$(4 \times 10) \times 2 = \underline{\qquad} \times 2 = \underline{\qquad}$$
$$10 \times (2 \times 4) = 10 \times \underline{\qquad} = \underline{\qquad}$$

They can be challenged to find all twelve ways of expressing the product of three numbers. As usual, manipulative activities will make this kind of problem solving more meaningful.

Problems of this sort for which the product of the fundamental fact is greater than 9, such as 3×40 or 5×200, should not be viewed as being essentially different from the easier ones, and in particular should not be treated as carrying situations. In solving $3 \times 40 = \square$, for example, the child should reason that since $3 \times 4 = 12$, 3×4 tens $= 12$ tens or 120, the '120' should be recorded in the "natural" way, i.e., not "put down '2' and carry '1'."

Teaching children to solve problems such as 20×30, 500×70, and so on (where *both* factors are multiples of powers of 10) is somewhat more difficult in that most of the models and manipulative devices appropriate for teaching the preceding type of problem are impractical. Instead, motivation may be supplied by raising such questions as, "How many pencils are there altogether in 30 boxes if there are 20 pencils in each box?" or "If 30 children each have 20 cents for lunch money, how much do they have altogether?" A *few* such problems should be solved by "brute force" (actually counting, adding, and so on) to generate interest in finding quicker methods of solution. Carefully arranged pictures can be suggestive (such as 3 rows of children, 10 children in each row, each with 2 dimes). Toy money, checkers, or other small counting devices, each representing a dime, can be carefully arranged to suggest various solutions. Six Dienes flats (or similar 10-by-10 models) can be arranged to form a 20-by-30 array, strongly

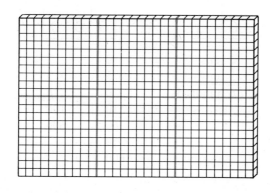

suggesting the role of both the fundamental fact, $2 \times 3 = 6$, and of the numeration-related concept, $10 \times 10 = 100$ in the solution of $20 \times 30 = \square$. Some children will need careful guidance in order to see the array in three ways; i.e., as a 20-by-30 array of units (ones); as a 2 tens-by-3 tens array; and as a 2-by-3 array of flats (hundreds).

Another useful device is the "stylized" array: one in which the individual objects are imagined and outlined, partitioned in terms of tens, hundreds, and so on. For example, a 20-by-30 array of objects, which would be difficult and time-consuming to construct or picture (and possibly confusing), can be represented as follows:

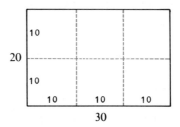

Like the Dienes type array above, this type of model strongly suggests the roles of fundamental facts and numeration in the solution of such problems.

Such activities, together with an understanding of factor rearrangement and place value skills, can lead to more abstract solutions, first in terms of equations, expanded forms, and place value charts:

$$20 \times 30 = 2 \text{ tens} \times 3 \text{ tens} = 6 \text{ hundreds}$$

$$\begin{aligned} 20 \times 30 &= (2 \times 10) \times (3 \times 10) \\ &= (2 \times 3) \times (10 \times 10) \\ &= 6 \times 100 \\ &= 600 \end{aligned}$$

H	T	O
	3	
×	2	
6		

H	T	O
	3	0
×	2	0
6	0	0

```
    2 tens
  × 3 tens
  6 hundreds
```

```
      2
    × 3
      6
   × 10
     60
   × 10
    600
```

```
      2
    × 3
      6
  × 100
    600
```

The child must ultimately be able to solve these problems mentally, without computation, reasoning, at least tacitly, that "since $2 \times 3 = 6$ and $10 \times 10 = 100$, 2 tens $\times$ 3 tens $= 6$ hundreds." Drill examples can be in both equation form and computational form:

$$
\begin{array}{llll}
30 \times 700 = 21000 & 700 & 30 & 90 \\
400 \times\ \ 30 = 12000 & \underline{\times\ \ 30} & \underline{\times\ 400} & \underline{\times\ 60} \\
\ 60 \times\ \ 90 = 5400 & 21000 & 12000 & 5400
\end{array}
$$

Multiplying Any Number by a Number Less Than 10

Finding products such as 3×32 or 6×278 is a skill that is used both by itself and as the first step in the algorithm for finding products such as, e.g., 23×32 or 346×278. It is used, too, in finding partial products beyond the first. For example, the second partial product for 36×32, i.e., 30×32 (which will be discussed in the next section) is *consciously* found in terms of 3×32. Thus the solution of such problems constitutes a key instructional stage.

The two skills involved in these problems are quite distinct: multiplying both ones and tens and "carrying." Initial problems should involve only the first of these, and "carrying" should be introduced only *after* this basic skill is understood. That is, initial problems should be those for which the fundamental facts being used have products less than 10 (except, perhaps, for the largest place of the larger number), e.g.,

$$
\begin{array}{llll}
32 & 634 & 21 & 3021 \\
\underline{\times\ 3} & \underline{\times\ \ 2} & \underline{\times\ 6} & \underline{\times\ \ \ \ 4}
\end{array}
$$

The essential mathematical principle used here is the distributive property, which should therefore first be reviewed in the context of fundamental facts (see Chapter 5). Also, of course, children need to be proficient in solving problems such as 2×30, 3×400, and so on. These, too, should be reviewed prior to introducing problems such as those above.

The already discussed basic teaching strategies, manipulative models, expanded forms, and so on, should all be used in teaching multiplication by a number less than 10. Since this is the first introduction to the distributive property beyond the fundamental facts stage, the teacher should be certain to focus the child's attention on the two (or more) multiplications and the addition that must be done (even though the addition is ultimately done automatically). Dimes and pennies, 10-blocks and 1-blocks, the abacus, stylized arrays, repeated addition, and place value charts can be used as before.

$$
\begin{array}{lll}
3 \times 32 = 32 + 32 + 32 & 32 & 30\quad 2 \\
 & 32 & 30\quad 2 \\
 & \underline{+\ 32} & \underline{+\ 30\quad 2}
\end{array}
$$

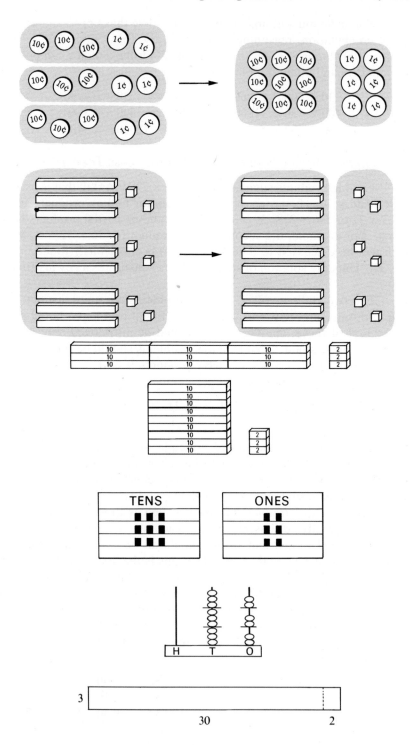

Equations and expanded computational forms are also comparable to previous ones:

$$3 \times (3 \text{ tens} + 2 \text{ ones}) = (3 \times 3 \text{ tens}) + (3 \times 2 \text{ ones})$$

$$3 \times (30 + 2) = (3 \times 30) + (3 \times 2)$$

$$\begin{array}{r} 30 + 2 \\ \times 3 \\ \hline 90 + 6 \end{array} \qquad \begin{array}{r} 3 \text{ tens} + 2 \text{ ones} \\ \times 3 \\ \hline 9 \text{ tens} + 6 \text{ ones} \end{array} \qquad \begin{array}{r} 32 \\ \times\ 3 \\ \hline 6 \\ +\ 90 \\ \hline 96 \end{array}$$

If the carrying process for addition is understood reasonably well, and if sufficient manipulative experience is provided, problems that involve carrying in multiplication present no major obstacle. Relevant activities, illustrated here for 3×26, are similar to those above.

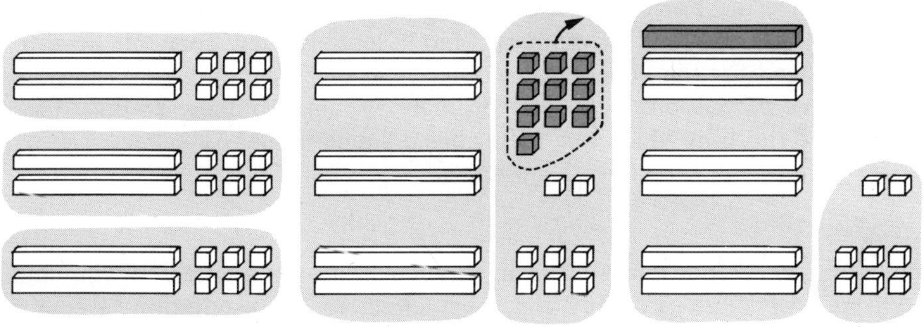

1 2 3

$$\begin{array}{rr} 20 & 6 \\ 20 & 6 \\ +\ 20 & 6 \\ \hline \multicolumn{2}{l}{60 + 18 = 78} \end{array} \qquad \begin{array}{r} 26 \\ 26 \\ +\ 26 \\ \hline 78 \end{array}$$

$$\begin{array}{r} 20 + 6 \\ \times 3 \\ \hline 60 + 18 = 78 \end{array} \qquad \begin{array}{rl} 26 & \\ \times\ 3 & \\ \hline 18 & \leftarrow 3 \times 6 \\ +\ 60 & \leftarrow 3 \times 20 \\ \hline 78 & \end{array} \qquad \begin{array}{rl} 26 & \\ \times\ 3 & \\ \hline \left.\begin{array}{r} 8 \\ 10 \end{array}\right\} & \leftarrow 3 \times 6 \\ 60 & \leftarrow 3 \times 20 \\ \hline 78 & \end{array}$$

Practice on problems of this sort should normally be in computational form, and the standard form should be introduced as soon as possible. As with addition, the use of a "reminder" of the carried number is helpful for many children, but they should be encouraged to do without it as soon as possible. Practice with higher decade addition facts will help them to do so. The "reminder" digit may be recorded in either of two places:

$$\begin{array}{r} \overset{\rightarrow\ 1}{26} \\ \times\ 3 \\ \hline 78 \end{array} \qquad \begin{array}{r} 26 \\ \times\ 3 \\ \hline 7\,{}^{|}8 \end{array}$$

Some children make the error of adding before they multiply; i.e.,

$$\text{``}1 + 2 = 3, \quad \text{then} \quad 3 \times 3 = 9\text{''} \qquad \begin{array}{r} \overset{|}{26} \\ \times\ 3 \\ \hline 98 \end{array}$$

This is usually caused by proceeding too quickly to the final form and can be remedied by returning to earlier instructional stages.

The General Case

Once the preceding stages have been mastered, children are ready for multiplying any pair of numbers. No essentially new concepts need to be introduced for the general case other than the procedure for recording and adding partial products. Accordingly, initial problems at this stage are usually those in which one factor has a single nonzero digit:

$$\begin{array}{r} 24 \\ \times\ 20 \\ \hline \end{array} \qquad \begin{array}{r} 27 \\ \times\ 40 \\ \hline \end{array} \qquad \begin{array}{r} 6254 \\ \times\ \ \ 300 \\ \hline \end{array}$$

Physical representations of such problems are impractical again, and stylized arrays are probably the most effective representation: Using a

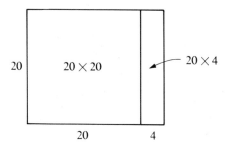

picture such as this, the teacher can ask how to find the number of elements in the entire 20-by-24 array (stories can be made up for interest, e.g., it could represent 20 rows of toy soldiers, with 24 in each row, trees planted in rows, and so on). Associating the parts of the array with 20×20 and 20×4, both of which the child can compute mentally, suggests that there are $400 + 80$, or 480 objects altogether in the array.

In using this algorithm, however, children need to be led to think of 20×24 in terms of 2×24. Using the factor rearrangement generalization, it is easy for them to see that 20×24, i.e., $(2 \times 10) \times 24$, can be found as $(2 \times 24) \times 10$ or as $(24 \times 10) \times 2$. Finding 2×24 is a familiar skill, as is multiplying by 10, which involves simply annexing a zero. Working a few problems in the expanded form below will demonstrate that multiplying 24 by 20, for example, can be accomplished either by multiplying by 2 and then by 10 or by reversing that order:

$$
\begin{array}{ccc}
\begin{array}{r} 24 \\ \times\ 2 \\ \hline 48 \\ \times\ 10 \\ \hline 480 \end{array}
& \text{or} &
\begin{array}{r} 24 \\ \times\ 10 \\ \hline 240 \\ \times\ 2 \\ \hline 480 \end{array}
\end{array}
$$

The standard form can be introduced as a short form in which multiplying by 10 is done *first* (by recording a 0 in ones place) and then multiplying by 2 is done in the usual way, recording the '48' to the left of the '0':

$$
\begin{array}{ccc}
\begin{array}{r} 24 \\ \times 20 \\ \hline 0 \end{array}
&
\begin{array}{r} 24 \\ \times 20 \\ \hline 80 \end{array}
&
\begin{array}{r} 24 \\ \times 20 \\ \hline 480 \end{array}
\\[4pt]
\uparrow & \uparrow & \uparrow \\
1 & 2 & 3
\end{array}
$$

Problems of the most general case can now be introduced. Here, again, stylized arrays prove a useful model. This 23×37 array, for example,

can be viewed in three ways: as *one* 23-by-37 array; as *two* arrays, one 3-by-37, and one 20-by-37; or as *four* arrays, 3-by-30, 3-by-7, 20-by-30, and 20-by-7. Thus the number of elements in the array can be viewed as

$$
\begin{array}{c}
23 \times 37, \quad \text{or} \\
(3 \times 37) + (20 \times 37), \quad \text{or} \\
(3 \times 30) + (3 \times 7) + (20 \times 30) + (20 \times 7)
\end{array}
$$

Since children have learned how to find all of these expanded products, the following equations and expanded forms, which can be related to the array, should pose no serious difficulties in leading up to the standard form:

$$23 \times 37 = (3 \times 37) + (20 \times 37)$$

$$
\begin{array}{cc}
37 & 37 \\
\underline{\times\ 3} & \underline{\times\ 20} \\
111\ + & 740\ \to
\end{array}
\qquad
\begin{array}{r}
111 \\
+\ 740 \\
\hline
851
\end{array}
$$

$$23 \times 37 = (3 \times 30) + (3 \times 7) + (20 \times 30) + (20 \times 7)$$
$$= \quad 90 \quad + \quad 21 \quad + \quad 600 \quad + \quad 140 \quad \to$$
$$= 851$$

$$
\begin{array}{r}
90 \\
21 \\
600 \\
+\ 140
\end{array}
$$

$$
\begin{array}{l}
37 \\
\underline{\times\ 23} \\
21 \leftarrow 3 \times 7\ \} \\
90 \leftarrow 3 \times 30 \\
140 \leftarrow 20 \times 7\ \} \\
\underline{600 \leftarrow 20 \times 30} \\
851
\end{array}
\qquad
\begin{array}{l}
3 \times 37 \to \\
\\
20 \times 37 \to
\end{array}
\qquad
\begin{array}{r}
37 \\
\underline{\times\ 23} \\
111 \\
\\
740 \\
\hline
851
\end{array}
$$

Once children become reasonably proficient with the solution of such problems, they are, of course, prepared to solve *any* multiplication problem involving whole numbers. Extensions include only larger numbers, more partial products, or both. Once children have practiced the algorithm for some time, they may discover − or be introduced to − a few familiar short cuts, mostly involving zero digits. None of these is essential and none should be introduced until the basic process is well understood.

$$
\begin{array}{cc}
\textit{Standard form} &
\begin{array}{r}
37 \\
\underline{\times\ 23} \\
111 \\
740 \\
\hline
851
\end{array}
\end{array}
\qquad
\begin{array}{cc}
\textit{Abbreviated form} &
\begin{array}{r}
37 \\
\underline{\times\ 23} \\
111 \\
74 \\
\hline
851
\end{array}
\end{array}
$$

This familiar "time-saver," for example, often causes problems with alignment and does not save enough time to be worth introducing unless children discover it on their own. On the other hand, this short cut reduces the

$$
\begin{array}{cc}
\textit{Standard form} &
\begin{array}{r}
327 \\
\underline{\times\ 802} \\
654 \\
0000 \\
261600 \\
\hline
262254
\end{array}
\end{array}
\qquad
\begin{array}{cc}
\textit{Abbreviated form} &
\begin{array}{r}
327 \\
\underline{\times\ 802} \\
654 \\
\underline{261600} \\
262254
\end{array}
\end{array}
$$

number of partial products to be added, and *can* save a significant amount of time. It is, therefore, a useful abbreviation. It is also an easy one for children to understand. A variation on it, for problems where the multiplier has one or more terminating zeroes, is illustrated in this example.

Standard form	*Abbreviated form*	

$$
\begin{array}{r}
5327 \\
\times\ 2800 \\
\hline
0000 \\
0000 \\
4261600 \\
10654000 \\
\hline
14915600
\end{array}
\qquad
\begin{array}{r}
5327 \\
\times\ 2800 \\
\hline
4261600 \\
10654 \\
\hline
14915600
\end{array}
\quad \text{or} \quad
\begin{array}{r}
5327 \\
\times\ 2800 \\
\hline
4261600 \\
10654000 \\
\hline
14915600
\end{array}
$$

For problems such as

$$
\begin{array}{r}
3206 \\
\times\quad 8 \\
\hline
\end{array}
$$

children generally discover by themselves that the "carrying" step can be abbreviated. That is, rather than think "$8 \times 6 = 48$, put down '8' and carry '4', $8 \times 0 = 0$, $0 + 4 = 4$," because of the zero, they think "$8 \times 6 = 48$, put down 48," and then continue. When carrying is not involved in the preceding step, as in

$$
\begin{array}{r}
3204 \\
\times\quad 2 \\
\hline
\end{array}
$$

they merely record the zero without consciously thinking "$2 \times 0 = 0$."

Our final example is also usually discovered and need not be introduced.

$$
\begin{array}{r}
237 \\
\times\ 424 \\
\hline
948 \\
4740 \\
94800
\end{array}
$$

Here, the digits, except for the terminal zeroes, are the same for the third partial product as for the first, so they can merely be repeated without conscious multiplication. This, again, is a useful time saver, easily understood by most children.

The Division Algorithms

Two quite distinct algorithms for division are commonly taught: The *quotient estimation* algorithm (see pp. 171–83) and the *repeated subtraction* algorithm. We will consider separately materials and activities for teaching each of these, although it may be noted that some are equally appropriate for both. Individual teachers' decisions as to which algorithm to teach and in what sequence to do so are again largely determined by the textbook series being used. Each teacher, particularly in the upper grades, should be familiar with both algorithms, however, since all the children in a given class may not have been taught the same method initially. The two methods will be compared briefly after we have examined both of them.

The Quotient Estimation Algorithm

The understandings and skills needed in order to use this algorithm can again most conveniently be described in terms of a sequence of instructional stages typically found in children's textbooks. In the case of division, the difficulty of a given problem, and thus the order in which the various types of problems are normally introduced, depends principally upon the divisor. Accordingly, we will first examine, in turn, divisors that are less than 10 and divisors that are multiples of a power of 10 but contain a single nonzero digit. The most general case, in which the divisor may be any nonzero number, is considered last.

Divisors Less Than 10. The four examples below, each with a divisor less than 10, represent the kinds of problems that can be used beyond the fundamental facts stage to develop some of the key ideas of the algorithm:

$$2\overline{)600} \quad 3\overline{)96} \quad 5\overline{)23} \quad 4\overline{)185}$$

Problems of the first type, such as $2\overline{)600}$, $3\overline{)90}$, $4\overline{)80}$, and $5\overline{)350}$, can be introduced when children are learning to solve corresponding multiplication problems, e.g., 300×2, 20×4, and 70×5. Solutions to these division problems should be one-step results, based only on the definition of division. That is, $600 \div 2$ is 300 *because* 300×2 is 600. Any manipulative materials used for the multiplication problems (see pp. 211–15) can be used with the division problems. Two things should be emphasized: First, the child should think of the dividend, e.g., 600, as six things, i.e., *6 hundreds,* so that he sees the relationship to fundamental facts. Models such as Dienes flats, tickets in the hundreds chart, or markers on the hundred strand of the abacus all help to emphasize this, as do expanded computational forms such as $2\overline{)6\text{ hundreds}}$ and $3\overline{)9\text{ tens}}$. For problems such as $5\overline{)350}$, where the dividend of the related fundamental fact is greater than 9, it will be necessary to think of 350 as 35 tens rather than 3 hundreds + 5 tens. Once a few problems are worked at the manipulative and semiabstract levels, the relationship to fundamental facts can be emphasized through exercises such as these:

$6 \div 2 = \underline{\qquad}$ $2\overline{)6}$

$60 \div 2 = \underline{\qquad}$ $2\overline{)60}$

$600 \div 2 = \underline{\qquad}$ or $2\overline{)600}$

$6000 \div 2 = \underline{\qquad}$ $2\overline{)6000}$

And second, the *partition* interpretation of division should be used, rather than *measurement.* That is, the child should think, "If 6 hundreds are separated into 2 matching parts, how many (hundreds) will be in each part?" rather than "How many 2s are there in 6 hundred?" (This emphasis on the partition interpretation is helpful for most of the subsequent stages of the development as well.) Once children understand the *computation* in terms of partition, they can, of course, be asked to solve related *problems* involving measurement.

The "long" form, below, is unnecessary with such problems, and can therefore be avoided at this time.

$$
\begin{array}{r}
300 \\
2\overline{)600} \\
\underline{600} \\
0
\end{array}
$$

The distributive principle for division over addition is involved in solving problems such as $3\overline{)96}$ or $2\overline{)846}$. In general, materials and activities

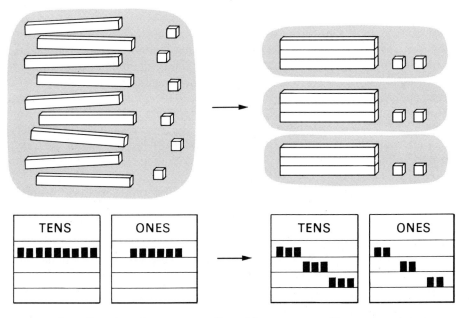

appropriate for the above type of problem are equally appropriate here, except that the results contain two or more steps — as demonstrated by these suggested activities for $3\overline{)96}$.

$$
\begin{array}{cc}
3 \text{ tens} + 2 \text{ ones} & 30 + 2 \\
3\overline{)9 \text{ tens} + 6 \text{ ones}} & 3\overline{)90 + 6}
\end{array}
$$

$$
\begin{aligned}
(9 \text{ tens} + 6 \text{ ones}) \div 3 &= (9 \text{ tens} \div 3) + (6 \text{ ones} \div 3) \\
&= \quad 3 \text{ tens} \quad + \quad 2 \text{ ones}
\end{aligned}
$$

$$
\begin{array}{cc}
\begin{array}{r}
32 \\
\overline{2} \\
30 \quad\uparrow \\
3\overline{)96}
\end{array}
&
\begin{array}{r}
32 \\
3\overline{)96}
\end{array}
\end{array}
$$

In this last example, the partial quotients can be recorded separately and then added above, (left), but most children quickly understand the more conventional form (right).

It is sometimes helpful to conceal those digits in the dividend that are irrelevant at a given step, to prevent distraction. A small piece of paper can be used, thus:

The next type of problem, exemplified by $5\overline{)23}$, is particularly important because it introduces the crucial *remainder* concept, which is central to understanding the algorithm. Many concrete examples—of both the measurement and the partition variety—should be explored, following the general practices suggested for teaching fundamental division facts. *Equation* forms should be avoided, however, since the only correct solution of an equation like $23 \div 5 = \square$ involves fractions or decimals, which, as a rule, the children have not yet encountered. It should be noted that the problems in this group are of the form $b\overline{)a}$, where b is any number from 2 to 9 and a is any number from $b + 1$ to $10b - 1$, except those numbers that are multiples of b. For example, if $b = 6$, it can include any of the forty-five examples $6\overline{)7}, 6\overline{)8}, 6\overline{)9}, \ldots, 6\overline{)59}$, excluding the fundamental facts $6\overline{)6}, 6\overline{)12}, 6\overline{)18}, \ldots, 6\overline{)54}$.

Both measurement and partition are appropriate to these problem situations, which should involve at least two questions.

Examples:

(a) "If Sam has 23 cents, how many 5-cent candy bars can he buy? How much money will he have left?" Familiarity with related problems involving fundamental facts will suggest the computation $5\overline{)23}$ and the physical manipulation to be used here:

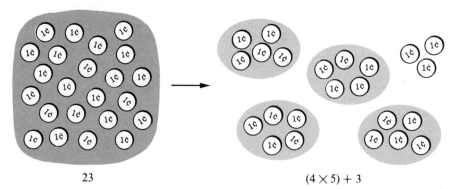

23                                    $(4 \times 5) + 3$

(b) "If 5 boys are to share 23 marbles equally, how many will each boy receive? How many marbles are left?"

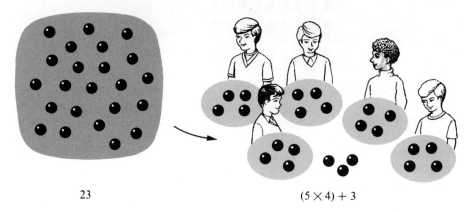

23 $(5 \times 4) + 3$

(c) "How many 5-inch pieces can be cut from a 23-inch length of string? How much string will be left?"

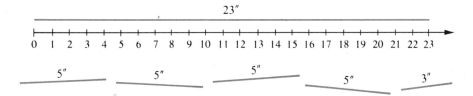

(d) "How many 5-car trains can be made from 23 cars? How many cars will be left?"

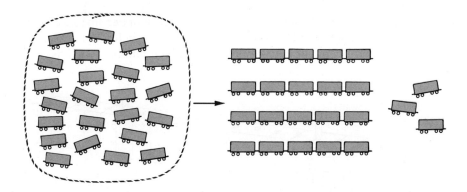

(e) "Arrange 23 1-blocks into an array with 5 blocks in each row (or 5 matching rows). How many rows can you form? How many of the blocks can you use? How many will be left over?"

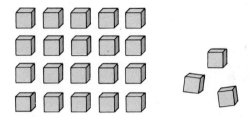

In exploring problems of this sort, it should be emphasized that each is related to a unique fundamental multiplication fact (e.g., $4 \times 5 = 20$, or its equivalent division form, $20 \div 5 = 4$), and that this related fact (here, with divisor of 5) is the one with the largest possible dividend, since otherwise the "leftover" quantity (marbles, string, and so on) could be further partitioned. In other words, this leftover quantity must always be *less* than the divisor.

Number line activities paralleling those for fundamental division facts are useful.

Examples:

(a) "How many 5-blocks will fit in the interval between 0 and 23 on the number line? What block will just fill the rest of the interval?" If the 5-blocks are set on the line beginning at '23' (rather than beginning at '0'), the child can determine the remainder by looking at the line.

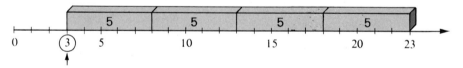

(b) For a given set of blocks, a wooden number line can be constructed with holes drilled to fit pegs at each point. When pegs are located at each multiple of a given number, such as 5, chil-

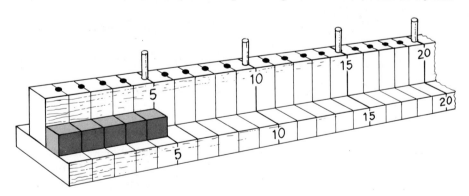

dren can be asked to express numbers between two successive pegs in terms of a multiple of 5, e.g., $19 = (3 \times 5) + 4$. Repeating this exercise in turn for *each* number from one peg to the next can help to reveal patterns, e.g.:

$$10 = (\underline{\quad} \times 5) + \underline{\quad}$$
$$11 = (\underline{\quad} \times 5) + \underline{\quad}$$
$$12 = (\underline{\quad} \times 5) + \underline{\quad}$$
$$13 = (\underline{\quad} \times 5) + \underline{\quad}$$
$$14 = (\underline{\quad} \times 5) + \underline{\quad}$$
$$15 = (\underline{\quad} \times 5) + \underline{\quad}$$

This activity develops the basic division relation, i.e., that *any* number a can be expressed uniquely as a multiple of *any* non-zero number b plus a number r which is less than b; if a is a multiple of b, then $r = 0$, e.g., $10 = (2 \times 5) + 0$.

At this point it is important to pursue the question of how many different remainders are possible for a given problem. Number line activities, such as the above, should reveal to children that this depends only on the divisor: if the divisor is b, there are b possible remainders, from 0 to $b - 1$. That is, for 6, the possible remainders are 0, 1, 2, 3, 4, and 5. It is also worthwhile to include examples where $a < b$, e.g.,

$$4 = (0 \times 5) + 4 \quad \text{and} \quad 3 = (0 \times 5) + 3$$

Activities like these can lead to a meaningful introduction to the standard "long" division form:

$$
\begin{array}{r}
4 \\
5{\overline{\smash{\big)}\,23}} \\
-20 \leftarrow (4 \times 5) \\
\hline
3
\end{array}
$$

At first, this new form should be directly related to the activities preceding it, so that children understand: that the '20' means 4×5; that it is recorded there so that the subtraction can be performed; and that this subtraction is performed to find the remainder (for example, how many of the 23 blocks are left after arranging them into as many rows of 5 as possible?). With practice, children can then solve similar problems by computation rather than manipulation. Once the form is understood, several activities are possible.

1. Introduce the word *remainder* and the words *divisor, quotient,* and *dividend* if they have not been introduced already. The conventional notation for the remainder can also be taught, being very careful that "4R3"

is interpreted correctly as *two* numbers, not one (again, be certain to avoid "equations" such as "23 ÷ 5 = 4R3.")

$$
\begin{array}{r}
4 \\
5\overline{)23} \\
-20 \\
\hline
3R
\end{array}
\qquad
\begin{array}{r}
4R3 \\
5\overline{)23} \\
-20 \\
\hline
3
\end{array}
$$

2. Occasionally include fundamental facts, examples where the quotient is zero, and those with divisors of 1, among practice problems:

$$
\begin{array}{r}
3R0 \\
5\overline{)15} \\
-15 \\
\hline
0
\end{array}
\qquad
\begin{array}{r}
0R4 \\
5\overline{)4} \\
-0 \\
\hline
4
\end{array}
\qquad
\begin{array}{r}
8R0 \\
1\overline{)8} \\
-8 \\
\hline
0
\end{array}
$$

The usual convention of not recording the remainder when it is zero should also be introduced. On the other hand, statements such as "There is no remainder" or "The division comes out even" are unnecessary and at least potentially misleading. The former contradicts the basic division relation, and the latter may conflict with the child's concept of even and odd numbers. Of course, the expressions *are* in common use, and can be used safely if they are introduced as figures of speech, not to be taken literally.

3. Problems of the preceding two types should be recalled and examined in terms of the new notation (physical models should definitely accompany this extension of the form at first).

$$
\begin{array}{r}
32 \\
3\overline{)96} \\
-90 \\
\hline
6 \\
-6 \\
\hline
0
\end{array}
\quad
\begin{array}{l}
\leftarrow \quad 30 \times 3 \\
\\
\leftarrow \quad 2 \times 3
\end{array}
$$

4. Consider expressions and computations such as the following, and ask children what is "wrong" about them (in terms of solving some of the preceding problems).

$$
28 = (4 \times 5) + 8
\qquad
\begin{array}{r}
4 \\
5\overline{)28} \\
-20 \\
\hline
8
\end{array}
$$

5. Use sequences of exercises where a given number is divided, in turn, by successively larger divisors.

$$2\overline{)15} \quad 3\overline{)15} \quad 4\overline{)15} \quad 5\overline{)15} \quad 6\overline{)15} \quad 7\overline{)15} \quad 8\overline{)15} \quad 9\overline{)15}$$

6. Introduce the technique of counting backward from the dividend to find the correct fundamental fact: For $9\overline{)58}$, for example, $58 \div 9$ is not a

fundamental fact, so try $57 \div 9$, $56 \div 9$, $55 \div 9$, and finally, $54 \div 9$. Since $54 \div 9 = 6$, the quotient is 6 and the remainder can be determined by the computation:

$$
\begin{array}{r}
6 \\
9\overline{)58} \\
-54 \\
\hline
4R
\end{array}
$$

7. Problem questions should be varied, some calling for the quotient only, some for the remainder only, some for both the quotient and remainder, some for the product of the quotient and divisor, and some requiring reasoning beyond the computation itself:
   (a) How many 5-inch pieces can be cut from a 23-inch length of string? (*Answer:* 4.)
   (b) Five brothers agree to share a bag of marbles equally and give any that are left to their sister, Susie. If there were 23 marbles in the bag, how many should Susie get? (*Answer:* 3.)
   (c) If 23 toy soldiers are lined up in rows of 5, how many rows of soldiers can be formed? (*Answer:* 4.) How many soldiers will be left? (*Answer:* 3.)
   (d) Sam had 23 books in a box. His five friends agree to help him. If Sam gives each friend the same number of books, how many books can he get rid of? (*Answer:* 20.)
   (e) If 23 children go on a field trip by car, and if each car can hold 5 children, how many cars are needed? (*Answer:* 5.)
   (f) If 23 children go in 5 cars, how many children should go in each car? (Answers can vary, e.g., 2 cars with 4 each and 3 cars with 5 each.)
   Note that problem questions that can only be answered correctly with fractions should be carefully avoided until that concept has been taught, e.g., "If a 23-inch string is cut into 5 pieces, each the same length, how long will each string be?" ($4\frac{3}{5}$ inches).
8. When computations are done in the context of problem solving, it is sometimes helpful to *label* the numbers according to the sense of the problem, e.g.,

$$
\begin{array}{rl}
4 & \text{marbles for each brother} \\
\text{brothers} \quad 5\overline{)23} & \text{marbles to begin with} \\
-20 & \text{marbles altogether for the boys} \\
\hline
3 & \text{marbles left for Susie}
\end{array}
$$

Once children become reasonably proficient with simple remainder problems, similar problems can be introduced in which the dividend figures are multiples of a power of ten:

$$
\begin{array}{r}
4 \text{ tens} \\
4\overline{)18 \text{ tens}} \\
-16 \text{ tens} \\
\hline
2 \text{ tens}
\end{array}
\qquad
\begin{array}{r}
7 \text{ hundreds} \\
8\overline{)58 \text{ hundreds}} \\
-56 \text{ hundreds} \\
\hline
2 \text{ hundreds}
\end{array}
$$

Such exercises must be treated carefully. If written in standard form, they will not satisfy the basic division relation, because the remainder is greater than the divisor:

$$
\begin{array}{r}
40 \\
4\overline{)180} \\
-160 \\
\hline
20
\end{array}
\qquad
\begin{array}{r}
700 \\
8\overline{)5800} \\
-5600 \\
\hline
200
\end{array}
$$

Computations of this form should not be viewed as "complete." They are introduced, in fact, only in preparation for the next step. On the other hand, the numbers of *tens* or *hundreds* in such quotients and remainders are correct according to the basic division relation. That is, the number of *tens* or *hundreds* in the remainder should be regarded as correct if it is less than the divisor. In subsequent problems, such intermediate remainders are renamed in terms of numeration, e.g., 2 tens is renamed as 20 ones and combined with (added to) the number in ones place.

The above activities should prepare students to divide *any* number by a nonzero number less than 10, e.g., $4\overline{)185}$. An appropriate *partition* problems can be used as an introduction, e.g., "If 185 blocks are separated into 4 equal piles, how many blocks will be in each pile and how many will be left?" The dividend could be presented in place value terms with a standard collection of Dienes blocks (not 185 units) and 4 loops. Children

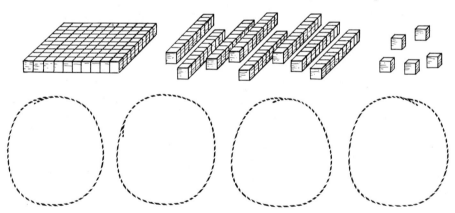

should then be allowed to try several possible solutions (e.g., they may put 2 longs and 1 unit in each pile but then face a dilemma with the remaining blocks). In time, they should see the feasibility of trading the flat for 10 longs. The collection then becomes 18 longs and 5 units. Four longs can be put into each of the 4 piles. This eliminates 16 longs from the original collection and leaves 2. These 2 longs can then each be traded for 10 units. Those 20 units are combined with the original 5 units, making 25 altogether. These can then be partitioned, putting 6 in each pile, with 1 unit left over. Each pile contains 4 longs and 6 units, so the quotient is 46 and the remainder is 1.

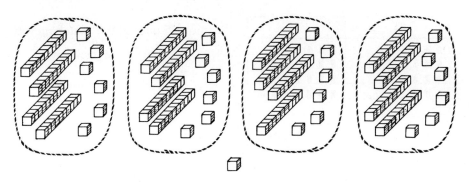

Manipulative activities can lead to, or be accompanied by, representation on place value devices, such as the place value chart:

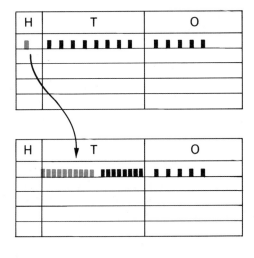

Express dividend in standard form:

1 hundred + 8 tens + 5 ones

Trade 1 hundred for 10 tens:

18 tens + 5 ones

Partition the tens into 4 matching rows:

$$\begin{array}{r} 4 \text{ tens} \quad \text{in each row} \\ 4\overline{)\,18 \text{ tens}} \\ \underline{16 \text{ tens}} \quad \text{used up} \\ 2 \text{ tens} \quad \text{left over} \end{array}$$

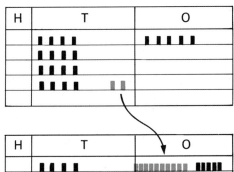

Trade the 2 leftover tens for 20 ones:

25 ones altogether

H	T	O
▮▮▮▮	▮▮▮▮▮▮	
▮▮▮▮	▮▮▮▮▮▮	
▮▮▮▮	▮▮▮▮▮▮	
▮▮▮▮	▮▮▮▮▮▮	

Partition 25 ones into 4 matching rows:

$$\begin{array}{r} \,6 \text{ ones} \quad \text{in each row} \\ \hline 4)\,\overline{25 \text{ ones}} \\ 24 \text{ ones} \quad \text{used up} \\ \hline 1 \qquad\quad \text{left over} \end{array}$$

Result: 4 tens and 6 ones in each row,
so the quotient is 46; 1 left over,
so the remainder is 1.

Various expanded computational forms *can* be used, but the renaming steps make them quite cumbersome; prior to the final form, however, it is helpful for some children to begin working such problems on a grid similar to a place value chart. "Irrelevant" places can be masked until they are to be considered:

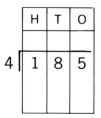

There are two quite distinct ways to proceed at this point in the computation; each has its advantages and limitations. One way is to use the method reviewed in section 1 of this chapter, whereby the child reasons that since he has multiplied 4 *tens* by 4, the product is not 16 but 160, so he annexes the necessary 0 and subtracts 160 from 185:

$$\begin{array}{r} 4 \\ 4)\overline{185} \\ -\ 160 \\ \hline 25 \end{array}$$

He then compares the '2' in '25' with the divisor, 4, to check for compliance with the basic division relation. The other approach is to record *only* the '16' (not the '0'), subtract 16 from 18, compare '2' with 4 to check the basic division relation, and then bring down the '5':

$$\begin{array}{r} 4 \\ 4)\overline{185} \\ -\ 16 \\ \hline 2 \end{array} \qquad \begin{array}{r} 4 \\ 4)\overline{185} \\ -\ 16 \\ \hline 2 \end{array} \ (2<4) \qquad \begin{array}{r} 4 \\ 4)\overline{185} \\ -\ 16 \\ \hline 25 \end{array}$$

Multiply;   Compare   Bring down '5'
subtract

Both methods can be made equally reasonable to children with sufficient reference to manipulative activities. The first is mathematically a little more straightforward (i.e., uses fewer "tricks") and is preferred by some on that basis; the second generally involves conscious manipulation with smaller numbers at each step, which is why some prefer it. The first method is sometimes introduced first and later replaced by the second.

Two special cases should be included in practice exercises. Although these should not be treated as being essentially different, some discussion accompanied by manipulative activity may be necessary, or at least helpful, when they are being presented. The first of these is the type of problem in which the remainder at the first step (or any step prior to the final one) is zero:

$$
\begin{array}{r}
41 \\
4\overline{)165} \\
-160 \\
\hline
5 \\
4 \\
\hline
1
\end{array}
\qquad
\begin{array}{r}
481 \\
3\overline{)1445} \\
-1200 \\
\hline
245 \\
240 \\
\hline
5 \\
3 \\
\hline
2
\end{array}
\qquad
\begin{array}{r}
311 \\
6\overline{)1867} \\
-1800 \\
\hline
67 \\
60 \\
\hline
7 \\
6 \\
\hline
1
\end{array}
$$

The second special case is concerned with problems in which zeroes occur in the quotient in one or more places after the first division:

$$
\begin{array}{r}
208 \\
4\overline{)835} \\
-800 \\
\hline
35 \\
32 \\
\hline
3
\end{array}
\qquad
\begin{array}{r}
3010 \\
6\overline{)18062} \\
-18000 \\
\hline
62 \\
60 \\
\hline
2
\end{array}
\qquad
\begin{array}{r}
300 \\
7\overline{)2105} \\
-2100 \\
\hline
5
\end{array}
\qquad
\begin{array}{r}
4002 \\
9\overline{)36025} \\
-36000 \\
\hline
25 \\
18 \\
\hline
7
\end{array}
$$

A rather common error children make in such problems is forgetting to record these zeroes in the quotient. Use of the place value chart kind of grid sometimes helps to prevent or correct this. Another technique is to identify the place of the first partial quotient and then mark off each remaining place with boxes before continuing the computation:

$$
\begin{array}{r}
3\,\boxed{}\boxed{}\boxed{} \\
6\overline{)18062}
\end{array}
$$

Since the first partial quotient is 3 *thousands,* there must be a digit in each of hundreds, tens, and ones places; the boxes serve as a reminder of this.

Checking, by the usual method of multiplying quotient times divisor and adding the remainder to see that the result is the dividend, is always a good habit, of course.

Multiples of 10 as Divisors. Two techniques were mentioned in the Mathematical Review section of this chapter: *estimating partial quotients,* which is unnecessary when divisors are less than 10 (the "count-ing down" procedure always yields the correct quotient); and *determining the place of the first partial quotient,* which is simple and straightforward when the divisor is less than 10. In the general case, however, both of these are necessary and both are potential sources of difficulty. The two skills can be introduced separately, the easier one first, by first considering divi-sors greater than 9 which contain only one nonzero digit, e.g., 20, 300, 5000. With such divisors, no guessing is necessary, but determining the place of the first partial quotient is "new."

Problems such as $10\overline{)530}$ or $20\overline{)460}$ can be introduced quite early. When multiplication problems such as 53 × 10 or 23 × 20 are considered, *readiness* for subsequent work with the corresponding division can be provided by recalling the inverse relationship. That is, because 53 × 10 = 530, it must be that 530 ÷ 10 = 53; and 460 ÷ 20 = 23 because 23 × 20 = 460. Both equations and computational forms can be used, although at this point, the division should be viewed only as a consequence of the multiplication, so the long form is unnecessary:

$$\begin{array}{c} 53 \\ \times\ 10 \\ \hline 530 \end{array} \quad \rightarrow \quad 10\overline{)530} \qquad \begin{array}{c} 23 \\ \times\ 20 \\ \hline 460 \end{array} \quad \rightarrow \quad 20\overline{)460}$$

Most of the activities used to solve the divisions directly parallel previously suggested ones. Measurement problems with fairly large divi-sors and small quotients can provide an effective, though limited, manipu-lative introduction, e.g., "If 240 blocks are to be put into boxes of 80 blocks each, how many boxes will be needed?" Dienes blocks (2 flats and 4 longs) can be easily manipulated, trading the flats for longs and then partitioning the 24 longs into piles of 80 (8 longs) each. Such problems, which can include

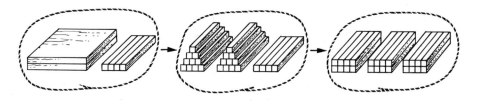

remainder situations if that concept has been developed, should be accom-panied by the various standard and expanded computational forms, including those for the related multiplication. Children should be encouraged to look for a relationship between 240 ÷ 80 = 3 and the fundamental fact 24 ÷ 8 = 3. To digress slightly, we note here that recognizing that 240 = 24 × 10 and 80 = 8 × 10 can lead to intuitive understanding of the very important general-ization that if $a \div b = c$, then

$$(a \times k) \div (b \times k) = c \qquad (k \neq 0)$$

and its converse. Although this theorem is not sufficient to explain all problems of the type we are considering here, it has numerous applications with whole numbers, fractions, and decimals, and is well worth exploring with children at this point, when it is convenient to do so. To this end, exercises such as these can be considered and discussed:

$8 \div 2 = 4$ $80 \div 20 = \underline{\quad}$ $800 \div 200 = \underline{\quad}$

$15 \div 3 = \underline{\quad}$ $150 \div 30 = \underline{\quad}$ $1500 \div 300 = \underline{\quad}$

$$5 \overline{)35}^{\,7} \qquad\qquad 50\overline{)350} \qquad\qquad 500\overline{)3500}$$

$$\overset{\nearrow \qquad \nwarrow}{\quad} \qquad\qquad \overset{\nearrow \qquad \nwarrow}{\quad}$$

$$5 \times 10 \quad 35 \times 10 \qquad\qquad 5 \times 100 \quad 35 \times 100$$

A useful equivalent of this theorem is that if $a \div b = c$ and if a and b are each divisible by a nonzero number k, then

$$(a \div k) \div (b \div k) = c$$

This, too, can be explored and discussed, e.g., given a problem such as $8\overline{)24}$, for which children know the quotient, ask what happens if we divide each of 8 and 24 by 2 (or 4, or 8) and *then* divide:

$$(8 \div 2) \, \overline{)24 \div 2} \rightarrow 4\overline{)12}$$

$$(8 \div 4) \, \overline{)24 \div 4} \rightarrow 2\overline{)6}$$

$$(8 \div 8) \, \overline{)24 \div 8} \rightarrow 1\overline{)3}$$

Similarly,

$$80\overline{)240} \rightarrow (80 \div 10) \, \overline{)240 \div 10} \rightarrow 8\overline{)24}^{\,3}$$

Many difficult computations can be simplified by using this generalization, e.g., given $192\overline{)3848}$, a child who understands this theorem can divide both terms by 2 (or 4, or 8) before dividing, which results in an easier problem. While this process yields the correct quotient, the remainder will differ unless treated as a fraction or unless *multiplied* by the same numbers:

$$192\overline{)3848} \qquad 96\overline{)924} \qquad 48\overline{)962} \qquad 24\overline{)481} \qquad 24\overline{)481}^{\,20}$$

$192\overline{)3848}$	$96\overline{)924}$	$48\overline{)962}$	$24\overline{)481}$	$24\overline{)481}$
	dividing	dividing	dividing	480
	by 2	by 2 again	by 2 again	1

Thus the quotient for $192\overline{)3848}$ is 20, and the remainder is $1 \times 2 \times 2 \times 2 = 8$. Now returning to the problems at hand, the place value grid and the technique of covering up extraneous places are useful in solving a problem such as $20)\overline{647}$:

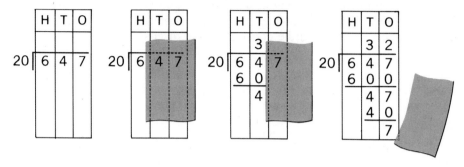

The new skill to be developed at this stage is that of determining the place of the first partial quotient (the rest is rather simple extension of earlier skills). Multiplying the divisor by successive powers of 10, which can be done mentally, can be used effectively, together with the basic division relation, to determine the place of the first partial quotient. Two activities are suggested, before this technique, which was discussed in the mathematical review section, is introduced: review and practice of the simple skill of multiplying a number by 10, 100, 1000, . . . ; and, using simple and familiar examples such as $3)\overline{58}$, comparison of several multiples of the divisor with the dividend, e.g.,

$3 \times 5 = 15$ and $15 < 58.$ Is the quotient *at least* 5?
$3 \times 10 = 30$ and $30 < 58.$ Is the quotient *at least* 10?
$3 \times 20 = 60$ and $60 > 58.$ Can the quotient be at least 20?

How do we know the quotient is between 10 and 20?

$$\begin{array}{r} 10 \\ 3\overline{)58} \\ -30 \leftarrow 10 \times 3 \\ \hline 28 \end{array} \qquad \begin{array}{r} 20 \\ 3\overline{)58} \\ -60 \leftarrow 20 \times 3 \\ \hline \end{array}$$

Some children will require many such examples to recognize (a) that the product of the quotient and the divisor is never greater than the dividend, and (b) that if *n* times the divisor is less than or equal to the dividend, then the quotient is at least *n*. A variety of questions should be asked. Again referring to $3)\overline{58}$, for example,

Is the quotient *at least* 19? Why?
Is the quotient at least 15 but less than 16? Why?
Is the quotient at least 1 but less than 100? Why?
Is the quotient greater than or equal to 10? 18? 19? 20? Why?
Is the quotient between 15 and 20? Why?

Larger dividends and divisors can be considered and powers of ten can replace numbers like 15, 16, 18, and so on, in the questions. In considering $8\overline{)2345}$, for example,

Is the quotient at least 1? 10? 100? 1000? Why?
Is the quotient between 1 and 10? Between 10 and 100?
Between 100 and 1000?

The use of inequality symbols is helpful, but not entirely necessary. If they are to be used, the number line can be helpful to give meaning — expressed in various ways — to mathematical sentences such as these:

(a) $1 < 7$ and $7 < 10$.
(b) $1 < 7 < 10$ (i.e., 7 is *between* 1 and 10).
(c) $1 < n < 10$.   (i.e., n is a number between 1 and 10;
                           n may be 2, 3, 4, 5, 6, 7, 8, or 9).
(d) $8 \leqslant n$ (i.e., 8 is less than *or* equal to n;
                           n may be 8, 9, 10, 11, . . . ;
                           n is *at least* 8;
                           n is greater than or equal to 8).
(e) $8 \leqslant n < 12$ (i.e., n is at least 8 but is less than 12;
                           n may be 8, 9, 10, or 11).
(f) $10 \leqslant q < 100$ (i.e., q is at least 10 but is less than 100).

Whether such *symbols* are used with children or whether the corresponding *words* are used, children should be led to recognize that all numbers between 2 successive powers of 10 have the same number of digits, e.g.:

If $1 \leqslant n < 10$,   then 'n' has one digit.
If $10 \leqslant n < 100$,   then 'n' has two digits.
If $100 \leqslant n < 1000$,   then 'n' has three digits.
                           etc.

Then, given examples such as $70\overline{)4325}$, children can be led to quickly determine that the quotient is at least 10 but is less than 100, so it will have 2 digits; a few exercises of this type may be helpful:

$$\begin{array}{r} \square \\ 70\overline{)4325} \\ \underline{70} \end{array}$$
     ← $1 \times 70 \leqslant 4325$, so the quotient is at least 1 and will have least one digit.

$$70\overline{)4325}$$
$$\underline{700} \quad \leftarrow \quad 10 \times 70 \leqslant 4325, \text{ so the quotient is at least 10 and will have at}$$
least 2 digits.

$$70\overline{)4325}$$
$$\underline{7000} \quad \leftarrow \quad 100 \times 70 > 4325, \text{ so the quotient is less than 100; it cannot}$$
have 3 or more digits.

Children quickly discover that this process can be abbreviated by writing (or imagining) the largest possible number of the form 70 . . . 0 under the dividend such that subtraction can occur, e.g.:

$$70\overline{)4325} \qquad 70\overline{)4325}$$
$$\underline{700}$$

This, in turn, can be further abbreviated later by considering only the first digit ('7') of the divisor and the first digit ('4') or the first two digits ('43') of the dividend.

Again, a variety of practice exercises should be provided at this stage, including problems with divisors or quotients of 2, 3, or more digits, and problems with both zero and nonzero remainders (both "intermediate" and final).

The General Case: Estimating Quotient Figures.   When problems of the preceding types are understood, the only new skill that needs to be developed is that of estimating partial quotients. The teaching of this skill has been the subject of considerable research. The major question has been: Which of several possible methods for estimating quotients is "best"? This, in turn, prompts three considerations: (1) Which method is *easiest*? (2) Which method is most *accurate,* i.e., most likely to yield the correct quotient? And (3) since overestimating is more quickly and easily detected after the multiplication step than is underestimating, which method is least likely to lead to underestimating?

All of these methods, basically, involve rounding the given divisor or dividend (or both) and using the fundamental fact suggested by the resulting significant (nonzero) digits. Numerous methods have been advocated —none totally reliable—and taught to children over the years. Before examining two of these, one point should be stressed: No matter what method children are taught, continued practice with the algorithm usually teaches them to discover their own modifications of it. The *simplest* method is probably the best, since most children will learn, by themselves, to improve upon it anyway.

The two most popular methods of quotient estimation are (1) The *apparent* method, in which the divisor and dividend are rounded "down" according to the first digit (that with largest place value) in the divisor and the first one or two digits in the dividend; and (2) the *rounding* method, in which the divisor and dividend are rounded to the *nearest* multiple of 10, determined by the digit in the second or third place. For example, the first partial quotient figure is determined as follows by these methods:

1. $732 \overline{)48376}$ Apparent: $7 \overline{)48}^{\,6}$ Correct figure: 6

   Rounding: $7 \overline{)48}^{\,6}$

2. $363 \overline{)9874}$ Apparent: $3 \overline{)9}^{\,3}$ Correct figure: 2

   Rounding: $4 \overline{)10}^{\,2}$

3. $264 \overline{)83572}$ Apparent: $2 \overline{)8}^{\,4}$ Correct figure: 3

   Rounding: $3 \overline{)8}^{\,2}$

Sometimes either method gives the correct result, sometimes neither does, and sometimes one does but the other doesn't. One common variation on each method is to use the fundamental fact whose dividend is *nearest* that obtained by the manipulation above. In the first example, since 48 is closer to 49 than 42, the fact $7 \overline{)49}$ would be used (giving an incorrect estimate in this case); and in the third example, since 8 is closer to 9 than to 6, the fact $3 \overline{)9}$ would be used, in the rounding case, which would be the correct choice. Note that the apparent method never leads to an underestimate, and is the simpler to use, whereas the rounding method is more accurate, but can produce either overestimates or underestimates. Considering these facts, the apparent method is generally preferred, at least as a beginning technique. Teaching children to do the necessary rounding for either method can be made meaningful via the number line, and later modified by considering the digit following the significant one: If that digit is 0, 1, 2, 3, or 4, the significant digit is used: otherwise it is increased by one:

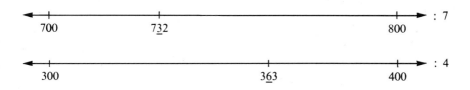

The Repeated Subtraction Algorithm

The repeated subtraction division algorithm is frequently taught in lieu of, or in addition to, the quotient estimation one. The basic division relation, the distributive generalization, estimating partial quotients, and determining their places are all relatively immaterial here. The basic mathematical ideas underlying this approach are, one, that a quotient can always be determined by repeatedly subtracting the divisor from the dividend, and two, that repeatedly subtracting a number b from a number a n times is equivalent to subtracting $(n \times b)$ from a. There is essentially no reason to develop the algorithm in stages—the only restriction on a child's ability to perform a particular computation is his ability to do the required multiplication and subtraction.

The basic principle of repeated subtraction can be illustrated by the fundamental fact $3\overline{)18}$. Interpreting this in the *measurement* sense, a child would think, essentially, "How many 3s are there in 18?"—i.e., if a set of 18 elements is partitioned into subsets of 3 elements each, how many such subsets can be formed? Recall from Chapter 5 that the answer to this

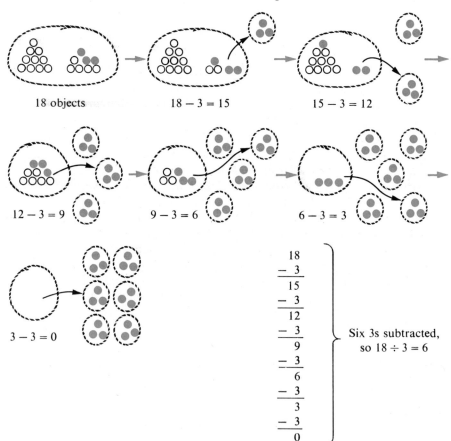

18 objects $18 - 3 = 15$ $15 - 3 = 12$

$12 - 3 = 9$ $9 - 3 = 6$ $6 - 3 = 3$

$3 - 3 = 0$

$$\begin{array}{r} 18 \\ -\ 3 \\ \hline 15 \\ -\ 3 \\ \hline 12 \\ -\ 3 \\ \hline 9 \\ -\ 3 \\ \hline 6 \\ -\ 3 \\ \hline 3 \\ -\ 3 \\ \hline 0 \end{array}$$

Six 3s subtracted, so $18 \div 3 = 6$

question can be determined, using physical objects, by starting with a collection of 18 things and removing 3 at a time, until either there are no objects left or there are fewer than 3 objects left. The quotient is the number of subsets of 3 that were removed, and the remainder is the number of objects (0, 1, 2) that are left. Physical manipulation can, of course, be replaced, or accompanied, by repeated subtractions.

A shorter approach involves taking away more than one subset of 3 at a time (or subtracting a multiple of 3 greater than 3 itself). There are, of course, many possible ways to do this.

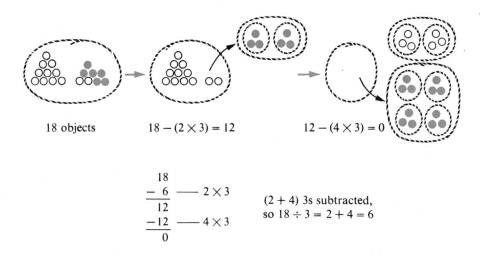

18 objects	$18 - (2 \times 3) = 12$	$12 - (4 \times 3) = 0$

$$
\begin{array}{r}
18 \\
- \ 6 \quad \text{---} \quad 2 \times 3 \\
\hline
12 \\
-12 \quad \text{---} \quad 4 \times 3 \\
\hline
0
\end{array}
$$

(2 + 4) 3s subtracted,
so $18 \div 3 = 2 + 4 = 6$

Although for larger dividends or divisors, or both, this *basic* interpretation is unchanged, given an example such as $264\overline{)89064}$, it is clearly unproductive to consider subtracting 264, or 2 or 3 times 264. Instead, the child can be led to think of a series of questions paralleling those of the quotient estimation algorithm that are used to determine the place of the first partial quotient:

Can I subtract 1×264 (264)?	(Yes)
Can I subtract 10×264 (2640)?	(Yes)
Can I subtract 100×264 (26,400)?	(Yes)
Can I subtract 1000×264 (264,000)?	(No)

Since it is possible to subtract (100×264) from 89,064, but it is not possible to subtract (1000×264), it is reasonable to ask, then, "Can I subtract (200×264)? (300×264)? (400×264)? . . . ? (900×264)?" *Tentative* answers to these questions can be obtained by the same kind of guessing techniques used for the quotient estimation algorithm. That is, rounding 264 and 89064 either to 200 and 80,000 or to 300 and 90,000, and then considering the related fundamental facts $(2\overline{)8}$ or $3\overline{)9})$, suggests that either

400 or 300 264s can be subtracted. *Conclusive* answers to the question can only be determined by multiplication:

$$400 \times 264 = 105{,}600 \quad \text{and} \quad 105{,}600 > 89064$$

so it is not possible to subtract 400 264s; but

$$300 \times 264 = 79200 \quad \text{and} \quad 79200 \leqslant 89064,$$

so it *is* possible to subtract 300 264's:

$$
\begin{array}{r}
264\,)\overline{89064} \\
- 79200 \leftarrow 300 \times 264 \\
\hline
9864
\end{array}
$$

Checking to see that it is not possible now to subtract another hundred 264s (26400), the child repeats the questions, using multiples of 10×264: "Can I subtract (10×264)? (20×264)? . . . ? (90×264)?" Trial and error establishes that it is possible to subtract at most 30×264 or 7920:

$$
\begin{array}{r}
264\,)\overline{89064} \\
- 79200 \leftarrow 300 \times 264 \\
\hline
9864 \\
- 7920 \leftarrow 30 \times 264 \\
\hline
1944
\end{array}
$$

Again repeating the questions with multiples of 1×264, i.e.: "Can I now subtract (1×264)? . . . ? (9×264)?" the child determines, by trial and error, that it is possible to subtract (7×264), but no more:

$$
\begin{array}{r}
264\,)\overline{89064} \\
- 79200 \leftarrow 300 \times 264 \\
\hline
9864 \\
- 7920 \leftarrow 30 \times 264 \\
\hline
1944 \\
- 1848 \leftarrow 7 \times 264 \\
\hline
96 \quad\quad 337 \times 264
\end{array}
$$

Thus a total of

$$(300 \times 264) + (30 \times 264) + (7 \times 264)$$

or $\quad (300 + 30 + 7) \times 264$

or $\quad (337 \times 264)$

has been subtracted, with 96 remaining. So the quotient is 337 and the remainder is 96.

No other skills are involved in the repeated subtraction division algorithm.

A Comparison of the Two Algorithms

Which algorithm — quotient estimation or repeated subtraction — should be taught? This is a question frequently raised. Repeated subtraction is, perhaps, easiest, since it does not require extensive understanding of the relatively complex mathematical generalizations that underlie the quotient estimation algorithm, nor is careful sequential development of the algorithm necessary through several stages. The problem of zeroes in the quotient, which is relatively difficult for children using quotient estimation, is quite simple with repeated subtraction (compare the solution of $24\overline{)48123}$ by each method, for example). And, also, if a child underestimates a partial quotient using repeated subtraction, the consequence is more easily corrected. For example, if in the first step of $264\overline{)89064}$, a child estimates that he can subtract at most (200×264), he can rectify his error by subtracting another 100×264, which involves a relatively simple maneuver compared with the erasing and remultiplying needed with quotient estimation:

$$
\begin{array}{r}
264\overline{)89064} \\
- 52800 \quad\quad 200 \times 264 \\
\hline
36264 \\
- 26400 \quad\quad 100 \times 264 \\
\hline
9864
\end{array}
$$

$$\vdots$$

Other factors need to be considered however. The repeated subtraction algorithm is essentially based on the measurement concept and the quotient estimation algorithm is based on partition. Thus it is more natural for children to use one algorithm than the other depending upon which type of problem situation exists. Research shows that children who can use both tend, in fact, to use repeated subtraction for measurement problems and quotient estimation for partition problems. Since both measurement and partition situations occur in problems, it can be argued that children should perhaps learn both algorithms. This, however, imposes a problem for some children. Many who can comprehend and succeed with repeated subtraction have considerable difficulty with quotient estimation. The teacher should recognize that while some children whose initial instruction has been with repeated subtraction can subsequently learn quotient estimation, others cannot. Finally, extensions of the division algorithm, in which the remainder is itself divided so that either fractions or decimals (or both) are used in expressing the quotient, are easier to rationalize with quotient estimation than with repeated subtraction.

Projects, Questions, and Suggested Activities

1. Try describing either of the division algorithms in general terms as was done for the other algorithms, e.g., $AB\overline{)CDEF}$.

2. Use a textbook series to trace the sequence of its development of one of the algorithms through the grades. In what sequence are new extensions developed? What strategies are used at each stage?

3. Use a set of Dienes blocks to show how to add, subtract, or divide in a base other than 10. What about multiplication? For division, use a small divisor and the partition interpretation.

4. Make a set of "Napier's bones" as described in some of the suggested readings. Practice using them and then demonstrate their use to your class.

5. Look up some unconventional algorithms (several are listed in the suggested readings, and most current mathematics books for elementary teachers describe some). Once you fully understand how and why they work, plan an enrichment lesson using one of them and try it with a child.

6. Make up a fairly comprehensive diagnostic computation test covering one operation, from fundamental facts to the most general kind of problem. Try it with a child and analyze his work. Similarly, make up a problem-solving test (word problems) covering all four operations and try it with a child.

Suggested Readings

Boykin, Wilfred E. "The Russian Peasant Algorithm: Rediscovery and Extension." *The Arithmetic Teacher,* January 1973, pp. 29–32.

> Variations on an old multiplication algorithm (sometimes called "doubling and halving") which middle-grade children usually enjoy. In the same issue, see also Reardin's article (pp. 33–35) for an explanation of the algorithm.

Brumfiel, Charles, and Vance, Irvin. "On Whole Number Computation." *The Arithmetic Teacher,* April 1969, pp. 253–57.

> Some interesting ideas from "The Trachtenberg System" for rapid mental computation, with suggestions for possible use in remedial teaching. In the same issue, Dilley and Rucker (pp. 306–8) provide some suggestions for taking the guesswork out of division during beginning instruction.

Carman, Robert A., and Carman, Marilyn J. "Number Patterns." *The Arithmetic Teacher,* December 1970, pp. 637–39.

> Forty ways to make addition and multiplication drill interesting!

Gardner, Martin. "Mathematical Games." *Scientific American,* March 1973, pp. 110–13.

> Describes "Napier's bones" and a related device.

Hamilton, E. W. "Subtraction by the 'Dribble Method'." *The Arithmetic Teacher,* May 1971, pp. 346–47.

Still another subtraction algorithm. Try it. Don't miss the editor's note.

Johnson, Paul B. "Finding the Missing Addend, or Checkbook Subtraction." *The Arithmetic Teacher,* November 1972, pp. 540–42.

The Austrian algorithm for solving problems of the form $a - (b + c + d) = \square$.

King, Irv. "Giving Meaning to the Addition Algorithm." *The Arithmetic Teacher,* May 1972, pp. 345–48.

A case for blocks like the Dienes MAB. Adaptable to other algorithms. In the same issue, see Cacka's description (pp. 349–54) of the array model for the multiplication algorithm.

Quast, W. G. "Method or Justification?" *The Arithmetic Teacher,* December 1972, pp. 617–22.

An analysis of important distinctions between algorithms and expanded computational forms. All four operations are considered. In the same issue, Zweng (pp. 623–27) makes a strong case for teaching division as multiplication rather than separately, based on the relative importance of problem solving and computational skill. Two good articles.

Sanders, Walter W. "Let's Go One Step Farther in Addition." *The Arithmetic Teacher,* October 1971, pp. 413–15.

A good technique to speed up the addition algorithm. Try it.

Sausjord, Gunnar. "What Is the Complementary Method of Subtraction?" *The Arithmetic Teacher,* May 1963, pp. 139–40.

A concise explanation of the method and an argument for using it.

Swart, William L. "Teaching the Division-by-Subtraction Process." *The Arithmetic Teacher,* January 1972, pp. 71–75.

Repeated subtraction as done by children at different levels of comprehension.

Traub, Raymond G. "Napier's Rods: Practice with Multiplication." *The Arithmetic Teacher,* May 1969, pp. 363–64.

Describing this old but still very interesting device for rapid multiplication. In the same issue are two articles on division: McLean (pp. 398–400) suggests an estimating technique for the repeated subtraction algorithm, and Schloff (pp. 403–4) describes a semiabstract representation for the quotient estimation algorithm.

Travers, Kenneth J. "Computation: Low Achiever's Stumbling Block or Stepping Stone?" *The Arithmetic Teacher,* November 1969, pp. 523–28.

Ways to involve students in mathematical problem solving in spite of their computational weaknesses via tables, charts, "slide rules," calculators, and so on.

7. Teaching Number Theory

1. What Is Number Theory and Why Teach It?

Topics from the theory of numbers have appeared with increasing frequency in elementary school textbooks, mathematical enrichment books for children, and the professional literature of elementary mathematics education during the past two decades. Before we consider the reasons for this, we will briefly examine the theory's general nature. The theory of numbers, or *number theory,* is an ancient branch of mathematics concerned mainly with certain properties of numbers. Specifically, the theory deals with the *integers.* Here, its use will be restricted to the *whole numbers* and the properties considered are mainly those related to multiplication (and division). A few familiar topics from elementary number theory are *primes* and *composites, factors* or *divisors, multiples, divisibility,* and *modular arithmetic.*

Number theory is regarded by many as basically "useless." There is perhaps some justification for this attitude, inasmuch as the theory lends itself to the solution of relatively few practical problems. But the study of such "pure," "impractical" subject matter has a strong appeal to many, and, almost in spite of itself, can lead to some *very* practical results. (At least two major mathematical topics evolved essentially from investigations in the theory of numbers: the theory of functions of complex variables grew out of the study of the distribution of primes, and investigations of "Fermat's last theorem" led to the theory of algebraic numbers.)

Topics such as complex variables and algebraic numbers are admittedly of no concern to most elementary teachers, but there *are* some very practical reasons for studying number theory in the elementary school. At least two topics, finding the *least common multiple* of two numbers and finding the *greatest common divisor* of two numbers, can be effectively used in teaching computational procedures with fractions. Many of the ideas studied provide intuitive background for the study of algebra. A third, more important reason, is that problems in number theory are easy to understand with very little background and lend themselves to solution through relatively unsophisticated methods; they provide, therefore, an excellent opportunity to develop, through discovery methods, mathematical and scientific problem-solving skills while simultaneously providing much drill in the context of learning new and interesting things. Finally, number theory, again because it can be studied in some depth very intuitively (as well as analytically), is a rich source of recreational mathematics. Through number theory, then, children can gain much insight into mathematics while getting valuable practice on skills — and having fun.

2. Mathematical Review

The subject matter of number theory is extensive and varied; we will only review here, however, those most rudimentary concepts that can either be taught directly to elementary school children or should be understood by their teachers. Interested readers can find many extensions in the references at the end of the chapter. With a few exceptions, we will omit proofs of generalizations, assuming one of two extremes — that they are quite easy and have probably been, or could be, provided by elementary teachers, or that they are too complicated to include here.

Factors and Multiples

A fundamental definition in number theory is the familiar meaning of "factor": A number a is a *factor* of a number b, if there is some number k such that $ka = b$. (We use the word "number" and variables, a, b, k, and so on, in this chapter to mean *whole* number). The word *divisor* is synonymous with *factor,* and if a is a factor of b, then b is said to be a *multiple* of a. The expressions *a divides b* and *b is divisible by a* mean also that a is a factor of b, and the notation $a\,|\,b$ is used to express this basic relationship. Many important generalizations, some quite obvious, follow directly from this definition and from rudimentary structural properties of the whole number system:

1. Every number is a factor of 0 $(a\,|\,0)$.
2. Every number is a factor of itself $(a\,|\,a)$.
3. 1 divides every number $(1\,|\,a)$.
4. If a divides b, then a also divides every multiple of b. (If $a\,|\,b$, then $a\,|\,bc$ for all numbers c.)
5. If a divides both b and c, then a divides the sum of b and c. (If $a\,|\,b$ and $a\,|\,c$, then $a\,|\,b+c$; furthermore if $b \geqslant c$, then $a\,|\,b-c$.)
6. Combining 4 and 5 above, if a divides both b and c, then a divides the sum of any multiples of b and c. (If $a\,|\,b$ and $a\,|\,c$, then $a\,|\,kb+mc$; if $kb \geqslant mc$, then also $a\,|\,kb-mc$.)

7. If a divides b, then a is less than b unless either $a = b$ or $b = 0$. (If $a|b$, $a \neq b$, and $b \neq 0$, then $a \leq b$.)
8. If a divides b and also b divides a, then a and b are identical. (If $a|b$ and $b|a$, then $a = b$.)
9. If $a|b$, then $a|a + b$; conversely if $a|a + b$, then $a|b$.
10. If $a > 1$ and a divides b, then a does not divide the successor of b. (If $a|b$, then $a \nmid b + 1$.)

Two is a very special divisor: If $2|a$, then a is called an *even* number; every number which is not even is called an *odd* number. Every even number is of the form $2k$ and every odd number is of the form $2k + 1$ (or $2k - 1$). Zero is, of course even, one is odd, and the evens and odds alternate in the natural sequence of numbers. If two numbers a and b are both even or both odd, they are said to be of the same *parity*. The relative parity of numbers is frequently used in logical reasoning and in game strategy. The parity of the sum and product of two numbers is dependent upon the parity of the numbers, as given in these two tables, where a and a' are any even numbers (E) and b and b' are any odd numbers (O):

+	a'	b'		$\times$	a'	b'
a	E	O		a	E	E
b	O	E		b	E	O

In words, the sum (or difference, when it exists) of two numbers is even if and only if the numbers have the same parity; the product of two numbers is odd if and only if both numbers are odd.

Greatest Common Factor and Least Common Multiple

Every number except zero has a finite number of factors (zero has infinitely many). Many problems depend on determining the set of all factors of a nonzero number or deciding whether one number is a factor of another. There are many ways of doing so. Using the basic definition of the preceding section, a is a factor of b if there is a number k such that $ka = b$; this is equivalent to saying that $b = ka + 0$, which suggests the *basic division relation*. So k, if it exists, can be found by the division algorithm. That is, to determine whether a is a factor of b, divide b by a (if $a \neq 0$). Then a is a factor of b if and only if the remainder is zero. (If $a = 0$, we cannot use division, of course, but we don't need to: Zero is not a factor of any number except itself, since the product of any number a and zero is always zero.) There are numerous familiar (and some not so familiar) "divisibility tests" to replace the division process for answering the question, and several general observations which can be made. One particularly useful one is that the factors of a number occur in *pairs*; if the remainder is zero in the division algorithm, then both the divisor and quotient are factors of the number. Also, one of these factors is less than the square root of the number and the other is greater than the square root. (If the number is a perfect square, of course, its square root is a factor, paired with itself.) Thus, in searching for the set of all factors of a number, it suffices to test as divisors only those numbers that are less than or equal to the square root of the number. This need not be calculated with any great degree of precision for numbers that are not perfect squares. If c is a number that is not a perfect square, it suffices to find a number d such that $d^2 < c$ and $(d+1)^2 > c$. For example, in searching for the set of all factors of 432, we need only divide 432 by numbers up to 20, since $20^2 = 400$, $21^2 = 441$, and $400 < 432 < 441$, so the square root of 432 is less than 21.

The number of factors a number has is of some interest, and several questions can be raised: What number has exactly 1 factor? What number has infinitely many factors? What numbers have exactly 2 factors? Which numbers have an odd number of factors? Another source of interesting problems is finding the sum of a number's factors. The ancient Greeks, who developed much of the theory of numbers, often associated numbers with physical or metaphysical attributes, and we still use some of their terms, e.g., square number, triangular number, perfect number, deficient number, abundant number, and amicable numbers. If the sum of the divisors of a number n is $2n$, then n is called a perfect number. The first perfect number is 6, and one of many famous unsolved problems is to determine whether any perfect number is odd. If the sum of n's factors is less than $2n$, then n is called *deficient* (e.g., 8), and if that sum is greater than $2n$, then n is an *abundant* number (e.g., 12). Typical, perhaps, of the appeal of "uscless" mathematics to some is this problem: What is the largest number that cannot be expressed as the sum of two (not necessarily distinct) abundant numbers? (The answer, 20,161, was actually found as an exercise to test the capabilities of a small computer. Thus, every number greater than 20,161 is the sum of 2 abundant numbers. For whatever that's worth!)

If we determine the set of all factors of a number a and the set of all factors of a number b, then we can find the set of all *common* factors of the two numbers by determining the intersection of the two sets. For example, the factor set of 36 is {1, 2, 3, 4, 6, 9, 12, 18, 36}, and the factor set of 24 is {1, 2, 3, 4, 6, 8, 12, 24}. The intersection of these sets is {1, 2, 3, 4, 6, 12}. In particular, the *greatest common factor* of 36 and 24 is 12, which is sometimes called their *greatest common divisor* [the abbreviations GCF and GCD are in common use, as are the notations $(36, 24) = 12$, or GCD $(36, 24) = 12$]. The set of *all* common factors of the two numbers is the set of all factors of their GCD, as can be seen in this case. The GCD of three or more numbers can be found by determining the GCD of any pair of them, then the GCD of that number and the third, and so on.

Every pair of numbers has 1 as a common factor. If 1 is the *greatest* common factor, then the numbers are said to be *relatively prime*. For example, GCD (8, 15) = 1, since

$$\{1, 2, 4, 8\} \cap \{1, 3, 5, 15\} = \{1\}$$

Finding the GCD of two numbers can be accomplished in several ways. One is by the so-called Euclidean algorithm. It is based on two generalizations:

1. If $a \mid b$, then GCD $(a, b) = a$.
2. If $a = bq + r$, then GCD $(a, b) =$ GCD $(a, b, r) =$ GCD (b, r).

The first of these should become clear by considering any specific case. For example, $4 \mid 8$, so 4 is a divisor of both 4 and 8, and is, of course, the largest divisor of itself and thus the largest possible *common* divisor of itself and *any* number, including 8. The second generalization follows from one of those previously mentioned (if $a \mid b$ and $a \mid c$, then $a \mid kb - mc$ if $kb \geq mc$) and can again be readily seen by an example. Consider this division:

$$
\begin{array}{r}
1 \\
26\overline{)38} \\
-26 \\
\hline
12
\end{array}
$$

Since $12 = 38 - 26$, then any number that divides both 38 and 26, i.e., *each* common divisor of 38 and 26, must also divide $38 - 26$, which is 12. Thus, in particular, GCD (38, 26) = GCD (38, 26, 12), which is the same as GCD (26, 12). Similarly, dividing 26 by 12 establishes that GCD (26, 12) = GCD (12, 2):

$$
\begin{array}{r}
2 \\
12\overline{)26} \\
-24 \\
\hline
2
\end{array}
$$

Since $2 \mid 12$, GCD (12, 2) = 2, so GCD (26, 12) = 2 and GCD (38, 26) = 2. In practice, these successive divisions are normally performed in this format:

$$
\begin{array}{r}
1 \\
26\overline{|38} \\
26 \quad 2 \\
\hline
12|26 \\
24 \quad 6 \\
\hline
2|12 \\
12 \\
\hline
0
\end{array}
$$

It should be clear that such successive divisions inevitably result in a zero remainder ultimately and that the final divisor, i.e., the last nonzero remainder, is the GCD of the original pair of numbers that were divided (38 and 26 here).

Another generalization, widely used in number theory, can be verified by considering the Euclidean algorithm: The GCD of 2 numbers can always be expressed as the difference of some multiples of those numbers, i.e., if $d = $ GCD (a, b), then there exist numbers x and y such that $d = xa - yb$ (or $d = yb - xa$). The numbers x and y, furthermore, are relatively prime. Here, GCD $(38, 26) = 2$, $2 = (3 \times 26) - (2 \times 38)$, and GCD $(3, 2) = 1$.

Common multiples of two numbers are also of interest, and the *least common multiple* (LCM) of two numbers is of particular importance. Every nonzero number, a, has infinitely many multiples, determined by multiplying a in turn by each whole number (the multiples of 3 are 0, 3, 6, 9, 12, 15, . . . , $3n$, . . .). And the set of all common multiples of two numbers is again the intersection of the sets of multiples of each. The LCM, then, is the least *nonzero* number in this intersection set. Each common multiple of two numbers is a multiple of the LCM. If m is the LCM of two numbers a and b, the notation LCM $[a, b] = m$ is commonly used. For example, the set of all multiples of 8 is {0, 8, 16, 24, 32, 40, 48, 56, 64, 72, . . . , $8n$, . . . } and the set of all multiples of 12 is {0, 12, 24, 36, 48, 60, 72, . . . , $12n$, . . . }; the intersection of these is {0, 24, 48, 72, . . . , $24n$, . . . }. The least nonzero number in this set is 24, so LCM $[8, 12] = 24$. A quicker way to find the LCM of a and b is to first find their GCD and then use the generalization that

$$\text{LCM } [a, b] = \frac{ab}{\text{GCD } (a, b)}$$

Thus,

$$\text{LCM } [8, 12] = \frac{8 \times 12}{4} = 24$$

A useful special case is: If $a|b$, then LCM $[a, b] = b$.

Primes and Composites

A prime (whole) number is one which has exactly 2 factors, itself and 1. A composite number, on the other hand, is a nonzero number which has more than two factors. Zero and 1 are neither prime nor composite according to these definitions (zero has infinitely many factors and 1 has only one factor). The least prime — and the only even one — is 2. Prime numbers are at the heart of number theory, and most of the preceding techniques, such as finding the GCD or LCM of two numbers, can be simplified by using primes.

The ancient Greeks proved that there are infinitely many primes, but they occur with decreasing frequency and with no regularity. There are 25 primes in the interval from 1 to 100, 21 from 101 to 200, and 16 from 201 to 300; this decrease is irregular, however (there are 17 in the interval from 1401 to 1500!). Two initial exploration questions are: "Is a given number n a prime?" and "What are all the primes from 2 to n?" The irregularity of the primes makes it generally necessary to use the basic division relation (or divisibility tests) to answer the first. For example, to determine whether 417 is prime, we need to determine whether there is at least one divisor of 417 other than itself and 1, by dividing 417 by each of 2, 3, 4, . . . , 416. This of course can be abbreviated by noting that 417 is between 20^2 and 21^2, so it suffices to check only those numbers from 2 through 20. But even this can be abbreviated by noting that every nonzero multiple of a prime is composite, so it suffices to divide 417 by the *primes,* in order, in the interval from 2 through 20. For example, there is no need to divide 417 by 4, a multiple of 2, once we have determined that 2 does not divide 417; since 2 does not divide 417, no multiple of 2 can divide it. Thus we must divide 417 by each of 2, 3, 5, 7, 11, 13, 17, and 19. If none of these is a factor, then 417 is prime. But we find that $3 \mid 417$ (i.e., $417 = 3 \times 139$), so the factors of 417 include 3 and 139; hence it is composite.

To find the number of primes up to a given number, n, a well-known technique is called the Sieve of Eratosthenes: List the numbers from 1 to n and identify the primes in *order*; once a prime has been identified, cross out its remaining multiples. The first number that has not been crossed out must be a prime, so the process is repeated with it. This must be continued up to $\sqrt{n}$. Thereafter, each remaining number is prime. If the numbers are arranged in a 6-row or 6-column array, it will be found that nearly

```
 1    2    3    4    5    6
 7    8    9   10   11   12
13   14   15   16   17   18
19   20   21   22   23   24
25   26   27   28   29   30
31   32   33   34   35   36
37   38   39   40   41   42
43   44   45   46   47   48
49   50   51   52   53   54
55   56   57   58   59   60
61   62   63   64   65   66
67   68   69   70   71   72
73   74   75   76   77   78
79   80   81   82   83   84
85   86   87   88   89   90
91   92   93   94   95   96
97   98   99  100
```

two-thirds of the numbers from 1 to n are crossed out in the first two steps. The process for the primes up to 100 is illustrated here. In detail, the sequence of the procedure is:

Step 1:

Cross out 1 (it is not prime).

Step 2:

Circle 2 (it is the first prime) and cross out the remaining multiples of 2. Note that these occur regularly in columns 2, 4, and 6, and include each number in those columns, except for 2 itself.

Step 3:

The next number not already crossed out is 3, so it is a prime. Although this is obvious in the case of 3, it should be noted that this is *generally* true since if it were not prime it would necessarily be a multiple of some prime less than itself. Cross out the remaining multiples of 3. Again, these occur regularly and include all the remaining numbers in the 3rd column. Another observation which can be made here is that in any such n-column (or n-row) array, if $m | n$, then each number in the m-column (or row) is a multiple of m, as is each number in the k-column (or row) where $m | k$, e.g., each number in columns 2, 4, and 6 is a multiple of 2, and each number in columns 3 and 6 is a multiple of 3.

Step 4:

The next number not crossed out is 5, so it is prime. Circle it and cross out any of its multiples that have not already been crossed out (every fifth number in column 1, beginning with 25, and every fifth number in column 5, beginning with 35).

Step 5:

The next prime is 7; circle it and cross out its multiples, which occur with predictable regularity. Another observation might be made here: If we consider any number n in this array, the number directly below it is $n + 6$ and the number below and to its right (if there is one) is $n + 7$. Hence if we begin at 7, we can think "down 1, right 1" to find the next multiple of 7, without multiplying. In the case of 7, this can be repeated up to 42, which occurs in the final (right-most) column; from there we can imagine another copy of the array to its right; again moving "down 1, right 1" leads us to 49, which is the next multiple of 7.

Step 6:

The next number that has not been crossed out is 11. Not only is *it* prime, but since it is greater than $\sqrt{100}$, so is *each* remaining number. Consider 97, for example. Since 97 is less than 100, its square root is less than $\sqrt{100}$, i.e., is less than 10. If 97 were not prime, it would have at least one factor in the interval from 2 to 10, i.e., it would be a multiple of at least one such number. But each multiple of 2, 3, 4, 5, . . . , 10 has already been crossed out, so since 97 has not been crossed out it must be prime. The same argument holds for each remaining number.

There have been many proofs that the number of primes is infinite. One of the classical ones, whose origins are uncertain, although it was reported by Euclid (about 300 B.C.), is based on one of the generalizations we have already considered: If $a > 1$ and if $a \mid b$, then $a \nmid b + 1$ (if we divide $b + 1$ by a, we will have a remainder of 1, not zero). If we were to assume there was a greatest prime, p, then we have the following contradiction: Consider the number n formed by multiplying each of the primes, then adding 1 to that product: $n = (2 \cdot 3 \cdot 5 \cdot \ldots \cdot p) + 1$. Clearly n is (much) larger than p, so by our *assumption* n must be composite. But each of the existing primes divides $(2 \cdot 3 \cdot 4 \cdot \ldots \cdot p)$, so none can divide n, which is 1 more than this number. Since n is composite, it must have at least one prime factor, but we have seen that *no* prime, according to our *assumption* divides p. Hence our assumption was wrong—there is no greatest prime.

A basic generalization about primes is appropriately called the *fundamental theorem of arithmetic*. It asserts that every composite number can be expressed, in exactly one way, as a product of primes (we have used this in some of the preceding arguments). The usual proof of the fundamental theorem rests on another important theorem, sometimes called the *prime product theorem*. It says that if a prime divides the product of two or more numbers, then it divides at least one of the numbers. When a number is expressed as a product of primes, that expression is called the prime factorization of the number. It can be obtained in various ways and of course the prime factors can be listed in any order. Usually, prime factorizations are obtained by repeated divisions. For example, to factor 135, first divide it by any *one* of its prime factors, then divide that quotient by any of *its* prime factors; continue until a prime quotient is obtained:

$$
\begin{array}{lll}
45 & 15 & 5 \\
3\overline{)135} & 3\overline{)45} & 3\overline{)15}
\end{array}
\qquad
\begin{aligned}
135 &= 3 \times 45 \\
&= 3 \times 3 \times 15 \\
&= 3 \times 3 \times 3 \times 5 \qquad \text{or} \qquad 3^3 \times 5
\end{aligned}
$$

The fundamental theorem provides alternate ways to find the GCD and LCM of two numbers: GCD (126, 135), for example, can be found by examining the prime factorizations of the numbers:

$$126 = 2 \times (3 \times 3) \times 7$$
$$135 = 3 \times (3 \times 3) \times 5$$

GCD $(126, 135) = 9$

Similarly LCM [126, 135] must contain all the prime factors of both numbers, without repetitions. Since 3×3 is common to both, it is listed only once:

$$\text{LCM } [126, 135] = (2 \times 3 \times 3 \times 7) \times 3 \times 5 \quad \text{or} \quad 2 \cdot 3^3 \cdot 5 \cdot 7$$

Two interesting conjectures should be mentioned before we continue: The first is that there are infinitely many "prime twins," that is primes that differ by 2, e.g., 3 and 5, 5 and 7, 11 and 13, . . . , 71 and 73, . . . , 1061 and 1063, . . . , 209,267 and 209,269. . . . The second, called Goldbach's conjecture, is that every even number greater than 4 is the sum of two odd primes. Neither has ever been proven.

Divisibility Tests

Factoring numbers is facilitated when it can be determined by inspection whether a number is divisible by another. Such "divisibility tests" exist and are well known by many children, but frequently without knowing why they work. We will briefly review those for the numbers up to 10 (except seven).

A number is divisible by 2 if its one's-place digit is even. There are numerous ways to verify this fact, which is usually discovered quite early by children. One way is to use the notation $ABCD$ as an arbitrary 4-digit numeral, i.e., as an abbreviation for

$$a \times 10^3 + b \times 10^2 + c \times 10^1 + d \times 10^0$$

where a, b, c, and d are each numbers less than 10 and $a \neq 0$ (the number of digits is immaterial, of course). Since $2|10$, $2|10^n$ for $n \geq 1$ and also $2|k \times 10^n$ according to our original generalizations about divisibility, so $2|A$, $2|B$, and $2|C$. Thus $2|ABC$. If also $2|D$, i.e., $2|d$, then $2|ABCD$. And of course $2|d$ only if d is even. Since $d < 10$, the number of cases to be considered is simple: 0, 2, 4, 6, and 8.

The same kind of argument holds for the familiar divisibility test for 5, i.e., $5|ABCD$ only if $d = 5$ or $d = 0$. Also, $10|ABCD$ only if $d = 0$.

A number is divisible by 3 if the sum of its digits is divisible by 3, and a number is divisible by 9 if the sum of its digits is divisible by 9. (For example, the sum of the digits of 243,768 is $2+4+3+7+6+8=30$. Thus, since $3|30$, $3|243,768$ and since $9\!\!\not|\,30$, $9\!\!\not|\,243,768$.) Both of these can be verified by noting that every power of ten (except 10^0) is 1 more than a "string of 9s":

$$10 = 9 + 1$$
$$100 = 99 + 1$$
$$1000 = 999 + 1$$
$$\text{etc.}$$

Thus, $ABCD$ can be expressed as

$$a \times (999 + 1) + b \times (99 + 1) + c \times (9 + 1) + d$$

or

$$(a \times 999) + a + (b \times 99) + b + (c \times 9) + c + d$$

and finally as

$$[(a \times 999) + (b \times 99) + (c \times 9)] + (a + b + c + d)$$

Since both 3 and 9 divide any "string of 9s," any multiple of such a "string," and any sum of such multiples,

$$3 \,|\, [(a \times 999) + (b \times 99) + (c \times 9)] \quad \text{and} \quad 9 \,|\, [(a \times 999) + (b \times 99) + (c \times 9)]$$

Hence

$$3 \,|\, [(a \times 999) + (b \times 99) + (c \times 9)] + (a + b + c + d)$$

providing $3 \,|\, (a + b + c + d)$. The same is true for 9.

Tests for 4 and 8 are similar to those for 2 and 5: $4 \,|\, ABCD$ if $4 \,|\, CD$, and $8 \,|\, ABCD$ if $8 \,|\, BCD$. (This test for 8 is practical only for fairly large numbers, of course). Since $4 \,|\, 100$, it divides any multiple of 100, e.g., 726,600; and since, for example, $725,624 = 725,600 + 24$, $4 \,|\, 725,624$ since $4 \,|\, 24$.

A number is divisible by 6 if it is divisible by both 2 and 3, i.e., $6 \,|\, ABCD$ if $3 \,|\, (a + b + c + d)$ and if d is even. (This test is based on the generalization that if $a \,|\, c$ and $b \,|\, c$ and if GCD $(a, b) = 1$, then $ab \,|\, c$. This same generalization can be used to justify the test for 10.)

There are numerous other divisibility tests, some of which are too complex to be very practical, and some, like that for 8, are not always helpful.

Several other topics from number theory will be discussed in the next section but need not be reviewed here.

3. Activities and Materials for Teaching Number Theory

Because most of the topics from number theory involve multiplication or division, relatively few teaching activities can include such topics prior to the introduction of those operations. One exception is the topic of even and odd numbers, which can be introduced quite early; another is that some interesting number sequences can be introduced with only an understanding of addition. Mathematical prerequisites for understanding a given topic should be rather obvious, as should their internal sequencing. Many of the topics are independent of each other and can be explored in any order, and at any time; and no particular order is implied in the listing of suggested activities that follows. In using most of these activities, teachers should primarily emphasize the search for pattern and hidden rules rather than the acquisition of skill. The development of computational skill, discovering some of the pleasures of mathematics, developing some of the fundamental concepts such as that of function, and growth in logical thinking are among the side benefits to be expected when topics in number theory are viewed from the standpoint of searching for patterns. The teacher's role should largely be that of posing problems, asking leading questions, and then letting children explore, raise their own questions, and so on. Many teachers set aside certain times on a regular basis for working on problems of the kind found in number theory, only to find that the children (and frequently the teacher) learn more in these quasi-recreational excursions than in more formal sessions. The activities that follow, in somewhat random order, can at best be regarded as beginnings. Many others can be found by examining some of the references at the end of the chapter, and others may suggest themselves.

Even and Odd Numbers

Children can be introduced to even and odd numbers as soon as they begin to learn the meanings and names of numbers themselves. As they develop numeration and computational skills, the even/odd concept can be extended with occasional specific activities.

Various collections of objects can be arranged in rows of two, for example, and the children asked, How many objects are there? Can they be separated into two subsets of the same size? Then, with the collections arranged randomly, Which collections can be arranged in twos? Which cannot be arranged in twos? How many are left over? Why?

When successive numbers are listed in 2 rows or 2 columns, children can look for patterns:

$$
\begin{array}{ccccc}
1 & 3 & 5 & 7 & 9 \\
2 & 4 & 6 & 8 & 10
\end{array}
\quad \cdots \quad
\begin{array}{cc}
1 & 2 \\
3 & 4 \\
5 & 6 \\
7 & 8 \\
9 & 10 \\
\vdots &
\end{array}
$$

The terms "even" and "odd" can be introduced here. As the list of numbers increases, the 0–2–4–6–8 and 1–3–5–7–9 ending patterns become apparent. Relevant questions at this point are: Is 10 even or odd? What about zero (it's not in the list)? What about 100? 1000? Is there a greatest even number? odd number? a least even number? a least odd number? What is the greatest odd number less than 100? even number? How many even numbers are there *between* 10 and 20? from 10 to 20 (inclusive)? How many odd numbers? How many of each are there from 1 to 9? 10?

Try skip counting by 2s, starting at 0, or 1, or 36, and so on. Or, having plotted the even numbers on a number line, ask, Where are they?

An addition or multiplication table can be used with questions such as, Which sums or products are even? Which are odd? What happens if you add two even numbers? an odd number and an even number? two odd numbers? Why is this true? Suppose the tables were extended beyond addends or factors of 9. Would these patterns continue? Why?

+	0	1	2	3	4	5 . . .
0	E	O	E	O	E	O . . .
1	O	E	O	E	O	E . . .
2	E	O	E	O	E	O . . .
3	O	E	O	E	O	E . . .
4	E	O	E	O	E	O . . .
5	O	E	O	E	O	E . . .

×	0	1	2	3	4	5 . . .
0	E	E	E	E	E	E . . .
1	E	O	E	O	E	O . . .
2	E	E	E	E	E	E . . .
3	E	O	E	O	E	O . . .
4	E	E	E	E	E	E . . .
5	E	O	E	O	E	O . . .

3-by-3 magic squares can give rise to such questions as: Which

2	9	4
7	5	3
6	1	8

8	1	6
3	5	7
4	9	2

6	7	2
1	5	9
8	3	4

numbers are even? Which are odd? Is it possible to change this pattern? Why or why not? How?

One final suggested activity using the odd/even concept is to arrange the numbers from 1 to n (say, 100) in 3 columns, 4 columns, . . . , 12 columns, . . . and ask: Where are the evens and where are the odds? Why? What other patterns can you find?

1	2	3
4	5	6
7	8	9
10	11	12
13	14	15
16	17	18
19	20	21

1	2	3	4
5	6	7	8
9	10	11	12
13	14	15	16
17	18	19	20
21	22	23	24
25	26	27	28

1	2	3	4	5
6	7	8	9	10
11	12	13	14	15
16	17	18	19	20
21	22	23	24	25
26	27	28	29	30
31	32	33	34	35

1	2	3	4	5	6
7	8	9	10	11	12
13	14	15	16	17	18
19	20	21	22	23	24
25	26	27	28	29	30
31	32	33	34	35	36
37	38	39	40	41	42

Factors, Multiples, and Primes

Families of factors of a given number are useful in teaching fundamental multiplication and division facts. One of the most effective beginning activities is to take a collection of small objects and arrange them in rows in the configuration of a rectangular array. For example, 8 objects can be arranged as a 1-by-8 array, a 2-by-4 array, a 4-by-2 array, or an 8-by-1 array; these arrays can be viewed in pairs or separately, and the word "factor" can be easily introduced in this context. Children should then try to arrange objects into 1 row, 2 rows, 3 rows, and so on. In addition to finding which numbers are factors of a given number and which are not, several other terms can be introduced and several discoveries can be made.

1. n objects can always be arranged in 1 row and in n rows (1 and n are always factors of n); similarly, it is never possible to arrange them in *zero* rows nor in more than n rows. It may sound "silly" to children to even consider these, particularly the zero case, but it provides a chance to discuss the ideas that zero is not a factor of any number (except itself) and that the greatest factor of n is itself.
2. If n objects can *only* be arranged in 1 row and in n rows, then n is a prime number (if $n > 1$).
3. Some numbers have many factors (e.g., 24) and others have fewer. Are there any patterns in this?
4. Some collections (e.g., of 4, 9, 16, and 25 objects) can be arranged in *square* arrays. These are the "square numbers." Which numbers have an even number of factors and which have an odd number?
5. Which numbers have 2 as a factor? 3? 4? If a number has 2 as a factor, does it also have 4 as a factor? Is the converse of this true? (If it has 4 as a factor, does it also have 2 as a factor?)

Factors, multiples, and related topics are all involved in the following activities.

Teacher and children can work together to list factors of a given number (24, for example) in an orderly way: First, put down the factors 1 and 24, side-by-side, to indicate that $24 = 1 \times 24$. Ask "Is 2 a factor of 24?" or "Is there a (whole number) solution for $2 \times \square = 24$?" or "Is 24 *divisible* by 2?" ("divisible" can be introduced quite early). Since $2 \times 12 = 24$, list this pair of factors next:

$$
\begin{array}{cc}
1 & 24 \\
2 & 12
\end{array}
$$

Repeat these questions *in turn,* and complete the list: "Is 3 a factor of 24?" "Is 4 a factor of 24?" "Is 5 a factor of 24?" and so on.

$$
\begin{array}{cc}
1 & 24 \\
2 & 12 \\
3 & 8 \\
4 & 6 \\
\vdots & \vdots
\end{array}
$$

At first, the questioning may continue all the way to 24, producing this list:

1	24
2	12
3	8
4	6
6	4
8	3
12	2
24	1

It will soon become clear that such a list is redundant (each factor appears twice), and that it can be condensed to:

1	24
2	12
3	8
4	6

Reading down the left column then up the right column gives all the factors in order. Children should be encouraged to look for patterns here, e.g., the numbers in the left column are less than 5, those in the right are greater than 5. ($\sqrt{24} < \sqrt{25}$.) Square numbers should be included in this activity; children will note the "double" listing of 6 in the factoring of 36, for example:

1	36
2	18
3	12
4	9
6	6

"Square root" can be casually introduced here, with numerous possibilities for discovery, e.g., square numbers have an odd number of factors, the square root of 24 is between 4 and 6 (but is not 5; Why?).

Factors of a number can be plotted, in pairs, on a number line.

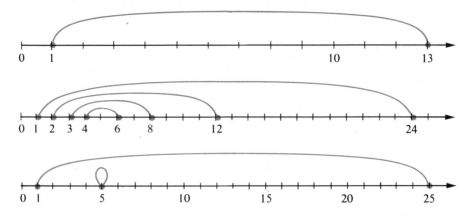

Several observations can be made with these visual representations: the factors occur with an "irregular symmetry" about the square root; for each factor less than the square root there is one greater than the square root; and the greatest factor of n which is less than n itself is never more than $\frac{1}{2}$ of n. Why?

Multiples of a given number can also be plotted on the number line. Common multiples of two numbers and their LCM in particular can be effectively visualized using a line with pegs such as was described in Chapter 6 (p. 226). Paint one collection of pegs blue and another collection black (any pair of contrasting colors will do, of course); paint a third collection with blue and black stripes. To demonstrate common multiples of, say, 3 and 5, have the children put a blue peg at each multiple of 3; when they have finished, within the physical limits of the model, have them put a black peg at each multiple of 5. At '15' they will discover that they need to put a black peg but there is already a blue one there, so suggest a blue and black peg, to indicate that 15 is a multiple of both 3 and 5 (actually zero is the first common multiple). It should be clear that if the line "went on and on" that there would be an *infinite* number of multiples of 3, of 5, and of their LCM. Similar activities could be used for common *factors*, of course, and paper-and-pencil number lines could replace the wooden one.

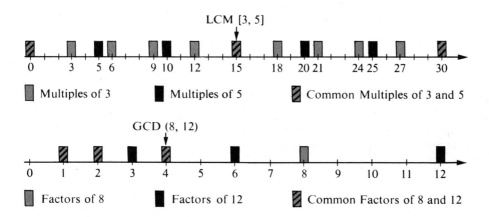

Prime factorization and the *fundamental theorem* are frequently introduced with "factor trees." A number, say 36, can be factored in *any* way, e.g., as 4×9, and diagramed as follows:

The process is then continued, by factoring those factors, until the only further factoring would involve 1s (i.e., until only primes remain):

If several children factor a number in this way and compare their results, they will soon discover that even though their "trees" may not be identical, they all end with the same primes, though perhaps in different order. (That is, they will discover the fundamental theorem of arithmetic.)

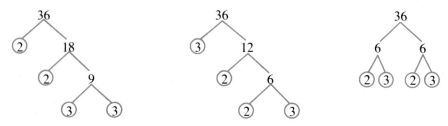

Prime factorization provides a natural setting in which to introduce power notation as a convenient short cut, e.g.,

$$2 \times 2 \times 2 \times 2 \times 2 = 2^5$$
$$2 \times 2 \times 3 \times 3 = 2^2 \times 3^2$$

In general, for bases and exponents greater than 1, an expression like 2^5, read "2 to the 5th power," can be introduced as the number which contains the factor 2 (the "base") 5 times. In helping children to find certain patterns it is worthwhile to introduce exponents of 1 and 0 as well. These must be interpreted somewhat differently, particularly the zero exponent. That $2^1 = 2$ and $2^0 = 1$ (and in general if $a \geq 1$, $a^0 = 1$) can be made reasonable by considering patterns in sequences such as these:

$2^4 = 16$	$3^4 = 81$	$10^4 = 10000$
$2^3 = 8$	$3^3 = 27$	$10^3 = 1000$
$2^2 = 4$	$3^2 = 9$	$10^2 = 100$
$2^1 = $ ____	$3^1 = $ ____	$10^1 = $ ____
$2^0 = $ ____	$3^0 = $ ____	$10^0 = $ ____

If the numbers are to decrease at the same rates, which they should, and since 8 is half of 16, and 4 is half of 8, then 2^1 ought to be half of 4, i.e., 2; so $2^1 = 2$ and then 2^0 should be half of 2, or 1; so $2^0 = 1$. Similarly $3^1 = 3$ and $3^0 = 1$, and so on.

Set intersection and its notation can be introduced in the meaningful context of exploring the GCD and LCM concepts. Both brace notation and Venn diagrams are possible (although Venn diagrams are less effective for LCM). For example, if A is the set of factors of 8 and if B is the set of factors of 12, then $A \cap B$ is the set of their common factors, in which the GCD, 4, can be found:

$A = \{1, 2, 4, 8\}$
$B = \{1, 2, 3, 4, 6, 12\}$
$A \cap B = \{1, 2, 4\}$

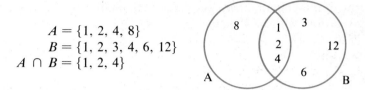

Looking for patterns in such things as the numbers of factors for various numbers and in the sums of those factors requires a great deal of computation, since most of the interesting patterns become apparent only when the list is fairly extensive. Such computational work can be distributed among several children to make a group project that can be very rewarding, once the data are accumulated, checked, and displayed in some sort of chart to be examined. A group of children can in time jointly list the numbers from 1 to 100, for example, and for each number, accumulate various data, such as its prime factorization, its factors expressed in standard form, the prime factorization of each of its factors, the sum of its factors, and so on. The number of possible discoveries and conjectures is virtually unlimited (as can be the enthusiasm).

Given a fairly lengthy list of numbers arranged in columns, as for the Eratosthenes Sieve activity, numerous ideas involving multiples of numbers can be explored. Multiples of a given number can be circled, for example, or joined by lines to reveal patterns. Multiples of one number can be circled and those of another enclosed by another shape (or circled with a contrasting color) to identify common multiples. This can be repeated with different numbers of columns to reveal relationships between factors and multiples, e.g., why the multiples of 3 occur in a *column* pattern in the 6-column array but in a *diagonal* pattern in the 8-column array. Multiples

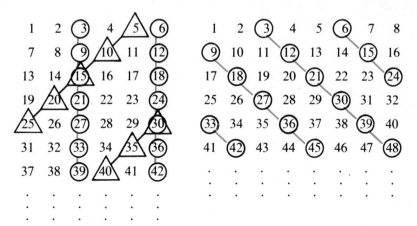

of what other numbers have column patterns in the 6-column array? What are the patterns of multiples of 2, 4, and 8 in the 8-column array? of 3, 5, 6, and 7? What are the patterns of multiples of 5 in a 12-column array? In which row of a 6-column array would the 50th multiple of 2 be found? Are there any arrays with all diagonal patterns? Why or why not? In which arrays is there only *one* column pattern? Where do you expect the next common multiple of 3 and 5 to occur? and the next? Check it. Endless questions of this sort can be raised by the teacher—and by children—to gain insight into the concepts of factors, multiples, primes, common factors and multiples, and relatively prime numbers.

Most of the generalizations and conjectures identified in the review section of this chapter can be discovered by children through similar questions. For example: What is the GCD of 8 and 12? Now divide 12 by 8. What is the remainder? What is the GCD of 8 and the remainder? (Several repetitions of this pattern of questioning, perhaps accompanied by displaying the results on a chart or number lines, can provide a meaningful introduction to the Euclidean algorithm.) Can you express 24 as the sum of 2 odd primes? Is there more than one way to do it $(5 + 19, 7 + 17, 11 + 13)$? Can you express 6 as the sum of 2 odd primes $(3 + 3)$? 8? 10? 12? Can you find an even number that can't be expressed like this? The persistent questions "Why?" or "Why not?" should always be raised by the teacher (in the unlikely event that they are not raised by children themselves). Children who become accustomed to looking for the rewards of finding patterns and being able to rationalize them are nearly always intrigued when, after much effort, their teacher finally reveals that, for example, Goldbach's conjecture is just that—a conjecture which never *has* been proven—or disproven.

The multiplication table can reveal many patterns, as suggested by questions such as these: Suppose the multiplication table were extended indefinitely: How many times would 0 appear? 1? 2? 3? 4? . . . Which numbers would appear only once? twice? three times? an even number of times? an odd number of times? four times? five times? Draw lines connecting the product 48 (or any fairly "abundant" number) each time it appears in the table opposite.

Many productive discussions can result from simple but thought-provoking questions: What would happen if we were to define 1 as a prime? Are there any successive primes other than 2 and 3? Why? Why isn't zero called the LCM of every pair of numbers? Why does no composite number have a proper factor that is more than half the number?

Arithmetic with Remainders

In this and in the next two sections, we will consider activities for teaching topics not included in the review section of the chapter. The first is *Modular* arithmetic (a topic which has many useful applications). There

×	0	1	2	3	4	5	6	7	8	9	10	11	12	13	14	15	
0	0	0	0	0	0	0	0	0	0	0	0	0	0	0	0	0	· · ·
1	0	1	2	3	4	5	6	7	8	9	10	11	12	13	14	15	· · ·
2	0	2	4	6	8	10	12	14	16	18	20	22	24	26	28	30	· · ·
3	0	3	6	9	12	15	18	21	24	27	30	33	36	39	42	45	· · ·
4	0	4	8	12	16	20	24	28	32	36	40	44	(48)	52	56	60	· · ·
5	0	5	10	15	20	25	30	35	40	45	50	55	60	65	70	75	· · ·
6	0	6	12	18	24	30	36	42	(48)	54	60	66	72	78	84	90	· · ·
7	0	7	14	21	28	35	42	49	56	63	70	77	84	91	98	105	· · ·
8	0	8	16	24	32	40	(48)	56	64	72	80	88	96	104	112	120	· · ·
9	0	9	18	27	36	45	54	63	72	81	90	99	108	117	126	135	· · ·
10	0	10	20	30	40	50	60	70	80	90	100	110	120	130	140	150	· · ·
11	0	11	22	33	44	55	66	77	88	99	110	121	132	143	154	165	· · ·
12	0	12	24	36	(48)	60	72	84	96	108	120	132	144	156	168	180	· · ·
13	0	13	26	39	52	65	78	91	104	117	130	143	156	169	182	195	· · ·
14	0	14	28	42	56	70	84	98	112	126	140	154	168	182	196	210	· · ·
15	0	15	30	45	60	75	90	105	120	135	150	165	180	195	210	225	· · ·
·	·	·	·	·	·	·	·	·	·	·	·	·	·	·	·	·	
·	·	·	·	·	·	·	·	·	·	·	·	·	·	·	·	·	

are numerous ways to introduce this topic: Assign to each child a pair of numbers, the first a unique counting number, e.g., if there are 30 children in a group, assign each a different counting number from 1 to 30. (These can be written on 3-by-5 cards or distributed orally, for example.) Then, following the same order, assign each a second number by "counting off" by twos, threes, fours, and so on. The second *number* could be replaced with letters, colors, or identifying symbols. For example,

First Number	Second Number	Or Color
1	1	White
2	2	Red
3	3	Green
4	1	White
5	2	Red
6	3	Green
7	1	White
8	2	Red
9	3	Green
10	1	White
11	2	Red
12	3	Green
13	1	White
⋮	⋮	⋮

Then ask all children whose second number was 1 to reveal their first number. This should be displayed for all to see; repeat for 2 and 3:

one: 1 4 7 10 13 16 19 22 25 28
two: 2 5 8 11 14 17 20 23 26 29
three: 3 6 9 12 15 18 21 24 27 30

Now various patterns can be sought; they may, for example, notice a regularity in the "sums of digits."

one: 1 4 7 1 4 7 1 4 7 1*
two: 2 5 8 2 5 8 2 5 8 2*
three: 3 6 9 3 6 9 3 6 9 3

(See page 270 for sums 1* and 2* here.) Different patterns will emerge depending on the "modulus"—in this case 3—used. Odd/even patterns, patterns of factors or multiples may be noticed. In case they don't notice it, ask each child to divide his first number by 3 and reveal the *remainder*; e.g., "If your remainder was 2, raise your hand."

one: 1 1 1 1 1 1 1 . . .
two: 2 2 2 2 2 2 2 . . .
three: 0 0 0 0 0 0 0 . . .

Alternately, an array of numbers, like those in the preceding section can be examined from the same viewpoint, noting particularly the remainder pattern. Columns can be labeled in any manner, e.g., with letters, colors, or the identifying remainders:

1	2	0
A	B	C
1	2	3
4	5	6
7	8	9
10	11	12
13	14	15
⋮	⋮	⋮

Numerous questions can now be raised: In which row will 100 appear if we extend the list? 150? 763? 827? Choose one number in column A and one in column B. Add the numbers. In which column is their sum? Choose another number from each of A and B. In which column is their sum? Repeating this with many examples from each of the various columns reveals a curious pattern. Can you tell without adding in which column the sum of 236 and 428 will be? Is it in the same column as is the sum of 2 and 2? Why or why not? Now multiply any number in column A by any number in column B. In which column is the answer? Repeating this again reveals similar patterns. A new "addition table" and "multiplication table" can be devised from these generalizations. The letters A, B, and C, the *remainders* 0, 1, and 2, or other symbols, can be used, referring to specific numbers in the lists, to develop these (carefully!).

Example:

+	A	B	C
A	B	C	A
B	C	A	B
C	A	B	C

×	A	B	C
A	A	B	C
B	B	A	C
C	C	C	C

or

+	0	1	2
0	0	1	2
1	1	2	0
2	2	0	1

×	0	1	2
0	0	0	0
1	0	1	2
2	0	2	1

These tables can be used to develop or review numerous concepts. If the remainders are used, it is important to frequently remind children that '2', for example, is used here as an abbreviation for "*any* number in the list 2, 5, 8, 11, 14, . . . " or "*some* number in the list 2, 5, 8, 11, 14, ..." For example, the expression "2 + 2 = 1" means "the sum of *any* pair of numbers in the '2' list is *some* number in the '1' list." The remainder of this section discusses the concepts that can be introduced and the discoveries children can make in the area of arithmetic with remainders.

The new operations have all the key properties of "regular" arithmetic. That is, the set of "numbers" {A, B, C} or {0, 1, 2} is closed with respect to both operations; both operations are commutative and associative; multiplication distributes over addition; there is an identity for each operation, and so on.

Using both sets of symbols {A, B, C} and {0, 1, 2} and both sets of tables is a natural way to introduce isomorphism (children enjoy learning such a sophisticated-sounding word!). That is, the system {A, B, C} and its operations may *look* different from the system {0, 1, 2} and its operations, but the only real difference is in the symbolism. Formally, there is a 1–1 correspondence between the elements of the two systems, under which the operations "behave" alike:

$$\{0, \ 1, \ 2\} \qquad\qquad A + B = C$$
$$\updownarrow \ \updownarrow \ \updownarrow \quad \text{e.g.} \quad \updownarrow \quad \updownarrow \quad \updownarrow$$
$$\{C, \ A, \ B\} \qquad\qquad 1 + 2 = 0$$

Not every 1–1 correspondence between the systems works this way, e.g.

$$\{0, \ 1, \ 2\} \qquad A + B = C$$
$$\updownarrow \ \updownarrow \ \updownarrow \qquad \updownarrow \quad \updownarrow \quad \updownarrow$$
$$\{A, \ B, \ C\} \qquad 0 + 1 = 2$$

Children enjoy inventing other systems isomorphic to this one, i.e., inventing new symbols and tables for the same system.

With older children at least, the standard notation of "congruences" can be introduced. Two numbers in the same column in the list from which the system was developed are said to be *congruent* (another impressive word). For example, in the 3-column list above, 5 and 14 are congruent, as are 4 and 10, 3 and 15, and so on. If a 4-column array had been used to develop the system, these would not be true, however, so we must specify the modulus. Standard notation for this is, for example: $5 \equiv 14 \pmod 3$, "5 is congruent to 14, modulus (or mod) 3." Whether or not this *notation* is used, some interesting questions can be raised.

1. If 2 numbers are congruent, what can you say about their difference? ($a - b$ or $b - a$ is a *multiple* of the modulus.)
2. $2 \equiv 2^3 \pmod 3$, $4 \equiv 4^3 \pmod 3$. Is this true for any number? (This turns out to be true when the modulus is *prime*, but not when it is composite. This — Fermat's theorem — and other differences between prime and composite moduli can be explored.)
3. Consider 2 congruent numbers, say 2 and 5 (mod 3). Multiply them each by some number, say 7. Are the products congruent? Multiply them each by different, but congruent numbers (e.g., 4 and 10). Are these new numbers congruent? That is, if $2 \equiv 5 \pmod 3$, is $2 \times 7 \equiv 5 \times 7 \pmod 3$? Is $2 \times 4 \equiv 5 \times 10 \pmod 3$?

The original numbers can be arranged, spiral fashion, in a circle instead of in columns (given plenty of space!). If the numbers are again

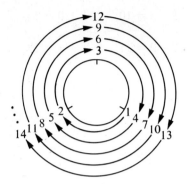

represented by their remainders, we have the equipment for a "clock arithmetic": a one-handed "clock" on which addition is interpreted as a singulary operation and multiplication is repeated addition. For example, $1 + 2 = \square$ means "Start at 1 and move 2 hours ahead." The ending point is 0, so $1 + 2 = 0$. Similarly $2 \times 1 = \square$ could be interpreted as "Start at 0 and make 2 moves, each of 1 hour." Thus $2 \times 1 = 2$. Many games and

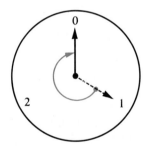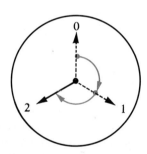

activities similar to this can be devised. An ordinary clock, with only its hour hand can be likened to a modulus 12 clock. Thus 37 hours after 7 o'clock is 8 o'clock (AM or PM?) because $37 \equiv 1 \pmod{12}$ and $7 + 1 \equiv 8 \pmod{12}$; 41 hours after 9 o'clock is 2 o'clock because $41 \equiv 5 \pmod{12}$ and $9 + 5 \equiv 2 \pmod{12}$. $86 \times 32 \equiv 4 \pmod{12}$ because $86 \equiv 2 \pmod{12}$, $32 \equiv 8 \pmod{12}$ and $2 \times 8 \equiv 4 \pmod{12}$.

In a 9-column array, it happens (Why?) that the sum of the digits of each number in a given column is the same:

1	2	3	4	5	6	7	8	9
10	11	12	13	14	15	16	17	18
19	20	21	22	23	24	25	26	27
28	29	30	31	32	33	34	35	36

.
.
.

Parenthetically, for numbers like 28, 29, 388, etc., the addition must be repeated to obtain a single digit, thus:

28:     $2 + 8 = 10;$ $1 + 0 = 1$

29:     $2 + 9 = 11;$ $1 + 1 = 2$

388: $3 + 8 + 8 = 19;$ $1 + 9 = 10;$ $1 + 0 = 1$

If, therefore, 2 numbers have the same "sum of digits," they are congruent, modulo 9, e.g., $388 \equiv 28$ (mod 9). Both are congruent to 1. If we label the columns in their natural way, 1, 2, 3, 4, 5, 6, 7, 8, and 9 (not zero), the observations we have made about congruences suggest that, for example, adding or multiplying 23 and 34 is equivalent, congruence-wise, to adding or multiplying 5 and 7, since $23 \equiv 5$ (mod 9) and $34 \equiv 7$ (mod 9). Thus

$$23 + 34 \equiv 5 + 7 \equiv 12 \equiv 3 \text{ (mod 9)}$$

$$23 \times 34 \equiv 5 \times 7 \equiv 35 \equiv 8 \text{ (mod 9)}$$

This can be used as one way of explaining the well-known technique of "casting out nines" for checking additions or multiplications (as well as subtractions and divisions). That is, suppose we perform these computations:

```
    34        34        34          1
  + 23      - 23      × 23      23) 34
  ----      ----      ----         23
    57        11       102         --
                        68         11
                       ---
                       728
```

As a check to see if our answers are correct, we can replace the addends, factors, products, remainders, and so on, with their "equivalents," mod 9, i.e., the "sum of their digits." If the results are consistent, our computation should be correct:

```
  34 →  7       34 → 7       34 →  7          1 →          1
+ 23 →  5     - 23 → 5     × 23 →  5      23) 34        5) 7
-------       ------       ----------        23 →          5
  57 → 12 → 3   11 → 2     728 → 35 → 8      --          --
                                            11 →          2
                                          23 → 5;  34 → 7
```

In case you were reading carelessly, note that we obtained the wrong answer in the multiplication problem, but it still "checked" — one problem with this otherwise useful "trick"! Of course, congruence-wise our answer is correct, since $728 \equiv 782$ (mod 9), but $728 \neq 782$. This suggests a similar, but even less reliable check: If two numbers of known parity are added (subtracted, multiplied, divided), the results should agree with corresponding problems involving their equivalents, mod 2 with the "0-class" expressed as "even," and "1-class" as "odd."

$34 \rightarrow$	even	$34 \rightarrow$	even	$34 \rightarrow$	even	$1 \rightarrow$	odd
$+\,23$	$+$ odd	$-\,23$	$-$ (odd)	$\times\,23$	$\times$ (odd)	$23\overline{)\,34}$	odd $\overline{)\,\text{even}}$
$57 \rightarrow$	odd	$11 \rightarrow$	odd	$782 \rightarrow$	even	23	$-$ (odd)
						$11 \rightarrow$	odd

Interesting extensions of this idea can be found by examining different moduli and various bases other than ten.

Patterns, Sequences, and Functions

One purpose of teaching topics from number theory is to develop problem-solving skills. These skills include that of finding patterns and relationships in a given set of data, such as a set of numbers. A concomitant skill is that of *using* these patterns and relationships to answer a question — which sometimes necessitates using the pattern to generate even more data. There are wide differences in children's *ability* to see relationships and to find patterns, to be sure, but developing skills from whatever innate ability children possess is one of our basic tasks as teachers. Sequences of numbers provide an excellent vehicle for developing these skills, while also teaching significant mathematical concepts as background for subsequent work, as well as computational practice — and intellectual satisfaction.

By "sequence" is meant here (though not universally) a list of numbers, at least potentially infinite, such that a given number in the list can normally be determined from preceding ones (normally the one *just* preceding it). More formally, we can describe a sequence as the elements in the *range* of a function whose *domain* is the set of natural numbers. Numbers in a sequence are called *terms* of the sequence, and since each term is paired with a natural number, we can speak of the *first* term, *second* term, etc.

Examples:

(a) Function: $S = \{(1, 1), (2, 4), (3, 9), (4, 16), \ldots, (n, n^2), \ldots\}$
 Sequence: $1, 4, 9, 16, \ldots, n^2, \ldots$
(b) Function: $F = \{(1, 1), (2, 1), (3, 2), (4, 3), (5, 5), (6, 8), \ldots,$
 $(n, F(n-1) + F(n-2)), \ldots\}$
 Sequence: $1, 1, 2, 3, 5, 8, \ldots$

Individual terms of a sequence are sometimes identified by a letter with a natural number subscript (the number in the domain with which the term is paired). Terms of the second sequence above could be labeled f_1 (first term), f_2 (second term), $\ldots, f_n$ (nth term). $\ldots$ In that sequence, then,

$$f_1 = 1$$
$$f_2 = 1$$
$$f_3 = 2$$
$$f_4 = 3$$

$$\vdots$$

$$f_n = f_{n-1} + f_{n-2} \qquad \text{(for } n > 2)$$

Moreover, f_n is called the *general* term of the sequence. It describes the pattern or rule which children are frequently asked to find, given the first few terms. Identifying this term correctly enables them to extend the sequence as far as they wish.

Among the things teachers can do to help children develop skill in finding number patterns such as those in sequences is to provide them with frequent and regular opportunities to find patterns and rules for sequences, functions, and arrays of numbers. Children enjoy and profit from brief games in which they are challenged to predict what number comes next or to find the rule when the teacher or a child, with a function rule in mind, either displays its first few terms or reveals the term associated with a given natural number. For example, the teacher thinks of a rule like $f(n) = n^2 + 1$. The first few terms, 2, 5, 10, 17, . . . , may be displayed and the children try to guess the next one. Or, a child may say "five," to which the teacher responds "twenty-six"; the children keep calling off numbers, trying to find a pattern in the teacher's responses. Another technique is to reveal one term at a time and ask them to guess the next. The first term doesn't provide much information, but it can suggest possibilities. For example, if the teacher writes 2 on the chalkboard as the first term of a sequence, children might think of the sequence of even numbers, of powers of two, of primes, of natural numbers, and so on. They should be encouraged to make these conjectures. When the next term is revealed, some of the original conjectures will be rejected and new ones may be made. Discretion is necessary in deciding when to reveal or confirm the pattern, or when to let a child reveal his discovery to others. While one child's description of how he reasoned may help others subsequently, intellectual productivity — and the fun — may end once the solution is revealed.

Children should be provided with problems of varied difficulty, ranging from easy ones to those that can be quite thought-provoking. More difficult sequences should be displayed, as on a bulletin board, sufficiently long for children to think about them, experiment, discuss them, and test resulting conjectures.

Charts and graphs are useful in helping children visualize possible relationships, e.g.,

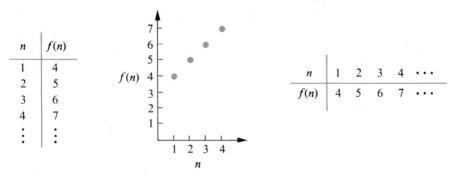

Provide general guidelines for generating successive terms of certain sequences (e.g., arithmetic progressions), then challenge children to determine a quicker way to generate subsequent terms. Thus, in the progression

$$t_1 = 1$$
$$t_2 = 1 + 2$$
$$t_3 = 1 + 2 + 3$$
$$t_4 = 1 + 2 + 3 + 4$$
$$t_5 = 1 + 2 + 3 + 4 + 5$$
$$t_6 = \ldots \ldots \ldots$$

the first five terms, 1, 3, 6, 10, 15, are obtained by addition. But addition becomes increasingly difficult. Is there a quick way to find say, t_{10}, without actually adding? Does this chart help?

n	t_n
1	1
2	3
3	6
4	10
5	15
⋮	⋮

Children may discover *several* ways to determine the next term, and the next, and so on. Those who can somehow determine the 6th term given the 5th should be challenged to determine, say, the 100th term without determining all those up to the 99th. This will be more difficult for many sequences. In this same regard, encourage children to think of alternate ways to *express* terms as a possible clue to finding patterns. For example, a child who guesses that the next term of the sequence 2, 4, 8, 16, . . . is 32, but cannot determine what the 100th term is, may get an idea by expressing the terms as 2^1, 2^2, 2^3, 2^4, . . . , particularly if these are recorded in a chart:

n	h_n
1	2^1
2	2^2
3	2^3
4	2^4
⋮	
100	$2^\square$

Children should be encouraged to "prove" that their conjectures are correct. There will be much variation, of course, and no particular format or degree of perfection should be expected. Rather, a child should be expected to show that his rule "works" for known terms (this is no "proof," of course) and that it seems to generate terms consistent with known ones in some way. Incidentally, a well-known geometric problem, easily solved for the first few terms, is this: If n distinct points are located on a circle, and if each point is connected to each other point to draw all possible segments, into how many regions will the circle be partitioned? Letting $n = 1, 2, 3, 4$, etc., in turn, produces the pictured sequence, 1, 2, 4, 8, which strongly suggests

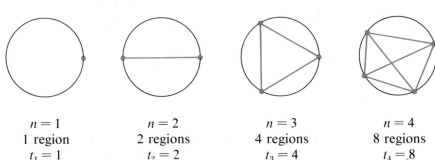

$n = 1$	$n = 2$	$n = 3$	$n = 4$
1 region	2 regions	4 regions	8 regions
$t_1 = 1$	$t_2 = 2$	$t_3 = 4$	$t_4 = 8$

the conjecture that the next term should be 2^5, or 16. Which it *is*. Armed with this verification (and faced with increasingly complicated drawings), it is easy to conjecture that t_6 should be 32. But alas, no matter how the picture is drawn, 32 is incorrect. In fact, it is possible to draw it in such a way that 30 regions result or 31. Never 32! By contrast, consider a related problem, that of counting the *segments* determined by the same constructions. For this problem, $t_1 = 0$, $t_2 = 1$, $t_3 = 3$, $t_4 = 6$, starting the sequence 0, 1, 3, 6, ... A child might reason from this *sequence* that $t_5 = 10$, for a variety of reasons. For example, the 2nd term can be obtained by adding 1 to the term before it, the 3rd term by adding 2 to the preceding one, then adding 3, and so on. Thus the next term must be obtained by adding 4 to 6, so $t_5 = 10$). This *result* is correct, but the child who reasons that when a fifth point is drawn in the picture, a segment can be drawn from that point to each of the 4 points already there (and that each such segment will be "new") so there will be 4 more segments than before, has supplied a valid *proof* for his conjecture (if not for the *general* case).

Encourage children to be on the lookout for the recurrence of a familiar sequence in new contexts. It can be really intriguing and exciting to discover that a sequence that emerges from one problem reappears in an entirely different one. Figuring out *why* is even more stimulating. (We have seen the sequence 1, 3, 6, 10, 15, . . . , in two quite different contexts here and will see it again shortly in at least two more.)

Many interesting discoveries can be made by examining "sequences of sequences," i.e., a set of sequences which are themselves related by some sort of pattern. One such, which we will consider in more detail soon, is this:

$$1, 3, \quad 6, 10, 15, 21, 28, 36, \ldots$$
$$1, 4, \quad 9, 16, 25, 36, 49, 64, \ldots$$
$$1, 5, 12, 22, 35, 51, 70, 92, \ldots$$

Once a sequence rule has been discovered, children frequently enjoy finding all the terms up to a given one, sometimes as a group project, e.g.:

$$1, 3, 6, 10, 15, 21, \ldots, 1275 \quad (a_{50})$$

It is helpful to provide them with occasional "check points" for this enterprise, i.e., tell them that the 10th term should be 55, the 20th should be 210, and so on.

Of the many sequences, number patterns, and arrays, there are three well-known ones both of particular interest to children and rich in patterns: *polygonal numbers,* the *Fibonacci sequence,* and *Pascal's triangle.*

Polygonal (or figurate) numbers originated with the ancient Greeks, who are believed by some to have recorded numbers with dots at a very early time in their history, perhaps like this:

Beginning with 3, any number can (theoretically) be expressed as a regular polygonal shape: Triangle, square, pentagon, hexagon, heptagon, octagon, and so on. The *words* become cumbersome rather quickly, so the *-gon* suffix, which refers in general to a "number of angles," is used. Hence a triangle could be called a 3-gon; a square a 4-gon; a decagon a 10-gon; and, in general, a regular *n*-sided polygon an *n*-gon. Each shape can be extended and enlarged in a systematic way, as suggested here. That is, each successive figure contains all its predecessors, with each side increased by

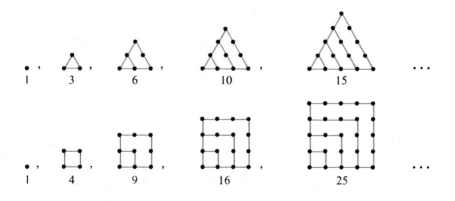

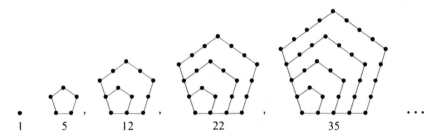

one. The numbers of dots form a sequence, each beginning with 1. (Since the smallest figure can be envisioned as starting with a single dot, that in the lower left-hand corner is sometimes called the initial point.) Hence the sequence of "triangular numbers," which we have encountered before, is:

$$1, 3, 6, 10, 15, 21, 28, \ldots$$

The square numbers; pentagonal numbers; hexagonal, septagonal, and octagonal numbers form these sequences:

$$1, 4, \ \ 9, 16, 25, 36, \ \ 49, \ \ 64, \ldots$$
$$1, 5, 12, 22, 35, 51, \ \ 70, \ \ 92, \ldots$$
$$1, 6, 15, 28, 45, 66, \ \ 91, 120, \ldots$$
$$1, 7, 18, 34, 55, 81, 112, 148, \ldots$$
$$1, 8, 21, 40, 65, 96, 133, 176, \ldots$$

The *triangular numbers* are particularly interesting and can be easily generated by children with a collection of any kind of small objects, such as poker chips. Any number of discoveries might be made — including perhaps how to find the nth triangular number — during activities concerned with describing the triangular numbers in sequence.

Examples:

(a) The second number can be found by adding 2 to the first number; the third can be found by adding 3 to the second one; the fourth can be found by adding 4 to the third; and so on.

$$1, \qquad 3, \qquad 6, \qquad 10, \qquad 15, \qquad \cdots$$
$$\searrow +2 \nearrow \searrow +3 \nearrow \searrow +4 \nearrow \searrow +5 \nearrow \searrow +6 \nearrow$$

(b) The second number is $1 + 2$; the third number is $1 + 2 + 3$; the fourth is $1 + 2 + 3 + 4$; and so on.

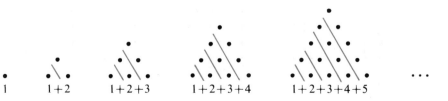

1   1+2   1+2+3   1+2+3+4   1+2+3+4+5

(c) The second number is half of 2×3; the third number is half of 3×4; the fourth is half of 4×5; and so on. Some children might even discover, then, that the nth triangular number is $\frac{1}{2}n(n+1)$ and thus, combined with the preceding observation

$$1 + 2 + 3 + \ldots + n = \frac{1}{2}n(n+1)$$

(d) The second number is half of $2^2 + 2$; the third is half of $3^2 + 3$; the fourth is half of $4^2 + 4$, and so on. The 15th triangular number, i.e., $1 + 2 + 3 + \ldots + 15$ can be found by considering the pattern of this array:

$$
\begin{array}{r|l}
1+ \ 2 & 3 \\
4+ \ 5+ \ 6 & 7+ \ 8 \\
9+ 10+ 11+ 12 & 13 + 14 + 15
\end{array}
$$

Can this be extended?

Similar descriptions result as children "build" the *square numbers*.

Examples:

(a) The second number can be found by adding 3 to the first; the third can be found by adding 5 to the second; the fourth is 7 more than the third, and so on.

$$1, \qquad 4, \qquad 9, \qquad 16, \qquad 25, \qquad \cdots$$

$$+3 \quad +5 \quad +7 \quad +9 \quad +11$$

(b) The second number is $1 + 3$, the third is $1 + 3 + 5$, the next is $1 + 3 + 5 + 7$, and so on.

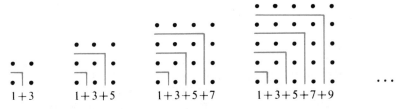

$$1 \qquad 1+3 \qquad 1+3+5 \qquad 1+3+5+7 \qquad 1+3+5+7+9 \qquad \cdots$$

(c) The second number is 2^2, the third is 3^2, the fourth is 4^2 and the nth is n^2, thus

$$1 + 3 + 5 + 7 + \ldots + (2n - 1) = n^2$$

(d) And a rather surprising discovery: Each square number (except 1) is the sum of two successive triangular numbers:

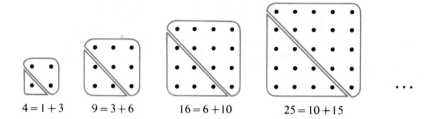

$4 = 1 + 3$ $9 = 3 + 6$ $16 = 6 + 10$ $25 = 10 + 15$ ...

(The nth square number is the sum of the nth and $(n-1)$st triangular numbers.)

(e) The square numbers are all in the main diagonal of a multiplication table:

×	0	1	2	3	4	5	6	7	8	9	...
0	0										
1		1									
2			4								
3				9							
4					16						
5						25					
6							36				
7								49			
8									64		
9										81	

Geometric forms made from cardboard, tile, wood, and so on, can be used to find the first few square numbers. Given any one of these shapes (and surely many others), we can ask "How many copies of these, set edge to edge, would it take to make a bigger figure with the same shape?" (In each case the answer is 4, or 9, or 16, or some square number.)

Some children may want to go beyond the triangular and square numbers. The procedure would be as follows: The terms of each sequence are sums, each with successive "skip intervals."

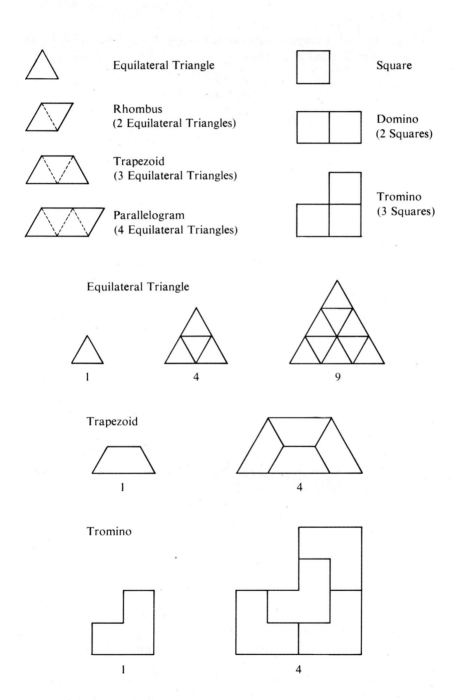

Examples:

(a) The nth triangular number is $1 + 2 + 3 + \ldots + n = \frac{n(n+1)}{2}$. The skip interval is 1. Thus:

$$a_1 = 1$$
$$a_2 = 1 + 2$$
$$a_3 = 1 + 2 + 3$$
$$a_4 = 1 + 2 + 3 + 4$$
$$\vdots$$

(b) The nth square number is $1 + 3 + 5 + \ldots + 2n - 1 = \frac{n(2n-0)}{2} = n^2$. The skip interval is 2. Thus:

$$a_1 = 1$$
$$a_2 = 1 + 3$$
$$a_3 = 1 + 3 + 5$$
$$a_4 = 1 + 3 + 5 + 7$$
$$\vdots$$

(c) The nth pentagonal number is $1 + 4 + 7 + \ldots + 3n - 2 = \frac{n(3n-1)}{2}$. The skip interval is 3. Thus:

$$a_1 = 1$$
$$a_2 = 5$$
$$a_3 = 12$$
$$a_4 = 22$$
$$\vdots$$

(d) The nth hexagonal number is $1 + 5 + 9 + \ldots + 4n - 3 = \frac{n(4n-2)}{2}$. The skip interval is 4. Thus:

$$a_1 = 1$$
$$a_2 = 6$$
$$a_3 = 15$$
$$a_4 = 28$$
$$\vdots$$

The general form of the final addend, e.g., $4n - 3$, and the general term, i.e., the nth sum and thus the nth term, e.g., $\frac{n(4n-2)}{2}$ have been included in the above examples for the teacher's benefit.

Children can get much meaningful practice in addition by constructing a table of polygonal numbers such as this (it can be of any dimensions, of course—the bigger the better; another opportunity for a group project).

	1	2	3	4	5	6	7	8 · · ·
Triangular	1	3	6	10	15	21	28	36 · · ·
Square	1	4	9	16	25	36	49	64 · · ·
Pentagonal	1	5	12	22	35	51	70	92 · · ·
Hexagonal	1	6	15	28	45	66	91	120 · · ·
Heptagonal	1	7	18	34	55	81	112	148 · · ·
Octagonal	1	8	21	40	65	96	133	176 · · ·
⋮	⋮	⋮	⋮	⋮	⋮	⋮	⋮	⋮
r-agonal								

Such a table is a rich source of curios. There are several questions which can be raised, some of which require computation—but with rewards!

1. Which numbers are odd and which are even? What patterns can you see?
2. What is the GCD of *all* the numbers in column 1? 2? 3? 4? . . . ?
3. Which numbers occur more than once in the table? Where?
4. Subtract pairs of adjacent numbers in column 1, 2, 3, ...
5. Is there any relationship between the triangular numbers and the pairs (square, pentagonal)? (pentagonal, hexagonal)? (hexagonal, heptagonal)? . . . ?
6. Choose any two successive rows, e.g., triangular, square. Consider the entries two columns at a time, in order, e.g.,

$$\triangle: \quad (1, 3) \quad (3, 6) \quad (6, 10) \quad (10, 15) \quad \cdots \quad (a, b)$$
$$\square: \quad (1, 4) \quad (4, 9) \quad (9, 16) \quad (16, 25) \quad \qquad (c, d)$$

and compute $ad - cb$.
7. Express each triangular number mod 3, each square number mod 4, and so on.

The well-known Fibonacci sequence is said to have originated with a hypothetical and amusing problem posed in the 1200s by an Italian mathematician called Fibonacci (also known as Leonardo Pisano): Suppose 2 rabbits are placed in a pen. It takes them a month to mature. At the beginning of the third month, and every month thereafter, they produce another pair. The new pair does likewise at the end of their second month, as does each successive pair. How many pairs of rabbits are in the pen at the end of each month? At the end of the first month: 1 pair; at the end of the second month: still 1 pair; at the end of the third month: 2 pairs; and thereafter at the end of each month (should you care to figure it out), there are as many as the preceding month (of course), increased by the number for the month before that:

$$1, \ 1, \ 2, \ 3, \ 5, \ 8, \ 13, \ 21, \ \cdots$$

This is a simple sequence and children can easily discover its rule and extend it as far as they like. It, too, has some interesting internal patterns to be discovered (while getting plenty of addition practice), e.g., finding the sum of the first *n* terms, or the first *n* *odd* terms, of the first *n* even terms, or of the squares of the first *n* terms (these patterns are a little more obscure than some of those for the polygonal numbers). A similar sequence, called the Lucas sequence, is 1, 3, 4, 7, 11, 18, . . . and there are relationships to be found between the Lucas and Fibonacci sequences.

One rather curious thing about the Fibonacci sequence is its occurrence in nature. If children *carefully* count the clockwise spirals in a sunflower (with just the seeds remaining) and then count the counterclockwise spirals, they obtain two successive terms of the Fibonacci sequence. The same will be found to be true for pineapples, for acorns, and for certain pine cones. Growth rates frequently follow the Fibonacci pattern: In some trees and bushes, the distance between a pair of branches or between a pair of leaves is frequently the same as the sum of the distances between the two pairs preceding them—the Fibonacci relationship. Distances between spirals on many shells follow this same pattern. Searching for instances of this relationship can provide children with valuable authentic scientific experience—gathering sufficient data, accurate counting and measuring, the excitement of occasional successes, and the acceptance of frequent failures.

If children can find the decimal equivalents of fractions, an interesting activity is to find, in turn, the ratio of each Fibonacci number to its predecessor:

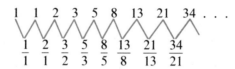

These are equivalent (or approximately equivalent—to the nearest thousandth), in order, to 1, 2, 1.5, 1.667, 1.6, 1.625, 1.615, 1.619, ... These numbers get closer and closer to the well-known irrational number sometimes designated as Φ [about 1.61803, actually $\frac{1}{2}(1 + \sqrt{5})$]. Artists and architects since the time of the Greeks have regarded the ratio $\Phi : 1$, the *golden ratio,* to be the most pleasing dimensions for the sides of a rectangle (it occurs frequently in famous artistic and architectural works). This ratio can be visualized—to any degree of precision—by constructing a set of squares whose dimensions are those of the Fibonacci numbers: Two 1-by-1 squares, and one each of size 2-by-2, 3-by-3, 5-by-5, and so on. The squares can be arranged to make successively larger rectangles, the dimensions of which get progressively closer to the golden ratio. The dimensions of these are, of course, 1-by-1, 1-by-2, 3-by-2, 3-by-5, 8-by-5, and 8-by-13—all adjacent Fibonacci numbers. On an $8\frac{1}{2}$-by-11″ sheet of graph paper, with

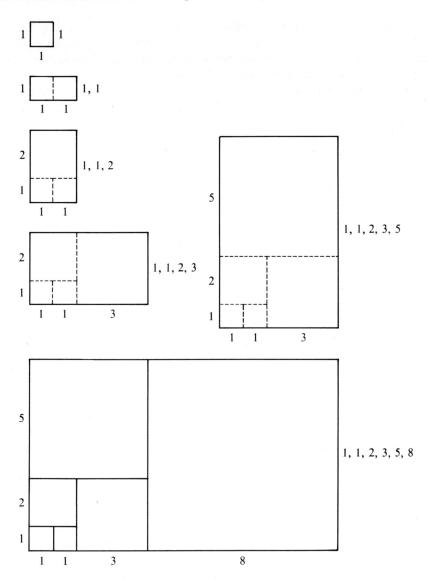

10 squares to the inch, a 55-by-89 unit rectangle (5.5-by-8.9″) can be constructed to visualize the ratio even better. The ratio of 89 to 55, two successive Fibonacci numbers, is 1.618−quite close to Φ. It may also be noted that the area of the largest rectangle pictured above, 8-by-13, is the sum $1^2 + 1^2 + 2^2 + 3^2 + 5^2 + 8^2$, suggesting one of the curious patterns to be found in the sequence, i.e.,

$$f_1^2 + f_2^2 + f_3^2 + \ldots + f_n^2 = f_n \times f_{n+1}$$

That this is true for *each* of the successive rectangles can be easily verified.

Before leaving (momentarily) this curious sequence, it may be of interest to some that in the early 1960s, a Fibonacci Association was formed; it now has at least 350 members and publishes the *Fibonacci Quarterly*; we have barely scratched the surface of this topic.

Our next pattern is not a sequence but a well-known triangular array of numbers, called Pascal's triangle (Pascal was a seventeenth-century mathematical giant).

```
                          1
                       1  2  1
                    1  3  3  1
                 1  4  6  4  1
              1  5  10  10  5  1
           1  6  15  20  15  6  1
        1  7  21  35  35  21  7  1
     1  8  28  56  70  56  28  8  1
   1  9  36  84  126 126 84  36  9  1
 1  10 45  120 210 252 210 120 45  10  1
1  11 55  165 330 462 462 330 165 55  11  1
 .  .  .  .  .  .  .  .  .  .  .  .
 .  .  .  .  .  .  .  .  .  .  .  .
 .  .  .  .  .  .  .  .  .  .  .  .
```

This array, which can continue as far as we wish, is a simple one to construct, and contains many patterns. In case the reader has not encountered it before, the top row contains a single 1; the next row contains two 1s; thereafter each row begins and ends with 1 and each intermediate number is the sum of the two numbers above it. Each row contains one more number than its predecessor. Children enjoy discovering this pattern in the triangle

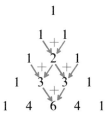

as the teacher constructs it, one row at a time, or part of a row at a time. Asked to identify any patterns they see, they will encounter many. If not, a few preliminary questions such as these may provoke some thought and reveal some patterns:

What is the first number in each row? the last?
Read the numbers in any row; then read them "backwards." What do you notice?

Add the numbers in each row. Is there a pattern?
Add all of the numbers in the first five rows. Can you express the sum of the first 10 rows without adding?
In which rows is each number in the row (except the 1s) divisible by the second number in the row?   (Several rows should be constructed to see the pattern here.)

The rows and diagonals in the triangle may be numbered in natural order, but there is some advantage to labeling them beginning with 0 instead of with 1, e.g.:

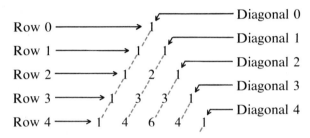

Thus the first number other than 1 in row 3 is 3, etc.
Also, the triangle may be "twisted" to form a right triangle; doing so helps to reveal certain patterns:

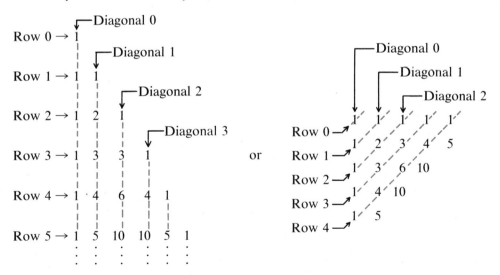

Another challenge is to find the patterns in diagonal 1 (the natural numbers); in diagonal 2 (the triangular numbers). Where else do these numbers occur in the triangle? Can they be seen by looking at the triangle in another way? Do the square numbers appear? Is there a pattern for each diagonal? Why does it work?

Consider this configuration of the triangle. Add the numbers along each of the dotted lines (note that these are neither rows nor diagonals).

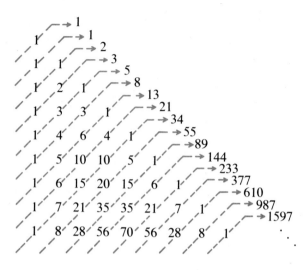

The Fibonacci numbers again! (It is interesting that this particular relation-ship went unnoticed—or at least unrecorded—for nearly 200 years after Pascal devised his triangle, though the Fibonacci sequence was over 400 years old when the triangle first appeared.)

Take any set of, say, 4 objects $\{1, 2, 3, 4\}$. How many 0-element subsets can you form? How many 1-element subsets can you form? How many 2-element subsets? How many 3-element subsets? How many 4-element subsets?

Example:

$\underline{1}$ 0-element subset: $\emptyset$
$\underline{4}$ 1-element subsets: $\{1\}$, $\{2\}$, $\{3\}$, $\{4\}$
$\underline{6}$ 2-element subsets: $\{1, 2\}$, $\{1, 3\}$, $\{1, 4\}$, $\{2, 3\}$, $\{2, 4\}$, $\{3, 4\}$
$\underline{4}$ 3-element subsets: $\{1, 2, 3\}$, $\{1, 2, 4\}$, $\{1, 3, 4\}$, $\{2, 3, 4\}$
$\underline{1}$ 4-element subset: $\{1, 2, 3, 4\}$

Do these numbers appear in Pascal's triangle? (Try this with a 1-element set, a 2-element set, a 3-element set, and so on.)

A related activity can be performed using blocks such as the Cuisenaire rods: In how many different ways can the length of, say, a 4-block be shown? In how many ways can this be done with one block? two blocks? three blocks? four blocks? This can be repeated with blocks of successive lengths: 1, 2, 3, 4, 5, ... Do you see the numbers in Pascal's triangle?

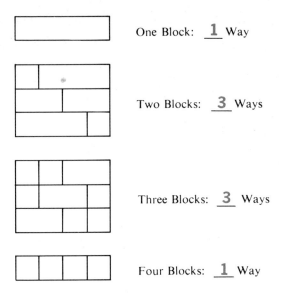

One Block: <u>**1**</u> Way

Two Blocks: <u>**3**</u> Ways

Three Blocks: <u>**3**</u> Ways

Four Blocks: <u>**1**</u> Way

     An interesting sequence of questions related to the last two activities is exemplified by this: In how many ways can 5 objects be chosen 3 at a time? How many 1-child committees can be formed from a group of 5 children? If any child can serve on several committees, how many 2-child committees can be formed? How many 3-child committees? 4-child committees? 5-child committees? (0-child committees??)

     If children are familiar with factorial notation (e.g., $5! = 5 \cdot 4 \cdot 3 \cdot 2 \cdot 1$) they may be interested in seeing how these questions – whose answers are successive entries in row 5 of the triangle: 1, 5, 10, 10, 5, 1 – can be answered by simple computation: A standard symbol $\binom{a}{b}$, which looks like a fraction without a bar, is used to represent the number which appears in row a and diagonal b and thus, for example, the number of possible b-element subsets of a set with a elements (or the number of b-child committees that can be formed from a group of a children. (Note that $b \leq a$). The number can be calculated as follows:

$$\binom{a}{b} = \frac{a!}{b!(a-b)!}$$

For example, $\binom{5}{3}$, the number in row 5, diagonal 3, is:

$$\binom{5}{3} = \frac{5!}{3!(2!)} = \frac{5 \cdot 4 \cdot 3 \cdot 2}{3 \cdot 2 \cdot 2} = \frac{5 \cdot 4 \cdot 3 \cdot 2}{3 \cdot 2 \cdot 2} = \frac{10}{1} = 10$$

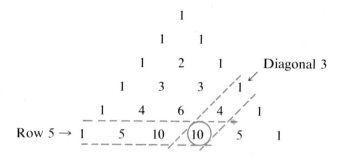

As might be expected, special exceptions must be made when a or b is zero or one (children can derive these from the triangle):

$$\binom{a}{0} = 1 \qquad \binom{a}{1} = a \qquad \binom{0}{0} = 1 \qquad 0! = 1$$

e.g.

$$\binom{5}{0} = 1 \qquad \binom{5}{1} = 5 \qquad \binom{5}{2} = 10 \qquad \binom{5}{3} = 10 \qquad \binom{5}{4} = 5 \qquad \binom{5}{5} = 1$$

The entire triangle can be represented with this new notation.

If there are thirty children in a class, how many committees of each size can be formed?

$$\binom{30}{0}, \binom{30}{1}, \binom{30}{2}, \ldots, \binom{30}{30}$$

How many committees could we have in our class? 2^{30} (a rather large number!)

A visual image of the successive powers of two can be obtained by constructing the first few rows of the Pascal triangle using blocks (Stern, Cuisenaire, Centimeter, or Unifix). A *few* additional rows can be shown if

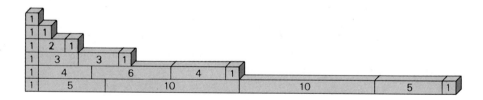

graph paper with quite small divisions is used; children are usually quite surprised when they first discover how rapidly the lengths of additional rows increase. This can lead to some interesting discussions. How much longer is the second row than the first? How much longer is the third row than the second? and so on. This question should be answered in two ways: The increases are 1, 2, 4, 8, 16, . . . ; and each row can be described as *twice* as long as the one before it. What if each row increased by *three* times its predecessor? What sequence of numbers would describe the increases? Is each increase three times as long as the one before it? How many rows could you build with a set of Cuisenaire rods? with a sheet of graph paper? How many rows would fit inside the classroom if you had enough rods? What if each increase were a power of 4? 5? 10? . . . ?

      Suppose we connect the numbers in Pascal's triangle with lines, as follows:

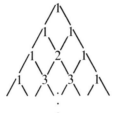

Now suppose we remove the numbers:

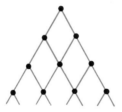

If these are thought of as (a network of) roads, in how many different ways can a car go from the "top" to any given intersection (no backing up)? If this pattern is used to cut grooves in a board large enough for a marble to roll through when the board is tilted, how many paths might the marble take in rolling from *A* to *B*? *A* to *C*? *A* to *D*? *A* to *E*? *A* to *F*?

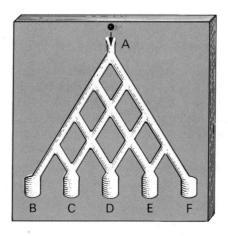

All physical aspects of the board being equal (smoothness of paths and intersection points, tilt of the board, and so on), if a marble were rolled 16 (2^4) times, how many times would you guess it would end at B? C? D? E? F? If such a board can be constructed, these guesses can be checked; if the marble is rolled $n \cdot 2^4$ times, where $n \geq 1$, it should arrive at each of B, C, D, E, and F *about* $n \cdot 1$, $n \cdot 4$, $n \cdot 6$, $n \cdot 4$ and $n \cdot 1$ times each, respectively. The larger n is, the "better the chances."

This theoretical probability can be deduced by multiplying each number in Pascal's triangle by n, say 3; many familiar (though modified) patterns are suggested:

$$
\begin{array}{ccccccc}
  &   &   & 3 &   &   &   \\
  &   & 3 &   & 3 &   &   \\
  & 3 &   & 6 &   & 3 &   \\
3 &   & 9 &   & 9 &   & 3 \\
\end{array}
$$

3   12   18   12   3

3   15   30   30   15   3

⋮ ⋮ ⋮ ⋮ ⋮ ⋮ ⋮

Children can look forward to meeting Pascal's triangle again in high school when they encounter the binomial theorem. Noting that the coefficients of the six terms in the expansion of $(a + b)^5$ are 1, 5, 10, 10, 5, and 1 may bring back curious memories.

$$
\begin{aligned}
(a + b)^0 &= 1 \\
(a + b)^1 &= 1a^1b^0 + 1a^0b^1 \\
(a + b)^2 &= 1a^2b^0 + 2a^1b^1 + 1a^0b^2 \\
(a + b)^3 &= 1a^3b^0 + 3a^2b^1 + 3a^1b^2 + 1a^0b^3 \\
(a + b)^4 &= 1a^4b^0 + 4a^3b^1 + 6a^2b^2 + 4a^1b^3 + 1a^0b^4 \\
(a + b)^5 &= 1a^5b^0 + 5a^4b^1 + 10a^3b^2 + 10a^2b^3 + 5a^1b^4 + 1a^0b^5
\end{aligned}
$$

(This is where Pascal—or was it Fibonacci?—*began* it all.)

Projects, Questions, and Suggested Activities

1. Numerous topics and activities have been suggested and many more can be found in the suggested readings. Pick out one that is new to you; try it, find out all you can about it, then try it with a child. These could include such topics as the sieve of Eratosthenes, the Euclidean algorithm, patterns in columns of numbers, Pascal's triangle, the Fibonacci sequence, and so on.

2. Examine a current elementary textbook series to determine which topics discussed in this chapter can be found there. Is number theory used in teaching other topics?

Suggested Readings

Ainsworth, Nathan. "An Introduction to Sequence: Elementary School Mathematics and Science Enrichment." *The Arithmetic Teacher,* February 1970, pp. 143–45.

Fibonaccia.

Association of Teachers of Mathematics. *Notes on Mathematics in Primary Schools.* Cambridge: Cambridge University Press, 1967.

Browse through this book for seemingly endless activities which can be carried out with children. A highly recommended source book.

Bush, Mary Thomas. "Seeking Little Eulers." *The Arithmetic Teacher,* February 1972, pp. 105–7.

Network games.

Clarkson, David M. "Taxicab Geometry, Rabbits, and Pascal's Triangle — Discoveries in a Sixth Grade Classroom." *The Arithmetic Teacher,* October 1962, pp. 308–13.

Pascal's Triangle, the Fibonacci sequence, and some interesting inventions (4 "plustorial" = 4 + 3 + 2 + 1) by children.

Dodge, Winston E. "Mathematical Spelunking." *The Arithmetic Teacher,* December 1967, pp. 665–67.

Several good ideas involving primes, divisors, and so on, which can be discovered by upper grade children.

Gardner, Martin. "Mathematical Games." *Scientific American,* December 1969, pp. 122–27.

Dominoes and network problems.

Gardner, Martin. "Mathematical Games." *Scientific American,* July 1970, pp. 117–19.

A discussion of Fermat's "Last Theorem" and other topics for the interested reader.

Gardner, Martin. "Mathematical Games." *Scientific American,* August 1970, pp. 110–13.

Palindromes. (See Brown's article in *The Arithmetic Teacher,* November, 1972, pp. 549–51.)

Goldenberg, E. Paul. "Scrutinizing Number Charts." *The Arithmetic Teacher,* December 1970, pp. 645–53.

A wide variety of activities using lists of numbers; in the same issue, Schafer (pp. 654–56) illustrates a graphic representation of primes, composites, multiples, and factors.

Hervey, Margaret A., and Litwiller, Bonnie H. "Polygonal Numbers: A Study of Patterns." *The Arithmetic Teacher,* January 1970, pp. 33–38.

> Just what the title suggests. Some good ideas.

Hicks, Carl D. "EOPDICA." *The Arithmetic Teacher,* January 1973, pp. 17–23.

> An electronic device which can be used to teach odd and even numbers, square numbers, and prime and composite numbers.

Hildebrand, Francis. "Experiment in Enrichment." *The Arithmetic Teacher,* February 1963, pp. 68–71.

> An approach to primes using modular arithmetic.

Hoffer, Alan R. "What You Always Wanted to Know About Six But Have Been Afraid to Ask." *The Arithmetic Teacher,* March 1973, pp. 173–80.

> Must be read to be appreciated. Perfect numbers, polygonal numbers and more. In the same issue, see also Neuner's article (pp. 214–15) on using a number line to teach clock arithmetic.

Hunter, J. A. H., and Madachy, Joseph S. *Mathematical Diversions.* Princeton, N.J.: Van Nostrand, 1963.

> Appropriately titled. A recreation and enrichment book from which ideas can be extracted for children's activities. Contains a wide variety of topics from number theory and other areas.

Loftus, Sonja. "Fibonacci Numbers: Fun and Fundamentals for the Slow Learner." *The Arithmetic Teacher,* March 1970, pp. 204–8.

> Don't let the title fool you. Many good ideas here for not-so-slow learners, too.

Meconi, L. J. "Discovering Structure Through Patterns." *The Arithmetic Teacher,* November 1972, pp. 531–33.

> Patterns and structural properties from games with columns of numbers. In the same issue, Brown (pp. 549–51) describes some interesting activities with "palindromic numbers"—those whose digits read the same forwards and backwards, such as 257752. Five more games are described by Trotter (pp. 558–60). Although easy games to play for enjoyable drill, they develop problem-solving skill. Some number theory and a use for the Fibonacci sequence.

Oliver, Charlene. "Gus's Magic Numbers: A Key to the Divisibility Test for Primes." *The Arithmetic Teacher,* March 1972, pp. 183–89.

> Divisibility tests derived by a sixth grader. Impressive. In the same issue, see Omejc's article (pp. 192–96) on the sieve of Eratosthenes, and Wardrop's article (pp. 218–20) on divisibility tests.

(See also p. 616 of the December 1972 issue for a reaction to Omejc's article.)

Rogers, Frank. "Divisibility Rule for Seven." *The Arithmetic Teacher,* January 1969, pp. 63–64.
> Just what the title suggests.

Sherzer, Laurence. "Adding Fractions Using the Definition of Addition of Rational Numbers and the Euclidean Algorithm." *The Arithmetic Teacher,* January 1973, pp. 27–28.
> Just what the title says.

Smith, Frank. "Divisibility Rules for the First Fifteen Primes." *The Arithmetic Teacher,* February 1971, pp. 85–87.
> Just what the title suggests. Possible enrichment for bright children.

Tassone, Sister Ann. "A Pair of Rabbits and a Mathematician." *The Arithmetic Teacher,* April 1967, pp. 285–88.
> The Fibonacci sequence and the golden ratio. Good enrichment ideas.

8. Teaching Geometry and Measurement

1. What Is Geometry and Why Teach It?

The word "geometry" no doubt still triggers in the minds of many readers memories of a tenth-grade experience involving axioms, definitions, proofs of theorems, drawings, compasses, rulers, protractors, and so on. (To many, the word has emotional associations as well. It is not at all uncommon to hear students say of their high school mathematics classes, "I loved algebra but hated geometry" or "I loved geometry but hated algebra.") First, it should be pointed out that the geometry in this chapter, and all geometry appropriate for elementary school, does *not* center around axioms, proofs, definitions, and the like. Second, the question at the head of this paragraph should have read "What are geometries and why teach them?" because, as we shall see, there are many geometries: We hear of metric geometry and nonmetric geometry, Euclidean geometry and non-Euclidean geometry, projective geometry, transformational geometry, topology, plane geometry, solid geometry, spherical geometry, affine geometry, coordinate geometry, motion geometry, and many others. We need not concern ourselves with any elaborate classification of geometries, but we should note that not all of the above labels refer to entirely different geometries. (Euclidean geometry, for example, is a particular kind of affine geometry.) There are, however, enough significant differences among geometries that it is not easy to state, in any but the broadest of terms, what they have in common, i.e., to identify "the meaning" of the now-generic term "geometry." Certainly the original derivation, from the Greek words for "earth" and "measure," is now inadequate. While no *definition* is implied, we can assert that geometry is a study of certain sets of points in space, frequently "idealized" models of physical objects, examined from various points of view, focusing on fundamental characteristics of those sets and relationships among them.

That geometry is now firmly entrenched in the elementary school mathematics program is obvious, at least if the professional journals and elementary textbooks for children can be used as an index: One sixth-grade textbook with a 1959 copyright date did not list "geometry" nor any geometric topics other than measures of area and volume in its index; a 1966 edition from the same publisher and grade level had nearly forty entries related to geometry alone, excluding measurement. The *Arithmetic Teacher,* in a four-year period in the 1950s had one article on geometry; in the comparable interval in the 1960s there were over seventy (curiously, perhaps, many of these were aimed at the preschool, kindergarten, and primary grades). Why is geometry, which for years had been relegated exclusively to the tenth grade, appearing as a major component of the elementary program? Several reasons, some more cogent than others, have been advanced to account for this:

1. There is abundant research evidence that children *can* learn a great deal of geometry at an early age; some claim that five-year-olds can, in fact, learn it easier than fifteen-year-olds.
2. It provides valuable background for numerical work, especially for that related to fractions.
3. It provides a welcome break—for both children and their teachers—from the routine of work with numbers.
4. It provides an opportunity for children to consider, interpret, organize, generalize, and thus better understand many aspects of their environments.
5. It provides many opportunities to develop logical thinking and reasoning, much of which can be expected to transfer to numerical problem-solving situations.
6. It can be aesthetically as well as intellectually pleasing and stimulating.
7. It provides a background that can make the more formal study of high school geometry meaningful; at the same time, its introduction in the elementary school affords an opportunity to broaden—considerably—the total K–12 exposure of children to this broad field of mathematics.
8. Geometry can be "fun" to children.

We emphasize once more—and shall, no doubt, again—that elementary school geometry is informal and intuitive, generally devoid of the formal axiomatic treatment that characterizes traditional high school work. Theorems, definitions, and axioms imposed "from above," i.e., by textbooks or teachers, are conspicuously absent at this level, although they may quite reasonably be expected to evolve—in children's terms—as a result of their curiosity and in response to their need and desire to talk about their observations and discoveries.

2. Mathematical Review

The mathematical review section of this chapter is sketchy; it will contain a little bit about several things but not much about any of them. While this may seem lamentable, it is necessary because of the scope of the subject matter. We have chosen to examine in more detail certain topics and ignore others. This, too, is unfortunate, but necessary. We will examine, in some detail, a few we believe may be "new" to many readers, and we will ignore some that are more common. Hopefully, the reader's previous study has included a significant number of the topics to be glossed over here (although experience suggests this may not be the case). No rigorous, in-depth previous study of all of the topics we shall review is essential (or feasible; perhaps not even desirable) for most readers, and it is to be expected that subsequent portions of the chapter, continued study, and work with children may supplement what will be covered here.

There is sometimes a fine line between "geometry" and "measurement" involving numbers. In the material that follows, we are inclined to take what we feel to be a *practical* rather than a rigorous view. That is, we prefer to consider the two topics together when it makes sense to do so, as we do in the classroom.

Fundamental Concepts

While geometries differ, sometimes dramatically, a few basic concepts and considerations are common to most of them, with varying degrees of emphasis. These include the following (we may think of "ordinary" Euclidean geometry in discussing them).

Dimension and Basic Geometric Entities

"Geometric objects" and their "real world" counterparts, when they exist, are commonly viewed as being "1 dimensional," "2 dimensional," or "3 dimensional." These terms refer roughly to the number of linearly *measurable* (though not necessarily measured) attributes of the object. One-dimensional objects are those that are classified as having only *length*. Lines and segments are 1 dimensional. Two-dimensional objects are those that have the attribute of *width* or breadth in addition to length. Triangles, squares, and shadows are 2 dimensional or "plane figures." Three-dimensional objects are those "solid figures" that possess a third attribute, *thickness*, depth, or height. (All physical objects are actually 3 dimensional, though we *think* of an uncrumpled sheet of paper, for example, as being 2 dimensional.) An additional "dimension," although we frequently do not think of it in these terms, is the absence of *any* dimension: zero-dimensional, if you will. A point is "0 dimensional"—it has nothing to measure; it is simply a location.

These are by no means definitions, but merely rough categorizations of the basic geometric entities: Most geometries concern themselves, then, with *points, lines, planes,* and *space.* "Geometric figures" are sets of discrete points; lines or subsets of lines, such as segments or rays; planes or subsets of planes, such as triangles, circles, and so on; or 3-dimensional figures such as cones, prisms, and pyramids.

The word "dimension" is frequently used in a slightly different way: We talk about the dimensions of a rectangle as being 3 and 4, for example; the numbers indicate the measured "lengths" of its length and width.

Incidence

A second common concern of geometries is the set of relationships among the entities (points, lines, planes, and space). Using the language and ideas of sets, we usually think of points as "basic" elements, and of lines, planes, and space as *sets* of points. Thus, a line is a particular set of points; a plane is a particular set of lines; and space is a set of planes. A "transitive" relationship holds between the entities: If a point is on (in) a particular line and that line is in a particular plane, then the point is on the plane. These statements mean the same thing:

Point *A* *is on* line *m*.
Line *m* *contains* point *A*.
Point *A* and line *m* are *incident*.
Point *A* *is incident with* line *m*.
Line *m* *is incident with* point *A*.

(The word "incident" is rarely used and we need not use it beyond this paragraph, since the set language is more familiar.) Some familiar relationships between points, lines, and planes involve the intersection of 2 lines, 2 planes, or a line and a plane. Parallelism of two lines, two planes, or a line and a plane, and perpendicular lines and planes are other general topics that may be thought of in this category.

Betweenness, Order, and Separation

Given several points on a line, the notion of order (e.g., "to the left of") is basic in many geometries, as is the notion of betweenness (e.g., "Point *C* is between points *A* and *B*"). There is no "order" of points in the *plane*. For example, in the picture below, we can say that *C* is between *A* and *B*, but it is meaningless to say that either *E* or *D* is between *A* and *B* (nor is *C* between *A* and *E*).

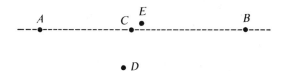

In some geometries, betweenness is meaningless. If we think of the earth as a "plane," and "great circles" (e.g., lines of longitude or the equator) as "lines," as in some spherical geometries, then each of three cities, *A*, *B*, *C* ("points") on the equator, for example, is "between" the other two. Think of these as widely separated along the equator; so "betweenness" becomes a useless notion (unless, perhaps, other definitions are imposed on the geometric theory).

Related to betweenness is the notion of separation: A point *separates* a line into 2 disjoint half-lines (neither of which contains the point); a line separates each plane on which it lies into 2 half-planes (neither containing the line); and each plane separates space into 2 half-spaces. When we think of a point separating a line, or of a line separating a plane, or of a plane separating space, the particular point, line, or plane is called the boundary (or border) of the half-lines, half-planes or half-spaces, respectively. A simple closed curve, such as a triangle, *separates* the plane into two parts, the *inside* and *outside* (or interior and exterior) of the triangle. Again the triangle borders each of these sets. Similarly, we can speak of the interior and exterior of an angle, since it separates the plane in which it lies. There are many relationships to examine whenever a set of points is separated. We do not think of segments, for example, as separating the plane, nor of solid figures like coffee cups as separating space (even though we colloquially speak of their "inside").

Separation is sometimes discussed in terms of partitioning. For example, we can say that a line partitions the plane into 3 subsets — the two half-planes and the line itself; each pair of these subsets is disjoint and the union of all three is the plane.

Angles

If a line is separated by a point, then the union of one of the determined half-lines and the point is usually called a *ray*. An angle is then usually defined as the set of points in the union of 2 rays which have a common endpoint. Angles are commonly classified as acute, right, obtuse, straight, and so on. We have previously mentioned the separation of the plane by an angle. The rays forming an angle are called the *sides* of the angle.

Curves

If, with a pencil, we draw any "line" without lifting the pencil (i.e., a *continuous* line), and do not retrace any portion of it, though possibly letting it cross itself, we have a model of a *curve* or *path*. A curve does not necessarily "wiggle" as in the ordinary usage of the word — a (straight) segment is a curve, for example. The classification of curves and relations among them is a major consideration of many geometries. The beginning and ending places of the pencil are the *endpoints* or *vertices* of the curve, which may be identical (coincident). A *simple* curve does not cross itself, and a *closed* curve has coincident endpoints. A *simple closed* curve, then, has both of these attributes. Properties of and relationships among particular simple closed curves, such as circles and polygons, especially triangles, are studied extensively in geometries.

Size and Shape

The relative sizes and shapes of geometric objects are major considerations in much of geometry. There are two ways of comparing the sizes and shapes of, say, two triangles: We can compare them in terms of making certain numerical measurements of the triangles with rulers or protractors, or we can compare them simply in terms of their *relative* sizes or shapes, without determining comparative numerical measures. Two figures are *similar* if they are the same shape. For example, a transparency drawing of a figure and its projected image on a screen, or a photograph and an enlargement of it, are pairs of similar figures. All circles are similar, as are all segments. If two similar objects are also of the same *size,* they are called *congruent.* Duplicate copies of a transparency or of a photograph, if they are the same size, are congruent figures. Two angles are congruent if one is a "tracing" of the other (without regard to how long we *draw* the sides) and two triangles are congruent if their "corresponding" angles and sides are congruent.

We usually think of measurement as the assignment of *numbers* to describe "size" or, in the case of angles, "shape" attributes of figures, compared either with some *standardized* sizes or shapes or with temporarily accepted "unit" sizes or shapes. The attributes we measure in geometry are *distances* between pairs of points, *openings* of angles, *areas* of simple closed curves, and *volumes* of solids. Imperfect measuring instruments are used, e.g., rulers, compasses, and protractors; and measurement always involves judgment. Inevitably, then, error must be acknowledged when measurements are made. (Even when we measure segments and angles *without* the assignment of numbers to them, i.e., to determine similarity or congruence with straightedge and compasses, we must accept the existence of error.) Precision in measurement can be increased by increasing our own skill, precaution, and judgment, or by improving the instruments. The former is largely a matter of practice and attitude. The latter can be accomplished in two significantly different ways: first, by choosing smaller and smaller *units* of measure; a ruler scaled in centimeters (only), for example, will provide a more precise measure of segment *AB* (the distance between

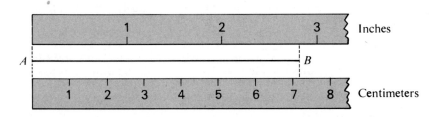

A and *B*) than will a ruler scaled in inches (only): 7 cm is a closer approximation of the length of $\overline{AB}$ than is 3 inches (this will not always occur, of course, but given *many* segments to measure, closer approximations are likely to occur more often when smaller units are used). Secondly, measuring instruments are improved by increasing the number of subdivisions of the unit of measure. If we subdivide the inch-ruler into sixteenths — or better, sixty-fourths — we obtain a more precise measure of $\overline{AB}$, above, than with the centimeter-ruler as it is. If we further subdivide the centimeter-ruler into millimeters, we can accomplish the same thing. By *sufficient* subdividing, we can measure distances or angles with any desired degree of precision. Judgment in measuring is involved even before measurements are made — in choosing an appropriate instrument and in choosing appropriate units. It would be as ridiculous to measure the distance between two towns with a 12-inch ruler as it would be to measure the thickness of a needle with it. In the first case, the *unit* is "wrong" (miles would be more appropriate), and in the second case the *instrument* is "wrong" (a micrometer would make more sense).

Change

Much of contemporary geometry is viewed in terms of changes or *transformations*, made in geometric figures as a result of "doing things" to them or of viewing them in various ways. Even much of conventional Euclidean geometry can be viewed in this way. If triangle $A'B'C'$ is congruent to triangle ABC, then we may think of $A'B'C'$ as a transformation — a change in position, perhaps — of ABC. In topology, some transformations we would normally think of as changes are not, topologically speaking, *basic* changes at all. A cup molded from a clay ball is topologically equivalent to the clay ball. Since many readers may be unfamiliar with this important topic, we will discuss a few of the basic ideas of transformations in some detail in the next section.

Transformations

Much of the geometry that is appropriate for the elementary school can be viewed in terms of transformations, just as much of more formal geometry can. While we intend to abide by our resolve to remain informal, we shall digress slightly here — and only momentarily. We implied in the last paragraph that a transformation is a change, and that is a reasonable but perhaps somewhat too general view. More formally, a transformation, for our purposes, can be viewed as a function whose *domain* and *range* are sets of points, i.e., geometric figures. Each point in the domain is associated with or *mapped with* a unique point in the range (called its "image") according to the *rule* of the function. The image of the entire domain is the range. That is, the image of the original figure is another figure, generally different (though not necessarily so) in some respect(s). One example of a transformation:

> Suppose we consider the three lines, ℓ_1, ℓ_2, and ℓ_3 below. On ℓ_1 is a segment, AB, with a few points, C, D, and E identified between A and B. On ℓ_2 is a point P. Suppose we let $\overline{AB}$ be the domain (our original figure) and let the function rule be:
>
> *For each point X in $\overline{AB}$, map it with the point X' in ℓ_3 such that X, P, and X' are collinear.*

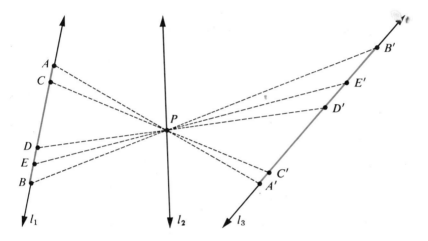

In the particular example above, we can note several things:

1. The image of segment AB is also a segment, $A'B'$ (the image is *similar* to the original).
2. $\overline{A'B'}$ is "upside down" relative to $\overline{AB}$ (it is oriented differently).
3. The two segments $\overline{AB}$ and $\overline{A'B'}$ are not congruent $-\overline{AB}$ is shorter (the original figure is "distorted").
4. The *relative* distance between points seems to be unchanged.

What would happen to these relationships between $\overline{AB}$ and its image (a) if ℓ_3 were parallel to ℓ_1? (b) if ℓ_3 were replaced with a circle? (c) if points in $\overline{AB}$ were "projected" through ℓ_2 along parallel rays? Suppose the lines were replaced by planes (viewed "edge on" in the picture) and segment AB were replaced by a triangle. If point P were a "pinhole," what would the image of $\overline{AB}$ look like? What if the third plane were the surface of a sphere?

When we consider any transformation, it is appropriate to consider two things: What characteristics of the original figure are *changed* (in the image) by the transformation and what characteristics remain *unchanged* (invariant)?

Rigid Motions

An important class of transformations are those in which the image of a figure is usually in a different location or oriented in a different way from the original, but in the same plane and undistorted (the image is congruent to the original). To represent this, cut out a small shape from a piece of cardboard (a square, triangle, circle, or an irregular shape — it makes no difference). Trace the outline of the shape on a sheet of paper to represent its "original" position. Then pick up the shape and toss it in the air, but let it fall on the paper. Trace its shape again, wherever it may have fallen, to represent an "image" position. Consider the possibilities in such a toss: The shape *might* land exactly where it started (unlikely, but not impossible — it probably will land in a different position); it might flip over and land "upside down" relative to its original position; and quite probably the image will be oriented differently from the original.

If we now try to describe, as succinctly as possible, how we could have taken the shape and moved it to its new position (without tossing), we could do so in at most 3 kinds of moves: *Slide* it along the paper in a straight line to the new location; *turn* it clockwise or counterclockwise as needed; and, if necessary, *flip* it over. These 3 "moves" represent the three "rigid motions," that is, transformations, which move the figure to a different location in the plane without distorting it. The technical names of these moves are: *translations* ("slides"), *rotations* ("turns"), and *reflections* ("flips"). These transformations can be described more precisely as follows:

Translations.   Translations (slides) can be conveniently described in terms of *vectors*. A vector is sometimes called a "directed line segment."

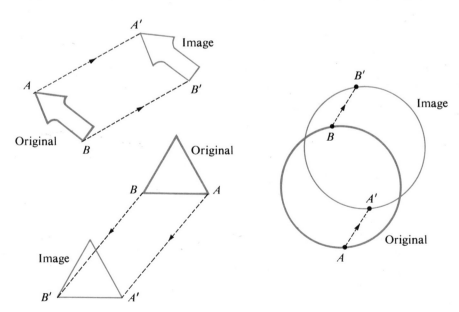

If we think of a straight path from a point A, which we can call the *initial* point, to a *terminal* point, B, that path is a vector. That is, a vector is a straight path from a point A to a point B. (If $A = B$, we have a "zero vector"). We can describe a translation, then, as follows: Choose any point, A, of the figure as the *initial* point of a vector. Let the *terminal* point of the vector be the image, A', of A. Then map each remaining point of the figure with the terminal point of a vector which is *parallel* to the original vector and which has the same *magnitude* (is the same length) as the original.

It should be clear that translations are rigid motions, i.e., that they preserve size and shape. Furthermore, they preserve *orientation*: The pairs of figures "point" the same way, and any lines in the image are parallel to the corresponding lines in the original.

Rotations.   Given any plane figure, any point O in the plane of the figure, and any angle measure, θ, a rotation ("turn") of the figure can be described by this function rule:

> *For each point X in the figure, the image of X, which we can call X', is that point on a circle with center at O, and with segment XO as a radius such that angle XOX' has measure θ. If O is on the figure, it is its own image.)*

We call O the *center* of rotation and θ (the measure of) the *angle* of rotation. Although angles can be measured either in a clockwise or counterclockwise direction, we will use only the latter here.

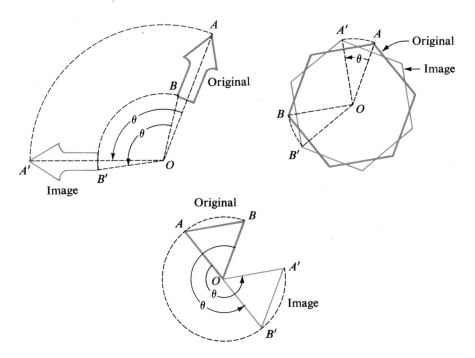

It can be seen that rotations, like translations, preserve congruence. Unlike translations, they change orientation. The distance from any
point X to the center of rotation is also preserved.

Reflections.   The image of a figure under a reflection, as the name
suggests, is like a mirror image of the figure. A function rule for reflections
can be described as follows:

> *Given any plane figure and any line ł in the plane of the figure, the
> image of any point X of the figure is the terminal point of a vector
> which has X as its initial point, which is perpendicular to and inter-
> sects ł, and whose length is twice the distance from X to ł. (If X
> is on ł, it is its own image.)*

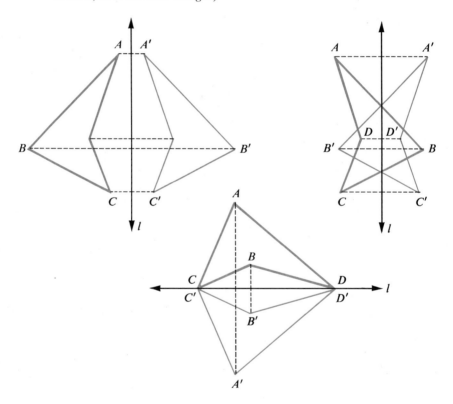

The line ł is called an axis of symmetry. The union of any figure and a reflection of it is a *symmetric* figure. Any connected figure is symmetric if
there exists at least one axis which intersects the figure so that the points
on either side of the line are a reflection of those on the other. A regular
polygon with n sides has n such axes. A circle has infinitely many. A figure
for which at least one such line can be found is said to be symmetric about
each of its axes of symmetry or to have bilateral symmetry.

Some Relationships Among Rigid Motions. For every rigid motion of a figure, there is another rigid motion of the same type which can be performed on the image so that the "image of the image" is the original figure. For translations and reflections this can be defined by reversing the direction of the original vector, and for rotations it can be defined by choosing θ, the corresponding angle measure, to be $360 - \theta$.

Every "pair" of translations, i.e., one translation followed by a second, can be accomplished by a single translation, e.g., the translation suggested by vector a, followed by the translation suggested by b, could be accomplished by the single translation suggested by vector c.

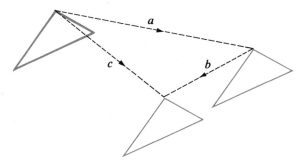

The same is true for any pair of rotations (but not for any pair of reflections).

A reflection in one axis followed by a reflection in a second axis perpendicular to the first is equivalent to a 180° rotation of the original figure, where the center of rotation is the point of intersection of the two axes.

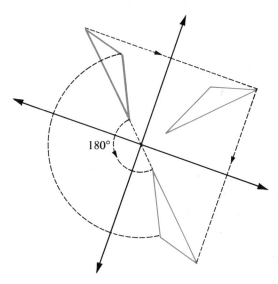

Any translation can be accomplished by, i.e., is equivalent to, a pair of reflections. One possibility for a particular translation is suggested here:

Figure 2 is the image of Figure 1 under the translation determined by vector *a*. Figure 3 is the reflection of Figure 1 in line ℓ_1 which is perpendicular to vector *a*. Line ℓ_2 is parallel to ℓ_1 and is midway between A and A', two corresponding points in Figures 2 and 3 respectively. Figure 2, then, is the image of Figure 3 under the reflection in ℓ_2. We could view this "in reverse" of course, i.e., if we first reflect a figure in one line, then reflect the image in a second line parallel to the first, the final image is equivalent to a single translation of the original figure.

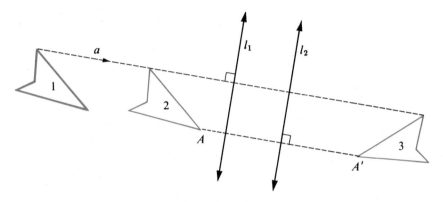

Similarly, a rotation is equivalent to a pair of reflections. Triangle *ABC* here, for example, can be transformed to $A'B'C'$ either by the single indicated rotation around point O, or by two successive reflections — lines ℓ_1 and ℓ_2 intersect at point O. If *ABC* is first reflected in ℓ_1 and then its image, $A''B''C''$, is reflected in ℓ_2, we have $A'B'C'$.

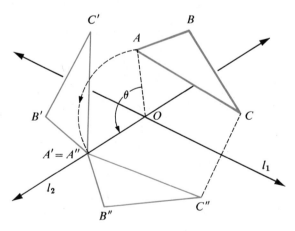

Numerous other generalizations can be made about rigid motions, but we will note just one more: If we consider any figure S and let T be the set of all possible translations of S, we can describe certain *geometric* properties of T in *algebraic* terms. Suppose we let *a*, *b*, *c*, and so on, be translations (elements of T) and let any symbol, say $+$, mean "followed by." Thus $a + b$ means "translation a followed by translation b." Set T, together with the operation $+$, is an example of an algebraic structure called a *group*, because it possesses these four properties:

1. The *closure* property: The sum of any two translations is a translation. (See p. 305).
2. The *associative* property: If a, b, and c are any translations, then $(a + b) + c = a + (b + c)$. The interested reader may easily demonstrate this characteristic.
3. The *identity* property: There exists a translation, which we can call 0 such that for any translation a, $a + 0 = a$ and $0 + a = a$. (This translation is determined by the "0 vector," i.e., no movement.)
4. The *inverse* property: For every translation a, there exists a translation, a^{-1}, such that $a + a^{-1} = 0$. A consequence of this (and the associative property) is that every equation of the form $a + \square = b$ has a unique solution, namely $a^{-1} + b$.

Can similar generalizations be made about the other rigid motions? Can other algebraic concepts describe the behavior of translations? (For example, is $a + b = b + a$?)

Projections

We will now consider briefly two transformations from one plane to another. These are among a class of transformations called projections. As the name "projection" suggests, we can think of these in terms of images or shadows cast by rays of light.

First, imagine a very powerful flashlight with a very tiny opening. This is a model of a *point source* of light. Suppose we cast light from a point source onto a figure drawn on a clear plastic or glass "plane" and then place

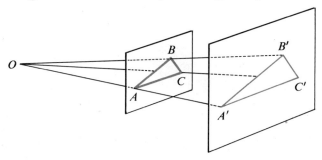

another plane parallel to the first. Such a transformation preserves similarity and orientation but not congruence. In fact the image is an *enlargement* of the original. If the point source is moved farther away from the original, the amount of enlargement is reduced, and if it is moved closer, the enlargement is greater. This projection can be viewed in one plane (imagine *drawing* the image, then transferring it to the plane of the original figure).

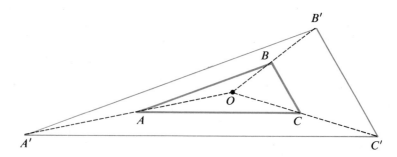

Which characteristics of the original would be preserved and which would change if the image plane were not parallel to the original? What would happen if the two planes remain parallel but move closer together or farther apart? How can we describe the appearance of the image viewed from "behind" (between the planes)? What would happen to the image if the point *O* were in a different position?

Before leaving this topic, we might note a relationship between it and art. (There are many surprising correlations between mathematics and the aesthetic worlds of art and music. Although they are not at all surprising to those who see mathematics as basically aesthetic, or art as basically mathematical.) In a representative painting of buildings, roads, trees, and so on, there is always perspective, especially where considerable depth is represented in the picture (painted on a flat, plane, surface). By extending pairs of segments representing *horizontal* ones, we can locate "vanishing points" (sometimes outside of the painting), analogous to point sources of light. Fronts of buildings are "images" of their backs, and so on.

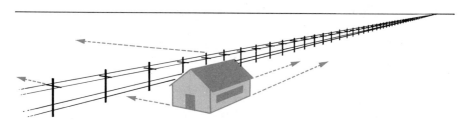

For the second kind of projection to be examined, suppose our source of light is enlarged so that *parallel* rays of light, perpendicular to the plane, shine on the figure. Under this transformation, not only similarity and orientation are preserved, but so is congruence. Such a transformation is analogous to a translation from one plane to another. Again we may ask which characteristics of the original would be preserved and which would

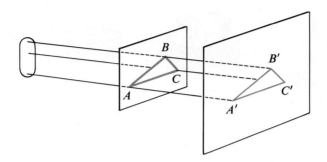

change if we were to alter the distance between planes, or arrange them so that they are not parallel. What would happen if the light rays were not perpendicular to the plane? We may view these "from above" to get an idea.

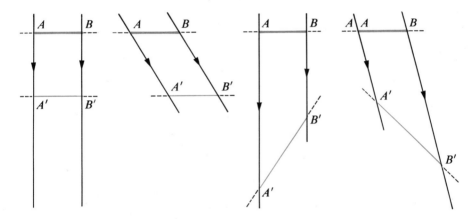

Solids

The study of parallel and point-source projections can lead to many things, including the study of solids. If we consider any simple closed curve and all the lines suggested by *parallel* light rays which intersect the curve, we have a model for a *surface*. If that surface is cut by two parallel planes, as in the previous section, then those points of the surface between the planes, together with both the points on the curve (and its image) and the points in the *interiors* of those curves, all join to form a *cylinder*. Several variations and combinations are possible: (a) If the light source is perpendicular to the two planes, it is a *right* cylinder. (b) The simple closed curve may be of *any* shape; if it is a circle, then the cylinder is a circular cylinder (people usually interpret "cylinder" to mean a right circular cylinder); if the curve is a polygon, the cylinder is called a *prism*. The tops and bottoms of cylinders are called *faces* (faces of prisms are sometimes called bases). The sides of a prism are called its *lateral faces*. The segment determined by the intersection of two adjacent lateral faces is an *edge*, as are the sides

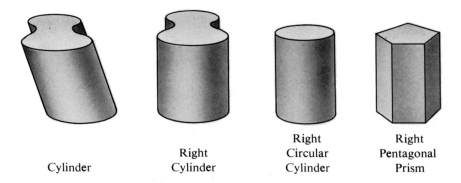

	Right	Right Circular	Right Pentagonal
Cylinder	Cylinder	Cylinder	Prism

of the polygon which form its base; and the *vertices* of a prism are those of
the polygons at the bases. An interesting relationship can be found between
the numbers of faces, edges, and vertices of a prism (and some other solids
which we will consider shortly). The pentagonal prism above has 7 faces
(2 bases and 5 lateral faces), 15 edges (5 on the sides, and 5 each on the top
and bottom), and 10 vertices. The sum of the numbers of faces and vertices,
7 + 10, differs from the number of edges, 15, by 2. While that in itself can
hardly be considered interesting, what *is* interesting is that this relationship
holds for *all* solids that have plane surfaces. If this idea is new to you, check
it out with various prisms. The relationship is called Euler's (pronounced
"oilers") formula:

$$F + V = E + 2$$

or $(F + V) - E = 2$, etc. We will consider other plane-faced solids later.
(Euler was another mathematical "giant" of the 1700s.)

  Just as parallel projections led to the notion of cylinders, the point-
source projection leads to that of *cones*. Without going through all the details, we usually think of a cone as the set of points from the source to the
first plane. The simple closed curve can be any shape, and we can have all
the variations as for cylinders, e.g., right circular cones (the ice-cream cone
shape), and so on. When the face (or base if you prefer) is a polygon, the
cone is called a *pyramid*. (The ancient Egyptian pyramids were in the shape
of cones with square bases, i.e., square right pyramids.) The lateral faces
of pyramids are always triangular, just as those of prisms are parallelograms

5 Faces
5 Vertices
8 Edges

Right Circular Cone   Right Square Pyramid

(rectangular in the case of right prisms). You may wish to check Euler's formula for other pyramids.

If two right circular cones are placed vertex-to-vertex with their faces parallel, an interesting thing to consider is the set of points obtained by the intersection of that "double napped cone" and a *plane*. Think of the various ways one could saw it in two parts using straight cuts (as shown here, for example), and then consider the shapes left on the edges of the cut

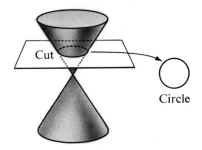

Circle

surface. You should be able to see how to "cut off" the shapes of the so-called *conic sections*. The circle we obtained here is one of them; the others are the parabola, ellipse, and hyperbola. (There are spherical, elliptical,

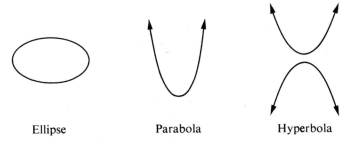

Ellipse   Parabola   Hyperbola

parabolic, and hyperbolic geometries.) How could the cut be made to produce a point? Two intersecting lines? Can you envision the intersection being a single line?

Before we look at a third (and our final) general kind of solid, we will consider a few attributes which a given 3-dimensional object may or may not possess. First, it may be solid in the sense of a block of wood or it may be hollow like a cardboard box. In geometry, we *usually* think of 3-dimensional objects in the latter sense though we *call* them "solids." Second, assuming it is hollow, it may or may not have an opening in its surface. If a cardboard box, for example, is sealed, then anything inside it is trapped, but if we open the box or cut a hole in one of its surfaces, then anything sufficiently small can get out of the box (or into it): We will consider the sealed kinds here, although the latter are of considerable interest in topology. Such a solid (one with no holes in its surface), like a simple

closed curve in a plane, has an unambiguous interior and exterior. It therefore separates space. We will consider only those figures in which any pair
of points in the interior can be connected by some path: A fly can go from
any inside point in a box to any other inside point of the box without touching the box or going outside it, but not so in a figure like the double cone
we considered above.

Third, a 3-dimensional object may or may not have a hole through
it, like a doughnut or an inner tube. Those shapes without such holes are
called *simply connected* solids. We will consider only simply connected
solids here, although the others are of considerable interest to children —
and topologists. (One way to think of this attribute is this: Imagine tying a
loop of elastic cord loosely around an inner tube through its hole and doing
the same with a closed solid like a cylinder. The cylinder is simply con-

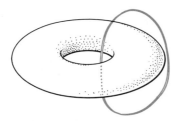

nected because we can always slip the loop off without breaking either it
or the solid. Finally, a simply connected solid may or may not be *convex*.
A convex solid is one in which the segment determined by any pair of
points on its interior is entirely contained in the interior, i.e., it is possible
to connect any pair of points in the interior with a *straight* path which doesn't
touch the surface or go outside. For example, consider cylinders A and B.
If we look at them from above, we can see that for *some* points inside cylinder A it is impossible to connect them with a straight path which is entirely
inside, whereas every pair of points inside B can be so connected. Thus
cylinder B is convex, but A is not. (Simple closed curves in a plane are
considered convex or not by this same criterion.)

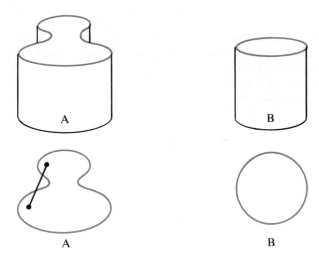

The final type of solid we will consider is called a *polyhedron*—a solid whose faces are polygonal (triangles, squares, and so on). Polyhedrons may or may not be simply connected or convex, and, of course, can take on a wide variety of shapes. Prisms and pyramids are polyhedrons, since their faces are all polygonal.

Of the many possible polyhedra there are five of particular interest. These are called the Platonic solids, after Plato. If we examine these 5

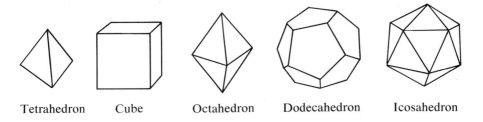

| Tetrahedron | Cube | Octahedron | Dodecahedron | Icosahedron |

polyhedrons several things can be noted: None has holes in its surface, each is simply connected (no doughnut-like holes), and each is convex. What makes them unique among polyhedrons, however, is that in each of them, every face is a *regular* polygonal region, congruent to each of the other faces: The tetrahedron, octahedron, and icosahedron are made of 4, 8, and 20 congruent equilateral triangles, respectively. The cube's 6 faces are congruent squares, and the 12 faces of the dodecahedron are congruent, regular pentagons. Furthermore, if we measure the *angles* at which two adjacent faces meet at an edge, they, too, are all congruent.

It is quite natural to consider whether there could be any other polyhedrons with both of these characteristics. When the ancient Greeks considered this, they discovered that it would be impossible for there to be any others. So important was this thought to be that these solids were associated with the five "basic" elements of nature—earth, air, water, fire, and the entire universe itself.

It is an interesting exercise to prove that no other solids could have these two properties of the Platonic solids. We will not do so here, but a few observations and questions may suggest a proof for the interested reader: Does the same number of polygons meet at each vertex of a given Platonic solid? Is this necessary? What is the *minimum* number? What is the measure of each angle of the polygon which determines the faces of a given Platonic solid? What is the minimum number of sides a polygon can have? What is the sum of the angle measures of all the polygons which meet at a vertex? Must this be less than 360°? Why?

Another project for the interested reader is to count (carefully!) the number of faces, edges, and vertices of the Platonic solids and show that Euler's formula holds for them, as it does for any simply connected polyhedron.

Networks

If a paper model of a cube is cut along some of its edges, it can be flattened out in one piece. One way to do so is shown. Each of the Platonic

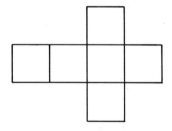

solids can similarly be cut apart. These can serve as patterns for constructing paper or cardboard models of the solids. (They may also help to answer some of the questions we raised about the possibility of constructing other regular polyhedrons.) If we examine these patterns, the segments that correspond to edges of the solids are seen to be *paths* in a plane, with a vertex at either end of each path. The faces of the solids become regions. This kind of figure is an example of a *network*.

A network is a set of connected paths (which need not be straight). If a path meets itself or another path, the point of intersection is called a vertex. A road map is one model of a network, with towns, cities, and crossroads as vertices and roads as paths. If one begins at any town (or crossroad) on a map, there may be one road out of town, 2 roads, 3 roads, or many roads. There may be "dead ends." (We would think of the end

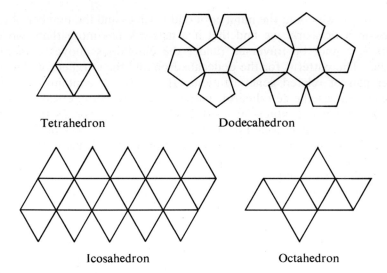

Tetrahedron   Dodecahedron

Icosahedron   Octahedron

of a dead-end path as a vertex, even though there is no crossroad there and possibly no town.)

We will consider here only two of the problems that occur in the study of networks. Both are counting problems.

In a network, a vertex is considered *odd* or *even* depending upon whether there are an odd or an even number of choices of paths one might take from that vertex. Consider these networks, for example. Can you

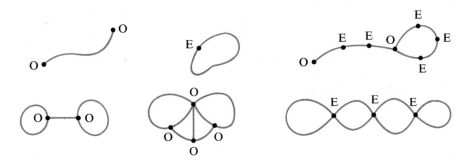

draw a network with only 1 odd vertex? With any odd number of odd vertices?

The first problem is to determine whether a given network can be traced without lifting the pencil and without traversing (tracing) any path more than once. When this can be done for a given network, that network is said to be "traversable." Before continuing, the reader may wish to determine which of the networks determined by the patterns of the Platonic solids are traversable and which are not (a *vertex* may be crossed any number of times), and which of the networks above are traversable.

When we count the number of odd vertices and the number of even vertices in a network, we find that if a network has more than two odd vertices it cannot be traversed (under the conditions above)—otherwise it can be. The patterns for the dodecahedron and the tetrahedron illustrate another pair of related generalizations: If a network contains only *even* vertices (such as the tetrahedron pattern), it can be traversed beginning at *any* vertex; if it contains at most 2 odd vertices (such as the dodecahedron pattern, which contains 36 even vertices and 2 odd ones), then it can be traversed *only* by beginning at one of the odd vertices. (Try it; where does the tracing end?)

The paths of a network may or may not *separate* the plane in which it lies. For example, these paths do *not* separate the plane. They do not bound (form the boundary of) any region. Only 1 region, the plane itself,

can be identified. Each of the networks below, however, determines (partitions the plane into) more than one region, that is, each has a region or regions inside the "loops" and an "outside" region (the rest of the plane).

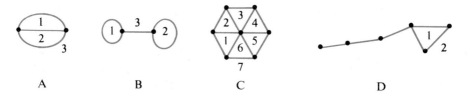

A   B   C   D

Our second counting problem with networks, then, is to determine the relationship between the numbers of vertices, paths, and regions in a given network. In the picture above, networks A and B each have 3 regions, 2 vertices, and 3 paths. Network C has 7 regions, 7 vertices, and 12 paths. How many regions, vertices, and paths are there in the patterns of each of the Platonic solids?

The relationship turns out, perhaps surprisingly, to be Euler's formula again. Using F, V, and E to represent the number of regions (faces), vertices, and paths (edges) in any network, we find again that

$$F + V - E = 2$$

One may be tempted to say, "Of course—if Euler's formula holds for the *solid*, why shouldn't it hold for the corresponding network?" True, but notice that the numbers of faces, vertices, and edges of the solid is *not* the same as the number of faces (regions), vertices, and edges (paths) of the network. The tetrahedron, for example, has 4 faces, 4 vertices, and 6 edges;

its network has 5 faces, 6 vertices, and 9 edges. (This is because some of
the edges and vertices are duplicated when we transfer it from 3 dimensions
to 2.) Relative to this, consider the problem of constructing a model of a
tetrahedron using plastic straws strung together with string (thin elastic
cord works nicely). We can lay out the network with 9 straws strung together by one *continuous* piece of string because the network has only
even vertices and so is traversable. But this would make a tetrahedron

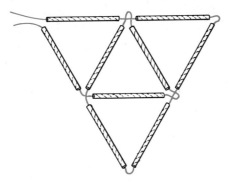

with some double edges. To get around this, we must remove some of the
straws (alternate "exterior" paths, e.g., 1, 6, 8). But this forms a network

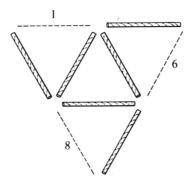

with 6 odd vertices, so it cannot be traced, i.e., there is no way to join the
vertices with one continuous piece of string! When we tie the appropriate
vertices together, we still have 4 odd vertices, so the edges of a tetrahedron
cannot be traced (continuously and without retracing).

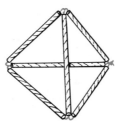

Coordinates

The patterns of the Platonic solids, except for the dodecahedron, are examples not only of networks, but of *tessellations*. If we take a sufficient number of equilateral triangles or squares, we can cover as large a plane surface as we wish, without any overlaps and without leaving any gaps. These shapes *tessellate* the plane. There are other shapes which do so, and there are many interesting things to do with this idea, some of which we will consider later. For now, we consider tessellation of *squares*, perhaps the most obvious one (it can go on and on, of course). This simple

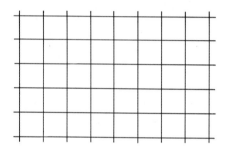

network can lead to many things, including a system for locating points — and sets of points — in the plane. Like a map of streets and avenues in a city, the *Cartesian coordinate system* (after Descartes) enables us to locate any point in the plane, or to describe its location, using pairs of numbers. We will review this system only very briefly since it is certainly familiar to most readers: Choosing an arbitrary vertex, 0, as a beginning point (origin), the square network enables us to identify two perpendicular lines, x and y,

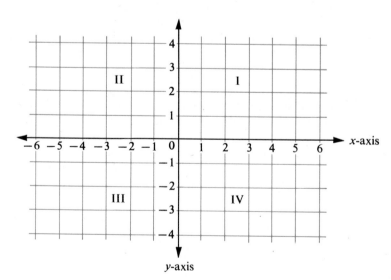

through 0. These lines are called the x-axis and the y-axis; the x-axis is usually horizontal and the y-axis vertical. Each vertex on each axis is then labeled with an integer (positive integers going up and to the right). The axes partition the network into 4 *quadrants*, traditionally labeled I, II, III, IV; the first quadrant is above the x-axis and to the right of the y-axis, and the remaining labels are assigned in order to the quadrants, counterclockwise about the origin.

From any vertex, A, on the network and not on one of the axes, we consider the two lines through A which are perpendicular to the axes. The two numbers a and b at the points of intersection of these lines and the x and y axes respectively are the *coordinates* of A (a is the x-coordinate and

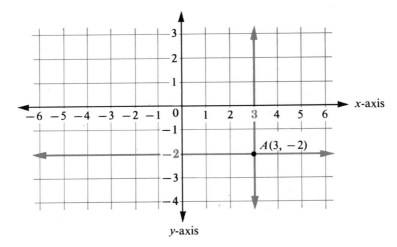

b is the y-coordinate), and the ordered pair of numbers (a, b) can then be used to identify the location of A.

A vertex C *on* the x-axis at the point labeled c has coordinates $(c, 0)$ and similarly a vertex D on the y-axis at the point labeled d has coordinates $(0, d)$. The coordinates of the origin are $(0, 0)$.

Several things about this particular coordinate system should be clear.

1. The coordinates of *any* point in the plane can be determined by extending the assignment of numbers to points on the axes to include the real numbers.
2. The size of the squares in the network is arbitrary as is the location of the origin. It is sometimes convenient to locate the origin and orient the axes in a particular way—as though the network were printed on a sheet of clear glass, superimposed over a plane.
3. The system can be designed around a nonsquare *rectangular* tessellation. It is sometimes convenient to use different scales for the two axes.

4. The system can be extended to three dimensions by a network of cubes and a third axis (the z-axis), perpendicular to the xy-plane through the origin. Thus, any point in space can be identified by an ordered triple (a, b, c) of real numbers.

There are other systems for locating points. In some geometries, the x and y axes are not perpendicular; on a sphere, for example, a network of great circles can be used as a coordinate system. One system that is particularly useful for certain topics is the *polar* coordinate system. Although we will not consider this in detail, in this system, a numbered *ray* called the *polar axis*, with endpoint 0 (the origin) is the single axis:

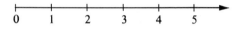

The coordinates (a, b) of a point P are the *distance, a,* of P from the origin as measured on the scale of the polar axis, and the measure, b, of the angle with vertex 0, with the polar axis as one side, and with the ray from 0 through P on the other.

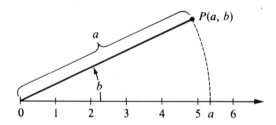

Measurement

The term "measurement" generally refers to processes that include the assignment of numbers to describe certain characteristics of things. These characteristics of concern to elementary school children include length, area, volume, mass or weight, temperature, and time. Other characteristics, beyond the interests of most elementary school children, include force, pressure, energy, power, acceleration, frequency, electrical current, voltage and resistance, and luminous intensity.

A measurement system includes a set of basic, standardized units of measure together with a set of agreed-upon procedures for naming multiples or subdivisions of those units. If more than one basic unit is employed to measure a given characteristic, the system also requires conversion tables to identify relationships among those units (e.g., 12 inches equal 1 foot). Appropriate tools or instruments such as rulers, scales, or thermometers are used to determine the number of units best describing the characteristic of interest in a given situation. The instrument is used, in effect, to *count* units (and multiples or fractional parts of units).

The system in common use in our country today was inherited in Colonial times and is usually called the English system. Its actual origins can be traced to a variety of ancient cultures, including Roman, Babylonian, Egyptian, Saxon, and Norman. It should not be surprising, therefore, that there exist in this system a wide and unwieldy assortment of units — and ratios relating those units. It is more surprising that we have persisted in the use of this antiquated, seemingly haphazard "system" for as long as we have.

The English system is now gradually being replaced in this country by the International System of Units, commonly abbreviated SI, and more generally referred to as the metric system. (SI is actually a modernized version of the metric system.) Before summarizing certain appropriate aspects of SI, let us briefly consider the natural and legitimate question, "Why change?" or, in particular, "Why change to SI?" After all, the English system works, we are accustomed to it, and changing to a different system will inevitably take a great deal of time and will entail some rather serious economic, educational, and psychological problems.

One argument for making this transition is that SI is much simpler to use than is the English system. For example, to convert 37 ounces into pounds, we must divide 37 by 16; to convert 37 inches into feet, we must divide 37 by 12; to convert 37 yards into feet, we must multiply 37 by 3. The list of conversion ratios goes on and on. Linear measure alone centers around seven different units — inch, foot, yard, rod, furlong, mile, and land league, with conversion ratios, in order, of 12 (to 1), 3, $5\frac{1}{2}$, 40, 8, and 3. By contrast, linear measure in SI is based essentially on a *single* unit, the meter. Larger or smaller units, such as the millimeter, centimeter, or kilometer are related to the meter on a decimal basis, so that all conversions can be quickly accomplished by "shifting" decimal points. Furthermore, the prefixes such as milli- (one-thousandth), centi- (one hundredth), and kilo- (one thousand times) are used consistently within the SI system for converting each of the basic units to larger or smaller ones, e.g., a *kilo*gram is 1000 grams.

To the argument of simplicity must be added the argument that the SI system is in virtual world-wide use. In 1965 Great Britain began a ten-year "metrication" plan, leaving the United States as the only major power not using the metric system. While this may not seem at first to be a convincing argument per se, the economic implications are in fact very convincing: International trade is simplified and stimulated when common units of weights and measures are used. A potential foreign purchaser of an American machine or product requiring servicing would quite naturally be hesitant to purchase anything that could not be maintained or repaired with his metric tools. Delays in converting to SI have no doubt already cost us millions of dollars in foreign trade.

Changing to SI is indeed a formidable task, and the transition is scheduled to occur gradually to ease many of the inevitable problems. We have for some time already been introduced to metric units in certain products, such as camera equipment and pharmaceuticals. Imported automobiles have long used parts and tools measured in metric terms and the major American automobile manufacturers have already begun to change over. The scientific community has, of course, employed metric weights and measures for many years.

Certainly, children will be able to learn the metric system much more quickly than it now takes to learn the English system.

Those SI base units with which elementary school children most need to become familiar are the meter, liter, and gram (SI units for measuring time and electricity are those we now use). Familiarity with these units requires first-hand experience with appropriate metric instruments, and exact conversions between English and metric units must be avoided if we hope to "think metric" (or "think SI"). However, the most common units are summarized here with some of their approximate equivalents in familiar terms:

Common Metric Terms

To Measure	Unit	Approximate Equivalent
Length	Kilometer (km)	A little more than $\frac{1}{2}$ mile (almost 0.6 mile)
	Meter (m)	A little more than 1 yard (almost 1.1 yard)
	Centimeter (cm)	About the width of a paper clip (almost 0.4 inch)
	Millimeter (mm)	About the diameter of a paper clip wire
Area	Square kilometer (km²)	About 247 acres
	Square meter (m²)	A little more than a square yard
	Square centimeter (cm²)	A little more than the head of a thumbtack
	Square millimeter (mm²)	A little less than the head of a straight pin
Volume	Cubic meter (m³)	Box large enough to hold a refrigerator
	Cubic centimeter (cm³)	Size of a white Cuisenaire rod (cm³ has, in the past, frequently been abbreviated cc.)

Common Metric Terms (continued)

To Measure	Unit	Approximate Equivalent
Fluid Volume	Kiloliter (kl)	About 265 gallons
	Liter (l)	A little more than a quart (actually .001m³)
	Centiliter (cl)	About 1 tablespoonful
	Milliliter (ml)	About ⅕ of a teaspoonful
Mass (weight)	Kilogram (kg)	A little more than 2 pounds (about 2.2 pounds)
	Gram (g)	About the weight of a paper clip
Temperature	Degrees Celsius (C)	0° C: Water freezes
		37° C: Body temperature (human)
		100° C: Water boils

More precise and complete summaries of the SI system can be obtained from sources listed in the Suggested Readings for this chapter (see entries for Frank Kendig and for the National Bureau of Standards).

3. Activities and Materials for Teaching Geometry and Measurement

A few general observations are in order before we consider specific activities for teaching geometric ideas. First, as has been noted before, elementary school geometry, like most of elementary school mathematics, should be kept informal. Geometric ideas evolve gradually from children's observations of natural and man-made things around them, through observing, thinking about, and discussing similarities and differences among those things, rather than from authoritatively imposed axioms or definitions. Definitions, in fact, should emerge, when the need arises, from children's discussions and debates as they try to describe things. Teachers should join in with children to challenge proposed descriptions (or conjectures) in order to gradually sharpen thinking; but children's terms need not be replaced by standard ones—"corner," for example, is just as meaningful as "vertex" (or "angle" if that is what is meant). The facts of geometry should be those which children accumulate themselves, under the teacher's guidance. Rigorous "proofs" are certainly out of the question, yet questions such as "Why?" or "Is there another way?" should persist. Generalizations and conjectures should result from, and be verified by *activity,* with constant search for patterns and relationships, again under the teacher's careful scrutiny. No drill is necessary in the sense of the skill-development aspects of the mathematics program; rather, the exploration of interesting problems ultimately leads to basic understandings.

Second, the sequence in which geometric activities are introduced is, with some obvious exceptions, of little importance. The activities listed in the remainder of this chapter are not sequential; much overlap will be observed among them. They can occur in nearly any order. Studying plane figures before solid ones makes some sense, for example, when viewed from a logical, deductive, adult point of view; but that sequence is unimportant from the pragmatic, inductive point of view that should characterize elementary school geometry. If anything, it is more reasonable to study 3-dimensional objects before 2-dimensional ones, since the shapes children encounter most naturally are 3-dimensional.

Third, the organizational procedures for teaching geometry can be very flexible. "Math time" can be devoted to geometry exclusively for several days at a time, for a few minutes each day, for one day a week, or between various arithmetic units. Activity cards prepared by the teacher can be available for individual or group spare-time projects. These and the necessary materials can be stored in an accessible place or displayed on a table or bulletin board. The nature of certain geometric topics is such that they may be integrated with art, social studies, or science work. The main consideration is that geometry should not be ignored; nor should it be presented as a single brief unit during the school year.

Finally, grade placement and ability levels per se should not stand in the way of providing children with the opportunity to learn geometry. For example, it has been shown that many primary grade children can learn to use rulers and compasses, albeit slowly and clumsily at first. Admittedly, young or generally low-achieving children are unlikely to grasp the ratio concept, are crude in their descriptions, or are unable to describe subtle relationships. But early and intuitive introduction to ideas, followed by frequent repetition, in spiral fashion throughout the grades, can lead to levels of comprehension of geometric ideas which could not be expected without exposure to those ideas. Most of the *content* of high school Euclidean geometry (without its formality) can and should be studied in the elementary school. Then, too, teachers can—and should expect to—learn along with their children.

In the following pages, we can only sample a small fraction of the many possible classroom activities that can in time be expected to lead to geometric maturity. References at the end of the chapter, continued study of journals such as *The Arithmetic Teacher,* and the teacher's own initiative should lead to many, many more.

Classifying

Classifying is a fundamental mathematical activity. Just as children classify *sets* in terms of 1–1 correspondence in arriving at the (whole) number concept, so do they classify various *objects* in terms of their physical attributes in arriving at geometric concepts. *Relative* concepts such as large or small, inside or outside, between, long or short (or tall and short), wide or narrow, heavy or light, fat or thin, parallel or nonparallel, perpendicular or nonperpendicular, similar or nonsimilar, straight or curved, sharp or smooth, are fundamental. Such concepts evolve subtly, largely subconsciously, and frequently without verbal association, through looking, touching, and thinking. They are more sharply delineated as a result of discussion, debate, and the mutual establishment of criteria for classifying objects in terms of certain attributes. The teacher's role is largely one of exposing children to numerous examples with gradually more subtle distinctions, asking them to describe objects, and helping them to decide on definitions.

The teacher can hold up or point to a given object, either solid or flat, e.g., a triangular-shaped block, a tin can, or a cardboard box, and ask children to describe it. After letting them pursue this, ask them to point to or tell about other things of that shape. "Find all the things in the room which look like it," or "Do you have any toys with this shape?" or "Are there any shapes like this in your mother's kitchen?" Given a collection of things which "look alike," they should then be asked to identify *differences* among them, e.g., "A drum looks like a tin can, except that it's bigger and flatter." "A pencil is like a crayon except it's longer and skinnier," and so on. Names of shapes can be introduced in such contexts, and finer distinctions can be gradually introduced, e.g., they can be asked to describe the similarities and differences between a triangle shaped from a wire coat hanger and one with the same size and shape cut out of cardboard.

Many kinds of *matching* exercises can be devised. At first, a given shape such as a square can be shown and the children asked to match it with the same shape among several—including triangles, circles, and so on. Gradually, less obvious distinctions can exist among the shapes from which the child must choose, e.g., matching a given square with the correct one among several that differ in size or orientation; or, matching a right triangle with the correct one among several which are not right. Irregular shapes, reflections, rotations, and polygons with many sides can all increase the difficulty of matching.

Some commercially available materials are designed to help develop children's classification skills. A particularly useful set of materials is the *Attribute Games and Problems,* developed originally by William P. Hull in the 1950s and now part of a collection of units called Elementary Science

Study (ESS). Four kinds of materials are included: A-blocks, people pieces, color cubes, and creature cards.

A-blocks are wooden blocks that can be sorted and classified according to as many as three attributes—shape, size, and color. There are 4 shapes, 4 colors, and 2 sizes; many activities are suggested in the teacher's guide and many more can be devised by teachers and children. A few examples: sort the blocks (here, a child chooses his own criterion); sort the blocks by shape, by color, or by size; pick out all the blocks that are red and triangles, red or triangles, yellow or blue, red but not circles, circles but not red or green, and so on; find the missing block (where several blocks are randomly displayed according to some rule, with one block missing); make a row of blocks where each block differs from the preceding one in exactly one way, e.g., if the first block is a small red square, then the next one may be a small red triangle, a large red square, a small blue square, and so on (the same game can be played with 2 differences or even 3 differences).

Creature cards each contain three sets of pictures (of geometric "creatures" with amusing names such as "Mokes," "Trugs," and "Wibbles"). A typical card says: (1) "All of these are Mokes" (followed by pictures of five or six objects which have some common attribute—geometric or otherwise). (2) "None of these are Mokes" (followed by another set of creatures, none of which has the *particular* attribute or attributes of Mokes). (3) "Which of these are Mokes?" (The child then tries to pick out the correct creatures by discovering the defining characteristic(s).) Numerous attributes are included, and the classification becomes increasingly difficult with each card.

Similar matching, sorting, and classifying activities can be devised with the *people pieces*, which are plastic tiles with pictures of people who are adult or child, fat or thin, male or female, and are wearing blue or red.

The *color cubes* consist of 60 wooden cubes, each the same size, painted in six colors (10 cubes of each color). They can be used for many interesting and challenging activities such as constructing Latin squares where each row and column contains one and only one cube of each color.

Classification skill can also be developed using a collection of wooden blocks called Poleidoblocs, developed by Margaret Lowenfeld. There are two collections of Poleidoblocs, labeled "A" and "G." The 140 A blocks are uncolored; each of the 54 G blocks is painted in one of four colors. There are several shapes—cubes, prisms, cones, cylinders, and so on—so that various sorting activities are possible. (Many additional geometric notions can be developed with these materials.)

The Dienes Algebraic Experience Materials (AEM), developed by Z. P. Dienes, who also developed the Multibase Arithmetic Blocks (MAB), include plain, thin wooden blocks of several sizes and shapes— equilateral triangles, squares, rectangles, trapezoids, and rhombuses. These, too, can be used for classifying activities.

Using such sets of blocks, various criteria should be used, singly or in pairs, to classify them — similarity, congruence, color, overall size, length, numbers of corners, and so on.

Another device that includes classification among its many uses is the *geoboard* (geometry board). This is a board on which there is a rectangular array of small pegs; rubber bands are stretched between two pegs to represent a segment, around 3 noncollinear pegs to represent a triangle, and so on. The board can be made of plywood and the pegs can be finishing nails (or escutcheon pins). Both wooden and molded plastic geoboards

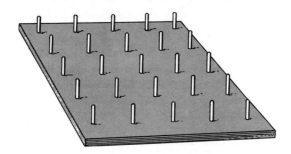

are available commercially. Most are 5-by-5 or 6-by-6 arrays; circular geoboards can be made or purchased (some commercial plastic models have pegs arranged in square arrays on one side of the board and in a circle on the other). Larger boards can be made from pegboard and dowels (or golf tees), and paper-and-pencil geoboards with more "pegs" can be simulated by printing an array of dots (a "lattice") on plain paper (this, too, is available commercially). We will consider several geoboard activities in subsequent sections of this chapter, but mention here that the geoboard can be used for certain activities related to teaching basic concepts involving classification. For example: (a) Given one segment represented on a geoboard or lattice paper, the child can be asked to make a segment which is longer, shorter, or the same length (possibly oriented differently). (b) Given a square, triangle, or other polygon, the child can be asked to make one like it, perhaps larger, or to see how many different shapes he can make which look like it. (c) Given a shape on one geoboard, see which shape — among several — it matches on a second one. (d) Given several pairs of lines, pick out the ones that are parallel (or perpendicular).

Solids

Children's first awareness of geometric ideas is related to solids — real, 3-dimensional objects that they can see and with which they are familiar. Making models of these objects in various ways can help to focus attention on the ideal attributes of actually imperfect things. For example, making a house, a church, a car or truck, the engine of a train, or a robot, from poleidoblocs, plasticine, cut and folded paper or cardboard, Tinkertoys, household objects such as spools, and so on, leads children to view or think about the real objects in relatively abstract ways; not-quite-straight lines become straight, ellipsoids become circles, and complex relationships or patterns must be simplified. This leads to consideration of the basic characteristics of and relationships among idealized solid figures, particularly when they are viewed from various angles and positions. Thus, free-play construction of this sort can lead to awareness of idealized characteristics of solids and to their organization and classification. Children should have abundant opportunity to engage in these activities, and to talk about what they see in their models. Names and attributes of basic, recurring shapes can be learned gradually. Children's names and descriptions can be replaced, in time, with standard ones, through guided discussions.

As children experiment with constructing solids from plane regions (paper or cardboard), they have the opportunity to discover many relationships. Designing, folding, cutting, and pasting a model such as the roof of a house or a church steeple can make them aware of the faces, edges, and vertices of a surface, as well as inside-outside surface and angle relationships. Mistakes—and some arguments, if more than one child is involved—are inevitable in any such project, and should be handled with patience, lest these learnings be interfered with. Skeleton constructions with straws and string or joined strips of wood or thin metal (such as Erector set parts or Tinkertoys) can lead to various discoveries; for example, that triangular shapes are rigid and strong, whereas all other polygonal shapes collapse unless they are braced by "triangulating" them (e.g., connecting one vertex to each of the others).

Teacher-made or commercially obtained models of various polyhedrons such as the Platonic solids, with directions to carefully count and record the numbers of faces, edges, and vertices, can lead to the discovery of Euler's formula.

Given patterns, children with reasonable dexterity can construct the Platonic (or other) solids. Heavy paper or thin cardboard (about the thickness of a file folder) should be used; the patterns on p. 315 can be used, but the dimensions should be relatively large. Once the patterns are carefully cut out, edges should be carefully traced with a heavy hand and a hard pencil, then prefolded before assembly. Edges can be joined with tape or tabs can be made on alternate outside edges of the pattern; rubber cement, paste, or glue holds them together (the last few edges are always a bit difficult). Before assembly, children may wish to color the pattern. Even this can lead to some interesting geometric ideas; for example, see if they can figure out the least number of different colors needed to color the pattern so that no two faces with a common edge are the same color. (A well-known unproven conjecture is that no more than 4 colors will be needed no matter how many regions are contained in a closed network such as this.) Children sometimes decorate the solids in ingenious ways.

The dodecahedron or icosahedron can be made from patches of different colored cloth and stuffed with cotton when the edges are sewed together.

Examining the surface of a classroom globe may lead to some interesting geometric discoveries, e.g.: (a) Every pair of lines of longitude intersect in *two* places (the north and south poles). (b) A triangle formed by two lines of longitude and the equator, with the north pole and two points on the equator as vertices, contains 2 right angles. (c) Each of 3 collinear points is between the other two. (d) There are many distinct lines each perpendicular to the equator through the north pole. Such discoveries are most interesting, of course, once children have encountered corresponding generalizations in Euclidean plane geometry (two lines meet in at most *one* point; a triangle can contain at most *one* right angle; of 3 collinear points, exactly one is between the other two; there is exactly *one* line perpendicular to a given line through a point not on the line, and so on).

Tessellations

As was indicated on p. 318, if a plane can be "covered" with copies of a single polygon so that there are no gaps and no overlaps, that polygon is said to *tessellate* the plane. A floor covered with square tiles is an example of a tessellation. The sum of the measures of the angles at each vertex of a tessellation must always be 360 degrees and at least three polygons must meet at each vertex. Various additional restrictions or various exceptions

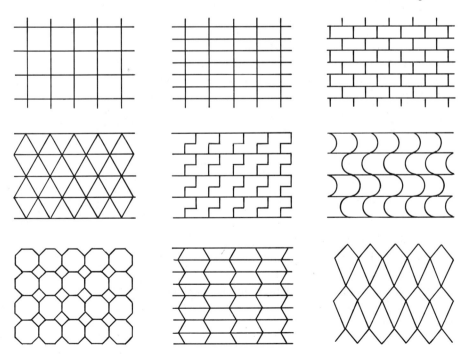

can be applied to this basic definition to create an assortment of tessellating patterns. There are many possibilities; for example, when two faces of a tessellation meet, their intersection must be either at least one *entire* common edge or a single point; or *two* or more figures may be used to form a tessellation; or curved figures may be used.

The edges of a bounded plane region are not necessarily covered by the tessellation, of course. In fact, any triangle or any quadrilateral — even quite irregular ones — can form the face of a tessellation, as can many irregular polygons (under certain conditions). However, it usually comes as somewhat of a surprise that of all the *regular* polygons (those whose angles are all congruent as are their sides) only the equilateral triangle, square, and equilateral hexagon will tessellate. (Note that a regular hexagon contains six equilateral triangles.) This is not difficult to verify, and we

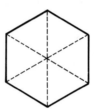

digress momentarily to do so, for the information of the teacher who may need to explain it to an inquisitive child — or, better yet, who may wish to help that child discover it.

First, if we measure the three angles of any triangle, the sum of those measures is always 180°. This can be verified intuitively by drawing an arbitrary triangle, then tearing off the corners and rearranging them in any order, using whatever rigid motions are necessary, to form a line.

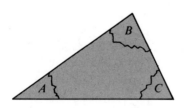
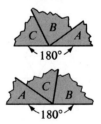

Next, if we consider any polygon with n vertices, it can always be triangulated, i.e., separated into triangles, by choosing any vertex, A of the polygon and joining it with each of the remaining $n - 2$ vertices, i.e., each vertex except the two which adjoin it (B and E, here).

This forms $n - 2$ triangles. Since the sum of the measures of the angles in each of the triangles is 180°, the sum of the measures of all the angles in the polygon is $(n - 2) \cdot 180$.

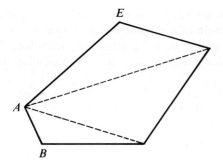

Example:

For this figure, $n = 5$, and if A, B, . . . , E and a, b, . . . , i are measures of the angles as shown, then

$$
\begin{aligned}
A + B + C + D + E &= (a + d + g) + h + (i + f) + (e + c) + b \\
&= (a + b + c) + (d + e + f) + (g + h + i) \\
&= \quad\quad 180 \quad\quad + \quad\quad 180 \quad\quad + \quad\quad 180 \\
&= 3 \times 180 \quad\quad\quad\quad \text{i.e., } (n - 2) \cdot 180
\end{aligned}
$$

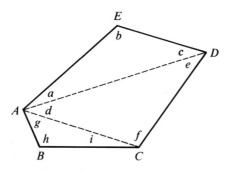

In the case of a quadrilateral, the sum of its angle measures is 360°. For any *regular* n-gon, the degree measure of *each* angle must be

$$\frac{(n - 2)\,180}{n}$$

e.g., for a square, the degree measure of each angle is $(2 \times 180) \div 4$ or 90; for a regular pentagon it is $(3 \times 180) \div 5$ or 108; for a regular hexagon it is $(4 \times 180) \div 6$ or 120; and for a regular (equilateral) triangle it is 60.

If we require that at least three polygons meet at each vertex of a tessellation, then, we can obtain the necessary degree measure of 360 for any vertex, using regular polygons, by constructing it so that 6 equilateral triangles meet at each vertex $(6 \times 60 = 360)$, or 4 squares $(4 \times 90 = 360)$, or 3 hexagons $(3 \times 120 = 360)$. If we try 3 pentagons, we have only 324°, and, of course, 4 pentagons would overlap (432 degrees). The degree measure of each angle of a regular *n*-gon, where $n > 6$, is greater than 120, so three of them together would exceed 360°; therefore the only tessellations possible with regular polygons are those with equilateral triangles, squares, and hexagons.

To see that *any* triangle will tessellate, suppose the vertices of an arbitrary triangle are A, B, and C; then, if at each vertex we arrange to have

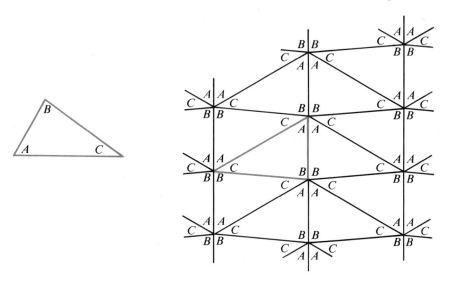

6 copies of the triangle meet so that each angle appears there twice, we have the necessary degree measure. The pattern of triangles shown here could obviously be repeated indefinitely. (Are other arrangements possible?)

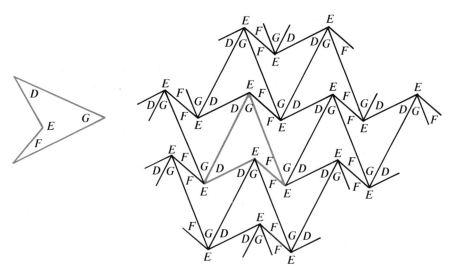

Tessellations can be formed by the quadrilateral $DEFG$ in a similar manner, with one of each of the angles D, E, F, and G at each vertex. One way of doing this is shown here.

With either the triangular or the quadrilateral tessellations above, could two or more of the basic faces be combined to form a tessellating face with more vertices? For example, will the pentagon whose angles are B, $A + C$, $2B$, C, and $2A + C$, or the hexagon whose angles are $G + F$, E, D, $G + F$, E, and D tessellate?

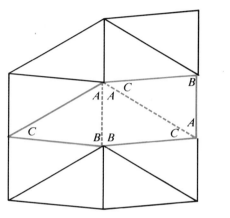 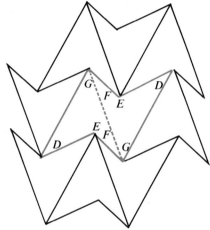

Children encounter many tessellations in their environment and are usually interested in the pleasing regularity of the patterns they see: bricks, cement blocks, and tiles of various shapes are arranged on walls, floors, and patios as tessellations; wire fences are tessellations of squares, rhombuses, or hexagons. While most examples are man-made, nature provides at least one tessellation children are likely to have seen, i.e., in the hexagonal pattern of honeycomb produced by bees.

There are many activities with tessellations that even quite young children enjoy; others intrigue quite mature children. For example, when asked to describe the patterns they see in a brick wall, a floor, or a fence, children find that even a simple tessellation can be rather difficult to describe, or that careful inspection reveals some otherwise unnoticed patterns. This can lead to all sorts of questions and activities: What are the dimensions of a brick? Why are they arranged in that way? Can you make a "brick wall" with a set of blocks? Can you draw a picture of another tessellation you have seen, such as a fence?

Given a pattern of a shape, e.g., a square or rectangle (or described by the teacher as a 3 cm square or a 3 cm by 9 cm rectangle), children enjoy cutting out many copies from colored construction paper, then pasting them on a large sheet of paper to form various patterns. The possibilities are virtually endless, even if all children use the same basic shape. The shapes can be oriented in various ways, and many interesting patterns in color will be found. The 4-color problem can be introduced: That is, given a particular shape, can you make a pattern using only 2 colors (so that no two adjacent shapes have the same color)? 3 colors? 4? Can anyone find a shape (from among several which *will* tessellate) that requires more than 4 colors?

Using a heavy tagboard cutout of an arbitrary triangle or quadrilateral, children can trace its outline over and over as a tessellation. This is easy for regular shapes, but can be a real challenge with irregular ones. Children will discover that what appears to start out as a tessellation sometimes leads to a "dead end." For example, a child might start an interesting pattern such as this, but shortly discover that no matter how he continues

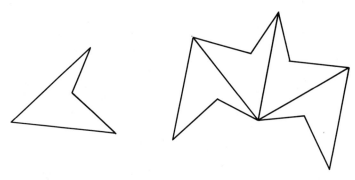

he cannot keep his pattern going. He may in time even come to think that tessellation with this shape is impossible. A few helpful hints are in order!

Using another piece of tagboard, cut out a random irregular quadrilateral, label the vertices *A*, *B*, *C*, and *D* (on both sides and preferably in contrasting colors), tear the corners off and see if the child can put the four pieces together to make one piece with no gaps, as in a tessellation. It may

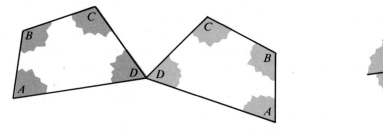

come as a surprise that the pieces fit together easily, and in any order, even when some of them are flipped over. Why? (If the child knows how to use a protractor, this would be a good time to suggest that he measure the angles of several "odd" quadrilaterals, then add those measures; if he is careful he will discover that the sum is 360 each time.) Whether he *measures* the angles or not, he should be led to think about the fact that when each of the four corners *A*, *B*, *C*, and *D* are put together, they "fit." Will this work with the original quadrilateral? If the child labels *its* vertices in the same way and traces its corners about a point, he should discover how to make a tessellation.

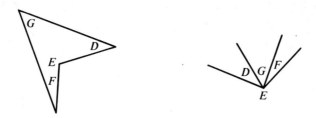

Another hint is to point out that since each side is of a different length, in order to make a tessellation, each edge must be adjacent to "itself"; but the model must be rotated so that no corner of one tracing meets the corresponding corners in the next. (For what kinds of quadrilaterals *could* a corner be placed next to itself?)

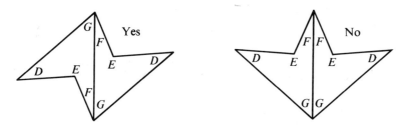

As the tessellation progresses, several interesting questions might be raised: If the vertices are labeled, as above, is there a regular pattern in the labeling? Do some lines seem to be parallel? *Are* they parallel? Why? How can you describe the relative positions of a given pair of copies of the "face"? (A good opportunity to introduce rigid motions.) Could you color it in a regular way with 2 colors? 3? 4? What would it look like if you colored a *pair* of faces (e.g., the entire figure above) the same color, then followed the "4-color rule"? Is it possible to make a *different* tessellation with this same shape?

Children can be led to discover which regular shapes tessellate and which do not by being supplied with (or, themselves, constructing, if they are skillful enough to do so) several cardboard copies of various regular shapes (wooden blocks such as the equilateral triangles in the Dienes AEM materials or Poleidoblocs work well). Four or five carefully constructed plywood or masonite blocks in each of the regular shapes with 3, 4, 5, 6, 7, and 8 sides would be very useful. Thin paper should be avoided since the pieces overlap so easily. Again, this idea can be probed as far as children's interest, skill, and maturity will permit, e.g., if they can measure angles, they may be led to see some of the "proof" discussed previously. Suppose two (or more) tessellating regular figures are combined. Will the new shape tessellate?

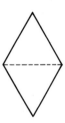 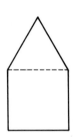 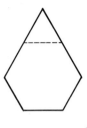

Given a tessellating shape on a geoboard, children can be asked to make the largest number of copies of it they can on their geoboards. The largest possible number is a tessellation of the geoboard (except possibly for its edges).

Once a tessellation has been made, ask children to count the number of copies of the face. An 8-by-10 cm sheet of paper covered with 1 cm squares can provide an opportunity to introduce the area concept and some generalizations regarding it, e.g., the lengths of two adjacent sides of the paper are 8 cm and 10 cm. The number of copies of the square on the paper is 80. Is there a relationship? What if the paper were cut in half along a diagonal? How many squares on each side of the diagonal are cut? Could

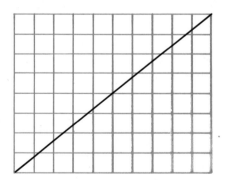

the pieces on one side of the cut be put back together to make squares? (This would be easier if we started with an 8-by-8 cm sheet of paper, of course.)

Among the many interesting patterns that can be created with tessellations, particularly by coloring them, are some 3-dimensional effects and optical illusions. Consider, for example, these patterns created by tessellating rhombuses.

Parts of tessellations can lead to other ideas. The triangular and square numbers can be represented in numerous ways with parts of tessellations, as suggested in Chapter 7.

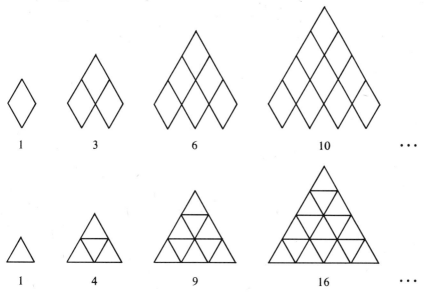

1   3   6   10   • • •

1   4   9   16   • • •

An informal introduction to the Pythagorean theorem can result from a discussion of these parts of tessellations.

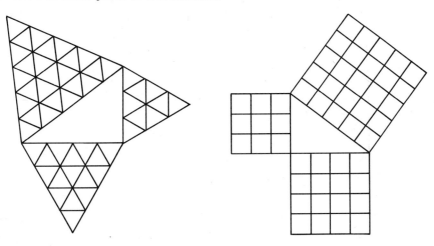

Maps and Networks

Most people readily acknowledge the importance of being able to read and to make maps. The importance of studying networks may be less obvious. The solutions of the two kinds of network problems we have examined here — relating the numbers of paths, regions, and vertices in a network, and determining whether a network is traversable — are little more than curios per se. Their importance at the elementary school level is their contribution to the development of general problem-solving skills (their importance beyond the elementary school is undeniable). The analysis of networks in the adult world is, however, very serious business — much of which can be understood by children. Systems of roads, telephone wires, airlines, and pipelines may be viewed as (rather expensive) networks; and many factors are considered in their design — particularly cost and reliability. Consider this hypothetical problem (easily understood by children) and the number of questions it can generate:

Example:

Three houses, A, B, and C are to be connected by telephone lines so that each can call the others and the operator at the telephone company — providing that the caller is connected to the telephone company and that there is a path (wire) connecting the two parties. Suppose, to make it convenient, they are located as shown, with the

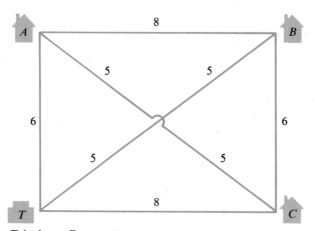

Telephone Company

indicated distances between expressed in kilometers. The illustrated network requires 48 km of wire. Are there any better ways to form the network? If the wire between A and B should break, is A cut off from B? Not at all: A is still connected to T and can reach B by way of C. Thus, we could do without the connection between *A* and *B,* saving 8 km of wire. Can we save any more wire? What if the wire from *A* to *C* were to break also? Still no problem: *A* is still connected to *T* and can reach either *C* or *B* through *T* — only 30 km of wire is really needed. Considering a problem such as this can lead to some very productive thinking. One child might suggest connecting the wires that cross in the middle: only 20 km are then needed and no house is cut off. Another

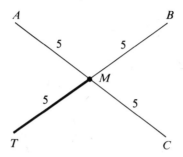

may argue that this is pretty risky, since now if a wire breaks, at least one house will be cut off — and if the line from *T* to *M* breaks, the whole system breaks down. Perhaps that particular wire should be extra strong. . . .

Quite young children enjoy making maps and decorating them to look "real." Making a map of the classroom, of the school, or of the locations of each child's house with respect to the school and other familiar landmarks can provide a wealth of geometric experience: Betweenness, relative distances, proportions, segments, points, planes, and similarity are all involved in a child's thinking as he makes a map. Actual measurement and drawing to scale are unnecessary, but provide valuable learnings for older children — and plenty of practice with fractions, division, and making judgments. Most towns have some streets that curve or intersect others at nonperpendicular angles. These can present real challenges — and opportunities for the teacher to introduce new ideas.

Making a map is only a beginning, however. Once it is finished (or given a professionally prepared one), numerous questions can be posed. For example: What is the shortest way to go from Bob's house to the school? Are there other reasonable ways? Are some ways as short as others? Who lives between Bob and Mary? Who lives closest to school? Who lives farthest away? What would be the best route for a school bus to take if it were to pick up only the children in our class? Could it do this without going down any street more than once? Would it cross its path? Where? How many times? These and many other questions can plant the seeds of important geometric learnings.

A regular road map can generate some interesting questions: What is the distance from A to Z by way of B and C? By way of B but not C? By airplane? Is B between A and Z by road? By airplane? Is B between A and Z? Could you drive from A to Z and back without going through B?

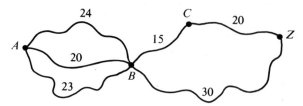

Could you drive from A to Z and come back a different way? How many ways are there to go from A to Z? From A to Z and back to A? How many roads are there out of A? B? C? Z? Could you plan a trip starting at A and going over each road just once? Where would you end up? Could you do this from B? From C? From Z? Could you plan a *round* trip from A and do this? From B?

Although most towns are not laid out with all streets parallel or perpendicular to each other, it is an easy situation for children to imagine. The teacher can draw such a make-believe map and suggest that the children name the streets. They will probably name them after streets they know, or after themselves (Smith Street, Jones Street, . . .). It makes no difference, of course. After some preliminary "games," the teacher will be renaming them as streets and avenues that are numbered 0, 1, 2, 3, . . . ("Zero Street" may be stranger sounding than "First Avenue," but it's basically make-believe at this point anyway.) Many questions similar to those previously discussed can be explored: How many (reasonable) ways

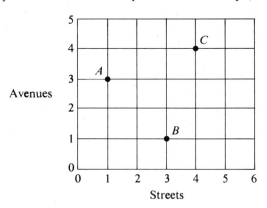

are there to go from A to B? From B to C? How far is it from A to B (in terms of blocks) by each path? From B to C? Is there a shortest path? (The teacher may need to fill each block with buildings to prevent the children from exercising their natural impulse to cut diagonally across "vacant lots"!) How can we describe the location of A? B? C? In time the standard ordered-pair notation can be introduced, e.g., the location of *A* is described by (1, 3), meaning the intersection of First Street and Third Avenue. This must be done carefully and some children need much practice before they correctly distinguish between (1, 3) and (3, 1) for example. Locate the intersection which is on the same street as *A* and the same avenue as *B*. What intersection is *between A* and *B* (as the crow flies)? Is there such an intersection between *B* and *C*?

   The maturity and interest of the children will influence the selection of the activities for which such a grid "map" can be used. A few examples will serve to illustrate their wide variety: (The geoboard or peg board can often be used here, with rubber bands connecting the desired points, as well as pencil and paper.) Draw segments connecting each of *A*, *B*, and *C*, or, using make-believe language, the path of a bird flying directly from *A* to *B*, then from *B* to *C*, and from *C* back to *A*; describe the shape of the figure. Draw the figure determined by (1, 1), (3, 1), (2, 3); and (4, 3) and name its shape. Name the coordinates of the corners of (a given figure). Name the coordinates of (the corners of) any square, hexagon, or rectangle. What is the sum of the two coordinates of *A*? How far is it—along streets and avenues—from (0, 0) to *A*? Draw a simple picture within the grid. Now make a larger, or smaller, grid and use the coordinates to help make a copy of the picture. (This can be facilitated by locating key points via their

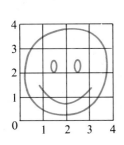
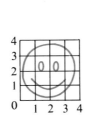
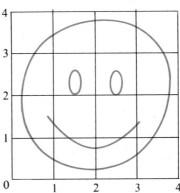

coordinates, and can be varied by making the "streets" farther apart than the "avenues"—or vice versa.) Can you predict the shape of the figure

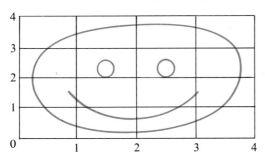
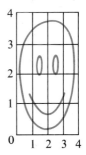

connecting the points whose coordinates are $(1, 2)$, $(2, 3)$, $(3, 4)$, $(4, 5)$?
Draw the figure and check your guess.

Various function rules can be given, from which children can determine coordinates of points and then graph them. For example, "the first
number is less than 6 and the second number is twice the first"; "both
numbers are the same"; "the second number is two"; or "the second number is the square of the first."

When negative numbers have been introduced, many of the preceding activities can be enriched by extending the coordinate system to include
all four quadrants. Eventually coordinates of points between whole num-
bers, e.g., $(\frac{1}{2}, 3\frac{1}{4})$, can be explored, and children can now begin to construct
many graphs based on data from various sources. The possibilities are
numerous.

The two network problems considered in Section 2 of this chapter
can be explored. We have suggested a few possibilities for doing so in the
preceding paragraphs, but might add that if a child or group of children is
interested in either of the problems, the best approach is to consider many
cases (provided by the teacher or invented by the children) and to keep
careful records, preferably in table form, in searching for patterns. Many
children *never* do discover Euler's formula or the traversability theorem,
but in *trying* to, they can learn much about attacking a problem — and as we
have said, that's the point of introducing them at this level. As in number
theory, it is sometimes interesting to pose geometric problems that cannot
be solved or whose solutions are unknown. One network problem of the
former kind is an old one which has appeared in many forms:

Example:

Suppose three houses, *A, B,* and *C,* are each to be connected to
three utility companies, water, telephone, and electricity, so that
the lines connecting them do not cross. Show how this can be done.
It sounds easy, and children will devise all sorts of "solutions."
Occasionally a child even discovers *why* it cannot be done — 8 of the
9 lines can be connected, but the last is impossible. One possible
attempt is shown here. Why cannot *C* be connected to *W*? Consider

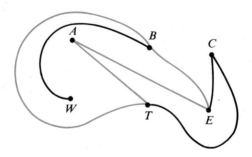

the closed path connecting the points B–T–A–E–B. It is a simple closed curve. W is on the interior of the curve and C is on the exterior, so any path from C to W must necessarily cross the curve, i.e., one of the lines already drawn.

Transformations

Children can engage in and enjoy many kinds of activities related to transformations, without the need for elaborate vocabulary, definitions, materials, or explanations. Symmetry, in particular, is very appealing and can be encountered in endless ways. Making ink blots by folding a sheet of paper in half, dropping a few drops of ink or paint on one side, then squeezing the two halves together, is a good way to start children thinking about bilateral symmetry. As they look at their results and talk about them, they begin an awareness of line symmetry. This can lead to a search for objects around them which "look alike on both sides." And the search proves to be surprisingly fruitful—nature is very symmetrical. Many leaves, plants, and most familiar animals—including butterflies, birds, pets, and children themselves—have bilateral symmetry. Symmetry can be found in countless man-made things as well. More mature children can identify *lines* of symmetry and even measure distances between corresponding points to verify the alleged symmetry of given objects.

Mirrors fascinate children and can be used effectively to introduce some of the basic ideas of bilateral symmetry. (Small plastic or metal mirrors are best, and to be most effective, should be silvered on both sides and should have no "edging" or case.) For example, children can be asked to make one of these shapes on their geoboards or dot paper, and then asked

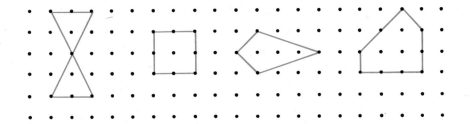

to try to put a mirror on the shape so that half of the shape, together with its image, looks like the whole shape. They should look for alternate ways of placing the mirror. They will discover that for some figures, there is only one way to do this, for some there are several ways, and for some it is impossible. Circles, equilateral triangles, or other figures that cannot be represented on the geoboard can be drawn on paper.

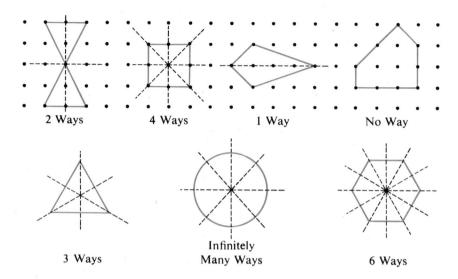

While experimenting with this task, they discover that they can make new shapes from the given ones, sometimes even making two shapes from one. Looking first in one side of the mirror and then the other, they see either the same "picture" on both sides, or two different "pictures," depending on whether they have located an axis of symmetry, but in either case, they see a symmetric figure.

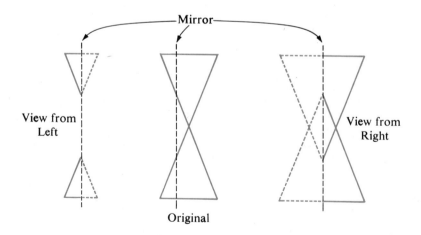

Show a simple figure, and tell the children to think of it as *half* of a shape; then ask them to draw the whole shape (without using a mirror). They will discover that there are several possibilities, depending on where they imagine the mirror:

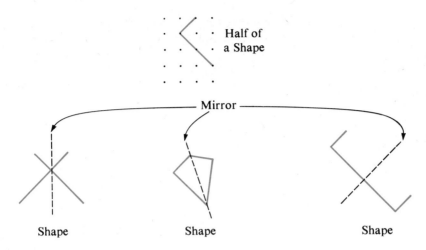

One of the units in the Elementary Science Study materials is called *Mirror Cards*. It consists of 21 sets of cards and several plastic mirrors. The cards are designed to be used for several kinds of tasks such as trying to make a particular shape from a given one. The tasks are progressive in difficulty, and include some which are impossible, illustrating for example, that mirrors cannot translate or rotate a shape (try, for example, to make shapes *B* or *C* by placing a mirror on shape *A*):

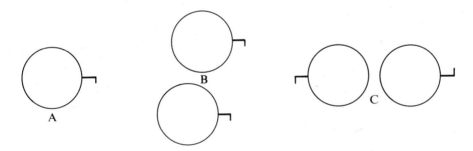

Paper folding and cutting can illustrate or start children thinking about bilateral symmetry. Children enjoy folding a piece of paper in half, then cutting out half-shapes of dolls, letters of the alphabet, snowflakes, and so on. Folding a paper twice, with the second fold along the first one,

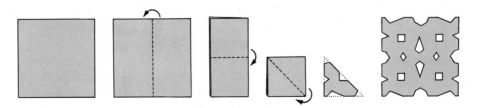

increases the possibilities (besides making a good model for a square corner) and three or four such folds, about the limit of most paper, can produce very interesting patterns, even with quite random cuts. Even the leftovers can make symmetric—and sometimes interesting—designs.

If perpendicular bisectors of two (or more) sides of a regular *n*-gon, e.g., equilateral triangle, square, or regular pentagon, are drawn, they will intersect in a point. If the polygon is rotated $\frac{1}{n}$th of a full revolution about that point, the image will appear to be in the same position as the original. This can be repeated up to (and beyond) a full revolution. For example, a regular pentagon will exhibit this *rotational symmetry* for turns of $\frac{1}{5}$, $\frac{2}{5}$, $\frac{3}{5}$, $\frac{4}{5}$, or $\frac{5}{5}$ of a full revolution (i.e., 72°, 144°, 216°, 288°, or 360°). One way to introduce this idea is to carefully cut out a regular figure—say a regular hexagon—from a sheet of paper, cardboard, or heavier material, and then ask children to fit the figure back into its hole in as many different ways as possible. Marking a key vertex on the figure and on the background facilitates keeping score. Children soon discover that not only can the cutout be

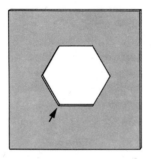

replaced by putting its marked corner in any of the six vertices of the background, but that there are six additional ways of replacing it if the figure is turned over.

A variation on this can be provided by drawing a regular shape on a background (of wood, paper, or masonite), then constructing a "spinner" of that same shape and size, loosely fastened to the background with a pin, nail, dowel, or paper fastener at the center of rotational symmetry. Many interesting games, such as "clock arithmetic" (see p. 269), can be devised

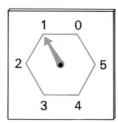

if, for example, the vertices of a background hexagon are numbered from 0 to 5 and a key vertex of a matching spinner is marked with a pointer. *Addition* can be interpreted in terms of say, counterclockwise turns, each one-sixth of a revolution. Thus 3 + 4 would mean, "start with the arrow at 3; make 4 counterclockwise turns; 3 + 4 is the number indicated by the pointer."

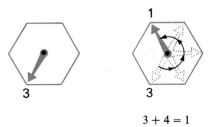

$$3 + 4 = 1$$

Multiplication can be interpreted similarly. For example, 3 × 4 could be interpreted: "Start at zero; make 3 moves of 4 turns each; 3 × 4 is the number indicated by the pointer."

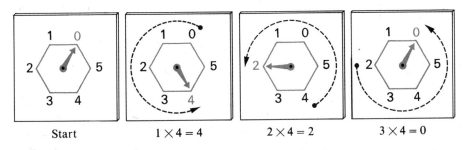

Start   1 × 4 = 4   2 × 4 = 2   3 × 4 = 0

Subtraction and *division* can be interpreted as turns in the opposite direction. Thus, rotational symmetry can be used to discover and enjoy the wonders of congruences and modular arithmetic, and to investigate important algebraic structural properties.

Rotations can be measured in terms of fractions or, later, in degrees. Many opportunities exist to introduce or extend the ideas of angle measure or addition and subtraction of fractions through rotational symmetry.

If the outline of a regular cardboard shape is traced on a piece of paper and then rotated through the center of rotational symmetry, using a pin to keep it intact, new shapes can be made. For example, an equilateral triangle can be traced, then rotated $\frac{1}{6}$ of a turn and retraced to produce a 6-pointed star, whose points can be connected to make a hexagon; tracing a square, then retracing it after $\frac{1}{8}$ of a turn produces an 8-pointed star or an octagon, and so on. Many interesting designs can be made in this way. *Half*-turn symmetry in particular can be interesting, and children enjoy finding objects with this property, such as playing cards, certain letters of

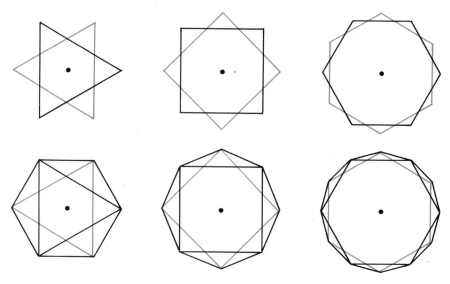

the alphabet (O, Z, N, H, I, S, X, properly drawn), and certain geometric figures (e.g., square or rectangle).

Projections can be explored by examining, discussing, and experimenting with shadows, something children always enjoy. Distortions in the image (shadow) of an opaque shape—or one drawn on a transparent plastic surface—in sunlight, or using point or parallel light sources (improvised with flashlights or with sources borrowed from a high school science department) can lead to many interesting discoveries. Observing, measuring, and recording the position and length of a vertical stick's shadow at different times of the day and at different seasons of the year can lead to many new ideas.

Translations can be found and discussed while making and coloring designs, such as those formed by tessellations or made with "rubber stamp" impressions (carved from wood, linoleum blocks, or potatoes).

Once children learn to identify points in terms of ordered pairs of numbers on a coordinate system, there are opportunities to study transformations, particularly translations or reflections, more formally. For example, a triangle with coordinates (2, 2), (5, 3), (4, 6) can be drawn on graph paper and then translated to a new position by a rule such as "right 7, up 3," i.e., increase each x-coordinate by 7 and each y-coordinate by 3, so that the image triangle is then determined by the coordinates (9, 5), (12, 6), (11, 9). Many variations are possible, e.g., a figure and its image under a translation may be shown and the child can be asked to name the "rules" for transforming each to the other. (This can lead, in turn, to discussions about positive and negative numbers, vectors, or slopes.)

Similar coordinate activities with reflections (in horizontal or vertical lines) are more difficult for most children to describe in terms of

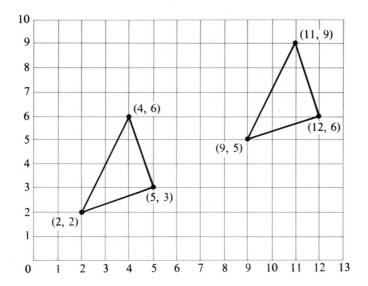

"rules," but given the coordinates of a figure and its image on reflection, they can construct both figures and try to locate, or describe coordinates of, the axis of reflection. For example, the triangles whose coordinates are $(1, 2)$, $(5, 3)$, $(4, 6)$ and $(11, 2)$, $(7, 3)$, $(8, 6)$ can be described as reflections in a mirror whose coordinates are, say, $(6, 0)$, $(6, 7)$. Much valuable practice can be provided in the context of such puzzles. Either graph paper or large geoboards can be used.

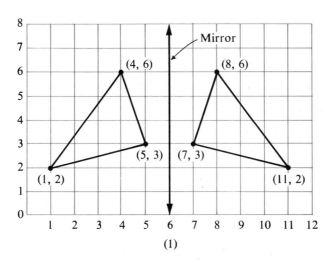

(1)

Geoboards provide an excellent vehicle for examining transformations that are not necessarily rigid motions:

1. Make a 3-sided figure on your geoboard. Stretch the rubber band to make it a 4-sided figure, then a 5-sided one, and so on.

2. Construct any shape. Then make one that "looks just like it" except that it is larger (an enlargement) or smaller. Can you describe how to do this?

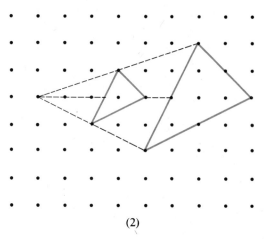

(2)

3. Make two diagonal paths, both the same length but in different positions. Construct rectangles around both paths so that the corners of the rectangles touch the paths, with the paths inside the rectangles. What can you say about the rectangles?

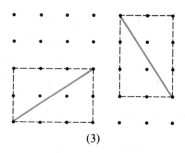

(3)

4. Construct this triangle (with a horizontal base). Move the vertex that is not on the horizontal base to the left or to the right; move it up or down. What can you say?

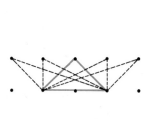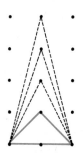

(4)

5. Construct this rectangle (with a horizontal base). Move each of the two vertices that are not on the base one (or two, . . .) pegs to the left (or right). What can you say?

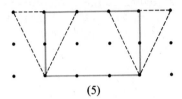

(5)

Transformations such as the above can lead to many geometric and measurement ideas. For example, the triangles in (2) above are *similar*; the sides of one are twice as long as the sides of the other; the area of the larger one is 4 times that of the smaller. The rectangles in (3) are congruent, so they have the same area; their relative positions may be described in terms of rigid motions. The area of each triangle formed in (4) by moving the top vertex to the left or right is unchanged; moving the vertex "up one" increases the area by one. The area of the parallelogram in (5) is the same as that of the rectangle, and so on.

Nonmetric Geometry

Many of the concepts and generalizations of Euclidean plane and solid geometry can be gradually introduced in the elementary school, and many elementary texts now include such relevant concepts as the following.

1. Identifying, naming, and classifying sets of points such as lines, segments, planes, rays, angles, paths, curves, regions, and classes of polygons and solids.
2. Relationships between the basic elements, such as:
   (a) Given 2 points, there is exactly one line which contains them.
   (b) The intersection of 2 lines contains at most one point.
   (c) Given a line, m, and a point, P, not on m, there is exactly one line through point P which is parallel to line m and exactly one line through P which is perpendicular to line m.
   (d) Every line is contained in infinitely many planes; two intersecting or parallel lines are contained in exactly one plane; and the intersection of two planes is a line or the Empty Set.
3. Similarity.
4. Congruence.
5. Interiors and exteriors of simple closed curves, angles, and solids.
6. Constructions using compass and straightedge, such as bisecting segments and angles or constructing parallel and perpendicular lines.

When concepts such as these are viewed without reference to measure, they are said to belong to the subject matter of *nonmetric* geometry.

Many of these ideas can best be introduced and developed by discussing questions or problems posed by the teacher (or sometimes by a child). Examining or drawing suitable pictures, or considering models found in the classroom is a must for most children. For example: "Describe the intersection of the floor and two adjacent walls in the classroom" leads to the conclusion that the intersection of 3 planes may be a single point. (Are there other possibilities?) Language must be kept simple and functional. Generalizations should be derived by children, through exploration and discovery, and expressed in their own terms. Discussion and debate will lead to gradual refinement of these expressions as children are challenged by their teacher and their peers. Discussion concerned with, for example, the notions of interior and exterior, might center on pictures such as these and questions like, Is *A* inside the curve or outside it? Is *B* inside

the angle or outside it? Both answers—"inside" and "outside"—can be expected from children, so much healthy debate can ensue: What do you *mean* when you say a point such as *A* is inside (or outside) the curve? How can I determine whether some *other* point I may draw is inside or outside the curve? Children may come up with *various* criteria (e.g., "if the curve were a fence and *A* were a bug, he could get "out" without crossing the fence"). The process of debating and finally agreeing upon mutually acceptable definitions in such activities is mathematical experience of a very valuable kind; children learn what definitions are, why they are needed, why they can be quite arbitrary, why they must be precise, and why they must sometimes be modified. As another example, the question of which points are "between" two given points may be resolved in various ways by chil-

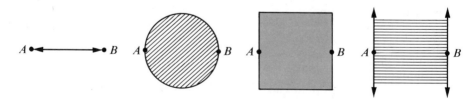

dren. If *A* and *B* are two points, they may decide that only points on open segment *AB* are between *A* and *B*, or that only points inside a particular circle or square, or between two lines are between *A* and *B*. There is nothing "wrong" with *any* of these decisions, as long as they are mutually *acceptable* to the children, i.e., as long as they survive the debates, are "well defined," and serve their purpose. There is plenty of time for children to learn the *standard* definitions (and undefined concepts). When children later encounter standard definitions, they will understand and appreciate them for what they are.

Many standard definitions must, of course, eventually be introduced. In doing so, the technique of the "creature cards" in the *Attribute* materials is a good one. For example, in defining *circle*, a teacher may show children several pictures, indicating what *are* called circles and what *are not*. Children can then be asked to pick out circles from among several pictures—here, again, is potential for debate—and to perhaps try to describe what a circle is. Their precision in doing so is unimportant at first, and will increase with maturity.

In probing questions such as "How many lines contain a given point?" or "How many points are there between 2 given points?" the question of "infinitely many" always comes up. Children frequently have (understandable) difficulty in expressing this idea. Expressions such as "more than can be counted" or even "lots" or "many, many" or "on and on" or "there is no end" are generally preferable to "infinite" or "infinitely many." The concept of infinity is a very elusive one, even for adults, and the word need not be introduced to children.

A related issue is that of undefined terms and models for them. Although teachers should certainly not attempt to *define* "point," "line," or "plane" with children, there is no need to burden them with *why* terms such as these cannot be defined. Those perceptive children who themselves raise this question can be referred to a dictionary to discover for themselves the circularity involved in trying to define all terms. Like most *defined* terms, words such as these should be handled intuitively and by example with children, though with as much precision as is consistent with their maturity. A *point*, for example, should be thought of as a very precise location, and children can understand its lack of dimension by discussing such questions as: Can you imagine a point which is exactly midway between this corner of the room and that one? Is there such a point? Where is it? Is it *exactly* there? If you look at a dot through a magnifying glass, where is the point it represents? What if we look at the dot through a microscope? Discussions such as these can lead children to think more and more carefully about such terms; and can help them to realize the importance of accuracy and precision in their drawings and their statements.

Many opportunities exist in geometry to increase children's skill in observation and to develop general problem-solving strategies.

Examples:

(a) How many segments do you see? (Name them.)

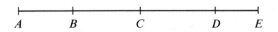

(b) How many triangles do you see?

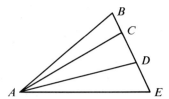 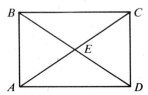

(c) How many segments are there with points A, B, . . . , H as endpoints?

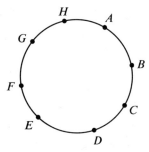

How many segments would be determined by 138 different points on a circle? By 138 different points on a line? Is there a relationship?

(d) Can you construct 2 triangles so they intersect in 1 point? 2 points? 3 points? 4 points? 0 points? More points than can be counted?

Various constructions are well within the capabilities of elementary school children. They include the straightedge and compass constructions of Euclidean geometry, paper-folding constructions, curve stitching, and constructions of "solids" from paper or cardboard. We have previously discussed the latter (pp. 327–9). An excellent source for Euclidean constructions is the 4-volume set *Geometry: Fun with Fundamentals* by Newton Hawley and Patrick Suppes (revised by George Gearhart). Some of the many constructions these volumes show children how to do with straightedge and compass are: bisect a given segment; construct a segment congruent to a given one; double, triple, etc., a given segment; construct an equilateral triangle with a given base; construct perpendiculars to a line from various points; construct a square; copy a given angle; draw a line parallel to a given one; bisect an angle; determine whether two angles are congruent; construct a triangle from three given segments or show why it cannot be done; construct a triangle similar to a given one, or congruent to a given one, etc. We will assume that the reader can do each of these — or find out how by examining a standard geometry text.

There are wide variations in children's ability to manipulate the tools for these constructions, of course, but with guidance most children can do a creditable job. Certainly one factor which affects the degree of their success is the quality of the tools they are using. A sharp, hard-leaded pencil and an inexpensive compass of the screw type are well worth the extra investment of time, effort, and money in terms of learning over a dull, soft-lead pencil and a 15-cent dime-store tension variety of compass. A major factor, of course, is teacher *guidance* in the use of their tools.

Many important geometric concepts and designs can be developed in paper folding activities. We have already mentioned the "square corner tester" and the many *symmetric* patterns obtainable from folding paper. Many others can be found in an NCTM booklet, *Paper Folding*, by Donovan Johnson. By simple folds, the Euclidean constructions — forming perpendiculars, parallel lines, bisectors of segments and angles, and so on — can all be formed. We will point out only a few here.

If a segment, AB, is drawn on a relatively translucent piece of paper (such as tracing paper or wax paper), the perpendicular bisector of $\overline{AB}$ can be seen in the crease formed by folding the paper so that points A and B are

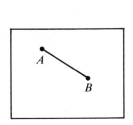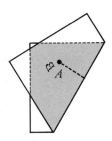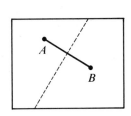

coincident. Ordinary paper can be used by making pinholes at A and B with the point of a compass and holding the paper up to a light.

This basic fold can be used to demonstrate several geometric generalizations and to provide a pattern for various curves such as the ellipse, hyperbola, and parabola. Children can see the shape of an ellipse, for example, by drawing a fairly large circle (about 6 inches in diameter) on a sheet of paper and marking many points on its circumference, say one every quarter inch or so. Then mark a point A inside the circle, and for each marked point X on the circumference, fold the paper to get the perpendicular bisector of $\overline{AX}$. Each of these folds is tangent to a point of an ellipse, so by forming enough of them, the shape of the ellipse emerges. Some children enjoy using the folds as a pattern for making a "curve stitching"—a design formed with colored yarn. The shape of a hyperbola can be formed in the same way, by choosing the point A to be *outside* the circle. The shape of a parabola can be formed by drawing a line and a point A not on the line; marking many points on the line; and, for each marked point, X, folding to obtain the perpendicular bisector of $\overline{AX}$.

An alternate way of forming a parabola is to draw a large angle on paper and on each leg label a number of points, say 1 or 2 cm apart. If there are, for example, 15 points on each leg, fold along the segment determined by point 1 on one leg and point 15 on the other, 2 and 14, 3 and 13, and so on (or label the points on one leg in opposite order from those on the other, then fold along points with corresponding numbers). The folds for the ellipse can be made easier by cutting out the circle. For the parabola, the edge of the paper is easier to use as the line than is drawing one; also, the angle can be cut out (or the *right* angle formed by the corner of a sheet of paper can be used).

Many other designs can be made by folding paper; children are often fascinated with the results—forming regular *curves* from *straight* lines.

Another way to construct an ellipse is to drive two pins through a piece of paper over a piece of plywood. Tie the ends of a short piece of heavy thread or light string together to form a loop; then using a pencil and the two pins to keep the loop tight (in the shape of a triangle), use the pencil to trace a path around the pins. The shape of the path will be elliptical, its exact shape depending on the length of the string and the distance between the pins. Trying to identify just *how* these two factors affect the shape of the ellipse can lead to some interesting and productive discoveries.

Activities such as paper folding, curve stitching, and so on, can be used essentially for recreation only, or simply to teach various shapes and how to make simple constructions; but for some inquisitive children (and alert teachers) they can lead to investigations into *why* they "work" as they do. The constructions themselves are only a beginning.

Measurement

The broad topic of measurement is often viewed separately from geometry, but since measurement so often involves geometric objects, we have chosen to discuss it here. We will also briefly consider some related topics.

The most important thing for the teacher to keep in mind about the teaching of measurement topics is almost too obvious to bear repeating, although it is too often neglected; that children learn the dual, and equally important, skills of estimating measures and measuring by doing so. Children from the very beginning of school should have frequent opportunities to learn and practice these skills, using the necessary measuring tools.

It should also be emphasized that if we expect children to think comfortably in metric terms, it will be necessary to use metric units virtually *exclusively* in measurement situations. Teaching an occasional "unit" on the metric system but normally measuring in English units will not suffice. Learning the SI system effectively requires virtual immersion in it, much as thinking in a foreign language is best accomplished by using that language exclusively. Of course, until the transition to general usage of SI has been accomplished, children will need to be familiar with both systems, but the two systems should be taught separately—with emphasis on metric units. Exercises involving both systems simultaneously, such as converting from inches to centimeters, are of questionable value in learning either system and should be avoided.

In the earliest grades, children must develop the prerequisite (premetric) concepts, and like prenumber and prenumeration concepts, these are developed largely by observing and discussing various measurable attributes of things in their environment. Such discussions should focus at first on relatively large differences between pairs of things, and thus gradually develop the essential premetric concepts of longer and shorter (for both length and time); larger and smaller (area); more and less (volume); hotter and colder (temperature); heavier and lighter (weight); and wider and narrower or duller and sharper (angles). Other "special" terms for linear measure include wider and narrower, or taller and shorter. Other terms occur sometimes even though they are not normally emphasized in elementary school, e.g., brighter and dimmer (luminous intensity) and stronger or weaker (power).

Once relatively large differences in these attributes are recognized by children, it is a quite natural step to begin measuring them. Usually length is the first attribute that is studied seriously, and there are good reasons for starting this with nonstandard units. Once children can count rationally, they enjoy choosing a unit of linear measure and finding out how long various things are, e.g., their desks, sheets of paper, tables, the classroom, the edge of a book, a shelf, the chalkboard or bulletin board, their own heights, the lengths of their arms, and so on. In choosing units, a few suggestions from the teacher will trigger many additional suggestions from the children: pencils, erasers, their feet, knuckles, outstretched fingers, paces—virtually anything. They should always be encouraged to guess before they measure and to compare their guesses with their measurements later. Four important discoveries are commonly made at this stage (or can be "planted" by the teacher): (1) that people disagree on what the length of a given object is (one child's pencil has been sharpened more often than another's, perhaps); (2) that the "laying off" process introduces a certain amount of error; (3) that measures don't always "come out even," e.g., the teacher's desk is a little less than 8 pencils wide; and (4) that shorter units usually come closer to "coming out even."

These discoveries pave the way for the introduction of standard units and the use of rulers. At first, teacher-made cardboard rulers scaled only in centimeters will suffice, and children must be carefully guided as they measure teacher-drawn segments which "come out even," i.e., which are as nearly exact multiples of 1 cm as possible. Quite soon, standard meter sticks and rulers (about 20 or 30 centimeters long) with millimeter markings can be introduced. Many objects in the classroom and at home can then be measured—pencils, erasers, tables, windows, desks, nails, paper clips, and so on. Measurements can first be expressed, for example, as "3 cm plus 4 mm" and later abbreviated to 3.4 cm or 34 mm. (This notation can be introduced strictly as an abbreviation—full understanding of the decimal system of notation is not a prerequisite.) Meter sticks and metric trundle wheels can be used for measuring larger objects and distances. Again, estimation should generally precede measurement and the two numbers should be compared.

As children gain more and more measuring experience, they can be exposed to special measurement problems. Indeed, they may encounter them quite naturally. How, for example, can we measure the depth of a hole too small for a ruler to fit in, or the crack between the door and the wall, or the thickness of a glass or the length of the school building, or the diameter of a round chair leg, or the distance around a large circular object such as a flower garden, or the length of a loop of string? As such special problems arise, children should be encouraged to devise techniques to solve them, e.g., we might measure the depth of a hole in a bowling ball by sticking a stiff wire in and marking it with our thumb, then measuring it with a ruler. Or we might measure the distance around a bicycle wheel or old automobile tire with a tape measure, then count the number of revolutions it makes as we roll it around the flower garden or along the wall of the school.

Special measuring tools and their uses can be introduced as the need arises: tape measures, calipers, feeler gauges, depth gauges, trundle wheels, micrometers (simplified but very functional and relatively inexpensive models of several such tools are available commercially—or perhaps they may be borrowed from a parent). Children always enjoy learning to use these.

The inevitable error factor in measurement should be emphasized repeatedly; the distance around a tree trunk, for example, should be measured three or four times (perhaps by three or four children) and the measurements recorded and compared. Older children can be introduced to the ideas of *greatest possible error* (half the length of the smallest unit of measure), *rounding off* measures to the nearest unit, and taking the *average* of several measurements.

Measurements other than linear should follow the same general guidelines, except that, in general, "homemade" units of measure are impractical, e.g., it is unlikely that children could devise their own units for measuring time and temperature. They should, however, be expected to measure time, for example, only in hours at first, then half-hours, quarter-hours, and then five-minute intervals before finally refining the skill to minutes and seconds.

Area and volume measures should be considered carefully. The standard "definitions" for these measures are in terms of squares or cubes whose dimensions are themselves measured in standard linear units. For example, the area of any simple closed curve is, by convention, the number of 1-by-1 squares (1 centimeter-by-1 centimeter, 1 kilometer-by-1 kilometer, and so on)—or fractional parts of such squares—required to tessellate the surface determined by the curve. The square shape is practical, but arbitrary, and in order to develop this standard convention with understanding, a useful activity is to consider several alternate shapes. For example, many simple closed shapes that can be constructed on a (square) geoboard can be covered with isosceles right triangles. It makes sense, therefore, as a pre-

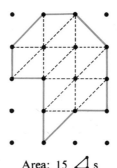

Area: 15 △ s

area exercise, to count the number of such triangles which cover various shapes. This avoids the need for fractions, while still teaching the essential concept of "area," i.e., the number of copies of a given shape which tessellate a particular region. The regular hexagon or equilateral triangle could similarly be used to approximate an "area," and the regular tetrahedron could serve as a measure of "volume" (individual servings of restaurant coffee cream are sometimes packaged in containers of this shape, perhaps in part because of the convenience in stacking and packaging them). The advantage of the square and cube lies chiefly in the convenience with which they can be counted and subdivided using fractions.

Beginning exercises in finding areas should involve such activities as pasting as many squares of uniform—though not necessarily standard—size, as needed to cover a region. At first the regions should be rectangular ones whose dimensions are multiples of those of the squares. After much experience of this kind, children can discover that the area of a rectangle can be found more quickly by measuring two adjacent dimensions and determining the product of those measures. Similarly, the volume of a box should be found first by filling it with cubes such as Cuisenaire unit cubes (each 1 cubic centimeter). The arithmetic procedure of multiplying the three dimensions should be left for them to discover.

Areas of right triangles — each half of a rectangle — should probably be considered next. The geoboard provides an excellent means for doing this.

Examples:

(a) If the unit square, i.e., area of 1, is defined to be this:

then the area of the rectangle shown here is 8, since it requires 8 unit squares to cover it.

(b) If a rectangle is cut diagonally, the area of each of the two right triangles formed is half that of the rectangle, i.e., 4 (some work with fractions is a prerequisite here, of course).

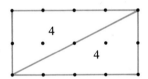

Areas of irregular triangles can then be found by enclosing them in rectangles, so that the vertices of the triangle meet the sides of the rectangle, and with at least one vertex of the two figures being coincident.

Example:

This triangle

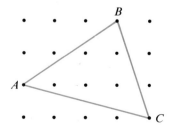

can be enclosed in rectangle *DECF* (with vertex *C* common to the two figures). The area of triangle *ABC* is the area of rectangle

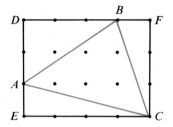

DECF minus the sum of the areas of triangles *DAB*, *BFC*, and *AEC*, each of which is easily determined: The area of triangle *DAB* is half the area of the rectangle whose adjacent sides measure 3 and 2 (the lengths of $\overline{DB}$ and $\overline{DA}$), i.e., 3. Similarly, the area of triangle *BFC* is $1\frac{1}{2}$ and that of *AEC* is 2. Thus since the area of rectangle *DECF* is 12, the area of triangle *ABC* is $12 - (3 + 1\frac{1}{2} + 2)$ or $5\frac{1}{2}$.

That the area of any triangle is half the product of the measures of its base and altitude can be discovered with the geoboard by constructing a right triangle with an easily measured base and altitude (i.e., horizontal and vertical, respectively), then finding the areas, as above, for several triangles with the same base and altitude, formed by transformations of the vertex opposite the base as suggested previously.

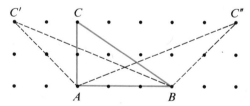

Area △ *ABC* = Area △ *ABC'* = Area △ *ABC"* = 3

Once they can find the areas of rectangles and right triangles, children can determine the areas of other polygons on the geoboard fairly easily, since any such polygon can be viewed in terms of rectangles and right triangles. Areas of certain parallelograms, trapezoids, or rhombuses can be found easily with the geoboard, and used as a basis for conjectures about formulas for finding areas of such figures in general.

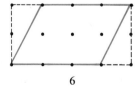

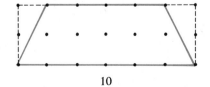

6   10   2

Other discoveries, such as the Pythagorean theorem, can be made from similar explorations.

Areas of curved regions such as circles are more complicated and generally beyond the elementary schoolchild, but can be approximated by counting techniques. For example, the curve below, drawn on lattice paper, has an area between $7\frac{1}{2}$ and $15\frac{1}{2}$, that is, between the area of the smallest and largest polygonal regions that can be drawn on its interior and exterior respectively (allowing for vertices which may touch the curve). The average of those two, $11\frac{1}{2}$, is a fairly close approximation.

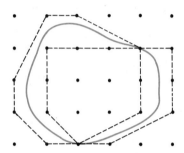

Learning to measure weights and fluid volume is relatively straightforward and teaching procedures and purposes should generally parallel those for teaching linear measure. That is, emphasis should be on familiarity with the basic units, based on grams and liters, and on developing skill with appropriate measuring devices. Estimation should again precede measurement. Liquids are measured best in graduated plastic containers with varying capacities, e.g., 10 ml, 250 ml, 500 ml, and 1 liter. Mass is measured on one or more of three kinds of devices. The pan balance is used with sets of weights of various standard sizes such as 1 g, 5 g, 10 g, or 50 g.

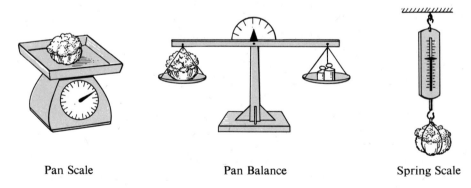

Pan Scale   Pan Balance   Spring Scale

Measuring angles is a relatively difficult task for elementary school children. The ordinary 180° semicircular protractor is difficult to handle and to read. Circular, 360°, clear plastic ones are a little easier and thus more useful, but even those are frequently confusing. Homemade protractors made by repeatedly folding a cut-out tracing-paper or wax-paper circle "in half" are sufficient for measuring most angles of interest at this stage. Angles can be measured roughly in terms of $\frac{1}{2}$-turns (180°), $\frac{1}{4}$-turns (90°), $\frac{1}{8}$-turns (45°) and $\frac{1}{16}$-turns ($22\frac{1}{2}$°) with such protractors until more precise, standardized instruments are introduced in junior high school or high school.

Gathering data through measurement or counting leads quite naturally to the question of recording and displaying that data in systematic ways. Any graph is a pictorial way of doing so. The old adage that "a picture is worth a thousand words" has much truth in it. The pictorial nature of a graph can reveal sometimes fascinating relationships among data which mere accumulation or even tabulation of it cannot.

Because of the extreme importance of emphasizing relationships and patterns in the teaching of elementary mathematics, children should be introduced to graphs early and use them constantly. They need to become familiar with several types of graphs—how to read them, how to use them, and how to make them. As a rule, children find graphing an interesting and sometimes challenging task. And, consideration of the problems involved in constructing their own graphs, beginning with pictographs, helps them in the subsequent task of reading those prepared by others, as found, for example, in their textbooks.

All kinds of real, and realistic, data can provide the impetus for making graphs, and the general nature of the relationship between kinds of data can lead to the rationale for constructing various kinds of graphs: pictographs, bar graphs, dot graphs, broken-line graphs, smooth-line graphs, and circle graphs. Each serves a unique purpose in emphasizing a particular type of relationship between the classes of data it portrays. Pictographs and bar graphs are useful for portraying absolute differences in measured or counted quantities such as populations of various political units or heights of mountains. Broken-line or smooth-line graphs emphasize changes and rates of change of a particular characteristic such as populations or a child's growth over a period of time. Circle graphs emphasize distributions of time, money, populations, and so on, as proportions devoted to each part of some totality such as a 24-hour day, or a budget, or a composite population.

Topics such as populations, budgets, and heights of mountains may not appeal to all children. But the resourceful teacher will find endless sources of data to graph, even in the first grade classroom: the number of children who come to school by car, on foot, on the school bus, and by public transportation; distances that various children travel to school; the amounts of time spent on various activities, in the classroom day or in a 24-hour day or in a week; progress on various achievement tests, such as fundamental facts tests; temperatures at various times of the day, various days of the weeks or months of the year; numbers of sunny days, rainy days, and so on, in a period of time; birth months of children in the room; heights or weights of children in the room, or changes in an individual child's height or weight; numerical data such as sum families, squares of numbers, dimensions of rectangles with a constant area, unit fractions, or factors of a given number; number of children absent each day, growth of a pet; and many, many more (see the Nuffield Mathematics Project, *Pictorial Representation* listed in the Suggested Readings for this chapter).

Interpreting a teacher-made or textbook graph, at least in broad, general terms, is generally an easier task than that of making one. A circle graph, in particular, is easy to interpret — broadly — but involves relatively sophisticated understandings of percentage and angle measure to prepare with any degree of accuracy. Thus, experience and guidance in reading graphs should generally precede attempts to make them.

The strategies and techniques used for helping children to construct graphs are governed by the nature of the data being graphed and the maturity of the children. Some of the problems children encounter as they learn to make various types of graphs include: deciding which type of graph is most appropriate; determining appropriate scales, including the problems of paper size and range of data; and determining whether to represent each piece of data or to group the data in a particular way. Some of these can be rather challenging and will require considerable help from the teacher. Sometimes a problem arising from trying to prepare a graph can provide excellent motivation for introducing a new topic such as finding averages or other measures of central tendency; the introduction of fractions, decimals, or percent; or using a protractor.

Tangrams and Soma Cubes

Many geometric problems and materials can be classified as "puzzles." These can be used purely for recreation at odd times, but they can also develop geometric visualization as well as lead to new ideas or to serious analysis. While there are hundreds of such puzzles available, we will consider here only two of the better known ones — Tangrams and Soma Cubes.

These two sets of materials have at least two things in common: both can be constructed by the teacher or by children in a few minutes, and both involve putting shapes together in virtually endless ways.

The *Tangram* puzzle, allegedly of ancient Chinese origin, consists of seven pieces (of heavy paper, cardboard, wood, masonite, plastic) shaped as shown here. It is possible to fit these shapes together in virtually endless ways, either to copy a given shape or to create a new one. Both can be challenging to children, yet at the same time both copying and creating shapes are attainable, rewarding, and fun. While Tangram puzzles and examples of shapes to be made are available from several commercial sources, the pieces can be easily made in the classroom and teachers or children can use them to invent shapes by the hundreds.

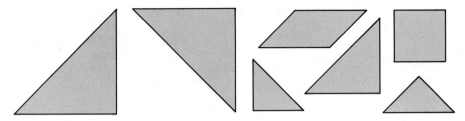

One of the more interesting shapes to make with the pieces is a square, and this can provide a model for constructing the pieces themselves. The picture below can be drawn on heavy paper or cardboard (or on a duplicator master to make multiple copies), then cut out. Any dimensions proportional to those shown can be used; lines that are parallel should be clear from the picture.

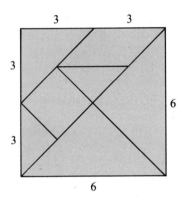

The Tangram pieces can be used in a variety of ways. At first, particularly with young children, use just the two largest pieces to see what shapes can be made, e.g., a large triangle or a square. Gradually add a few of the pieces at a time to create more shapes, until finally all seven pieces are used. Activity cards or a bulletin board can be prepared showing silhouettes or outlines of shapes to be made, either in the actual size or in a different scale. (Children, too, can make such silhouettes or outlines to display their creations or to challenge their peers.) Older children can be challenged to make their own set of pieces, perhaps by paper folding.

Several standard geometric shapes besides the square can be made using all seven pieces: A large (right) triangle, a rectangle, a hexagon, a parallelogram, and a trapezoid. (There are 7 other convex shapes that can be made.) In addition to these, a full set can be used to make numerals, letters of the alphabet, or various caricatures, e.g., of a cat, a dog, a chicken, a horse, a candle, a house. (A good reference is Ronald C. Read's paperback, listed at the end of this chapter.)

Children who have learned to find areas of the shapes can be asked to measure the dimensions and determine the individual areas, and the relationships among them. Alternately, and perhaps easier and more interesting, an arbitrary area, say 1, can be assigned to each of the smallest triangles, and the children can be challenged to then determine the areas of each of the other pieces and of the square. This may suggest the task of making each of the pieces from a tessellation of the smallest triangle, and identifying various rotations, reflections, and translations in that tessellation.

Soma Cubes, originally developed by Piet Hein of Denmark, consist of seven blocks, each of which can be constructed by gluing together small cubes so that their faces match as shown here. These, too, can be

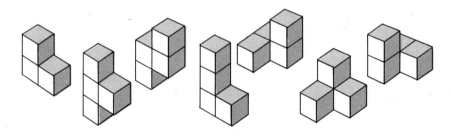

purchased commercially. Notice that the smallest block is the only way that 3 cubes can be glued together so that faces fit together and so that the blocks are not all in a straight line (it could be rotated or reflected to *view* another way). The remaining 6 blocks are the only 6 ways in which 4 cubes may be arranged face-to-face, other than in a straight line.

Like Tangrams, Soma Cubes can be assembled to make many interesting shapes, either suggestive of familiar things (e.g., a cube, tunnel, sofa, or stairway) or simply as creative designs. Either part or all of the set can be used. Of all the shapes, perhaps the most interesting is the cube (3 by 3 by 3 of course, since there are 27 small cubes altogether.) The most curious thing about the construction of the cube, particularly to the child who finally figures it out for the first time, is that it can be done in *many* ways—in fact, in more than a quarter of a million ways! (This was demonstrated by a Swedish astrophysicist, which shows that such materials lend themselves to rather serious analysis as well as to recreation.) Children generally use trial and error at first, as they do with Tangrams, but as their spatial visualization develops they gradually develop strategies, such as deciding which block could *not* be used in a particular corner.

Techniques for using Soma Cubes are basically the same as for Tangrams. For example, show a picture of a shape on an activity card or on a bulletin board and challenge the children to make it; have them make their own sets using the *conditions* for the constructions rather than pictures of them; or have them create their own constructions. As with Tangrams, one should begin with a few pieces at a time.

Both Soma Cubes and Tangrams, with booklets suggesting many things to do with them, are available commercially from several sources, including Creative Publications, Cuisenaire, and McGraw–Hill (see Appendix B). Several block puzzles similar to the Soma Cubes are also available.

Incidentally, other interesting activities related to Soma Cubes revolve around *polyominoes*—sets of squares joined edge-to-edge. While there is only one *monomino* and one *domino,* it is interesting to see in how many different ways, including straight lines but excluding reflections or rotations, 3, 4, 5, or more squares can be put together. Hundreds of interesting pastimes can be derived from these, the most popular being with the 12 pentominoes (5 squares each). We leave that for you to explore if it appeals to you—it will to some of your students.

Projects, Questions, and Suggested Activities

1. Select a topic or activity, either in this chapter or in some of the suggested readings, which is new to you. Try it, find out all you can about it, and then, if possible, try teaching it to a child.
2. Examine a current elementary school textbook series for its geometric content. List the topics and concepts emphasized at each grade level.

Suggested Readings

"All You Will Need to Know About Metric." Metric Information Office, U.S. Department of Commerce, National Bureau of Standards, Washington, D.C. 20234.

A free, one-page summary of most common metric units.

Alspaugh, Carol Ann. "Kaleidoscopic Geometry." *The Arithmetic Teacher,* February 1970, pp. 116–17.

Several geometric topics developed from hinged mirrors. In the same issue, four other articles of interest are Forseth and Adams' (pp. 119–21) discussion of symmetry in children's art activities; Liedtke and Kieren's (pp. 123–26) discussion of some geoboard activities for very young children; Wardrop's (pp. 127–28) description of eleven ways to make a pattern for a cube, with some interesting questions to consider; and Buchman's (pp. 129–32) description of several enrichment experiments with the Pythagorean theorem.

Association of Teachers of Mathematics. *Notes on Mathematics in Primary Schools.* Cambridge: Cambridge University Press, 1967.

If you examined this book in conjunction with Chapter 7, you will recall the wide range of geometric activities that appear also. An excellent source book.

Bachrach, Beatrice. "No Time on Their Hands." *The Arithmetic Teacher,* February 1973, pp. 102–3.

>On teaching children to tell time, which we have not discussed much in this chapter. In the same issue, see Trimble's article (pp. 129–33) which gives excellent suggestions on teaching approximations in measurement.

Brydegaard, Marguerite. "Flight to Reality." *The Arithmetic Teacher,* February 1972, pp. 83–84.

>A fitting introduction to an issue which features several articles on geometry. In the same issue, see also the articles by Bruni (pp. 85–87); Knight and Schweitzer (pp. 88–89); Wong (pp. 91–95); Williford (pp. 97–104); Coltharp (pp. 117–22); Strangman (pp. 123–25); Lulli (pp. 127–30); Backman and Smith (pp. 156–57). Many good ideas.

Denmark, Thomas, and Kalin, Robert. "Suitability of Teaching Geometric Construction in Upper Elementary Grades—A Pilot Study." *The Arithmetic Teacher,* February 1964, pp. 73–80.

>Report of a study conducted with fifth- and sixth-grade students using Hawley and Suppes' *Geometry For Primary Grades.* Other reports on the use of these materials can be found in *The Arithmetic Teacher;* April 1963 (pp. 191–94), October 1962 (pp. 314–16), and November 1961 (pp. 374–76).

Dickoff, Steven S. "Paper Folding and Cutting a Set of Tangram Pieces." *The Arithmetic Teacher,* April 1971, pp. 250–52.

>Just what the title suggests.

Dienes, Zolten P., and Golding, E. W. *Geometry Through Transformations.* 3 vols. New York: Herder and Herder, 1967.

>A good source book for teachers on this topic.

Farrell, Margaret A. *Geoboard Geometry.* Palo Alto, Calif.: Creative Publications, 1971.

>Excellent source book of geoboard activities for all grade levels.

Gardner, Martin. "Mathematical Games." *Scientific American,* September 1971, pp. 204–12.

>Constructing the Platonic solids from strips of paper.

Gardner, Martin. "Mathematical Games." *Scientific American,* November 1971, pp. 114–21.

>Puzzles of the Tangram sort.

Gardner, Martin. "Mathematical Games." *Scientific American,* June 1972, pp. 114–18.

>The four-color map problem.

Gardner, Martin. "Mathematical Games." *Scientific American*, September 1972, pp. 176–80.

> Soma cubes and some extensions.

Grant, Nicholas, and Tobin, Alexander. "Let Them Fold." *The Arithmetic Teacher*, October 1972, pp. 420–25.

> Seven paper-folding activities.

Hall, Gary D. "A Pythagorean Puzzle." *The Arithmetic Teacher*, January 1972, pp. 67–70.

> Teaching the Pythagorean theorem in the sixth grade using a puzzle.

Hallerberg, Arthur E. "The Metric System: Past, Present — Future?" *The Arithmetic Teacher*, April 1973, pp. 247–55.

> A concise summary of significant historical events leading to the 1972 Metric Conversion Act. This issue features several articles on metrication, including many classroom activities.

Hawley, Newton, and Suppes, Patrick. *Geometry: Fun with Fundamentals*, 4 vols. Rev. by George Gearhart. San Francisco: Holden-Day, 1972.

> Compass and straightedge constructions.

Helgren, Fred J. "Metric Supplement to Mathematics." Waukegan, Illinois: Metric Association, 1967.

> A collection of exercises for children in Grades 3–8 to provide experience with estimating and measuring with metric units. This and other educational aids are available from Metric Association, Inc., 2004 Ash Street, Waukegan, Illinois 60085.

Hoffer, Alan R. "What You Always Wanted to Know About Six But Have Been Afraid to Ask." *The Arithmetic Teacher*, March 1973, pp. 173–80.

> An interesting property of hexagons (p. 179).

Ibe, Milagros D. "Better Perception of Geometric Figures Through Folding and Cutting." *The Arithmetic Teacher*, November 1970, pp. 583–86.

> Interesting paper-folding and cutting activities for teaching conservation of area.

Ibe, Milagros D. "Drawing 3-D Figures from 2-D Templates." *The Arithmetic Teacher*, March 1971, pp. 180–82.

> An application of translations in art. The author suggests other designs from translations and rotations of simple shapes in a second article in this issue (pp. 183–84).

Inskeep, James E., Jr. "Primary Grade Instruction in Geometry." *The Arithmetic Teacher*, May 1968, pp. 422–26.

> An excellent summary of arguments for teaching geometry in the elementary school as well as practical suggestions for doing so. Should be read.

Johnson, Donovan A. *Paper Folding for the Mathematics Class*. Washington: National Council of Teachers of Mathematics, 1957.

> Many good ideas for elementary schools can be extracted from this, even though it is intended principally for secondary classes.

Kendig, Frank. "Coming of the Metric System." *Saturday Review*, December 1972, pp. 40–44.

> A comprehensive review of efforts to adopt the metric system in America, and reasons why they may now suceed. Includes a summary of metric units. Good background material.

Liedtke, Werner. "What Can You Do with a Geoboard?" *The Arithmetic Teacher*, October 1969, pp. 491–93.

> Many practical ideas: graphing, area, perimeter, networks, and others.

McClintic, Joan. "Capacity Comparisons by Children." *The Arithmetic Teacher*, January 1970, pp. 19–25.

> Measurement activities (area and volume) in the Kindergarten. In the same issue, Biggs (pp. 25–32) provides anecdotal records of measurement activities tried with children (and teachers) in England.

National Bureau of Standards, "Brief History of Measurement Systems with a Chart of the Modernized Metric System." Revised October 1972.

> A concise summary of SI. For sale by the Superintendent of Documents, U.S. Government Printing Office, Washington, D.C. 20402 (25 cents). Special publication 304A.

Niman, John, and Postman, Robert D. "Probability on the Geoboard." *The Arithmetic Teacher*, March 1973, pp. 167–70.

> Another use for the geoboard.

Nuffield Mathematics Project. *Pictorial Representation*. New York: Wiley, 1967.

> Many examples of graphs that children have made and ideas for sources of data that can be graphed.

Pierson, Robert C. "Elementary Graphing Experiences." *The Arithmetic Teacher*, March 1969, pp. 199–201.

> Several ideas for topics that lend themselves to graphing experiences in the lower grades.

Read, Ronald C. *Tangrams: 330 Puzzles*. New York: Dover, 1965.

> Just what the title suggests. A wide variety.

Schloff, Charles E. "Rolling Tetrahedrons." *The Arithmetic Teacher*, December 1972, pp. 657–59.

An idea for a construction activity with much opportunity for learning geometry—plus a finished product that can be used for several games.

Steinhaus, H. *Mathematical Snapshots.* New York: Oxford University Press, 1969.

> A delightful book which anyone interested in geometry will enjoy rambling through.

Walter, Marion. "A Common Misconception About Area." *The Arithmetic Teacher*, April 1970, pp. 286–89.

> The interesting misconception about relationships between perimeter and area.

Walter, Marion. "An Example of Informal Geometry: Mirror Cards." *The Arithmetic Teacher*, October 1966, pp. 448–52.

> Some ideas for using this device created by the author. See corrections, May 1967 issue, p. 372, and a sequel, "Some Mathematical Ideas Involved in the Mirror Cards," by the same author in the February 1967, issue (pp. 115–25).

Walter, Marion. "A Second Example of Informal Geometry: Milk Cartons." *The Arithmetic Teacher*, May 1969, pp. 368–70.

> Excellent beginning activities with polyominoes, using milk cartons, scissors, and construction paper. In the same issue (pp. 371–78), Junge gives many suggestions for teaching about graphs.

Witt, Sarah M. "A Snip of the Scissors." *The Arithmetic Teacher*, November 1971, pp. 496–99.

> Making 3-, 4-, 5-, . . . pointed stars with folded paper and scissors. Interesting.

9. Teaching Numbers Beyond the Whole Numbers

Elementary school children encounter at least the beginnings of two number systems beyond the whole numbers. A rather thorough study of fractional numbers, including the concept of fractional number, equivalence of fractions, computational procedures, and structural properties, is usually undertaken in the elementary grades, beginning as early as the first grade. Integers are studied in less detail, but are usually introduced as background for more serious study later on. Thus, studies of the *system of integers* and the *system of rational numbers* originate in the elementary grades. Additionally, three important topics, related particularly to rational numbers, are begun here: the notation of *decimals*, the language of *percentage*, and the concept of *ratio*.

We will discuss each of these topics in this chapter. Considering fractions, decimals, percentage, and ratio as "separate" topics would be unwise, we believe, because they are so interrelated by their very nature — and activities for teaching them should reflect this.

Before beginning a mathematical review of these topics, a note should be made about the relative emphasis of fractions and decimals in schools. Historically, the invention of fractions preceded that of decimals by many centuries, and schools have apparently reflected this to a large extent in the teaching of them. Fractions have received by far the greater emphasis, and decimals have been treated in many cases as a side topic or as a notation for special fractions. We concur with many who believe the emphasis should be reversed, or at least modified considerably. Computations with decimals are generally easier than are those with fractions (which was the basic reason for their invention). This is particularly true for computations related to measurements made with metric instruments. In fact, the advent of widespread metric measurement may one day relegate the study of fractions — especially the computations we now do with them — to an insignificant role. Fractions themselves may one day be viewed as an interesting historical topic.

As a simple example, suppose a child needs to divide a standard $8\frac{1}{2}$-by-11 inch sheet of paper into, say 7 columns. How wide should each column be? $8\frac{1}{2} \div 7 = 1\frac{3}{14}$. But how much is $\frac{3}{14}$ of an inch? Assuming he is using a ruler scaled in sixteenths of an inch, he has two options: Make each line "a little more" than $1\frac{3}{16}$ inch apart (which may be close enough, depending on his needs and on how much of a perfectionist he is) or perform some rather complicated interpolation, such as $\frac{3}{14} = \frac{x}{16}$, to find that 3-fourteenths is $3\frac{3}{7}$-sixteenths, i.e., about midway between $\frac{3}{16}$ and $\frac{4}{16}$. By contrast, if the paper were measured in centimeters, it would be found to measure about 21.6 cm; dividing this by 7 reveals that each column should be about 3.09 cm wide, "just under" 3.1 cm. Both results, $1 + 3\frac{1}{2}$-sixteenths in. and 3.09 cm are close enough to do the job respectably, but there can be little question that the metric approach is easier and quicker. (Dividing the paper into 8 columns would be equally easy with inches and fractions or with centimeters and decimals, of course.)

1. Mathematical Review

Integers

There are at least two common ways of describing or defining those numbers we call the integers. The first, which is probably the more authentic historically, is by postulating the existence of an opposite for each natural number, n, called quite arbitrarily "negative n" or "the opposite of n" and designated ^-n. On a number line, the natural number n and its opposite, ^-n, can be represented as endpoints of vectors with equal magnitude but with opposite direction, both vectors beginning at zero. The natural numbers may then be called *positive* integers and their opposites *negative* integers. Zero is considered to be an integer, but is classified by itself, neither positive nor negative.

The second approach grows out of the change or difference represented by a given ordered pair of natural numbers. Under this interpretation, an ordered pair, (a, b) of natural or whole numbers arbitrarily represents a positive change if $a > b$, a "negative" change if $b > a$, and no change if $a = b$. Positive changes are represented by positive integers, and so on. The absolute difference of a and b, i.e., either $a - b$ or $b - a$, whichever is defined for natural or whole numbers, is used to indicate the "magnitude" of the integer. For example, any of the pairs $(3, 0)$, $(4, 1)$, $(5, 2)$, $(6, 3)$, $(7, 4)$, . . . , $(n, n - 3)$, . . . , could represent the integer *positive* 3 ($^+3$); any of $(0, 3)$, $(1, 4)$, $(2, 5)$, $(3, 6)$, $(4, 7)$, . . . , $(n, n + 3)$, . . . , could represent *negative* 3 ($^-3$). Both $^+3$ and $^-3$ have the same magnitude, or *absolute value*, 3. Any of $(0, 0)$, $(1, 1)$, $(2, 2)$, $(3, 3)$, . . . , (n, n), . . . , could represent zero. In general, two pairs of natural (or whole) numbers, (a, b) and (c, d) represent the *same* integer if $a + d = b + c$. This relationship can be used to define an equivalence relation in a formal view of the system of integers. The interested reader who has not done so may wish to pursue this; we shall not do so here.

    The basic operations of addition and multiplication of integers can be defined and represented, as can the numbers themselves, in various ways. The sum, $a + b$, of two integers, a and b, for example, can be defined in at least three ways.

1. Start at the point on the number line represented by a; move in the *direction* on the line represented by b (to the right if b is positive, to the left if b is negative, or not at all if b is zero) and the *distance* on the line represented by the magnitude, or absolute value, of b, e.g.:

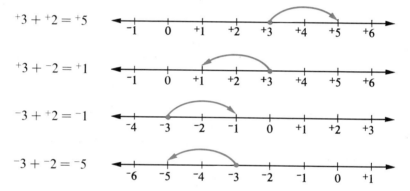

2. Start at *any* point on the number line. Move in the direction indicated by the sign of a (right if a is positive, left if a is negative, or not at all if a is zero) and the distance indicated by $|a|$, the absolute value of a; from that point, move in the direction and distance indicated by b. The net result of the two trips, i.e., the distance equivalent to a trip from the starting point of the first trip to the ending point of the second trip, represents the sum:

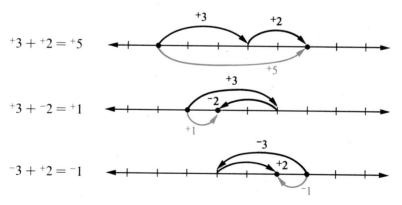

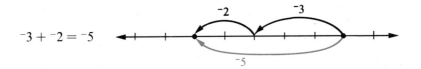

$$^-3 + {}^-2 = {}^-5$$

3. If $a = (w, x)$ and $b = (y, z)$, then
$$a + b = (w + y, x + z),$$
e.g., if $a = {}^+3 = (3, 0)$ and if $b = {}^-2 = (0, 2)$, then
$$a + b = (3, 0) + (0, 2) = (3 + 0, 0 + 2) = (3, 2) = {}^+1$$

   Similarly, the product of two integers, a and b, can be defined in at least two ways.

1. The absolute value of a multiplied by the absolute value of b, is a whole number c. The magnitude of $a \times b$ can be defined as c. And the sign of $a \times b$ is positive if a and b are either both positive or both negative; negative if either of a or b is positive and the other negative; and neither positive nor negative, i.e. zero, if either a or b is zero. For example,
$$^-3 \times {}^+2 = {}^-6$$
$$^-4 \times {}^-5 = {}^+20$$
$$^-2 \times 0 = 0$$

2. If $a = (w, x)$ and $b = (y, z)$, then
$$a \times b = (wy + xz, xy + wz)$$
e.g., if $a = {}^+3$ and $b = {}^-2$,
$$a \times b = (3, 0) \times (0, 2) = (3 \cdot 0 + 0 \cdot 2, 0 \cdot 0 + 3 \cdot 2) = (0, 6) = {}^-6$$

   No matter which way addition and multiplication are defined, it is easily established that the basic properties of the whole number operations are also true in the system of integers — the commutative, associative, and distributive properties hold; and the additive and multiplicative identities are zero and (positive) one, respectively. Additionally, when subtraction and division are defined in the usual way, as the "inverse operations" of addition and multiplication, respectively, each integer has an additive inverse, so that the difference of each pair of integers is an integer, i.e., the set of integers is closed with respect to subtraction. In fact, if a and b are integers, then $a - b$ is $a + {}^-b$ (a plus the opposite of b). This characteristic is the principal reason for the invention of the integers, and is the major advantage of the system of integers over the whole number system.

Several new generalizations, not appropriate for whole numbers, can be proven, based on the above definitions. They include these, which are true for all integers, a, b, and c (in reading these, note that, for example, if a is a variable representing some integer — positive, negative, or zero — then ^-a should be thought of as "the *opposite* of a," not "negative a," e.g., if a is negative, then ^-a is positive):

$$(^-a) - b = ^-(a + b)$$
$$^-(a - b) = ^-a + b$$
$$^-(^-a) = a$$
$$(^-a) + (^-b) = ^-(a + b)$$
$$a(^-b) = ^-(ab) \qquad \text{and} \qquad (^-a)b = ^-(ab)$$
$$(^-a)(^-b) = ab$$
$$a(b - c) = ab - ac, \qquad \text{and} \qquad (b - c)a = ba - ca$$

The system of integers also inherits all of the generalizations that are true in the whole number system. Those involving subtraction, as the last equation above, which must be *restricted* for whole numbers [e.g., $a(b - c) = ab - ac$ is true for whole numbers only if $b \geq c$], are true without restriction with integers.

The relative order of any pair of integers can also be defined in various ways. For example:

1. $a < b$ if the coordinate of a on the number line is to the left of the co-ordinate of b (assuming the line is oriented horizontally in the usual way).
2. $a < b$ if $b - a$ is a positive integer.
3. $a < b$ if there is a positive integer c such that $a + c = b$.

Several basic order generalizations can then be shown:

1. If $a < b$, then $a + c < b + c$.
2. If $a < b$, and if $c < 0$, then $a \cdot c > b \cdot c$.
3. If $a < b$, and if $c > 0$, then $a \cdot c < b \cdot c$.
4. If $a < b$ and $b < c$, then $a < c$.

Fractions, Decimals, Percent, and Ratio

The number system we associate with the fractions of everyday arithmetic was, like all number systems, invented by man. Perhaps "evolved" is a more appropriate term than "invented." We can't pinpoint any inventor (though much credit is commonly given to the ancient Egyptians); but we can conjecture about *why* fractions were invented.

The evolution of this system of numbers is commonly attributed to two inadequacies of the system of whole numbers. The first of these concerns *measurement*; the second involves *division*. One may argue that the two are not really different, but it will be instructive to consider them separately.

The measurement problem can be illustrated by a hypothetical situation involving linear measurement. Suppose we were assigned the task of determining the distance from the front wall of a room to the rear wall, and suppose that we had only whole numbers with which to work (no fractional number concepts). We would probably choose some appropriate standardized unit (e.g., meter, decimeter, centimeter) and proceed in the familiar manner. Suppose that the distance is not an exact multiple of the chosen unit; for example, suppose the distance is greater than 6 meters but less than 7 meters. Then we must decide whether 6 or 7 is more descriptive of the distance. In order to obtain a more precise measurement, we could change to some shorter unit (e.g., the decimeter) and report the distance, for example, as 6 meters, 2 decimeters, or 62 decimeters (6.2 meters). This process could be continued (6 meters, 2 decimeters and 7 centimeters, for example), but the precision of our measure would always be restricted by the lengths of our standard units: the shorter the unit, the more precise the measurement would be. We would need to repeatedly invent newer and shorter units in order to comply with increased demands for more and more precise measurements.

The second limitation of the whole number system involves division. Many situations arise which suggest dividing a pair of whole numbers but for which no whole number quotient exists and for which the quotient-remainder approach is not appropriate. Consider these questions and the division equations which they suggest:

1. If 2 hungry boys are to share 7 cookies, how many cookies should each boy receive? $(7 \div 2 = x)$
2. What is the average cost per can of cat food that sells at 2 cans for 35 cents? $(35 \div 2 = x)$
3. If 4 boys are to share 2 candy bars, how much candy should each boy receive? $(2 \div 4 = x)$

Appropriate answers to questions such as these could not be determined by division without the use of fractions.

Basic Definition of Fractional Numbers

There are various ways to describe or define fractional numbers, all of which involve division in one way or another. The simplest definition, and the basic one, is that a fractional number is the quotient, $a \div b$, of two whole numbers, a and b, where b is nonzero. The standard form for expressing that quotient is the fraction $\frac{a}{b}$. A more general definition is that of a *rational number*: The quotient, $x \div y$, of two *integers* x and y, where $y \neq 0$, is by definition a rational number, expressed by the fraction $\frac{x}{y}$. Fractional numbers, then, are a special restriction of rational numbers — they include all the rational numbers except the negative ones. We will consider here only the fractional numbers, since these are the fractions of most elementary school programs.

Fraction vs. Fractional Number

Before considering other definitions for fractional numbers and other aspects of the fractional number system, it should be noted that the expressions "fraction" and "fractional number" are sometimes used interchangeably. We will not generally do so here, so we must specify what we mean by each. We have already said that a fraction, $\frac{a}{b}$ is an expression of the quotient, $a \div b$, of two particular whole numbers, a and b. (That b cannot be zero is well known to the reader, so we will not continually repeat that restriction.) If fractions are to be viewed as quotients, then they should conform with all of the properties of division. One essential property is that the quotient $a \div b$ is unaffected, i.e., is identical, if a and b are each multiplied or divided by the same nonzero number, k. For example, the quotient $32 \div 8$ is the same as the quotients $64 \div 16$, $16 \div 4$, $8 \div 2$, or $4 \div 1$. To be consistent, we must then agree that the *fractions* $\frac{32}{8}$, $\frac{64}{16}$, $\frac{16}{4}$, $\frac{8}{2}$, and $\frac{4}{1}$ are equivalent, since $\frac{32}{8} = \frac{64}{16} = \frac{16}{4} = \frac{8}{2} = \frac{4}{1}$. There are infinitely many more expressions of this same quotient, and it is that entire *collection* of fractions that we designate as a fractional number. That is, we may think of a fractional number as the set of all fractions that are equivalent to a given one. Thus, when we work with a particular fraction, as in addition or subtraction, we could replace it with any other to which it is equivalent. Although the fractions $\frac{1}{2}$ and $\frac{2}{4}$ are different, they are equivalent and therefore interchangeable. It can be observed that if two quotients $a \div b$ and $c \div d$ are the same, then $a \times d = b \times c$. For example, given the quotients $8 \div 2$ and $4 \div 1$, we see that $8 \times 1 = 2 \times 4$. This can be verified in general: If $a \div b$ and $c \div d$ name the same number x, i.e., if $a \div b = x$ and $c \div d = x$, then by the definition of division $xb = a$ and $xd = c$. Multiplying each side of the first equation by d and each side of the second by b (both are nonzero) gives $xbd = ad$ and $xdb = cb$. Since $xbd = xdb$, $ad = cb$ by the transitive property of equality.

This, then, can be used as a criterion for determining whether two fractions are equivalent, i.e.,

$$\frac{a}{b} = \frac{c}{d} \qquad \text{if and only if} \qquad a \times d = b \times c$$

Reduced Fractions

Since fractions are defined in terms of division, and since division is a basic concept of number theory, it should not be surprising that many characteristics of fractions can be viewed in terms of number theory. One of several such connections is this: given any fractional number, there is exactly *one* fraction expressing that number such that its terms (numerator and denominator, i.e., dividend and divisor) are relatively prime. The proof of this is too lengthy to include here, but is not particularly complicated (although it is not trivial). This single fraction is usually singled out as the simplest form of the number and is used as its standard name. Each fraction which names the number can be reduced to this simplest one.

Ratio, Proportion, and Percentage

Let us now return to some variations on the basic definition of fractional numbers. A second definition is in terms of ratios. A ratio is a quotient, so there is no essential difference between defining a fraction as a quotient and defining it as a ratio. Rather, the distinction is only in the various ways we think of and *use* fractions. We usually think of a ratio as a pair of numbers, and we use ratios in *comparison* situations. For example, if we consider a set of 20 rabbits, 8 black and 12 white, we can make several comparisons, including these: (a) The ratio of black rabbits to white ones is 8 to 12; there are $\frac{8}{12}$ as many black rabbits as white ones; conversely, the ratio of white rabbits to black ones is 12 to 8; there are $\frac{12}{8}$ as many white rabbits as blacks. (b) The ratio of black rabbits to the entire hutch is 8 to 20; $\frac{8}{20}$ of the rabbits are black. Similarly, $\frac{12}{20}$ of them are white.

Ratios are often used in pairs. In the rabbit situation above, when we say that there is an 8-to-12 ratio of black rabbits to white, we can think of this as an 8-to-12 *correspondence* between the elements of the two subsets. In general, an *a*-to-*b* correspondence between the elements of two sets is a pairing of each *a* elements of one set with exactly *b* elements of the other. (1–1 correspondence is a special case of this.) But we frequently need to, or wish to, consider other correspondences which express the same *rate*. For example, the rabbits can be paired on a 4-to-6 basis (each 4 black rabbits is paired with 6 white ones) or on a 2-to-3 basis. These correspondences or ratios are "at the same rate" and are therefore "equivalent," e.g., to say that there are $\frac{8}{12}$ as many black rabbits as white ones is equivalent to saying that there are $\frac{2}{3}$ as many black ones as white ones. A *proportion* is an expression or assertion that two ratios are equivalent, e.g., $\frac{8}{12} = \frac{2}{3}$.

The ratio and proportion ideas have many applications in problem solving. Typical of one kind of problem is the question, If our rabbit population were to increase at the same rate, how many white rabbits would there be if the population of black rabbits increased to 20?

$$\frac{8}{12} = \frac{20}{x}$$

The same equivalence relationship holds for ratios as with fractions in general, so $8x = 240$, or $x = 30$, i.e., we would have 30 white rabbits. Ratio and proportion are also involved in solving problems such as, If one brand

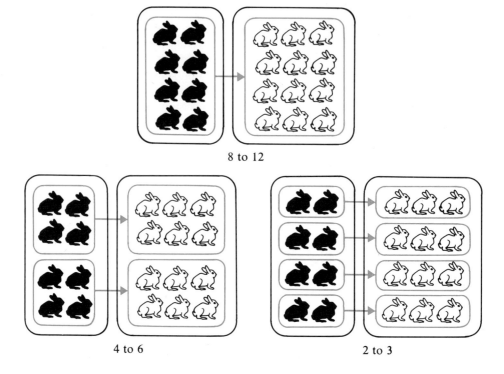

8 to 12

4 to 6   2 to 3

of cat food sells at 2 cans for 35 cents, what is the (average) cost per can? How much would 6 cans cost? Is this a better price than another brand selling at 3 cans for 54 cents? What would be the difference in the unit cost if I buy the larger size can, which sells for 25 cents? All of these, and of course many like them which involve comparisons of rates, can be solved by using ratios.

One must be cautious about relating fractions to ratios when *addition* is considered. For example, if Mr. Jones has 3 black rabbits and 5 white ones in one pen, and if in a second pen he has 4 black rabbits and 2 white ones, the ratio of black rabbits to white ones altogether is

$$\frac{7}{7}$$

or 1 to 1. The "sum" of the two *ratios*

$$\frac{3}{5} \text{ and } \frac{4}{2}$$

is

$$\frac{7}{7}$$

whereas the sum of the two *fractions* $\frac{3}{5}$ and $\frac{4}{2}$ is $\frac{26}{10}$.

Percentage is a particular ratio, which has many familiar uses. The expression "24 percent" is an expression of the ratio of 24 to 100, $\frac{24}{100}$. We say 40 percent of our rabbits are black, since the ratio 8 to 20 is at the same rate as the ratio 40 to 100; there are $66\frac{2}{3}$ percent as many black rabbits as white ones, etc.

Other Interpretations of Fractional Numbers

A second variation on the definition of fractions is a measurement one, using geometric ideas: If a given region, segment, or solid is considered as a unit, i.e., if we agree to call its measure 1, then if we partition that region into n congruent parts ($n > 0$), the measure of each part is expressed by the *unit* fraction, $\frac{1}{n}$. The measure of any collection of m of these $\frac{1}{n}$s, i.e., $m \times \frac{1}{n}$, is expressed by the fraction $\frac{m}{n}$. This "part of a whole" interpretation is commonly used to introduce children to fractions and will be more fully discussed in that context subsequently.

A related measurement interpretation involves coordinates of points on a line: If a unit segment is partitioned into n congruent parts, then each of the dividing points is associated with a fraction. For example, if a unit segment is partitioned into 10 congruent parts, the coordinate of the first point is $\frac{0}{10}$, the next point is associated with the fraction $\frac{1}{10}$, and the 14th point from 0 (if additional copies of the partitioned segment are annexed to the first) is $\frac{14}{10}$ or $1\frac{4}{10}$.

Decimal Notation for Fractional Numbers

If we as teachers ask children to solve $3\overline{)36}$, we expect them to *replace* $36 \div 3$ with the standard numeral 12. We would probably be surprised if a child's solution were $\frac{36}{3}$! Yet this *expression* of the quotient is perfectly correct if we accept the foregoing definitions of fractions. We may view the expected *computed* response, 12, as part of a ratio: The ratio of 36 to 3 is equivalent to the ratio 12 to 1. Similar computation, rather than mere expression, is involved when we express fractions in decimal notation. That is, given an expression such as $2 \div 5$, we can *express* it as $\frac{2}{5}$ or we can compute it, using decimals, to be .4. Thus the ratio 2-to-5 is equivalent to the ratio .4-to-1.

Every fraction can be expressed as a decimal via division. The procedure, which is probably well known by the reader, is to divide the numerator by the denominator, annex a decimal point and as many zeroes as required (or desired) to the dividend, and divide as with whole numbers.

Example:

$$\frac{3}{8} = 8\overline{)3.0}$$ We think of 3 as "3 and 0 tenths" or 30 *tenths*.

$$= 8\overline{)\,3.0}^{\,.3}$$
$$\underline{2.4}$$
$$.6$$

30 (tenths) = [3 (tenths) × 8] + 6 (tenths).

$$= 8\overline{)\,3.00}^{\,.37}$$
$$\underline{2.4}$$
$$.60$$
$$\underline{.56}$$
$$.04$$

6 tenths = 60 hundredths;
60 (hundredths) = [7 (hundredths) × 8]
    + 4 (hundredths).

$$\doteq 8\overline{)\,3.000}^{\,.375}$$
$$\underline{2.4}$$
$$.60$$
$$\underline{.56}$$
$$.040$$
$$\underline{.040}$$
$$0$$

4 hundredths = 40 thousandths;
40 (thousandths) = 5 (thousandths) × 8.

Thus $\tfrac{3}{8} = .375$.

The decimal .375 is an example of a *terminating* decimal; we all know that some such divisions do not terminate, e.g., $3\overline{)\,2} = .6666$ . . . , or $33\overline{)\,4} = .121212$ . . . . These are *repeating* decimals. What is not so widely understood is which fractions correspond to terminating decimals and which correspond to repeating decimals? (and why?) The surprisingly simple answer is that the decimal equivalent of a fraction $\tfrac{a}{b}$ terminates if and only if, either a is a multiple of b or the prime factors of b are only 2s and/or 5s. This can be related to the fact that the prime factors of our *base*, ten, are 2 and 5. If we were to determine the decimal equivalents of fractions in base six, for example, the terminating decimals would correspond to those whose denominators contained prime factors of 2s or 3s, e.g., $\tfrac{2}{3} = .4$ in base six.

Basic Operations and Their Properties

The basic operations, addition and multiplication, of fractional numbers are usually defined in the following manner.

If x and y are fractional numbers expressed as fractions, i.e. if

$$x = \frac{a}{b} \quad \text{and} \quad y = \frac{c}{d}$$

then

$$\frac{a}{b} + \frac{c}{d} = \frac{ad + bc}{bd} \quad \text{and} \quad \frac{a}{b} \times \frac{c}{d} = \frac{ac}{bd}$$

If two fractions have the *same* denominator, addition may be alternately defined as

$$\frac{a}{b} + \frac{c}{b} = \frac{a+c}{b}$$

Fractions with *different* denominators can be renamed and the above definition used, e.g.,

$$\frac{a}{b} = \frac{ad}{bd} \quad \text{and} \quad \frac{c}{d} = \frac{bc}{bd}$$

so

$$\frac{a}{b} + \frac{c}{d} = \frac{ad}{bd} + \frac{bc}{bd} = \frac{ad+bc}{bd}$$

If x and y are fractional numbers expressed as decimals, then addition is accomplished as a simple extension of the whole number addition algorithm, with the same kind of alignment of corresponding places, e.g.,

$$\begin{array}{r} 3.20 \\ + 0.57 \\ \hline 3.77 \end{array} \text{ (3 ones + 7 tenths + 7 hundredths)}$$

Multiplication (of terminating decimals) is likewise accomplished by the whole number multiplication algorithm. Place values for the product, and thus the location of the decimal point, can be determined in various ways. One way is illustrated below:

Example: $1.7 \times .32$

$$\begin{array}{r} 32 \\ \times 17 \\ \hline 224 \\ 32 \\ \hline 544 \end{array}$$

then

$.32 = 32 \times \frac{1}{100}$ and $1.7 = 17 \times \frac{1}{10}$, so

$.32 \times 1.7$
$= (32 \times 17) \times (\frac{1}{100} \times \frac{1}{10})$
$= 544 \times \frac{1}{1000}$
$= .544$

The structural properties of the whole number system are inherited by the fractional number system: closure, commutativity, the associative and distributive properties, the roles of zero ($\frac{0}{1}$) and one ($\frac{1}{1}$), and all of the basic theorems are identical. These are most easily verified by expressing the fractions as decimals, but can of course be shown in fractional form as well.

Order

The concept of order is very important with fractional numbers. The basic definition is the same as with whole numbers, i.e., if x and y are fractional numbers, then $x < y$ if there exists some nonzero fractional number z such that $x + z = y$. If x and y are expressed as decimals, determining the relative order of two fractional numbers is a simple extension of whole number numeration, e.g., $.8 < .875$ because $.8 = 8$ tenths or $.800$, and $.875 = 8$ tenths *plus* 75 thousandths. Expressed as fractions, $\frac{4}{5}$ and $\frac{7}{8}$, the relative order is less apparent: The *digits* 7, 8, or 4, 5, give no clue, and the definition is unwieldy per se, e.g., $\frac{7}{8} < \frac{4}{5}$ if there is a fractional number $\frac{a}{b}$ such that $\frac{7}{8} + \frac{a}{b} = \frac{4}{5}$; and $\frac{4}{5} < \frac{7}{8}$ if there is a fractional number $\frac{c}{d}$ such that $\frac{4}{5} + \frac{c}{d} = \frac{7}{8}$. The latter is true, because $\frac{4}{5} + \frac{3}{40} = \frac{7}{8}$, but finding such a number is troublesome. There is a theorem, however, which is valid for fractional numbers (but which must be modified for *rational* numbers):

$$\frac{a}{b} < \frac{c}{d} \quad \text{if} \quad ad < bc \quad \text{and} \quad \frac{a}{b} > \frac{c}{d} \quad \text{if} \quad ad > bc$$

for example

$$\frac{4}{5} < \frac{7}{8} \quad \text{since} \quad 4 \cdot 8 < 5 \cdot 7$$

One major distinction between the whole number system and the fractional number system is related to order: If x and y are fractional numbers and if $x < y$, then there exists a fractional number z which is between x and y, i.e., $x < z < y$. For example $\frac{1}{2}(x + y)$ is between x and y (it is their average). In fact, then, there are infinitely many fractional numbers between x and y, since this generalization can be reapplied as often as we wish. This is sometimes called the *density property*. It, of course, does not hold for either the whole numbers or the integers.

Again, the procedure for *identifying* a fractional number between two given ones is simple with decimals: $.801, .802, .803, \ldots, .874$ are all between $.800$ and $.875$, as are $.8011, .8021, .8031, \ldots, .8741$ and as many others as we care to identify. On the other hand, finding such a large collection of numbers between $\frac{4}{5}$ and $\frac{7}{8}$ using fractions is much more tedious.

Fractional numbers are frequently viewed as being partitioned into two classes: those which are less than 1 and those which are greater than or equal to 1:

$$\frac{a}{b} < 1 \quad \text{if} \quad a < b$$

$$\frac{a}{b} = 1 \quad \text{if} \quad a = b$$

$$\frac{a}{b} > 1 \quad \text{if} \quad a > b$$

Fractions naming numbers less than 1 have been called "proper" fractions and those greater than or equal to one "improper." (These expressions are now rarely used, as are expressions like "vulgar" or "common" fractions.) A fractional number greater than 1 has an alternate form, traditionally called a "mixed" numeral: A whole number plus a fractional number less than 1. For example, $\frac{23}{4}$ can be expressed as $5\frac{3}{4}$, an abbreviation for $5 + \frac{3}{4}$. The basic division relation of number theory suggests the usual procedure for determining this form: $\frac{23}{4}$ means $23 \div 4$, and the basic division relation guarantees that there are unique whole numbers n and r such that $23 = (4 \cdot n) + r$ and $r < 4$ ($n = 5$ and $r = 3$). Since $r < 4$, $\frac{r}{4} < 1$ ($\frac{3}{4} < 1$). Thus to find the mixed numeral corresponding to $\frac{23}{4}$, we divide 23 by 4. (In some computations, mixed numerals occur when the fraction part is greater than 1, but this is not standard form, e.g., $5\frac{13}{4} = 5 + \frac{13}{4} = 5 + 3\frac{1}{4} = 8\frac{1}{4}$).

Subtraction and Division

The inverse operations, subtraction and division, can be defined in a manner exactly analogous to the usual definitions of subtraction and division of whole numbers, i.e.:

If $\quad \frac{a}{b} \geqslant \frac{c}{d}$, $\quad$ then $\quad \frac{a}{b} - \frac{c}{d} = \frac{x}{y}$ $\quad$ if $\quad \frac{x}{y} + \frac{c}{d} = \frac{a}{b}$

If $\quad \frac{c}{d} \neq \frac{0}{1}$, $\quad$ then $\quad \frac{a}{b} \div \frac{c}{d} = \frac{n}{r}$ $\quad$ if $\quad \frac{n}{r} \times \frac{c}{d} = \frac{a}{b}$

Techniques for these operations again are seemingly remote from the definitions, and again are simpler if decimal notation is used than if fraction notation is. In the case of subtraction, using fraction notation, the procedure parallels that for addition, i.e.:

$$\frac{a}{b} - \frac{c}{b} = \frac{a - c}{b}$$

$$\frac{a}{b} - \frac{c}{d} = \frac{ad - bc}{bd}$$

With decimals, whole number techniques are used, as with addition.

Division, with fractions, rests on a second major distinction between the system of fractional numbers and the whole number system: In the fractional number system, each nonzero number $\frac{a}{b}$ has a multiplicative inverse (or reciprocal). That is, for each nonzero number, there is a nonzero number such that the product of the two is the multiplicative identity, $\frac{1}{1}$. If $\frac{a}{b}$ is such a nonzero number, its reciprocal is $\frac{b}{a}$, since

$$\frac{a}{b} \times \frac{b}{a} = \frac{1}{1}$$

for example,

$$\frac{2}{3} \times \frac{3}{2} = \frac{6}{6} = \frac{1}{1}$$

The reciprocal idea is used in division as follows: The definition of division states that

$$\frac{a}{b} \div \frac{c}{d} = \frac{x}{y} \qquad \text{if} \qquad \frac{x}{y} \cdot \frac{c}{d} = \frac{a}{b}$$

If we choose $\frac{x}{y}$ to be $\frac{a}{b} \cdot \frac{d}{c}$, i.e., the product of $\frac{a}{b}$ and the reciprocal of $\frac{c}{d}$, then the basic relationship holds, i.e., if $\frac{x}{y} = \frac{ad}{bc}$, then

$$\frac{x}{y} \cdot \frac{c}{d} = \left(\frac{a}{b} \cdot \frac{d}{c}\right) \cdot \frac{c}{d} = \frac{a}{b} \cdot \left(\frac{d}{c} \cdot \frac{c}{d}\right) = \frac{a}{b} \cdot \frac{1}{1} = \frac{a}{b}$$

Perhaps not at first glaringly apparent is that because all nonzero fractional numbers have multiplicative inverses, the quotient of two fractional numbers always exists and is a fractional number providing zero is, as usual, excluded as a divisor. Except for zero divisors, then, the set of fractional numbers is closed with respect to division.

With decimals, finding the quotient of two fractional numbers when the divisor is a natural number has already been discussed; if the divisor is *not* a natural number, it can always be multiplied by a power of ten (providing that the dividend is multiplied by that same power) without affecting the quotient so that the resulting divisor *is* a natural number. For example, given $3.7\overline{)2.34}$, we can multiply each of 3.7 and 2.34 by 10 to obtain $37\overline{)23.4}$, which can be computed by the previously mentioned method.

Several additional mathematical features of the fractional number system will be considered in the next section.

2. Activities and Materials for Teaching Integers and Fractional Numbers

Objectives

What should the elementary school child know about — and be able to do with — integers and fractional numbers? The answers to these questions should certainly guide our selection of activities and materials for teaching these subjects.

In the case of integers, we should expect children to acquire, quite early, the concept of what integers *are*. Although the whole number concept must be reasonably well developed before the integers are introduced, there is no reason to postpone this important topic until, say, the middle grades, and certainly not until junior or senior high school. The concept of integers can and should be developed from *several* (intuitive) points of view, particularly those of number lines, vectors, and ordered pairs. We will suggest how to do this subsequently.

A second objective with respect to the integers should be an intuitive introduction to addition and subtraction, through problem solving, discovery, and manipulative experience. Formal rules for these operations should be avoided. Although many children will certainly discover these rules as they work with materials and keep records of their findings, no pressure should be put on them to verbalize the rules they discover. Multiplication and division with integers is probably best left alone or explored only with those children who raise questions about these operations. We will not consider those operations here.

In the case of fractional numbers, we should expect a little more. Each child should in time acquire the concept of fractional numbers, both as decimals and as fractions. This should include geometric interpretations, ratios and percentage, equivalence, order, numeration, and conversions between notations (e.g., the decimal equivalents of fractions and the fraction equivalent of a percent).

Children need to learn to solve problems involving fractional numbers, again including each of the notations, so they may acquire both understanding of and skill with (in that order, of course) all four operations with these numbers.

Common Difficulties and Some Remedies

Before considering specific activities for teaching integers and fractional numbers to children, a few potential pitfalls should be acknowledged, so that they may be either avoided or compensated for.

First, it should be noted that the definitions (concepts) of the numbers themselves are somewhat more complicated than for whole numbers, and in the case of fractional numbers, more crucial. Each whole number has only one standard name, i.e., there is a single *numeral* which names it (although there are many *expressions* which do so); fractional numbers, on the other hand, have infinitely many standard names, and children need to make use of them in computation, especially addition and subtraction. For example, in adding $\frac{1}{2}$ and $\frac{3}{4}$ we usually first choose another name for $\frac{1}{2}$, namely $\frac{2}{4}$.

Related to this, there are several quite distinct interpretations of the numerals, each of which must be learned so that they can be selected and used appropriately in various contexts. This is true of whole numbers as well, of course. Children need to use whole numbers in both the cardinal and ordinal senses, and to associate them with quantities such as distance, weight, time, points on a line, and so on. Integers are used in some of the same ways but must be interpreted in a dual way, i.e., each integer is associated with both a magnitude and a *direction*. Children must, of course, learn all the multiple meanings of fractions; but, the *duality* of fractions— that they involve *pairs* of numbers—must be acknowledged as a potential stumbling block for at least some children.

There are no easy remedies for these problems. The best advice is probably obvious: Expose children to many *problems* involving each of the various interpretations, spend sufficient time on developing these number concepts, and be patient with children's efforts and mistakes as they gradually develop the concepts. In the case of fractional numbers, emphasis on decimal notation rather than fractions, once it is understood, can alleviate many difficulties.

A second source of difficulty is language. Children tend to interpret words more literally than adults do, and some of the traditional vocabulary of fractions is misleading at least. Words such as "cancel," "reduce," "invert," "part of a whole (number)," "mixed" number, "proper" and "improper" fractions should either be replaced or used with caution (their appearance in textbooks is rarer now than before, but they are still perpetrated by word of mouth). Either choice can be made with equal effectiveness. For example, the process traditionally called "reducing" is now sometimes called "simplifying," which is probably some improvement. The main thing is that the process should be understood first and *then* labeled. There is nothing wrong with the "reduce" label as long as children are led to understand that it is a sort of tongue-in-cheek expression, i.e., that a "reduced fraction" is *not* "smaller," i.e., less than the original one. Teachers who retain these rather colorful expressions should discuss them rather carefully to prevent misunderstandings.

The cancelling process is one children find so appealing (because it can save much hard work) that they frequently apply it haphazardly (high school teachers sometimes speak of these children as "happy cancellers"). For example:

$$\frac{3}{8} + \frac{4}{8} = \frac{3 + 4^1}{8_2} = \frac{4}{2} = 2$$

Two things can be done to prevent "happy cancellers." First, carefully teach children to understand *why* it "works" when it does, and second, pre-expose them to potential errors. That is, once children understand the process, explore with them what happens when it is used in other settings. For example, have them solve an addition problem such as $\frac{3}{5} + \frac{5}{6} = \square$ in the conventional way, then try cancelling:

$$\frac{\overset{1}{\cancel{3}}}{\underset{1}{\cancel{5}}} + \frac{\overset{1}{\cancel{5}}}{\underset{2}{\cancel{6}}} = 1\frac{1}{2}$$

Compare the two answers. Are they equivalent? Shouldn't they be? Why aren't they? Which is correct? Can we cancel when we add? Such an experience can prevent or at least reduce the likelihood of future occurrence of the error.

The major language problem with integers is with the dual use of the + and − symbols as symbols for operations and for direction. One approach to preventing this confusion is to *raise* the sign slightly and/or make it small when it is used to indicate the direction of an integer, e.g., $^-3$ rather than -3. Another is to use parentheses rather extensively, e.g., $(+5) - (-3)$. But the best way to prevent confusion is for the *teacher* to verbalize the symbols correctly and to continually insist that children do so: $^+4$ is "*positive* 4," not "*plus* 4"; $^-7$ is "*negative* 7," not "*minus* 7." The expression "$^+3 - ^-2$" should be read "positive 3 minus negative 2." An additional difficulty emerges when variables are introduced. Is ^-n a negative integer? Should we read it "negative n"? The answer is, of course, that out of context we cannot tell whether n is positive, negative, or zero, so the best way to verbalize $-n$ is "the opposite of n." The teacher can help children with this by using expressions such as "the opposite of negative 5 is positive 5." A similar problem arises when two or more minus signs are used together: "$-(^-4)$" should be read "the opposite of negative 4."

A final source of potential difficulty with integers and fractional numbers is that the algorithms (except with decimals) are more difficult to rationalize than are those for whole number operations. The interpretations that children have associated with the operations for whole numbers do not always apply and help them with other numbers. For example, multiplication of *whole* numbers can be interpreted in terms of set union, repeated addition, the number line, and Cartesian products; but none of these is useful in interpreting multiplication of fractional numbers. Addition and subtraction of whole numbers can be interpreted as moves to the right and to the left respectively on the number line, but this must be modified with integers since the numbers themselves are "directed." *None* of the usual models for division of whole numbers (partition of sets, repeated subtraction, and so on) is applicable to division of fractional numbers in the *general* sense.

It will be more appropriate to discuss possible solutions of these particular problems subsequently rather than here, but we should note two related areas for which it *is* appropriate to suggest remedies here.

First, relationships between relative sizes of factors and products, both in multiplication and division, change with fractional numbers. The product of two whole numbers is always greater than (or equal to, in the case of zero or one) either factor; but the product of two fractional numbers may be greater than, less than, *or* equal to either, or both, of the factors.

Examples:

$\frac{2}{3} \times \frac{5}{8}$ is less than either $\frac{2}{3}$ or $\frac{5}{8}$.

$\frac{2}{3} \times \frac{8}{5}$ is greater than $\frac{2}{3}$ but less than $\frac{8}{5}$.

$\frac{3}{2} \times \frac{8}{5}$ is greater than either $\frac{3}{2}$ or $\frac{8}{5}$.

Similarly, the quotient of two fractional numbers may be greater than the dividend. Probably the best approach to follow here is, as for cancelling, to call this to children's attention early, discuss it, find out why it makes sense, and possibly analyze it. When is the product of two fractional numbers less than either of them? When is it greater? When could it be greater than one of them but less than the other? When will it equal one of the factors?

Second, it can be argued that the usual sequence in which the operations for fractional numbers are taught is both logically and psychologically wrong (though not seriously). It *is* logically reasonable to teach addition of *whole* numbers before multiplication because we usually *use* addition in teaching multiplication, and it is psychologically reasonable to do so because addition is generally easier. Neither of these arguments is valid when we consider the sequence for teaching fractional numbers, and as a matter of fact, it would make sense to reverse them: Multiplication of fractional numbers is easier than addition (at least to *do,* if not also to understand); and not only do we not use addition to teach multiplication, but we could use multiplication to teach some of the renaming involved in addition. While this may not be a serious problem, and while teachers frequently feel bound to prescribed sequences in some textbook or curriculum guide, some teachers may wish to try reversing the sequence for these two operations.

Introducing the Integers

Elementary school introduction to integers should be early, varied, and informal. Children quite naturally encounter number situations for which a directed number scale is or could be employed, with numbers "on either side of" a key number or event: Temperatures are measured with respect to 0°, and children—at least those in cold climates—are quite familiar with expressions like −5° (or 5 below zero). Events leading up to and following the ignition and lift off of a rocket are timed and recorded in similar terms. Every child is familiar with "10–9–8–7–6–5–4–3–2–1 lift off" and expressions such as "T minus 2 minutes and holding." Time lines measure historical events in terms of B.C. and A.D. Many games children play involve scoring procedures that can either increase or decrease the player's score or position, which can sometimes lead to negative scores. Lines of longitude are labeled with reference to the prime meridian and lines of latitude with reference to the equator. Stocks and bonds, national debts, unemployment rates, and the cost of living—which children hear about, even though they don't fully understand—are measured in "ups" and "downs." These and other *natural* situations can be used to motivate the introduction of integers.

Several classroom activities can lead to the introduction of signed numbers, and sometimes *simultaneously* to the introduction of addition. For example, a line on the floor or playground can be marked off with points each about one pace apart. These can be labeled with whole numbers at first or be left unlabeled (children will very likely suggest labeling). Children can take turns drawing previously written instructions from a hat. Such an instruction might read, "Take 5 steps forward and 2 steps backward" in a "race" to a given finishing point. They can quite easily be led to see the meaning of abbreviating such directions to "+5, −2" or "(5, 2)", where it is agreed that the first number tells how many forward steps to take and the second indicates steps in reverse. They will quickly discover how to save steps, i.e., (5, 2) is equivalent to 3 steps forward. In time, some child whose position is at point 3 will draw the direction (2, 7). Should he be out of the race? Why not extend the line in the other direction? What could we call the points if we do that? While children may choose any names they like, it is a simple matter to label them with negative integers.

Such games can be played with markers on a number line and even on a coordinate grid, e.g., a child whose position at some stage of a game is, say, the point whose coordinates are (1, 4) might receive the direction ($\leftarrow$3, $\uparrow$ 2), i.e., "left 3, up 2," which would require him to move to the point whose coordinates are ($^-$2, 6).

A supply of checkers, marbles, paper tickets, or similar small objects of uniform size but of two contrasting colors (e.g., black and red) can be used to introduce the same idea. Interesting two-person or small-group games can be played by placing the checkers in a box. Each player takes his turn reaching into the box (without looking) and taking out as many checkers as he wishes. Suppose a child takes 8 checkers and they turn out to be 6 black and 2 red. If it is agreed that black checkers each represent a gain of one point and red ones a loss of one, the child's score is 4 (or 4 more than his previous score, and so on). Many variations can be invented for this activity and children soon discover important relationships: The total number of checkers drawn is unimportant—a small number of checkers might yield a greater gain than a large number; many pairs produce the same gain, e.g., (5, 3), (9, 7), (2, 0), etc.; an equal number of blacks and reds results in no change. The standard notation of integers can easily be introduced, and keeping cumulative scores can lead to background for, or an introduction to, addition. The teacher can raise many questions: What is the greatest possible gain or loss if a player draws 5 checkers? Is a player assured of either gaining or losing by drawing an odd number of checkers? An even number? What are *all* the possibilities if 5 checkers are drawn? Are gains and losses always equally *likely* to occur? If you have 7 blacks and 3 reds and I take away 2 of each color, how is your score affected? If I give you some checkers—2 more reds than blacks—can you tell how your score will be affected without knowing how many I give you? What if I take away 2 more reds than blacks?

Other activities might include graphing *changes* over a period of time of something like temperatures relative to some fixed temperature; changes in weight (although with children and some of the rest of us, this might provide meagre opportunity to introduce negative numbers); or differences from the average of some set of data. Hypothetical stories can be invented about increasing and decreasing bank balances, or increases and decreases in all sorts of things—the number of pages in the daily paper, daily attendance, numbers of births reported in the hospital column of the paper—any statistic that can actually, theoretically, or hypothetically vary from some reasonable fixed number can serve to introduce "positive" and "negative" values, including positive and negative fractions.

    Probably the best model for introducing addition and particularly subtraction of integers is the number line. Here, again, due care must be taken to distinguish between the "negative" and "minus" interpretations of the $-$ sign. One effective technique is to use a set of blocks and a matching scale, such as Cuisenaire or Centimeter rods, with a centimeter scale reproduced on a piece of paper. A set of rods can be labeled, each with a numeral, an arrow, and possibly a dot (using a felt pen or small stick-on labels) so that the rods can be used as models of vectors or directed segments, with the dot and arrow representing the beginning and terminal points respectively and the numeral representing the magnitude. When a rod is oriented so the arrow points to the right, it can be interpreted as positive, and when it is inverted, so the arrow points left, it is negative (colors will help to compensate for the upside-down numerals). Rules for

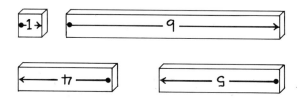

both addition and subtraction on the line should be expressed in terms of addition: first addend, second (sometimes unknown) addend, and sum, e.g., $a - b = \square$ should be interpreted as $b + \square = a$, where a is the sum, b is the first addend, and $\square$ is the second addend; and $c + d = \triangle$ means c is the first addend, d is the second addend, and $\triangle$ is the sum. Thus either the second addend or the sum is to be determined in each case.

    If both addends are given, i.e., for an *addition* such as $a + b = \square$, the solution can be found by starting at the point on the line designated by a, placing the initial point (dot) of the b block at that point, and oriented according to the direction of b: The sum is the number indicated by the terminal point of the vector.

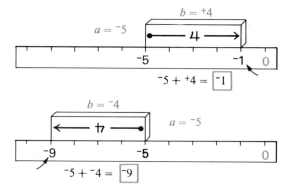

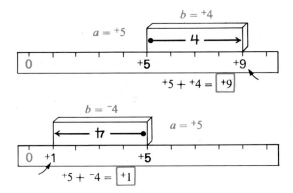

For subtractions such as $d + \triangle = c$ or $c - d = \triangle$, the same basic rules apply except that this time the sum (ending point on the scale) is known and the second addend must be determined, i.e., the block with correct magnitude and direction must be found to fit the gap from the point designated by the first addend to that designated by the sum.

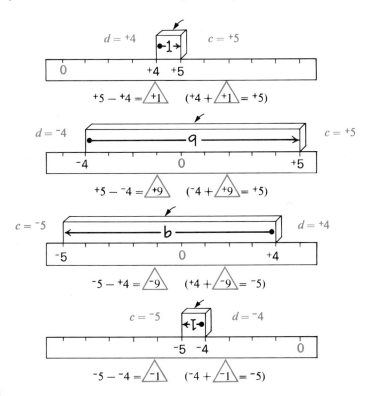

Several things should be noted about this model: (1) The teacher should practice it several times before introducing it to children. (2) The blocks are useful but not entirely necessary. (3) The same basic model, i.e., with the first addend representing the beginning point, the sum representing the ending point, and the second addend representing the distance traveled is one of the several basic number-line models for addition and subtraction of *whole* numbers and should be the model receiving primary emphasis if the transition from whole numbers to integers is to be achieved most smoothly. (4) Neither skill nor "rules" for addition and subtraction or integers should be emphasized with this sort of activity. Both will evolve quite naturally as children solve repeated problems and seek short cuts to the use of blocks and the number line. The technique of paired problems will encourage this, e.g.:

$$^+5 + {}^+4 = \underline{\hspace{1cm}} \qquad ^-3 + {}^-6 = \underline{\hspace{1cm}} \qquad ^+8 + {}^-3 = \underline{\hspace{1cm}}$$
$$^+5 - {}^-4 = \underline{\hspace{1cm}} \qquad ^-3 - {}^+6 = \underline{\hspace{1cm}} \qquad ^+8 - {}^+3 = \underline{\hspace{1cm}}$$

Fractional Numbers

In this final section, we consider activities and materials for teaching the meanings of fractional numbers and the usual operations with them. In the first five subsections, the emphasis is on fractional numbers expressed as fractions. The remaining sections deal with decimals, relationships between the two notations, and the related topics of percentage and ratio.

The child's first introduction to fractional numbers is usually in the context of candy or other treats—he is admonished to eat only *half* of a cookie now and save the rest until after dinner or to give *half* of it to his brother. The parent's primary concern is more nutritional or social than mathematical, but the child nonetheless begins developing a vague concept of fractional numbers at home. Most children at this stage think of "half" and "part" as synonymous, and often speak of the "bigger half" and "smaller half" of a cookie.

Teaching the Meaning of Fractions

In school, these homegrown notions are gradually refined and expanded, first in terms of simple *unit* fractions ($\frac{1}{2}, \frac{1}{3}$, and $\frac{1}{4}$) and later in terms of nonunit fractions such as $\frac{2}{3}$ or $\frac{3}{4}$. Fractions such as $\frac{1}{2}, \frac{1}{3}$, and $\frac{1}{4}$ take on more precise meanings as solids, regions, segments, and sets are partitioned into 2, 3, or 4 parts of the same size and shape. And ideas about the "smaller half" of a cookie develop into understandings that expressions like "one-half" are used only when the unit has been partitioned into parts of the same size; that "one-half" of something may take various forms; and, that a fraction, or a pair of fractions, is always considered relative to a particular *unit*. Materials such as the figures illustrated here can provoke interesting debates and ultimately lead to agreements and understandings.

Which of these shaded parts represent one-half?

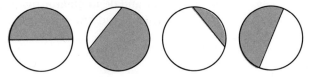

Are these shaded parts each one-half?

Which is the bigger half?

Is $\frac{1}{3}$ greater than $\frac{1}{2}$?

Initial experience with fractions should be with real things such as geometric forms cut out of cardboard, wood, masonite, or heavy paper. (Material with some thickness—on the order of $\frac{1}{8}''$ or $\frac{1}{4}''$—is preferable to paper, since the edges of paper overlap too easily.) A variety of regular shapes should be used (squares, rectangles, circles, hexagons, triangles) as well as sets of things such as checkers, coins, books, children, and so on. Slicing a real apple "in half" can lead to discussions about precision and the children's vernacular use of "half" before they had refined their notion of fractions. When a physical model of a region has been disassembled into two or more parts, a child should have access to a copy of the unit whenever he is asked to associate a given piece or set of pieces with a fraction.

With teacher guidance, the concept of unit fractions can be developed in the early grades by folding paper in half, into four parts, and so on. Various shapes provide different opportunities here, e.g., an $8\frac{1}{2}''$ by $11''$ sheet can be folded in half horizontally or vertically, but a square piece can also be folded diagonally. Pictures provide a variety of activities in this area: children can color "one-half," "one-third," or "one-fourth" of various regions partitioned into halves, thirds, or fourths. Or, given a picture of 3 circles, for example, they can be asked to color one-third of the objects. Pictures of three or four candy bars, pies, oranges, and so on, each of which has been separated into 4 noncongruent parts or more or fewer than 4 parts, can be used with such questions as "which picture shows one-fourth?"

When children first learn to write the numerals, they should be helped to see the roles of the numerator and denominator by discussing and labeling them. Once they have learned to read and write the numerals for

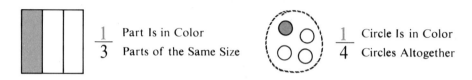

$\dfrac{1}{3}$ Part Is in Color
Parts of the Same Size

$\dfrac{1}{4}$ Circle Is in Color
Circles Altogether

fractions, they should be given much opportunity to use these skills in such activities as these.

What Part Is in Color?

What Part of the Set Is a Square?

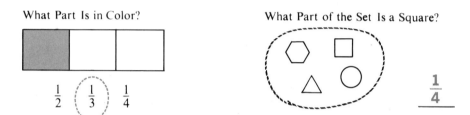

$\dfrac{1}{2}$ $\dfrac{1}{3}$ $\dfrac{1}{4}$

$\dfrac{1}{4}$

Cuisenaire or Centimeter rods can be used as models to introduce a slightly different role of fractions: Comparing two different things. A 10-rod and two 5-rods can be put side by side (*color* names for the rods rather than number names should be used with children, although we will use number names here, since the color schemes of the two sets of rods are different). Since two 5-rods match one 10-rod, the 5-rod is identified as $\frac{1}{2}$ as long as the 10-rod. Several such comparisons are possible with the rods: Each rod can be compared with those whose lengths are its factors, e.g., the 10-rod can be compared with 1-rods ($\frac{1}{10}$), 2-rods ($\frac{1}{5}$), and 5-rods ($\frac{1}{2}$), and so on. Unifix cubes can be used in the same way; or they can be used

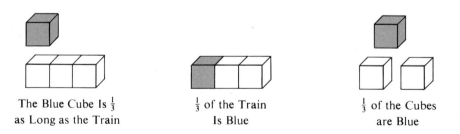

The Blue Cube Is $\frac{1}{3}$
as Long as the Train

$\frac{1}{3}$ of the Train
Is Blue

$\frac{1}{3}$ of the Cubes
are Blue

in the sense of parts of regions or sets. A set of homemade rods will be described in the next section.

Work with rods can lead quite naturally to viewing fractions in terms of segments, e.g.:

$\frac{1}{5}$ of the Segment Is in Color

The Top Segment Is $\frac{1}{5}$ as Long as the Bottom One

Once unit fractions are understood in the various contexts above, nonunit fractions can be introduced using similar activities. These need not be repeated here, but it should be noted that when children can identify nonunit fractions meaningfully, several new ideas can be explored:

Example:

$\frac{2}{5}$ of the Squares Are in Color

$\frac{3}{5}$ of the Squares Are White

What Part of the Circles Are Colored in Each Picture?

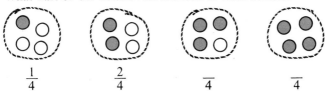

$\frac{1}{4}$ $\frac{2}{4}$ $\overline{4}$ $\overline{4}$

Points on a segment can now be identified with fractions by relating them to the endpoints of segments that are $\frac{1}{4}$, $\frac{2}{4}$, etc., as long as the unit segment. Fractions with numerator of 0 can be introduced best in this context, as can fractions greater than 1.

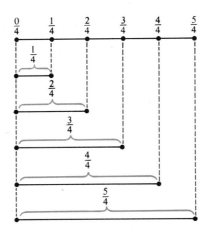

While children can usually correctly identify, say, $\frac{1}{3}$ of a set of 3 things, they sometimes have difficulty with identifying $\frac{1}{3}$ of 6, 9, 12, or some larger *multiple* of 3, especially if these are arranged randomly. This can be

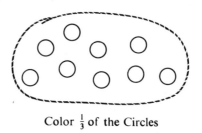

Color $\frac{1}{3}$ of the Circles

anticipated by activities related to the partition interpretation of division, such as this: Given 12 red checkers, the child can be asked to arrange them

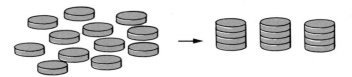

in three matching stacks. Each stack is then seen as $\frac{1}{3}$ of the collection. If 1 stack is replaced with black checkers and the 12 checkers then arranged randomly, the child may more easily identify that part of the collection with the fraction $\frac{1}{3}$.

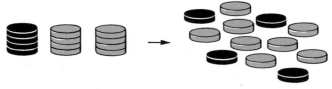

$\frac{1}{3}$ of the Checkers are Black

This is the most difficult meaning of a fraction (ratio) and must be developed carefully, slowly, and with close supervision and guidance. In time children should be able to answer questions about more complex

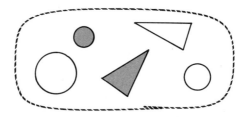

situations. What part of this set of figures is circles? Triangles? Colored? White? What part of the subset of circles is colored? What part of the subset of triangles is colored? What part of the subset of colored figures is circles? Triangles? What part of the subset of white figures is circles? Triangles? A more difficult challenge can follow: There are _____ as many triangles as circles; or, there are _____ as many colored figures as white ones.

Equivalent Fractions and Order

There are a number of activities that can develop concepts related to equivalent and nonequivalent fractions, including renaming a given fractional number (e.g., reducing it or expressing it in larger terms), determining whether one fractional number is less than another, and so on.

As children experiment with regions, solids, segments, and sets while learning names of fractions, they frequently discover, for example, that $\frac{2}{4}$ is "the same size as" $\frac{1}{2}$. Eventually, activities should be structured to emphasize and extend these discoveries. An old but still very effective device for stimulating such discoveries is a set of blocks made to represent various fractions based on a common unit. For example, an 18-cm square can be cut into two 18-by-9–cm rectangles, each of which then represents one-half. Another can be cut into three 6-by-18–cm pieces to represent thirds, and so on. These can be purchased commercially or made at home. Quarter-inch plywood, masonite, or tile is more effective and permanent than paper even though more time is required for construction. When constructing such blocks, it is well to keep in mind that one dimension should remain constant for all of the blocks. Fractions with composite denominators such as 4 *could* be represented by partitioning the square either along two dimensions or along one. However, experience suggests that children

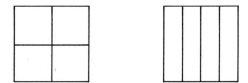

can make many comparisons more easily, and storage is simplified, if the latter form is used. Precision in construction is important if children are to be able to use these blocks effectively and easily. Note particularly, that if an 18-cm square of plywood is sawed into ten 1.8-cm strips to represent tenths, it will be found that when put together the strips do not form a square because of the wood lost by the thickness of the saw cut. The pieces should be cut from a long strip, with each measurement made after the preceding cut has been accomplished. A reasonably careful craftsman with a good saw should be entrusted to do the work. (The square unit pattern is much easier to construct accurately — and for children to use — than is the popular circular shape often made from paper plates, although these are easy to make and have their place.) Each set of blocks should be painted a different color. Labeling the blocks, at least on one side, is often helpful.

In the lower grades, blocks representing units, halves, thirds, and fourths are usually sufficient; whereas upper grade children should also have access to fifths, sixths, eighths, tenths, and twelfths. Two fractions are equivalent if the blocks representing them are congruent of course.

Numerous questions can be explored with these blocks: How many fractions equivalent to $\frac{1}{2}$ can you find? How many sixths match $\frac{2}{3}$? Is there a single block which matches $\frac{4}{8}$? In how many ways can you match $\frac{9}{12}$? Which of these ways uses the fewest blocks? Can you match $\frac{3}{4}$ using $\frac{1}{5}$-blocks? Can you represent both $\frac{2}{3}$ and $\frac{1}{2}$ with blocks of the same size? Arrange one block of each color in order of their size. What can you say about the fractions they represent? Which is more, $\frac{3}{4}$ or $\frac{2}{3}$?

Once manipulative explorations of this sort have been carried out, pictures can be used. Children usually "see" the equivalence of $\frac{1}{2}$ and $\frac{2}{4}$ in pictures such as these after they have had some manipulative experience.

Related experiences can be structured with segments, preceded by manipulative exercises with Cuisenaire rods, Centimeter rods, or home-made rods cut to appropriate lengths, as with the blocks (a long strip of $\frac{3}{4}$-by-$\frac{3}{4}$ wood, with cuts based on a unit of 36 cm is very effective).

Sets of objects like checkers can be manipulated (and later pictured) to discover equivalence. For example, if 1 red checker and 2 black ones are arranged on a table, the child will agree that $\frac{1}{3}$ of the set is red; when two such sets are combined, the child can identify the red checkers either in terms of $\frac{1}{3}$ or $\frac{2}{6}$. The basis for deciding that $\frac{1}{3} = \frac{2}{6}$ is not congruence this time, and some children will have more difficulty and need more practice with this interpretation than with region or segment models.

Once equivalence has been explored through experience, children can begin to examine it on a more abstract level. One effective activity is to ask a group of children to call off several names for a familiar fractional number such as $\frac{1}{2}$, while the teacher or a child records them on the board. They will usually include $\frac{2}{4}, \frac{5}{10}, \frac{4}{8}, \frac{3}{6}, \frac{6}{12}$, etc. Ask them then to suggest a way to list these in some kind of order to see if they can find any patterns. While several orders may be suggested and considered, the most likely suggestion will be

$$\frac{1}{2}, \frac{2}{4}, \frac{3}{6}, \frac{4}{8}, \frac{5}{10}, \frac{6}{12}$$

This sequence can then be studied and many useful discoveries can be made. Questions and suggestions can stimulate discoveries not observed at first by the children: Read the numerators only — in order. What do you notice?

Now read the denominators in order. Do you think there is a "next" fraction? ($\frac{7}{14}$ will probably be suggested even though it may not be familiar.) *Is* $\frac{7}{14}$ equivalent to $\frac{1}{2}$? (A quick sketch may help.) Is there a "next" fraction and a "next" . . . ? Eventually they will probably propose that the list can go on and on and will enjoy continuing it to some extent. If, for some reason, a fraction, say $\frac{5}{10}$, had not been on the original list, reading the numerators or denominators will suggest that "something is missing" (1, 2, 3, 4, __, 6 or 2, 4, 6, 8, __, 12). Now choose any two fractions in the list. Multiply one numerator by the other denominator. Now multiply the first denominator by the second numerator. What happens? As this is repeated for many examples, they discover that the two products are the same each time.

$$\frac{1}{2}, \frac{3}{6} \qquad 1 \times 6 = 2 \times 3$$

$$\frac{2}{4}, \frac{5}{10} \qquad 2 \times 10 = 4 \times 5$$

$$\frac{3}{6}, \frac{4}{8} \qquad 3 \times 8 = 6 \times 4$$

This can lead in time to a rule, which they can derive themselves, to tell whether two fractions are equivalent, i.e.,

$$\frac{a}{b} = \frac{c}{d} \qquad \text{if} \qquad a \times d = b \times c$$

Have the children consider the fraction $\frac{1}{2}$ and any other fraction in the list, say $\frac{6}{12}$. How are the two numerators related? How are the denominators related? Two responses are likely: 6 is 5 more than 1, and 12 is 10 more than 2 (5 and 10 are the numerator and denominator of the fraction just before $\frac{6}{12}$ in the list). While this is of some interest, a more useful discovery is that 6 is 1×6 and 12 is 2×6. After considering many more examples of this kind, they will conclude, or can be easily led to see, that multiplying both terms of a fraction by the same (nonzero) number results in an equivalent fraction. Conversely, *dividing* both terms by the same nonzero number produces an equivalent fraction.

$$\frac{6}{12} = \frac{6 \div 2}{12 \div 2} = \frac{6 \div 3}{12 \div 3} = \frac{6 \div 6}{12 \div 6}$$

$$\frac{1}{2} = \frac{1 \times 3}{2 \times 3} = \frac{1 \times 4}{2 \times 4} = \frac{1 \times 7}{2 \times 7}$$

$$\frac{2}{4} = \frac{2 \times 3}{4 \times 3} = \frac{2 \div 2}{4 \div 2} = \frac{2 \times 4}{4 \times 4}$$

These discoveries are very useful since they can be used later when the operations of addition and subtraction are introduced and when fractions are simplified. In fact, this latter topic can be explored at this time: Can we divide the numerator and denominator of $\frac{1}{2}$ both by the same number? (Dividing them each by 1 is soon rejected, since it results in the same fraction.) Thus, $\frac{1}{2}$ is the "simplest" fraction in the list.

Once some of these basic generalizations have been discovered and reinforced, a related activity using frames can be pursued. Expressions such as the following can be presented and children challenged to name the missing numerators or denominators:

$$\frac{2}{3} = \frac{\square}{6} \qquad \frac{5}{6} = \frac{20}{\triangle} \qquad \frac{3}{\triangledown} = \frac{\bigcirc}{6} \qquad \frac{\square}{\triangle} = \frac{6}{\triangledown} \qquad \frac{\bigcirc}{15} = \frac{12}{\diamondsuit}$$

If several children do these and compare results, they will discover that several answers are possible, e.g.,

$$\frac{3}{\triangle} = \frac{\bigcirc}{6} \qquad \text{is} \qquad \frac{3}{3} = \frac{6}{6} \qquad \text{or} \qquad \frac{3}{9} = \frac{2}{6} \qquad \text{or} \qquad \frac{3}{2} = \frac{9}{6}, \text{ etc.}$$

(The missing terms are factors of 18, the cross product is 3×6.)

The relative order of two nonequivalent fractions can be determined by methods closely related to those suggested in the preceding paragraphs. For example, $\frac{a}{b} < \frac{c}{d}$ if the region represented by $\frac{a}{b}$ is smaller than that represented by $\frac{c}{d}$; if $a \cdot d < b \cdot c$; and if the point corresponding to $\frac{a}{b}$ is to the left of that corresponding to $\frac{c}{d}$.

Returning to the topic of simplifying fractions, there are several techniques children can use to determine whether a given fraction is in simplest form or to simplify it if it is not. These range in sophistication from awkward and brute-force methods to using set intersection and prime factorizations. At the earliest stages, a fraction is simplified by simply trying, eventually in a systematic way, to find a common factor by which both numerator and denominator can be divided. The first systematic approach is to try 2, then 3, then 4, and so on. As understanding grows, the *factors* of the smaller term can be tried, beginning with the term itself, then its next smaller factor, and so on. For example, to reduce $\frac{12}{20}$, try 12, then 6, and so on, until a factor of 12 is found which divides 20.

Finding the GCD of the numerator and denominator is the most sophisticated approach. To reduce $\frac{12}{64}$, for example, the intersection of the factor sets of 12 and 64; the Euclidean algorithm; or prime factorization can each be used to determine that the GCD of 12 and 64 is 4. Thus

$$\frac{12}{64} = \frac{12 \div 4}{64 \div 4} = \frac{3}{16}$$

$$\{1, 2, 3, 4, 6, 12\} \cap \{1, 2, 4, 8, 16, 32, 64\} = \{1, 2, 4\}$$

or

$$
\begin{array}{r}
5 \\
12\overline{)64} \\
\underline{60} \quad 3 \\
\overline{④)\,12} \\
\underline{12} \\
0
\end{array}
$$

or

$$\frac{12}{64} = \frac{\cancel{2 \times 2} \times 3}{\cancel{2 \times 2} \times 2 \times 2 \times 2 \times 2}$$

When fractions are of the form $\frac{a}{b}$, where $a > b$, i.e., where $\frac{a}{b} > 1$, mixed numerals are frequently considered to be "simpler" than the corresponding fractions. For example, $2\frac{3}{4}$ is commonly regarded as simpler than the equivalent $\frac{11}{4}$ (although mathematically, and for some pedagogical purposes, $\frac{11}{4}$ is simpler and more appropriate). The usual process for renaming $\frac{11}{4}$ as $2\frac{3}{4}$ is to divide 11 by 4. If children have become familiar with this basic meaning for fractions, and if they have discovered how to handle the remainder appropriately, this poses little difficulty:

$$\begin{array}{r} 2 \\ 4\overline{)11} \\ -8 \\ \hline 3 \end{array}$$

This treatment of remainders can be introduced once children understand that $\frac{a}{b}$ means $a \div b$, providing also that they understand the right distributive property of division over addition, i.e., that

$$11 \div 4 = (8 + 3) \div 4 = (8 \div 4) + (3 \div 4) = 2 + \tfrac{3}{4} = 2\tfrac{3}{4}$$

This can be introduced at a more manipulative level by considering a problem such as, "If 11 candy bars are to be shared by 4 boys, how much should each boy receive?" Clearly each boy would receive 2 full candy bars but 3 candy bars are "left over," certainly not to be disregarded! There is not quite enough for each boy to receive another full candy bar, but if each of the three bars is cut into fourths and if $\frac{1}{4}$ of each bar is given to each boy, then they each receive $\frac{3}{4}$ of an additional candy bar. Thus, each boy receives $2\frac{3}{4}$ candy bars altogether. There is no "remainder."

Other equivalence problems, e.g., renaming $3\frac{2}{3}$ as $\frac{11}{3}$ or as $2\frac{5}{3}$ arise in subtraction and multiplication situations and will be discussed subsequently.

Addition and Subtraction

Many of the things children learn about addition and subtraction with whole numbers can be easily transferred to help them understand addition and subtraction of fractional numbers. These include, in particular, the basic interpretations of *sum* and *difference*.

The *sum* of two numbers has been conceptualized via sets and via linear measure. That is, for whole numbers x and y, their sum, $x + y$, is the number of elements in $A \cup B$, where $n(A) = x$ and $n(B) = y$ and where $A \cap B = \phi$. Alternately, $x + y$ has been thought of as the distance on a number line from the 0 endpoint to the point corresponding to the end of a "trip" of length x followed by a "trip" of length y. These can be (cautiously) extended. Given two *fractional* numbers, x and y, we can associate

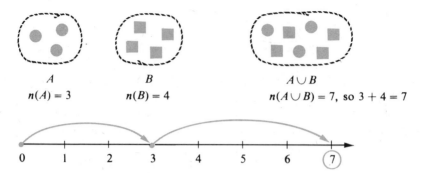

A B $A \cup B$

$n(A) = 3$ $n(B) = 4$ $n(A \cup B) = 7$, so $3 + 4 = 7$

each with the measure of something, put the two "somethings" together to form a single "thing" and determine its number. This somewhat parallels the set model for addition of whole numbers (e.g., 3 is the "measure" of set A, above, and so on). We will start with a simple example.

Example:

Consider $\frac{1}{5} + \frac{2}{5}$. We can obtain a region whose measure is $\frac{1}{5}$, and a region whose measure is $\frac{2}{5}$ (both measures must be based on the *same unit,* of course), put the regions together, and determine the measure of the resulting combination. Or we can use the number line, appropriately scaled, and represent the sum as the *resultant* of two "trips."

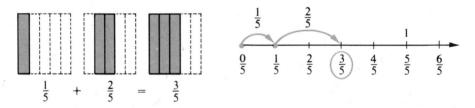

$$\frac{1}{5} \quad + \quad \frac{2}{5} \quad = \quad \frac{3}{5}$$

In a like manner, the basic meanings children associate with *subtraction* of whole numbers can be readily extended to subtraction of fractional numbers. That is, for fractional numbers x and y, if $x \geqslant y$, they can "take away" y from x, determine how much greater x is than y, or compare the two numbers. The number line, again, is a useful model.

A few general guidelines for teaching addition and subtraction of fractional numbers include these:

1. Begin with relatively easy problems that can be easily solved by manipulation of appropriate models, and proceed gradually to the more difficult ones (a suggested sequence follows).

2. Vary the manipulative models used—use circular regions, rectangular regions, triangular regions, sets, number line, and so on.
3. Be certain that children have models of the *unit* to guide them. Even if a child knows that a given region supposedly corresponds to some fraction, he has little basis for determining that fraction without a copy of the unit to guide him.
4. Be sure that children have had sufficient experience with "trading" and that they accept the fact that a fraction can be replaced by another equivalent to it.

The usual approach to addition or subtraction of fractions is to rename the fractions, if necessary, so that both have a common denominator. The first stage in teaching these operations is, therefore, to teach how to add or subtract fractions that have the same denominator.

$$\frac{2}{5}+\frac{1}{5} \qquad \frac{7}{8}-\frac{2}{8} \qquad \text{etc.}$$

After the manipulative stage, various "expanded algorithms" are useful:

$$\begin{array}{r} 2 \text{ fifths} \\ + 1 \text{ fifth} \\ \hline \end{array} \qquad \text{or} \qquad \frac{2}{5}+\frac{1}{5}=\frac{2+1}{5}$$

These emphasize the key idea that only the numerators are added or subtracted. There is no particular *need* for vertical notation at this time; and, in fact, it may be argued that the horizontal (equation) form is a bit easier (at least until the algorithm is extended to include mixed numerals). Since this is a key step in that all subsequent addition or subtraction problems involving fractional numbers are done in this manner, it is imperative that children understand the process before continuing. In the early stages, it is probably better not to confound the difficulty by expecting children to reduce their answers.

Probably the next easiest type of problem is that where one of the denominators is a factor of the other, e.g.,

$$\frac{1}{2}+\frac{3}{4} \qquad \frac{7}{8}-\frac{3}{4} \qquad \frac{3}{5}+\frac{1}{10} \qquad \frac{5}{6}-\frac{1}{2}$$

Again, manipulation of models should precede introduction to the abstract (final) form, as should skill in the preceding type of problem. Here, of course, is where a child needs to be comfortable with the notion that every fraction has infinitely many interchangeable names. A good approach to the introduction of such problems is to consider a given problem, like $\frac{3}{4}+\frac{5}{8}=\triangle$, and ask them to explain how this problem is unlike preceding ones. ("These fractions don't have the same denominator.") One effective introductory activity is to list a few names of the numbers to be added, as was done with $\frac{1}{2}$ before:

$$\frac{3}{4} \quad \frac{6}{8} \quad \frac{9}{12} \quad \frac{12}{16} \quad \frac{15}{20} \quad \frac{18}{24} \quad \frac{21}{28} \quad \cdots$$

$$\frac{5}{8} \quad \frac{10}{16} \quad \frac{15}{24} \quad \frac{20}{32} \quad \frac{25}{40} \quad \frac{30}{48} \quad \frac{35}{56} \quad \cdots$$

By inspection, the child can determine *several* pairs of fractions (there are infinitely many, of course) which could be used to change the problem to the familiar type:

$$\frac{3}{4} + \frac{5}{8} = \frac{6}{8} + \frac{5}{8} \qquad \text{or} \qquad \frac{12}{16} + \frac{10}{16} \qquad \text{or} \qquad \frac{18}{24} + \frac{15}{24} \qquad \text{etc.}$$

While there is certainly no need to find the *least* common denominator, such an activity should motivate children to *want* to do so (it is easier to simplify $6 + 5$ than $10 + 12$ or $15 + 18$). When using this method, the fractions are replaced *in toto,* i.e., $\frac{3}{4}$ is replaced with, say, $\frac{6}{8}$ by examining the list of fractions, *not* by first determining a common denominator and then determining the corresponding numerators. Vertical notation can reasonably be introduced at this time, although it certainly isn't necessary. A similar argument holds for reducing answers, which is an entirely different skill and need not plague children who are trying to learn this addition/subtraction skill.

Once these two problem types have been reasonably well understood, the child is ready for the general case, i.e., $\frac{a}{b} + \frac{c}{d}$ where b and d are not restricted. There are two possibilities: b and d may have a common factor but one is not a multiple of the other ($\frac{2}{15} + \frac{7}{9}$) or b and d may be relatively prime. In any event, it is time to move from the awkward technique of the preceding stages (although they are still valid and useful conceptually). The emphasis should be on finding the least common denominator (LCD), which is, of course, the least common multiple (LCM) of the denominators. Here, some careful development of ideas from number theory can pay off, especially the notions of *multiple, common multiples* of two (or more) numbers, and finally the *LCM* of two (or more) numbers. There are a number of useful approaches to finding the LCM of two numbers.

Given two natural numbers, k and n, the LCM of k and n (abbreviated LCM$[k, n]$) is equal to or greater than the *larger* of k and n, so it suffices to consider the multiples of that number *only* until we find one which is also a multiple of the other. For example, to find LCM$[15, 9]$, we would consider only the multiples of 15, i.e., 15, 30, 45, 60, 75, etc., until we find in the list a multiple of 9 (we usually do this by division). Since 45 is the *first* such number, LCM$[15, 9] = 45$, so to add or subtract fractions with denominators of 15 and 9, we use 45 as the LCD. Thus, for $\frac{2}{15} + \frac{7}{9}$, we have LCM$[15, 9] = 45$; and therefore (vertical notation is now useful),

Step 1 **Step 2**

$$\frac{2}{15} = \frac{}{45} \qquad \frac{2}{15} = \frac{6}{45}$$

$$+ \frac{7}{9} = \frac{}{45} \qquad + \frac{7}{9} = \frac{35}{45}$$

Note that the denominators are listed first, then the numerators are determined, based on the generalization (for whole numbers a, b, k),

$$\frac{a}{b} = \frac{ak}{bk} \qquad (b > 0, k > 0)$$

i.e., since $a = 2$, $b = 15$, and $bk = 45 = 15 \times 3$, $k = 3$ and so the numerator, ak, must be $2 \times 3 = 6$.

An alternate approach is to use the product of the denominators as the common denominator, since the product of 2 numbers is a common multiple of the numbers, although not necessarily their *least* common multiple. This number serves perfectly well as a common denominator, of course, but can be cumbersome:

$$\frac{2}{15} = \frac{18}{135}$$

$$+ \frac{7}{9} = \frac{105}{135}$$

So, to (possibly) find a smaller common multiple we can try dividing 135 by 2, by 3, by 4, etc. We find that although $135 \div 2$ isn't a whole number, $135 \div 3 = 45$, which "works." This approach uses the theorem from number theory that

$$\text{LCM}[a, b] = \frac{a \cdot b}{\text{GCD}(a, b)}$$

for natural numbers a and b. Recall that $\text{GCD}(a, b)$ is the greatest common divisor (or factor) of a and b, i.e., $\text{GCD}(15, 9) = 3$ so

$$\text{LCM}[15, 9] = \frac{15 \times 9}{3} = \frac{135}{3} = 45$$

A third approach, based essentially on the same theorem, involves prime factorization. To find $\text{LCM}[15, 9]$, for example, a child would think:

$$9 = 3 \times 3 \qquad \text{or} \qquad 3^2$$
$$15 = 3 \times 5 \qquad \text{or} \qquad 3^1 \times 5^1$$

The LCM is the product of the *largest* power of each distinct prime in the two factorizations, i.e.,

$$\text{LCM}[15, 9] = 3^2 \times 5^1 = 45$$

Children need to extend their skill in adding or subtracting fractional numbers to include those involving mixed numerals. This is generally accomplished at *each* stage of the development of the algorithm, after the "new" work—adding or subtracting the fractions—has been reasonably well mastered. There is nothing new conceptually in doing so. The process completely parallels that for adding or subtracting whole numbers, i.e., we first add (or subtract) the *fractions*, then ones, then tens, and so on. The only real complications arise where renaming (borrowing and carrying) is necessary. In the case of *addition,* this is less of a problem than in adding whole numbers, because if the sum of the fractions is greater than 1, the carrying need *not* be done until the sum has been determined completely, e.g.,

$$23\tfrac{2}{3}$$
$$+\,14\tfrac{2}{3}$$
$$\overline{37\tfrac{4}{3}=37+1\tfrac{1}{3}=38\tfrac{1}{3}}$$

Not

$$\overset{1}{23\tfrac{2}{3}}$$
$$+\,14\tfrac{2}{3}$$
$$\overline{38\tfrac{1}{3}}$$

The most common mistake children make in such problems seems to result from trying to do too much in one step, especially when fractions need to be renamed. It is generally a good idea to rewrite the entire example, as follows:

$$3\tfrac{2}{3}=\quad 3\tfrac{4}{6}$$
$$+\,1\tfrac{5}{6}=+\,1\tfrac{5}{6}$$
$$\overline{\qquad 4\tfrac{9}{6}=4+1\tfrac{1}{2}=5\tfrac{1}{2}}$$

Subtraction problems that require renaming the minuend (borrowing) are generally of two kinds (assuming the fractions have common denominators): those where the minuend fraction is less than the subtrahend fraction, and those where the minuend is a whole number:

$$12\tfrac{1}{3}$$
$$-\ 6\tfrac{2}{3}$$

and

$$12$$
$$-\ 6\tfrac{2}{3}$$

In the first case, the basic understanding is that 1 can be renamed as $\tfrac{k}{k}$, for any natural number k. Briefly, the approach would be to rename (mentally) 12 as $11+1$, then rename 1 as $\tfrac{3}{3}$, and finally associate that $\tfrac{3}{3}$ with the given $\tfrac{1}{3}$:

$$12\tfrac{1}{3}=12+\tfrac{1}{3}=(11+1)+\tfrac{1}{3}=(11+\tfrac{3}{3})+\tfrac{1}{3}=11+(\tfrac{3}{3}+\tfrac{1}{3})=11\tfrac{4}{3}$$

Each of these steps is easy to demonstrate with manipulative materials and to explain mathematically, using the associative property of addition. Children can accomplish this rather complicated renaming in a single step, particularly if the renaming is practiced per se before encountering it in subtraction situations, e.g.,

$$9\tfrac{2}{3}=\ 8\tfrac{}{3}$$
$$10\tfrac{1}{4}=\ 9\tfrac{}{4}$$
$$12\tfrac{2}{5}=11\tfrac{}{5}$$

Much potential difficulty can be avoided by encouraging children to do only one thing at a time, particularly when working with subtraction examples such as this:

$$5\tfrac{2}{5}$$
$$-2\tfrac{7}{8}$$

This is best rewritten twice. In the first step, the fractions are renamed with common denominators, and in the second step, the minuend is renamed as needed.

Step 1   Step 2

$$5\tfrac{2}{5} = 5\tfrac{16}{40} = 4\tfrac{56}{40}$$
$$-2\tfrac{7}{8} = 2\tfrac{35}{40} = 2\tfrac{35}{40}$$

The difficulty in problems such as $12 - 6\tfrac{2}{3}$ is analogous to that of zero in the minuend in subtraction of whole numbers:

$$120$$
$$- 62$$

The usual approach to resolving the impasse for $12 - 6\tfrac{2}{3}$ is, as before, to rename 12 first as $11 + 1$, then as $11 + \tfrac{3}{3}$ or $11\tfrac{3}{3}$.

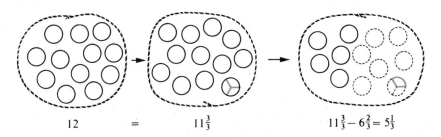

$$12 \qquad = \qquad 11\tfrac{3}{3} \qquad\qquad 11\tfrac{3}{3} - 6\tfrac{2}{3} = 5\tfrac{1}{3}$$

Children should be led to see the parallels between impasse situations involving whole numbers and those involving fractions: Understanding the former helps in discovering how to resolve similar situations when they occur with fractions. Children will require extra guidance, generally in the form of checking via addition or of returning to manipulative activity, if they make this common error:

$$12$$
$$- 6\tfrac{2}{3}$$
$$\overline{6\tfrac{2}{3}}$$

Multiplication

One measurement activity discussed in Chapter 8 was that of finding areas of regions by tessellating those regions with squares of some uniform size. This activity can be used to lead children to discovery of a rule for multiplying fractional numbers. They can be challenged, for example, to find the area of a rectangular region whose dimensions are not both exact multiples of the unit, such as a $\frac{3}{4}$-by-$\frac{2}{3}$ region, a $2\frac{1}{2}$-by-$3\frac{2}{3}$ region, or a 4-by-$2\frac{3}{5}$ region.

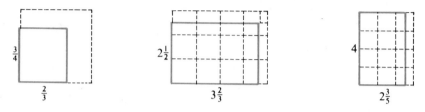

Before proposing such tasks, it is well to be certain that the children have at least these prerequisite understandings:

1. The *meaning* of area, i.e., the area of a region is the number of copies of the unit square which cover it.
2. Finding the area of a region may require (fractional) *parts* of units squares, e.g., the area of this figure is $8 + \frac{5}{2}$ or $10\frac{1}{2}$.

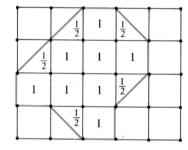

3. The area of a *rectangular* region can be found without covering it or counting squares; the product of two adjacent dimensions of a rectangle is the same number as the area, since if the dimensions are, say, 3 and 4, the region will be covered with a 3-by-4 *array* of squares.

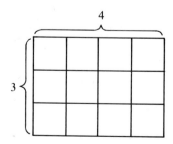

This last concept, which is easily discovered in the context of rectangles with *whole number* dimensions, is the one that needs to be extended to rectangles with fractional dimensions. That is, if children can find the area of a $\frac{3}{4}$-by-$\frac{2}{3}$ rectangle, or a $2\frac{1}{2}$-by-$3\frac{1}{3}$ one, and so on, and if they realize that the same generalization ($A = l \cdot w$) is true for fractional numbers, then they will have discovered the *products* $\frac{3}{4} \times \frac{2}{3}$ and $2\frac{1}{2} \times 3\frac{1}{3}$. This may lead them to conjectures about a general way to find similar products, i.e., how to multiply any fractional numbers, $\frac{a}{b} \times \frac{c}{d} = \square$.

It is best to explore rectangles with fractional dimensions first with some easier problems involving unit fractions or whole numbers. For example: Find the area of a 2-by-$\frac{1}{3}$ rectangle and of a $\frac{1}{2}$-by-$\frac{1}{3}$ rectangle. If these are constructed on a *grid* of unit squares, their areas can be found easily. That is, the area of the 2-by-$\frac{1}{3}$ rectangle is $\frac{2}{3}$; that of the $\frac{1}{2}$-by-$\frac{1}{3}$

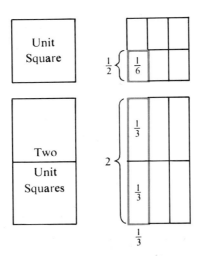

rectangle is $\frac{1}{6}$, since the unit square is partitioned into 6 parts, each of the same size and shape. If the generalization relating the area of a rectangle to the products of its dimensions holds for *all* rectangles, then $2 \times \frac{1}{3} = \frac{2}{3}$ and $\frac{1}{2} \times \frac{1}{3} = \frac{1}{6}$. Does this seem reasonable? If, in general $n \times \frac{1}{3}$ suggests "n thirds" (as $n \times 3$ means "n 3s"), i.e., n suggests "how many times," then "how many times" is $\frac{1}{3}$ contained in each picture? Two times in one case, and "half a time" in the other. The latter may require a little extra exploration with some children. For example, it may be necessary to consider pictures that contain 3 thirds, $2\frac{1}{2}$ thirds, then $1\frac{1}{2}$ thirds before "half a third" will seem reasonable.

Children may, with only these preliminary explorations, propose the general rule

$$\frac{a}{b} \times \frac{c}{d} = \frac{a \times c}{b \times d}$$

since it fits $\frac{1}{2} \times \frac{1}{3}$ and $\frac{2}{1} \times \frac{1}{3}$ at least. If it "works," it will be used to find areas of other rectangles, such as those originally suggested; if not, most will quickly discover so as they proceed. Either of two general approaches might be followed in finding areas of rectangles with dimensions such as $\frac{3}{4}$-by-$\frac{2}{3}$, $2\frac{1}{2}$-by-$3\frac{2}{3}$, or 4-by-$2\frac{3}{5}$. Some children may find one easier than the other, and some may need to try both: The first approach is to outline the given rectangle, then cover it with unit squares (and/or *parts* of unit squares), then count. Careful measurements are necessary and should probably be provided by the teacher in most cases. This approach can be rather difficult

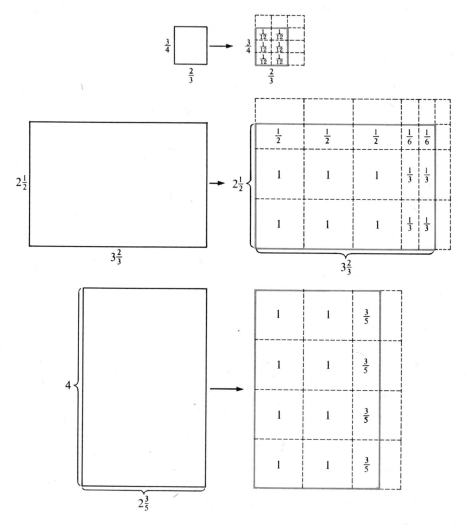

and in fact requires considerable skill with addition. Furthermore, the results will not necessarily suggest the algorithm, although if we express the factors and product as fractions, we get a clue: If $2\frac{1}{2} \times 3\frac{2}{3} = 9\frac{1}{6}$ is expressed as $\frac{5}{2} \times \frac{11}{3} = \frac{55}{6}$, the algorithm is suggested.

The second, and preferable, approach is to start with a grid of unit squares partitioned according to the denominators of the two factors, then construct the rectangle on that grid. These can be constructed in advance by the teacher on transparencies to be used either over a piece of clean paper or projected. For example, to solve the three problems above, five transparencies would be needed. These can be made as follows: Starting with five sheets of standard $8\frac{1}{2}$-by-11″ white paper (from which the transparencies are later made), draw heavy margins 3 cm above the bottom of each page and 3 cm from the left edge. Now mark off unit points along the bottom margin 4.5 cm apart and draw a *heavy* ray from each parallel to the left margin (the points along the horizontal margin correspond to 0, 1, 2, 3, and 4, but should not be labeled). Leave one of these constructions alone; on

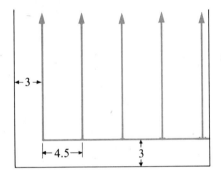

the second, draw a *light* ray midway between each heavy one (2.25 cm from each). The points on the horizontal ray now correspond to 0, $\frac{1}{2}$, 1, $1\frac{1}{2}$, 2, . . . , 4. On the third paper, draw (light) rays to partition the units into thirds (1.5 cm apart); similarly, partition the remaining two copies into fourths and fifths, respectively. Now cut off and discard the tops of each sheet 18.5 cm from the bottom margin and make the five transparencies.

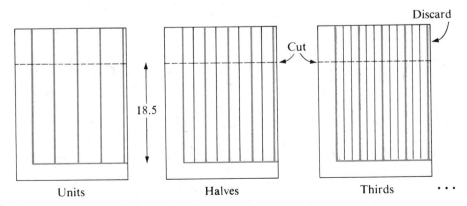

To construct a $\frac{3}{4}$-by-$\frac{2}{3}$ rectangle, we can flip and rotate the model for *fourths* over that for *thirds* to make a 4-by-4 grid of unit squares (heavy lines) each partitioned horizontally into fourths and vertically into thirds. On this grid we can outline the desired rectangle, using a grease pencil, and determine its area. The two transparencies may be pinned together on a

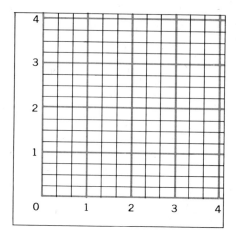

board and the intersecting number lines may be labeled, with grease pencil, to emphasize the desired rectangle (the extraneous part of the grid can be masked to prevent distraction).

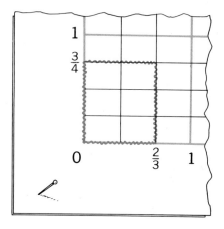

The $\frac{3}{4}$-by-$\frac{2}{3}$ rectangle, outlined in wavey lines here, is a 3-by-2 array of $\frac{1}{12}$s (since the unit square is partitioned into 12 congruent parts). Thus, its area is *six* $\frac{1}{12}$s, or $\frac{6}{12}$. Thus $\frac{3}{4} \times \frac{2}{3} = \frac{6}{12}$. The $2\frac{1}{2}$-by-$3\frac{2}{3}$ rectangle can be similarly constructed by superimposing the "halves" model over the "thirds" model; the key vertices of the rectangle should be labeled $\frac{5}{2}$ and $\frac{11}{3}$; the grid will reveal a 5-by-11 array of sixths, so its area is $\frac{55}{6}$, suggesting $\frac{5}{2} \times \frac{11}{3} = \frac{55}{6}$.

There are several other approaches to teaching multiplication of fractional numbers. One is to first establish the generalization for unit fractions, much as was previously suggested, e.g., $\frac{1}{4} \times \frac{1}{3} = \frac{1}{12}$, then view any fraction $\frac{a}{b}$ as the product $a \times \frac{1}{b}$. By using the commutative and associative properties of multiplication (which most children readily accept as valid for fractional numbers since they are valid for whole numbers), the multiplication algorithm can then be established as suggested here:

$$\frac{3}{4} \times \frac{2}{3} = (3 \times \tfrac{1}{4}) \times (2 \times \tfrac{1}{3})$$
$$= (3 \times 2) \times (\tfrac{1}{4} \times \tfrac{1}{3})$$
$$= 6 \times \tfrac{1}{12}$$
$$= \tfrac{6}{12}$$

$$\frac{5}{2} \times \frac{11}{3} = (5 \times \tfrac{1}{2}) \times (11 \times \tfrac{1}{3})$$
$$= (5 \times 11) \times (\tfrac{1}{2} \times \tfrac{1}{3})$$
$$= 55 \times \tfrac{1}{6}$$
$$= \tfrac{55}{6}$$

A third approach is to interpret, for example, $\frac{3}{4} \times \frac{2}{3}$ as $\frac{3}{4}$ *of* $\frac{2}{3}$ and to then proceed much as with the model above using intersecting grids (which need not be square). Our experience suggests that while children can quite

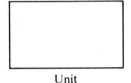

Unit

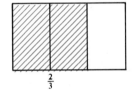

$\frac{2}{3}$

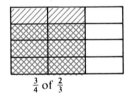

$\frac{3}{4}$ of $\frac{2}{3}$

easily see that $\frac{3}{4}$ of $\frac{2}{3}$ is, indeed, $\frac{6}{12}$, they are less willing to accept that therefore $\frac{3}{4}$ *times* $\frac{2}{3}$ is $\frac{6}{12}$. On the other hand, if they *first* discover that $\frac{3}{4} \times \frac{2}{3}$ is $\frac{6}{12}$, they can later discover that if they wish to find $\frac{3}{4}$ of $\frac{2}{3}$, they can do so by applying the multiplication algorithm.

In any event, no matter how the algorithm is developed, it should be used in many problem situations, such as finding areas of various rectangular regions, "halving" recipes, finding volumes, and so on. Various structural properties should be explored, such as establishing what the commutative, associative, identity, and distributive (if they have also learned to add) properties hold for fractional numbers.

In time, these structural properties can be used to carefully derive some computational short cuts.

Examples:

(a) $8 \times \dfrac{3}{4} = \dfrac{8}{1} \times \dfrac{3}{4} = \dfrac{24}{4} = 6$

$\therefore 8 \times \dfrac{3}{4} = \dfrac{8 \times 3}{4} = \dfrac{24}{4} = 6$

(b) $\dfrac{5}{6} \times \dfrac{18}{25} = \dfrac{5 \times 18}{6 \times 25} = \dfrac{18 \times 5}{6 \times 25} = \dfrac{18}{6} \times \dfrac{5}{25} = \dfrac{3}{1} \times \dfrac{1}{5} = \dfrac{3}{5}$

$\therefore \quad \dfrac{{}^1 5}{{}_1 6} \times \dfrac{18^3}{25_5} = \dfrac{3}{5}$ (cancelling)

(c) $2\frac{3}{5} \times 12 = (2 + \frac{3}{5}) \times 12 = (2 \times 12) + (\frac{3}{5} \times 12)$

$\qquad = 24 + \frac{36}{5} = 24 + 7\frac{1}{5} = 31\frac{1}{5}$

$$\therefore \quad \begin{array}{r} 12 \\ \times\ 2\frac{3}{5} \\ \hline 5\overline{)36} \\ 7\frac{1}{5} \\ 24 \\ \hline 31\frac{1}{5} \end{array}$$

Division

There are several common approaches to teaching division of fractional numbers. This topic is frequently introduced with problems involving
"special" cases, such as "How many $\frac{1}{2}$-pound packages of hamburger can
be made from 6 pounds?" We call this a "special" case because it can be
quite easily solved by "brute force," using manipulative or visual aids. As
such, it can lead to an awareness of the *need* to divide fractional numbers
and can provide some insight into possible approaches to the solution of
similar problems. The special case also provides an opportunity to review
and apply some of the basic properties the children have learned about
division, its relationship to multiplication, and so on. On the other hand,
the strategies (e.g., repeated subtraction) a child may use to solve such
relatively easy problems simply don't "work" when applied to other division
problems. We believe that it is pedagogically sound to move very quickly
from such problems to those whose solutions can lead to a *general* algorithm.
That is, pose a problem; have the children explore possible solutions (this
can be time-consuming, of course); and, when it is finally solved, try to help
them use their solution to discover a pattern or general algorithm that can
be relied on for *any* division problem. After they understand and feel secure
with the *basic* approach, problems such as the hamburger problem can be
used to introduce helpful — but not necessary — alternatives, i.e., short cuts
that *sometimes* can be used. This was also our recommended approach to
multiplication.

Unlike multiplication, however, and unlike virtually every other
topic in arithmetic, we know of no *manipulative* or *visual* model for division
problems with fractions that satisfies the two important criteria of *reliability*
(i.e., it "works" for *any* problem) and *simplicity* (children can use it independently). The various approaches we will suggest here for the general
case of division rely more on mathematical or intellectual models than on
manipulative, visual ones.

Fortunately, these mathematical models can be developed either while children are discovering the properties of division for *whole* numbers; from their introductory work with fractions; or as a result of independent explorations with fractions using basically the concepts of whole number division. These models — or generalizations — include the following:

1. The definition of division: $a \div b$ is that number x which when multiplied by b equals a (where $b \neq 0$).
2. The relationship between division and fractions: The fraction $\frac{a}{b}$ is the quotient, $a \div b$, of a and b;
3. The reciprocal or multiplicative inverse concept: Two nonzero numbers are reciprocals of each other if their product is 1, the multiplicative identity. For any natural number n, its reciprocal is $\frac{1}{n}$, since $n \cdot \frac{1}{n} = 1$; and for any nonzero fractional number $\frac{a}{b}$, its reciprocal is $\frac{b}{a}$, since $\frac{a}{b} \cdot \frac{b}{a} = 1$.
4. The property of 1 as a divisor: For any natural number n, $n \div 1 = n$ since $n \cdot 1 = n$.
5. Any natural number n divided by itself equals 1: $n \div n = 1$; thus, since also $n \div n$ means $\frac{n}{n}$, $\frac{n}{n} = 1$.
6. Multiplying both dividend and divisor (or numerator and denominator) by the same nonzero number k leaves the quotient unchanged, i.e., results in an equivalent fraction: $a \div b = (a \cdot k) \div (b \cdot k)$ or $\frac{a}{b} = \frac{ak}{bk}$.

Many adult problems involving division of fractional numbers originate in the grocery store. Although their solutions are less interesting to children than to adults, the problems can be *meaningful* to children and therefore can be used as reasonable ways to introduce the topic. A "raid," a few moments before this writing, on the family pantry disclosed 5 cans of tomatoes of different sizes, prices, and brands. A few questions arise quite naturally: Assuming that a can of tomatoes is a can of tomatoes (a hypothetical question since some brands are more satisfactory than others) and assuming that the size of the can is immaterial (again hypothetical, since some recipes require only a small can, so that opening a large one would be wasteful), we can ask: What is the cost per ounce of each can? Which is the best buy?

While answers to these questions may be less than interesting to fifth- or sixth-grade children, they suggest possible problems that *can* be of interest to them. Let us take one such sample problem and consider several approaches to its solution — leading to some algorithms for dividing fractional numbers. Suppose a child measures the capacity of his favorite glass by pouring a glassful of milk or water into a measuring cup. The glass holds $1\frac{1}{4}$ cups; now if he is admonished to drink a quart (4 cups) of milk each day, how many glasses of milk should he drink?

Translating the question into multiplicative terms, it becomes, "How many times $1\frac{1}{4}$ is 4?" or "$1\frac{1}{4}$ times what is 4?" or "How many $1\frac{1}{4}$s are there in 4?", e.g., $\square \times 1\frac{1}{4} = 4$. By the definition of division, this becomes $4 \div 1\frac{1}{4} = \square$ or, in terms of fractions, $\frac{4}{1} \div \frac{5}{4} = \square$.

One approach, sometimes called the least common multiple (LCM) method, is to multiply both dividend and divisor by the LCM of the two denominators, which always tranforms the two numbers to whole numbers.

$$\text{LCM}[1, 4] = 4 \qquad \text{and} \qquad (\tfrac{4}{1} \times 4) \div (\tfrac{5}{4} \times 4) = 16 \div 5$$

Since $16 \div 5$ means $\frac{16}{5}$ or $3\frac{1}{5}$, $\frac{4}{1} \div \frac{5}{4} = 3\frac{1}{5}$. Thus, $3\frac{1}{5}$ glasses of milk are required. Assuming that a child has experienced enough number theory to be able to find the LCM of any (reasonable) pair of numbers, and that he sufficiently understands that $a \div b = ak \div bk$ and that $x \div y = \frac{x}{y}$, this is an easy algorithm to discover (with guidance), to learn, and to use.

A related approach, sometimes called the least common denominator (LCD) method calls for first expressing each number with a common denominator, as is done for addition and subtraction: $\frac{4}{1} \div \frac{5}{4} = \frac{16}{4} \div \frac{5}{4}$. The quotient can then be found by dividing the numerators, much as a comparable sum or difference would be found by adding or subtracting them. That is,

$$\tfrac{16}{4} \div \tfrac{5}{4} = 16 \div 5 = \tfrac{16}{5}$$

This can be rationalized by again multiplying each of $\frac{16}{4}$ and $\frac{5}{4}$ by 4, the common denominator:

$$\tfrac{16}{4} \div \tfrac{5}{4} = (\tfrac{16}{4} \times 4) \div (\tfrac{5}{4} \times 4) = 16 \div 5 = \tfrac{16}{5}$$

Both the LCM and LCD approaches are easy to justify, easy to use, and (with careful guidance) are easy for the child to discover. There is no need to employ more complicated algorithms such as the traditional "invert the divisor and multiply" (reciprocal) approach. However, some interesting insights into the structure of the fractional number system can be obtained by exploring the notion of reciprocals. One approach is suggested here:

First, assuming children have learned to multiply fractional numbers (an assumption which underlies each of the division algorithms), they can be given pairs of problems to solve:

(a)	$8 \div 2 =$	(b)	$8 \times \frac{1}{2} =$
(a)	$15 \div 3 =$	(b)	$15 \times \frac{1}{3} =$
(a)	$10 \div 5 =$	(b)	$10 \times \frac{1}{5} =$
(a)	$9 \div 3 =$	(b)	$9 \times \frac{1}{3} =$
(a)	$24 \div 4 =$	(b)	$24 \times \frac{1}{4} =$

Once the solutions are obtained and simplified, a number of questions can be raised: What does each pair of problems have in common? How does each problem on the left (a) differ from the corresponding problem on the right (b)? Are the answers the same for each pair of problems? From such questions, children will quickly observe that the "first" numbers of each pair of problems are the same; for each pair of problems, the first is a division problem and the second is a multiplication problem; the answers for each pair of problems are the same; and that if the "second" number (the divisor) of the first problem is n, the "second" number of the corresponding problem is $\frac{1}{n}$.

This final observation, whether it is discovered first, last, or otherwise, can then be explored: What can you tell about these pairs of numbers — $(2, \frac{1}{2})$, $(3, \frac{1}{3})$, $(5, \frac{1}{5})$, $(4, \frac{1}{4})$? Although various responses may be forthcoming and several hints may be necessary, it should ultimately emerge that the *product* of each pair is 1.

$$2 \times \tfrac{1}{2} = 3 \times \tfrac{1}{3} = 5 \times \tfrac{1}{5} = 4 \times \tfrac{1}{4} = 1$$

This, then, can lead to a definition: Two numbers whose product is 1 are called *reciprocals* of each other, e.g., 2 is the reciprocal of $\frac{1}{2}$; $\frac{1}{3}$ is the reciprocal of 3; 4 and $\frac{1}{4}$ are reciprocals, and so on. It is a simple matter then to identify reciprocals of various natural numbers and unit fractions.

Two important questions can then be explored: (1) If a and b are natural numbers, what is the relationship between $a \div b$ and $a \times \frac{1}{b}$ (when $a \div b$ is a natural number, as in the examples given)? (2) If $\frac{x}{y}$ is a *non*unit fraction, what is its reciprocal? For example, what is the reciprocal of $\frac{2}{3}$ or of $\frac{3}{4}$? That is, what is the solution of

$$\tfrac{2}{3} \times \square = 1 \qquad \text{or} \qquad \tfrac{3}{4} \times \triangle = 1$$

While this question is a bit more difficult, the hint that $1 = \frac{2}{2} = \frac{3}{3} = \frac{4}{4} = \frac{5}{5} = \ldots$ eventually leads to correct solutions:

$$\frac{2}{3} \times \boxed{\frac{3}{2}} = \frac{6}{6} = 1 \qquad \frac{3}{4} \times \triangle\!\!\frac{4}{3} = \frac{12}{12} = 1$$

In general,

$$\frac{a}{b} \times \frac{b}{a} = 1$$

i.e., the reciprocal of any (nonzero) fraction $\frac{a}{b}$ is $\frac{b}{a}$, the fraction obtained by inverting the terms of $\frac{a}{b}$.

Putting these several observations together can lead to such questions as, if the quotient $a \div b$ is the same as the product of a and the reciprocal of b, i.e., if

$$a \div b = a \times \frac{1}{b}$$

where a and b are natural numbers (or whole numbers with $b \neq 0$), then is the quotient $x \div y$, where x and y are *fractional* numbers, equal to the product of x and the reciprocal of y? For example, is $\frac{4}{1} \div \frac{5}{4} = \frac{4}{1} \times \frac{4}{5}$? Since $\frac{4}{1} \times \frac{4}{5}$

$= \frac{16}{5}$, this question is equivalent to, Is $\frac{4}{1} \div \frac{5}{4}$ equal to $\frac{16}{5}$? The answer is "yes" *if* $\frac{16}{5} \times \frac{5}{4} = \frac{4}{1}$, which can be easily verified. Several such problems can readily establish the algorithm that, for any fractional numbers $\frac{a}{b}$ and $\frac{c}{d}$ ($\frac{c}{d} \neq 0$),

$$\frac{a}{b} \div \frac{c}{d} = \frac{a}{b} \times \frac{d}{c}$$

This, then, provides a third algorithm for dividing fractional numbers.

Related questions include: Are there any fractional numbers which are their own reciprocals? Are there any fractional numbers which do not have reciprocals? (Only $\frac{1}{1}$ is its own reciprocal; only $\frac{0}{1}$ has no reciprocal.) If a fractional number is between zero and one, what can you say about its reciprocal? If a fractional number is greater than one, what can you say about its reciprocal?

There are various reciprocal algorithms for dividing fractional numbers, all of which can lead to the standard algorithm above. All are based on the same idea, already used several times, i.e., that

$$a \div b = a \cdot k \div b \cdot k \qquad (b \neq 0,\ k \neq 0)$$

One of these is based on the "dividing by one" idea:

A problem such as $\frac{4}{1} \div \frac{5}{4}$ can be transformed to a "dividing by one" problem if each of $\frac{4}{1}$ and $\frac{5}{4}$ is multiplied by the reciprocal of the divisor, $\frac{5}{4}$:

$$\frac{4}{1} \div \frac{5}{4} = \left(\frac{4}{1} \times \frac{4}{5}\right) \div \left(\frac{5}{4} \times \frac{4}{5}\right)$$
$$= \left(\frac{4}{1} \times \frac{4}{5}\right) \div 1$$
$$= \frac{4}{1} \times \frac{4}{5}$$
$$= \frac{16}{5}$$

Another reciprocal algorithm, usually viewed as too abstract for elementary school children, but nonetheless worth mentioning briefly, is a "complex fraction" method. (A complex fraction is one whose numerator and/or denominator is a fraction):

Example:

Since

$a \div b$	means	$\dfrac{a}{b}$
$\dfrac{4}{1} \div \dfrac{5}{4}$	means	$\dfrac{\frac{4}{1}}{\frac{5}{4}}$

Multiplying this last fraction by 1 in the form of the complex fraction $\dfrac{\frac{4}{5}}{\frac{4}{5}}$ (the reciprocal of $\frac{5}{4}$ divided by itself) produces this:

$$\frac{4}{1} \div \frac{5}{4} = \frac{\frac{4}{1}}{\frac{5}{4}} = \frac{\frac{4}{1}}{\frac{5}{4}} \times \frac{\frac{4}{5}}{\frac{4}{5}} = \frac{\frac{4}{1} \times \frac{4}{5}}{\frac{5}{4} \times \frac{4}{5}} = \frac{\frac{4}{1} \times \frac{4}{5}}{1} = \frac{4}{1} \times \frac{4}{5} = \frac{16}{5}$$

All of this eventually leads, as do other reciprocal methods, to discovery of the algorithm, $\frac{a}{b} \div \frac{c}{d} = \frac{a}{b} \times \frac{d}{c}$, which can then be used without all the intervening steps.

Many other explorations might be undertaken in the search for a division algorithm, for children can make many discoveries about this interesting topic. For example, children frequently note that since $\frac{2}{3} \times \frac{4}{5} = \frac{8}{15}$, it should be true that $\frac{8}{15} \div \frac{4}{5} = \frac{2}{3}$, according to the basic meaning of division (as the opposite of multiplication); and this suggests a potential algorithm:

$$\frac{8}{15} \div \frac{4}{5} = \frac{8 \div 4}{15 \div 5}$$

While this observation is correct, it must be explored further to make it useful. Can it be used, for example, for $\frac{2}{3} \div \frac{4}{5}$? If the terms of $\frac{2}{3}$ are each multiplied by the LCM of 4 and 5, then $\frac{2}{3}$ can be replaced with $\frac{40}{60}$; and then

$$\frac{40}{60} \div \frac{4}{5} = \frac{40 \div 4}{60 \div 5}$$

Similarly, given a problem that calls for solving

$$\frac{3}{4} \div \frac{2}{3} = \frac{x}{y}$$

if we write it as

$$\frac{x}{y} \cdot \frac{2}{3} = \frac{3}{4}$$

can we find whole numbers x and y such that $x \cdot 2 = 3$ and $y \cdot 3 = 4$? Of course not! But suppose we replace $\frac{3}{4}$ with an equivalent fraction. There are many possibilities; e.g., $\frac{6}{8}, \frac{9}{12}, \frac{12}{16}, \frac{15}{20}, \frac{18}{24}, \frac{21}{28}, \ldots$, but $\frac{18}{24}$ "works":

$$\frac{x}{y} \cdot \frac{2}{3} = \frac{18}{24} \qquad \text{is solved by} \qquad \frac{x}{y} = \frac{9}{8}$$

Is there an easy way to do this? Is there a pattern we can find that will help us to use this with other problems?

A fifth-grade girl, after having been taught a reciprocal method for dividing fractional numbers, showed this writer (then her teacher) a discovery she had made:

Given an expression like $\frac{a}{b} \div \frac{c}{d}$, why rewrite it as $\frac{a}{b} \times \frac{d}{c}$? Why not just use this algorithm:

$$\frac{a}{b} \div \frac{c}{d} = \frac{a \times d}{b \times c}$$

Furthermore, she had found that she could "cancel" a pair of numerators or a pair of denominators in a division expression to save work, e.g.,

$$\frac{\overset{2}{4}}{5} \div \frac{\overset{3}{6}}{7} = \frac{2 \times 7}{5 \times 3}$$

(Her explanation of why her algorithm and her short cut both "work" was flawless.)

As we have seen, there are numerous algorithms for division of fractional numbers, some of them quite simple, others requiring more insight. Of far more importance than *how* to divide fractional numbers is the skill of correctly associating a given *problem* situation with a particular division expression. Does a given problem suggest division? If so, what is the divisor? What is the dividend? This skill is best developed by providing children with plenty of opportunity to solve problems — and plenty of guidance. The sense of a division problem involving fractional numbers is no different from the sense of one with whole numbers. Teachers can help by pointing out similarities, patterns, analogies, and relationships to whole number division so that in time children will form the habit of seeing these themselves — routinely. Among these habits, as always, is the question, Does the answer "make sense"? Many problems require interpolation. For example, how many $\frac{3}{4}$-inch-wide strips of wood can be cut from a board $5\frac{3}{4}$ inches wide? The *computation* yields $7\frac{2}{3}$, but the *answer* is 7 (remember the saw cut!).

Decimals

Many of the complicated problems considered in the past several pages do not arise when fractional numbers are expressed as decimals. Once the SI system of measures receives widespread acceptance, so that measurements are made only in terms of metric units, and tenths, hundredths, or thousandths of metric units, the problem of equivalent fractional numbers will become of relatively little importance, and most computational procedures will become simple extensions of those for whole numbers.

Although the time may come when fractions as we now think of them will become obsolete (or virtually so), we currently live in an era when *both* fractions and decimals are important, and both are commonly used — even simultaneously — in "mixed" notation. The two notational systems are related, of course, yet are, in a sense, independent of each other. Here, we shall look at decimals first as independent of fractional notation and then consider relationships between the two systems.

The first task is that of introducing children to the concept of fractional numbers expressed as decimals, and the numeration of that system. This can start when children are first beginning to experiment with linear measurement, even before they are introduced to standard units of measure. For example, given Cuisenaire, Centimeter, Dienes, or Stern 10-blocks, they can lay down a string of the blocks to obtain a rough measure of things around them—their desks, pencils, books, the floor, the chalkboard, and so on. As the need for more accuracy becomes evident, which is inevitable, the 1-blocks can be introduced. Dimensions can be recorded as two-part numerals.

Dimensions of My Math Book

	How Many Orange Rods?	+	How Many White Rods?
Width	2		2
Height	2		8
Thickness	0		2

Questions of precision are certain to arise with such relatively large measuring units but this serves to develop the very concept of error and precision in measurement: The child must decide whether the width of his book is nearer to 2 orange rods and 1 white rod or 2 orange rods and 2 white rods. There are no alternatives, given only these measuring instruments.

Noting that 10 rods of the smaller size match 1 of the larger can lead to considering various ways of *recording* measurements. The height of the math book may either be described as 28 white rods or 2 orange rods and 8 white rods. The latter can lead to the consideration of notations such as 2, 8 or 2:8 or 2/8 or 2.8, the latter being the *standard* form and thus "pushed" by the teacher. Children, even if their experience with fraction *notation* is meagre or nonexistent, have little difficulty in accepting 2.8 as meaning "2 and 8-*tenths*," since it takes ten 1-blocks to match one 10-block.

Measurement situations such as these can be extended considerably before any standard units of measure need to be used. Simple addition and subtraction situations involving measures can be introduced (e.g., What is the combined length of two math books? or, How much wider is your math book than your spelling book?). Cardboard rulers, scaled in tenths, can be made by the teacher for children to use. These need not be based on standard units, although *some* sort of name for a basic unit will need to be adopted and agreed upon by the children. In time, of course, the words meter, decimeter, centimeter, and millimeter would be used and things will be measured with rulers, meter sticks, or tape measures scaled in these standard units. In any event, children should have rather extensive experience with *tenths only*, before hundredths and thousandths are introduced, just as in learning the numeration of whole numbers considerable experience with ones and *tens* should precede introduction to hundreds and thousands.

The various materials and activities used to develop whole number numeration concepts can be adapted to develop fractional number concepts: Place value charts can be relabeled as "Ones" and "Tenths"; the first strand of an abacus can be used as the "tenths" strand; the counting board, counting man, and various sets of blocks can be redesignated in "decimal" terms. In each case, as with fractions, the *unit* concept must be emphasized. The child must know what is to represent *one* before he can correctly identify tenths. And the unit should be represented in a wide variety of ways: as segments of different lengths, in terms of particular points on a line, as blocks of different sizes and shapes (e.g., sometimes a Dienes long should be 1, sometimes a flat should play this role, and so on), as plane regions of varying sizes and shapes, as dimes or dollars, even as a set of 10 discrete things such as checkers. The counting, trading, comparing, and rounding activities discussed in Chapter 4 can all be modified and repeated using tenths, then hundredths, and so on.

Once children understand the addition and subtraction algorithms for whole numbers and the equivalence of 1 and 10 tenths, the activities in Chapter 6 can be adapted to solve corresponding problems with decimals. The extension is a very natural one, but manipulative representations, expanded algorithms, and the like should not be overlooked. Although the algorithms with decimals can be related to those for fractions (with denominators of ten), it is not necessary to do so. In fact, it would seem more reasonable to first relate the addition and subtraction algorithms with decimals to those for whole numbers and then use those understandings in *introducing* addition and subtraction with fractions, than to introduce the decimal computations in terms of fractions, as is commonly done.

Multiplication and division with decimals is best delayed until the general structure of the decimal notation system has been fairly well established. Experiences with hundredths and thousandths, including addition and subtraction as well as the basic numeration activities, can exactly parallel those with tenths. Again, the extension from tenths to hundredths, and beyond, can evolve quite naturally out of previously suggested activities. For example, if a Dienes *flat* is chosen as unit, then *longs* become tenths; and a natural question is, What shall we call the *units*? As children perform linear measurement tasks with a fairly long unit, they may not be satisfied with the degree of precision that can be obtained with tenths of that unit. This can lead to the suggestion that each *tenth* be further partitioned into tenths. What should the smaller subdivisions be called? How many of these smaller lengths are in a unit? This would be a good time to introduce the metric ruler, using the decimeter as unit, centimeters as *tenths,* and millimeters as hundredths. If children are accustomed to accepting a *variety* of units, as proposed above, they will have little difficulty redesignating millimeters as thousandths of a *meter*, centimeters as hundredths, and decimeters as tenths.

The roles of the numeral 0 in decimals should be discussed and experienced carefully. In recording "3 hundredths," for example, children should be helped to see the need for a zero in tenths place, and the analogy to whole number numeration. A second important role, which has no parallel in ordinary usage of whole number numeration, but which becomes important in understanding division and in comparing decimals, is that annexing one or more zeroes to a decimal does not affect its value. This should be examined carefully and ample practice should be provided with comparing decimals such as .035 and .12, .4 and .04, etc.

In time, starting with such devices as place value charts, the child should be led to explore patterns and relationships in the decimal extension of the whole number place value structure, such as the relative positions of tens place and tenths place, hundreds place and hundredths place, and so on. In particular, equivalent numerals such as .2, .20, and .200 or .03, .030 and .0300 should be examined. As a prelude to multiplication, children should note that if a unit square is partitioned into tenths along each dimension, it may be viewed as a 10-by-10 array of smaller squares, so that the area of each small square region is one hundredth.

Multiplication is frequently introduced in terms of repeated addition with one factor a whole number, e.g., "How much string is required to cut 5 lengths, each 2.3 meters long?" Linear measurement models such as the various sets of blocks can make this reasonable and children who understand the role of the distributive property for whole number multiplication will quickly recognize its analogous role with decimals. Expanded forms corresponding to those for the whole number algorithm should again be employed.

Since problems with a whole number multiplier, however, do not introduce children to the significant problem of locating decimal points in products, it is important to provide an early introduction to this more general case. The area model described previously for fractions can be used, beginning with unit squares partitioned into tenths, along both dimensions. At first, areas of rectangles with dimensions less than 1, e.g., .3-by-.7, .4-by-.5, .2-by-.3, etc., should be considered. As children discover that $.3 \times .7 = .21$, $.4 \times .5 = .20$, and $.2 \times .3 = .06$, they will of course note both the parallel with whole number multiplication and the difference between multiplication and the first two operations with regard to the decimal point. Care should be taken to help children to see that both patterns make sense, each for their respective operations.

Gradually, areas of larger regions can be determined and the algorithms extended. The area of the region shown here, for example, is found to be 351 hundredths since it is a 13-by-27 array of hundredths. That this is equivalent to 3.51 can be established in various ways, such as constructing

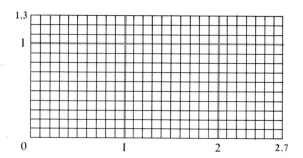

it with Dienes' base ten flats, longs, and units, or similar models that can be shifted around. The relationship to whole number multiplication should again be confirmed quite readily after a very few examples, as should the rule relating the number of "decimal places" in the factors and the product. The distributive property can be used in various ways, e.g., the rectangle can be viewed as partitioned into smaller rectangles such as $(1 \times 2) + (.3 \times 2) + (1 \times .7) + (.3 \times .7)$, or $2 + .6 + .7 + .21 = 3.51$.

Much practice should be provided on estimating and mentally rounding numbers so that children recognize that an answer makes sense. The area, say, of a 3.1 by 5.2 rectangle will be "a little more than 15" since the two dimensions are a little more than 3 and 5 respectively. Thus, for example, 161.2 or 1.612 would be viewed as "obviously" wrong answers. This can be practiced with exercises such as

If $\quad 48 \times 2 = 96,\quad$ then $\quad .48 \times 2 =$ _____ , $4.8 \times 2 =$ _____ , $4.8 \times .2 =$ _____

This becomes an important and useful habit as the algorithm is extended to include additional places. It should be supplemented by more careful analysis, however, by considering sequences of problems.

$$\begin{array}{rcl}
1 \text{ tenth} \times 1 \text{ tenth} = & 1 & \rule{2cm}{0.4pt} \\
2 \text{ tenths} \times 3 \text{ tenths} = & 6 & \rule{2cm}{0.4pt} \\
12 \text{ tenths} \times 2 \text{ tenths} = & 24 & \rule{2cm}{0.4pt} \\
\vdots & & \\
n \text{ tenths} \times m \text{ tenths} = n \times m & & \rule{2cm}{0.4pt}
\end{array}$$

and

$$\begin{array}{rcl}
1 \text{ tenth} \times 1 \text{ hundredth} = & 1 & \rule{2cm}{0.4pt} \\
2 \text{ tenths} \times 3 \text{ hundredths} = & 6 & \rule{2cm}{0.4pt} \\
12 \text{ tenths} \times 2 \text{ hundredths} = & 24 & \rule{2cm}{0.4pt} \\
\vdots & & \\
n \text{ tenths} \times m \text{ hundredths} = n \times m & & \rule{2cm}{0.4pt}
\end{array}$$

The familiar rule of counting decimal places in the factors should be left as a discovery for children to make on their own *after* they have such opportunities to understand why it works.

The very useful skill of mentally multiplying a decimal by a power of ten can similarly be discovered by providing problems such as:

$$.32 \times \quad 10 = \underline{\hspace{1.5cm}}$$
$$1.6 \times \quad 100 = \underline{\hspace{1.5cm}}$$
$$4.687 \times 1000 = \underline{\hspace{1.5cm}}$$

Similarities and differences between "moving the decimal point" and "adding zeroes" should be considered once children discover these short cuts, to be certain that they understand why each works. The two "tricks" are essentially the same, i.e., multiplying any number (whole number *or* fractional number expressed as a decimal) by 10^n can be accomplished by shifting each digit n places to the left (1 place for 10, 2 places for 100, and so on). In the case of a whole number like 24, each digit can be shifted by annexing zeroes; in the case of a fractional number like 2.4, digits are shifted by shifting the reference (decimal) point which identifies places. Place-value charts can be used to help visualize this.

Division with decimals is usually introduced with problems involving a natural number divisor, much as addition with fractions is introduced with common denominators such as $\frac{2}{5} + \frac{1}{5}$. The reason in both cases is the same: The general case is usually solved by first renaming the given numbers in these terms. When we need to add or subtract two numbers expressed as fractions, we first rename one or both of them (if necessary) so that they are expressed with a common denominator; when we need to divide a pair of numbers expressed as decimals we multiply each by a power of ten, if necessary, so that the divisor is a natural number.

Children quickly discover that the algorithm for whole number division can be used with decimals also, with a few added features. Before these "new" features are introduced, problems corresponding to the "zero remainder" case with whole numbers are usually considered, so that children can discover how the basic algorithm parallels that for the whole numbers.

Example:

"If 4 boys share $1.28, how much will each receive?" The dividend can be represented either with real or play money (1 dollar, 2 dimes, and 8 pennies) or with more generalized models such as Dienes blocks (1 flat, 2 longs, and 8 units). The partitioning into 4 equivalent parts is represented exactly as with whole number division, i.e., the 1 is first traded for 10 tenths, then the 12 tenths and 8 hundredths are partitioned. Thus, each boy receives 3 tenths and 2 hundredths or 32 hundredths ($.32).

After several such relatively easy problems—accompanied by concrete representation with blocks, semiconcrete representation with

place value devices, and semiabstract representation with expanded forms —
and after numerous opportunities to observe and discuss such things as
relationships to whole number division, relationships to multiplication of
decimals, and apparent rules for decimal points in the quotients, children
will be ready for some new discoveries. Most of these are related to nonzero
remainder situations with whole numbers. In time, children will combine
these discoveries into two key generalizations:

1. Given *any* numbers a and b (where $b \neq 0$), there is a number c such that
   $c \times b = a$, i.e., we can find the quotient of any two numbers (with the
   usual nonzero divisor restriction), without any remainder.
2. Given any such numbers a and b, we can always find a number d such
   that $d \times b$ is as close to a as we wish. That is, the process of finding the
   actual quotient of a and b sometimes "goes on and on" but we can
   terminate the process at any point to get an approximation of the quotient that is close enough for *practical* considerations. (Although this
   concept will probably not be fully developed until beyond the elementary
   school, it can certainly be born there.)

   One of the first discoveries leading to these generalizations is related
to the discovery that annexing zeroes to a decimal numeral does not affect
its value, e.g., .3 = .30 = .300, or 43 = 43. = 43.0 = 43.00, etc. This concept
can be used to extend the usefulness of division. For example, given a
problem such as 2.3 ÷ 4, suppose a Dienes block is chosen as the unit.
Then 2 blocks and 3 flats can be separated into 4 piles (after trading 2 blocks
for 20 flats), with 5 flats (tenths) in each pile, and with 3 flats (tenths) left
over. Can any of the leftovers be distributed among the four piles? With

$$
\begin{array}{r}
.5 \\
4\overline{\smash{\big)}\,2.3} \\
\underline{2.0} \\
.3
\end{array}
$$

some reflection on this, children should eventually suggest that the 3 flats
be traded for 30 longs—7 longs can then be put in each pile. (If 3 flats
represent 3 tenths, then 30 longs represent 30 hundredths.) There will
then be only 2 longs left over. This manipulation can ultimately lead, with

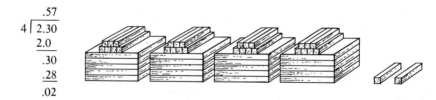

$$
\begin{array}{r}
.57 \\
4\overline{\smash{\big)}\,2.30} \\
\underline{2.0} \\
.30 \\
\underline{.28} \\
.02
\end{array}
$$

discussion and guidance, to understanding the corresponding computation. By trading the 2 longs (hundredths) each for 10 units (thousandths) and distributing them among the four piles, the process will be completed and the corresponding computation made meaningful.

$$
\begin{array}{r}
.575 \\
4{\overline{\smash{)}}\,2.300} \\
-\,2.0 \\
\hline
.30 \\
-\,.28 \\
\hline
.020 \\
-\,.020 \\
\hline
0
\end{array}
$$

.575 ← Each pile contains 5 tenths (flats), 7 hundredths (longs), and 5 thousandths (units), the equivalent of 575 thousandths (units).

0 ← There is nothing left over.

The usefulness of annexing zeros is also revealed in problems with divisors that are not natural numbers, e.g., "If a glass holds 1.6 cups of milk, how many glasses of milk can be poured from a quart (4 cups) of milk?"

$$1.6{\overline{\smash{)}}\,4}$$

Several manipulative experimentations may lead to the solution, and such an approach is recommended as a first step. (The reader should be able to envision them without our help.) In time, the child can be led to recall two generalizations he has previously learned as a technique for solving problems of this sort: first, that a quotient such as $4 \div 1.6$ is unaffected if both numbers are multiplied by any nonzero number, and second, that multiplying a number by 10, 100, 1000, etc. can be accomplished by shifting places. Using these, the quotient $4 \div 1.6$ can be renamed to the equivalent $40 \div 16$ and then solved by previously learned techniques.

$$
1.6{\overline{\smash{)}}\,4} \rightarrow
\begin{array}{r}
2.5 \\
16{\overline{\smash{)}}\,40.0} \\
32 \\
\hline
8.0 \\
8.0 \\
\hline
0
\end{array}
$$

Rather than rewrite the expression, various short cuts for locating the decimal point in the quotient can eventually be introduced:

$$1.6{\overline{\smash{)}}\,4.0}$$

The divisors in the preceding examples, 4 and 1.6, were carefully chosen, as they should be at first, to avoid introducing too many new ideas at once. That is, when 1.6 is multiplied by 10, the result has only 2s in its prime factorization and divisors whose only prime factors are 2 and/or 5 correspond to terminating decimals. Until children are ready for the next step, divisors should be restricted to powers of 2 or powers of 5 (or such numbers multiplied or divided by powers of 10, e.g., .02 or 1.25). Alternately, *both* dividend and divisor can be chosen so that the dividend (or 10^n times the dividend) is a multiple of the divisor, e.g., $3.6 \div 3$, $.21 \div .7$, etc.

In time, arbitrary divisors and dividends should be introduced. This is when children will discover that sometimes the division process "goes on and on." Introduction of repeating decimals in quotients involves no new skill in the division process, but leads to the question of rounding quotients and settling for approximations when solving practical problems. (Notation such as 1.3333 . . . or $1.\overline{3}$ can be introduced, if children are interested; but are not normally used to represent solutions of ordinary problems.) The question of rounding should not be new to children by this time, so it is not particularly difficult to use the number line, Dienes blocks, or related materials to establish the notion that in the problem below, for example, the quotient $3.2 \div 7$ is between .45 and .46 but is closer to .46.

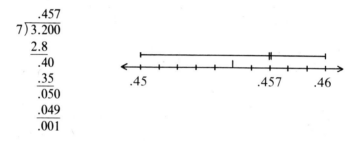

If accuracy to the nearest hundredth will do, then .46 is an acceptable answer; but if more accuracy is desired, the process can be continued indefinitely. Most children grasp this idea quite slowly, after much practice; and it is not uncommon for some to really understand it only after the elementary school years.

Some children, however, find that repeating decimals generated by division provides interesting enrichment topics for exploration. A few such problems are therefore suggested here.

Thus, for which divisions does the quotient repeat and for which does it terminate? We have already noted that the key to this is the divisor: Those divisors whose prime factors include only 2s or 5s will always terminate, while others repeat (unless the dividend is a multiple of the divisor). This can be discovered by dividing 1 in turn by 2, 3, 4, 5, 6, etc. (that is, finding the decimal equivalents of successive unit fractions) and noting which terminate and which repeat. For those who need a hint, prime factorization of the divisors (denominators) may help. Children who are proficient with bases other than ten can repeat this exercise in different bases to see that the distinction between terminating and repeating "decimals" is indeed dependent on the prime factors of the base. For example, in base six, the fractions $\frac{1}{2}$, $\frac{1}{3}$, $\frac{1}{4}$, $\frac{1}{6}$, $\frac{1}{8}$, and $\frac{1}{9}$ have terminating "decimal" (hexigesimal?) equivalents, whereas $\frac{1}{5}$, $\frac{1}{10}$, $\frac{1}{20}$, etc., do not, since the prime factors of 6 are 2 and 3.

In doing the preceding exercise (in base ten), one question that arises is this: If a decimal does not terminate, how long is the block of repeating digits? How long *could* it be? A few primes are particularly interesting in this regard. For example, the decimal equivalent of $\frac{1}{7}$, $0.\overline{142857}$, contains 6 digits in its repeating block; a curious pattern emerges with the decimal equivalents of $\frac{2}{7}, \frac{3}{7}, \frac{4}{7}, \frac{5}{7}$, and $\frac{6}{7}$: The digits for each of these decimals repeat in the same cycle as for $\frac{1}{7}$, e.g., $\frac{2}{7} = 0.\overline{285714}$. If we add the first 3 digits of one of these blocks to the second 3 digits, another interesting pattern emerges:

$$\frac{1}{7}: \quad \begin{array}{r} 142 \\ + 857 \\ \hline 999 \end{array} \qquad \frac{2}{7}: \quad \begin{array}{r} 285 \\ + 714 \\ \hline 999 \end{array} \qquad \frac{3}{7}: \quad \begin{array}{r} 428 \\ + 571 \\ \hline 999 \end{array}$$

The same pattern can be found for certain other primes, including 17, 19, 23, 29, and 47, e.g., $\frac{1}{17} = .\overline{0588235294117647}$.

If we plot both $\frac{1}{3}$ and .3 on a number line, we note that the coordinate of .3 is to the left of that of $\frac{1}{3}$, i.e., $.3 < \frac{1}{3}$. This can be verified numerically, i.e., $\frac{3}{10} < \frac{1}{3}$ or $.3 < .3\frac{1}{3}$. If the unit distance is sufficiently large, or if we view an enlarged "close up" of the interval from .3 to $\frac{1}{3}$ ($\frac{1}{30}$ of the unit), it can be noted that $.3 < .33 < \frac{1}{3}$. Again, this can be verified numerically: $.30 < .33 < .33\frac{1}{3}$ or $\frac{3}{10} < \frac{33}{100} < \frac{1}{3}$. The coordinate of .33 is .03 units closer to $\frac{1}{3}$ than the coordinate of .3. (It is located at the point .9 of the distance between the coordinates of .3 and $\frac{1}{3}$.) This may be repeated several times, either with the number line or numerically and it can be noted that as the number of 3s in the decimal .333 . . . 3 is increased, the number gets closer and closer to $\frac{1}{3}$—but never quite gets there. While few elementary school children, if any, can be expected to fully understand this, it can start them thinking, intuitively, about the *limit* concept: The number $\frac{1}{3}$ is the *limit* of the sequence .3, .33, .333, .333, ... That is, by extending the number of digits sufficiently in a decimal of the form .333 . . . 3, we can get closer and closer to $\frac{1}{3}$, though no *finite* number of such digits ever yields a number that *equals* $\frac{1}{3}$.

Some children enjoy adding repeating decimals. This must be done left to right, with any necessary carrying done by some sort of "scratch" method. For example, consider the sum of $\frac{1}{7}$ and $\frac{2}{7}$, each expressed as decimals:

Step 1	**Step 2**	**Step 3**
.142857 . . .	.142857 . . .	.142857 . . .
+ .285714 . . .	+ .285714 . . .	+ .285714 . . .
.3	.3̸2	.3̸27
	4	4

Step 4	**Final step**	
.142857 . . .	.142857 . . .	
+ .285714 . . .	+ .285714 . . . = .428571 . . . = $\frac{3}{7}$	
.3̸27̸5	.3̸27̸5̸61	
4 8	4 8 7	

Adding the decimal equivalents of $\frac{1}{3}$ and $\frac{2}{3}$ in this way, we have:

$$.3333 \ldots$$
$$+ .6666 \ldots$$
$$\overline{.9999 \ldots}$$

Since $\frac{1}{3} + \frac{2}{3} = 1$, this shows the rather curious fact that $1 = .9999. \ldots$ (Again, 1 is the *limit* of the sequence .9, .99, .999, ...)

Each terminating decimal *can*, in fact, be written in three ways. For example:

$$.275 \qquad \text{(the conventional way)}$$
$$.27500000 \ldots \qquad \text{or} \qquad .275\overline{0}$$
$$.27499999 \ldots \qquad \text{or} \qquad .274\overline{9}$$

A familiar technique for suggesting the equivalence of, say, .5 and $.4\overline{9}$ is this:

Example:

Let

$$n = .4\overline{9}$$

Then

$$10n = 4.\overline{9}$$

and

$$10n - n = 9n = 4.\overline{9} - .4\overline{9} = 4.5$$

Since

$$9n = 4.5, \qquad n = 4.5 \div 9 = .5$$
$$\therefore .4\overline{9} = .5$$

Although most children find this difficult to accept, some at least find it interesting and curious. This would, of course, normally be regarded as an enrichment topic and only for certain children.

Percentage, Ratio, and Relationships Between Notations

Fraction and decimal notations for fractional numbers can be developed independently; but when both are taught, relationships between the notations should be emphasized, particularly when decimals are introduced in terms of fractions. Both of the two basic ideas commonly taught are relatively simple. The first is that of conversion — expressing a given number in one notation, given the other. That is, given a (terminating) decimal, express it as a fraction; or given a fraction, express it as a decimal. The second idea involves intermixing the notations used most frequently in certain division situations, e.g., expressing a quotient as $.45\frac{5}{7}$.

The conversion skill is basically one of understanding the meanings of the two kinds of numerals, and if these understandings have been carefully developed, children have little difficulty in shifting back and forth between notations whenever it is convenient to do so. If children recognize that .35 *means* 35 hundredths (and are accustomed to reading it as such, rather than "point three five"), then assuming that they also have learned to associate "n-hundredths" with the fraction $\frac{n}{100}$, the fact that $.35 = \frac{35}{100}$ (or $\frac{7}{20}$) is obvious. Models for developing the concepts underlying the two notation systems are basically identical. Similarly, if children associate the fraction $\frac{7}{20}$ with the quotient $7 \div 20$, i.e., the result of dividing 7 "things" into 20 parts, and if they are also familiar with the algorithm for determining the quotient $20\overline{)7.00}$, then again the fact that $\frac{7}{20} = .35$ is easy to see. When converting a fraction greater than 1, such as $2\frac{3}{4}$, to decimal notation, children can readily discover two options: Either think of $2\frac{3}{4}$ as $\frac{11}{4}$ and divide $(11 \div 4)$ or think of $2\frac{3}{4}$ as 2 plus $\frac{3}{4}$, divide 3 by 4 and add 2. Only when a fraction $\frac{a}{b}$ is to be expressed as a decimal and either a is not a multiple of b or $a \cdot 10^n$ is not a multiple of b, e.g., $\frac{2}{3}$, does the more difficult (but in some ways more interesting) question of repeating decimals arise.

The second skill, the intermixing of notations, is more difficult to develop but again depends basically on understanding both of the two notations. Mature children can understand at least fairly simple instances of mixed notation, e.g., $.3\frac{1}{2}$ means three and one-half tenths. The number line or blocks can be used to verify that $3\frac{1}{2}$ tenths is equivalent to 35 hundredths. Also, once children understand how remainders can be divided

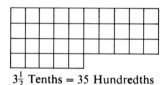

$3\frac{1}{2}$ Tenths = 35 Hundredths

and added to the rest of the quotient, and once they understand division with decimals, these ideas can be combined to intermix the two notations.

$$
\begin{array}{ccc}
3\frac{1}{2} & .3\frac{1}{2} & .35 \\
2\overline{)7} & 2\overline{).7} & 2\overline{).70} \\
\underline{6} & \underline{.6} & \underline{.60} \\
1 & .1 & .10 \\
& & \underline{.10} \\
\end{array}
$$

Headlines such as "3.5 Billion Dollar Budget Approved" provide still another mixture of notations similar to that used in scientific notation, where a number less than ten is multiplied by a power of ten to express a very large or very small number. This notation is generally beyond the capabilities (and interest) of elementary school children, although many can understand the meaning of such expressions if they are carefully examined.

Children frequently hear numerical relationships expressed as percentages and as ratios. "Three out of four doctors recommend such-and-such," or "Automobile sales are up 40 percent over last year" are typical of messages received from TV commercials and newspaper head-lines. So, too, "60 miles per hour" and "3 for 35 cents" are typical of the household expressions children begin to understand, intuitively, before studying them more formally, although the common characteristic tacitly described by such diverse expressions is usually not fully understood until much later. In each case, these expressions involve pairs of numbers whose quotients express a *rate*. The pair is either stated explicitly (3 out of 4, 3 for 35 cents) or implied (40 percent means 40 out of 100, and 60 miles per hour means 60 miles in 1 hour). Since the indicated rate is the quotient of two numbers, it may be expressed as a fraction or as a decimal. A second implied but unstated idea of the ratio concept is that a *given* pair of numbers is one ordered pair of a particular linear function, all of whose pairs are related "at the same rate," i.e., have the same quotient. This is an important idea, which teachers need to help children develop (gradually). The exercises below belong to one general "class" of problems to which this concept can be applied.

Examples:

Given an ordered pair of numbers (a, b) and a number c, determine the number d such that either

$$\frac{a}{b} = \frac{c}{d} \qquad \text{or} \qquad \frac{a}{b} = \frac{d}{c}$$

(a) If $\frac{3}{4}$ of all the children in a school bring their lunches and there are 400 children in the school, how many bring their lunches?

$$a = 3$$
$$b = 4 \qquad\qquad \frac{3}{4} = \frac{d}{400} \qquad\qquad d = 300$$
$$c = 400$$

(b) If 300 children bring their lunches and this is 75 percent of the children in the school, how many children are there altogether in the school?

$$a = 75$$
$$b = 100 \qquad\qquad \frac{75}{100} = \frac{300}{d} \qquad\qquad d = 400$$
$$c = 300$$

(c) If a car travels at 60 miles per hour for 3 hours, how far will it go?

$$a = 60$$
$$b = 1 \qquad\qquad \frac{60}{1} = \frac{d}{3} \qquad\qquad d = 180$$
$$c = 3$$

(d) If a car travels at 60 miles per hour, how long does it take to go 180 miles?

$$a = 60$$
$$b = 1 \qquad \frac{60}{1} = \frac{180}{d} \qquad d = 3$$
$$c = 180$$

(e) If candy sells at 3 pieces for 5 cents, how many pieces can you buy for a quarter?

$$a = 3$$
$$b = 5 \qquad \frac{3}{5} = \frac{d}{25} \qquad d = 15$$
$$c = 25$$

(f) If candy sells at 3 pieces for 5 cents, how much would a dozen pieces cost?

$$a = 3$$
$$b = 5 \qquad \frac{3}{5} = \frac{12}{d} \qquad d = 20$$
$$c = 12$$

(g) 3 is what percent of 5?

$$a = 3$$
$$b = 5 \qquad \frac{3}{5} = \frac{d}{100} \qquad d = 60$$
$$c = 100$$

(h) If a child sleeps 10 hours every night, what percent of his time does he spend asleep?

$$a = 10$$
$$b = 24 \qquad \frac{10}{24} = \frac{d}{100} \qquad d = 41\tfrac{2}{3}$$
$$c = 100$$

(i) How much is saved if a 25 dollar coat is bought at a "10 percent off" sale?

$$a = 10$$
$$b = 100 \qquad \frac{10}{100} = \frac{d}{25} \qquad d = 2.50$$
$$c = 25$$

It should be clear that various approaches can be used to solve such problems; the equivalent-fractions format is only one. It should also be clear that *order* is important: The two rate pairs must be expressed in the same order. But this order is arbitrary. For example, in (e) above, a child may think "5 cents for 3 pieces," i.e.,

$$a = 5$$
$$b = 3 \qquad \frac{5}{3} = \frac{25}{d} \qquad d = 15$$
$$c = 25$$

Also, some of the "given" numbers may be obscure and it may require varying degrees of insight to find them, e.g., (e) through (i) above.

Many of the activities proposed for developing the equivalent-fractions concept provide a background for helping children to solve rate pair problems. Early introduction and frequent exposure to problem situations of this kind are necessary, of course, if children are to develop gradual insight into the rate concept. Physical manipulation of objects, pictures, graphs, tables, and number lines can help lead to understanding.

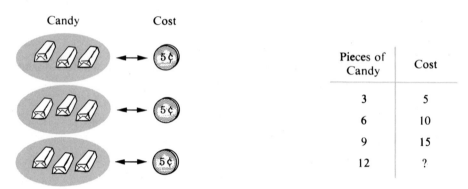

Pieces of Candy	Cost
3	5
6	10
9	15
12	?

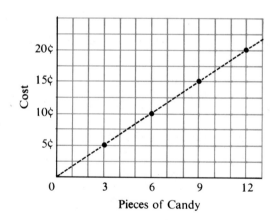

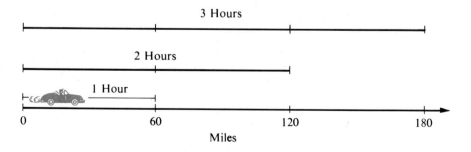

When ratios are expressed as fractions, an effective technique is to *label* the data, e.g.,

$$\frac{\text{pieces of candy}}{\text{cost}} \qquad \frac{3}{5} \qquad \frac{\square}{25}$$

$$\frac{\text{miles}}{\text{hours}} \qquad \frac{60}{1} \qquad \frac{180}{\triangle}$$

When percentage is introduced, care should be taken to ensure that children understand its meaning, and some practice will be required per se on conversion exercises among the *three* notations—fractions, decimals, and percents. Special attention should be given to the meaning of percents less than 10 (3%), those greater than 100 (150%), and those expressed in mixed notations using fractions or decimals ($4\frac{1}{2}$%, 40.7%, $\frac{1}{2}$%). Ten-by-ten arrays, or models such as money can help. In time, various applications such as finding percentages of increase or decrease will be within the capabilities of some, but not all, elementary school children. As always, teachers need to progress gradually, carefully assess children's readiness before extending the idea, and provide a wide variety of problems and visual assistance.

Projects, Questions, and Suggested Activities

1. In case you did not try exercise 6 from Chapter 4, you may wish to try it now.
2. Find the "decimal" equivalents of $\frac{1}{2}$, $\frac{1}{3}$, $\frac{1}{4}$, . . . , $\frac{1}{10}$ in bases 2, 3, 4, . . . , 10. What patterns can you find? What are the decimal equivalents of $\frac{1}{9}$, $\frac{2}{9}$, $\frac{3}{9}$, . . . , $\frac{8}{9}$? Of $\frac{1}{11}$, $\frac{2}{11}$, $\frac{3}{11}$, . . . , $\frac{10}{11}$ (in base ten)?
3. Add a pair of repeating decimals with "cycles" of different lengths, e.g., $.\overline{09} + .\overline{027}$. How long is the block of repeating digits in the sum? Try $.\overline{12} + .\overline{3456}$. What is $.\overline{5} \times .\overline{3}$? How many digits are in the cycle?
4. Make sets of blocks to represent fractions as suggested on pp. 399–400. Try them with children in teaching order, equivalence, addition, and subtraction.
5. Which form of fractional numbers, fraction or decimal, is easier to use for computation? Consider these:

$$\begin{array}{r} .250 \\ + .375 \\ \hline \end{array} \quad \text{vs.} \quad \frac{1}{4} + \frac{3}{8} \qquad\qquad \begin{array}{r} .333 \ldots \\ + .666 \ldots \\ \hline \end{array} \quad \text{vs.} \quad \frac{1}{3} + \frac{2}{3}$$

$$\begin{array}{r} .25 \\ + .60 \\ \hline \end{array} \quad \text{vs.} \quad \frac{1}{4} + \frac{3}{5} \qquad\qquad \begin{array}{r} .142857142857 \ldots \\ + .428571428571 \ldots \\ \hline \end{array} \quad \text{vs.} \quad \frac{1}{7} + \frac{3}{7}$$

or

$$\begin{array}{r} .375 \\ + .700 \\ \hline \end{array} \quad \text{vs.} \quad \frac{3}{8} + \frac{7}{10} \qquad\qquad \begin{array}{r} .333333 \ldots \\ + .833833 \ldots \\ \hline \end{array} \quad \text{vs.} \quad \frac{1}{3} + \frac{5}{6}$$

$$\begin{array}{c} .4375 \\ +\ .4000 \end{array} \quad \text{vs.} \quad \tfrac{7}{16} + \tfrac{2}{5} \qquad\qquad \begin{array}{c} .161616\ldots \\ +\ .858585\ldots \end{array} \quad \text{vs.} \quad \tfrac{16}{99} + \tfrac{85}{99}$$

Can you devise a division algorithm for repeating decimals?

6. Examine several textbook series to find out where decimals are first introduced and how much is done with them at each grade level. Do the same for fractions. Compare your findings. Where is the metric system of linear measure introduced?

7. Start a file of fraction and decimal games and activities by surveying past issues of *The Arithmetic Teacher*. You will find many.

8. Consider this model for the rational number system: Construct a set of lattice points and a conventional coordinate system on those points, as follows:

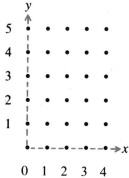

Associate each *point,* whose coordinates are (x, y), $x \in N$, $y \in W$, with the fraction $\frac{y}{x}$. Use this model to answer the following:

(a) Describe geometrically the relationship between *equivalent* fractions. In any set of equivalent fractions, which point corresponds to the one *reduced* fraction? Given an arbitrary fraction, how can one tell, geometrically, whether it is reduced? Which points must be "deleted," i.e., which points cannot correspond to fractions?

(b) Find a geometric meaning for *order.*

$$\frac{a}{b} < \frac{c}{d}$$

(c) Which set of points represents the fractions equivalent to $\frac{1}{1}$? Describe the geometric relationship between this set of points and those corresponding to pairs of reciprocals (e.g., $\frac{2}{3}$ and $\frac{3}{2}$).

(d) Find geometric interpretations for addition, subtraction, multiplication, and division of fractional numbers.

(e) Extend the model to include negative coordinates. Describe geometrically the relationship between

$$\frac{a}{b} \qquad \text{and} \qquad -\!\left(\frac{a}{b}\right)$$

(f) Extend the model to include rational coordinates and thus complex fractions, e.g.,

$$\frac{\frac{2}{3}}{\frac{4}{5}}.$$

Show geometrically that

$$\frac{\frac{2}{3}}{\frac{4}{5}} = \frac{5}{6}$$

Suggested Readings

Armstrong, Charles. "'Fradécent'—A Game Using Equivalent Fractions, Decimals, and Percents." *The Arithmetic Teacher*, March 1972, pp. 222–23.

> Just what the title implies. A card game.

Cotler, Stanley. "Charged Particles: A Model for Teaching Operations with Directed Numbers." *The Arithmetic Teacher*, May 1969, pp. 349–53.

> Another model for integer operations: Positively and negatively charged particles in a field. Other games and strategies for these operations can be found in this issue in the articles by Mauthe (pp. 354–56), Mehl and Mehl (pp. 357–59), Sherzer (pp. 360–62), Frank (pp. 395–97), and Milne (pp. 397–98).

Gardner, Martin. "Mathematical Games." *Scientific American*, March 1970, pp. 121–24.

> Cyclic numbers, e.g., 142857 ($\frac{1}{7} = .\overline{142857}$).

Green, George F., Jr. "A Model for Teaching Multiplication of Fractional Numbers." *The Arithmetic Teacher*, January 1973, pp. 5–9.

> More detail on the algorithm for multiplication of fractional numbers discussed in this chapter. In the same issue, see Sherzer's article (pp. 27–28) on addition of fractional numbers, and Sister Marijane Werner's article (pp. 61–64) which describes a number line model for subtracting integers.

Mayor, John R. "Science and Mathematics: 1970's—A Decade of Change." *The Arithmetic Teacher*, April 1970, pp. 293–97.

> Presenting, among other things, a strong case for teaching decimals before common fractions.

10. Teaching Probability and Statistics

There are strong arguments for introducing elementary school children to certain basic elements of probability and statistics. As with number theory and geometry, these topics are appealing to young children. There is an element of intrigue to such statements as, "It will probably rain today" or "I'll bet Miss Jones wears her red dress tomorrow" or "The chances of having chocolate ice cream for dessert are pretty good." Such nonfactual statements become more interesting as children encounter confirmations of their predictions—or those of others. There is a further appeal in dealing with mathematical situations for which the answer is speculative and empirically determined rather than exact and precisely predictable. Children enjoy guessing and then testing their guesses against experimentally accumulated evidence. This motivation can gradually and subtly lead them to intuitive understanding of some of the not-so-imprecise "laws" of probability and of some of the basics of statistics; and in the process, many valuable mathematical skills (searching for patterns, evaluating evidence, making conjectures, computation) are developed.

That probability and statistics are of vital importance in such diverse adult endeavors as medical research, insurance, marketing, agriculture, manufacturing, traffic, and politics cannot be denied, but can probably be ignored insofar as children are concerned. There is plenty of time beyond the elementary years to be concerned about that. Yet, as with geometry, if some of the basic ideas are encountered intuitively at an early age, subsequent, more serious encounters with the topic are likely to appear more plausible to them than if early experience were lacking.

1. Mathematical Review

What are "probability" and "statistics" and how are they related? Precise definitions are unnecessary here, but basically we usually think of probability as that branch of mathematics dealing with the likelihood of certain events occurring under certain circumstances and under certain basic assumptions. A probability model provides a basis for making predictions about the outcome of a repetitive experiment or experience. Probability is the basic tool of statistics. Given a probability model to "describe" the probable outcomes of an experiment, statistics deals with accumulated data which is analyzed for the purpose of (a) describing a situation or (b) making decisions, on the basis of information obtained from samples of a very large collection. We need not concern ourselves with all the complexities of probability theory or statistical theory; rather, it suffices to examine a few rudimentary ideas and relationships from the two fields.

Probability

Basic Concepts

Probability is usually introduced in the context of rather common games of chance. (Indeed, Pascal and Fermat are commonly credited with systematizing the theory in the course of their correspondence about a problem posed by an active French gambler.) Typical experiments include rolling dice, flipping coins, or drawing cards from a deck. There are several significant common features of such experiments: Each can be repeated as frequently as one desires; the set of all possible *outcomes* is finite and easily identifiable. For example, when a coin is tossed, 2 and only 2 possibilities exist—heads or tails. There is no certainty which outcome will occur on a particular trial, yet the structural nature of the apparatus and the assumptions about its use suggest intuitively that if the experiment is repeated enough times, each outcome is likely to occur with a particular frequency. If a single, perfectly balanced, die is rolled many times, for example, any given number (from 1 to 6) will *probably* occur *about* once in every six rolls. The more times the die is rolled, the closer the actual ratio is to this theoretical ratio, until, finally, each possible outcome (i.e., each number from 1 to 6) will occur with equal frequency.

The term *sample space* (SS) is commonly used to denote the set of all possible outcomes of a particular experiment. For example, if a coin is tossed, the sample space is $\{H, T\}$. The sample space depends on the experiment, of course: If the experiment is tossing 2 coins, say a penny and a nickel, the sample space might be designated (H, h), (H, t), (T, h), (T, t), (where H and T designate, say, the penny and h and t the nickel). If a red die and a white die are tossed, either simultaneously or consecutively, the sample space is frequently portrayed on a coordinate grid, where each point represents one of 36 ordered pairs of numbers (see top of p. 442).

Each outcome of an experiment is sometimes called a (simple) *event*. For example, in the experiment of rolling a single die there are 6 simple events: rolling a '1', rolling a '2', etc. But there are other, more

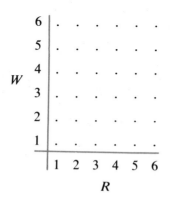

interesting events that can be considered for this or other experiments. For example, rolling an even number, rolling a number greater than 2, rolling a prime, and so on, are all events. An event, then, can be described as a subset of the sample space; a few events (subsets of $\{1, 2, 3, 4, 5, 6,\}$), which we label $A, B, C, \ldots$, include:

A: Rolling a two: $\{2\}$
B: Rolling an even number: $\{2, 4, 6\}$
C: Rolling a prime: $\{2, 3, 5\}$
D: Rolling a number greater than 2: $\{3, 4, 5, 6\}$
E: Rolling a number greater than 6: $\emptyset$
F: Rolling a number less than 7: $\{1, 2, 3, 4, 5, 6\}$
G: Rolling an odd number: $\{1, 3, 5\}$

It should be noted from examples E and F that an event might range from including *no* elements of the sample space (E is impossible) to including *all* of them (F is certain to occur).

Furthermore, it is often of interest to consider two or more events. Using the above subsets of the sample space $\{1, 2, 3, 4, 5, 6\}$, the event "rolling an even number or rolling a prime" can be designated $B \cup C = \{2, 3, 4, 5, 6\}$; the event "rolling a prime greater than 2" could be described as $C \cap D = \{3, 5\}$; or we may be interested in events such as "rolling a number which is not prime" $\bar{C} = \{1, 4, 6\}$. Events that cannot both occur such as B and G are called *mutually exclusive* events ($B \cap G = \emptyset$).

For a given experiment with sample space SS, if E is an event in that sample space, then the probability of E, designated $P(E)$, is a rational number in the interval from 0 to 1 (a fractional number, sometimes expressed as a decimal or percent). The assignment of probabilities to events is made according to certain basic agreements:

1. If an event E cannot occur, i.e., if E is not in the sample space of the experiment, then

$$P(E) = 0$$

2. If an event is certain to occur, i.e., if E is the entire sample space, then

$$P(E) = 1$$

3. If two events E_1 and E_2 are mutually exclusive (i.e., disjoint), then the probability that E_1 *or* E_2 will occur is

$$P(E_1 \cup E_2) = P(E_1) + P(E_2)$$

This can be extended, of course, to include 3, 4, or more events. In fact, implicit in these agreements is that the sum of the probabilities of all outcomes in the sample space must be 1, for if $E_1, E_2, \ldots, E_n$ are *all* the outcomes in a sample space, then they are mutually exclusive and their union is the sample space, whose probability is 1.

    If the nature of an experiment is such that there are n outcomes in the sample space and if each outcome is assumed to be equally likely to occur on any trial, then each outcome has probability $\frac{1}{n}$. Thus, if an event includes m possible outcomes, the probability of that event is $\frac{m}{n}$. For the experiment of rolling a single die, then, we have, for events A through G:

$$
\begin{aligned}
P(A) &= \tfrac{1}{6} \\
P(B) &= \tfrac{3}{6} \quad \text{or} \quad \tfrac{1}{2} \\
P(C) &= \tfrac{3}{6} \quad \text{or} \quad \tfrac{1}{2} \\
P(D) &= \tfrac{4}{6} \quad \text{or} \quad \tfrac{2}{3} \\
P(E) &= 0 \\
P(F) &= 1 \\
P(G) &= \tfrac{3}{6} \quad \text{or} \quad \tfrac{1}{2}
\end{aligned}
$$

Furthermore,

$$P(A \cup D) = P(A) + P(D) = \tfrac{1}{6} + \tfrac{4}{6} = \tfrac{5}{6}$$

since A and D are mutually exclusive, whereas

$$P(B \cup C) \neq P(B) + P(C)$$

because B and C are not mutually exclusive.

$$P(B \cup C) = \tfrac{5}{6} \qquad \text{but} \qquad P(B) + P(C) = \tfrac{3}{6} + \tfrac{3}{6} = 1$$

Since

$$B \cap C = \{2\} \qquad P(B \cap C) = \tfrac{1}{6}$$

and we may note that

$$P(B \cup C) = P(B) + P(C) - P(B \cap C)$$

i.e., $\frac{5}{6} = \frac{3}{6} + \frac{3}{6} - \frac{1}{6}$. This is true in general for any pair of events for an experiment.

    The nature of some experiments is such that we cannot "automatically" predict that each outcome is equally likely to occur. For example, consider the experiment of tossing a thumbtack on a table. There are two

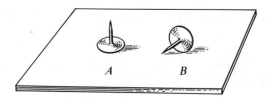

outcomes, A and B, in the sample space. What is $P(A)$? *If* we assume that A and B are equally likely to occur, then $P(A) = P(B) = \frac{1}{2}$. Although we are at liberty to make such an assumption, the model may be inconsistent with reality. The best way to determine such probabilities is to replicate the experiment many times, record the frequency of each outcome, and *then* decide on a theoretical probability for each. When this procedure is followed for theoretically predictable experiments such as flipping a coin or rolling a die, the observed frequencies may be inconsistent with the theoretical frequencies. In fact, they are quite *likely* to be different because of various physical sources of bias. It is difficult to structure completely unbiased experiments.

We are sometimes concerned in experiments with questions like this: If an event A occurs, what is the probability that event B will occur? Such a question is commonly phrased, "What is the probability of B, given A?" The probability of B, given A, is symbolized $P(B \mid A)$. If A and B are *independent* of each other, that is, if $P(B)$ is unaffected by the occurrence of A, then, of course, $P(B \mid A) = P(B)$. But this is not always the case. Consider the experiment of tossing a pair of dice, and these events:

A: The sum of the two numbers is 7.
B: The '2' on at least one die.

We can picture the sample space of the experiment as before and identify subsets A and B.

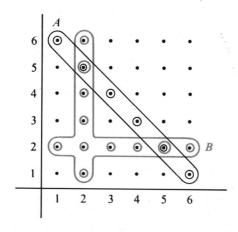

What is $P(B \mid A)$? That is, if the sum of the numbers on the dice is 7, what is the probability that there is a '2' on at least one of the dice? The sample space for this question is A, which has 6 elements; and since $B \cap A$ contains 2 elements, there are 2 chances out of 6 that B will occur. Thus, $P(B \mid A) = \frac{2}{6}$. Since $P(B) = \frac{11}{36}$ and $\frac{11}{36} \neq \frac{2}{6}$, $P(B \mid A) \neq P(B)$. We can note in this case that $P(B \cap A) = \frac{2}{36}$, that $P(A) = \frac{6}{36}$, and that

$$P(B \mid A) = \frac{P(A \cap B)}{P(A)}$$

i.e., $\frac{2}{36} \div \frac{6}{36} = \frac{2}{6}$. This relationship is true in general. Thus also

$$P(A \cap B) = P(A) \cdot P(B \mid A)$$

In general, if A and B are independent (which they are *not* in this case), then

$$P(A \cap B) = P(A) \cdot P(B)$$

Whether two events are independent is often intuitively obvious, although it may not always be so. Consider the following three events in an experiment in which both a coin is flipped and a die is rolled.

A: A '2' or a '3' appears on the die.
B: Neither '1' nor '2' appears on the die (i.e., '3', '4', '5', or '6' appears).
C: A coin lands "heads up."

In this case A and C would seem to be "independent" as would B and C, and both of these intuitive assertions are correct, as can be verified; it can also be verified that A and B are not independent. That is:

$$P(A \cap C) = P(A) \cdot P(C), \quad \text{i.e.,} \quad P(C) = P(C \mid A)$$
$$P(B \cap C) = P(B) \cdot P(C), \quad \text{i.e.,} \quad P(C) = P(C \mid B)$$
$$P(A \cap B) \neq P(A) \cdot P(B), \quad \text{i.e.,} \quad P(B) \neq P(B \mid A)$$

When the sample space and the events are illustrated as before, we see that

$$A \cap C = \{(2, H), (3, H)\}$$

$$P(A \cap C) = \tfrac{1}{6} \qquad P(A) = \tfrac{1}{3} \qquad P(C) = \tfrac{1}{2}$$

and $\frac{1}{3} \times \frac{1}{2} = \frac{1}{6}$, that is,

$$P(A) \cdot P(C) = P(A \cap C)$$

Similarly,

$$A \cap B = \{(3, T), (3, H)\}$$

$$P(A \cap B) = \tfrac{1}{6} \qquad P(A) = \tfrac{1}{3} \qquad P(B) = \tfrac{2}{3}$$

and $\tfrac{1}{6} \neq \tfrac{1}{3} \times \tfrac{2}{3}$, that is

$$P(A \cap B) \neq P(A) \cdot P(B)$$

On the other hand, $P(B \mid A) = \tfrac{1}{2}$, and since $\tfrac{1}{3} \times \tfrac{1}{2} = \tfrac{1}{6}$,

$$P(A) \cdot P(B \mid A) = P(A \cap B)$$

The reader should be able to verify that B and C are independent, i.e., that $P(C) = P(C \mid B)$ and thus

$$P(B \cap C) = P(B) \cdot P(C)$$

Suppose that X, Y, and Z are running for office and their chances of winning are $\tfrac{5}{10}$, $\tfrac{3}{10}$, and $\tfrac{2}{10}$, respectively. If Z withdraws, then what are X's new chances (the probability of X winning, given that Z cannot win)? $P(Z')$, the (original) probability that Z will *not* win, is $1 - \tfrac{2}{10}$ or $\tfrac{8}{10}$, so

$$P(X|Z') = \frac{P(X \cap Z')}{P(Z')} = \frac{p(x)}{p(z')} \qquad \text{(Why?)}$$

that is,

$$P(X|Z') = \tfrac{5}{10} \div \tfrac{8}{10} = \tfrac{5}{8}$$

Repetitive Experiments

In the case of repetitive or multistep experiments, analogous events are generally independent; for example, if the experiment of tossing a single die is repeated twice, the second toss is unaffected by the first. If events A and B, above, are considered separately for each of two repetitions of the experiment, we can ask such questions as, What is the probability of

> A on each trial?
> B on each trial?
> A on the first trial and B on the second?
> A on the first trial and A or B on the second?
> A on the first trial and A and B on the second?

The *fundamental counting principle* states that if there are x ways to do one thing and y ways to do a second, then there are $x \cdot y$ ways to do the first followed by the second. An analogous principle applies in probability: If, as here, events A and B have probabilities $\tfrac{2}{6}$ and $\tfrac{4}{6}$ respectively, then the probability of A on the first stage and B on the second stage is $\tfrac{2}{6} \times \tfrac{4}{6} = \tfrac{8}{36} = \tfrac{2}{9}$. Such results can be represented as ordered pairs, or with "tree diagrams" in which all paths satisfying the condition in question are singled out. Here we see that the number of paths satisfying A on the first trial and B on the second is 8 out of 36 or $\tfrac{2}{9}$.

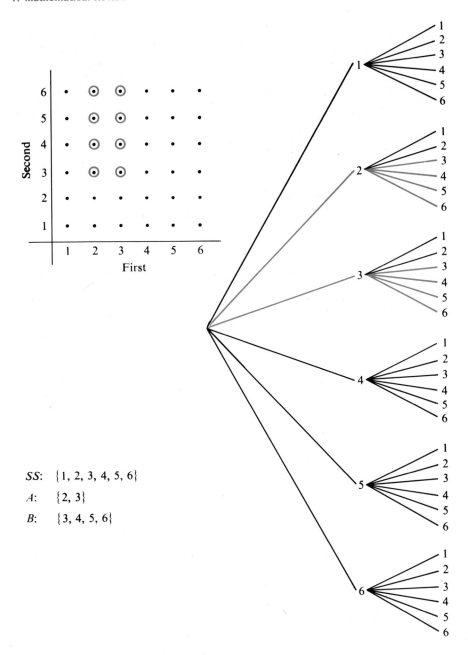

SS: {1, 2, 3, 4, 5, 6}

A: {2, 3}

B: {3, 4, 5, 6}

If we consider the probability of "B on the first and A or B on the second," we have $P(B) \cdot P(A \cup B)$ or

$$P(B) \cdot [P(A) + P(B) - P(A \cap B)] = \tfrac{2}{3}[\tfrac{1}{3} + \tfrac{2}{3} - \tfrac{1}{6}] = \tfrac{2}{3} \times \tfrac{5}{6} = \tfrac{10}{18} = \tfrac{20}{36}$$

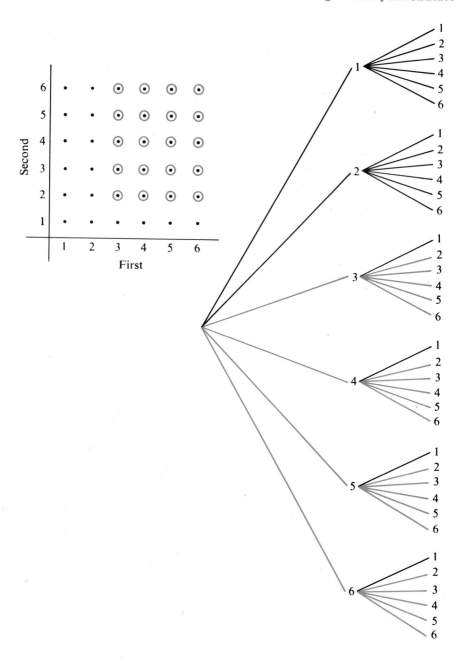

Similarly, the probability of "A on the first, and A and B on the second" is

$$P(A) \cdot [P(A) \cdot P(B \mid A)] = P(A) \cdot \left[P(A) \cdot \frac{P(A \cap B)}{P(B)} \right]$$

$$= \frac{1}{3} \times \left[\frac{1}{3} \times \frac{1}{2}\right] = \frac{1}{18}$$

or $\frac{2}{36}$.

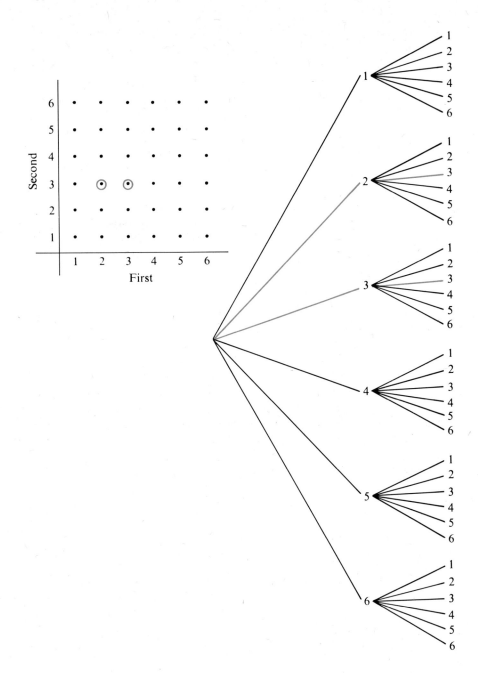

Some multistage experiments are such that the sample space for one stage is affected by that of its predecessor.

Examples:

(a) Draw a card from a deck of playing cards, then, without replacing it, draw a second card. While the sample space for the first stage contains 52 elements, that for the second contains only 51. Thus, for example, the probability of drawing a heart on the first draw and a spade on the second is $\frac{13}{52} \times \frac{13}{51} = \frac{13}{204}$.

(b) A box contains 10 colored cubes, 6 red, 3 white, and 1 black. Draw one cube at random; keep it, and then draw a second cube; keep it, and draw a third. What is the probability that the first cube was red, the second was also red, and the third was white? At the first step, there are 6 chances out of 10, so its probability is $\frac{6}{10}$; assuming that the first *was* red, there are 5 red cubes among the remaining 9, so the second-stage probability is $\frac{5}{9}$; since there are 3 white cubes among the 8 cubes remaining in the box, the third-stage probability is $\frac{3}{8}$. The three stages were independent, so the desired probability is $\frac{6}{10} \times \frac{5}{9} \times \frac{3}{8}$ or $\frac{1}{8}$.

When we draw 3 cubes from the box of colored cubes used in the last example, our concern may not be one of order. Consider, for example, the probability that *some* two of the cubes are red and the other is white. First, what is the sample space and how many elements does it contain? We may think of the experiment as one of choosing a 3-element subset from a set of 10 elements. How many such subsets are there? This can be determined in various ways—by trial and error, for example, although the process would be tedious. Recall that the entries in row 10 of Pascal's triangle are, respectively, the numbers of 0-element, 1-element, 2-element, . . . , 10-element subsets that can be formed from a 10-element set. But even constructing 10 rows of the triangle is rather time-consuming. The symbol $\binom{10}{3}$ is used to designate the number of 3-element subsets that can be formed from a 10-element set, and since in general $\binom{a}{b}$ can be evaluated as

$$\frac{a!}{b!(a-b)!} \qquad (0 \leqslant b \leqslant a,\ 0! = 1! = 1)$$

we have

$$\binom{10}{3} = \frac{10!}{3!7!} = \frac{10 \times 9 \times 8 \times 7 \times 6 \times 5 \times 4 \times 3 \times 2}{(3 \times 2)(7 \times 6 \times 5 \times 4 \times 3 \times 2)}$$

With judicious cancelling, this quickly simplifies to 120. Thus, the sample space for the experiment contains 120 elements (there are 120 possible ways to draw 3 cubes from a box of 10 cubes). How many of these subsets contain 2 reds and 1 white? Since there are 6 reds altogether and 3 whites, we can think, How many 2-element subsets are there in a set of 6 red cubes and how many 1-element subsets are there in a set of 3 white ones?

$$\binom{6}{2} = \frac{6!}{2!(4!)} \qquad \text{and} \qquad \binom{3}{1} = \frac{3!}{2!}$$

i.e., 15 and 3 respectively. So there are 15 ways to pick 2 reds and 3 ways to pick 1 white, i.e., 15×3 or 45 ways to pick 2 reds and 1 white. Thus, the probability is

$$\frac{\binom{6}{2} \cdot \binom{3}{1}}{\binom{10}{3}} = \frac{15 \cdot 3}{120} = \frac{45}{120} \qquad \text{or} \qquad \frac{3}{8}$$

Statistics

Sampling

Basic statistical notions center around the accumulation, tabulation, representation, and analysis of data. Some kinds of data are accessible enough that we can easily collect *all* of it (e.g., How tall are the children in Miss Jones' fourth grade class?). But more interesting questions are such that accumulating all necessary data would be either impractical or impossible. For example, suppose a machine is designed to produce say 1000 items each hour, and that there are important reasons for wanting those items to have certain measurable characteristics such as a particular size or weight. Since machines are subject to wear, it becomes necessary to *inspect* the products. But the inspection of each item may be impossible, so a random sample, say ten items each half-hour, might be inspected and decisions made about the entire (universal) batch (population) on the basis of that sample.

Many important and sometimes delicate questions must be considered in such sampling processes before we can place much confidence in decisions about the uncertain universal population based on the smaller sample population: What is the sample size? Was the sample actually chosen at random or was there some possible (albeit unintentional) bias involved? How diverse are the sample items? What extent of deviation from the desired standard is acceptable?

Answers to such questions can be highly technical and varied, depending in part upon the nature of the activity or experiment, its materials, and their intended use. While there are situations, some medical research or production, for example, where very small deviations from the accepted standard could be gravely important, an intuitive understanding of the technical aspects of sampling can be attained by considering relatively simple situations.

Suppose, for example, that a box is known to contain 1000 marbles but that nothing is known about their colors. If we are interested in predicting how many marbles there are of each color, we might pick a random sample of, say, 10 marbles. If 4 of them are red and 6 are black, we might make several conjectures: (1) Each marble in the box is either black or red. (2) There are more black marbles than red ones. Or (3) to be more "exact," $\frac{4}{10}$ of the marbles in the box are red and $\frac{6}{10}$ of them are black, i.e., the box contains 400 red and 600 black marbles.

Each of these is of course a guess, and our confidence in any of them might be either strengthened or weakened by repeating the experiment, thus, in effect, increasing the sample size. This may lead to new conjectures, but each remains a guess unless we choose to examine the entire population of 1000 marbles.

Analysis of Data

Once data for an experiment have been accumulated and recorded directly, they need to be organized in some effective way for analysis. If a large number of outcomes are to be accumulated, this can begin while the data are being gathered. For example, consider the experiment of rolling 2 dice and recording the sum of the resulting numbers. Since the outcomes predictably range from 2 to 12, this potential range of scores can be written down in advance, and the individual outcomes can be recorded with tally marks. This technique can be useful even in experiments for which the range is less predictable. For certain kinds of data, other preliminary steps might include *ranking*, i.e., listing outcomes in order from one extreme to the other, or grouping them in terms of intervals.

Percentile. At this stage, individual data, such as scores on a test, are frequently classified with respect to the entire collection of data. One statistic commonly employed for ranking such data is the *percentile*. To illustrate, suppose 10 children take a test and make the following scores:

$$32, 29, 28, 28, 27, 27, 27, 26, 20, 18$$

If we assume that *any* score is possible, the set of all possible scores could be represented (graphed) as a continuous line. It is useful, then, to think of each particular score as an *interval*: The score 29, for example, would be represented by the interval from 28.5 to 29.5. Since *two* children scored 28, each of these scores would be represented by *half* of the interval from 27.5 to 28.5, and since there are three 27s, each would be represented by $\frac{1}{3}$ of the interval from 26.5 to 27.5. The entire set of scores can be represented as shown here. The *n*th percentile for a given set of such scores, then, can be interpreted as the coordinate of the first point on the line below

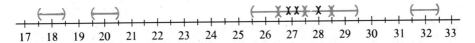

which n percent of the scores lie. For example, the 10th percentile for this set of scores is 18.5; the 25th percentile is 26 (25 percent of 10 is $2\frac{1}{2}$ so we must think in terms of "$2\frac{1}{2}$ scores"; the third score, represented by the interval from 25.5 to 26.5, is "divided in half" at the point whose coordinate is 26). The 50th percentile is 27.17 (correct to the nearest hundredth), since the lower 50 percent (half) of the ten scores include the three below the point labeled 26.5 and the first two of the three from 26.5 to 27.5. The coordinate of the 50th percentile point, then, is $26.5 + \frac{2}{3}$, or approximately $26.5 + 0.67$, i.e., 27.17. Similarly, the 75th percentile is 28.25.

The percentile rank of a particular score, such as 26, can be interpreted as the percentage of the scores (intervals) which lie to the left of the point labeled 26. In this case, then, the percentile rank of the score 26 is 25, since $2\frac{1}{2}$ of the 10 scores, i.e., 25 percent of them, are to the left of the point whose coordinate is 26. Even though no person scored 21, 22, 23, 24, or 25 in this case, the percentile rank of *each* of these scores would be 20, since 20 percent of the scores, i.e., 2 of the 10 scores, are to the left of each of these points.

Central Tendency. One of the most useful, and common, analyses of data is the measurement of the *central tendency* of those data. This measure is a single "typical" score which in some sense is considered representative of all of the data. Three different statistics are used for this purpose: The *mean, median,* and *mode.* Of these, the mean (arithmetic mean or average) is used most. By definition, the mean, generally designated as $\bar{x}$, of a set of scores (or other data) is the *sum* of those scores divided by the *number* of scores. For the scores 32, 29, 28, 28, 27, 27, 27, 26, 20, 18, then, the mean is $262 \div 10$ or 26.2.

The mode is the most frequently appearing score. In the case of the above data, the mode is 27. Frequently, a set of data is multimodal, i.e., two or more scores occur more frequently than others, although not necessarily with exactly *equal* frequency; in other cases, a set of data may have *no* mode, of course.

The median score is the 50th percentile. That is, it is the "middle" score, which is exactly midway between the scores that separate the upper and lower 50 percent of the scores. In the case of the data above, the median is 27, since the lower half of the scores are less than or equal to 27 and the upper half of the scores are greater than or equal to 27. In this particular case, then, the median happens to be the same as the mode; in the case of an odd number of scores, the median would simply be the middle one; whereas for an even number of scores, it is midway between the largest of the lower half of the scores and the least of the upper half.

Variability. A second important class of statistics deals with the extent to which a set of data varies, i.e., with the distribution of the data. The simplest such statistic is the *range*. In the case of the data 32, 29, 28, 28, 27, 27, 27, 26, 20, 18, the scores range from 32 to 18, a "distance" of $(32 - 18) + 1$ or 15. Of more interest, however, is the *deviation* of a particular score from the mean. If X_i is a particular score and $\bar{X}$ is the mean, then the deviation of X_i from $\bar{X}$ is $(X_i - \bar{X})$. It is of some interest to consider the average of these deviations, the *mean deviation*. In determining this statistic, we disregard signs and use the absolute value of each deviation, i.e., for those scores below the mean, we use the opposite of the deviation, e.g., 6.2 rather than −6.2. A still more useful statistic of variability is the *variance*, sometimes abbreviated s^2, which is found by squaring each deviation and then averaging those squared deviations. Finally, the *standard deviation*, abbreviated σ (Greek lower-case sigma) is the square root of the variance. The standard deviation is the most commonly used measure of deviation: If the standard deviation is relatively small, then the scores are relatively homogeneous or close together, whereas a high standard deviation reflects wider differences among them. In general, about two-thirds (68.26 percent) of a set of scores occur in the interval from $\bar{X} - \sigma$ to $\bar{X} + \sigma$, and almost all (95.46 percent) of the scores are between $\bar{X} - 2\sigma$ and $\bar{X} + 2\sigma$.

The mean deviation, variance, and standard deviation for our sample data are summarized in the table.

X	$X_i - \bar{X}$	$(X_i - \bar{X})^2$
32	5.8	33.62
29	2.8	7.84
28	1.8	3.24
28	1.8	3.24
27	0.8	0.64
27	0.8	0.64
27	0.8	0.64
26	0.2	0.04
20	6.2	38.44
18	8.2	67.24
Sum 262	29.2	155.60
Mean 26.2	2.92	15.56

$\bar{X} = 26.2$
$s^2 = 15.56$
$\sigma = \sqrt{15.56} \doteq 3.94$

2. Activities and Materials for Teaching Probability and Statistics

The preceding mathematical review contains considerably more than most elementary school children can be expected to comprehend.

Some of that content was reviewed as background material for occasional enrichment experiences, and some for the teacher's own use (e.g., the statistical material related to the analysis of test scores). However, many ideas from that section can be used directly with children, particularly in the upper grades. In the remainder of this chapter we will summarize a few activities and materials appropriate for exploration of these ideas with children.

General Guidelines

A few general guidelines should be kept in mind when teaching probability and statistics; before specific materials and activities are discussed, these will be summarized.

Much of the mathematics of probability and statistics rests on the concept of ratio, which is a relatively sophisticated concept for elementary school children. At the same time, experiences with probability and statistics can contribute to *developing* the ratio concept, and, therefore, should not be automatically ruled out simply because children have not *thoroughly* developed all the prerequisite concepts.

Basic vocabulary and notation must be introduced in order to develop key ideas, of course, but this can and should be done gradually and with relaxed informality. Children may in fact invent their own notation— with the teacher's careful guidance. Certainly, intuition, informality, pictorial representations, and empirically derived evidence should predominate over formal definitions, handed-down formulas, and the like. With guidance, probability provides a rich source of discovery experience.

Unlike some mathematical topics to which we introduce children, basic concepts of probability and statistics (especially probability) can only be developed via genuine experimentation, beginning, of course, with relatively simple situations. The more times an experiment is repeated, the closer will its results be likely to reflect ideal or theoretic generalizations. If several children each flip a coin 30 times and average their *collective* data, the results are much more likely to approach the theoretic 50–50 ratio than if each child considers only his own 30 results.

Every experiment requires accurate, unbiased observation and record keeping. The principle of random sampling depends in part on appropriate attitudes. If children work in pairs, they can check the accuracy of each other's tallies, decide when a particular trial should be ignored, and be on the lookout for potential sources of bias or "unfairness." Questions raised by the teacher can generate a questioning attitude on the part of students and help them account for deviations from predicted results. Children in fact sometimes become more sensitive to sources of bias than they need to be! Questions such as the following, posed by the teacher, are likely to help develop appropriate attitudes: What are all the possible outcomes? Are they equally likely to occur? Why or why not? Why do you suppose your observed results are different from your predictions? Should your prediction be modified? Did you forget to consider some factor? Are your trials completely fair? Can you graph your results? Can you diagram the results you expect?

Basic Probability Materials

Beginning experience with probability should be based on materials for which sample spaces contain a small number, n, of outcomes, each of which is equally likely to occur on a given trial, so that the probability of each can be predicted to be about $\frac{1}{n}$. Some of the more common materials and their basic uses are noted below. (All are simple and inexpensive; many were discussed in the mathematical review.)

Coins. Any ordinary coin, or in fact any flat disc, such as a checker, for which the two sides are distinguishable, can be flipped as a basis for numerous experiments. Here there are two equally likely outcomes, so the probability of each is $\frac{1}{2}$. (Specific experiments will be discussed subsequently.)

Dice. Rolling an ordinary cubical die, or several of them, is familiar to many children through such board games as *Monopoly*. Each of the six faces of the familiar die is stamped with 1, 2, 3, 4, 5, or 6 dots, and the number of dots that appears "up" on a given roll is an outcome. The probability of each of these six outcomes is, of course, $\frac{1}{6}$. The particular numbers 1 through 6 are irrelevant to the basic concepts to be developed: The faces on a die may be distinguished from each other by labeling them with any numbers, letters, colors, words, and so on, by means of stick-on labels (available from a stationery store). At first, each face should have a unique label, but in time experiments can be conducted with dice labeled so that the same symbol appears on more than one face, e.g., the faces might be labeled a, b, b, c, c, c. Cuisenaire, centimeter, Stern, or Dienes unit cubes — or any other cubes, such as those found in the Attribute materials — can be labeled and used as dice. The number of faces on the usual die is not crucial; any of the five platonic solids (tetrahedron, hexahedron, octahedron, dodecahedron, or icosahedron) can be used as a die by appropriately labeling the faces, and inexpensive plastic models of such dice are available commercially.

Spinners. Many children's games employ spinners for generating random outcomes; the usual spinner consists of a light metal arrow mounted loosely to rotate at the center of a circular cardboard disc which is partitioned into several sectors.

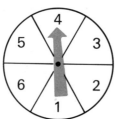

The arrow is set in motion by a flip of the finger and the outcome is determined by the label assigned to that sector of the cardboard on which the arrowhead comes to rest ('4' in the illustration above). The number of outcomes for a particular spinner depends on the number of regions marked off on the cardboard base, which can vary widely, of course. The probability of each outcome depends on the area of the corresponding sector of the base. If the base is partitioned into 8 congruent sectors, for example, each labeled in a distinct way, then the probability of each is $\frac{1}{8}$. On the other hand, if the areas of the sectors are not congruent, probabilities of the possible outcomes depend on the relative areas of each. For example, using a spinner for sectors A, B, C as shown here, $P(A) = \frac{1}{2}$, $P(B) = \frac{1}{4}$, and $P(C) = \frac{1}{4}$.

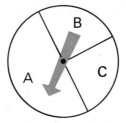

Theoretic probabilities can thus be manipulated either by varying the number of sectors or by varying their relative areas.

A variation on the usual spinner can be made from a pencil and a piece of fairly rigid cardboard (e.g., a file folder). The cardboard is cut in the shape of a regular polygonal region, and angle bisectors are drawn from each vertex to the point at which they meet. That point is pierced with a pencil, which can then be spun like a top; outcomes are identified by labels assigned to the various edges on which the cardboard might come to rest. Again, probabilities can be varied, depending on the number of edges and on the way in which they are labeled.

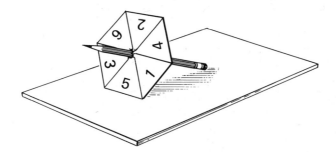

Pencils. If an ordinary pencil with hexagonal cross sections is rolled along a smooth table top, and if its six faces are each marked, e.g., with dots, the face "up" when the pencil comes to rest can identify an outcome. If each face is labeled uniquely (and if the pencil's cross section is quite close to being a true regular hexagon—which is not always the case), then the probability of each outcome is again $\frac{1}{6}$.

Targets. A surface such as a sheet of paper can be partitioned into several regions and each region identified by a particular label (such as a number or a color); such a target can be randomly touched at some point, e.g., with the point of a pencil, much as an unskilled dart player might hit a target. If, for example, it is known that the target is $\frac{1}{3}$ blue, $\frac{1}{3}$ white, and $\frac{1}{3}$ black, then the probability of touching each color can be predicted (if the color ratio is unknown, then it can be estimated or predicted by a large sample of "hits"). Colors or other labels should be distributed randomly.

Cards. Decks of cards of various types, when properly shuffled, provide an exceptionally good source of random data generation. An ordinary deck of bridge cards has an advantage over the preceding materials in that it provides a relatively large number of possible outcomes; and those outcomes can be subdivided, e.g., in terms of suit, numbers, face cards, and so on. Furthermore, both independent and dependent situations can be easily introduced, depending on whether a card drawn on a particular trial is replaced before the next trial.

Marbles and Cubes. A collection of marbles, ball bearings, small cubes, or other similar objects that can be partitioned into a relatively small number of subsets according to some attribute other than size and shape (e.g., color), can be used for many experiments. Children can be told the number of marbles of each color in a box and asked to determine the probability of randomly selecting one of a given color, or they can be told only the total number of marbles and asked to predict the number of each color by sampling processes.

Simple Experiments

What can be done with coins, dice, cards, spinners, and so on, to introduce children to basic ideas of probability and statistics? Let us consider instructions and possible questions for some very basic experiments.

1. Flip a coin. How many different ways can it land? Is it as likely to land "heads up" as it is "tails up"? If a coin is flipped 30 times, about how many heads will occur? Tails? Try it. Did your experiment produce exactly the results you expected? Why? How many heads would you expect in 300 flips? Have nine friends each flip a coin 30 times. Find the *average* number of heads obtained by you and your friends. The terms *probability, frequency,* and *sample space* can be introduced early in such an experiment: If 1 out of every 2 flips is expected to be a head, then the *probability* of heads is $\frac{1}{2}$. The *observed* frequency of heads may be, say, 12 out of 30 or $\frac{12}{30}$. Is this close to the theoretic frequency of $\frac{15}{30}$? The *sample space* is {Heads, Tails}.

2. Roll a die. What are the possible outcomes (sample space)? What is the probability that a 1 will occur? 2? 3? . . . ? 6? What is the theoretic frequency of '1' in 30 rolls? In 300 rolls? What is your observed frequency of each outcome in 30 rolls? What is the average observed frequency of each possible outcome when you and several friends each roll a die 30 times?

3. Given a spinner with, say, 8 congruent sectors, labeled 1 through 8, what is the sample space? What is $P(1)$? $P(2)$? Spin the arrow 50 times. What is the observed frequency of each outcome, 1 through 8? How does this compare with your expected (theoretic) frequency? Again, find the average frequency for each outcome for several students. If the arrowhead lands on a line, what should be done?

4. Mark the faces of a hexagonal pencil with dots (1 through 6). Roll the pencil along a desk many times and record the frequency of each outcome. Determine the proportion of each observed outcome and compare it with its expected probability.

5. Given a "target" which is known to be $\frac{1}{3}$ red, $\frac{1}{3}$ black, and $\frac{1}{3}$ white, if you close your eyes and touch the target with the point of a pencil, what is $P(R)$? $P(B)$? $P(W)$? Try it. How many times *should* you touch red in 300 trials?

6. A box contains 100 marbles, 60 of them white and 40 of them red. Close your eyes and pick a marble. What is the probability that it is white? Red? What *is* it? Repeat 50 times. Have several friends do the same experiment. What are your *average* findings?

7. Take an ordinary deck of bridge cards (52 cards). How many elements are in the sample space of the experiment, "Draw one card"? (There are too many elements — 52 — to list them separately.) Draw a card. Look at it, then put it back in the deck and reshuffle the deck. Suppose you now draw cards from the deck until you draw that same card again (replacing and reshuffling each time). How many cards do you think you would draw before drawing that same card again? Try it. Have several friends try it and average your findings.

Not-So-Simple Experiments

The experiments above were all very similar, even though the particular materials were different; each was directed at determining the theoretic probability of one *outcome* (from among several) of a simple experiment, and at comparing the *observed* frequency for that experiment with the *predicted* (theoretic) frequency for a given number of trials. Many similar experiments can be devised by the resourceful teacher.

For many children, this may be the limit of the kind of probability experiments that can be meaningfully performed. For many others, however, more complex events can be considered – those that may be thought of as combinations of simple events. For example, if A and B are simple events, what is the probability of A or B? of A and B? For such questions, it is helpful to focus attention on the sample space and its subsets A, B, etc. This may be done by listing the elements of those sets or by drawing graphs of ordered pairs or tree diagrams. In general, experiments should be restricted to those for which events are independent. For such experiments it should become clear, in time, that if A and B are subsets of the sample space, SS, then $P(A$ or $B)$ is

$$\frac{N(A \cup B)}{N(SS)}$$

while $P(A$ and $B)$ is

$$\frac{N(A \cap B)}{N(SS)}$$

The following representative experiments are restricted to the materials already suggested.

1. Roll a die. What is $P(2$ or $3)$? The sample space, SS, is $\{1, 2, 3, 4, 5, 6\}$. If $A = \{2\}$ and $B = \{3\}$, then A, B, and $A \cup B$ are subsets of SS. Since $A \cup B = \{2, 3\}$, $P(2$ or $3)$ is 2 out of 6 or $\frac{2}{6}$. Many similar questions can be raised, e.g., What is the probability of rolling an even number? An odd number? A prime? A '1' or an even number? An odd prime? A number greater than 4?

2. Roll two dice and determine the sum of the two numbers. What is the sample space? Some children may need guidance in understanding coordinate grid representations of the sample space; but once such a representation is understood, numerous questions can be posed: What is the range of outcomes? What is $P(2)$? $P(3)$? $P(4)$? . . . ? $P(12)$? What is the most likely sum? Least likely? Which sums have the same probability? What is the probability of a sum of 7? 8? 6 or 4? A sum greater than 7? Less than 7? Similar questions can be raised about the product of the two numbers or the (absolute value of the) differences of

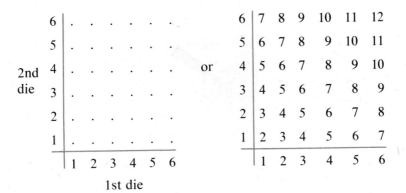

the two numbers. More astute children can be asked to find the probability that one of the dice reads '2' if the sum is 7, and so on.

3. Toss two coins, a dime and a penny. What is the sample space? This may be represented in several ways:

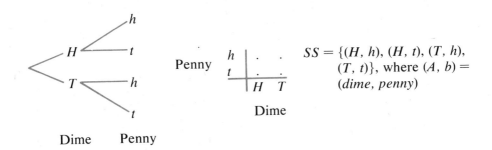

What is the probability of exactly 2 heads? At least 1 head? A head on the dime? A head on the dime and a tail on the penny? A tail and a head? A head on the dime given that at least one of the coins is a head?

4. Roll a hexagonal pencil, marked as before. What is the probability of an even number? An odd number? A number less than or equal to 3? Greater than 3? An odd prime?

5. Draw a card from a standard deck. What is the probability of a heart? A 7? A red king? A face card? An ace or a king? A black card less than 8? A 7, 8, or 9? A king or a queen? The ace of spades?

6. Given a spinner with 8 equivalent sectors labeled 1–8, what is the probability of an even number? A prime number? A number greater than 5? An even number greater than 4?

7. Suppose a spinner is $\frac{1}{2}$ blue, $\frac{1}{4}$ black, and $\frac{1}{4}$ white (as shown)? What is $P(Blu)$? $P(W)$? $P(Bla)$? $P(Bla$ or $W)$? $P(Blu$ or $Bla)$? $P($not $Blu)$? $P($neither W nor $Blu)$?

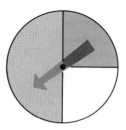

8. Draw a card from a standard deck. Without replacing it, draw a second card. How many elements are in the sample space for the second choice? Why? If the first card were the 7 of spades, what is the probability that the second card is a 7? A spade? The 6 of hearts? If I draw a card and tell you it is a club, what is the probability that it is the 7, 8, or 9 of clubs?

9. Put 3 red marbles and 2 black marbles in a box. Pick out 2 marbles at random. What is the probability that both are red? Black? One red and one black?

10. Think of five marbles as being labeled R_1, R_2, R_3, W_1, W_2. How many 2-element subsets can be formed from this set? How many of those subsets contain two reds? Two blacks? One of each color?

$$\{(R_1, R_2), (R_1, R_3), (R_1, W_1), (R_1, W_2), (R_2, R_3)$$
$$(R_2, W_1), (R_2, W_2), (R_3, W_1), (R_3, W_2), (W_1, W_2)\}$$

As children begin to determine probabilities of more complex events by intuition and by considering diagrams, charts, histograms, or lists, some of them may discover some of the computational generalizations discussed previously, e.g., if A and B are particular events, then

$$P(A \text{ or } B) = P(A) + P(B)$$
$$P(A \text{ and } B) = P(A) \cdot P(B)$$

Some children can even be led to see why these generalizations depend on relationships between the events and the more general situations

$$P(A \text{ or } B) = P(A) + P(B) - P(A \mid B)$$
$$P(A \text{ and } B) = P(A) \cdot P(A \mid B)$$

With most elementary children, however, the formalization of these notions should probably be avoided.

Sampling Experiments

All of the preceding experiments were based on identifiable sample spaces. Another class of experiments that most elementary school children can understand (at some level) includes those for which the sample space is uncertain. There are at least three typical kinds of situations for which probability predictions are made based on *sampling* an uncertain space. We may know nothing of the contents of a container, for example, except that it contains "many" things; we may know that it contains exactly n things, where n is fairly large; or we may know that it contains exactly m kinds of things, where m is fairly small. If we take random samples from the contents of the container, we can formulate a *guess* as to the exact contents of the container on the basis of the contents of the sample. A few representative experiments of each type will be considered here. It should be consistently emphasized with children that statements made on the basis of sampling are conjectures rather than facts, and that two important questions should be raised about such statements: What was the sample size (relative to the total "population")? Was the sample actually chosen randomly or was there some possible source of *bias* in the sampling? It is not difficult to find examples of statements whose validity is subject to question on these grounds: "Two out of three doctors recommend Blotto," or "Most of the kids in my school wear jeans." (How many doctors, or kids, were sampled? How many doctors or kids are there altogether who *could* have been sampled?) A wide variety of sampling experiments can be conducted, a small "sample" of which are suggested below. Before considering them, it should be noted that there are two possible ways to sample a collection. Suppose, for example, we wish to draw 10 marbles from a container as a means of predicting the colors of all the marbles. We could draw the ten simultaneously or we could draw one, record its color and *replace* it before drawing the next. The latter is generally preferable, since each sampled marble is then drawn from the collection under essentially identical circumstances. Children may try both sampling methods and look for differences in the results.

1. A box contains several things. Reach in the box and take out 10 of them. Guess at the entire contents of the box. For example, suppose the box contains some of the Attribute blocks: Wooden blocks of several shapes, colors and sizes. Shapes may be triangular, circular, or square; colors may be red, blue, green, or yellow; and sizes may be small or large. By randomly choosing 10 pieces, one at a time, the child's conjectures may progressively range, depending on his choice, from, "The box contains wooden blocks," "Some blocks are red, some are blue, some are yellow, and some are green," and "Some blocks are large and some are small," to more specific statements such as, "There are as many large ones as small ones," or "There are as many small green triangles as there are small yellow squares."

2. Put 100 or so marbles or cubes of 2 or 3 colors in a box. Tell the child only the total number of objects and have him guess the number of each color, based on progressively larger samples of, say, 5, 10, or 20. It is not difficult to establish that the larger the sample, the more confidence

can be placed in predictions based on the samples (children should be allowed to establish the actual ratio by counting, after making several predictions). The same kind of experiment can be repeated, given both the total number of marbles (or cubes) and the number of different colors.

3. Children can take surveys of their peers regarding their opinions about some topic of current interest, e.g., opinions about a TV program, movie, popular record, or style of dress. Encourage them to play "devil's advocate" in challenging the validity and reliability of each other's data and conclusions.

4. Show the child a two- or three-color target for which the distribution of colors is not revealed — and not obvious. Have him close his eyes and touch regions of the target several times with the point of a pencil. Using this sample as a guide, have him guess the color ratio.

5. Choose some subset of a deck of cards (e.g., all but the hearts, or all but the 8s, 9s, and 10s). Have the child guess which cards are missing on the basis of sampling the remaining cards.

6. Use a die which has been labeled in an unorthodox way or with an unconventional number of faces, such as a dodecahedron. Have one child roll the die several times and, on the basis of the results obtained, have other children try to guess the labeling pattern or the number of faces.

7. Choose a book and carefully tally the distribution of 100 or 200 letters in a randomly chosen sequence of pages (e.g., the third line of every seventh page). Use this tally to predict the frequency of various letters in ordinary discourse. Use that prediction to decode a message in which letters are regularly transposed (e.g., each 'A' is replaced by a 'T', and so on). Certain skills and techniques will enhance the value and enjoyment of this activity: Order the letters according to the frequency of their occurrence, and then determine what *percent* of the letters in the passage were 'E', and so on. Now do the same for the coded message and try to match the two. A certain amount of error must be expected, of course, but much insight and satisfaction can result from this rather lengthy experiment. Secret codes have always fascinated children.

Miscellaneous Experiments

1. Construct a triangular game board using a pattern such as that shown here.

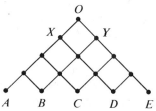

Put a marker at O and flip a coin; if the coin lands heads up, move the marker to the next intersection point to the left (X); if it lands tails, move to the right (Y). Repeat until the marker is at A, B, C, D, or E (i.e., a total of 4 moves). Repeat this procedure 16 times and record the number of markers that end up at each point. In theory, the distribution would be the same as row 4 of Pascal's triangle:

A	B	C	D	E
1	4	6	4	1

The averaged results of many repetitions of this experiment will, of course, lead to distributions more nearly like the theoretically predicted one than will the results of a single experiment. Many variations can be introduced, e.g., the number of rows or trials can be varied (using 3 rows would suggest 2^3 repetitions or, better, multiples of 2^3).

Dropping marbles, beads, or ball bearings in a home-made or commercially obtained board like that suggested at the end of Chapter 7 provides a visual approximation of the "normal" (bell-shaped) distribution curve. Graphing either the empirically derived distribution or the actual numbers in Pascal's triangle can be an interesting activity:

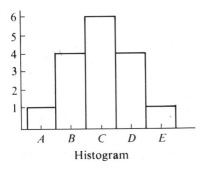

Histogram

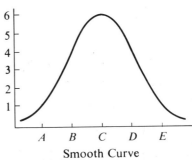

Smooth Curve

2. Put a collection of thumb tacks (of uniform size and shape) in a container, shake, and spill the tacks on a flat table. Count the number of tacks that land in each of the two possible positions (point up and point not up) and, after a large number of repetitions, arrive at a ratio you would be willing to use to predict the probability of each outcome. Similar experiments can be designed with small matchboxes, paper cups, cylinders of varying heights, irregularly shaped dice, and so on.

3. Give the child a sample space and associated probabilities for a regular (though not necessarily cubical) die. Ask him to determine the shape and labeling of the die from the data provided, e.g.,

Sample space: $\{a, b, c\}$

Probabilities: $P(a) = \dfrac{3}{8}$ $P(b) = \dfrac{1}{8}$ $P(c) = \dfrac{1}{2}$

Here the data suggests that the die has 8 faces, 3 of which are labeled *a;* 1 face is labeled *b* and 4 are labeled *c.* If a blank octahedron is available, label its faces in that way and check the probabilities by experimenting. A slightly more difficult task would be to provide the child with only a hypothetical set of data and questions such as: A die was rolled 48 times, with the results that $a = 18$ times, $b = 6$ times, $c = 24$ times. What is the probable shape and labeling pattern of the die? (A similar problem was previously suggested, using empirically derived data.)

Statistics

Statistical topics appropriate for most elementary school children include finding averages, ranges, and frequencies; making, reading, and interpreting graphs of various kinds; and very *intuitive* consideration of deviations from the mean.

These topics can be introduced informally, either in the context of performing probability experiments such as already suggested, or in the context of other classroom experiences. Techniques for teaching these topics should need little discussion here. Statistical ideas and their names can be simply introduced as data are being collected (e.g., "range" and "frequency").

The Average

Children frequently hear, and sometimes use, the word "average" long before they are aware of how to *compute* averages. An intuitive idea of the meaning of the term can and should be established before the computational procedure is introduced. This can be accomplished in endless ways and contexts. Quite natural questions posed by children (or teachers) frequently give rise to the basic idea: How tall are fourth graders? What do they weigh? How warm is it (usually) at noon? How fast does a plant or a pet grow? How did we do on yesterday's spelling test? These and countless other questions quite naturally lead to gathering data and then trying to use it to answer the questions. The data-gathering process itself provides many opportunities for developing careful, accurate, and unbiased measurements. Even quite young children can make and interpret simple pictographs, which can be used to introduce the notions of range, variability, and central tendency. Suppose, for example, the heights of 10 girls are determined (in cm):

Ann	123	Fay	133
Beth	135	Gail	122
Chris	126	Heather	123
Doris	130	Iris	124
Elsie	126	Jean	138

Several alternative activities and questions can now be pursued: Arrange the girls' names in order according to their heights:

Ann,   Elsie,

Gail, Heather, Iris, Chris, Doris, Fay, Beth, Jean

Who is tallest? Shortest? "In the middle"? How much taller is Jean than Gail? Make a pictograph of the heights (this should be done as carefully and as closely to scale as possible, and may require considerable help from the teacher). From the graph, if you were asked to draw a "middle" line to represent all the girls, where would you draw it? Which girl—or girls— would you select as most "typical" of the group?

The idea of average can be made more precise by arranging several sets of blocks or other objects of uniform size in a given number of columns or stacks of varying heights, then rearranging them so that, insofar as possible, all columns or stacks have about the *same* height. If, for example, each girl's height were represented by a stack of blocks such as Cuisenaire unit cubes,

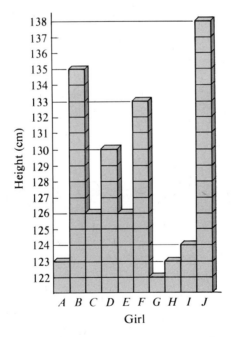

the blocks could be rearranged by trial and error, taking blocks from taller stacks and putting them on shorter ones, until each stack was the same height. For this particular collection, that height would be found to be 128. Thus, 128 can reasonably be accepted as an "average."

From such a manipulative activity it is not difficult to introduce the standard computational procedure.

Example:

Imagine a row of Cuisenaire rods as long as the height of each girl, i.e., 123 rods to represent Ann, 135 for Beth, and so on. Suppose the rows were then arranged end-to-end. How long would the resulting row be? (1280 cm, which can be determined by *adding* the number of rods in each row.) Now imagine rearranging those 1280 rods into 10 *equivalent* rows (since there are 10 girls). How many rods would be in each row?

$$1280 \div 10 = \underline{128}$$

Several such experiments, with a variety of data and materials can lead to an understanding of the mathematical determination of the average, or arithmetic mean. Sometimes (in fact, in general) a nonzero remainder will be encountered; this can provide a motivation for introducing the fraction or decimal treatment.

Example:

When the numbers representing each of 15 scores are added, the sum is 183. Divide that sum by the number of scores. What is the average score?

$$
\begin{array}{r}
12 \\
15\overline{)183} \\
15 \\
\hline
33 \\
30 \\
\hline
3(R)
\end{array}
\rightarrow
\begin{array}{r}
12\frac{3}{15} = 12\frac{1}{5} \\
15\overline{)183} \\
15 \\
\hline
33 \\
30 \\
\hline
3
\end{array}
\quad \text{or} \quad
\begin{array}{r}
12.2 \\
15\overline{)183.0} \\
15 \\
\hline
33 \\
30 \\
\hline
3.0 \\
3.0
\end{array}
$$

Thus the average of 15 scores totaling 183 is $12\frac{1}{5}$ or 12.2.

Children will note that the average "score" is not necessarily, nor generally, one of the actual scores (none of the 10 girls was 128 cm tall). Also, for some collections of data the average is more representative of the individual scores than for others. (Only three of the girls in the example were fairly close to the average height.) Other things should sometimes be taken into consideration, e.g., deviations from the mean.

Some children may even realize that, in order to simplify computation, a constant can be subtracted from each score before computing averages, then added back to the computed average. For example, in the illustration above, 70 blocks were used to represent the girls' heights; in effect, 121 blocks were subtracted from each height. The average of the 70 blocks is 7, which, when we add back the 121, gives the true average, 128.

Projects, Questions, and Suggested Activities

1. Several experiments for children, and some for teachers, have been suggested within the chapter. Try them. Have some friends replicate them in those cases where it has been suggested that several students average their findings. Construct any necessary materials that are not readily available.
2. Take a set of actual test scores and calculate various percentiles, the mean, range, variance, and standard deviation.
3. Examine some contemporary elementary school textbooks and determine the extent to which they include topics from probability and statistics; do the same for some older texts.
4. Make a collection of experiments for children patterned after those suggested in the chapter; write the instructions on 5-by-8 cards designed for children to use independently.
5. Look up "binomial distribution," and the "chi-square distribution" in statistics books. How are they related to topics in this chapter?
6. Predict, then determine empirically, the probability that on a random toss a red Cuisenaire rod will land on some one of its four 1 cm-by-2 cm faces; some one of its two 1 cm-by-1 cm faces.

Suggested Readings

Berkeley, Edmund C. *Probability and Statistics: An Introduction Through Experiments*. Newtonville, Mass.: Berkeley Enterprises, 1961.

> As the title suggests, numerous experiments leading to key ideas are included; simple materials, available in a kit, are used for some experiments.

Burt, Bruce C. "Drawing Conclusions from Samples (An Activity for the Low Achiever)." *The Arithmetic Teacher*, November 1969, pp. 539–41.

> Several sampling activities with inexpensive materials.

Campbell, Irene. *Statistics*. Boston: Houghton Mifflin, 1970.

> A small book for children with many good examples to illustrate basic ideas of probability and statistics.

Flory, D. W. "What Are the Chances?" *The Arithmetic Teacher*, November 1969, pp. 581–82.

> Simple problems using tacks, coins, beads, and corks.

Girard, Ruth A. "Development of Critical Interpretation of Statistics and Graphs." *The Arithmetic Teacher*, April 1967, pp. 272–77.

> A class project, which began with reading simple graphs, led to discovery and understanding of many statistical concepts.

Grass, Benjamin A. "Statistics Made Simple." *The Arithmetic Teacher*, March 1965, pp. 196–98.

> How a group of fourth graders learned some important ideas about experimentation, making hypotheses, and gathering and interpreting data — starting with their curiosity about extrasensory perception.

Higgins, James E. "Probability with Marbles and a Juice Container." *The Arithmetic Teacher*, March 1973, pp. 165–66.

> Drawing marbles from a container can lead to skills in making predictions. In the same issue, Niman and Postman (pp. 167–70) discuss interesting ways to use a geoboard to develop basic concepts of probability.

Hildebrand, Francis H., and Johnson, Nellie. "An Ordered Pair Approach to Addition of Rational Numbers in Second Grade." *The Arithmetic Teacher,* February 1965, pp. 106–8.

> How second graders' experiments with dice led to an algorithm for adding fractions (probabilities), using such questions as, "What are the chances of getting either a sum of 4 or a sum of 9?"

Immerzeel, George, and Wiederanders, Don. "Ideas." *The Arithmetic Teacher,* April 1971, pp. 239–42.

> Two activities involving collecting and recording data that could lead to ideas about probability and statistics.

Page, Donald, and Beattie, Ian D. *Probability: A Programmed Supplement.* Prindle, Weber and Schmidt, 1969.

> A brief programed unit, designed for self-instruction, covering some basic concepts of probability: sample space, events, simple probabilities, the probability of events *A* and *B* both occurring, the probability of event *A* or event *B* occurring, and conditional probability. In the same series of programed units by the same authors, see also *Some Basic Statistics: A Programmed Supplement,* which covers the topics of mean, median, mode, percentile, variance, standard deviation, and representation of data by histograms and frequency polygons.

Ruchlis, Hy, and Marcus, Esther. *Hextstat.* New York: Harcourt, Brace and World, 1965.

> Teacher's manual for using a device designed to roll 256 (2^8) small steel balls into channels representing the first eight rows of Pascal's triangle.

Schaefer, Anne W., and Mauthe, Albert H. "Problem Solving With Enthusiasm — The Mathematics Laboratory." *The Arithmetic Teacher*, January 1970, pp. 7–14.

> Includes some probability experiments with dice and coins.

Schell, Leo M. "Horizontal Enrichment with Graphs." *The Arithmetic Teacher,* December 1967, pp. 654–56.

> Four short enrichment lessons to develop concepts of sampling, graphing, and predicting.

School Mathematics Study Group (SMSG), *Probability for Primary Grades,* and *Probability for Intermediate Grades,* Stanford: SMSG, 1965 and 1966.

> Two volumes for elementary school students, with accompanying teacher's editions; includes basic topics such as sample space, events, independent events, and mutually exclusive events. Many experiments, especially with spinners.

Sherrill, James M. "Egg Cartons Again?" *The Arithmetic Teacher*, January 1973, pp. 13–16.

> Dropping disks (such as coins) into egg cartons can lead to preliminary ideas of probability.

Wilkinson, Jack D., and Nelson, Owen. "Probability and Statistics — Trial Teaching in Sixth Grade." *The Arithmetic Teacher,* February 1966, pp. 100–106.

> Description of several classroom activities using probability, some interesting ideas children had (e.g., "A quarter isn't a fair coin to flip"), and some good advice from the teacher-experimenters.

APPENDIXES

Appendix A
Games and Problems

This appendix is a small *potpourri* of little problems, games, activities, and puzzles; some of them quite young children could enjoy; others are fairly challenging (some could be *modified* for children). They were chosen in an attempt to suggest a variety of types of problems rather than to present a complete collection (Appendix B, Section 2 is a list of sources of such problems). We have excluded most types of classroom activities fashioned after games like "Bingo," baseball, spelling bees, and so on, since the reader is probably familiar with them or could invent them easily. We have also excluded riddles for which the solutions are (generally) nonmathematical "tricks." Excluding these two should not be construed as rejection of them—children enjoy them and can learn from them.

No order of difficulty is intended by the listing, and only a few related problems are listed together.

Sources of the problems are given where possible, although these may or may not be original sources. Where only a name is given, it is that of a former student or a colleague who brought the problem to our attention. Many sources are frankly unknown; somehow the material got into our files from some book, journal, conversation, or whatever. A diligent perusal of the sources in Appendix B would probably uncover some of these, whether they were our sources or not: interesting problems seem to "get around."

1. Fill each ◯ with one of the digits 1–8 so that no two adjacent ◯'s contain successive numbers:

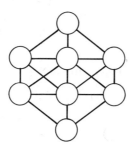

2. Make a magic circle by filling in each ⃝ with a different digit, using each of 1 through 9 exactly once.

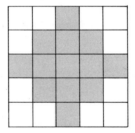

3. Construct a 5-by-5 magic square using each of the numbers from 1 to 25 exactly once so that the odd numbers are all in the shaded region.

(After H. E. Dudeney, *536 Puzzles and Curious Problems*, Charles Scribner's Sons, 1967, p. 145.)

4. [*Note:* The *order* of a magic square is the number of rows (or columns) it contains. Thus 3-by-3, 5-by-5, 7-by-7, or 9-by-9 magic squares are "odd ordered." A normal (or perfect) magic square of order n contains each of the numbers from 1 to n^2 exactly once.] One of several ways to construct an odd-ordered normal magic square is to begin with 1 in the middle cell of the top row. Thereafter, each number from 2 to n^2 is entered *in order* according to the following two rules:

Rule 1:
Enter the next number in the cell that is up 1, then 1 to the right (diagonally). If this is "off the board," simply imagine a second copy of the grid above or to the right (or both) and enter the next number there, then transfer to the original grid in the same relative position.

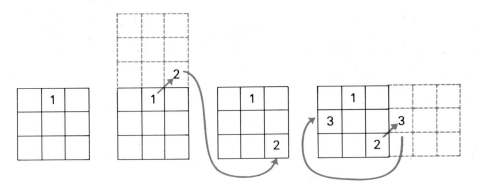

Rule 2:
If and only if rule 1 fails, i.e., if the cell up 1 and right 1 is already occupied, enter the next number down 1.

Using these rules you should be able to construct any odd-ordered magic square. Construct a few (orders 3, 5, 7, 9, and 11 at least), then consider some of these questions:

(a) In which cell is n^2?
(b) How frequently must you use rule 2?
(c) What is the "magic constant" (the sum of any row, column, or major diagonal) in terms of n?
(d) What number, in terms of n, is in the middle cell?
(e) What can you say about the major diagonal from lower left to upper right?
(f) Where in the grid is n? $n + 1$? $2(n + 1)$? $3(n + 1)$? . . .
(g) When are the numbers in the upper left and upper right both odd? Both even? What about the corresponding numbers in the bottom row?
(h) [If you "reflect" the square in any of the four axes of symmetry of the square or "rotate" it in quarter turns about the middle cell, you will still have a magic square, of course.] In how many different ways could the same configuration occur? Describe "Rule 1" and "Rule 2" for each different configuration.
(i) Follow the above rules for a perfect magic square of order n (n odd) except enter each number "mod n" (enter the remainder when the

number is divided by n). Do you get a Latin square, i.e., does each number from 0 to $n - 1$ appear in each row, each column and each major diagonal exactly once? What other patterns can you find?

5. (a) $\dfrac{1}{1 \times 2} + \dfrac{1}{2 \times 3} + \dfrac{1}{3 \times 4} + \cdots + \dfrac{1}{49 \times 50} =$

 (b) $\dfrac{1}{2} + \dfrac{1}{4} + \dfrac{1}{8} + \cdots + \dfrac{1}{2^{100}} =$

 (C. A. Reeves)

6. See how many successive numbers you can express using exactly four 4's. (Addition, subtraction, multiplication, division, square root, decimals — including repeating ones — raising to the fourth power, 4 factorial, and so on, are permitted.) Can you get to 60?

 Example: $60 = \dfrac{4! \sqrt{4}}{.4 \sqrt{4}}$

7. (a) $\quad (1 \times 8) + 1 =$
 $\quad (12 \times 8) + 2 =$
 $\quad (123 \times 8) + 3 =$
 $(1234 \times 8) + 4 =$
 $\vdots$

 (b) $\quad (1 \times 9) + 2 =$
 $\quad (12 \times 9) + 3 =$
 $\quad (123 \times 9) + 4 =$
 $(1234 \times 9) + 5 =$
 $\vdots$

8. For successive values of N, list all the *reduced* fractions from $\frac{0}{1}$ to $\frac{1}{1}$, *in order*, with denominators no greater than N, e.g., for $N \leqslant 4$:

N							
1	$\frac{0}{1}$,	$\frac{1}{1}$					
2	$\frac{0}{1}$,	$\frac{1}{2}$,	$\frac{1}{1}$				
3	$\frac{0}{1}$,	$\frac{1}{3}$,	$\frac{1}{2}$,	$\frac{2}{3}$,	$\frac{1}{1}$		
4	$\frac{0}{1}$,	$\frac{1}{4}$,	$\frac{1}{3}$,	$\frac{1}{2}$,	$\frac{2}{3}$,	$\frac{3}{4}$,	$\frac{1}{1}$

Find the sequences for $N = 5, 6, 7, \ldots$ and look for patterns in these sequences (called Farey sequences).

(a) Do the denominators in each sequence follow any pattern?

(b) Can you find an easy way to determine the terms of any "next" sequence? Can you find a relationship between the Farey sequences and Suggested Activity 8(b) for Chapter 9?

(c) If $\frac{a}{b}$ and $\frac{c}{d}$ are successive fractions in some sequence, what can you say about the numbers ad and bc? What can you say about the fraction $\frac{a+c}{b+d}$?

(d) An equation of the form

$$ax + by = c$$

where a, b, and c are integers, is called a linear Diophantine equation. If a and b are relatively prime, there are infinitely many pairs of integers (x, y) such that $ax + by = c$. For example, the equation $2x + 3y = 1$ has solutions (x, y) including $(2, -1)$, $(5, -3)$, $(8, -5)$, $(11, -7)$, and $(14, -9)$. Can you find any relationships between linear Diophantine equations and Farey sequences?

9. Pick a number.

      Multiply by 6
      Add 12
      Divide by 2
      Subtract 6
      Divide by 3

Where are you? Why?

(Many variations on this are possible.)

10. Write down any large number. Reverse the digits and add; repeat until a palindromic number occurs.

$$
\begin{array}{r}
843207 \\
+\ 702348 \\
\hline
1545555 \\
+\ 5555451 \\
\hline
7101006 \\
+\ 6001017 \\
\hline
13102023 \\
+\ 32020131 \\
\hline
45122154 \\
\end{array}
$$

11. Write down any three-digit number such that each digit is one less than the one to its left, e.g., 987, 876, 765, 654, 543, 432, 321, or 210. Reverse the digits and subtract. Your answer is 198. Why? Repeat with 2 digits, 4 digits, 5 digits. What do you get? Why?

12. Multiply 12345679 by

1×9	5×9
2×9	6×9
3×9	7×9
4×9	9×9

What happens? Why? What about 8?

13. What is the sum of the first 213 terms of each of these sequences?
    (a) $^-1, ^+2, ^-3, ^+4, ^-5, \ldots$
    (b) $^+1, ^-2, ^+3, ^-4, ^+5, \ldots$
    (Robert J. Kansky)

14. What is the relationship between B, the number of boundary points; I, the number of interior points; and A, the area of any polygon constructed on a geoboard? (Area of $\square$ = 1.)

Example:

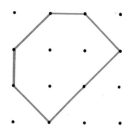

B: 7 boundary points
I: 3 interior points
A: Area $= 5\frac{1}{2}$

(Pick's formula)

15. If a square geoboard has 501 pegs along each outer edge, how many "shortest" segments (as long as $\overline{AB}$ below) are determined by all of the pegs? How many "next-to-shortest" segments (as long as $\overline{AC}$)?

(C. A. Reeves)

16. Consider entering consecutive numbers on a sheet of squared graph paper following the clockwise spiral pattern suggested by 1 through 18 here.

	7 → 8	9	10	
	6 (1)→ 2	11		
18	5 ← 4 ← 3	12		
17	16	15	14	13

Instead of starting at 1, start at the first of a pair of prime twins (e.g., 3, 5, 11, 17, 29, 41, 59, 71, 101, 107, 137, etc.). Which numbers along the diagonal from upper left to lower right (passing through the starting number) are primes?
(Lawrence Couvillon)

17. To square a number ending in 5:
    (a) The last 2 digits are '25'.
    (b) The remaining digits are $n(n + 1)$ where n is the "number" preceding the 5:

$$35^2 = 1225$$
$$\quad\quad\llcorner\!\!\!-3 \times 4$$

$$85^2 = 7225$$
$$\quad\quad\llcorner\!\!\!-8 \times 9$$

$$115^2 = 13225$$
$$\quad\quad\llcorner\!\!\!-11 \times 12$$

Why?

18. Arrange 16 toothpicks to make 5 squares as shown:

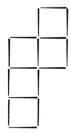

Remove 2 toothpicks so that 4 squares remain.

19. Without lifting pencil from the paper, connect the 9 dots with exactly 4 segments.

      •   •   •

      •   •   •

      •   •   •

(Tom Denmark)

20. In how many different ways can you go from A to B below, following a continuous path of segments (with dots as endpoints) which never crosses or retraces itself? (Any horizontal, vertical, or diagonal segment is permitted; *one* possible path is shown.)

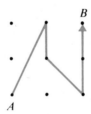

21. How many distinct factors does $5^{99} \cdot 7^{48}$ have? 560^{99}? (Ruth Hauseal)

22. Add the first n numbers along any *diagonal* of Pascal's triangle. Where, in the triangle, is the sum?

23. The triangular numbers can be represented by dot patterns. (See Chapter 7, p. 275.)
    (a) If the base of a triangular dot pattern has 25 dots, what triangular number does it represent?
    (b) How many dots are at the base of the triangular dot pattern for 20,100?

24. Given any regular polygon, a second polygon of the same kind can be nested within it by joining the midpoints of consecutive sides. This can be repeated indefinitely.
    The numbers 3, 5, and $^-2$ are assigned to the vertices of a first triangle; thereafter, numbers are assigned at each vertex of the next triangle by adding the numbers at the two vertices for which it is the midpoint. The process is repeated again and again:

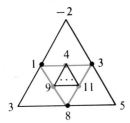 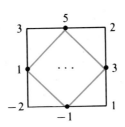 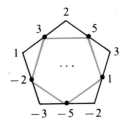

(a) What is the sum of the numbers at the vertices of the 78th nested triangle?

(b) What is the sum of the numbers at the vertices of the 78th nested square?

(c) What is the sum of the numbers at the vertices of the 78th nested pentagon?

(d) What are the numbers at the vertices of the 99th and 100th nested triangle beginning with

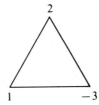

(Robert J. Kansky)

25. Fill each ◯ with one of the digits 1–9 so that the sum is the same in each diagonal.

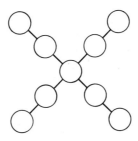

26. Replace each letter with a digit so that the resulting computation is correct (repetitions of a letter in the same problem must be replaced by the same digit).

XMAS	SEND	THREE	FOOT
MAIL	+ MORE	THREE	FOOT
+ EARLY	MONEY	+ ONE	+ FOOT
PLEASE		SEVEN	YARD

```
        FOUR            TEN
         ONE            TEN
       THREE           NINE
     + THREE          EIGHT
      ELEVEN        + THREE
                      FORTY
```

(From J. A. H. Hunter and Joseph S. Madachy, *Mathematical Diversions,* Van Nostrand, 1963, pp. 90–95.)

27. Battleship (a game for two):

Two players each have an 8-by-8 coordinate grid which the other player cannot see. Each player has 4 battleships, located at secret points (represented by ordered pairs of whole numbers). Players take turns calling off coordinates; if one player names the location of one of the other's battleships, he sinks it. Game continues until all 4 ships of one player are sunk.

(NCTM, *Experiences in Mathematical Discovery,* NCTM, 1963.)

28. In how many different ways can the numbers 1 through 9 be arranged in 3-by-3 array so that the number in each cell is less than the number to its right and the number below it (where these exist)?

29. (a) Write down the word name of any number. Count the letters in that word name. Count the letters in *that* word name. Continue until you keep getting the same word. What is it?

    Example:

    > thirty-seven (11 letters)
    > eleven   (6 letters)
    > six   (3 letters)
    > .
    > .
    > .

    (b) Begin a sequence with any number K. If K is odd, the next number is $3K + 1$; if K is even, the next number is $\frac{K}{2}$; continue, using these same rules, until you get into a cycle. What is the cycle?

    Example:

    > 17, 52, 26, 13, 40, . . .
    > 18, 9, 28, 14, 7, . . .

(Lawrence Couvillon)

30. In a certain bank, the positions of cashier, manager, and teller are held by Brown, Jones, and Smith, though not necessarily in that order. The teller, who is an only child, earns the least. Smith, who married Brown's sister, earns more than the manager. What position does each man fill? (From C. R. Wylie, Jr., *101 Puzzles in Thought and Logic*, Dover, 1957.)

31. Construct an 8-by-8 array of squares. Remove the lower left square and the upper right square. Can the remaining 62 squares be covered with 31 dominoes. Why or why not?
    (From J. A. H. Hunter and Joseph S. Madachy, *Mathematical Diversions*, Van Nostrand, 1963, p. 77.)

32. Six players *A*, *B*, *C*, *D*, *E*, and *F* sit around a table with a numbered disk which spins (see picture). The disk is spun 5 times and each player's score for each spin is determined by the numbers on the disk. The person with the highest cumulative score wins. (If the arrows land on the lines between players, the spin is redone.)

    The result of the first spin is pictured. On the second spin, *D* was ahead. *A* won the game. What was each person's score at the end of the game?

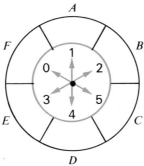

    (From Martin Gardner, "Mathematical Games," *Scientific American*, April 1972, pp. 100–101.)

33. There are five different houses, each of a different color and inhabited by men of different nationalities, with different pets, drinks, and cigarettes.
    (a) The Englishman lives in the red house.
    (b) The Spaniard owns the dog.
    (c) Coffee is drunk in the green house.
    (d) The Ukranian drinks tea.
    (e) The green house is immediately to the right of the ivory house.
    (f) The Old Golds smoker owns snails.
    (g) Kools are smoked in the yellow house.

(h) Milk is drunk in the middle house.
(i) The Norwegian lives in the first house.
(j) The man who smokes Chesterfields lives two houses to the right of the man with the fox.
(k) Kools are smoked two houses from the house where the horse is kept.
(l) The Lucky Strike smoker drinks orange juice.
(m) The Japanese smokes Parliaments.
(n) The Norwegian lives next door to the blue house.
Now who's the teetotaler who drinks H_2O? And who owns the zebra?

34. A Baseball Problem:
Brown, White, Adams, Miller, Green, Hunter, Knight, Jones, and Smith are members of a baseball team. What position does each play?
(a) Smith and Brown each won $10 playing poker with the pitcher.
(b) Hunter is taller than Knight and shorter than White, but each of these players weighs more than the 1st baseman.
(c) The 3rd baseman lives across the corridor from Jones in the same apartment house.
(d) Miller and the outfielders play bridge in their spare time.
(e) White, Miller, Brown, and the right fielder and the center fielder are the only bachelors.
(f) One of Adams and Knight is an outfielder.
(g) The right fielder is shorter than the center fielder.
(h) The pitcher's wife is the 3rd baseman's sister.
(i) Green is taller than the infielders or battery, except for Jones, Smith, and Adams.
(j) The 2nd baseman beat Jones, Brown, Hunter, and the catcher at cards.
(k) The shortstop, 3rd baseman, and Hunter made $150 each on the stock market.
(l) The 2nd baseman is engaged to Miller's sister.
(m) Adams lives in the same house with his sister. He hates the catcher.
(n) Adams, Brown, and the shortstop lost $150 each on the stock market.
(o) The catcher has 3 daughters, the 3rd baseman has two sons, and Green had a fight with his wife last night.
(Wendall Wyatt)

Appendix B
Materials and Their Sources

We have referred to various instructional materials throughout this text; most of these are available commercially. The main purpose of this appendix is to help the reader locate specific and recent information on such materials. It is recommended that the prospective or beginning teacher begin accumulating a file of catalogues from various suppliers. The addresses we have provided below, a supply of post cards, and a few hours' work should bring a useful collection of (generally free) catalogues. Three things should be kept in mind: (1) No such list can be "complete." New devices and materials are introduced continually. The lists below can be expanded as new sources appear in professional literature or at professional meetings. (2) Although the addresses below should be correct, these sometimes change. (3) Catalogue materials frequently suggest ideas for home-made variations on commercially produced materials. It should be kept in mind, of course, that some materials require quite precise workmanship to be effective. Poorly constructed models *can* lead to misconceptions.

In the October 1968 issue of *The Arithmetic Teacher*, Patricia A. Davidson presented "An Annotated Bibliography of Suggested Manipulative Devices" (pp. 509–24). Although now several years old, this comprehensive listing is still useful. There are fifteen categories of materials (blocks, measuring devices, games, and so on) and each entry includes a description, suggested uses, price, grade level, and source. It is highly recommended.

1. Suppliers of Basic Materials

The following list indicates some (15) sources of materials mentioned in this text. This brief list is presented as a starter. Materials are cross-referenced at the end of the list. A list of other suppliers, many of whom offer comparable materials, is provided at the end of this section.

Suppliers	Selected Materials Available
1. Activity Resources Company 24827 Calaroga Avenue Hayward, California 94545	Games, tangrams, enrichment books.
2. Childcraft Education Corporation 964 Third Avenue New York, New York 10022	Prenumber, number mate- rials; mathematical balance; measurement tools.
3. Creative Publications P. O. Box 10328 Palo Alto, California 94303	Tangrams, enrichment books, Dienes blocks, Unifix materials, attribute games, mathematical balance, measurement tools, geo- boards, activity cards, metric materials, games, geometric solids, abacus, Soma Cubes.
4. Creative Teaching Associates P. O. Box 293 Fresno, California 93708	Games, tangrams, geoboard, mathematical balance.
5. Cuisenaire Company of America 12 Church Street New Rochelle, New York 10805	Cuisenaire rods, geoboards, geometric solids, activity cards, games, Soma Cubes, enrichment books.
6. Edmund Scientific Company EDSCORP Building Barrington, New Jersey 08007	Geometric solids, point light source, Soma Cubes.
7. Geyer Instructional Aids Co., Inc. P. O. Box 7306 Fort Wayne, Indiana 46807	Geometric solids, abacus, enrichment books, measurement tools.
8. Houghton Mifflin Co. 53 W. 43rd Street New York, New York 10036	Stern materials, Centimeter rods, activity cards.
9. The Macmillan Company 866 Third Avenue New York, New York 10022	Papy's Minicomputer
10. Mind/Matter Corp. P. O. Box 345 Danbury, Connecticut 06810	Measuring tools, geometric solids, geoboard, attribute blocks, tangrams, curve stitching, Napier's Bones, mathematical balance, Unifix materials.
11. Scott Resources, Inc. P. O. Box 2121 Fort Collins, Colorado 80521	Tangrams, geoboards, enrichment books, activity cards.

12. Selective Educational Equipment, Inc. (SEE)
    3 Bridge Street
    Newton, Massachusetts 02195

    Poleidoblocks, geometric solids, mathematical balance.

13. Silver Burdett
    Box 362
    Morristown, New Jersey 07960

    Enrichment books, attribute blocks, tangrams, abacus, mathematical balance.

14. Walker Educational Book Corp.
    720 Fifth Avenue
    New York, New York 10019

    Geoboard

15. Webster/McGraw-Hill
    Manchester Road
    Manchester, Missouri 63011

    Elementary Science Study Units (attribute games and problems, mirror cards, and so on).

Cross Reference	(Numbers Refer to Above Suppliers)
1. Abacus	3, 7, 13
2. Activity cards	3, 5, 8, 11
3. Attribute blocks	3, 10, 13, 15
4. Centimeter rods	8
5. Cuisenaire rods	5
6. Curve stitching	10
7. Dienes blocks	3
8. Enrichment books	1, 3, 5, 7, 11, 13
9. Games	1, 3, 4, 5
10. Geoboards	3, 4, 5, 10, 11, 14
11. Geometric Solids	3, 5, 6, 7, 10, 12
12. Mathematical balance	2, 3, 4, 10, 12, 13
13. Measurement tools	2, 3, 7, 10
14. Metric materials	3
15. Mirror cards	15
16. Napier's Bones	10
17. Papy's Minicomputer	9
18. Point light source	6
19. Poleidoblocks	12
20. Prenumber, number materials	2
21. Soma Cubes	3, 5, 6
22. Stern materials	8
23. Tangrams	1, 3, 4, 10, 11, 13
24. Unifix materials	3, 10

Additional Suppliers

Cadaco, Inc.
310 West Polk Street
Chicago, Illinois 60607

Fearon Publishers
2165 Park Boulevard
Palo Alto, California 94306

Gel-Sten Supply Company, Inc.
911–913 South Hill Street
Los Angeles, California 90015

Gerrard Publishing Company
123 West Park Avenue
Champaign, Illinois 61820

D. C. Heath and Company
125 Spring Street
Lexington, Massachusetts 02173

Holt, Rinehart and Winston, Inc.
Box 2334, Grand Central Station
New York, New York 10017

Ideal School Supply Company
1100 South Lavergne Avenue
Oak Lawn, Illinois 60453

Kenworthy Educational Service
45 North Division Street
Buffalo, New York 14205

Mainco School Supply Company
Canton, Massachusetts 02021

Charles E. Merrill Publishing Co.
1300 Alum Creek Drive
Columbus, Ohio 43216

Midwest Publications Co., Inc.
P. O. Box 307
Birmingham, Michigan 48012

Miles Kimball Company
41 West 8th Avenue
Oshkosh, Wisconsin 54901

Milton Bradley Company
Springfield, Massachusetts 01101

Minnesota Mining &
Manufacturing Co. (3M)
2501 Hudson Road
St. Paul, Minnesota 55119

Motivational Research, Inc.
4216 Howard Avenue
Kensington, Maryland

Nifty Division
St. Regis Paper Company
3300 Pinson Valley Parkway
Birmingham, Alabama 35217

Playskool Manufacturing Company
3720 North Kedzie Avenue
Chicago, Illinois 60618

Products of the Behavioral Sciences
1140 Dell Avenue
Campbell, California 95008

Responsive Environmental Corp.
(REC)
Learning Materials Division
Englewood Cliffs, New Jersey
07632

G. W. School Supply
5626 East Belmont Avenue
P. O. Box 14
Fresno, California

Schoolhouse Visuals, Inc.
816 Thayer Avenue
Silver Springs, Maryland 20910

Science Research Associates, Inc.
259 East Erie Street
Chicago, Illinois 60611

Scott Foresman and Company
Glenview, Illinois 60025

Stanley Bowman Company, Inc.
4 Broadway
Valhalla, New York 10595

TUF
P. O. Box 173
Rowayton, Connecticut 06853

WFF'N PROOF
P. O. Box 71
New Haven, Connecticut 06501

2. Sources of Problems

The following is a list of sources, mostly books, many of them paperbacks, of problems, games, and puzzles. (Many of the problems and activities in Appendix A can be traced to these sources.) They are not categorized; some are aimed primarily at children, but most are for adults. Some of the problems are quite challenging. This incomplete list is intended as a resource for the reader who is interested in recreational mathematics. The National Council of Teachers of Mathematics has published *A Bibliography of Recreational Mathematics* (2 volumes), by William L. Schaaf, which is an excellent, and certainly much more extensive, treatment of this topic. A free list of such NCTM publications can be obtained from the council, 1906 Association Drive, Reston, Va. 22091.

Adler, Irving. *The Magic House of Numbers.* New York: Signet Books, 1913.

Andree, Josephine, P., ed. *Chips from the Mathematical Log.* Norman, Oklahoma: Mu Alpha Theta, University of Oklahoma, 1966.

Andree, Josephine P. *More Chips from the Mathematical Log.* Norman, Oklahoma, Mu Alpha Theta, University of Oklahoma, 1970.

Ball, W. W. Rouse. *Mathematical Recreations and Essays.* New York: The Macmillan Company, 1956.

Barr, Stephen. *A Miscellany of Puzzles.* New York: Thomas Y. Crowell Company, 1965.

Barr, Stephen. *2nd Miscellany of Puzzles.* New York: The Macmillan Company, 1969.

Beiler, Albert H. *Recreations in the Theory of Numbers.* New York: Dover Publications, 1964.

Dudeney, H. E. *536 Puzzles and Curious Problems.* New York: Charles Scribner's Sons, 1967.

Dunn, Angelo. *Mathematical Bafflers.* New York: McGraw-Hill, 1964.

Fujii, John N. *Puzzles and Graphs.* Reston, Va.: NCTM, 1966.

Gardner, Martin. "Mathematical Games." *Scientific American* (monthly).

Gardner, Martin. *Mathematics, Magic and Mystery.* New York: Dover Publications, 1956.

Gardner, Martin. *New Mathematical Diversions from Scientific American.* New York: Simon and Schuster, 1966.

Heath, Royal V. *Mathemagic.* New York: Dover Publications, 1953.

Hunter, J. A. H. *Fun with Figures.* New York: Dover Publications, 1956.

Hunter, J. A. H., and Madachy, Joseph S. *Mathematical Diversions.* Princeton: D. Van Nostrand Co., Inc., 1963.

Jacoby, Oswald. *Mathematics for Pleasure.* Greenwich, Conn.: Fawcett Publications, Inc., 1962.

Kraitchik, Maurice. *Mathematical Recreations.* New York: Dover Publications, 1953.

Longley-Cook, L. H. *Work This One Out.* Greenwich, Conn.: Fawcett Publications, Inc., 1963.

Mach, Joseph S. *Mathematics on Vacation.* New York: Charles Scribner's Sons, 1966.

Mott-Smith, Geoffrey. *Mathematical Puzzles.* New York: Dover Publications, 1954.

National Council of Teachers of Mathematics. *Enrichment Mathematics for the Grades* (27th Yearbook). Reston, Va.: NCTM, 1963.

O'Beirne, T. H. *Puzzles and Paradoxes.* New York: Oxford University Press, 1965.

Peck, Lyman C. *Secret Codes, Remainder Arithmetic, and Matrices.* Reston, Va.: NCTM, 1961.

Phillips, Hubert. *My Best Puzzles in Logic and Reasoning.* New York: Dover Publications, 1961.

Steinhaus, H. *Mathematical Snapshots.* New York: Oxford University Press, 1969.

The Little Puzzle Book. Mt. Vernon, N. Y.: Peter Pauper Press, 1955.

Wylie, C. R., Jr. *101 Puzzles in Thought and Logic.* New York: Dover Publications, 1957.

3. "Ideas"

Since January, 1971, each issue of *The Arithmetic Teacher* has included a section entitled "IDEAS," prepared by George Immerzeel and Donald Wiederanders. Each issue contains several activity sheets designed to be cut out, duplicated, and distributed to children. On the back of each page are the objectives, suggested grade levels, directions for teachers, directions for students, comments, and answers. We have not included these excellent sources of activities within the suggested readings for various chapters of this book, although they certainly are appropriate. Instead we list here the topics included in each of the issues up to the time of this writing. The reader is encouraged to examine and make use of some of these excellent "IDEAS."

It should be noted also that a regular feature of *The Arithmetic Teacher* is "Things You Can Try," now edited by Arnold N. Chandler. These are normally very brief articles, describing ideas other teachers have tried. If the reader is surveying older issues of *The Arithmetic Teacher*, he will find that this feature was edited by Charlotte W. Junge up to May 1972, and was previously called "In the Classroom."

Issue	Pages	Objectives and Grade Levels
Jan. 1971	30–36	Practice with addition basic facts (Grades 1–3). Computation practice with multiplication (Grades 4–6). Computational practice with addition and multiplication of fractions (Grades 6–8).
Feb. 1971	94–98	Experience in addition that relates to simple number patterns (Grades 1–3). Experience in seeing a pattern that relates multiplication to addition (Grades 4–8).
Mar. 1971	164–70	Experience in visualization of three dimensions (Grades 1–3) (Grades 4–6) (Grades 6–8).
Apr. 1971	238–42	Experience in recording data (Grades 1–3). Experience in reading data (Grades 4–8).
May 1971	310–16	Experience with identification of congruent polygons (Grades 1–8). Experiences with perimeter of polygons and identification of the edges of a solid (Grades 3–8). Experience with surface area of prisms (Grades 5–8).
Oct. 1971	390–98	Experience with the number line (Grades 1–2) (Grades 2–4) (Grades 4–6). Number line experience with fractions (Grades 6–8).
Nov. 1971	480–90	Experience with numeration patterns (Grades 1–2). Experience with computation patterns involving the associative and commutative properties for addition (Grades 2–3). Experiences with patterns that focus on the distributive property (Grades 4–6). Experience with patterns in solving the sums of basic arithmetic series (Grades 5–8).
Dec. 1971	576–84	Experience in identification of the standard number symbols (Grade 1). Experience with addition and subtraction patterns at the basic fact level (Grades 2–3). Experience with patterns in factors and products (grades 4–5). Experience with patterns that involve the concept of exponents (Grades 6–8).
Jan. 1972	38–44	Experience in constructing polygons out of triangles (Grades 1–3). Experience in constructing a square from a variety of polygons, each containing at least one right angle (Grades 4–6). Experience with the area concept using a standard unit that is not a square (Grades 6–8).
Feb. 1972		None
Mar. 1972	201–8	Experience with equations and inequalities (Grades 1–7). Experience with ordered pairs of numbers (Grades 7–8).
Apr. 1972	284–92	Experience with patterns in number pairs (Grades 1–2) (Grades 3–4) (Grades 5–6) (Grades 7–8).

Issue	Pages	Objectives and Grade Levels
May 1972	362–73	Experience with the metric system of weight (Grades 1–3). Experience with weight and length using the metric system (Grades 3–4). Experience in using conversion tables: English system to metric system and metric system to English system (Grades 5–6). Experience in using conversion tables: English system to metric system (Grades 6–8).
Oct. 1972	457–65	Experience with the concept of equals (Levels 1–2) (Levels 2–3) (Levels 4–6) (Levels 7–8). (Also a "problem poster" involving a balance situation.)
Nov. 1972	561–68	Experience in matching pictures of like shapes (similar polygons) when the pictures show different orientations of the shape (Levels 1–3). Experience in matching pictures of a geometric solid when the pictures show a different orientation of the solid (Levels 2–4). Experience in investigation of a physical geometry situation that involves constant ratio (Levels 5–7). Experience in the investigation of a physical geometry situation that involves constant ratio and invariance of angle measures (Levels 6–8).
Dec. 1972	649–56	Experience with basic numeration patterns (Levels 1–2). Experience with estimating the sum (Levels 2–3). Experience with estimating sums (Levels 4–5). Experience with estimating products (Levels 6–8).
Jan. 1973	38–43	Experience with counting patterns (Levels 1–8).
Feb. 1973	116–21	Experience with basic concepts of geometry (Levels 1–3) (Levels 3–5) (Levels 6–8).
Mar. 1973	194–207	Experience with ordering numbers identified by their basic facts names (Levels 1–2). Experience in ordering numbers that encourages estimation rather than computation (Levels 2–3). Experience in ordering numbers that encourages estimation rather than computation, using a modification of the number line (Levels 4–5) (Levels 5–6) (Levels 6–8). (Also two "problem posters," one involving probability, the other involving a water-pouring problem; and a bulletin board idea related to order.)
Apr. 1973	280–87	Experience in relating basic units of linear measure using a metric number line (Levels 1–3). Experience in relating basic metric units of weight using a number line model (Levels 2–3). Experience with equivalent English and metric measures (Levels 4–8).

4. Homemade Equipment

Many manipulative and visual devices can be made at home or in the classroom either to save money or to modify the designs of commercially manufactured materials. Several suggestions have been made throughout this text and many more can be found in books, pamphlets, and journals. In this section we will present a few suggestions, but first a few general reminders.

First, many highly effective teaching aids need not be "made" at all. They already exist and are available with virtually no effort or expense. In addition to the many obvious classroom and household items that can be recruited, resourceful teachers often find that local businesses or manufacturers routinely throw away things that can be easily put to use either "as is" or with a minimum of work. One of this writer's students discovered, for example, that a local record manufacturing company discarded the round plastic centers punched from 45 RPM records; these made excellent counters. Paper companies, too, are an excellent source.

Many aids depend, for their effectiveness, on precision workmanship (many do not). But frequently a parent, PTA member, student, or high school shop teacher has the right combination of tools, time, talent, and interest in children's education to voluntarily provide the necessary labor (and sometimes even the material) to construct useful aids, given only an idea of what is needed. In connection with this, it should be kept in mind that discretion is necessary when children are conscripted to make their own apparatus. Many times, under careful guidance, significant learning can take place as children construct their own instructional materials, but at other times precision beyond what can reasonably be expected of children is necessary.

One final reminder is that storage and usage should be given careful consideration. Frequently one device can be shared by several teachers, to be used at different times and stored in a central facility. Sometimes a device can be reproduced so easily and quickly that storing it is unnecessary — it can be recreated as needed. Still other materials are needed so frequently and so spontaneously that they should be accessibly stored in each classroom.

Things to Collect

While there are differences among grade levels and topics being studied at a given time, the following list suggests some of the kinds of everyday household items frequently used for various projects:

Beads	Cardboard and cardboard boxes
Beans (dry)	Checkers
Blocks	Cigar boxes
Buttons	Clay

Coat hangers
Coffee cans (and other tin cans)
Dowels
Egg cartons
Jars
Magnets
Match boxes
Measuring cups and spoons
Meter sticks
Milk cartons
Mirrors
Plastic straws

Poker chips
Popsicle sticks
Rulers
Scales
Spools (thread, wire, etc.)
String, thread, and wire
Tape measures (cloth and steel)
Thermometers
Tiles
Washers
Yardsticks

Things to Make

The following are items the teacher may wish to make or, in some cases, to have made by someone who has the necessary tools. The items have been previously mentioned in the text. Materials and dimensions are only suggestions, of course, and can be modified as desired. (Dimensions are generally given in English measures, since most suppliers are not yet "thinking metric.")

Abacus

To make a spike abacus (See Chapter 4, p. 90) first obtain a supply of wooden or plastic spools (from thread), each the same size. You might even buy new spools, at 20–40 cents each, and varnish the thread to get uniform colors and sizes, or use emptied spools. Measure the height and hole size of the spools and decide whether to make 9-, 10- or 18-spool spikes. Obtain some dowel accordingly; drill the appropriate size holes in a base of $\frac{3}{4}$-inch plywood or 1-by-6 pine or fir, about 3 inches apart. Glue the dowels and, if the diameters of the spool holes and the dowels are quite close, wax the dowels. The illustrated example will hold 18 spools. Beads, thick washers, loops of pipe cleaner, plastic rings (used for knitting), and so on, can replace the spools, with appropriate adjustments in the length and diameter of the dowels. A small model can be made with long finishing nails as spikes and washers for counters.

A frame abacus (See Chapter 4, p. 89) can be made on a $\frac{1}{4}$-inch plywood base, with frame (A, B) and divider (C) made of $\frac{3}{4}$-inch wood, glued and nailed or screwed to the base (D). Choose a wire diameter to match that of the beads to be used. Drill holes in both ends of the frame according to the diameter of the wire and an equal distance apart. Tie a washer on one end of the wire, string the 9 or 10 beads for ones place, loop the wire into the hole for tens place, string those beads and tighten the ones

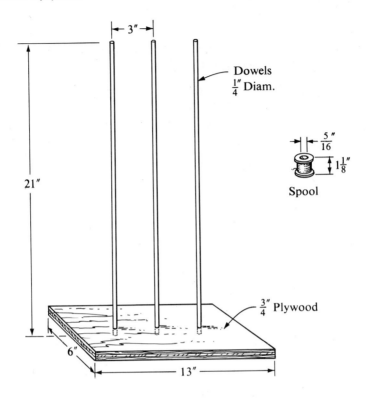

place wire; continue until each place is finished, then tie another washer
on the other end of the wire (this may be a little tricky if your wire is quite
thick, but it can be done).

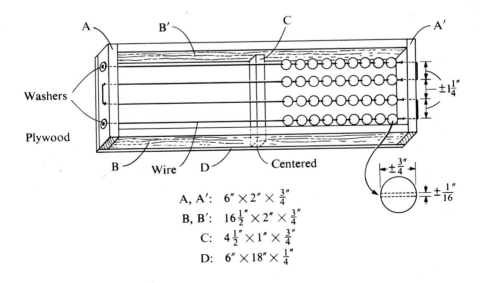

$$A, A': \quad 6'' \times 2'' \times \tfrac{3}{4}''$$
$$B, B': \quad 16\tfrac{1}{2}'' \times 2'' \times \tfrac{3}{4}''$$
$$C: \quad 4\tfrac{1}{2}'' \times 1'' \times \tfrac{3}{4}''$$
$$D: \quad 6'' \times 18'' \times \tfrac{1}{4}''$$

Mathematical Balance

A sturdy mathematical balance (See Chapter 5, p. 158) can be constructed of $\frac{3}{4}$-inch wood, and dowels as shown here.

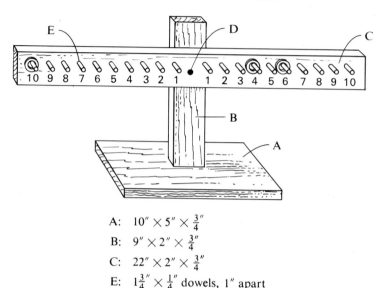

A: $10'' \times 5'' \times \frac{3''}{4}$

B: $9'' \times 2'' \times \frac{3''}{4}$

C: $22'' \times 2'' \times \frac{3''}{4}$

E: $1\frac{3}{4}'' \times \frac{1}{4}''$ dowels, 1″ apart

At D, use a short ($\frac{5}{8}''$) piece of tubing, as small in diameter as possible, as a bushing and a 2″ bolt to match it. The bolt should have no thread for at least $\frac{3}{4}$ of an inch from the head. Drill a hole in C so that the bushing will be a snug fit and tap it in. Polish the bolt carefully with steel wool, lubricate it lightly. Drill a hole in B to receive the bolt and connect B and C using two nuts and washers; C must swing freely, of course.

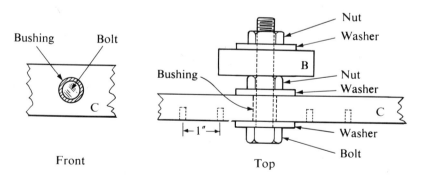

Front   Top

Twenty $\frac{1}{4}$-inch dowels, spaced 1 inch apart, are attached by drilling $\frac{1}{4}$-inch holes in C, applying white glue and tapping in. A supply of fairly heavy washers of uniform size are used for weights. If the finished product does not quite balance, either adding thumbtacks to the light end or whittling the heavy end will help.

Blocks

A set of blocks similar to the Stern, Cuisenaire, or centimeter rods, i.e., 1-blocks, 2-blocks, . . . , 10-blocks can be constructed as suggested in Chapter 5 (Projects, Questions, and Suggested Activities, number 6). Obtain a supply of good 1-by-6 or 1-by-8 lumber (straight, free of knots) such as fir. (Hard wood is better, but is more expensive and harder to find.) Have it sliced into strips $\frac{3}{4}$ inch wide at the lumber yard, unless you have access to a power saw that will do this accurately. Then cut the blocks, measuring very carefully *after* each cut as follows:

Block	Length (inches)
1	$\frac{3}{4}$
2	$1\frac{1}{2}$
3	$2\frac{1}{4}$
4	3
5	$3\frac{3}{4}$
6	$4\frac{1}{2}$
7	$5\frac{1}{4}$
8	6
9	$6\frac{3}{4}$
10	$7\frac{1}{2}$

A set of 10 blocks of each size will require about 35 feet of the $\frac{3}{4}$-by-$\frac{3}{4}$ inch material; this allows for the waste from saw cuts, knots, and so on. Starting with a 1-by-8-inch board 8 feet long should be sufficient to allow for this.

After the blocks are sanded (children enjoy doing this), they can be painted with nontoxic paint. If calibrations are desired, they can be notched in with a thin-bladed saw or drawn with India ink (either way is a big job).

Similar "blocks" can be constructed from heavy tagboard, and paper companies will sometimes cut sheets into whatever width strips you wish (or a small printing shop may oblige). The "grooves" for such blocks can be made by drawing a grid with lines $\frac{3}{4}$-inch apart on a mimeograph stencil, then using the stencil to print several colors of mimeograph paper; these can then be cut to the desired lengths and attached to the tagboard strips with rubber cement.

Counting Board

Counting boards such as those shown in Chapter 4 (p. 98) are easy to make of either tagboard, $\frac{1}{4}$-inch plywood, or $\frac{1}{8}$-inch masonite (masonite is best). Two pieces are needed: The grid is printed on the bottom piece (with India ink over white paint, for example); the second piece, with the opening cut out, acts as a frame. A $1\frac{1}{2}$-inch margin is adequate. Be sure the grid matches the blocks you use, and make the opening loose enough to allow for manipulation. Fasten the two pieces together with white glue.

Fraction Parts

Two sets of fraction parts, as described in Chapter 9 (pp. 399–400), can be made quite easily with a good power saw. For the square unit, $\frac{1}{8}$-inch masonite is best: The number of desired parts of each size will determine the amount of material required, of course, but usually 2 units of each size is sufficient (e.g., 4 halves, 6 thirds, etc.). Metric dimensions are easiest to use, and each piece should be measured *after* the preceding cut, as noted in Chapter 9. For example, if an 18-by-18 cm square is chosen as the unit size, start with a *strip* 18 cm wide and perhaps 1.2 m (4 ft) long. Mark the desired width of the first block, cut it, then mark the next, and so on. Sizes of the blocks can be as follows:

Fraction	Width (each 18 cm long)
unit	18 cm
halves	9 cm
thirds	6 cm
fourths	4.5 cm
fifths	3.6 cm
sixths	3 cm
sevenths	2.57 cm (approx.)
eighths	2.25 cm
ninths	2 cm
tenths	1.8 cm
twelfths	1.5 cm
sixteenths	1.125 cm

The linear model (Chapter 9, p. 400) can be constructed from $\frac{3}{4}$-by-$\frac{3}{4}$-inch strips as suggested for making blocks (#2 above). If a 36-cm unit is chosen, the lengths would be as follows:

Fraction	Length (cm)
unit	36
halves	18
thirds	12
fourths	9
fifths	7.2
sixths	6
sevenths	5.14 (approx.)
eighths	4.5
ninths	4
tenths	3.6
twelfths	3
sixteenths	2.25

Geoboard

Geoboards (see Chapter 8, p. 327) are really quite simple to construct. A useful one can be made by drawing a square grid on a piece of $\frac{3}{4}$-inch plywood with lines 1 inch apart to locate the nails. One-inch finishing nails, driven $\frac{1}{2}$ inch into the plywood work well, and if a classroom set of boards is to be made, it will be worthwhile to make a template out of $\frac{1}{2}$-inch plywood, drilling holes just slightly larger than the nail heads. The template can then be set over the block and the nails tapped in flush with the surface of the template. If the boards are to be painted or have grids printed on them, this should be done first.

Hundred Boards

Several types of hundred boards were suggested in Chapter 4 (pp. 97–8). One- or two-inch spacing is effective for the pegs, which can be either nails or dowels, depending on what type of marker is desired. Round tagboard key labels make good markers, and the suggestions in Chapter 4 should be sufficient for construction. Plywood, $\frac{3}{4}$ inch thick is recommended; and if nails are used as pegs, they need only extend about $\frac{1}{4}$ inch, so $\frac{3}{4}$-inch finishing nails would serve well. A scrap piece of $\frac{1}{4}$-inch masonite with a hole drilled just larger than the nail heads will help to tap the nails in to a uniform depth.

Number Line. There are many ways to design a number line to match a given set of blocks. For Cuisenaire or centimeter rods, a meter stick is ideal. A track similar to that of the Stern materials can be made from two $\frac{3}{4}$-by-$\frac{3}{4}$-by-75-inch strips (A) of wood glued and nailed to a $\frac{3}{4}$-by-$2\frac{1}{4}$-by-75-inch plywood base (B), painted white, and marked with India ink at $\frac{3}{4}$-inch intervals. A $1\frac{1}{2}$-by-$2\frac{1}{4}$-inch block of $\frac{1}{8}$-inch masonite (C) should be fastened at the 0 end.

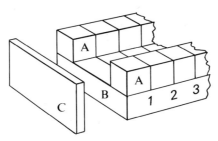

The line described in Chapter 6 (p. 226) can be made on a base of the same size, with a center piece measuring about 2-by-$\frac{3}{4}$-by-75 inches, painted and marked as above. If holes are drilled to match pegs, as shown in Chapter 6, a piece of scrap wood should be used with the drill to be certain that the holes are a uniform depth. Three-inch-long $\frac{1}{4}$-inch dowels in

1-inch-deep holes work well. These can be painted on the top two inches as suggested in Chapter 7, (p. 261) i.e., some red, some black, and some with black-and-red stripes. The 1-inch section that fits into the board can be waxed to make the pegs fit easily.

Place Value Charts

There are many ways to construct place value charts. As suggested in Chapter 4 (pp. 83–9), these charts may contain pockets to hold tickets or may be constructed with brass fasteners or pegs (e.g., finishing nails) on which tickets may be hung. Two types are considered here, both designed around 1-by-3-inch paper markers. A pocket chart can be folded from a 20-by-25-inch sheet of heavy construction paper as shown here. Sides of the pockets are stapled, holding the pockets as flat as possible, and the chart can then be labeled (Ones, Tens, and so on) and taped to a 13-by-20 piece of $\frac{1}{8}$-inch masonite or heavy cardboard.

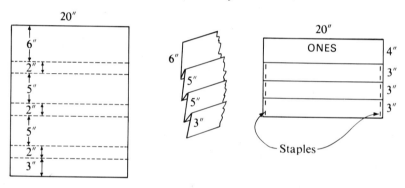

A chart on which markers hang (as pictured on page 85) can be made from a piece of $\frac{1}{2}$-inch plywood and small finishing nails or $1\frac{1}{2}$-inch lengths of $\frac{1}{4}$-inch (or less) dowel glued into holes drilled about $1\frac{1}{2}$ inches apart. Four rows of ten hangers each, spaced 4 inches between rows, with a 4-inch margin at top and bottom and 2-inch margin on each side, would require a 20-by-$17\frac{1}{2}$-inch base. A cardboard base with brass paper fasteners as hangers works quite well. Holes need to be punched in the markers with this type of chart.

Miscellaneous Constructions

A few other devices have been mentioned in the text or are commonly used. Some of those which have been mentioned and which should require no special directions for construction include the following:

1. Counting man (Chapter 4, p. 101)
2. Counting rods (Chapter 4, pp. 69–70)

3. Flannel board (Chapter 4, p. 61)
4. Geometric forms (Chapter 7, p. 279; Chapter 8, pp. 332, 335)
5. Grid for multiplying fractions (Chapter 9, pp. 413–14)
6. Individual abaci (Chapter 4, p. 89)
7. Individual place value charts (Chapter 4, p. 87)
8. Number lines (Chapter 4, p. 71)
9. Papy's Minicomputer (Chapter 4, pp. 85–87)
10. Pascal's triangle board (Chapter 7, p. 289)
11. Platonic solids (Chapter 8, pp. 313–15)
12. Playing board for Dienes blocks (Chapter 4, p. 96)
13. Some Cubes (Chapter 8, p. 366)
14. Tangrams (Chapter 8, p. 365)

Many more can be found in articles in *The Arithmetic Teacher*, or will occur to the reader as he examines suppliers' catalogues.

INDEX

1 2 3 4 5 6 7 8 9 10